The Editor

PHILLIP MALLETT is Senior Lecturer in English at the University of St Andrews. He is the author of chapters and articles on a number of Victorian and earlier writers, and editor of several texts and collections of essays, including *Kipling Considered, Rudyard Kipling: Limits and Renewals, A Spacious Vision: Essays on Thomas Hardy* (with Ronald Draper), *Satire,* and *The Achievement of Thomas Hardy.*

A NORTON CRITICAL EDITION

Thomas Hardy

THE MAYOR OF CASTERBRIDGE

AN AUTHORITATIVE TEXT
BACKGROUNDS AND CONTEXTS
CRITICISM

SECOND EDITION

Edited by

PHILLIP MALLETT
UNIVERSITY OF ST ANDREWS

W • W • NORTON & COMPANY • *New York* • *London*

Copyright © 2001, 1977 by W. W. Norton & Company, Inc.

The text of this book is composed in Electra
with the display set in Bernhard Modern.
Composition by Publishing Synthesis, Ltd.
Manufacturing by Courier Companies.
Book design by Antonina Krass.

Library of Congress Cataloging-in-Publication Data

Hardy, Thomas, 1840–1928.
The Mayor of Casterbridge : an authoritative text, backgrounds and contexts,
criticism / Thomas Hardy ; edited by Phillip Mallett.—2nd ed.
p. cm. — (A Norton critical edition)
Includes bibliographical references (p.   ).

ISBN 0-393-97498-7 (pbk.)

1. Fathers and daughters—Fiction.   2. Hardy, Thomas, 1840–1928. Mayor of
Casterbridge.   3. Wessex (England)—Fiction.   4. Men—England—Fiction.   5.
Mayors—Fiction.   I. Mallett, Phillip, 1946– II. Title. III. Series.

PR4750.M25 2000
823'.8—dc21   00-03798

W. W. Norton & Company, Inc., 500 Fifth Avenue, New York, N.Y. 10110
www.wwnorton.com

W. W. Norton & Company Ltd., Castle House, 75/76 Wells Street,
London W1T 3QT

5 6 7 8 9 0

For Louisa, Roger, Imogen, and Mollie

Contents

The Text of *The Mayor of Casterbridge*

Backgrounds and Contexts

Criticism

Preface to the Second Edition

"Henchard is a great fellow, and Dorchester is touched in with the hand of a master. Do you think you would let me try to dramatize it?" So wrote Robert Louis Stevenson to Thomas Hardy, shortly after the first publication of *The Mayor of Casterbridge* in book form, in May 1886. Elsewhere the novel had a more cautious reception. Hardy himself thought he had damaged it in his struggle to pack in the amount of incident required of a weekly serial. His publishers, Smith, Elder, were lukewarm, no doubt influenced by their reader, James Payn, who warned them that a novel that did not deal with the gentry would not attract an audience. Moreover, it was four years since Hardy had last appeared before the public, with *Two on a Tower* (1882), and the year before that with *A Laodicean*, neither of them among the best of his works. Smith, Elder eventually offered Hardy a disappointing one hundred pounds for the two-volume edition, half what they had paid for *The Trumpet-Major* (1880), and were in their turn disappointed with the sales, with fewer than seven hundred copies sold. The transaction had been unsatisfactory all round, and novelist and publisher severed their connection.

The reviews, however, were broadly favorable. Like Stevenson, the reviewers applauded the presentation of Wessex, and the towering figure of Henchard at the center of the novel—though the writer in the *Saturday Review* (possibly George Saintsbury) affected not to know which part of the country Hardy was writing about. With hindsight, it is clear that *The Mayor of Casterbridge* represented a crucial stage in Hardy's sense of himself as a Wessex novelist. He had moved back to Dorchester in 1883, and then into his house there, Max Gate, in 1885. For much of that period he was systematically reading through and making notes on old issues of the *Dorset County Chronicle* for the years 1826–30, immersing himself as a reader in a world he also knew by report from his family, especially from his mother and grandmother. One of the strengths of the novel is the way pieces of material arrived at by different routes sit together so well. When in Chapter 31 the bankrupt Henchard offers his creditors his watch, and "a silent, reserved young man named Boldwood" commends the gesture, Hardy is drawing on the *Chronicle* for the incident, but he had already recounted, in *Far from the Madding Crowd* (1874), the story of Boldwood's later life. The town of Casterbridge, discontented because the bread made from Henchard's wheat is inedible, can be seen as a city suffering because of its ruler's sins—as it were, Thebes in rural England—but it remains a credible town in Victorian Dorset. The question demanded of Henchard in Chapter 5—"But what are you going to do to repay us for the past?"—has a wonderful resonance, but it is spoken by a baker or miller, who has lost out in his financial dealings with a corn factor whose business has outgrown his capacity to supervise it. Henchard's "roaring din-

ners" are as palpable a sign of hubris as the red carpet on which Agamem-
non walks into his house in Aeschylus's play, but they too are to be found in
old copies of the *Dorset County Chronicle*. Hardy's claim, in the first chapter of his next novel, The Woodlanders, that "dramas of a grandeur and unity
truly Sophoclean" might from time to time be enacted in the real in some
remote spot, "outside the gates of the world," followed directly from the experience of writing The Mayor.

The Mayor himself, Michael Henchard, is one of the great male figures
of Victorian fiction. As many critics have observed, the novel explores the
processes of social change, as a community beginning to tire of the volcanic
energies of one Mayor of Casterbridge turns with relief to the more cautious
and prudent management of another. It has often proved tempting to go on
to suggest that this is a novel about the clash between an older, greater, and
somehow more truly rural way of life, and a newer, smaller, and essentially
mechanical one. But this is to simplify the novel. Henchard is a speculator,
gambling on the weather and the consequent fluctuations in the markets, not
a peasant who embodies an idealized traditional way of life. He is not defeated by the coming of new machinery, but by the recklessness of his own
financial dealings. But he is at the same time a man who fears his own unruly nature, and whom we see in search of a moral order: by turns fetichistic, defiant, aloof, self-destructive, penitent. Within the novel, Hardy quotes
or alludes to the stories of Cain, Job, Saul, Oedipus, and King Lear. These
are among the great tragic stories of Western literature, dealing with the violation of moral law; with love, loss, and belonging; and with the intertwined
themes of friendship, power, and rivalry. It is a mark of Hardy's extraordinary
achievement that it does not seem preposterous to invoke these stories in
tracing the fortunes of an out-of-work hay-trusser in the southwestern counties of England in the early nineteenth century.

In the twentieth century, *The Mayor of Casterbridge* has taken its place
alongside *Tess of the d'Urbervilles* and *Jude the Obscure* as one of Hardy's
most successful novels. It has been televised, prescribed for reading in
schools and universities, and made the subject of academic monographs. It
has also been brought out in a number of scholarly editions. The first published text of the novel seen by Hardy, however, was of a very different kind.
Like almost all of Hardy's novels, *The Mayor of Casterbridge* was first published in serial form, with the book edition appearing as the serial was drawing to an end. The first two chapters came out in the *Graphic*, an illustrated
weekly newspaper, on 2 January 1886. These chapters, together with an illustration by Robert Barnes of the conversation on the road between Henchard and the turnip-hoer, occupied just over two A3 pages (roughly 16.5 by
11.5 inches), printed in three densely set columns, with about ten lines of
type to the inch. On the previous page are advertisements for everything from
Broadwood pianos to chandeliers, turret-clocks, and cures for dyspepsia; on
the page following, an article on children's fashions and a series of short reviews written with all the confidence of the editorial "we." These seemingly
trivial matters are pertinent because, as N. N. Feltes has pointed out in a
study of *Modes of Production of Victorian Novels* (Chicago, 1986), part of the
meaning of a novel published in a magazine was established by the meanings that were already there, in its layout, blend of fiction and nonfiction, and

so forth, and in the readership these implied. This issue of the *Graphic*, for example, included under the heading "Topics of the Week" articles opposing Home Rule for Ireland, discussing "the Arab menace" in the Sudan, and denouncing the "predatory habits, ferocity, and cowardice" of the dacoits in Burma. The illustrations, some of them full-page engravings, showed war abroad, between Serbia and Bulgaria; and at home, a new production of *Faust* at the Lyceum theater, the visit of the Prince of Wales to the Doulton pottery works, and views of "The Royal River—The Thames from Source to Sea." If Hardy wished to challenge the complacency of late-Victorian England, he was trying to do so in a magazine that embodied it.

The present edition too carries its own cultural meanings, but it is not the part of an editor to comment on these. The first aim of this Norton Critical Edition has been to provide a reliable text. Here I have largely agreed with James K. Robinson, who edited the novel for Norton in 1977, in basing the text on that of the Wessex Edition of 1912. The reasons for doing so, and a list of the places where I have departed from the Wessex Edition, are set out in a Note on the Text. While I have profited by James Robinson's work in preparing the annotation, I have sometimes differed from him, and at others have chosen to annotate what he left without comment. No doubt the level of annotation in each case reflects our experience as readers of Hardy, and as teachers of English literature. I have also been able, in the section on "Backgrounds and Contexts," to include rather more of Hardy's nonfiction writings, in particular passages from his essay on "The Dorsetshire Labourer" of 1883, in which he commented directly on the social changes he had observed in his native county—one of the rare occasions when he set aside his usual insistence that his work offered only "impressions."

The other main differences between the two editions are to be found in the sections on modern criticism of the novel. I have included some or all of five essays that appeared after 1977, from (in chronological order) Elaine Showalter, George Levine, William Greenslade, Suzanne Keen and H. M. Daleski, together with two passages from Michael Millgate's *Thomas Hardy: His Career as a Novelist*. In order to do so I have had to exclude some pieces that Robinson had included; I have done so with regret, but in the confidence that the issues they raised are taken up and reexamined, in varying ways, by the passages included here for the first time.

I am grateful to Jill Gamble in the School of English in St Andrews for her help in preparing this edition, and to Carol Bemis, Ben Reynolds, Kate Lovelady, and Christa Grenawalt at Norton for their patient assistance throughout.

PHILLIP MALLETT

A Note on the Text

Like its predecessor, this Norton edition of *The Mayor of Casterbridge* is based on the Macmillan Wessex Edition of 1912, departing from it in three respects: in the correction of obvious misprints, in regularizing the use of double quotation marks within quoted speech, and in the admission of some variants from the Mellstock Edition of 1920. These changes, 26 in all, are listed at the end of this note. But Hardy was an inveterate reviser, and there are accordingly a number of texts that an editor of *The Mayor* might choose to consult. It may be helpful to describe these briefly here.

There is first the surviving manuscript, which Hardy presented to the Dorset County Museum in 1911. It consists of 374 pages; 108 pages are missing, and 5 are fragmentary. Simon Gatrell has suggested, plausibly, that Hardy himself excised the missing portions of the manuscript because they had been written in by his wife, Emma.[1] Since whatever notes or plans Hardy had made for the novel before he began writing have not survived, part of the interest of the manuscript is the evidence it provides of various cancelled plotlines. Taken together these suggest that as Hardy began writing, large areas of the action were still to be decided: at one stage there were to be two daughters, one staying with Henchard, the other going with Susan and Newson; the Elizabeth-Jane of the opening chapters was not to die, so the figure we meet in the body of the novel was to be Henchard's real daughter; Newson, on the other hand, was to die, instead of returning in the final chapters to supplant Henchard. It is hard to square any of these possibilities with the novel as we now have it, and Hardy's hesitation in working out the family relationships perhaps supports the suggestion that the center of the novel, at least at the outset, was to be Henchard's relationship with Farfrae. This would be consistent with the narrator's comment in Chapter Six that if Farfrae had not overheard and reacted to the townspeople's complaints about the damaged grain, "this history had never been enacted" (see p. 31). Whatever the reasoning that led Hardy to his final decisions about the plot, the effect of these decisions was to distribute the interest of the novel more evenly, with the story of Henchard's baffled attempt to undo the past, and of his shifting relationship with Elizabeth-Jane, interweaving with the crises brought about by the rivalry of the older and the younger man.

The manuscript was the basis for both the English and the American serial versions of the novel, in the *Graphic* and in *Harper's Weekly*, which ran concurrently over the nineteen-week period from 2 January to 15 May 1886. There are no major differences between the serial versions, except that for reasons of space *Harper's* omitted some passages, which were restored in

---

1. Simon Gatrell, *Hardy the Creator: A Textual Biography* (Oxford, 1988), p. 48.

later editions. The serial versions show about 300 changes from the manuscript, essentially minor local improvements: a decrease in the number of Latinisms, modifications to the dialect, and some bowdlerization (for example, in the *Graphic*, "damn it" becomes "hang it"; *Harper's* appears to have been less persnickety).

The novel also appeared in book form in 1886, as the serial publication was drawing to a close, published in two volumes in Britain by Smith, Elder, and in a one-volume edition in America by Henry Holt. Hardy made further changes for both of these editions. In later years he wrote that *The Mayor* "was a story he had damaged more recklessly as an artistic whole, in the interest of the newspaper in which it appeared serially, than perhaps any other of his novels,"[2] and in revising it for publication in volume form he set out to streamline the plot, cutting back on episodes whose main purpose was to grab the attention of the serial reader. Among the incidents he removed were the marriage of Henchard and Lucetta two weeks before Susan's return; a chance encounter between Lucetta and Susan, which Henchard observes; and another chance meeting, with Farfrae coming across Henchard and Lucetta, now Mrs. Farfrae, in the dusk, but failing to recognize her. In addition, two episodes in which letters were passed through intermediaries were greatly simplified. No doubt Hardy felt that enough of the action already turned on the misdelivery or the untimely opening of letters.

But there are also significant differences between the two book versions. In the serial and in the American editions, Elizabeth-Jane knows that Newson is still alive, and she has in fact been meeting him for some time without Henchard's knowledge. In the English edition, the situation is reversed: Henchard knows of Newson's return but Elizabeth-Jane does not. In effect, in the American edition Elizabeth-Jane deceives Henchard, while in the English edition he deceives her. Consequently, in the English edition it is the realization that she is about to be reunited with her real father, rather than her forthcoming marriage to Farfrae, that causes Henchard to leave Casterbridge. This edition also omitted Henchard's return to see the wedding, bringing the goldfinch as a present, only to be rejected by Elizabeth-Jane; this episode was retained in the American edition. Taken together, these changes cause Elizabeth-Jane to appear in a less sympathetic light in the American version.

A second English edition, in 1887, by Sampson Low, Marston, this time in one volume, had comparatively few changes from the Smith, Elder edition, of which the most notable is the addition of Farfrae's unfeeling remark that to spend the night away from home in the search for Henchard would "make a hole in a sovereign." For the first Collected Edition of his novels, however, the Osgood, McIlvaine Edition of 1895, Hardy made over 600 revisions. A number of these followed from his decision to embed all his novels more firmly in the world of "Wessex," with locations and distances made more consistent with those in other novels. Many of the other changes were modifications to the dialect. There is a typical example of these in the first conversation in the novel. In the earlier versions the turnip-hoer laments that "fokes" have nowhere to live in Weydon-Priors; in 1895 Hardy amended this

2. *The Life and Work of Thomas Hardy,* by Thomas Hardy, ed. Michael Millgate (London, 1984), p. 185.

to "volk," nearer to the softer forms of speech in the south and southwest of England. Farfrae's Scots, too, underwent some revision, following the advice of Hardy's friend Sir George Douglas. But there were also more substantial changes, including the reinstatement of the goldfinch episode and a return to Hardy's original plan for an irregular sexual liaison between Henchard and Lucetta—not, as in the serial, a marriage entered into on the assumption that Susan is dead, nor, as in the earlier book versions, a nonsexual relationship. By 1895, the novel had reached in all essentials the shape in which it has most often been reprinted.

The last sustained process of revision was for the Wessex Edition of 1912, with approximately 150 minor changes, many of them further modifications to the dialect. The Mellstock Edition of 1920 shows only minor changes, but in a few instances these provide support for correcting what can reasonably be seen as typographical errors in the 1912 text.

The case for using the 1912 Wessex Edition as the copy text is a strong one. It has been suggested, however, that while this edition should be used for substantives, the accidentals—essentially, the punctuation—should be checked against the manuscript, on the grounds that in these areas this represents Hardy's intentions, whereas the printed text reflects the hand of a number of compositors and their varying and sometimes inconsistent interpretations of the house styles adopted by different publishers.[3] This argument has been rejected in this edition for two reasons.

First, *The Mayor* was Hardy's tenth published novel; he was familiar with the ways of compositors, and to the extent that he did not insist on his own punctuation it may be assumed that he was not unwilling to allow the compositors to regularize it. In this edition I have followed the ancient legal principle that in the absence of other evidence, silence should be taken to imply consent.

The second point is perhaps the more compelling. Since the manuscript of *The Mayor* is incomplete, it would be necessary to refer also to the *Graphic*, as the text nearest to the manuscript. But where these two can be compared, there is a significant number of differences between them. For example, in folio 17 of the manuscript (reproduced in facsimile as part of Christine Winfield's essay in this volume [see p. 267]), there are the following differences:

Manuscript	Graphic
'Very well—	'Very well,
swear?	swears?
temper.	temper!
hay trusser's	hay-trusser's
and the child both	and the child, both
good-bye	good bye

3. For fuller discussion of these issues, see Simon Gatrell, *Hardy the Creator*, pp. 209–22, and his "Hardy, House-style, and the Aesthetics of Punctuation," in Anne Smith, ed., *The Novels of Thomas Hardy* (London, 1979), pp. 169–92; Michael Millgate, "The Making and Unmaking of Hardy's Wessex Edition," in Jane Millgate, ed., *Editing Nineteenth-Century Fiction* (New York, 1978), pp. 61–82; Robert Schweik and Michael Piret, "Editing Hardy," *Browning Institute Studies* 9 (1981): 15–41.

Two of these changes are merely trivial, one introducing and the other removing a hyphen, but the rest are not. Three of them, in altering the punctuation, also affect the rhythm and movement of the sentence: for example, the hyphen after "Very well" invites a longer pause than the comma. The fourth suggests that Newson too speaks in dialect, in using the third person form of the verb with the second person pronoun ("that you swears?"). But the broader point is that a comparison of one page of the manuscript with the corresponding passage in the *Graphic* reveals no fewer than six differences. It seems difficult, on this basis, to justify the use of the *Graphic* for the 108 pages missing from the manuscript, if the intention is to get close to Hardy's preferred text.

This is not to dismiss the point, made by Simon Gatrell and others, that an over-fussy compositor can damage Hardy's prose. Describing Susan's brief moment of defiance in the opening chapter, as she pauses by the door of the tent before leaving with Newson, the manuscript has:

> On reaching it she turned, and pulling off her wedding ring flung it across the room in the hay trusser's face.

In the Wessex Edition this becomes:

> On reaching it, she turned, and pulling off her wedding-ring, flung it across the booth in the hay-trusser's face.

The change from "room" to "booth" is logical (it also reveals that when he came to revise the text Hardy paused over this sentence), but the added commas, though grammatically correct, are surely out of key with the passionate nature of Susan's gesture. It is tempting to go with the earlier version. But there are other sentences where a compositor has added or adjusted punctuation in a way that seems to be required by the sense, and where most modern editors might also feel inclined to do so. Even if we had it complete, to transcribe Hardy's manuscript might create as many problems as it resolved. But since we do not have it complete, and it therefore cannot be used consistently, I have preferred to work from the edition of 1912, and to make the smallest possible number of changes.

The following are the changes made from the 1912 Wessex Edition:

Wessex Edition		Norton Edition	
14.7	od send	13.30	'od send
23.7	whity-brown	19.19	whitey-brown
35.16	agitated,	26.36	agitated.
84.17	makes	58.21	make
88.17	Laocoons	60.25	Laocoöns
97.8	Shinar's	66.28	Shiner's
118.9	hands	80.14	hands.
127.31	caligraphy	86.12	calligraphy
158.25	to day	106.32	to-day
183.1	Ay,	122.15	'Ay,
191.38	grasshoper	127.34	grasshopper
238.27	you	157.40	your
241.12	you	159.28	your

301.8	landlady,	198.1	landlady.
302.12	way,	198.25	way.
304.26	day,	200.5	day.
310.14	lappel	204.5	lapel
329.31	Henchard	216.16	Henchard,
337.11	'Since	221.5	"Since
337.12	bide,'	221.6	bide,"
337.12	' 'twill	221.6	" 'twill
337.14	for,'	221.7	for,"
337.14	'while	221.7	"while
337.17	home.'	221.9	home."
344.14	imag eo'	225.35	image o'
356.18	eclat	233.4	éclat

The Text of
THE LIFE AND DEATH OF THE MAYOR OF CASTERBRIDGE

A Story of a Man of Character

by
THOMAS HARDY

PERSONAL CHARACTER

PUBLIC STANDING

Preface

Readers of the following story who have not yet arrived at middle age are asked to bear in mind that, in the days recalled by the tale, the home Corn Trade, on which so much of the action turns, had an importance that can hardly be realized by those accustomed to the sixpenny loaf of the present date, and to the present indifference of the public to harvest weather.

The incidents narrated arise mainly out of three events, which chanced to range themselves in the order and at or about the intervals of time here given, in the real history of the town called Casterbridge[1] and the neighbouring country. They were the sale of a wife by her husband,[2] the uncertain harvests which immediately preceded the repeal of the Corn Laws,[3] and the visit of a Royal personage[4] to the aforesaid part of England.

The present edition of the volume,[5] like the previous one,[6] contains nearly a chapter which did not at first appear in any English copy,[7] though it was printed in the serial issue of the tale, and in the American edition. The restoration was made at the instance of some good judges across the Atlantic, who strongly represented that the home edition[8] suffered from the omission. Some shorter passages and names, omitted or altered for reasons which no longer exist, in the original printing of both English and American editions, have also been replaced or inserted.

The story is more particularly a study of one man's deeds and character than, perhaps, any other of those included in my Exhibition of

---

1. The name Hardy gave in his fiction to Dorchester, county town of Dorset. See pp. 302–3 for a key to the place names in *The Mayor of Casterbridge*.
2. Hardy found instances of wife-selling in the *Dorset County Chronicle* and elsewhere; see Christine Winfield, "Factual Sources of Two Episodes in *The Mayor of Casterbridge*," *Nineteenth-Century Fiction* 25 (1970): 224–27; and Michael Millgate, *Thomas Hardy: His Career as a Novelist* (London, 1971), pp. 240–42.
3. Laws introduced in 1815 restricting the import of foreign grain in order to protect home producers. They were finally repealed in 1846. See p. 304 for a fuller account of these laws.
4. Prince Albert, who in fact passed through Dorchester in July 1849, some years after the action of the novel.
5. The Wessex Edition, published in London by Macmillan in 1912.
6. The edition published in London by Osgood, McIlvaine & Co. in 1895.
7. Chapter 44 of this Norton Critical Edition was not included in either of the first English editions, brought out by Smith, Elder & Co. in 1886, and by Sampson Low, Marston in 1887. It was reinstated at the suggestion of Rebekah and Catherine Owen of New York City.
8. The novel was serialized in Britain in the *Graphic*, and in America in *Harper's Weekly*; the first American edition was by Henry Holt & Co. of New York, in 1886.

Wessex life.[9] Objections have been raised to the Scotch language of Mr. Farfrae, the second character; and one of his fellow-countrymen went so far as to declare that men beyond the Tweed did not and never could say "warrld," "cannet," "advairrtisment," and so on. As this gentleman's pronunciation in correcting me seemed to my Southron[1] ear an exact repetition of what my spelling implied, I was not struck with the truth of his remark, and somehow we did not get any forwarder in the matter. It must be remembered that the Scotchman of the tale is represented not as he would appear to other Scotchmen, but as he would appear to people of outer regions. Moreover, no attempt is made herein to reproduce his entire pronunciation phonetically, any more than that of the Wessex speakers. I should add, however, that this new edition of the book has had the accidental advantage of a critical overlooking by a professor of the tongue in question[2]—one of undoubted authority:—in fact he is a gentleman who adopted it for urgent personal reasons in the first year of his existence.

Furthermore, a charming non-Scottish lady, of strict veracity and admitted penetration, the wife of a well-known Caledonian, came to the writer shortly after the story was first published, and inquired if Farfrae were not drawn from her husband, for he seemed to her to be the living portrait of that (doubtless) happy man. It happened that I had never thought of her husband in constructing Farfrae. I trust therefore that Farfrae may be allowed to pass, if not as a Scotchman to Scotchmen, as a Scotchman to Southerners.

The novel was first published complete, in two volumes, in May 1886.

T. H.

February 1895 — May 1912.[3]

---

9. Hardy introduced the term Wessex in Chapter 50 of *Far from the Madding Crowd*, in 1874. It covers an area of the south and southwest of England comprising most of Cornwall, Devon, Somerset, Dorset, Hampshire, Wiltshire, and Berkshire.
1. Southern.
2. Sir George Douglas (1856–1935), whom Hardy first met in 1881.
3. The Preface was originally written in February 1895 for the Osgood, McIlvaine Edition, where it appeared in volume III, and then slightly revised for the Wessex Edition of 1912, where it appeared in volume V.

I

One evening of late summer, before the nineteenth century had reached one-third of its span, a young man and woman, the latter carrying a child, were approaching the large village of Weydon-Priors,[1] in Upper Wessex, on foot. They were plainly but not ill clad, though the thick hoar of dust which had accumulated on their shoes and garments from an obviously long journey lent a disadvantageous shabbiness to their appearance just now.

The man was of fine figure, swarthy, and stern in aspect; and he showed in profile a facial angle so slightly inclined as to be almost perpendicular. He wore a short jacket of brown corduroy, newer than the remainder of his suit, which was a fustian[2] waistcoat with white horn buttons, breeches of the same, tanned leggings, and a straw hat overlaid with black glazed canvas. At his back he carried by a looped strap a rush basket, from which protruded at one end the crutch of a hay-knife, a wimble[3] for hay-bonds being also visible in the aperture. His measured, springless walk was the walk of the skilled countryman as distinct from the desultory shamble of the general labourer; while in the turn and plant of each foot there was, further, a dogged and cynical indifference personal to himself, showing its presence even in the regularly interchanging fustian folds, now in the left leg, now in the right, as he paced along.

What was really peculiar, however, in this couple's progress, and would have attracted the attention of any casual observer otherwise disposed to overlook them, was the perfect silence they preserved. They walked side by side in such a way as to suggest afar off the low, easy, confidential chat of people full of reciprocity; but on closer view it could be discerned that the man was reading, or pretending to read, a ballad sheet[4] which he kept before his eyes with some difficulty by the hand that was passed through the basket strap. Whether this apparent cause were the real cause, or whether it were an assumed one to escape an intercourse that would have been irksome to him, nobody but himself could have said precisely; but his taciturnity was unbroken, and the woman enjoyed no society whatever from his presence. Virtually she walked the highway alone, save for the child she bore. Sometimes the man's bent elbow almost touched her shoulder, for she kept as close to his side as was possible without actual contact; but she seemed to have no idea of taking his arm, nor he of offering it; and far from exhibiting surprise at his ignoring silence she appeared to receive it as a natural thing. If any word at all were uttered by the little group, it was an occasional whisper of the woman to the child—a tiny girl

---

1. Weyhill, a village near Andover in Hampshire ("Upper Wessex").
2. Thick cotton material, usually dark in color.
3. Tool used to wind strands of hay into cords.
4. Broadsheet, printed on one side only, usually with verses of topical interest.

in short clothes and blue boots of knitted yarn—and the murmured bab
ble of the child in reply.

The chief—almost the only—attraction of the young woman's face
was its mobility. When she looked down sideways to the girl she became
pretty, and even handsome, particularly that in the action her features
caught slantwise the rays of the strongly coloured sun, which made
transparencies of her eyelids and nostrils and set fire on her lips. When
she plodded on in the shade of the hedge, silently thinking, she had the
hard, half-apathetic expression of one who deems anything possible at
the hands of Time and Chance except, perhaps, fair play. The first phase
was the work of Nature, the second probably of civilization.

That the man and woman were husband and wife, and the parents of
the girl in arms, there could be little doubt. No other than such relationship would have accounted for the atmosphere of stale familiarity
which the trio carried along with them like a nimbus[5] as they moved
down the road.

The wife mostly kept her eyes fixed ahead, though with little interest—the scene for that matter being one that might have been matched
at almost any spot in any county in England at this time of the year; a
road neither straight nor crooked, neither level nor hilly, bordered by
hedges, trees, and other vegetation, which had entered the blackened-
green stage of colour that the doomed leaves pass through on their way
to dingy, and yellow, and red. The grassy margin of the bank, and the
nearest hedgerow boughs, were powdered by the dust that had been
stirred over them by hasty vehicles, the same dust as it lay on the road
deadening their footfalls like a carpet; and this, with the aforesaid total
absence of conversation, allowed every extraneous sound to be heard.

For a long time there was none, beyond the voice of a weak bird
singing a trite old evening song that might doubtless have been heard on
the hill at the same hour, and with the self-same trills, quavers, and
breves, at any sunset of that season for centuries untold. But as they
approached the village sundry distant shouts and rattles reached their
ears from some elevated spot in that direction, as yet screened from view
by foliage. When the outlying houses of Weydon-Priors could just be
descried, the family group was met by a turnip-hoer with his hoe on his
shoulder, and his dinner-bag suspended from it. The reader promptly
glanced up.

'Any trade doing here?' he asked phlegmatically, designating the village in his van by a wave of the broadsheet. And thinking the labourer
did not understand him, he added, 'Anything in the hay-trussing line?'

The turnip-hoer had already begun shaking his head. 'Why, save the
man, what wisdom's in him that 'a should come to Weydon for a job of
that sort this time o' year?'

5. In classical painting, the band of light shown around the heads of saints or divine figures.

'Then is there any house to let—a little small new cottage just a build-ed, or such like?' asked the other.

The pessimist still maintained a negative. 'Pulling down is more the nater of Weydon. There were five houses cleared away last year, and three this; and the volk nowhere to go—no, not so much as a thatched hurdle;[6] that's the way o' Weydon-Priors.'

The hay-trusser, which he obviously was, nodded with some supercil-iousness. Looking towards the village, he continued, 'There is some-thing going on here, however, is there not?'

'Ay. 'Tis Fair Day.[7] Though what you hear now is little more than the clatter and scurry of getting away the money o' children and fools, for the real business is done earlier than this. I've been working within sound o't all day, but I didn't go up—not I. 'Twas no business of mine.'

The trusser and his family proceeded on their way, and soon entered the Fair-field, which showed standing-places and pens where many hun-dreds of horses and sheep had been exhibited and sold in the forenoon, but were now in great part taken away. At present, as their informant had observed, but little real business remained on hand, the chief being the sale by auction of a few inferior animals, that could not otherwise be dis-posed of, and had been absolutely refused by the better class of traders, who came and went early. Yet the crowd was denser now than during the morning hours, the frivolous contingent of visitors, including journey-men[8] out for a holiday, a stray soldier or two home on furlough, village shopkeepers, and the like, having latterly flocked in; persons whose activities found a congenial field among the peep-shows, toy-stands, wax-works, inspired monsters, disinterested medical men who travelled for the public good, thimble-riggers,[9] nick-nack vendors, and readers of Fate.

Neither of our pedestrians had much heart for these things, and they looked around for a refreshment tent among the many which dotted the down. Two, which stood nearest to them in the ochreous haze of expir-ing sunlight, seemed almost equally inviting. One was formed of new, milk-hued canvas, and bore red flags on its summit; it announced 'Good Home-brewed Beer, Ale, and Cyder.' The other was less new; a little iron stove-pipe came out of it at the back, and in front appeared the plac-ard, 'Good Furmity Sold Hear.' The man mentally weighed the two inscriptions, and inclined to the former tent.

'No—no—the other one,' said the woman. 'I always like furmity; and so does Elizabeth-Jane; and so will you. It is nourishing after a long hard day.'

---

6. Frame made of hazel wood, used for shelter or to pen animals.
7. September 15.
8. Men who had completed their apprenticeship to a trade or craft, but who worked for daily wages rather than becoming self-employed.
9. Professional swindlers, exponents of the shell and pea game.

'I've never tasted it,' said the man. However, he gave way to her representations, and they entered the furmity booth forthwith.

A rather numerous company appeared within, seated at the long narrow tables that ran down the tent on each side. At the upper end stood a stove, containing a charcoal fire, over which hung a large three-legged crock, sufficiently polished round the rim to show that it was made of bell-metal.[1] A haggish creature of about fifty presided, in a white apron, which, as it threw an air of respectability over her as far as it extended, was made so wide as to reach nearly round her waist. She slowly stirred the contents of the pot. The dull scrape of her large spoon was audible throughout the tent as she thus kept from burning the mixture of corn in the grain, flour, milk, raisins, currants, and what not, that composed the antiquated slop in which she dealt. Vessels holding the separate ingredients stood on a white-clothed table of boards and trestles close by.

The young man and woman ordered a basin each of the mixture, steaming hot, and sat down to consume it at leisure. This was very well so far, for furmity, as the woman had said, was nourishing, and as proper a food as could be obtained within the four seas; though, to those not accustomed to it, the grains of wheat swollen as large as lemon-pips, which floated on its surface, might have a deterrent effect at first.

But there was more in that tent than met the cursory glance; and the man, with the instinct of a perverse character, scented it quickly. After a mincing attack on his bowl, he watched the hag's proceedings from the corner of his eye, and saw the game she played. He winked to her, and passed up his basin in reply to her nod; when she took a bottle from under the table, slily measured out a quantity of its contents, and tipped the same into the man's furmity. The liquor poured in was rum. The man as slily sent back money in payment.

He found the concoction, thus strongly laced, much more to his satisfaction than it had been in its natural state. His wife had observed the proceeding with much uneasiness; but he persuaded her to have hers laced also, and she agreed to a milder allowance after some misgiving.

The man finished his basin, and called for another, the rum being signalled for in yet stronger proportion. The effect of it was soon apparent in his manner, and his wife but too sadly perceived that in strenuously steering off the rocks of the licensed liquor-tent she had only got into maelstrom depths[2] here amongst the smugglers.

The child began to prattle impatiently, and the wife more than once said to her husband, 'Michael, how about our lodging? You know we may have trouble in getting it if we don't go soon.'

But he turned a deaf ear to those bird-like chirpings. He talked loud to the company. The child's black eyes, after slow, round, ruminating

---

1. Alloy of copper and tin, used in bell-making.
2. Bottomless depths.

gazes at the candles when they were lighted, fell together; then they opened, then shut again, and she slept.

At the end of the first basin the man had risen to serenity; at the second he was jovial; at the third, argumentative; at the fourth, the qualities signified by the shape of his face, the occasional clench of his mouth, and the fiery spark of his dark eye, began to tell in his conduct; he was overbearing—even brilliantly quarrelsome.

The conversation took a high turn, as it often does on such occasions. The ruin of good men by bad wives, and, more particularly, the frustration of many a promising youth's high aims and hopes and the extinction of his energies by an early imprudent marriage, was the theme.

'I did for myself that way thoroughly,' said the trusser, with a contemplative bitterness that was well-nigh resentful. 'I married at eighteen, like the fool that I was; and this is the consequence o't.' He pointed at himself and family with a wave of the hand intended to bring out the penuriousness of the exhibition.

The young woman his wife, who seemed accustomed to such remarks, acted as if she did not hear them, and continued her intermittent private words on tender trifles to the sleeping and waking child, who was just big enough to be placed for a moment on the bench beside her when she wished to ease her arms. The man continued—

'I haven't more than fifteen shillings in the world, and yet I am a good experienced hand in my line. I'd challenge England to beat me in the fodder business; and if I were a free man again I'd be worth a thousand pound before I'd done o't. But a fellow never knows these little things till all chance of acting upon 'em is past.'

The auctioneer selling the old horses in the field outside could be heard saying, 'Now this is the last lot—now who'll take the last lot for a song? Shall I say forty shillings? 'Tis a very promising broodmare, a trifle over five years old, and nothing the matter with the hoss at all, except that she's a little holler in the back and had her left eye knocked out by the kick of another, her own sister, coming along the road.'

'For my part I don't see why men who have got wives and don't want 'em, shouldn't get rid of 'em as these gipsy fellows do their old horses,' said the man in the tent. 'Why shouldn't they put 'em up and sell 'em by auction to men who are in need of such articles? Hey? Why, begad, I'd sell mine this minute if anybody would buy her!'

'There's them that would do that,' some of the guests replied, looking at the woman, who was by no means ill-favoured.

'True,' said a smoking gentleman, whose coat had the fine polish about the collar, elbows, seams, and shoulder-blades that long-continued friction with grimy surfaces will produce, and which is usually more desired on furniture than on clothes. From his appearance he had possibly been in former time groom or coachman to some neighbouring county family. 'I've had my breedings in as good circles, I may say, as any man,' he added, 'and I know true cultivation, or nobody do; and I can declare she's got it—in the bone, mind ye, I say—as much as any female in the fair—though it may want a little bringing out.' Then, crossing his legs, he resumed his pipe with a nicely-adjusted gaze at a point in the air.

The fuddled young husband stared for a few seconds at this unexpected praise of his wife, half in doubt of the wisdom of his own attitude towards the possessor of such qualities. But he speedily lapsed into his former conviction, and said harshly—

'Well, then, now is your chance; I am open to an offer for this gem o' creation.'

She turned to her husband and murmured, 'Michael, you have talked this nonsense in public places before. A joke is a joke, but you may make it once too often, mind!'

'I know I've said it before; I meant it. All I want is a buyer.'

At the moment a swallow, one among the last of the season, which had by chance found its way through an opening into the upper part of the tent, flew to and fro in quick curves above their heads, causing all eyes to follow it absently. In watching the bird till it made its escape the assembled company neglected to respond to the workman's offer, and the subject dropped.

But a quarter of an hour later the man, who had gone on lacing his furmity more and more heavily, though he was either so strong-minded or such an intrepid toper that he still appeared fairly sober, recurred to the old strain, as in a musical fantasy the instrument fetches up the original theme. 'Here—I am waiting to know about this offer of mine. The woman is no good to me. Who'll have her?'

The company had by this time decidedly degenerated, and the renewed inquiry was received with a laugh of appreciation. The woman whispered; she was imploring and anxious: 'Come, come, it is getting dark, and this nonsense won't do. If you don't come along, I shall go without you. Come!'

She waited and waited; yet he did not move. In ten minutes the man broke in upon the desultory conversation of the furmity drinkers with, 'I asked this question, and nobody answered to 't. Will any Jack Rag or Tom Straw among ye buy my goods?'

The woman's manner changed, and her face assumed the grim shape and colour of which mention has been made.

'Mike, Mike,' said she; 'this is getting serious. O!—too serious!'

'Will anybody buy her?' said the man.

'I wish somebody would,' said she firmly. 'Her present owner is not at all to her liking!'

'Nor you to mine,' said he. 'So we are agreed about that. Gentlemen, you hear? It's an agreement to part. She shall take the girl if she wants to, and go her ways. I'll take my tools, and go my ways. 'Tis simple as Scripture history. Now then, stand up, Susan, and show yourself.'

'Don't, my chiel,' whispered a buxom staylace[3] dealer in voluminous petticoats, who sat near the woman; 'yer good man don't know what he's saying.'

The woman, however, did stand up. 'Now, who's auctioneer?' cried the hay-trusser.

'I be,' promptly answered a short man, with a nose resembling a copper knob, a damp voice, and eyes like button-holes. 'Who'll make an offer for this lady?'

The woman looked on the ground, as if she maintained her position by a supreme effort of will.

'Five shillings,' said some one, at which there was a laugh.

'No insults,' said the husband. 'Who'll say a guinea?'

Nobody answered; and the female dealer in staylaces interposed.

'Behave yerself moral, good man, for Heaven's love! Ah, what a cruelty is the poor soul married to! Bed and board is dear at some figures, 'pon my 'vation[4] 'tis!'

'Set it higher, auctioneer,' said the trusser.

'Two guineas!' said the auctioneer; and no one replied.

'If they don't take her for that, in ten seconds they'll have to give more,' said the husband. 'Very well. Now, auctioneer, add another.'

'Three guineas—going for three guineas!' said the rheumy man.

'No bid?' said the husband. 'Good Lord, why she's cost me fifty times the money, if a penny. Go on.'

'Four guineas!' cried the auctioneer.

'I'll tell ye what—I won't sell her for less than five,' said the husband, bringing down his fist so that the basins danced. 'I'll sell her for five guineas to any man that will pay me the money, and treat her well; and he shall have her for ever, and never hear aught o' me. But she shan't go for less. Now then—five guineas—and she's yours. Susan, you agree?'

She bowed her head with absolute indifference.

'Five guineas,' said the auctioneer, 'or she'll be withdrawn. Do anybody give it? The last time. Yes or no?'

'Yes,' said a loud voice from the doorway.

All eyes were turned. Standing in the triangular opening which formed the door of the tent was a sailor, who, unobserved by the rest, had arrived there within the last two or three minutes. A dead silence followed his affirmation.

'You say you do?' asked the husband, staring at him.

'I say so,' replied the sailor.

'Saying is one thing, and paying is another. Where's the money?'

The sailor hesitated a moment, looked anew at the woman, came in, unfolded five crisp pieces of paper, and threw them down upon the table-

3. Lace used to fasten a woman's corset ("stays").
4. Salvation.

cloth. They were Bank-of-England notes for five pounds. Upon the face of this he chinked down the shillings severally—one, two, three, four, five.

The sight of real money in full amount, in answer to a challenge for the same till then deemed slightly hypothetical, had a great effect upon the spectators. Their eyes became riveted upon the faces of the chief actors, and then upon the notes as they lay, weighted by the shillings, on the table.

Up to this moment it could not positively have been asserted that the man, in spite of his tantalizing declaration, was really in earnest. The spectators had indeed taken the proceedings throughout as a piece of mirthful irony carried to extremes; and had assumed that, being out of work, he was, as a consequence, out of temper with the world, and society, and his nearest kin. But with the demand and response of real cash the jovial frivolity of the scene departed. A lurid colour seemed to fill the tent, and change the aspect of all therein. The mirth-wrinkles left the listeners' faces, and they waited with parting lips.

'Now,' said the woman, breaking the silence, so that her low dry voice sounded quite loud, 'before you go further, Michael, listen to me. If you touch that money, I and this girl go with the man. Mind, it is a joke no longer.'

'A joke? Of course it is not a joke!' shouted her husband, his resentment rising at her suggestion. 'I take the money: the sailor takes you. That's plain enough. It has been done elsewhere—and why not here?'

"'Tis quite on the understanding that the young woman is willing,' said the sailor blandly. 'I wouldn't hurt her feelings for the world.'

'Faith, nor I,' said her husband. 'But she is willing, provided she can have the child. She said so only the other day when I talked o't!'

'That you swear?' said the sailor to her.

'I do,' said she, after glancing at her husband's face and seeing no repentance there.

'Very well, she shall have the child, and the bargain's complete,' said the trusser. He took the sailor's notes and deliberately folded them, and put them with the shillings in a high remote pocket, with an air of finality.

The sailor looked at the woman and smiled. 'Come along!' he said kindly. 'The little one too—the more the merrier!' She paused for an instant, with a close glance at him. Then dropping her eyes again, and saying nothing, she took up the child and followed him as he made towards the door. On reaching it, she turned, and pulling off her wedding-ring, flung it across the booth in the hay-trusser's face.

'Mike,' she said, 'I've lived with thee a couple of years, and had nothing but temper! Now I'm no more to 'ee; I'll try my luck elsewhere. 'Twill be better for me and Elizabeth-Jane, both. So good-bye!'

Seizing the sailor's arm with her right hand, and mounting the little girl on her left, she went out of the tent sobbing bitterly.

A stolid look of concern filled the husband's face, as if, after all, he had not quite anticipated this ending; and some of the guests laughed.

'Is she gone?' he said.

'Faith, ay; she's gone clane enough,' said some rustics near the door.

He rose and walked to the entrance with the careful tread of one conscious of his alcoholic load. Some others followed, and they stood looking into the twilight. The difference between the peacefulness of inferior nature and the wilful hostilities of mankind was very apparent at this place. In contrast with the harshness of the act just ended within the tent [*auction* — handwritten annotation] was the sight of several horses crossing their necks and rubbing each other lovingly as they waited in patience to be harnessed for the homeward journey. Outside the fair, in the valleys and woods, all was quiet. The sun had recently set, and the west heaven was hung with rosy cloud, which seemed permanent, yet slowly changed. To watch it was like looking at some grand feat of stagery from a darkened auditorium. In presence of this scene after the other there was a natural instinct to abjure man as the blot on an otherwise kindly universe; till it was remembered that all terrestrial conditions were intermittent, and that mankind might some night be innocently sleeping when these quiet objects were raging loud.

'Where do the sailor live?' asked a spectator, when they had vainly gazed around.

'God knows that,' replied the man who had seen high life. 'He's without doubt a stranger here.'

'He came in about five minutes ago,' said the furmity woman, joining the rest with her hands on her hips. 'And then 'a stepped back, and then 'a looked in again. I'm not a penny the better for him.'

'Serves the husband well be-right,' said the staylace vendor. 'A comely respectable body like her—what can a man want more? I glory in the woman's sperrit. I'd ha' done it myself—'od send[5] if I wouldn't, if a husband had behaved so to me! I'd go, and 'a might call, and call, till his keacorn[6] was raw; but I'd never come back—no, not till the great trumpet,[7] would I!'

'Well, the woman will be better off,' said another of a more deliberative turn. 'For seafaring natures be very good shelter for shorn lambs, and the man do seem to have plenty of money, which is what she's not been used to lately, by all showings.'

'Mark me—I'll not go after her!' said the trusser, returning doggedly to his seat. 'Let her go! If she's up to such vagaries she must suffer for 'em. She'd no business to take the maid—'tis my maid; and if it were the doing again she shouldn't have her!'

5. God send.
6. Throat (dialect).
7. The trumpet announcing the Day of Judgment.

Perhaps from some little sense of having countenanced an indefensible proceeding, perhaps because it was late, the customers thinned away from the tent shortly after this episode. The man stretched his elbows forward on the table, leant his face upon his arms, and soon began to snore. The furmity seller decided to close for the night, and after seeing the rum-bottles, milk, corn, raisins, etc., that remained on hand, loaded into the cart, came to where the man reclined. She shook him, but could not wake him. As the tent was not to be struck that night, the fair continuing for two or three days, she decided to let the sleeper, who was obviously no tramp, stay where he was, and his basket with him. Extinguishing the last candle, and lowering the flap of the tent, she left it, and drove away.

II

The morning sun was streaming through the crevices of the canvas when the man awoke. A warm glow pervaded the whole atmosphere of the marquee, and a single big blue fly buzzed musically round and round it. Besides the buzz of the fly there was not a sound. He looked about—at the benches—at the table supported by trestles—at his basket of tools—at the stove where the furmity had been boiled—at the empty basins—at some shed grains of wheat—at the corks which dotted the grassy floor. Among the odds and ends he discerned a little shining object, and picked it up. It was his wife's ring.

A confused picture of the events of the previous evening seemed to come back to him, and he thrust his hand into his breast-pocket. A rustling revealed the sailor's bank-notes thrust carelessly in.

This second verification of his dim memories was enough; he knew now they were not dreams. He remained seated, looking on the ground for some time. 'I must get out of this as soon as I can,' he said deliberately at last, with the air of one who could not catch his thoughts without pronouncing them. 'She's gone—to be sure she is—gone with that sailor who bought her, and little Elizabeth-Jane. We walked here, and I had the furmity, and rum in it—and sold her. Yes, that's what's happened, and here am I. Now, what am I to do—am I sober enough to walk, I wonder?' He stood up, found that he was in fairly good condition for progress unencumbered. Next he shouldered his tool basket, and found he could carry it. Then lifting the tent door he emerged into the open air.

Here the man looked around with gloomy curiosity. The freshness of the September morning inspired and braced him as he stood. He and his family had been weary when they arrived the night before, and they had observed but little of the place; so that he now beheld it as a new thing. It exhibited itself as the top of an open down, bounded on one extreme by a plantation, and approached by a winding road. At the bottom stood the village which lent its name to the upland and the annual fair that was held thereon. The spot stretched downward into valleys, and onward to other uplands, dotted with barrows,[1] and trenched with the remains of prehistoric forts. The whole scene lay under the rays of a newly risen sun, which had not as yet dried a single blade of the heavily dewed grass, whereon the shadows of the yellow and red vans were projected far away, those thrown by the felloe of each wheel[2] being elongated in shape to the orbit of a comet. All the gipsies and showmen who had remained on the ground lay snug within their carts and tents, or wrapped in horse-cloths under them, and were silent and still as death, with the exception of an occasional snore that revealed their presence. But the Seven Sleepers[3] had a dog; and dogs of the mysterious breeds that vagrants own, that are as much like cats as dogs and as much like foxes as cats, also lay about here. A little one started up under one of the carts, barked as a matter of principle, and quickly lay down again. He was the only positive spectator of the hay-trusser's exit from the Weydon Fair-field.

This seemed to accord with his desire. He went on in silent thought, unheeding the yellowhammers which flitted about the hedges with straws in their bills, the crowns of the mushrooms, and the tinkling of local sheep-bells, whose wearers had had the good fortune not to be included in the fair. When he reached a lane, a good mile from the scene of the previous evening, the man pitched his basket and leant upon a gate. A difficult problem or two occupied his mind.

'Did I tell my name to anybody last night, or didn't I tell my name?' he said to himself; and at last concluded that he did not. His general demeanour was enough to show how he was surprised and nettled that his wife had taken him so literally—as much could be seen in his face, and in the way he nibbled a straw which he pulled from the hedge. He knew that she must have been somewhat excited to do this; moreover, she must have believed that there was some sort of binding force in the transaction. On this latter point he felt almost certain, knowing her freedom from levity of character, and the extreme simplicity of her intellect. There may, too, have been enough recklessness and resentment beneath her ordinary placidity to make her stifle any momentary doubts. On a previous occasion when he had declared during a fuddle that he would dispose of her as he had done, she had replied that she would not hear him say that many times more before it happened, in the resigned tones of a fatalist. . . . 'Yet she knows I am not in my senses when I do that!' he exclaimed. 'Well, I must walk about till I find her. . . . Seize her, why didn't she know better than bring me into this disgrace!' he roared out. 'She wasn't queer[4] if I was. 'Tis like Susan to show such idiotic sim-

1. Ancient burial mounds.
2. Rim of wheel.
3. Seven young Christians who fell asleep in a cave in Ephesus during the persecution of Decius (250 C.E.), and woke two centuries later to find Christianity the accepted religion.
4. Drunk.

plicity. Meek—that meekness has done me more harm than the bitterest temper!'

When he was calmer he turned to his original conviction that he must somehow find her and his little Elizabeth-Jane, and put up with the shame as best he could. It was of his own making, and he ought to bear it. But first he resolved to register an oath, a greater oath than he had ever sworn before: and to do it properly he required a fit place and imagery; for there was something fetichistic[5] in this man's beliefs.

He shouldered his basket and moved on, casting his eyes inquisitively round upon the landscape as he walked, and at the distance of three or four miles perceived the roofs of a village and the tower of a church. He instantly made towards the latter object. The village was quite still, it being that motionless hour of rustic daily life which fills the interval between the departure of the field-labourers to their work, and the rising of their wives and daughters to prepare the breakfast for their return. Hence he reached the church without observation, and the door being only latched he entered. The hay-trusser deposited his basket by the font, went up the nave till he reached the altar-rails, and opening the gate entered the sacrarium,[6] where he seemed to feel a sense of the strangeness for a moment; then he knelt upon the foot-pace.[7] Dropping his head upon the clamped book which lay on the Communion-table, he said aloud—

'I, Michael Henchard, on this morning of the sixteenth of September do take an oath before God here in this solemn place that I will avoid all strong liquors for the space of twenty-one years to come, being a year for every year that I have lived. And this I swear upon the book before me; and may I be strook dumb, blind, and helpless, if I break this my oath!'

When he had said it and kissed the big book, the hay-trusser arose, and seemed relieved at having made a start in a new direction. While standing in the porch a moment he saw a thick jet of wood smoke suddenly start up from the red chimney of a cottage near, and knew that the occupant had just lit her fire. He went round to the door, and the housewife agreed to prepare him some breakfast for a trifling payment, which was done. Then he started on the search for his wife and child.

The perplexing nature of the undertaking became apparent soon enough. Though he examined and inquired, and walked hither and thither day after day, no such characters as those he described had anywhere been seen since the evening of the fair. To add to the difficulty he could gain no sound of the sailor's name. As money was short with him he decided, after some hesitation, to spend the sailor's money in the prosecution of this search; but it was equally in vain. The truth was that

---

5. Superstitious, inclined to reverence inanimate objects.
6. Area around the altar in a church, traditionally a place of sanctuary.
7. The raised platform on which the altar stands.

a certain shyness of revealing his conduct prevented Michael Henchard from following up the investigation with the loud hue-and-cry such a pursuit demanded to render it effectual; and it was probably for this reason that he obtained no clue, though everything was done by him that did not involve an explanation of the circumstances under which he had lost her.

Weeks counted up to months, and still he searched on, maintaining himself by small jobs of work in the intervals. By this time he had arrived at a seaport, and there he derived intelligence that persons answering somewhat to his description had emigrated a little time before. Then he said he would search no longer, and that he would go and settle in the district which he had had for some time in his mind. Next day he started, journeying south-westward, and did not pause, except for nights' lodgings, till he reached the town of Casterbridge, in a far distant part of Wessex.

III

The highroad into the village of Weydon-Priors was again carpeted with dust. The trees had put on as of yore their aspect of dingy green, and where the Henchard family of three had once walked along, two persons not unconnected with that family walked now.

The scene in its broad aspect had so much of its previous character, even to the voices and rattle from the neighbouring village down, that it might for that matter have been the afternoon following the previously recorded episode. Change was only to be observed in details; but here it was obvious that a long procession of years had passed by. One of the two who walked the road was she who had figured as the young wife of Henchard on the previous occasion; now her face had lost much of its rotundity; her skin had undergone a textural change; and though her hair had not lost colour it was considerably thinner than heretofore. She was dressed in the mourning clothes of a widow. Her companion, also in black, appeared as a well-formed young woman about eighteen, completely possessed of that ephemeral precious essence youth, which is itself beauty, irrespective of complexion or contour.

A glance was sufficient to inform the eye that this was Susan Henchard's grown-up daughter. While life's middle summer had set its hardening mark on the mother's face, her former spring-like specialities were transferred so dexterously by Time to the second figure, her child, that the absence of certain facts within her mother's knowledge from the girl's mind would have seemed for the moment, to one reflecting on those facts, to be a curious imperfection in Nature's powers of continuity.

They walked with joined hands, and it could be perceived that this was the act of simple affection. The daughter carried in her outer hand a withy basket[1] of old-fashioned make; the mother a blue bundle, which contrasted oddly with her black stuff gown.[2]

Reaching the outskirts of the village they pursued the same track as formerly, and ascended to the fair. Here, too, it was evident that the years had told. Certain mechanical improvements might have been noticed in the roundabouts and highfliers, machines for testing rustic strength and weight, and in the erections devoted to shooting for nuts. But the real business of the fair had considerably dwindled. The new periodical great markets of neighbouring towns were beginning to interfere seriously with the trade carried on here for centuries. The pens for sheep, the tie-ropes for horses, were about half as long as they had been. The stalls of tailors, hosiers, coopers,[3] linen-drapers, and other such trades had almost disappeared, and the vehicles were far less numerous. The mother and daughter threaded the crowd for some little distance, and then stood still.

'Why did we hinder our time by coming in here? I thought you wished to get onward?' said the maiden.

'Yes, my dear Elizabeth-Jane,' explained the other. 'But I had a fancy for looking up here.'

'Why?'

'It was here I first met with Newson—on such a day as this.'

'First met with father here? Yes, you have told me so before. And now he's drowned and gone from us!' As she spoke the girl drew a card from her pocket and looked at it with a sigh. It was edged with black, and inscribed within a design resembling a mural tablet were the words, 'In affectionate memory of Richard Newson, mariner, who was unfortunately lost at sea, in the month of November 184—, aged forty-one years.'

'And it was here,' continued her mother, with more hesitation, 'that I last saw the relation we are going to look for—Mr. Michael Henchard.'

'What is his exact kin to us, mother? I have never clearly had it told me.'

'He is, or was—for he may be dead—a connection by marriage,' said her mother deliberately.

'That's exactly what you have said a score of times before!' replied the young woman, looking about her inattentively. 'He's not a near relation, I suppose?'

'Not by any means.'

'He was a hay-trusser, wasn't he, when you last heard of him?'

'He was.'

'I suppose he never knew me?' the girl innocently continued.

1. Basket woven from willow branches.
2. Gown made from woollen cloth.
3. Barrel-makers.

Mrs. Henchard paused for a moment, and answered uneasily, 'Of course not, Elizabeth-Jane. But come this way.' She moved on to another part of the field.

'It is not much use inquiring here for anybody, I should think,' the daughter observed, as she gazed round about. 'People at fairs change like the leaves of trees; and I daresay you are the only one here to-day who was here all those years ago.'

'I am not so sure of that,' said Mrs. Newson, as she now called herself, keenly eyeing something under a green bank a little way off. 'See there.'

The daughter looked in the direction signified. The object pointed out was a tripod of sticks stuck into the earth, from which hung a three-legged crock, kept hot by a smouldering wood fire beneath. Over the pot stooped an old woman, haggard, wrinkled, and almost in rags. She stirred the contents of the pot with a large spoon, and occasionally croaked in a broken voice, 'Good furmity sold here!'

It was indeed the former mistress of the furmity tent—once thriving, cleanly, white-aproned, and chinking with money—now tentless, dirty, owning no tables or benches, and having scarce any customers except two small whitey-brown boys, who came up and asked for 'A ha'p'orth,[4] please—good measure,' which she served in a couple of chipped yellow basins of commonest clay.

'She was here at that time,' resumed Mrs. Newson, making a step as if to draw nearer.

'Don't speak to her—it isn't respectable!' urged the other.

'I will just say a word—you, Elizabeth-Jane, can stay here.'

The girl was not loth, and turned to some stalls of coloured prints while her mother went forward. The old woman begged for the latter's custom as soon as she saw her, and responded to Mrs. Henchard-Newson's request for a pennyworth with more alacrity than she had shown in selling six-pennyworths in her younger days. When the *soi-disant*[5] widow had taken the basin of thin poor slop that stood for the rich concoction of the former time, the hag opened a little basket behind the fire, and looking up slily, whispered, 'Just a thought o' rum in it?—smuggled, you know—say two penn'orth—'twill make it slip down like cordial!'[6]

Her customer smiled bitterly at this survival of the old trick, and shook her head with a meaning the old woman was far from translating. She pretended to eat a little of the furmity with the leaden spoon offered, and as she did so said blandly to the hag, 'You've seen better days?'

'Ah, ma'am—well ye may say it!' responded the old woman, opening the sluices of her heart forthwith. 'I've stood in this fair-ground, maid, wife, and widow, these nine-and-thirty year, and in that time have known

4. Half-penny's worth.
5. Self-styled (from the French).
6. Stimulating drink.

what it was to do business with the richest stomachs in the land! Ma'am, you'd hardly believe that I was once the owner of a great pavilion-tent that was the attraction of the fair. Nobody could come, nobody could go, without having a dish of Mrs. Goodenough's furmity. I knew the clergy's taste, the dandy gent's taste; I knew the town's taste, the country's taste. I even knowed the taste of the coarse shameless females. But Lord's my life—the world's no memory; straightforward dealings don't bring profit—'tis the sly and the underhand that get on in these times!'

Mrs. Newson glanced round—her daughter was still bending over the distant stalls. 'Can you call to mind,' she said cautiously to the old woman, 'the sale of a wife by her husband in your tent eighteen years ago to-day?'

The hag reflected, and half shook her head. 'If it had been a big thing I should have minded it in a moment,' she said. 'I can mind every serious fight o' married parties, every murder, every manslaughter, even every pocket-picking—leastwise large ones—that 't has been my lot to witness. But a selling? Was it done quiet-like?'

'Well, yes. I think so.'

The furmity woman half shook her head again. 'And yet,' she said, 'I do. At any rate, I can mind a man doing something o' the sort—a man in a cord jacket, with a basket of tools; but, Lord bless ye, we don't gi'e it head-room, we don't, such as that. The only reason why I can mind the man is that he came back here to the next year's fair, and told me quite private-like that if a woman ever asked for him I was to say he had gone to—where?—Casterbridge—yes—to Casterbridge, said he. But, Lord's my life, I shouldn't ha' thought of it again!'

Mrs. Newson would have rewarded the old woman as far as her small means afforded had she not discreetly borne in mind that it was by that unscrupulous person's liquor her husband had been degraded. She briefly thanked her informant, and rejoined Elizabeth, who greeted her with, 'Mother, do let's go on—it was hardly respectable for you to buy refreshments there. I see none but the lowest do.'

'I have learned what I wanted, however,' said her mother quietly. 'The last time our relative visited this fair he said he was living at Casterbridge. It is a long, long way from here, and it was many years ago that he said it; but there I think we'll go.'

With this they descended out of the fair, and went onward to the village, where they obtained a night's lodging.

IV

Henchard's wife acted for the best, but she had involved herself in difficulties. A hundred times she had been upon the point of telling her daughter Elizabeth-Jane the true story of her life, the tragical crisis of which had been the transaction at Weydon Fair, when she was not much older than the girl now beside her. But she had refrained. An innocent maiden had thus grown up in the belief that the relations between the genial sailor and her mother were the ordinary ones that they had always appeared to be. The risk of endangering a child's strong affection by disturbing ideas which had grown with her growth was to Mrs. Henchard too fearful a thing to contemplate. It had seemed, indeed, folly to think of making Elizabeth-Jane wise.[1]

But Susan Henchard's fear of losing her dearly loved daughter's heart by a revelation had little to do with any sense of wrong-doing on her own part. Her simplicity—the original ground of Henchard's contempt for her—had allowed her to live on in the conviction that Newson had acquired a morally real and justifiable right to her by his purchase—though the exact bearings and legal limits of that right were vague. It may seem strange to sophisticated minds that a sane young matron could believe in the seriousness of such a transfer; and were there not numerous other instances of the same belief the thing might scarcely be credited. But she was by no means the first or last peasant woman who had religiously adhered to her purchaser, as too many rural records show.

The history of Susan Henchard's adventures in the interim can be told in two or three sentences. Absolutely helpless she had been taken off to Canada, where they had lived several years without any great worldly success, though she worked as hard as any woman could to keep their cottage cheerful and well-provided. When Elizabeth-Jane was about twelve years old the three returned to England, and settled at Falmouth, where Newson made a living for a few years as boatman and general handy shoreman.

He then engaged in the Newfoundland trade,[2] and it was during this period that Susan had an awakening. A friend to whom she confided her history ridiculed her grave acceptance of her position; and all was over with her peace of mind. When Newson came home at the end of one winter he saw that the delusion he had so carefully sustained had vanished for ever.

There was then a time of sadness, in which she told him her doubts if she could live with him longer. Newson left home again on the Newfoundland trade when the season came round. The vague news of his loss at sea a little later on solved a problem which had become torture to her meek conscience. She saw him no more.

Of Henchard they heard nothing. To the liege subjects of Labour,[3] the England of those days was a continent, and a mile a geographical degree.[4]

---

1. Echo of the last two lines of Thomas Gray's "Ode on a Distant Prospect of Eton College" (1747): "where ignorance is bliss, / 'Tis folly to be wise."
2. Fishing.
3. Those obliged to work for a living.
4. Measure of distance (72 miles).

Elizabeth-Jane developed early into womanliness. One day, a month or so after receiving intelligence of Newson's death off the Bank of Newfoundland, when the girl was about eighteen, she was sitting on a willow chair in the cottage they still occupied, working twine nets for the fishermen. Her mother was in a back corner of the same room, engaged in the same labour; and dropping the heavy wood needle she was filling[5] she surveyed her daughter thoughtfully. The sun shone in at the door upon the young woman's head and hair, which was worn loose, so that the rays streamed into its depths as into a hazel copse. Her face, though somewhat wan and incomplete, possessed the raw materials of beauty in a promising degree. There was an under-handsomeness in it, struggling to reveal itself through the provisional curves of immaturity, and the casual disfigurements that resulted from the straitened circumstances of their lives. She was handsome in the bone, hardly as yet handsome in the flesh. She possibly might never be fully handsome, unless the carking[6] accidents of her daily existence could be evaded before the mobile parts of her countenance had settled to their final mould.

The sight of the girl made her mother sad—not vaguely, but by logical inference. They both were still in that strait-waistcoat of poverty from which she had tried so many times to be delivered for the girl's sake. The woman had long perceived how zealously and constantly the young mind of her companion was struggling for enlargement; and yet now, in her eighteenth year, it still remained but little unfolded. The desire— sober and repressed—of Elizabeth-Jane's heart was indeed to see, to hear, and to understand. How could she become a woman of wider knowledge, higher repute—'better,' as she termed it—this was her constant inquiry of her mother. She sought further into things than other girls in her position ever did, and her mother groaned as she felt she could not aid in the search.

The sailor, drowned or no, was probably now lost to them; and Susan's staunch, religious adherence to him as her husband in principle, till her views had been disturbed by enlightenment, was demanded no more. She asked herself whether the present moment, now that she was a free woman again, were not as opportune a one as she would find in a world where everything had been so inopportune, for making a desperate effort to advance Elizabeth. To pocket her pride and search for the first husband seemed, wisely or not, the best initiatory step. He had possibly drunk himself into his tomb. But he might, on the other hand, have had too much sense to do so; for in her time with him he had been given to bouts only, and was not a habitual drunkard.

At any rate, the propriety of returning to him, if he lived, was unquestionable. The awkwardness of searching for him lay in enlightening

5. Threading with twine.
6. Harassing, wearing.

Elizabeth, a proceeding which her mother could not endure to contemplate. She finally resolved to undertake the search without confiding
to the girl her former relations with Henchard, leaving it to him if they
found him to take what steps he might choose to that end. This will
account for their conversation at the fair and the half-informed state in
which Elizabeth was led onward.

In this attitude they proceeded on their journey, trusting solely to the
dim light afforded of Henchard's whereabouts by the furmity woman.
The strictest economy was indispensable. Sometimes they might have
been seen on foot, sometimes on farmers' waggons, sometimes in carriers' vans; and thus they drew near to Casterbridge. Elizabeth-Jane discovered to her alarm that her mother's health was not what it once had
been, and there was ever and anon in her talk that renunciatory tone
which showed that, but for the girl, she would not be very sorry to quit a
life she was growing thoroughly weary of.

It was on a Friday evening, near the middle of September, and just
before dusk, that they reached the summit of a hill within a mile of the
place they sought. There were high-banked hedges to the coach-road
here, and they mounted upon the green turf within, and sat down. The
spot commanded a full view of the town and its environs.

'What an old-fashioned place it seems to be!' said Elizabeth-Jane,
while her silent mother mused on other things than topography. 'It is
huddled all together; and it is shut in by a square wall of trees, like a plot
of garden ground by a box-edging.'

Its squareness was, indeed, the characteristic which most struck the
eye in this antiquated borough, the borough of Casterbridge—at that
time, recent as it was, untouched by the faintest sprinkle of modernism.
It was compact as a box of dominoes. It had no suburbs—in the ordinary
sense. Country and town met at a mathematical line.

To birds of the more soaring kind Casterbridge must have appeared
on this fine evening as a mosaic-work of subdued reds, browns, greys,
and crystals, held together by a rectangular frame of deep green. To the
level eye of humanity it stood as an indistinct mass behind a dense stockade of limes and chestnuts, set in the midst of miles of rotund down and
concave field. The mass became gradually dissected by the vision into
towers, gables, chimneys, and casements, the highest glazings shining
bleared and bloodshot with the coppery fire they caught from the belt of
sunlit cloud in the west.

From the centre of each side of this tree-bound square ran avenues
east, west, and south into the wide expanse of corn-land and coomb[7] to
the distance of a mile or so. It was by one of these avenues that the pedestrians were about to enter. Before they had risen to proceed two men
passed outside the hedge, engaged in argumentative conversation.

7. Deep hollow or valley.

'Why, surely,' said Elizabeth, as they receded, 'those men mentioned the name of Henchard in their talk—the name of our relative?'

'I thought so too,' said Mrs. Newson.

'That seems a hint to us that he is still here.'

'Yes.'

'Shall I run after them, and ask them about him——'

'No, no, no! Not for the world just yet. He may be in the workhouse, or in the stocks, for all we know.'

'Dear me—why should you think that, mother?'

''Twas just something to say—that's all! But we must make private inquiries.'

Having sufficiently rested they proceeded on their way at evenfall. The dense trees of the avenue rendered the road dark as a tunnel, though the open land on each side was still under a faint daylight; in other words, they passed down a midnight between two gloamings. The features of the town had a keen interest for Elizabeth's mother, now that the human side came to the fore. As soon as they had wandered about they could see that the stockade of gnarled trees which framed in Casterbridge was itself an avenue, standing on a low green bank or escarpment, with a ditch yet visible without. Within the avenue and bank was a wall more or less discontinuous, and within the wall were packed the abodes of the burghers.

Though the two women did not know it these external features were but the ancient defences of the town, planted as a promenade.

The lamplights now glimmered through the engirdling trees, conveying a sense of great snugness and comfort inside, and rendering at the same time the unlighted country without strangely solitary and vacant in aspect, considering its nearness to life. The difference between burgh and champaign[8] was increased, too, by sounds which now reached them above others—the notes of a brass band. The travellers returned into the High Street, where there were timber houses with overhanging stories, whose small-paned lattices were screened by dimity[9] curtains on a drawing-string, and under whose barge-boards[1] old cobwebs waved in the breeze. There were houses of brick-nogging,[2] which derived their chief support from those adjoining. There were slate roofs patched with tiles, and tile roofs patched with slate, with occasionally a roof of thatch.[3]

The agricultural and pastoral character of the people upon whom the town depended for its existence was shown by the class of objects displayed in the shop windows. Scythes, reap-hooks, sheep-shears, bill-hooks,[4] spades, mattocks, and hoes at the iron-monger's; bee-hives, butter-

8. Town and countryside.
9. Cotton fabric, made to appear patterned by the use of two threads woven together.
1. Boards used to conceal jutting roof-timbers, and usually decorated by carvings.
2. Brickwork filled between wooden frames.
3. Most of these old houses have now been pulled down [Hardy's note].
4. Heavy knives with hooked ends.

firkins,[5] churns, milking stools and pails, hay-rakes, field-flagons,[6] and seed-lips[7] at the cooper's; cart-ropes and plough-harness at the saddler's; carts, wheel-barrows, and mill-gear at the wheelwright's and machinist's; horse-embrocations at the chemist's; at the glover's and leather-cutter's, hedging-gloves, thatchers' knee-caps, ploughmen's leggings, villagers' pattens[8] and clogs.

They came to a grizzled church, whose massive square tower rose unbroken into the darkening sky, the lower parts being illuminated by the nearest lamps sufficiently to show how completely the mortar from the joints of the stonework had been nibbled out by time and weather, which had planted in the crevices thus made little tufts of stone-crop and grass almost as far up as the very battlements. From this tower the clock struck eight, and thereupon a bell began to toll with a peremptory clang. The curfew[9] was still rung in Casterbridge, and it was utilized by the inhabitants as a signal for shutting their shops. No sooner did the deep notes of the bell throb between the house-fronts than a clatter of shutters arose through the whole length of the High Street. In a few minutes business at Casterbridge was ended for the day.

Other clocks struck eight from time to time—one gloomily from the gaol, another from the gable of an almshouse, with a preparative creak of machinery, more audible than the note of the bell; a row of tall, varnished case-clocks from the interior of a clock-maker's shop joined in one after another just as the shutters were enclosing them, like a row of actors delivering their final speeches before the fall of the curtain; then chimes were heard stammering out the Sicilian Mariners' Hymn;[1] so that chronologists of the advanced school were appreciably on their way to the next hour before the whole business of the old one was satisfactorily wound up.

In an open space before the church walked a woman with her gown-sleeves rolled up so high that the edge of her under-linen was visible, and her skirt tucked up through her pocket hole. She carried a loaf under her arm from which she was pulling pieces of bread, and handling them to some other women who walked with her; which pieces they nibbled critically. The sight reminded Mrs. Henchard-Newson and her daughter that they had an appetite; and they inquired of the woman for the nearest baker's.

'Ye may as well look for manna-food[2] as good bread in Casterbridge just now,' she said, after directing them. 'They can blare their trumpets

---

5. Small casks.
6. Bottles (of beer) used by fieldworkers.
7. Baskets used to carry seed when sowing by hand.
8. Wooden-soled overshoes.
9. In medieval times, the bell rung as a signal to extinguish household fires.
1. These chimes, like those of other country churches, have been silenced for many years [Hardy's note]. Hymn beginning "Lord, dismiss us with thy blessing," used to close a religious service.
2. Food provided miraculously for the Israelites in the wilderness; see Exodus 16.14–26.

and thump their drums, and have their roaring dinners'—waving her hand towards a point further along the street, where the brass band could be seen standing in front of an illuminated building—'but we must needs be put-to for want of a wholesome crust. There's less good bread than good beer in Casterbridge now.'

'And less good beer than swipes,'[3] said a man with his hands in his pockets.

'How does it happen there's no good bread?' asked Mrs. Henchard.

'Oh, 'tis the corn-factor[4]—he's the man that our millers and bakers all deal wi', and he has sold 'em growed wheat,[5] which they didn't know was growed, so they *say*, till the dough ran all over the ovens like quicksilver; so that the loaves be as flat as toads, and like suet pudden inside. I've been a wife, and I've been a mother, and I never see such unprincipled bread in Casterbridge as this before.—But you must be a real stranger here not to know what's made all the poor volks' insides plim[6] like blowed bladders this week?'

'I am,' said Elizabeth's mother shyly.

Not wishing to be observed further till she knew more of her future in this place, she withdrew with her daughter from the speaker's side. Getting a couple of biscuits at the shop indicated as a temporary substitute for a meal, they next bent their steps instinctively to where the music was playing.

V

A few score yards brought them to the spot where the town band was now shaking the window-panes with the strains of 'The Roast Beef of Old England.'[1]

The building before whose doors they had pitched their music-stands was the chief hotel in Casterbridge—namely, the King's Arms. A spacious bow-window projected into the street over the main portico, and from the open sashes came the babble of voices, the jingle of glasses, and the drawing of corks. The blinds, moreover, being left unclosed, the whole interior of this room could be surveyed from the top of a flight of stone steps to the road-waggon office opposite, for which reason a knot of idlers had gathered there.

'We might, perhaps, after all, make a few inquiries about—our relation Mr. Henchard,' whispered Mrs. Newson who, since her entry into Casterbridge, had seemed strangely weak and agitated. 'And this, I think, would be a good place for trying it—just to ask, you know, how he stands

3. Weak or poor-quality beer.
4. Dealer in corn or grain.
5. Wheat that has sprouted before harvesting.
6. Swell up.
1. Song from *The Grub-Street Opera* (1731), words by Henry Fielding, music by Richard Leveridge.

in the town—if he is here, as I think he must be. You, Elizabeth-Jane, had better be the one to do it. I'm too worn out to do anything—pull down your fall[2] first.'

She sat down upon the lowest step, and Elizabeth-Jane obeyed her directions and stood among the idlers.

'What's going on to-night?' asked the girl, after singling out an old man and standing by him long enough to acquire a neighbourly right of converse.

'Well, ye must be a stranger sure,' said the old man, without taking his eyes from the window. 'Why, 'tis a great public dinner of the gentle-people and such like leading volk—wi' the Mayor in the chair. As we plainer fellows bain't invited, they leave the winder-shutters open that we may get jist a sense o't out here. If you mount the steps you can see 'em. That's Mr. Henchard, the Mayor, at the end of the table, a facing ye; and that's the Council men right and left. . . . Ah, lots of them when they begun life were no more than I be now!'

'Henchard!' said Elizabeth-Jane, surprised, but by no means suspect-ing the whole force of the revelation. She ascended to the top of the steps.

Her mother, though her head was bowed, had already caught from the inn-window tones that strangely riveted her attention, before the old man's words, 'Mr. Henchard, the Mayor,' reached her ears. She arose, and stepped up to her daughter's side as soon as she could do so without showing exceptional eagerness.

The interior of the hotel dining-room was spread out before her, with its tables, and glass, and plate, and inmates. Facing the window, in the chair of dignity, sat a man about forty years of age; of heavy frame, large features, and commanding voice; his general build being rather coarse than compact. He had a rich complexion, which verged on swarthiness, a flashing black eye, and dark, bushy brows and hair. When he indulged in an occasional loud laugh at some remark among the guests, his large mouth parted so far back as to show to the rays of the chandelier a full score or more of the two-and-thirty sound white teeth that he obviously still could boast of.

That laugh was not encouraging to strangers; and hence it may have been well that it was rarely heard. Many theories might have been built upon it. It fell in well with conjectures of a temperament which would have no pity for weakness, but would be ready to yield ungrudging admi-ration to greatness and strength. Its producer's personal goodness, if he had any, would be of a very fitful cast—an occasional almost oppressive generosity rather than a mild and constant kindness.

Susan Henchard's husband—in law, at least—sat before them, matured in shape, stiffened in line, exaggerated in traits; disciplined,

2. Veil attached to a woman's bonnet.

thought-marked—in a word, older. Elizabeth, encumbered with no recollections as her mother was, regarded him with nothing more than the keen curiosity and interest which the discovery of such unexpected social standing in the long-sought relative naturally begot. He was dressed in an old-fashioned evening suit, an expanse of frilled shirt showing on his broad breast; jewelled studs, and a heavy gold chain. Three glasses stood at his right hand; but, to his wife's surprise, the two for wine were empty, while the third, a tumbler, was half full of water.

When last she had seen him he was sitting in a corduroy jacket, fustian waistcoat and breeches, and tanned leather leggings, with a basin of hot furmity before him. Time, the magician, had wrought much here. Watching him, and thus thinking of past days, she became so moved that she shrank back against the jamb of the waggon-office doorway to which the steps gave access, the shadow from it conveniently hiding her features. She forgot her daughter till a touch from Elizabeth-Jane aroused her. 'Have you seen him, mother?' whispered the girl.

'Yes, yes,' answered her companion hastily. 'I have seen him, and it is enough for me! Now I only want to go—pass away—die.'

'Why—O what?' She drew closer, and whispered in her mother's ear, 'Does he seem to you not likely to befriend us? I thought he looked a generous man. What a gentleman he is, isn't he? and how his diamond studs shine! How strange that you should have said he might be in the stocks, or in the workhouse, or dead! Did ever anything go more by contraries! Why do you feel so afraid of him? I am not at all; I'll call upon him—he can but say he don't own such remote kin.'

'I don't know at all—I can't tell what to set about. I feel so down.'

'Don't be that, mother, now we have got here and all! Rest there where you be a little while—I will look on and find out more about him.'

'I don't think I can ever meet Mr. Henchard. He is not how I thought he would be—he overpowers me! I don't wish to see him any more.'

'But wait a little time and consider.'

Elizabeth-Jane had never been so much interested in anything in her life as in their present position, partly from the natural elation she felt at discovering herself akin to a coach;[3] and she gazed again at the scene. The younger guests were talking and eating with animation; their elders were searching for titbits, and sniffing and grunting over their plates like sows nuzzling for acorns. Three drinks seemed to be sacred to the company—port, sherry, and rum; outside which old-established trinity few or no palates ranged.

A row of ancient rummers[4] with ground figures on their sides, and each primed with a spoon, was now placed down the table, and these

---

3. Related to someone of wealth or importance enough to ride in an official coach (here, the mayoral coach).
4. Large drinking glasses.

were promptly filled with grog[5] at such high temperatures as to raise serious considerations for the articles exposed to its vapours. But Elizabeth-Jane noticed that, though this filling went on with great promptness up and down the table, nobody filled the Mayor's glass, who still drank large quantities of water from the tumbler behind the clump of crystal vessels intended for wine and spirits.

'They don't fill Mr. Henchard's wine-glasses,' she ventured to say to her elbow acquaintance, the old man.

'Ah, no; don't ye know him to be the celebrated abstaining worthy of that name? He scorns all tempting liquors; never touches nothing. O yes, he've strong qualities that way. I have heard tell that he sware a gospel oath in by-gone times, and has bode by it ever since. So they don't press him, knowing it would be unbecoming in the face of that; for yer gospel oath is a serious thing.'

Another elderly man, hearing this discourse, now joined in by inquiring, 'How much longer have he got to suffer from it, Solomon Longways?'

'Another two year, they say. I don't know the why and the wherefore of his fixing such a time, for 'a never has told anybody. But 'tis exactly two calendar years longer, they say. A powerful mind to hold out so long!'

'True. . . . But there's great strength in hope. Knowing that in four-and-twenty months' time ye'll be out of your bondage, and able to make up for all you've suffered, by partaking without stint—why, it keeps a man up, no doubt.'

'No doubt, Christopher Coney, no doubt. And 'a must need such reflections—a lonely widow man,' said Longways.

'When did he lose his wife?' asked Elizabeth.

'I never knowed her. 'Twas afore he came to Casterbridge,' Solomon Longways replied with terminative emphasis, as if the fact of his ignorance of Mrs. Henchard were sufficient to deprive her history of all interest. 'But I know that 'a's a banded[6] tee-totaller, and that if any of his men be ever so little overtook by a drop he's down upon 'em as stern as the Lord upon the jovial Jews.'[7]

'Has he many men, then?' said Elizabeth-Jane.

'Many! Why, my good maid, he's the powerfullest member of the Town Council, and quite a principal man in the country round besides. Never a big dealing in wheat, barley, oats, hay, roots, and such-like but Henchard's got a hand in it. Ay, and he'll go into other things too; and that's where he makes his mistake. He worked his way up from nothing when 'a came here; and now he's a pillar of the town. Not but what he's

5. Rum or other spirit diluted with water.
6. Bound by a pledge.
7. A reference to Jehovah's anger at the Israelites, who made and worshipped a golden calf while Moses was receiving the Ten Commandments on Mount Sinai. See Exodus 32.

been shaken a little to-year[8] about this bad corn he has supplied in his contracts. I've seen the sun rise over Durnover Moor these nine-and-sixty year, and though Mr. Henchard has never cussed me unfairly ever since I've worked for'n, seeing I be but a little small man, I must say that I have never before tasted such rough bread as has been made from Henchard's wheat lately. 'Tis that growed out that ye could a'most call it malt, and there's a list[9] at bottom o' the loaf as thick as the sole of one's shoe.'

The band now struck up another melody, and by the time it was ended the dinner was over, and speeches began to be made. The evening being calm, and the windows still open, these orations could be distinctly heard. Henchard's voice arose above the rest; he was telling a story of his hay-dealing experiences, in which he had outwitted a sharper who had been bent upon outwitting him.

'Ha-ha-ha!' responded his audience at the upshot of the story; and hilarity was general till a new voice arose with, 'This is all very well; but how about the bad bread?'

It came from the lower end of the table, where there sat a group of minor tradesmen who, although part of the company, appeared to be a little below the social level of the others; and who seemed to nourish a certain independence of opinion and carry on discussions not quite in harmony with those at the head; just as the west end of a church is sometimes persistently found to sing out of time and tune with the leading spirits in the chancel.

This interruption about the bad bread afforded infinite satisfaction to the loungers outside, several of whom were in the mood which finds its pleasure in others' discomfiture; and hence they echoed pretty freely, 'Hey! How about the bad bread, Mr. Mayor?' Moreover, feeling none of the restraints of those who shared the feast, they could afford to add, 'You rather ought to tell the story o' that, sir!'

The interruption was sufficient to compel the Mayor to notice it.

'Well, I admit that the wheat turned out badly,' he said. 'But I was taken in in buying it as much as the bakers who bought it o' me.'

'And the poor folk who had to eat it whether or no,' said the inharmonious man outside the window.

Henchard's face darkened. There was temper under the thin bland surface—the temper which, artificially intensified, had banished a wife nearly a score of years before.

'You must make allowances for the accidents of a large business,' he said. 'You must bear in mind that the weather just at the harvest of that corn was worse than we have known it for years. However, I have mended my arrangements on account o't. Since I have found my business too large to be well looked after by myself alone, I have advertised for a thorough good man as manager of the corn department. When I've got him you will find these mistakes will no longer occur—matters will be better looked into.'

'But what are you going to do to repay us for the past?' inquired the man who had before spoken, and who seemed to be a baker or miller. 'Will you replace the grown flour we've still got by sound grain?'

Henchard's face had become still more stern at these interruptions, and he drank from his tumbler of water as if to calm himself or gain time. Instead of vouchsafing a direct reply, he stiffly observed—

'If anybody will tell me how to turn grown wheat into wholesome wheat I'll take it back with pleasure. But it can't be done.'

Henchard was not to be drawn again. Having said this, he sat down.

VI

Now the group outside the window had within the last few minutes been reinforced by new arrivals, some of them respectable shopkeepers and their assistants, who had come out for a whiff of air after putting up the shutters for the night; some of them of a lower class. Distinct from either there appeared a stranger—a young man of remarkably pleasant aspect—who carried in his hand a carpet-bag of the smart floral pattern prevalent in such articles at that time.

He was ruddy and of a fair countenance,[1] bright-eyed, and slight in build. He might possibly have passed by without stopping at all, or at most for half a minute to glance in at the scene, had not his advent coincided with the discussion on corn and bread; in which event this history had never been enacted. But the subject seemed to arrest him, and he whispered some inquiries of the other bystanders, and remained listening.

When he heard Henchard's closing words, 'It can't be done,' he smiled impulsively, drew out his pocket-book, and wrote down a few words by the aid of the light in the window. He tore out the leaf, folded and directed it, and seemed about to throw it in through the open sash upon the dining-table; but, on second thoughts, edged himself through the loiterers, till he reached the door of the hotel, where one of the waiters who had been serving inside was now idly leaning against the door-post.

'Give this to the Mayor at once,' he said, handing in his hasty note.

Elizabeth-Jane had seen his movements and heard the words, which attracted her both by their subject and by their accent—a strange one for those parts. It was quaint and northerly.

---

1. An echo of descriptions of David, at first the friend but later the rival of Saul. See 1 Samuel 16.12 and 17.42.

The waiter took the note, while the young stranger continued—

'And can ye tell me of a respectable hotel that's a little more moderate than this?'

The waiter glanced indifferently up and down the street.

'They say the Three Mariners, just below here, is a very good place,' he languidly answered; 'but I have never stayed there myself.'

The Scotchman, as he seemed to be, thanked him, and strolled on in the direction of the Three Mariners aforesaid, apparently more concerned about the question of an inn than about the fate of his note, now that the momentary impulse of writing it was over. While he was disappearing slowly down the street the waiter left the door, and Elizabeth-Jane saw with some interest the note brought into the dining-room and handed to the Mayor.

Henchard looked at it carelessly, unfolded it with one hand, and glanced it through. Thereupon it was curious to note an unexpected effect. The nettled, clouded aspect which had held possession of his face since the subject of his corn-dealings had been broached, changed itself into one of arrested attention. He read the note slowly, and fell into thought, not moody, but fitfully intense, as that of a man who has been captured by an idea.

By this time toasts and speeches had given place to songs, the wheat subject being quite forgotten. Men were putting their heads together in twos and threes, telling good stories, with pantomimic laughter which reached convulsive grimace. Some were beginning to look as if they did not know how they had come there, what they had come for, or how they were going to get home again; and provisionally sat on with a dazed smile. Square-built men showed a tendency to become hunchbacks; men with a dignified presence lost it in a curious obliquity of figure, in which their features grew disarranged and one-sided; whilst the heads of a few who had dined with extreme thoroughness were somehow sinking into their shoulders, the corners of their mouth and eyes being bent upwards by the subsidence. Only Henchard did not conform to these flexuous changes; he remained stately and vertical, silently thinking.

The clock struck nine. Elizabeth-Jane turned to her companion. 'The evening is drawing on, mother,' she said. 'What do you propose to do?'

She was surprised to find how irresolute her mother had become. 'We must get a place to lie down in,' she murmured. 'I have seen—Mr. Henchard; and that's all I wanted to do.'

'That's enough for to-night, at any rate,' Elizabeth-Jane replied soothingly. 'We can think to-morrow what is best to do about him. The question now is—is it not?—how shall we find a lodging?'

As her mother did not reply Elizabeth-Jane's mind reverted to the words of the waiter, that the Three Mariners was an inn of moderate charges. A recommendation good for one person was probably good for another. 'Let's go where the young man has gone to,' she said. 'He is respectable. What do you say?'

Her mother assented, and down the street they went.

In the meantime the Mayor's thoughtfulness, engendered by the note as stated, continued to hold him in abstraction; till, whispering to his neighbour to take his place, he found opportunity to leave the chair. This was just after the departure of his wife and Elizabeth.

Outside the door of the assembly-room he saw the waiter, and beckoning to him asked who brought the note which had been handed in a quarter of an hour before.

'A young man, sir—a sort of traveller. He was a Scotchman seemingly.'

'Did he say how he had got it?'

'He wrote it himself, sir, as he stood outside the window.'

'Oh—wrote it himself. . . . Is the young man in the hotel?'

'No, sir. He went to the Three Mariners, I believe.'

The Mayor walked up and down the vestibule of the hotel with his hands under his coat tails, as if he were merely seeking a cooler atmosphere than that of the room he had quitted. But there could be no doubt that he was in reality still possessed to the full by the new idea, whatever that might be. At length he went back to the door of the dining-room, paused, and found that the songs, toasts, and conversation were proceeding quite satisfactorily without his presence. The Corporation,[2] private residents, and major and minor tradesmen had, in fact, gone in for comforting beverages to such an extent that they had quite forgotten, not only the Mayor, but all those vast political, religious, and social differences which they felt necessary to maintain in the daytime, and which separated them like iron grills. Seeing this the Mayor took his hat, and when the waiter had helped him on with a thin holland[3] overcoat, went out and stood under the portico.

Very few persons were now in the street; and his eyes, by a sort of attraction, turned and dwelt upon a spot about a hundred yards further down. It was the house to which the writer of the note had gone— the Three Mariners—whose two prominent Elizabethan gables, bow-window, and passage-light could be seen from where he stood. Having kept his eyes on it for a while he strolled in that direction.

This ancient house of accommodation for man and beast, now, unfortunately, pulled down, was built of mellow sandstone, with mullioned[4] windows of the same material, markedly out of perpendicular from the settlement of foundations. The bay window projecting into the street, whose interior was so popular among the frequenters of the inn, was closed with shutters, in each of which appeared a heart-shaped aperture, somewhat more attenuated in the right and left ventricles than is seen in

2. Members of the Town Council.
3. Linen.
4. Divided by vertical stone uprights.

Nature. Inside these illuminated holes, at a distance of about three inches, were ranged at this hour, as every passer knew, the ruddy polls[5] of Billy Wills the glazier, Smart the shoe-maker, Buzzford the general dealer, and others of a secondary set of worthies, of a grade somewhat below that of the diners at the King's Arms, each with his yard of clay.[6]

A four-centered Tudor arch was over the entrance, and over the arch the signboard, now visible in the rays of an opposite lamp. Hereon the Mariners, who had been represented by the artist as persons of two dimensions only—in other words, flat as a shadow—were standing in a row in paralyzed attitudes. Being on the sunny side of the street the three comrades had suffered largely from warping, splitting, fading, and shrinkage, so that they were but a half-invisible film upon the reality of the grain, and knots, and nails, which composed the signboard. As a matter of fact, this state of things was not so much owing to Stannidge the landlord's neglect, as from the lack of a painter in Casterbridge who would undertake to reproduce the features of men so traditional.

A long, narrow, dimly-lit passage gave access to the inn, within which passage the horses going to their stalls at the back, and the coming and departing human guests, rubbed shoulders indiscriminately, the latter running no slight risk of having their toes trodden upon by the animals. The good stabling and the good ale of the Mariners, though somewhat difficult to reach on account of there being but this narrow way to both, were nevertheless perseveringly sought out by the sagacious old heads who knew what was what in Casterbridge.

Henchard stood without the inn for a few instants; then lowering the dignity of his presence as much as possible by buttoning the brown holland coat over his shirt-front, and in other ways toning himself down to his ordinary everyday appearance, he entered the inn door.

VII

Elizabeth-Jane and her mother had arrived some twenty minutes earlier. Outside the house they had stood and considered whether even this homely place, though recommended as moderate, might not be too serious in its prices for their light pockets. Finally, however, they had found courage to enter, and duly met Stannidge the landlord; a silent man, who drew and carried frothing measures to this room and to that, shoulder to shoulder with his waiting-maids—a stately slowness, however, entering into his ministrations by contrast with theirs, as became one whose service was somewhat optional. It would have been altogether optional but for the orders of the landlady, a person who sat in the bar, corporeally motionless, but with a flitting eye and quick ear, with which she observed and heard through the open door and hatchway the press-

5. Heads.
6. Long clay pipe for tobacco.

ing needs of customers whom her husband overlooked though close at hand. Elizabeth and her mother were passively accepted as sojourners, and shown to a small bedroom under one of the gables, where they sat down.

The principle of the inn seemed to be to compensate for the antique awkwardness, crookedness, and obscurity of the passages, floors, and windows, by quantities of clean linen spread about everywhere, and this had a dazzling effect upon the travellers.

'Tis too good for us—we can't meet it!' said the elder woman, looking round the apartment with misgiving as soon as they were left alone.

'I fear it is, too,' said Elizabeth. 'But we must be respectable.'

'We must pay our way even before we must be respectable,' replied her mother. 'Mr. Henchard is too high for us to make ourselves known to him, I much fear; so we've only our own pockets to depend on.'

'I know what I'll do,' said Elizabeth-Jane after an interval of waiting, during which their needs seemed quite forgotten under the press of business below. And leaving the room, she descended the stairs and penetrated to the bar.

If there was one good thing more than another which characterized this single-hearted girl it was a willingness to sacrifice her personal comfort and dignity to the common weal.

'As you seem busy here to-night, and mother's not well off, might I take out part of our accommodation by helping?' she asked of the landlady.

The latter, who remained as fixed in the arm-chair as if she had been melted into it when in a liquid state, and could not now be unstuck, looked the girl up and down inquiringly, with her hands on the chair-arms. Such arrangements as the one Elizabeth proposed were not uncommon in country villages; but, though Casterbridge was old-fashioned, the custom was well-nigh obsolete here. The mistress of the house, however, was an easy woman to strangers, and she made no objection. Thereupon Elizabeth, being instructed by nods and motions from the taciturn landlord as to where she could find the different things, trotted up and down stairs with materials for her own and her parent's meal.

While she was doing this the wood partition in the centre of the house thrilled to its centre with the tugging of a bell-pull upstairs. A bell below tinkled a note that was feebler in sound than the twanging of wires and cranks that had produced it.

'Tis the Scotch gentleman,' said the landlady omnisciently; and turning her eyes to Elizabeth, 'Now then, can you go and see if his supper is on the tray? If it is you can take it up to him. The front room over this.'

Elizabeth-Jane, though hungry, willingly postponed serving herself awhile, and applied to the cook in the kitchen, whence she brought forth the tray of supper viands, and proceeded with it upstairs to the apartment indicated. The accommodation of the Three Mariners was far from spacious, despite the fair area of ground it covered. The room demanded by intrusive beams and rafters, partitions, passages, staircases, disused ovens, settles,[1] and four-posters, left comparatively small quarters for human beings. Moreover, this being at a time before home-brewing was abandoned by the smaller victuallers, and a house in which the twelve-bushel strength[2] was still religiously adhered to by the landlord in his ale, the quality of the liquor was the chief attraction of the premises, so that everything had to make way for utensils and operations in connection therewith. Thus Elizabeth found that the Scotchman was located in a room quite close to the small one that had been allotted to herself and her mother.

When she entered nobody was present but the young man himself— the same whom she had seen lingering without the windows of the King's Arms Hotel. He was now idly reading a copy of the local paper, and was hardly conscious of her entry, so that she looked at him quite coolly, and saw how his forehead shone where the light caught it, and how nicely his hair was cut, and the sort of velvet-pile or down that was on the skin at the back of his neck, and how his cheek was so truly curved as to be part of a globe, and how clearly drawn were the lids and lashes which hid his bent eyes.

She set down the tray, spread his supper, and went away without a word. On her arrival below the landlady, who was as kind as she was fat and lazy, saw that Elizabeth-Jane was rather tired, though in her earnestness to be useful she was waiving her own needs altogether. Mrs. Stannidge thereupon said with a considerate peremptoriness that she and her mother had better take their own suppers if they meant to have any.

Elizabeth fetched their simple provisions, as she had fetched the Scotchman's, and went up to the little chamber where she had left her mother, noiselessly pushing open the door with the edge of the tray. To her surprise her mother, instead of being reclined on the bed where she had left her, was in an erect position, with lips parted. At Elizabeth's entry she lifted her finger.

The meaning of this was soon apparent. The room allotted to the two women had at one time served as a dressing-room to the Scotchman's chamber, as was evidenced by signs of a door of communication between them—now screwed up and pasted over with the wall paper. But, as is frequently the case with hotels of far higher pretensions than the Three Mariners, every word spoken in either of these rooms was distinctly audible in the other. Such sounds came through now.

1. High-backed wooden seats for two or more people.
2. Good quality (the strength of beer is measured by the amount of malt used in the brewing process).

Thus silently conjured Elizabeth deposited the tray, and her mother whispered as she drew near, ''Tis he.'

'Who?' said the girl.

'The Mayor.'

The tremors in Susan Henchard's tone might have led any person but one so perfectly unsuspicious of the truth as the girl was, to surmise some closer connection than the admitted simple kinship as a means of accounting for them.

Two men were indeed talking in the adjoining chamber, the young Scotchman and Henchard, who, having entered the inn while Elizabeth-Jane was in the kitchen waiting for the supper, had been deferentially conducted upstairs by host Stannidge himself. The girl noiselessly laid out their little meal, and beckoned to her mother to join her, which Mrs. Henchard mechanically did, her attention being fixed on the conversation through the door.

'I merely strolled in on my way home to ask you a question about something that has excited my curiosity,' said the Mayor, with careless geniality. 'But I see you have not finished supper.'

'Ay, but I will be done in a little! Ye needn't go, sir. Take a seat. I've almost done, and it makes no difference at all.'

Henchard seemed to take the seat offered, and in a moment he resumed: 'Well, first I should ask, did you write this?' A rustling of paper followed.

'Yes, I did,' said the Scotchman.

'Then,' said Henchard, 'I am under the impression that we have met by accident while waiting for the morning to keep an appointment with each other? My name is Henchard; ha'n't you replied to an advertisement for a corn-factor's manager that I put into the paper—ha'n't you come here to see me about it?'

'No,' said the Scotchman, with some surprise.

'Surely you are the man,' went on Henchard insistingly, 'who arranged to come and see me? Joshua, Joshua, Jipp—Jopp—what was his name?'

'You're wrong!' said the young man. 'My name is Donald Farfrae. It is true I am in the corren trade—but I have replied to no advairrtisment, and arranged to see no one. I am on my way to Bristol—from there to the other side of the warrld, to try my fortune in the great wheat-growing districts of the West! I have some inventions useful to the trade, and there is no scope for developing them heere.'

'To America—well, well,' said Henchard, in a tone of disappointment, so strong as to make itself felt like a damp atmosphere. 'And yet I could have sworn you were the man!'

The Scotchman murmured another negative, and there was a silence, till Henchard resumed: 'Then I am truly and sincerely obliged to you for the few words you wrote on that paper.'

'It was nothing, sir.'

'Well, it has a great importance for me just now. This row about my grown wheat, which I declare to Heaven I didn't know to be bad till the people came complaining, has put me to my wits' end. I've some hundreds of quarters[3] of it on hand; and if your renovating process will make it wholesome, why, you can see what a quag[4] 'twould get me out of. I saw in a moment there might be truth in it. But I should like to have it proved; and of course you don't care to tell the steps of the process sufficiently for me to do that, without my paying ye well for't first.'

The young man reflected a moment or two. 'I don't know that I have any objection,' he said. 'I'm going to another country, and curing bad corn is not the line I'll take up there. Yes, I'll tell ye the whole of it— you'll make more out of it heere than I will in a foreign country. Just look heere a minute, sir. I can show ye by a sample in my carpet-bag.'

The click of a lock followed, and there was a sifting and rustling; then a discussion about so many ounces to the bushel, and drying, and refrigerating, and so on.

'These few grains will be sufficient to show ye with,' came in the young fellow's voice; and after a pause, during which some operation seemed to be intently watched by them both, he exclaimed, 'There, now, do you taste that.'

'It's complete!—quite restored, or—well—nearly.'

'Quite enough restored to make good seconds out of it,' said the Scotchman. 'To fetch it back entirely is impossible; Nature won't stand so much as that, but heere you go a great way towards it. Well, sir, that's the process; I don't value it, for it can be but of little use in countries where the weather is more settled than in ours; and I'll be only too glad if it's of service to you.'

'But hearken to me,' pleaded Henchard. 'My business, you know, is in corn and in hay; but I was brought up as a hay-trusser simply, and hay is what I understand best, though I now do more in corn than in the other. If you'll accept the place, you shall manage the corn branch entirely, and receive a commission in addition to salary.'

'You're liberal—very liberal; but no, no—I cannet!' the young man still replied, with some distress in his accents.

'So be it!' said Henchard conclusively. 'Now—to change the subject—one good turn deserves another; don't stay to finish that miserable supper. Come to my house; I can find something better for 'ee than cold ham and ale.'

Donald Farfrae was grateful—said he feared he must decline—that he wished to leave early next day.

'Very well,' said Henchard quickly, 'please yourself. But I tell you,

---

3. Eight bushels (one bushel is eight gallons).
4. Quagmire or bog.

young man, if this holds good for the bulk, as it has done for the sample, you have saved my credit, stranger though you be. What shall I pay you for this knowledge?'

'Nothing at all, nothing at all. It may not prove necessary to ye to use it often, and I don't value it at all. I thought I might just as well let ye know, as you were in a difficulty, and they were harrd upon ye.'

Henchard paused. 'I shan't soon forget this,' he said. 'And from a stranger! . . . I couldn't believe you were not the man I had engaged! Says I to myself "He knows who I am, and recommends himself by this stroke." And yet in turns out, after all, that you are not the man who answered my advertisement, but a stranger!'

'Ay, ay; that's so,' said the young man.

Henchard again suspended his words, and then his voice came thoughtfully: 'Your forehead, Farfrae, is something like my poor brother's—now dead and gone; and the nose, too, isn't unlike his. You must be, what—five foot nine, I reckon? I am six foot one and a half out of my shoes. But what of that? In my business, 'tis true that strength and bustle build up a firm. But judgment and knowledge are what keep it established. Unluckily, I am bad at science, Farfrae; bad at figures—a rule o' thumb sort of man. You are just the reverse—I can see that. I have been looking for such as you these two year, and yet you are not for me. Well, before I go, let me ask this: Though you are not the young man I thought you were, what's the difference? Can't ye stay just the same? Have you really made up your mind about this American notion? I won't mince matters. I feel you would be invaluable to me—that needn't be said—and if you will bide and be my manager, I will make it worth your while.'

'My plans are fixed,' said the young man, in negative tones. 'I have formed a scheme, and so we need na say any more about it. But will you not drink with me, sir? I find this Casterbridge ale warreming to the stomach.'

'No, no; I fain would, but I can't,' said Henchard gravely, the scraping of his chair informing the listeners that he was rising to leave. 'When I was a young man I went in for that sort of thing too strong—far too strong—and was well-nigh ruined by it! I did a deed on account of it which I shall be ashamed of to my dying day. It made such an impression on me that I swore, there and then, that I'd drink nothing stronger than tea for as many years as I was old that day. I have kept my oath; and though, Farfrae, I am sometimes that dry in the dog days[5] that I could drink a quarter-barrel to the pitching,[6] I think o' my oath, and touch no strong drink at all.'

'I'll no' press ye, sir—I'll no' press ye. I respect your vow.'

---

5. The hottest period of the summer.
6. To the bottom of the barrel (these were lined with pitch). A quarter-barrel held nine gallons.

'Well, I shall get a manager somewhere, no doubt,' said Henchard, with strong feeling in his tones. 'But it will be long before I see one that would suit me so well!'

The young man appeared much moved by Henchard's warm convictions of his value. He was silent till they reached the door. 'I wish I could stay—sincerely I would like to,' he replied. 'But no—it cannet be! it cannet! I want to see the warrld.'

VIII

Thus they parted; and Elizabeth-Jane and her mother remained each in her thoughts over their meal, the mother's face being strangely bright since Henchard's avowal of shame for a past action. The quivering of the partition to its core presently denoted that Donald Farfrae had again rung his bell, no doubt to have his supper removed; for humming a tune, and walking up and down, he seemed to be attracted by the lively bursts of conversation and melody from the general company below. He sauntered out upon the landing, and descended the staircase.

When Elizabeth-Jane had carried down his supper tray, and also that used by her mother and herself, she found the bustle of serving to be at its height below, as it always was at this hour. The young woman shrank from having anything to do with the groundfloor serving, and crept silently about observing the scene—so new to her, fresh from the seclusion of a seaside cottage. In the general sitting-room, which was large, she remarked the two or three dozen strong-backed chairs that stood round against the wall, each fitted with its genial occupant; the sanded floor; the black settle which, projecting endwise from the wall within the door, permitted Elizabeth to be a spectator of all that went on without herself being particularly seen.

The young Scotchman had just joined the guests. These, in addition to the respectable master-tradesmen occupying the seats of privilege in the bow-window and its neighbourhood, included an inferior set at the unlighted end, whose seats were mere benches against the wall, and who drank from cups instead of from glasses. Among the latter she noticed some of those personages who had stood outside the windows of the King's Arms.

Behind their backs was a small window, with a wheel ventilator in one of the panes, which would suddenly start off spinning with a jingling sound, as suddenly stop, and as suddenly start again.

While thus furtively making her survey the opening words of a song greeted her ears from the front of the settle, in a melody and accent of peculiar charm. There had been some singing before she came down; and now the Scotchman had made himself so soon at home that, at the request of some of the master-tradesmen, he, too, was favouring the room with a ditty.

Elizabeth-Jane was fond of music; she could not help pausing to listen; and the longer she listened the more she was enraptured. She had
never heard any singing like this; and it was evident that the majority of
the audience had not heard such frequently, for they were attentive to a
much greater degree than usual. They neither whispered, nor drank, nor
dipped their pipe-stems in their ale to moisten them, nor pushed the
mug to their neighbours. The singer himself grew emotional, till she
could imagine a tear in his eye as the words went on:—

> 'It's hame, and it's hame, hame fain would I be,
> O hame, hame, hame to my ain countree!
> There's an eye that ever weeps, and a fair face will be fain,
> As I pass through Annan Water with my bonnie bands again;
> When the flower is in the bud, and the leaf upon the tree,
> The lark shall sing me hame to my ain countree!'[1]

There was a burst of applause, and a deep silence which was even
more eloquent than the applause. It was of such a kind that the snapping
of a pipe-stem too long for him by old Solomon Longways, who was one
of those gathered at the shady end of the room, seemed a harsh and
irreverent act. Then the ventilator in the window-pane spasmodically
started off for a new spin, and the pathos of Donald's song was temporarily effaced.

"'Twas not amiss—not at all amiss!' muttered Christopher Coney, who
was also present. And removing his pipe a finger's breadth from his lips,
he said aloud, 'Draw on with the next verse, young gentleman, please.'

'Yes. Let's have it again, stranger,' said the glazier, a stout, bucket-
headed man, with a white apron rolled up round his waist. 'Folks don't
lift up their hearts like that in this part of the world.' And turning aside,
he said in undertones, 'Who is the young man?—Scotch, d'ye say?'

'Yes, straight from the mountains of Scotland, I believe,' replied
Coney.

Young Farfrae repeated the last verse. It was plain that nothing so
pathetic had been heard at the Three Mariners for a considerable time.
The difference of accent, the excitability of the singer, the intense local
feeling, and the seriousness with which he worked himself up to a climax, surprised this set of worthies, who were only too prone to shut up
their emotions with caustic words.

'Danged if our country down here is worth singing about like that!'
continued the glazier, as the Scotchman again melodized with a dying
fall, 'My ain countree!' 'When you take away from among us the fools
and the rogues, and the lammigers,[2] and the wanton hussies, and the

---

1. From a Jacobite song, collected by (and sometimes attributed to) Allan Cunningham
   (1784–1842).
2. Cripples.

slatterns, and such like, there's cust few left to ornament a song with in Casterbridge, or the country round.'

'True,' said Buzzford, the dealer, looking at the grain of the table. 'Casterbridge is a old, hoary place o' wickedness, by all account. 'Tis recorded in history that we rebelled against the King[3] one or two hundred years ago, in the time of the Romans, and that lots of us was hanged on Gallows Hill,[4] and quartered, and our different jints sent about the country like butcher's meat; and for my part I can well believe it.'

'What did ye come away from yer own country for, young maister, if ye be so wownded about it?' inquired Christopher Coney, from the background, with the tone of a man who preferred the original subject. 'Faith, it wasn't worth your while on our account, for, as Maister Billy Wills says, we be bruckle[5] folk here—the best o' us hardly honest sometimes, what with hard winters, and so many mouths to fill, and God-a'mighty sending his little taties[6] so terrible small to fill 'em with. We don't think about flowers and fair faces, not we—except in the shape o' cauliflowers and pigs' chaps.'[7]

'But, no!' said Donald Farfrae, gazing round into their faces with earnest concern; 'the best of ye hardly honest—not that surely? None of ye has been stealing what didn't belong to him?'

'Lord! no, no!' said Solomon Longways, smiling grimly. 'That's only his random way o' speaking. 'A was always such a man of under-thoughts.' (And reprovingly towards Christopher): 'Don't ye be so over-familiar with a gentleman that ye know nothing of—and that's travelled a'most from the North Pole.'

Christopher Coney was silenced, and as he could get no public sympathy, he mumbled his feelings to himself: 'Be dazed, if I loved my country half as well as the young feller do, I'd live by claning my neighbour's pigsties afore I'd go away! For my part I've no more love for my country than I have for Botany Bay!'[8]

'Come,' said Longways; 'let the young man draw onward with his ballet, or we shall be here all night.'

'That's all of it,' said the singer apologetically.

'Soul of my body, then we'll have another!' said the general dealer.

'Can you turn a strain to the ladies, sir?' inquired a fat woman with a

3. After Monmouth's unsuccessful rebellion against James II in 1685, many of the rebels were sentenced to be hanged and quartered at the "Bloody Assizes," held in Dorchester under Judge Jeffreys. Buzzford's "the time of the Romans" may be a confused reference to James II's Roman Catholicism.
4. Hill at the junction of Icen Way and South Walk in Dorchester.
5. Rough.
6. Potatoes.
7. Part of pigs' cheeks, used for food.
8. An inlet on the coast of New South Wales, Australia, used by the British as a convict settlement.

figured purple apron, the waist-string of which was overhung so far by her sides as to be invisible.

'Let him breathe—let him breathe, Mother Cuxsom. He hain't got his second wind yet,' said the master glazier.

'O yes, but I have!' exclaimed the young man; and he at once rendered 'O Nannie'[9] with faultless modulations, and another or two of the like sentiment, winding up at their earnest request with 'Auld Lang Syne.'[1]

By this time he had completely taken possession of the hearts of the Three Mariners' inmates, including even old Coney. Notwithstanding an occasional odd gravity which awoke their sense of the ludicrous for the moment, they began to view him through a golden haze which the tone of his mind seemed to raise around him. Casterbridge had sentiment—Casterbridge had romance; but this stranger's sentiment was of differing quality. Or rather, perhaps, the difference was mainly superficial; he was to them like the poet of a new school who takes his contemporaries by storm; who is not really new, but is the first to articulate what all his listeners have felt, though but dumbly till then.

The silent landlord came and leant over the settle while the young man sang; and even Mrs. Stannidge managed to unstick herself from the framework of her chair in the bar and get as far as the door-post, which movement she accomplished by rolling herself round, as a cask is trundled on the chine[2] by a drayman without losing much of its perpendicular.

'And are you going to bide in Casterbridge, sir?' she asked.

'Ah—no!' said the Scotchman, with melancholy fatality in his voice, 'I'm only passing thirrough! I am on my way to Bristol, and on frae there to foreign parts.'

'We be truly sorry to hear it,' said Solomon Longways. 'We can ill afford to lose tuneful wynd-pipes like yours when they fall among us. And verily, to mak' acquaintance with a man a-come from so far, from the land o' perpetual snow, as we may say, where wolves and wild boars and other dangerous animalcules[3] be as common as blackbirds hereabout—why, 'tis a thing we can't do every day; and there's good sound information for bide-at-homes like we when such a man opens his mouth.'

'Nay, but ye mistake my country,' said the young man, looking round upon them with tragic fixity, till his eye lighted up and his cheek kindled with a sudden enthusiasm to right their errors. 'There are not perpetual snow and wolves at all in it!—except snow in winter, and—well—a little in summer just sometimes, and a "gaberlunzie"[4] or two stalking

---

9. A traditional song, collected by Bishop Percy in his *Reliques of Ancient English Poetry* (1765), and set to music by Thomas Carter (1769–1800).
1. A poem and song by Robert Burns (1759–1796), celebrating friendship.
2. Projecting rim at the edge of a cask.
3. Minute animals: a malapropism for wild animals.
4. Beggar (Scots).

about here and there, if ye may call them dangerous. Eh, but you should take a summer jarreny to Edinboro', and Arthur's Seat,[5] and all round there, and then go on to the lochs, and all the Highland scenery—in May and June—and you would never say 'tis the land of wolves and perpetual snow!'

'Of course not—it stands to reason,' said Buzzford.. ''Tis barren ignorance that leads to such words. He's a simple home-spun man, that never was fit for good company—think nothing of him, sir.'

'And do ye carry your flock bed,[6] and your quilt, and your crock, and your bit of chiney? or do ye go in bare bones, as I may say?' inquired Christopher Coney.

'I've sent on my luggage—though it isn't much; for the voyage is long.' Donald's eyes dropped into a remote gaze as he added: 'But I said to myself, "Never a one of the prizes of life will I come by unless I undertake it!" and I decided to go.'

A general sense of regret, in which Elizabeth-Jane shared not least, made itself apparent in the company. As she looked at Farfrae from the back of the settle she decided that his statements showed him to be no less thoughtful than his fascinating melodies revealed him to be cordial and impassioned. She admired the serious light in which he looked at serious things. He had seen no jest in ambiguities and roguery, as the Casterbridge toss-pots[7] had done; and rightly not—there was none. She disliked those wretched humours of Christopher Coney and his tribe; and he did not appreciate them. He seemed to feel exactly as she felt about life and its surroundings—that they were a tragical rather than a comical thing; that though one could be gay on occasion, moments of gaiety were interludes, and no part of the actual drama. It was extraordinary how similar their views were.

Though it was still early the young Scotchman expressed his wish to retire, whereupon the landlady whispered to Elizabeth to run upstairs and turn down his bed. She took a candlestick and proceeded on her mission, which was the act of a few moments only. When, candle in hand, she reached the top of the stairs on her way down again, Mr. Farfrae was at the foot coming up. She could not very well retreat; they met and passed in the turn of the staircase.

She must have appeared interesting in some way—notwithstanding her plain dress—or rather, possibly, in consequence of it, for she was a girl characterized by earnestness and soberness of mien, with which simple drapery accorded well. Her face flushed, too, at the slight awkwardness of the meeting, and she passed him with her eyes bent on the candle-flame that she carried just below her nose. Thus it happened that when

---

5. The hill overlooking Edinburgh from the east.
6. Bed stuffed with wool.
7. Drunkards, sots.

confronting her he smiled; and then, with the manner of a temporarily light-hearted man, who has started himself on a flight of song whose momentum he cannot readily check, he softly tuned an old ditty that she seemed to suggest—

> 'As I came in by my bower door,
>   As day was waxin' wearie,
> Oh wha came tripping down the stair
>   But bonnie Peg my dearie.'[8]

Elizabeth-Jane, rather disconcerted, hastened on; and the Scotchman's voice died away, humming more of the same within the closed door of his room.

Here the scene and sentiment ended for the present. When, soon after, the girl rejoined her mother, the latter was still in thought—on quite another matter than a young man's song.

'We've made a mistake,' she whispered (that the Scotchman might not overhear). 'On no account ought ye to have helped serve here to-night. Not because of ourselves, but for the sake of *him*. If he should befriend us, and take us up, and then find out what you did when staying here, 'twould grieve and wound his natural pride as Mayor of the town.'

Elizabeth, who would perhaps have been more alarmed at this than her mother had she known the real relationship, was not much disturbed about it as things stood. Her 'he' was another man than her poor mother's. 'For myself,' she said, 'I didn't at all mind waiting a little upon him. He's so respectable, and educated—far above the rest of 'em in the inn. They thought him very simple not to know their grim broad way of talking about themselves here. But of course he didn't know— he was too refined in his mind to know such things!' Thus she earnestly pleaded.

Meanwhile, the 'he' of her mother was not so far away as even they thought. After leaving the Three Mariners he had sauntered up and down the empty High Street, passing and repassing the inn in his promenade. When the Scotchman sang his voice had reached Henchard's ears through the heart-shaped holes in the window-shutters, and had led him to pause outside them a long while.

'To be sure, to be sure, how that fellow does draw me!' he had said to himself. 'I suppose 'tis because I'm so lonely. I'd have given him a third share in the business to have stayed!'

---

8. From the song "Bonnie Peg," possibly by Burns; see *Burns: Poems and Songs*, ed. James Kinsley (London, 1969), p. 726.

IX

When Elizabeth-Jane opened the hinged casement next morning the mellow air brought in the feel of imminent autumn almost as distinctly as if she had been in the remotest hamlet. Casterbridge was the complement of the rural life around; not its urban opposite. Bees and butterflies in the cornfields at the top of the town, who desired to get to the meads at the bottom, took no circuitous course, but flew straight down High Street without any apparent consciousness that they were traversing strange latitudes. And in autumn airy spheres of thistledown floated into the same street, lodged upon the shop fronts, blew into drains; and innumerable tawny and yellow leaves skimmed along the pavement, and stole through people's doorways into their passages with a hesitating scratch on the floor, like the skirts of timid visitors.

Hearing voices, one of which was close at hand, she withdrew her head and glanced from behind the window-curtains. Mr Henchard—now habited no longer as a great personage, but as a thriving man of business—was pausing on his way up the middle of the street, and the Scotchman was looking from the window adjoining her own. Henchard, it appeared, had gone a little way past the inn before he had noticed his acquaintance of the previous evening. He came back a few steps, Donald Farfrae opening the window further.

'And you are off soon, I suppose?' said Henchard upwards.

'Yes—almost this moment, sir,' said the other. 'Maybe I'll walk on till the coach makes up on me.'

'Which way?'

'The way ye are going.'

'Then shall we walk together to the top o' town?'

'If ye'll wait a minute,' said the Scotchman.

In a few minutes the latter emerged, bag in hand. Henchard looked at the bag as at an enemy. It showed there was no mistake about the young man's departure. 'Ah, my lad,' he said, 'you should have been a wise man, and have stayed with me.'

'Yes, yes—it might have been wiser,' said Donald, looking microscopically at the houses that were furthest off. 'It is only telling ye the truth when I say my plans are vague.'

They had by this time passed on from the precincts of the inn, and Elizabeth-Jane heard no more. She saw that they continued in conversation, Henchard turning to the other occasionally, and emphasizing some remark with a gesture. Thus they passed the King's Arms Hotel, the Market House, St. Peter's churchyard wall, ascending to the upper end of the long street till they were small as two grains of corn; when they bent suddenly to the right into the Bristol Road, and were out of view.

'He was a good man—and he's gone,' she said to herself. 'I was nothing to him, and there was no reason why he should have wished me good-bye.'

The simple thought, with its latent sense of slight, had moulded itself out of the following little fact: when the Scotchman came out at the door he had by accident glanced up at her; and then he had looked away again without nodding, or smiling, or saying a word.

'You are still thinking, mother,' she said, when she turned inwards.

'Yes; I am thinking of Mr. Henchard's sudden liking for that young man. He was always so. Now, surely, if he takes so warmly to people who are not related to him at all, may he not take as warmly to his own kin?'

While they debated this question a procession of five large waggons went past, laden with hay up to the bedroom windows. They came in from the country, and the steaming horses had probably been travelling a great part of the night. To the shaft of each hung a little board, on which was painted in white letters, 'Henchard, corn-factor and hay-merchant.' The spectacle renewed his wife's conviction that, for her daughter's sake, she should strain a point to rejoin him.

The discussion was continued during breakfast, and the end of it was that Mrs. Henchard decided, for good or for ill, to send Elizabeth-Jane with a message to Henchard, to the effect that his relative Susan, a sailor's widow, was in the town; leaving it to him to say whether or not he would recognize her. What had brought her to this determination were chiefly two things. He had been described as a lonely widower; and he had expressed shame for a past transaction of his life. There was promise in both.

'If he says no,' she enjoined, as Elizabeth-Jane stood, bonnet on, ready to depart; 'if he thinks it does not become the good position he has reached to in the town, to own—to let us call on him as—his distant kinsfolk, say, "Then, sir, we would rather not intrude; we will leave Casterbridge as quietly as we have come, and go back to our own country." . . . I almost feel that I would rather he did say so, as I have not seen him for so many years, and we are so—little allied to him!'

'And if he say yes?' inquired the more sanguine one.

'In that case,' answered Mrs. Henchard cautiously, 'ask him to write me a note, saying when and how he will see us—or *me*.'

Elizabeth-Jane went a few steps towards the landing. 'And tell him,' continued her mother, 'that I fully know I have no claim upon him—that I am glad to find he is thriving; that I hope his life may be long and happy—there, go.' Thus with a half-hearted willingness, a smothered reluctance, did the poor forgiving woman start her unconscious daughter on this errand.

It was about ten o'clock, and market-day, when Elizabeth paced up the High Street, in no great hurry; for to herself her position was only that of a poor relation deputed to hunt up a rich one. The front doors of the private houses were mostly left open at this warm autumn time, no thought of umbrella stealers disturbing the minds of the placid burgess-es. Hence, through the long, straight, entrance passages thus unclosed could be seen, as through tunnels, the mossy gardens at the back, glow-ing with nasturtiums, fuchsias, scarlet geraniums, 'bloody warriors,'[1] snap-dragons, and dahlias, this floral blaze being backed by crusted grey stone-work remaining from a yet remoter Casterbridge than the venera-ble one visible in the street. The old-fashioned fronts of these houses, which had older than old-fashioned backs, rose sheer from the pave-ment, into which the bow-windows protruded like bastions, necessitat-ing a pleasing *chassez-déchassez*[2] movement to the time-pressed pedes-trian at every few yards. He was bound also to evolve other Terpsichorean figures[3] in respect of door-steps, scrapers, cellar-hatches, church buttresses, and the over-hanging angles of walls which, original-ly unobtrusive, had become bow-legged and knock-kneed.

In addition to these fixed obstacles which spoke so cheerfully of indi-vidual unrestraint as to boundaries, movables occupied the path and roadway to a perplexing extent. First the vans of the carriers in and out of Casterbridge, who hailed from Mellstock, Weatherbury, The Hintocks, Sherton-Abbas, Kingsbere, Overcombe, and many other towns and villages round. Their owners were numerous enough to be regarded as a tribe, and had almost distinctiveness enough to be regard-ed as a race. Their vans had just arrived, and were drawn up on each side of the street in close file, so as to form at places a wall between the pave-ment and the roadway. Moreover every shop pitched out half its con-tents upon trestles and boxes on the kerb, extending the display each week a little further and further into the roadway, despite the expostula-tions of the two feeble old constables,[4] until there remained but a tortu-ous defile for carriages down the centre of the street, which afforded fine opportunities for skill with the reins. Over the pavement on the sunny side of the way hung shopblinds so constructed as to give the passenger's hat a smart buffet off his head, as from the unseen hands of Cranstoun's Goblin Page,[5] celebrated in romantic lore.

Horses for sale were tied in rows, their forelegs on the pavement, their hind legs in the street, in which position they occasionally nipped little boys by the shoulder who were passing to school. And any inviting recess in front of a house that had been modestly kept back from the general line was utilized by pig-dealers as a pen for their stock.[6]

---

1. Wallflowers.
2. Dance steps to the right and the left (from the French).
3. Dance steps. Terpsichore was the Greek muse of dance.
4. Officers appointed by magistrates to maintain law and order.
5. In Sir Walter Scott's *The Lay of the Last Minstrel* (1805), one of Lord Cranstoun's servants is a malicious practical joker.
6. The reader will scarcely need to be reminded that time and progress have obliterated from the town that suggested these descriptions many or most of the old-fashioned features here enu-merated [Hardy's note].

The yeomen, farmers, dairymen, and townsfolk, who came to transact business in these ancient streets, spoke in other ways than by articulation. Not to hear the words of your interlocutor in metropolitan centres is to know nothing of his meaning. Here the face, the arms, the hat,
the stick, the body throughout spoke equally with the tongue. To express
satisfaction the Casterbridge market-man added to his utterance a
broadening of the cheeks, a crevicing of the eyes, a throwing back of the
shoulders, which was intelligible from the other end of the street. If he
wondered, though all Henchard's carts and waggons were rattling past
him, you knew it from perceiving the inside of his crimson mouth, and
a target-like circling of his eyes. Deliberation caused sundry attacks on
the moss of adjoining walls with the end of his stick, a change of his hat
from the horizontal to the less so; a sense of tediousness announced
itself in a lowering of the person by spreading the knees to a lozenge-
shaped aperture and contorting the arms. Chicanery, subterfuge, had
hardly a place in the streets of this honest borough to all appearance;
and it was said that the lawyers in the Court House hard by occasionally threw in strong arguments for the other side out of pure generosity
(though apparently by mischance) when advancing their own.

Thus Casterbridge was in most respects but the pole, focus, or nerve-
knot of the surrounding country life; differing from the many manufacturing towns which are as foreign bodies set down, like boulders on a
plain, in a green world with which they have nothing in common.
Casterbridge lived by agriculture at one remove further from the fountain-
head than the adjoining villages—no more. The townsfolk understood
every fluctuation in the rustic's condition, for it affected their receipts as
much as the labourer's; they entered into the troubles and joys which
moved the aristocratic families ten miles round—for the same reason.
And even at the dinner-parties of the professional families the subjects
of discussion were corn, cattle-disease, sowing and reaping, fencing and
planting; while politics were viewed by them less from their own standpoint of burgesses[7] with rights and privileges than from the standpoint of
their county neighbours.

All the venerable contrivances and confusions which delighted the
eye by their quaintness, and in a measure reasonableness, in this rare old
market-town, were metropolitan novelties to the unpractised eyes of
Elizabeth-Jane, fresh from netting fish-seines[8] in a seaside cottage. Very
little inquiry was necessary to guide her footsteps. Henchard's house was
one of the best, faced with dull red-and-grey old brick. The front door
was open, and, as in other houses, she could see through the passage to
the end of the garden—nearly a quarter of a mile off.

Mr. Henchard was not in the house, but in the store-yard. She was

7. Members of a borough with full municipal rights.
8. Large fishing-nets.

conducted into the mossy garden, and through a door in the wall, which was studded with rusty nails speaking of generations of fruit-trees that had been trained there. The door opened upon the yard, and here she was left to find him as she could. It was a place flanked by hay-barns, into which tons of fodder, all in trusses, were being packed from the waggons she had seen pass the inn that morning. On other sides of the yard were wooden granaries on stone staddles,[9] to which access was given by Flemish ladders,[1] and a store-house several floors high. Wherever the doors of these places were open, a closely packed throng of bursting wheat-sacks could be seen standing inside, with the air of awaiting a famine that would not come.

She wandered about this place, uncomfortably conscious of the impending interview, till she was quite weary of searching; she ventured to inquire of a boy in what quarter Mr. Henchard could be found. He directed her to an office which she had not seen before, and knocking at the door she was answered by a cry of 'Come in.'

Elizabeth turned the handle; and there stood before her, bending over some sample-bags on a table, not the corn-merchant, but the young Scotchman Mr. Farfrae—in the act of pouring some grains of wheat from one hand to the other. His hat hung on a peg behind him, and the roses of his carpet-bag glowed from the corner of the room.

Having toned her feelings and arranged words on her lips for Mr. Henchard, and for him alone, she was for the moment confounded.

'Yes, what is it?' said the Scotchman, like a man who permanently ruled there.

She said she wanted to see Mr. Henchard.

'Ah, yes; will you wait a minute? He's engaged just now,' said the young man, apparently not recognizing her as the girl at the inn. He handed her a chair, bade her sit down, and turned to his sample-bags again. While Elizabeth-Jane sits waiting in great amaze at the young man's presence we may briefly explain how he came there.

When the two new acquaintances had passed out of sight that morning towards the Bath and Bristol road they went on silently, except for a few commonplaces, till they had gone down an avenue on the town walls called the Chalk Walk, leading to an angle where the North and West escarpments met. From this high corner of the square earthworks a vast extent of country could be seen. A footpath ran steeply down the green slope, conducting from the shady promenade on the walls to a road at the bottom of the scarp.[2] It was by this path the Scotchman had to descend.

'Well, here's success to 'ee,' said Henchard, holding out his right hand and leaning with his left upon the wicket which protected the descent.

9. Stone pillars used to raise the floor of the granary above ground level.
1. Rope ladders.
2. Steep bank or slope.

In the act there was the inelegance of one whose feelings are nipped and wishes defeated. 'I shall often think of this time, and of how you came at the very moment to throw a light upon my difficulty.'

Still holding the young man's hand he paused, and then added deliberately: 'Now I am not the man to let a cause be lost for want of a word. And before ye are gone for ever I'll speak. Once more, will ye stay? There it is, flat and plain. You can see that it isn't all selfishness that makes me press 'ee; for my business is not quite so scientific as to require an intellect entirely out of the common. Others would do for the place without doubt. Some selfishness perhaps there is, but there is more; it isn't for me to repeat what. Come bide with me—and name your own terms. I'll agree to 'em willingly and 'ithout a word of gainsaying; for, hang it, Farfrae, I like thee well!'

The young man's hand remained steady in Henchard's for a moment or two. He looked over the fertile country that stretched beneath them, then backward along the shaded walk reaching to the top of the town. His face flushed.

'I never expected this—I did not!' he said. 'It's Providence! Should any one go against it? No; I'll not go to America; I'll stay and be your man!'

His hand, which had lain lifeless in Henchard's, returned the latter's grasp.

'Done,' said Henchard.

'Done,' said Donald Farfrae.

The face of Mr. Henchard beamed forth a satisfaction that was almost fierce in its strength. 'Now you are my friend!' he exclaimed. 'Come back to my house; let's clinch it at once by clear terms, so as to be comfortable in our minds.' Farfrae caught up his bag and retraced the North-West Avenue in Henchard's company as he had come. Henchard was all confidence now.

'I am the most distant fellow in the world when I don't care for a man,' he said. 'But when a man takes my fancy he takes it strong. Now I am sure you can eat another breakfast? You couldn't have eaten much so early, even if they had anything at that place to gi'e thee, which they hadn't; so come to my house and we will have a solid, staunch tuck-in, and settle terms in black-and-white if you like; though my word's my bond. I can always make a good meal in the morning. I've got a splendid cold pigeon-pie going just now. You can have some home-brewed if you want to, you know.'

'It is too airly in the morning for that,' said Farfrae with a smile.

'Well, of course, I didn't know. I don't drink it because of my oath; but I am obliged to brew for my work-people.'

Thus talking they returned, and entered Henchard's premises by the back way or traffic entrance. Here the matter was settled over the breakfast, at which Henchard heaped the young Scotchman's plate to a prodigal fulness. He would not rest satisfied till Farfrae had written for his luggage from Bristol, and despatched the letter to the post-office. When it was done this man of strong impulses declared that his new friend should take up his abode in his house—at least till some suitable lodgings could be found.

He then took Farfrae round and showed him the place, and the stores of grain, and other stock; and finally entered the offices where the younger of them has already been discovered by Elizabeth.

X

While she still sat under the Scotchman's eyes a man came up to the door, reaching it as Henchard opened the door of the inner office to admit Elizabeth. The new-comer stepped forward like the quicker cripple at Bethesda,[1] and entered in her stead. She could hear his words to Henchard: 'Joshua Jopp, sir—by appointment—the new manager.'

'The new manager!—he's in his office,' said Henchard bluntly.

'In his office!' said the man, with a stultified air.

'I mentioned Thursday,' said Henchard; 'and as you did not keep your appointment, I have engaged another manager. At first I thought he must be you. Do you think I can wait when business is in question?'

'You said Thursday or Saturday, sir,' said the new-comer, pulling out a letter.

'Well, you are too late,' said the corn-factor. 'I can say no more.'

'You as good as engaged me.' murmured the man.

'Subject to an interview,' said Henchard. 'I am sorry for you—very sorry indeed. But it can't be helped.'

There was no more to be said, and the man came out, encountering Elizabeth-Jane in his passage. She could see that his mouth twitched with anger, and that bitter disappointment was written in his face everywhere.

Elizabeth-Jane now entered, and stood before the master of the premises. His dark pupils—which always seemed to have a red spark of light in them, though this could hardly be a physical fact—turned indifferently round under his dark brows until they rested on her figure. 'Now then, what is it, my young woman?' he said blandly.

'Can I speak to you—not on business, sir?' said she.

'Yes—I suppose.' He looked at her more thoughtfully.

'I am sent to tell you, sir,' she innocently went on, 'that a distant relative of yours by marriage, Susan Newson, a sailor's widow, is in the town; and to ask whether you would wish to see her.'

The rich *rouge-et-noir*[2] of his countenance underwent a slight change. 'Oh—Susan is—still alive?' he asked with difficulty.

---

1. In the New Testament story, the pool at Bethesda was from time to time stirred by an angel; the first person to enter the pool thereafter was cured of any disease. See John 5.2–9.
2. Red and black (from the French).

CHAPTER X

'Yes, sir.'

'Are you her daughter?'

'Yes, sir—her only daughter.'

'What—do you call yourself—your Christian name?'

'Elizabeth-Jane, sir.'

'Newson?'

Elizabeth-Jane Newson.'

This at once suggested to Henchard that the transaction of his early married life at Weydon Fair was unrecorded in the family history. It was more than he could have expected. His wife had behaved kindly to him in return for his unkindness, and had never proclaimed her wrong to her child or to the world.

'I am—a good deal interested in your news,' he said. 'And as this is not a matter of business, but pleasure, suppose we go indoors.'

It was with a gentle delicacy of manner, surprising to Elizabeth, that he showed her out of the office and through the outer room, where Donald Farfrae was overhauling bins and samples with the inquiring inspection of a beginner in charge. Henchard preceded her through the door in the wall to the suddenly changed scene of the garden and flowers, and onward into the house. The dining-room to which he introduced her still exhibited the remnants of the lavish breakfast laid for Farfrae. It was furnished to profusion with heavy mahogany furniture of the deepest red-Spanish hues. Pembroke tables,[3] with leaves hanging so low that they well-nigh touched the floor, stood against the walls on legs and feet shaped like those of an elephant, and on one lay three huge folio volumes—a Family Bible, a 'Josephus,'[4] and a 'Whole Duty of Man.'[5] In the chimney corner was a fire-grate with a fluted semicircular back, having urns and festoons[6] cast in relief thereon; and the chairs were of the kind which, since that day, has cast lustre upon the names of Chippendale and Sheraton,[7] though, in point of fact, their patterns may have been such as those illustrious carpenters never saw or heard of. 'Sit down—Elizabeth-Jane—sit down,' he said, with a shake in his voice as he uttered her name; and sitting down himself he allowed his hands to hang between his knees, while he looked upon the carpet. 'Your mother, then, is quite well?'

'She is rather worn out, sir, with travelling.'

'A sailor's widow—when did he die?'

---

3. Small drop-leaf tables.
4. Probably *The Antiquity of the Jews* by Flavius Josephus (37–93 C.E.), historian of the Jews.
5. A popular devotional book, first published in 1658 and often reprinted, possibly written by Richard Allestree. See Ecclesiastes 12.13: "Fear God, and keep his commandments: for this is the whole duty of man."
6. Garlands of flowers.
7. Thomas Chippendale and Thomas Sheraton, famous furniture designers of the eighteenth century.

'Father was lost last spring.'[8]

Henchard winced at the word 'father,' thus applied. 'Do you and she come from abroad—America or Australia?' he asked.

'No. We have been in England some years. I was twelve when we came here from Canada.'

'Ah; exactly.' By such conversation he discovered the circumstances which had enveloped his wife and her child in such total obscurity that he had long ago believed them to be in their graves. These things being clear, he returned to the present. 'And where is your mother staying?'

'At the Three Mariners.'

'And you are her daughter Elizabeth-Jane?' repeated Henchard. He arose, came close to her, and glanced in her face. 'I think,' he said, suddenly turning away with a wet eye, 'you shall take a note from me to your mother. I should like to see her. . . . She is not left very well off by her late husband?' His eye fell on Elizabeth's clothes, which, though a respectable suit of black, and her very best, were decidedly old-fashioned even to Casterbridge eyes.

'Not very well,' she said, glad that he had divined this without her being obliged to express it.

He sat down at the table and wrote a few lines; next taking from his pocket-book a five-pound note, which he put in the envelope with the letter, adding to it, as by an after-thought, five shillings. Sealing the whole up carefully, he directed it to 'Mrs. Newson, Three Mariners Inn,' and handed the packet to Elizabeth.

'Deliver it to her personally, please,' said Henchard. 'Well, I am glad to see you here, Elizabeth-Jane—very glad. We must have a long talk together—but not just now.'

He took her hand at parting, and held it so warmly that she, who had known so little friendship, was much affected, and tears rose to her aerial-grey eyes. The instant that she was gone Henchard's state showed itself more distinctly; having shut the door he sat in his dining-room stiffly erect, gazing at the opposite wall as if he read his history there.

'Begad!' he suddenly exclaimed, jumping up. 'I didn't think of that. Perhaps these are impostors—and Susan and the child dead after all!'

However, a something in Elizabeth-Jane soon assured him that, as regarded her, at least, there could be little doubt. And a few hours would settle the question of her mother's identity; for he had arranged in his note to see her that evening.

'It never rains but it pours!' said Henchard. His keenly excited interest in his new friend the Scotchman was now eclipsed by this event; and Donald Farfrae saw so little of him during the rest of the day that he wondered at the suddenness of his employer's moods.

8. In Chapter III, Elizabeth-Jane carries a card that reports Newson's death as occurring in November (see p. 18).

In the meantime Elizabeth had reached the inn. Her mother, instead of taking the note with the curiosity of a poor woman expecting assistance, was much moved at sight of it. She did not read it at once, asking Elizabeth to describe her reception, and the very words Mr. Henchard used. Elizabeth's back was turned when her mother opened the letter. It ran thus:—

> 'Meet me at eight o'clock this evening, if you can, at the Ring[9] on the Budmouth road. The place is easy to find. I can say no more now. The news upsets me almost. The girl seems to be in ignorance. Keep her so till I have seen you.
>
> M. H.'

He said nothing about the enclosure of five guineas. The amount was significant; it may tacitly have said to her that he bought her back again. She waited restlessly for the close of the day, telling Elizabeth-Jane that she was invited to see Mr. Henchard; that she would go alone. But she said nothing to show that the place of meeting was not at his house, nor did she hand the note to Elizabeth.

XI

The Ring at Casterbridge was merely the local name of one of the finest Roman Amphitheatres, if not the very finest, remaining in Britain.

Casterbridge announced old Rome in every street, alley, and precinct. It looked Roman, bespoke the art of Rome, concealed dead men of Rome. It was impossible to dig more than a foot or two deep about the town fields and gardens without coming upon some tall soldier or other of the Empire, who had lain there in his silent unobtrusive rest for a space of fifteen hundred years. He was mostly found lying on his side, in an oval scoop in the chalk, like a chicken in its shell; his knees drawn up to his chest; sometimes with the remains of his spear against his arm; a fibula[1] or brooch of bronze on his breast or forehead; an urn at his knees, a jar at his throat, a bottle at his mouth; and mystified conjecture pouring down upon him from the eyes of Casterbridge street boys and men, who had turned a moment to gaze at the familiar spectacle as they passed by.[2]

Imaginative inhabitants, who would have felt an unpleasantness at the discovery of a comparatively modern skeleton in their gardens, were quite unmoved by these hoary shapes. They had lived so long ago, their time was so unlike the present, their hopes and motives were so widely

---

9. Maumbury Ring, a neolithic fort or earthworks to the southwest of Dorchester, later enlarged by the Romans and used for circuses and gladiatorial combat.
1. Clasp or buckle (Latin).
2. Three Roman skeletons were discovered during the excavations for Hardy's house outside Dorchester, Max Gate, in 1883.

removed from ours, that between them and the living there seemed to stretch a gulf too wide for even a spirit to pass.

The Amphitheatre was a huge circular enclosure, with a notch at opposite extremities of its diameter north and south. From its sloping internal form it might have been called the spittoon of the Jötuns.[3] It was to Casterbridge what the ruined Coliseum is to modern Rome, and was nearly of the same magnitude. The dusk of evening was the proper hour at which a true impression of this suggestive place could be received. Standing in the middle of the arena at that time there by degrees became apparent its real vastness, which a cursory view from the summit at noon-day was apt to obscure. Melancholy, impressive, lonely, yet accessible from every part of the town, the historic circle was the frequent spot for appointments of a furtive kind. Intrigues were arranged there; tentative meetings were there experimented after divisions and feuds. But one kind of appointment—in itself the most common of any—seldom had place in the Amphitheatre: that of happy lovers.

Why, seeing that it was pre-eminently an airy, accessible, and sequestered spot for interviews, the cheerfullest form of those occurrences never took kindly to the soil of the ruin, would be a curious inquiry. Perhaps it was because its associations had about them something sinister. Its history proved that. Apart from the sanguinary nature of the games originally played therein, such incidents attached to its past as these: that for scores of years the town-gallows had stood at one corner; that in 1705 a woman who had murdered her husband[4] was half-strangled and then burnt there in the presence of ten thousand spectators. Tradition reports that at a certain stage of the burning her heart burst and leapt out of her body, to the terror of them all, and that not one of those ten thousand people ever cared particularly for hot roast after that. In addition to these old tragedies, pugilistic encounters almost to the death had come off down to recent dates in that secluded arena, entirely invisible to the outside world save by climbing to the top of the enclosure, which few townspeople in the daily round of their lives ever took the trouble to do. So that, though close to the turnpike-road, crimes might be perpetrated there unseen at mid-day.

Some boys had latterly tried to impart gaiety to the ruin by using the central arena as a cricket-ground. But the game usually languished for the aforesaid reason—the dismal privacy which the earthen circle enforced, shutting out every appreciative passer's vision, every commendatory remark from outsiders—everything, except the sky; and to play at games in such circumstances was like acting to an empty house. Possibly, too, the boys were timid, for some old people said that at cer-

3. Giants of Norse mythology.
4. Mary Channing, wife of a Dorchester grocer. For much of the eighteenth century the town gallows was sited in the Ring. See Hardy's article of 1908 on "Maumbury Ring," in *Thomas Hardy's Personal Writings*, ed. Harold Orel (London, 1967), pp. 225–32.

tain moments in the summer time, in broad daylight, persons sitting with a book or dozing in the arena had, on lifting their eyes, beheld the slopes lined with a gazing legion of Hadrian's soldiery[5] as if watching the gladiatorial combat; and had heard the roar of their excited voices; that the scene would remain but a moment, like a lightning flash, and then disappear.

It was related that there still remained under the south entrance excavated cells for the reception of the wild animals and athletes who took part in the games. The arena was still smooth and circular, as if used for its original purpose not so very long ago. The sloping pathways by which spectators had ascended to their seats were pathways yet. But the whole was grown over with grass, which now, at the end of summer, was bearded with withered bents[6] that formed waves under the brush of the wind, returning to the attentive ear Æolian modulations,[7] and detaining for moments the flying globes of thistledown.

Henchard had chosen this spot as being the safest from observation which he could think of for meeting his long-lost wife, and at the same time as one easily to be found by a stranger after nightfall. As Mayor of the town, with a reputation to keep up, he could not invite her to come to his house till some definite course had been decided on.

Just before eight he approached the deserted earthwork, and entered by the south path which descended over the *débris* of the former dens. In a few moments he could discern a female figure creeping in by the great north gap, or public gateway. They met in the middle of the arena. Neither spoke just at first—there was no necessity for speech—and the poor woman leant against Henchard, who supported her in his arms.

'I don't drink,' he said in a low, halting, apologetic voice. You hear, Susan?—I don't drink now—I haven't since that night.' Those were his first words. → JUDGEMENTAL NARRATIVE

He felt her bow her head in acknowledgment that she understood. After a minute or two he again began:

'If I had known you were living, Susan! But there was every reason to suppose you and the child were dead and gone. I took every possible step to find you—travelled—advertised. My opinion at last was that you had started for some colony with that man, and had been drowned on your voyage out. Why did you keep silent like this?'

'O Michael! because of him—what other reason could there be? I thought I owed him faithfulness to the end of one of our lives—foolishly I believed there was something solemn and binding in the bargain; I thought that even in honour I dared not desert him when he had paid

---

5. Hadrian was emperor of Rome, 117-38 C.E.
6. Stalks of stiff grass.
7. The phrase is from Shelley's poem *Prometheus Unbound*, IV. i. 186–88. Aeolus was the Greek god of the wind; an Aeolian harp is a musical instrument made to sound by the wind blowing across its strings.

so much for me in good faith. I meet you now only as his widow—I consider myself that, and that I have no claim upon you. Had he not died I
should never have come—never! Of that you may be sure.'

'Ts-s-s! How could you be so simple?'

'I don't know. Yet it would have been very wicked—if I had not
thought like that!' said Susan, almost crying.

'Yes—yes—so it would. It is only that which makes me feel 'ee an
innocent woman. But—to lead me into this!'

'What, Michael?' she asked, alarmed.

'Why, this difficulty about our living together again, and Elizabeth-
Jane. She cannot be told all—she would so despise us both that—I
could not bear it!'

'That was why she was brought up in ignorance of you. I could not
bear it either.'

'Well—we must talk of a plan for keeping her in her present belief,
and getting matters straight in spite of it. You have heard I am in a large
way of business here—that I am Mayor of the town, and churchwarden,
and I don't know what all?'

'Yes,' she murmured.

'These things, as well as the dread of the girl discovering our disgrace,
make it necessary to act with extreme caution. So that I don't see how
you two can return openly to my house as the wife and daughter I once
treated badly, and banished from me; and there's the rub o't.'[8]

'We'll go away at once. I only came to see——'

'No, no, Susan; you are not to go—you mistake me!' he said, with
kindly severity. 'I have thought of this plan: that you and Elizabeth take
a cottage in the town as the widow Mrs. Newson and her daughter; that
I meet you, court you, and marry you, Elizabeth-Jane coming to my
house as my step-daughter. The thing is so natural and easy that it is half
done in thinking o't. This would leave my shady, headstrong, disgrace-
ful life as a young man absolutely unopened; the secret would be yours
and mine only; and I should have the pleasure of seeing my own only
child under my roof, as well as my wife.'

'I am quite in your hands, Michael,' she said meekly. 'I came here for
the sake of Elizabeth; for myself, if you tell me to leave again to-morrow
morning, and never come near you more, I am content to go.'

'Now, now; we don't want to hear that,' said Henchard gently. 'Of
course you won't leave again. Think over the plan I have proposed for a
few hours; and if you can't hit upon a better one we'll adopt it. I have to
be away for a day or two on business, unfortunately; but during that time
you can get lodgings—the only ones in the town fit for you are those over
the china-shop in High Street—and you can also look for a cottage.'

---

8. "There's the problem." The phrase has become proverbial from its use in Shakespeare's
   Hamlet, III.1.67.

'If the lodgings are in High Street they are dear, I suppose?'

'Never mind—you *must* start genteel if our plan is to be carried out. Look to me for money. Have you enough till I come back?'

'Quite,' said she.

'And are you comfortable at the inn?'

'O yes.'

'And the girl is quite safe from learning the shame of her case and ours?—that's what makes me most anxious of all.'

'You would be surprised to find how unlikely she is to dream of the truth. How could she ever suppose such a thing?'

'True!'

'I like the idea of repeating our marriage,' said Mrs. Henchard, after a pause. 'It seems the only right course, after all this. Now I think I must go back to Elizabeth-Jane, and tell her that our kinsman, Mr. Henchard, kindly wishes us to stay in the town.'

'Very well—arrange that yourself. I'll go some way with you.'

'No, no. Don't run any risk!' said his wife anxiously. 'I can find my way back—it is not late. Please let me go alone.'

'Right,' said Henchard. 'But just one word. Do you forgive me, Susan?' NEEDS VALIDATION

She murmured something; but seemed to find it difficult to frame her answer.

'Never mind—all in good time,' said he. 'Judge me by my future works—good-bye!'

He retreated, and stood at the upper side of the Amphitheatre while his wife passed out through the lower way, and descended under the trees to the town. Then Henchard himself went homeward, going so fast that by the time he reached his door he was almost upon the heels of the unconscious[9] woman from whom he had just parted. He watched her up the street, and turned into his house.

XII

On entering his own door after watching his wife out of sigh, the Mayor walked on through the tunnel-shaped passage into the garden, and thence by the back door towards the stores and granaries. A light shone from the office-window, and there being no blind to screen the interior Henchard could see Donald Farfrae still seated where he had left him, initiating himself into the managerial work of the house by overhauling the books. Henchard entered, merely observing, 'Don't let me interrupt you, if ye will stay so late.'

He stood behind Farfrae's chair, watching his dexterity in clearing up the numerical fogs which had been allowed to grow so thick in

9. Unaware.

Henchard's books as almost to baffle even the Scotchman's perspicacity. The corn-factor's mien was half admiring, and yet it was not without a dash of pity for the tastes of any one who could care to give his mind to such finnikin[1] details. Henchard himself was mentally and physically unfit for grubbing subtleties from soiled paper; he had in a modern sense received the education of Achilles,[2] and found penmanship a tantalizing art.

'You shall do no more to-night,' he said at length, spreading his great hand over the paper. 'There's time enough to-morrow. Come indoors with me and have some supper. Now you shall! I am determined on't.' He shut the account-books with friendly force.

Donald had wished to get to his lodgings; but he already saw that his friend and employer was a man who knew no moderation in his requests and impulses, and he yielded gracefully. He liked Henchard's warmth, even if it inconvenienced him; the great difference in their characters adding to the liking.

They locked up the office, and the young man followed his companion through the private little door which, admitting directly into Henchard's garden, permitted a passage from the utilitarian to the beautiful at one step. The garden was silent, dewy, and full of perfume. It extended a long way back from the house, first as lawn and flower-beds, then as fruit-garden, where the long-tied espaliers,[3] as old as the old house itself, had grown so stout, and cramped, and gnarled that they had pulled their stakes out of the ground and stood distorted and writhing in vegetable agony, like leafy Laocoöns.[4] The flowers which smelt so sweetly were not discernible; and they passed through them into the house.

The hospitalities of the morning were repeated, and when they were over Henchard said, 'Pull your chair round to the fireplace, my dear fellow, and let's make a blaze—there's nothing I hate like a black grate, even in September.' He applied a light to the laid-in fuel, and a cheerful radiance spread around.

'It is odd,' said Henchard, 'that two men should meet as we have done on a purely business ground, and that at the end of the first day I should wish to speak to 'ee on a family matter. But, damn it all, I am a lonely man, Farfrae: I have nobody else to speak to; and why shouldn't I tell it to 'ee?'

'I'll be glad to hear it, if I can be of any service,' said Donald, allowing his eyes to travel over the intricate wood-carvings of the chimney-piece, representing garlanded lyres, shields, and quivers, on either side of a draped ox-skull, and flanked by heads of Apollo and Diana in low relief.

---

1. Finicking, trivial.
2. Achilles, the hero of Homer's *Iliad*, was trained in martial and practical skills, not in literary ones.
3. Fruit trees trained to grow flat against a wall or wooden frame.
4. The Trojan priest Laocoön and his sons were killed by sea-serpents; the scene, from Virgil's *Aeneid*, Book II, is represented in a famous sculpture in the Vatican.

'I've not been always what I am now,' continued Henchard, his firm deep voice being ever so little shaken. He was plainly under the strange influence which sometimes prompts men to confide to the newfound friend what they will not tell to the old. 'I began life as a working hay-trusser, and when I was eighteen I married on the strength o' my calling. Would you think me a married man?'

'I heard in the town that you were a widower.'

'Ah, yes—you would naturally have heard that. Well, I lost my wife nineteen years ago or so—by my own fault. . . . This is how it came about. One summer evening I was travelling for employment, and she was walking at my side, carrying the baby, our only child. We came to a booth in a country fair. I was a drinking man at that time.'

Henchard paused a moment, threw himself back so that his elbow rested on the table, his forehead being shaded by his hand, which, how-ever, did not hide the marks of introspective inflexibility on his features as he narrated in fullest detail the incidents of the transaction with the sailor. The tinge of indifference which had at first been visible in the Scotchman now disappeared.

Henchard went on to describe his attempts to find his wife; the oath he swore; the solitary life he led during the years which followed. 'I have kept my oath for nineteen years,' he went on; 'I have risen to what you see me now.'

'Ay!'

'Well—no wife could I hear of in all that time; and being by nature something of a woman-hater, I have found it no hardship to keep most-ly at a distance from the sex. No wife could I hear of, I say, till this very day. And now—she has come back.'

'Come back, has she!'

'This morning—this very morning. And what's to be done?'

'Can ye no' take her and live with her, and make some amends?'

'That's what I've planned and proposed. But, Farfrae,' said Henchard gloomily, 'by doing right with Susan I wrong another innocent woman.'

'Ye don't say that?'

'In the nature of things, Farfrae, it is almost impossible that a man of my sort should have the good fortune to tide through twenty years o' life without making more blunders than one. It has been my custom for many years to run across to Jersey in the way of business, particularly in the potato and root season. I do a large trade wi' them in that line. Well, one autumn when stopping there I fell quite ill, and in my illness I sank into one of those gloomy fits I sometimes suffer from, on account o' the loneliness of my domestic life, when the world seems to have the black-ness of hell, and, like Job,[5] I could curse the day that gave me birth.'

---

5. See Job 3.3: "Let the day perish wherein I was born, and the night in which it was said, There is a man child conceived."

'Ah, now, I never feel like it,' said Farfrae.

'Then pray to God that you never may, young man. While in this state I was taken pity on by a woman—a young lady I should call her, for she was of good family, well bred, and well educated—the daughter of some harum-scarum[6] military officer who had got into difficulties and had his pay sequestrated.[7] He was dead now, and her mother too, and she was as lonely as I. This young creature was staying at the boarding-house where I happened to have my lodging; and when I was pulled down she took upon herself to nurse me. From that she got to have a foolish liking for me. Heaven knows why, for I wasn't worth it. But being together in the same house, and her feelings warm, we got naturally intimate. I won't go into particulars of what our relations were. It is enough to say that we honestly meant to marry. There arose a scandal, which did me no harm, but was of course ruin to her. Though, Farfrae, between you and me, as man and man, I solemnly declare that philandering with womankind has neither been my vice nor my virtue. She was terribly careless of appearances, and I was perhaps more, because o' my dreary state; and it was through this that the scandal arose. At last I was well, and came away. When I was gone she suffered much on my account, and didn't forget to tell me so in letters one after another; till, latterly, I felt I owed her something, and thought that, as I had not heard of Susan for so long, I would make this other one the only return I could make, and ask her if she would run the risk of Susan being alive (very slight as I believed) and marry me, such as I was. She jumped for joy, and we should no doubt soon have been married—but, behold, Susan appears!'

Donald showed his deep concern at a complication so far beyond the degree of his simple experiences.

'Now see what injury a man may cause around him! Even after that wrong-doing at the fair when I was young, if I had never been so selfish as to let this giddy girl devote herself to me over at Jersey, to the injury of her name, all might now be well. Yet, as it stands, I must bitterly disappoint one of these women; and it is the second. My first duty is to Susan—there's no doubt about that.'

'They are both in a very melancholy position, and that's true!' murmured Donald.

'They are! For myself I don't care—'twill all end one way. But these two.' Henchard paused in reverie. 'I feel I should like to treat the second, no less than the first, as kindly as a man can in such a case.'

'Ah, well, it cannet be helped!' said the other, with philosophic woefulness. 'You mun write to the young lady, and in your letter you must put it plain and honest that it turns out she cannet be your wife, the

6. Reckless, irresponsible.
7. Seized for payment of debts.

first having come back; that ye cannet see her more; and that—ye wish her weel.'

'That won't do. 'Od seize it, I must do a little more than that! I must—though she did always brag about her rich uncle or rich aunt, and her expectations from 'em—I must send a useful sum of money to her, I suppose—just as a little recompense, poor girl. . . . Now, will you help me in this, and draw up an explanation to her of all I've told ye, breaking it as gently as you can? I'm so bad at letters.'

'And I will.'

'Now, I haven't told you quite all yet. My wife Susan has my daughter with her—the baby that was in her arms at the fair; and this girl knows nothing of me beyond that I am some sort of relation by marriage. She has grown up in the belief that the sailor to whom I made over her mother, and who is now dead, was her father, and her mother's husband. What her mother has always felt, she and I together feel now—that we can't proclaim our disgrace to the girl by letting her know the truth. Now what would you do?—I want your advice.'

'I think I'd run the risk, and tell her the truth. She'll forgive ye both.'

'Never!' said Henchard. 'I am not going to let her know the truth. Her mother and I be going to marry again; and it will not only help us to keep our child's respect, but it will be more proper. Susan looks upon herself as the sailor's widow, and won't think o' living with me as formerly without another religious ceremony—and she's right.'

Farfrae thereupon said no more. The letter to the young Jersey woman was carefully framed by him, and the interview ended, Henchard saying, as the Scotchman left, 'I feel it a great relief, Farfrae, to tell some friend o' this! You see now that the Mayor of Casterbridge is not so thriving in his mind as it seems he might be from the state of his pocket.'

'I do. And I'm sorry for ye!' said Farfrae.

When he was gone Henchard copied the letter, and, enclosing a cheque, took it to the post-office, from which he walked back thoughtfully.

'Can it be that it will go off so easily!' he said. 'Poor thing—God knows! Now then, to make amends to Susan!'

XIII

The cottage which Michael Henchard hired for his wife Susan under her name of Newson—in pursuance of their plan—was in the upper or western part of the town, near the Roman wall, and the avenue which overshadowed it. The evening sun seemed to shine more yellowly there than anywhere else this autumn—stretching its rays, as the hours grew later, under the lowest sycamore boughs, and steeping the ground-floor of the dwelling, with its green shutters, in a substratum of radiance which the foliage screened from the upper parts. Beneath these sycamores on the town walls could be seen from the sitting-room the tumuli[1] and earth forts of the distant uplands; making it altogether a pleasant spot, with the usual touch of melancholy that a past-marked prospect lends.

As soon as the mother and daughter were comfortably installed, with a white-aproned servant and all complete, Henchard paid them a visit, and remained to tea. During the entertainment Elizabeth was carefully hoodwinked by the very general tone of the conversation that pre-vailed—a proceeding which seemed to afford some humour to Henchard, though his wife was not particularly happy in it. The visit was repeated again and again with business-like determination by the Mayor, who seemed to have schooled himself into a course of strict mechanical rightness towards this woman of prior claim, at any expense to the later one and to his own sentiments.

One afternoon the daughter was not indoors when Henchard came, and he said drily, 'This is a very good opportunity for me to ask you to name the happy day, Susan.'

The poor woman smiled faintly; she did not enjoy pleasantries on a situation into which she had entered solely for the sake of her girl's rep-utation. She liked them so little, indeed, that there was room for wonder why she had countenanced deception at all, and had not bravely let the girl know her history. But the flesh is weak;[2] and the true explanation came in due course.

'O Michael!' she said, 'I am afraid all this is taking up your time and giving trouble—when I did not expect any such thing!' And she looked at him and at his dress as a man of affluence, and at the furniture he had provided for the room—ornate and lavish to her eyes.

'Not at all,' said Henchard, in rough benignity. 'This is only a cot-tage—it costs me next to nothing. And as to taking up my time'—here his red and black visage kindled with satisfaction—'I've a splendid fellow to superintend my business now—a man whose like I've never been able to lay hands on before. I shall soon be able to leave everything to him, and have more time to call my own than I've had for these last twenty years.'

Henchard's visits here grew so frequent and so regular that it soon became whispered, and then openly discussed in Casterbridge that the masterful, coercive Mayor of the town was captured and enervated by the genteel widow Mrs. Newson. His well-known haughty indifference to the society of womankind, his silent avoidance of converse with the sex, contributed a piquancy to what would otherwise have been an unro-mantic matter enough. That such a poor fragile woman should be his

---

1. Mounds of earth, usually to mark a grave (from the Latin).
2. See Mark 14.38: "The spirit truly is ready, but the flesh is weak."

choice was inexplicable, except on the ground that the engagement was a family affair in which sentimental passion had no place; for it was known that they were related in some way. Mrs. Henchard was so pale that the boys called her 'The Ghost.' Sometimes Henchard overheard this epithet when they passed together along the Walks—as the avenues on the walls were named—at which his face would darken with an expression of destructiveness towards the speakers ominous to see; but he said nothing.

He pressed on the preparations for his union, or rather reunion, with this pale creature in a dogged, unflinching spirit which did credit to his conscientiousness. Nobody would have conceived from his outward demeanour that there was no amatory fire or pulse of romance acting as stimulant to the bustle going on in his gaunt, great house; nothing but three large resolves—one, to make amends to his neglected Susan; another, to provide a comfortable home for Elizabeth-Jane under his paternal eye; and a third, to castigate himself with the thorns[3] which these restitutory acts brought in their train; among them the lowering of his dignity in public opinion by marrying so comparatively humble a woman.

Susan Henchard entered a carriage for the first time in her life when she stepped into the plain brougham[4] which drew up at the door on the wedding-day to take her and Elizabeth-Jane to church. It was a windless morning of warm November rain, which floated down like meal, and lay in a powdery form on the nap of hats and coats. Few people had gathered round the church door though they were well packed within. The Scotchman, who assisted as groomsman, was of course the only one present, beyond the chief actors, who knew the true situation of the contracting parties. He, however, was too inexperienced, too thoughtful, too judicial, too strongly conscious of the serious side of the business, to enter into the scene in its dramatic aspect. That required the special genius of Christopher Coney, Solomon Longways, Buzzford, and their fellows. But they knew nothing of the secret; though, as the time for coming out of church drew on, they gathered on the pavement adjoining, and expounded the subject according to their lights.

"'Tis five-and-forty years since I had my settlement in this here town,' said Coney; 'but daze me if ever I see a man wait so long before to take so little! There's a chance even for thee after this, Nance Mockridge.' The remark was addressed to a woman who stood behind his shoulder— the same who had exhibited Henchard's bad bread in public when Elizabeth and her mother entered Casterbridge.

'Be cust if I'd marry any such as he, or thee either,' replied that lady.

3. The apostle Paul described his human infirmities as "a thorn in the flesh," warning him against the sin of pride. See 2 Corinthians 12.7.
4. Closed carriage drawn by a single horse, with the driver sitting outside.

'As for thee, Christopher, we know what ye be, and the less said the better. And as for he—well, there—(lowering her voice) 'tis said 'a was a poor parish 'prentice—I wouldn't say it for all the world—but 'a was a poor parish 'prentice, that began life wi' no more belonging to 'en than a carrion crow.'

'And now he's worth ever so much a minute,' murmured Longways. 'When a man is said to be worth so much a minute, he's a man to be considered!'

Turning, he saw a circular disc reticulated with creases, and recognized the smiling countenance of the fat woman who had asked for another song at the Three Mariners. 'Well, Mother Cuxsom,' he said, 'how's this? Here's Mrs. Newson, a mere skellinton,[5] has got another husband to keep her, while a woman of your tonnage have not.'

'I have not. Nor another to beat me. . . . Ah, yes, Cuxsom's gone, and so shall leather breeches!'[6]

'Yes; with the blessing of God leather breeches shall go.'

''Tisn't worth my old while to think of another husband,' continued Mrs. Cuxsom. 'And yet I'll lay my life I'm as respectable born as she.'

'True; your mother was a very good woman—I can mind her. She were rewarded by the Agricultural Society[7] for having begot the greatest number of healthy children without parish assistance, and other virtuous marvels.'

''Twas that that kept us so low upon ground—that great hungry family.'

'Ay. Where the pigs be many the wash[8] runs thin.'

'And dostn't mind how mother would sing, Christopher?' continued Mrs. Cuxsom, kindling at the retrospection; 'and how we went with her to the party at Mellstock, do ye mind?—at old Dame Ledlow's, farmer Shiner's aunt, do ye mind?—she we used to call Toad-skin, because her face were so yaller and freckled, do ye mind?'

'I do, hee-hee, I do!' said Christopher Coney.

'And well do I—for I was getting up husband-high at that time—one-half girl, and t'other half woman, as one may say. And canst mind'—she prodded Solomon's shoulder with her finger-tip, while her eyes twinkled between the crevices of their lids—'canst mind the sherry-wine, and the zilver-snuffers,[9] and how Joan Dummett was took bad when we were coming home, and Jack Griggs was forced to carry her through the mud; and how 'a let her fall in Dairyman Sweetapple's cow-barton,[1] and we had to clane her gown wi' grass—never such a mess as 'a were in?'

'Ay—that I do—hee-hee, such doggery as there was in them ancient

---

5. Skeleton.
6. Trousers made of long-lasting but not indestructible material.
7. A number of such societies were formed in and around the 1830s to promote good farming practices.
8. Pig-swill.
9. Devices for trimming or putting out candles.
1. Cow-yard.

days, to be sure! Ah, the miles I used to walk then; and now I can hardly step over a furrow!'

Their reminiscences were cut short by the appearance of the reunited
pair—Henchard looking round upon the idlers with that ambiguous
gaze of his, which at one moment seemed to mean satisfaction, and at
another fiery disdain.

'Well—there's a difference between 'em, though he do call himself a
teetotaller,' said Nance Mockridge. 'She'll wish her cake dough[2] afore
she's done of him. There's a bluebeardy[3] look about 'en; and 'twill out
in time.'

'Stuff—he's well enough! Some folk want their luck buttered. If I had
a choice as wide as the ocean sea I wouldn't wish for a better man. A
poor twanking[4] woman like her—'tis a godsend for her, and hardly a pair
of jumps or night-rail[5] to her name.'

The plain little brougham drove off in the mist, and the idlers dispersed. 'Well, we hardly know how to look at things in these times!' said
Solomon. 'There was a man dropped down dead yesterday, not so very
many miles from here; and what wi' that, and this moist weather, 'tis
scarce worth one's while to begin any work o' consequence to-day. I'm
in such a low key with drinking nothing but small table ninepenny[6] this
last week or two that I shall call and warm up at the Mar'ners as I pass
along.'

'I don't know but that I may as well go with 'ee, Solomon,' said
Christopher; 'I'm as clammy as a cockle-snail.'[7]

XIV

A Martinmas summer[1] of Mrs. Henchard's life set in with her entry into
her husband's large house and respectable social orbit; and it was as
bright as such summers well can be. Lest she should pine for deeper
affection than he could give he made a point of showing some semblance of it in external action. Among other things he had the iron rail-
ings, that had smiled sadly in dull rust for the last eighty years, painted a
bright green, and the heavy-barred, small-paned Georgian sash windows
enlivened with three coats of white. He was as kind to her as a man,
mayor, and churchwarden could possibly be. The house was large, the
rooms lofty, and the landings wide; and the two unassuming women
scarcely made a perceptible addition to its contents.

To Elizabeth-Jane the time was a most triumphant one. The freedom

2. She'll wish she had not changed her condition (i.e., from supposed widow to married woman).
3. Resembling Bluebeard, who in the folktale married and then murdered a succession of wives.
4. Miserable, peevish.
5. Old-fashioned bodice worn instead of stays; *night-rail*: night-dress.
6. Weak beer that cost nine pence a gallon.
7. Edible marine mollusk.
1. Unusually warm autumn weather. St. Martin's Day is on November 11.

she experienced, the indulgence with which she was treated, went beyond her expectations. The reposeful, easy, affluent life to which her mother's marriage had introduced her was, in truth, the beginning of a great change in Elizabeth. She found she could have nice personal possessions and ornaments for the asking, and, as the mediæval saying puts it, 'Take, have, and keep, are pleasant words.' With peace of mind came development, and with development beauty. Knowledge—the result of great natural insight—she did not lack; learning, accomplishments—those, alas, she had not; but as the winter and spring passed by her thin face and figure filled out in rounder and softer curves; the lines and contractions upon her young brow went away; the muddiness of skin which she had looked upon as her lot by nature departed with a change to abundance of good things, and a bloom came upon her cheek. Perhaps, too, her grey, thoughtful eyes revealed an arch gaiety sometimes; but this was infrequent; the sort of wisdom which looked from their pupils did not readily keep company with these lighter moods. Like all people who have known rough times, light-heartedness seemed to her too irrational and inconsequent to be indulged in except as a reckless dram now and then; for she had been too early habituated to anxious reasoning to drop the habit suddenly. She felt none of those ups and downs of spirit which beset so many people without cause; never—to paraphrase a recent poet[2]—never a gloom in Elizabeth-Jane's soul but she well knew how it came there; and her present cheerfulness was fairly proportionate to her solid guarantees for the same.

It might have been supposed that, given a girl rapidly becoming good-looking, comfortably circumstanced, and for the first time in her life commanding ready money, she would go and make a fool of herself by dress. But no. The reasonableness of almost everything that Elizabeth did was nowhere more conspicuous than in this question of clothes. To keep in the rear of opportunity in matters of indulgence is as valuable a habit as to keep abreast of opportunity in matters of enterprise. This unsophisticated girl did it by an innate perceptiveness that was almost genius. Thus she refrained from bursting out like a water-flower that spring, and clothing herself in puffings[3] and knick-knacks, as most of the Casterbridge girls would have done in her circumstances. Her triumph was tempered by circumspection; she had still that fieldmouse fear of the coulter[4] of destiny despite fair promise, which is common among the thoughtful who have suffered early from poverty and oppression.

'I won't be too gay on any account,' she would say to herself. 'It would

---

2. Probably Matthew Arnold (1822–1888), whose essay on Wordsworth includes the comment "no line in Goethe's poetry . . . but its maker well knew how it came there" (*Essays in Criticism: Second Series*, 1888). The word "recent" was added in the 1895 edition of the novel.
3. Trimmings of ruffs or frills.
4. The blade of a plough. Hardy is probably referring to Robert Burns's poem "To a Mouse, On turning her up in her Nest, with the Plough."

be tempting Providence to hurl mother and me down, and afflict us again as He used to do.'

We now see her in a black silk bonnet, velvet mantle or silk spencer,[5] dark dress, and carrying a sunshade. In this latter article she drew the line at fringe, and had it plain edged, with a little ivory ring for keeping it closed. It was odd about the necessity for that sunshade. She discovered that with the clarification of her complexion and the birth of pink cheeks her skin had grown more sensitive to the sun's rays. She protected those cheeks forthwith, deeming spotlessness part of womanliness.

Henchard had become very fond of her, and she went out with him more frequently than with her mother now. Her appearance one day was so attractive that he looked at her critically.

'I happened to have the ribbon by me, so I made it up,' she faltered, thinking him perhaps dissatisfied with some rather bright trimming she had donned for the first time.

'Ay—of course—to be sure,' he replied in his leonine way. 'Do as you like—or rather as your mother advises ye. 'Od send—I've nothing to say to't!'

Indoors she appeared with her hair divided by a parting that arched like a white rainbow from ear to ear. All in front of this line was covered with a thick encampment of curls; all behind was dressed smoothly, and drawn to a knob.

The three members of the family were sitting at breakfast one day, and Henchard was looking silently, as he often did, at this head of hair, which in colour was brown—rather light than dark. 'I thought Elizabeth-Jane's hair—didn't you tell me that Elizabeth-Jane's hair promised to be black when she was a baby?' he said to his wife.

She looked startled, jerked his foot warningly, and murmured, 'Did I?'

As soon as Elizabeth was gone to her own room Henchard resumed. 'Begad, I nearly forgot myself just now! What I meant was that the girl's hair certainly looked as if it would be darker, when she was a baby.'

'It did; but they alter so,' replied Susan.

'Their hair gets darker, I know—but I wasn't aware it lightened ever?'

'O yes.' And the same uneasy expression came out on her face, to which the future held the key. It passed as Henchard went on:

'Well, so much the better. Now, Susan, I want to have her called Miss Henchard—not Miss Newson. Lot's o' people do it already in carelessness—it is her legal name—so it may as well be made her usual name—I don't like t'other name at all for my own flesh and blood. I'll advertise it in the Casterbridge paper—that's the way they do it. She won't object.'

'No. O no. But——'

'Well, then, I shall do it,' said he, peremptorily. 'Surely, if she's willing, you must wish it as much as I?'

5. Close-fitting short jacket.

'O yes—if she agrees let us do it by all means,' she replied.

Then Mrs. Henchard acted somewhat inconsistently; it might have been called falsely, but that her manner was emotional and full of the earnestness of one who wishes to do right at great hazard. She went to Elizabeth-Jane, whom she found sewing in her own sitting-room upstairs, and told her what had been proposed about her surname. 'Can you agree—is it not a slight upon Newson—now he's dead and gone?'

Elizabeth reflected. 'I'll think of it, mother,' she answered.

When, later in the day, she saw Henchard, she adverted to the matter at once, in a way which showed that the line of feeling started by her mother had been persevered in. 'Do you wish this change so very much, sir?' she asked.

'Wish it? Why, my blessed fathers, what an ado you women make about a trifle! I proposed it—that's all. Now, 'Lizabeth-Jane, just please yourself. Curse me if I care what you do. Now, you understand, don't 'ee go agreeing to it to please me.'

Here the subject dropped, and nothing more was said, and nothing was done, and Elizabeth still passed as Miss Newson, and not by her legal name.

Meanwhile the great corn and hay traffic conducted by Henchard throve under the management of Donald Farfrae as it had never thriven before. It had formerly moved in jolts; now it went on oiled castors. The old crude *vivâ voce*[6] system of Henchard, in which everything depended upon his memory, and bargains were made by the tongue alone, was swept away. Letters and ledgers took the place of 'I'll do't,' and 'you shall hae't'; and, as in all such cases of advance, the rugged picturesqueness of the old method disappeared with its inconveniences.

The position of Elizabeth-Jane's room—rather high in the house, so that it commanded a view of the hay-stores and granaries across the garden—afforded her opportunity for accurate observation of what went on there. She saw that Donald and Mr. Henchard were inseparables. When walking together Henchard would lay his arm familiarly on his manager's shoulder, as if Farfrae were a younger brother, bearing so heavily that his slight figure bent under the weight. Occasionally she would hear a perfect cannonade of laughter from Henchard, arising from something Donald had said, the latter looking quite innocent and not laughing at all. In Henchard's somewhat lonely life he evidently found the young man as desirable for comradeship as he was useful for consultations. Donald's brightness of intellect maintained in the corn-factor the admiration it had won at the first hour of their meeting. The poor opinion, and but ill-concealed, that he entertained of the slim Farfrae's physical girth, strength, and dash was more than counterbalanced by the immense respect he had for his brains.

6. By word of mouth rather than in writing (from the Latin).

Her quiet eye discerned that Henchard's tigerish affection for the younger man, his constant liking to have Farfrae near him, now and then resulted in a tendency to domineer, which, however, was checked in a moment when Donald exhibited marks of real offence. One day, looking down on their figures from on high, she heard the latter remark, as they stood in the doorway between the garden and yard, that their habit of walking and driving about together rather neutralized Farfrae's value as a second pair of eyes, which should be used in places where the principal was not. "Od damn it,' cried Henchard, 'what's all the world! I like a fellow to talk to. Now come along and hae some supper, and don't take too much thought about things, or ye'll drive me crazy.'

When she walked with her mother, on the other hand, she often beheld the Scotchman looking at them with a curious interest. The fact that he had met her at the Three Mariners was insufficient to account for it, since on the occasions on which she had entered his room he had never raised his eyes. Besides, it was at her mother more particularly than at herself that he looked, to Elizabeth-Jane's half-conscious, simple-minded, perhaps pardonable, disappointment. Thus she could not account for this interest by her own attractiveness, and she decided that it might be apparent only—a way of turning his eyes that Mr. Farfrae had.

She did not divine the ample explanation of his manner, without personal vanity, that was afforded by the fact of Donald being the depositary of Henchard's confidence in respect of his past treatment of the pale, chastened mother who walked by her side. Her conjectures on that past never went further than faint ones based on things casually heard and seen—mere guesses that Henchard and her mother might have been lovers in their younger days, who had quarrelled and parted.

Casterbridge, as has been hinted, was a place deposited in the block upon a corn-field. There was no suburb in the modern sense, or transitional intermixture of town and down. It stood, with regard to the wide fertile land adjoining, clean-cut and distinct, like a chess-board on a green table-cloth. The farmer's boy could sit under his barley-mow[7] and pitch a stone into the office-window of the town-clerk; reapers at work among the sheaves nodded to acquaintances standing on the pavement-corner; the red-robed judge, when he condemned a sheep-stealer, pronounced sentence to the tune of Baa, that floated in at the window from the remainder of the flock browsing hard by; and at executions the waiting crowd stood in a meadow immediately before the drop, out of which the cows had been temporarily driven to give the spectators room.

The corn grown on the upland side of the borough was garnered by farmers who lived in an eastern purlieu called Durnover. Here wheat-ricks overhung the old Roman street, and thrust their eaves against the

7. Stack of unthreshed barley.

church tower; green-thatched barns, with doorways as high as the gates of Solomon's temple,[8] opened directly upon the main thoroughfare. Barns indeed were so numerous as to alternate with every half-dozen houses along the way. Here lived burgesses who daily walked the fallow;[9] shepherds in an intra-mural squeeze. A street of farmers' homesteads— a street ruled by a mayor and corporation, yet echoing with the thump of the flail, the flutter of the winnowing-fan, and the purr of the milk into the pails—a street which had nothing urban in it whatever—this was the Durnover end of Casterbridge.

Henchard, as was natural, dealt largely with this nursery or bed of small farmers close at hand—and his waggons were often down that way. One day, when arrangements were in progress for getting home corn from one of the aforesaid farms, Elizabeth-Jane received a note by hand, asking her to oblige the writer by coming at once to a granary on Durnover Hill. As this was the granary whose contents Henchard was removing, she thought the request had something to do with his business, and proceeded thither as soon as she had put on her bonnet. The granary was just within the farm-yard, and stood on stone staddles, high enough for persons to walk under. The gates were open, but nobody was within. However, she entered and waited. Presently she saw a figure approaching the gate—that of Donald Farfrae. He looked up at the church clock, and came in. By some unaccountable shyness, some wish not to meet him there alone, she quickly ascended the step-ladder leading to the granary door, and entered it before he had seen her. Farfrae advanced, imagining himself in solitude; and a few drops of rain beginning to fall he moved and stood under the shelter where she had just been standing. Here he leant against one of the staddles, and gave himself up to patience. He, too, was plainly expecting some one; could it be herself? if so, why? In a few minutes he looked at his watch, and then pulled out a note, a duplicate of the one she had herself received.

The situation began to be very awkward, and the longer she waited the more awkward it became. To emerge from a door just above his head and descend the ladder, and show she had been in hiding there, would look so very foolish that she still waited on. A winnowing machine stood close beside her, and to relieve her suspense she gently moved the handle; whereupon a cloud of wheat husks flew out into her face, and covered her clothes and bonnet, and stuck into the fur of her victorine.[1] He must have heard the slight movement for he looked up, and then ascended the steps.

'Ah—it's Miss Newson,' he said as soon as he could see into the granary. 'I didn't know you were there. I have kept the appointment, and am at your service.'

8. The temple is described in 1 Kings 6, though its height is not mentioned.
9. Farmland allowed to lie idle for a season.
1. Fur scarf or cape.

'O Mr. Farfrae,' she faltered; 'so have I. But I didn't know it was you who wished to see me, otherwise I ——'

'I wished to see you? O no — at least, that is, I am afraid there may be a mistake.'

'Didn't you ask me to come here? Didn't you write this?' Elizabeth held out her note.

'No. Indeed, at no hand would I have thought of it! And for you — didn't you ask me? This is not your writing?' And he held up his.

'By no means.'

'And is that really so! Then it's somebody wanting to see us both. Perhaps we would do well to wait a little longer.'   ·

Acting on this consideration they lingered, Elizabeth-Jane's face being arranged to an expression of preternatural composure, and the young Scot, at every footstep in the street without, looking from under the granary to see if the passer were about to enter and declare himself their summoner. They watched individual drops of rain creeping down the thatch of the opposite rick — straw after straw — till they reached the bottom; but nobody came, and the granary roof began to drip.

'The person is not likely to be coming,' said Farfrae. 'It's a trick perhaps, and if so, it's a great pity to waste our time like this, and so much to be done.'

''Tis a great liberty,' said Elizabeth.

'It's true, Miss Newson. We'll hear news of this some day, depend on't, and who it was that did it. I wouldn't stand for it hindering myself; but you, Miss Newson' ——

'I don't mind — much,' she replied.

'Neither do I.'

They lapsed again into silence. 'You are anxious to get back to Scotland, I suppose, Mr. Farfrae?' she inquired.

'O no, Miss Newson. Why would I be?'

'I only supposed you might be from the song you sang at the Three Mariners — about Scotland and home, I mean — which you seemed to feel so deep down in your heart; so that we all felt for you.'

'Ay — and I did sing there — I did —— But, Miss Newson' — and Donald's voice musically undulated between two semitones, as it always did when he became earnest — 'it's well you feel a song for a few minutes, and your eyes they get quite tearful; but you finish it, and for all you felt you don't mind it or think of it again for a long while. O no, I don't want to go back! Yet I'll sing the song to you wi' pleasure whenever you like. I could sing it now, and not mind at all?'

'Thank you, indeed. But I fear I must go — rain or no.'

'Ay! Then, Miss Newson, ye had better say nothing about this hoax, and take no heed of it. And if the person should say anything to you, be civil to him or her, as if you did not mind it — so you'll take the clever person's laugh away.' In speaking his eyes became fixed upon her dress, still sown with wheat husks. 'There's husks and dust on you. Perhaps you don't know it?' he said, in tones of extreme delicacy. 'And it's very bad to let rain come upon clothes when there's chaff on them. It washes in and spoils them. Let me help you—blowing is the best.'

As Elizabeth neither assented nor dissented Donald Farfrae began blowing her back hair, and her side hair, and her neck, and the crown of her bonnet, and the fur of her victorine, Elizabeth saying, 'O, thank you,' at every puff. At last she was fairly clean, though Farfrae, having got over his first concern at the situation, seemed in no manner of hurry to be gone.

'Ah—now I'll go and get ye an umbrella,' he said.

She declined the offer, stepped out and was gone. Farfrae walked slowly after, looking thoughtfully at her diminishing figure, and whistling in undertones, 'As I came down through Cannobie.'[2]

XV

At first Miss Newson's budding beauty was not regarded with much interest by anybody in Casterbridge. Donald Farfrae's gaze, it is true, was now attracted by the Mayor's so-called step-daughter, but he was only one. The truth is that she was but a poor illustrative instance of the prophet Baruch's sly definition: 'The virgin that loveth to go gay.'[1]

When she walked abroad she seemed to be occupied with an inner chamber of ideas, and to have slight need for visible objects. She formed curious resolves on checking gay fancies in the matter of clothes, because it was inconsistent with her past life to blossom gaudily the moment she had become possessed of money. But nothing is more insidious than the evolution of wishes from mere fancies, and of wants from mere wishes. Henchard gave Elizabeth-Jane a box of delicately-tinted gloves one spring day. She wanted to wear them to show her appreciation of his kindness, but she had no bonnet that would harmonize. As an artistic indulgence she thought she would have such a bonnet. When she had a bonnet that would go with the gloves she had no dress that would go with the bonnet. It was now absolutely necessary to finish; she ordered the requisite article, and found that she had no sunshade to go with the dress. In for a penny in for a pound; she bought the sunshade, and the whole structure was at last complete.

Everybody was attracted, and some said that her bygone simplicity was the art that conceals art, the 'delicate imposition' of Rochefoucauld;[2] she had produced an effect, a contrast, and it had been done on purpose. As a matter of fact this was not true, but it had its result; for as soon as

2. Unidentified, but possibly a variant on Robert Burns's "Bonnie Peg."
1. In fact the words of the prophet Jeremiah, quoted in the Apocryphal book of Baruch; see Baruch 6.9.
2. François, Duc de la Rochefoucauld (1613–1680). Number 289 of his *Maximes* can be translated "a feigned simplicity is a delicate imposition" (i.e., deception).

Casterbridge thought her artful it thought her worth notice. 'It is the first time in my life that I have been so much admired.' she said to herself; 'though perhaps it is by those whose admiration is not worth having.'

But Donald Farfrae admired her, too; and altogether the time was an exciting one; sex had never before asserted itself in her so strongly, for in former days she had perhaps been too impersonally human to be distinctively feminine. After an unprecedented success one day she came indoors, went upstairs, and leant upon her bed face downwards, quite forgetting the possible creasing and damage. 'Good Heaven,' she whispered, 'can it be? Here am I setting up as the town beauty!'

When she had thought it over, her usual fear of exaggerating appearances engendered a deep sadness. 'There is something wrong in all this,' she mused. 'If they only knew what an unfinished girl I am—that I can't talk Italian, or use globes, or show any of the accomplishments they learn at boarding-schools, how they would despise me! Better sell all this finery and buy myself grammar-books and dictionaries and a history of all the philosophies!'

She looked from the window and saw Henchard and Farfrae in the hay-yard talking, with that impetuous cordiality on the Mayor's part, and genial modesty on the younger man's, that was now so generally observable in their intercourse. Friendship between man and man; what a rugged strength there was in it, as evinced by these two. And yet the seed that was to lift the foundation of this friendship was at that moment taking root in a chink of its structure.

It was about six o'clock; the men were dropping off homeward one by one. The last to leave was a round-shouldered, blinking young man of nineteen or twenty, whose mouth fell ajar on the slightest provocation, seemingly because there was no chin to support it. Henchard called aloud to him as he went out of the gate. 'Here—Abel Whittle!'

Whittle turned, and ran back a few steps. 'Yes, sir,' he said, in breathless deprecation, as if he knew what was coming next.

'Once more—be in time to-morrow morning. You see what's to be done, and you hear what I say, and you know I'm not going to be trifled with any longer.'

'Yes, sir.' Then Abel Whittle left, and Henchard and Farfrae; and Elizabeth saw no more of them.

Now there was good reason for this command on Henchard's part. Poor Abel, as he was called, had an inveterate habit of over-sleeping himself and coming late to his work. His anxious will was to be among the earliest; but if his comrades omitted to pull the string that he always tied round his great toe and left hanging out of the window for that purpose, his will was as wind. He did not arrive in time.

As he was often second hand at the hay-weighing, or at the crane which lifted the sacks, or was one of those who had to accompany the waggons into the country to fetch away stacks that had been purchased, this affliction of Abel's was productive of much inconvenience. For two mornings in the present week he had kept the others waiting nearly an hour; hence Henchard's threat. It now remained to be seen what would happen to-morrow.

Six o'clock struck, and there was no Whittle. At half-past six Henchard entered the yard; the waggon was horsed that Abel was to accompany; and the other man had been waiting twenty minutes. Then Henchard swore, and Whittle coming up breathless at that instant, the corn-factor turned on him, and declared with an oath that this was the last time; that if he were behind once more, by God, he would come and drag him out o' bed.

'There is sommit wrong in my make, your worshipful!' said Abel, 'especially in the inside, whereas my poor dumb brain gets as dead as a clot afore I've said my few scrags of prayers. Yes—it came on as a stripling, just afore I'd got man's wages, whereas I never enjoy my bed at all, for no sooner do I lie down than I be asleep, and afore I be awake I be up. I've fretted my gizzard green[3] about it, maister, but what can I do? Now last night, afore I went to bed, I only had a scantling[4] o' cheese and——'

'I don't want to hear it!' roared Henchard. 'To-morrow the waggons must start at four, and if you're not here, stand clear. I'll mortify[5] thy flesh for thee!'

'But let me clear up my points, your worshipful——'

Henchard turned away.

'He asked me and he questioned me, and then 'a wouldn't hear my points!' said Abel, to the yard in general. 'Now, I shall twitch like a moment-hand[6] all night to-night for fear o' him!'

The journey to be taken by the waggons next day was a long one into Blackmoor Vale, and at four o'clock lanterns were moving about the yard. But Abel was missing. Before either of the other men could run to Abel's and warn him, Henchard appeared in the garden doorway. 'Where's Abel Whittle? Not come after all I've said? Now I'll carry out my word, by my blessed fathers—nothing else will do him any good! I'm going up that way.'

Henchard went off, entered Abel's house, a little cottage in Back Street, the door of which was never locked because the inmates had nothing to lose. Reaching Whittle's bedside the corn-factor shouted a bass note so vigorously that Abel started up instantly, and beholding Henchard standing over him, was galvanized into spasmodic movements which had not much relation to getting on his clothes.

---

3. Worried myself sick.
4. Morsel.
5. Literally, put to death. An echo of St. Paul's words on demanding strict self-denial; see Colossians 3.5.
6. Minute hand on a clock, which makes a visible jump each minute.

'Out of bed, sir, and off to the granary, or you leave my employ to-day! 'Tis to teach ye a lesson. March on; never mind your breeches!'

The unhappy Whittle threw on his sleeve waistcoat, and managed to get into his boots at the bottom of the stairs, while Henchard thrust his hat over his head. Whittle then trotted on down Back Street, Henchard walking sternly behind.

Just at this time Farfrae, who had been to Henchard's house to look for him, came out of the back gate, and saw something white fluttering in the morning gloom, which he soon perceived to be the part of Abel's shirt that showed below his waistcoat.

'For maircy's sake, what object's this?' said Farfrae, following Abel into the yard, Henchard being some way in the rear by this time.

'Ye see, Mr. Farfrae,' gibbered Abel with a resigned smile of terror, 'he said he'd mortify my flesh if so be I didn't get up sooner, and now he's a-doing on't! Ye see it can't be helped, Mr. Farfrae; things do happen queer sometimes! Yes—I'll go to Blackmoor Vale half naked as I be, since he do command; but I shall kill myself afterwards; I can't outlive the disgrace; for the women-folk will be looking out of their winders at my mortification all the way along, and laughing me to scorn as a man 'ithout breeches! You know how I feel such things, Maister Farfrae, and how forlorn thoughts get hold upon me. Yes—I shall do myself harm— I feel it coming on!'

'Get back home, and slip on your breeches, and come to wark like a man! If ye go not, you'll ha'e your death standing there!'

'I'm afeard I mustn't! Mr. Henchard said——'

'I don't care what Mr. Henchard said, nor anybody else! 'Tis simple foolishness to do this. Go and dress yourself instantly, Whittle.'

'Hullo, hullo!' said Henchard, coming up behind. 'Who's sending him back?'

All the men looked towards Farfrae.

'I am,' said Donald. 'I say this joke has been carried far enough.'

'And I say it hasn't! Get up in the waggon, Whittle.'

'Not if I am manager,' said Farfrae. 'He either goes home, or I march out of this yard for good.'

Henchard looked at him with a face stern and red. But he paused for a moment, and their eyes met. Donald went up to him, for he saw in Henchard's look that he began to regret this.

'Come,' said Donald quietly, 'a man o' your position should ken better, sir! It is tyrannical and no worthy of you.'

''Tis not tyrannical!' murmured Henchard, like a sullen boy. 'It is to make him remember!' He presently added, in a tone of one bitterly hurt: 'Why did you speak to me before them like that, Farfrae? You might have stopped till we were alone. Ah—I know why! I've told ye the secret o' my life—fool that I was to do't—and you take advantage of me!'

'I had forgot it,' said Farfrae simply.

Henchard looked on the ground, said nothing more, and turned away. During the day Farfrae learnt from the men that Henchard had kept Abel's old mother in coals and snuff all the previous winter, which made him less antagonistic to the corn-factor. But Henchard continued moody and silent, and when one of the men inquired of him if some oats should be hoisted to an upper floor or not, he said shortly, 'Ask Mr. Farfrae. He's master here!'

Morally he was; there could be no doubt of it. Henchard, who had hitherto been the most admired man in his circle, was the most admired no longer. One day the daughters of a deceased farmer in Durnover wanted an opinion on the value of their haystack, and sent a messenger to ask Mr. Farfrae to oblige them with one. The messenger, who was a child, met in the yard not Farfrae, but Henchard.

'Very well,' he said. 'I'll come.'

'But please will Mr. Farfrae come?' said the child.

'I am going that way . . . Why Mr. Farfrae?' said Henchard, with the fixed look of thought. 'Why do people always want Mr. Farfrae?'

'I suppose because they like him so — that's what they say.'

'Oh — I see — that's what they say — hey? They like him because he's cleverer than Mr. Henchard, and because he knows more; and, in short, Mr. Henchard can't hold a candle to him — hey?'

'Yes — that's just it, sir — some of it.'

'Oh, there's more? Of course there's more! What besides? Come, here's sixpence for a fairing.'[7]

'"And he's better-tempered, and Henchard's a fool to him," they say. And when some of the women were a-walking home they said, "He's a diment[8] — he's a chap o' wax[9] — he's the best — he's the horse for my money," says they. And they said, "He's the most understanding man o' them two by long chalks.[1] I wish he was the master instead of Henchard," they said.'

'They'll talk any nonsense,' Henchard replied with covered gloom. 'Well, you can go now. And *I* am coming to value the hay, d'ye hear? — I.' The boy departed, and Henchard murmured, 'Wish he were master here, do they?'

He went towards Durnover. On his way he overtook Farfrae. They walked on together, Henchard looking mostly on the ground.

'You're no yoursel' the day?' Donald inquired.

'Yes, I am very well,' said Henchard.

'But ye are a bit down — surely ye are down? Why, there's nothing to be angry about! 'Tis splendid stuff that we've got from Blackmoor Vale. By the by, the people in Durnover want their hay valued.'

7. Cake or gift sold at a fair.
8. Diamond.
9. Man of ability.
1. By a long way.

'Yes. I am going there.'

'I'll go with ye.'

As Henchard did not reply Donald practised a piece of music *sotto voce*,[2] till, getting near the bereaved people's door, he stopped himself with —

'Ah, as their father is dead I won't go on with such as that. How could I forget?'

'Do you care so very much about hurting folks' feelings?' observed Henchard with a half sneer. 'You do, I know — especially mine!'

'I am sorry if I have hurt yours, sir,' replied Donald, standing still, with a second expression of the same sentiment in the regretfulness of his face. 'Why should you say it — think it?'

The cloud lifted from Henchard's brow, and as Donald finished the corn-merchant turned to him, regarding his breast rather than his face.

'I have been hearing things that vexed me,' he said. ''Twas that made me short in my manner — made me overlook what you really are. Now, I don't want to go in here about this hay — Farfrae, you can do it better than I. They sent for 'ee, too. I have to attend a meeting of the Town Council at eleven, and 'tis drawing on for't.'

They parted thus in renewed friendship, Donald forbearing to ask Henchard for meanings that were not very plain to him. On Henchard's part there was now again repose; and yet, whenever he thought of Farfrae, it was with a dim dread; and he often regretted that he had told the young man his whole heart, and confided to him the secrets of his life.

XVI

On this account Henchard's manner towards Farfrae insensibly became more reserved. He was courteous — too courteous — and Farfrae was quite surprised at the good breeding which now for the first time showed itself among the qualities of a man he had hitherto thought undisciplined, if warm and sincere. The corn-factor seldom or never again put his arm upon the young man's shoulder so as to nearly weigh him down with the pressure of mechanized friendship. He left off coming to Donald's lodgings and shouting into the passage, 'Hoy, Farfrae, boy, come and have some dinner with us! Don't sit here in solitary confinement!' But in the daily routine of their business there was little change.

Thus their lives rolled on till a day of public rejoicing was suggested to the country at large in celebration of a national event[1] that had recently taken place.

For some time Casterbridge, by nature slow, made no response. Then one day Donald Farfrae broached the subject to Henchard by asking if

2. In an undertone (from the Italian).
1. Possibly the birth of Princess Alice (1843) or Prince Alfred (1844).

he would have any objection to lend some rick-cloths[2] to himself and a few others, who contemplated getting up an entertainment of some sort on the day named, and required a shelter for the same, to which they might charge admission at the rate of so much a head.

'Have as many cloths as you like,' Henchard replied.

When his manager had gone about the business Henchard was fired with emulation. It certainly had been very remiss of him, as Mayor, he thought, to call no meeting ere this, to discuss what should be done on this holiday. But Farfrae had been so cursed quick in his movements as to give old-fashioned people in authority no chance of the initiative. However, it was not too late; and on second thoughts he determined to take upon his own shoulders the responsibility of organizing some amusements, if the other Councilmen would leave the matter in his hands. To this they quite readily agreed, the majority being fine old crusted characters who had a decided taste for living without worry.

So Henchard set about his preparations for a really brilliant thing— such as should be worthy of the venerable town. As for Farfrae's little affair, Henchard nearly forgot it; except once now and then when, on it coming into his mind, he said to himself, 'Charge admission at so much a head—just like a Scotchman!—who is going to pay anything a head?' The diversions which the Mayor intended to provide were to be entirely free.

He had grown so dependent upon Donald that he could scarcely resist calling him in to consult. But by sheer self-coercion he refrained. No, he thought, Farfrae would be suggesting such improvements in his damned luminous way that in spite of himself he, Henchard, would sink to the position of second fiddle, and only scrape harmonies to his manager's talents.

Everybody applauded the Mayor's proposed entertainment, especially when it became known that he meant to pay for it all himself.

Close to the town was an elevated green spot surrounded by an ancient square earthwork—earthworks square, and not square, were as common as blackberries hereabout—a spot whereon the Casterbridge people usually held any kind of merry-making, meeting, or sheep-fair that required more space than the streets would afford. On one side it sloped to the river Froom, and from any point a view was obtained of the country round for many miles. This pleasant upland was to be the scene of Henchard's exploit.

He advertised about the town, in long posters of a pink colour, that games of all sorts would take place here; and set to work a little battalion of men under his own eye. They erected greasy-poles for climbing, with smoked hams and local cheeses at the top. They placed hurdles in rows for jumping over; across the river they laid a slippery pole, with a

2. Waterproof covers used to protect grain-ricks from bad weather.

live pig of the neighborhood tied at the other end, to become the property of the man who could walk over and get it. There were also provided wheelbarrows for racing, donkeys for the same, a stage for boxing, wrestling, and drawing blood generally; sacks for jumping in. Moreover, not forgetting his principles, Henchard provided a mammoth tèa, of which everybody who lived in the borough was invited to partake without payment. The tables were laid parallel with the inner slope of the rampart, and awnings were stretched overhead.

Passing to and fro the Mayor beheld the unattractive exterior of Farfrae's erection in the West Walk, rick-cloths of different sizes and colours being hung up to the arching trees without any regard to appearance. He was easy in his mind now, for his own preparations far transcended these.

The morning came. The sky, which had been remarkably clear down to within a day or two, was overcast, and the weather threatening, the wind having an unmistakable hint of water in it. Henchard wished he had not been quite so sure about the continuance of a fair season. But it was too late to modify or postpone, and the proceedings went on. At twelve o'clock the rain began to fall, small and steady, commencing and increasing so insensibly that it was difficult to state exactly when dry weather ended or wet established itself. In an hour the slight moisture resolved itself into a monotonous smiting of earth by heaven, in torrents to which no end could be prognosticated.

A number of people had heroically gathered in the field, but by three o'clock Henchard discerned that his project was doomed to end in failure. The hams at the top of the poles dripped watered smoke in the form of a brown liquor, the pig shivered in the wind, the grain of the deal tables showed through the sticking tablecloths, for the awning allowed the rain to drift under at its will, and to enclose the sides at this hour seemed a useless undertaking. The landscape over the river disappeared; the wind played on the tent-cords in Æolian improvisations; and at length rose to such a pitch that the whole erection slanted to the ground, those who had taken shelter within it having to crawl out on their hands and knees.

But towards six the storm abated, and a drier breeze shook the moisture from the grass bents. It seemed possible to carry out the programme after all. The awning was set up again; the band was called out from its shelter, and ordered to begin, and where the tables had stood a place was cleared for dancing.

'But where are the folk?' said Henchard, after the lapse of half-an-hour, during which time only two men and a woman had stood up to dance. 'The shops are all shut. Why don't they come?'

'They are at Farfrae's affair in the West Walk,' answered a Councilman who stood in the field with the Mayor.

'A few, I suppose. But where are the body o' 'em?'

'All out of doors are there.'

'Then the more fools they!'

Henchard walked away moodily. One or two young fellows gallantly came to climb the poles, to save the hams from being wasted; but as there were no spectators, and the whole scene presented the most melancholy appearance, Henchard gave orders that the proceedings were to be suspended, and the entertainment closed, the food to be distributed among the poor people of the town. In a short time nothing was left in the field but a few hurdles, the tents, and the poles.

Henchard returned to his house, had tea with his wife and daughter, and then walked out. It was now dusk. He soon saw that the tendency of all promenaders was towards a particular spot in the Walks, and eventually proceeded thither himself. The notes of a stringed band came from the enclosure that Farfrae had erected—the pavilion as he called it—and when the Mayor reached it he perceived that a gigantic tent had been ingeniously constructed without poles or ropes. The densest point of the avenue of sycamores had been selected, where the boughs made a closely interlaced vault overhead; to these boughs the canvas had been hung, and a barrel[3] roof was the result. The end towards the wind was enclosed, the other end was open. Henchard went round and saw the interior.

In form it was like the nave of a cathedral with one gable removed, but the scene within was anything but devotional. A reel or fling of some sort was in progress; and the usually sedate Farfrae was in the midst of the other dancers in the costume of a wild Highlander, flinging himself about and spinning to the tune. For a moment Henchard could not help laughing. Then he perceived the immense admiration for the Scotchman that revealed itself in the women's faces; and when this exhibition was over, and a new dance proposed, and Donald had disappeared for a time to return in his natural garments, he had an unlimited choice of partners, every girl being in a coming-on disposition towards one who so thoroughly understood the poetry of motion as he.

All the town crowded to the Walk, such a delightful idea of a ballroom never having occurred to the inhabitants before. Among the rest of the onlookers were Elizabeth and her mother—the former thoughtful yet much interested, her eyes beaming with a longing lingering light, as if Nature had been advised by Correggio[4] in their creation. The dancing progressed with unabated spirit, and Henchard walked and waited till his wife should be disposed to go home. He did not care to keep in the light, and when he went into the dark it was worse, for there he heard remarks of a kind which were becoming too frequent:

'Mr. Henchard's rejoicings couldn't say good morning to this,' said

3. Concave.
4. Italian painter (1494–1534) noted for his subtle use of light and shade.

one. 'A man must be a headstrong stunpoll[5] to think folk would go up to that bleak place to-day.'

The other answered that people said it was not only in such things as those that the Mayor was wanting. 'Where would his business be if it were not for this young fellow? 'Twas verily Fortune sent him to Henchard. His accounts were like a bramblewood when Mr. Farfrae came. He used to reckon his sacks by chalk strokes all in a row like garden-palings, measure his ricks by stretching with his arms, weigh his trusses by a lift, judge his hay by a chaw,[6] and settle the price with a curse. But now this accomplished young man does it all by ciphering[7] and mensuration. Then the wheat—that sometimes used to taste so strong o' mice when made into bread that people could fairly tell the breed—Farfrae has a plan for purifying, so that nobody would dream the smallest four-legged beast had walked over it once. O yes, everybody is full of him, and the care Mr. Henchard has to keep him, to be sure!' concluded this gentleman.

'But he won't do it for long, good-now,'[8] said the other.

'No!' said Henchard to himself behind the tree. 'Or if he do, he'll be honeycombed[9] clean out of all the character and standing that he's built up in these eighteen year!'

He went back to the dancing pavilion. Farfrae was footing a quaint little dance with Elizabeth-Jane—an old country thing, the only one she knew, and though he considerately toned down his movements to suit her demurer gait, the pattern of the shining little nails in the soles of his boots became familiar to the eyes of every bystander. The tune had enticed her into it; being a tune of a busy, vaulting, leaping sort—some low notes on the silver string of each fiddle, then a skipping on the small, like running up and down ladders—'Miss M'Leod of Ayr'[1] was its name, so Mr. Farfrae had said, and that it was very popular in his own country.

It was soon over, and the girl looked at Henchard for approval; but he did not give it. He seemed not to see her. 'Look here, Farfrae,' he said, like one whose mind was elsewhere, 'I'll go to Port-Bredy Great Market to-morrow myself. You can stay and put things right in your clothes-box, and recover strength to your knees after your vagaries.' He planted on Donald an antagonistic glare that had begun as a smile.

Some other townsmen came up, and Donald drew aside. 'What's this, Henchard,' said Alderman Tubber, applying his thumb to the corn-factor like a cheese-taster. 'An opposition randy[2] to yours, eh? Jack's as good as his master, eh? Cut ye out quite, hasn't he?'

5. Fool.
6. By chewing it.
7. Doing arithmetic.
8. That's for sure (dialect).
9. Hollowed out, like the cells in a honeycomb.
1. One of Hardy's favorite dance tunes.
2. Party, entertainment.

'You see, Mr. Henchard,' said the lawyer, another good-natured friend, 'where you made the mistake was in going so far afield. You should have taken a leaf out of his book, and have had your sports in a sheltered place like this. But you didn't think of it, you see; and he did, and that's where he's beat you.'

'He'll be top-sawyer[3] soon of you two, and carry all afore him,' added jocular Mr. Tubber.

'No,' said Henchard gloomily. 'He won't be that, because he's shortly going to leave me.' He looked towards Donald, who had again come near. 'Mr. Farfrae's time as my manager is drawing to a close—isn't it, Farfrae?'

The young man, who could now read the lines and folds of Henchard's strongly-traced face as if they were clear verbal inscriptions, quietly assented; and when people deplored the fact, and asked why it was, he simply replied that Mr. Henchard no longer required his help.

Henchard went home, apparently satisfied. But in the morning, when his jealous temper had passed away, his heart sank within him at what he had said and done. He was the more disturbed when he found that this time Farfrae was determined to take him at his word.

XVII

Elizabeth-Jane had perceived from Henchard's manner that in assenting to dance she had made a mistake of some kind. In her simplicity she did not know what it was till a hint from a nodding acquaintance enlightened her. As the Mayor's step-daughter, she learnt, she had not been quite in her place in treading a measure amid such a mixed throng as filled the dancing pavilion.

Thereupon her ears, cheeks, and chin glowed like live coals at the dawning of the idea that her tastes were not good enough for her position, and would bring her into disgrace.

This made her very miserable, and she looked about for her mother; but Mrs. Henchard, who had less idea of conventionality than Elizabeth herself, had gone away, leaving her daughter to return at her own pleasure. The latter moved on into the dark dense old avenues, or rather vaults of living woodwork, which ran along the town boundary, and stood reflecting.

A man followed in a few minutes, and her face being towards the shine from the tent he recognized her. It was Farfrae—just come from the dialogue with Henchard which had signified his dismissal.

'And it's you, Miss Newson?—and I've been looking for ye everywhere!' he said, overcoming a sadness imparted by the estrangement with the corn-merchant. 'May I walk on with you as far as your street-corner?'

3. Superior person (literally, the man using the upper end of a two-handled saw mounted over a pit).

She thought there might be something wrong in this, but did not utter any objection. So together they went on, first down the West Walk, and then into the Bowling Walk, till Farfrae said, 'It's like that I'm going to leave you soon.'

She faltered 'Why?'

'Oh—as a mere matter of business—nothing more. But we'll not concern ourselves about it—it is for the best. I hoped to have another dance with you.'

She said she could not dance—in any proper way.

'Nay, but you do! It's the feeling for it rather than the learning of steps that makes pleasant dancers. . . . I fear I offended your father by getting up this! And now, perhaps, I'll have to go to another part o' the warrld altogether!'

This seemed such a melancholy prospect that Elizabeth-Jane breathed a sigh—letting it off in fragments that he might not hear her. But darkness makes people truthful, and the Scotchman went on impulsively—perhaps he had heard her after all:

'I wish I was richer, Miss Newson; and your stepfather had not been offended; I would ask you something in a short time—yes, I would ask you to-night. But that's not for me!'

What he would have asked her he did not say, and instead of encouraging him she remained incompetently silent. Thus afraid one of another they continued their promenade along the walls till they got near the bottom of the Bowling Walk; twenty steps further and the trees would end, and the street-corner and lamps appear. In consciousness of this they stopped.

'I never found out who it was that sent us to Durnover granary on a fool's errand that day,' said Donald, in his undulating tones. 'Did ye ever know yourself, Miss Newson?'

'Never,' said she.

'I wonder why they did it!'

'For fun, perhaps.'

'Perhaps it was not for fun. It might have been that they thought they would like us to stay waiting there, talking to one another? Ay, well! I hope you Casterbridge folk will not forget me if I go.'

'That I'm sure we won't!' she said earnestly. 'I—wish you wouldn't go at all.'

They had got into the lamplight. 'Now, I'll think over that,' said Donald Farfrae. 'And I'll not come up to your door; but part from you here; lest it make your father more angry still.'

They parted, Farfrae returning into the dark Bowling Walk, and Elizabeth-Jane going up the street. Without any consciousness of what she was doing she started running with all her might till she reached her father's door. 'O dear me—what am I at?' she thought, as she pulled up breathless.

Indoors she fell to conjecturing the meaning of Farfrae's enigmatic words about not daring to ask her what he fain would. Elizabeth, that silent observing woman, had long noted how he was rising in favour among the townspeople; and knowing Henchard's nature now she had feared that Farfrae's days as manager were numbered; so that the announcement gave her little surprise. Would Mr. Farfrae stay in Casterbridge despite his words and her father's dismissal? His occult breathings to her might be solvable by his course in that respect.

The next day was windy—so windy that walking in the garden she picked up a portion of the draft of a letter on business in Donald Farfrae's writing, which had flown over the wall from the office. The useless scrap she took indoors, and began to copy the calligraphy, which she much admired. The letter began 'Dear Sir,' and presently writing on a loose slip 'Elizabeth-Jane,' she laid the latter over 'Sir,' making the phrase 'Dear Elizabeth-Jane.' When she saw the effect a quick red ran up her face and warmed her through, though nobody was there to see what she had done. She quickly tore up the slip, and threw it away. After this she grew cool and laughed at herself, walked about the room, and laughed again; not joyfully, but distressfully rather.

It was quickly known in Casterbridge that Farfrae and Henchard had decided to dispense with each other. Elizabeth-Jane's anxiety to know if Farfrae were going away from the town reached a pitch that disturbed her, for she could no longer conceal from herself the cause. At length the news reached her that he was not going to leave the place. A man following the same trade as Henchard, but on a very small scale, had sold his business to Farfrae, who was forthwith about to start as corn and hay merchant on his own account.

Her heart fluttered when she heard of this step of Donald's, proving that he meant to remain; and yet, would a man who cared one little bit for her have endangered his suit by setting up a business in opposition to Mr. Henchard's? Surely not; and it must have been a passing impulse only which had led him to address her so softly.

To solve the problem whether her appearance on the evening of the dance were such as to inspire a fleeting love at first sight, she dressed herself up exactly as she had dressed then—the muslin, the spencer, the sandals, the parasol—and looked in the mirror. The picture glassed back was, in her opinion, precisely of such a kind as to inspire that fleeting regard, and no more—'just enough to make him silly, and not enough to keep him so,' she said luminously; and Elizabeth thought, in a much lower key, that by this time he had discovered how plain and homely was the informing spirit of that pretty outside.

Hence, when she felt her heart going out to him, she would say to herself with a mock pleasantry that carried an ache with it, 'No, no, Elizabeth-Jane—such dreams are not for you!' She tried to prevent herself from seeing him, and thinking of him; succeeding fairly well in the former attempt, in the latter not so completely.

Henchard, who had been hurt at finding that Farfrae did not mean to put up with his temper any longer, was incensed beyond measure when he learnt what the young man had done as an alternative. It was in the town-hall, after a council meeting, that he first became aware of Farfrae's *coup*[1] for establishing himself independently in the town; and his voice might have been heard as far as the town-pump expressing his feelings to his fellow councilmen. Those tones showed that, though under a long reign of self-control he had become Mayor and churchwarden and what not, there was still the same unruly volcanic stuff beneath the rind of Michael Henchard as when he had sold his wife at Weydon Fair.

'Well, he's a friend of mine, and I'm a friend of his—or if we are not, what are we? 'Od send, if I've not been his friend, who has, I should like to know? Didn't he come here without a sound shoe to his voot?[2] Didn't I keep him here—help him to a living? Didn't I help him to money, or whatever he wanted? I stuck out for no terms—I said "Name your own price." I'd have shared my last crust with that young fellow at one time, I liked him so well. And now he's defied me! But damn him, I'll have a tussle with him now—at fair buying and selling, mind—at fair buying and selling! And if I can't overbid such a stripling as he, then I'm not wo'th a varden![3] We'll show that we know our business as well as one here and there!'

His friends of the Corporation did not specially respond. Henchard was less popular now than he had been when, nearly two years before, they had voted him to the chief magistracy on account of his amazing energy. While they had collectively profited by this quality of the corn-factor's they had been made to wince individually on more than one occasion. So he went out of the hall and down the street alone.

Reaching home he seemed to recollect something with a sour satis-faction. He called Elizabeth-Jane. Seeing how he looked when she entered she appeared alarmed.

'Nothing to find fault with,' he said, observing her concern. 'Only I want to caution you, my dear. That man, Farfrae—it is about him. I've seen him talking to you two or three times—he danced with 'ee at the rejoicings, and came home with 'ee. Now, now, no blame to you. But just hearken: Have you made him any foolish promise? Gone the least bit beyond sniff and snaff[4] at all?'

'No. I have promised him nothing.'

'Good. All's well that end's well. I particularly wish you not to see him again.'

1. Move (from the French: literally, a strike or blow).
2. Foot.
3. Worth a farthing.
4. Casual conversation.

'Very well, sir.'

'You promise?'

She hesitated for a moment, and then said —

'Yes, if you much wish it.'

'I do. He's an enemy to our house!'

When she had gone he sat down, and wrote in a heavy hand to Farfrae thus: —

> SIR, — I make request that henceforth you and my step-daughter be as strangers to each other. She on her part has promised to welcome no more addresses from you; and I trust, therefore, you will not attempt to force them upon her.
>
> M. HENCHARD.

One would almost have supposed Henchard to have had policy to see that no better *modus vivendi*[5] could be arrived at with Farfrae than by encouraging him to become his son-in-law. But such a scheme for buying over a rival had nothing to recommend it to the Mayor's headstrong faculties. With all domestic *finesse* of that kind he was hopelessly at variance. Loving a man or hating him, his diplomacy was as wrongheaded as a buffalo's; and his wife had not ventured to suggest the course which she, for many reasons, would have welcomed gladly.

Meanwhile Donald Farfrae had opened the gates of commerce on his own account at a spot on Durnover Hill — as far as possible from Henchard's stores, and with every intention of keeping clear of his former friend and employer's customers. There was, it seemed to the younger man, room for both of them and to spare. The town was small, but the corn and hay-trade was proportionately large, and with his native sagacity he saw opportunity for a share of it.

So determined was he to do nothing which should seem like trade-antagonism to the Mayor that he refused his first customer — a large farmer of good repute — because Henchard and this man had dealt together within the preceding three months.

'He was once my friend,' said Farfrae, 'and it's not for me to take business from him. I am sorry to disappoint you, but I cannot hurt the trade of a man who's been so kind to me.'

In spite of this praiseworthy course the Scotchman's trade increased. Whether it were that his northern energy was an over-mastering force among the easy-going Wessex worthies, or whether it was sheer luck, the fact remained that whatever he touched he prospered in. Like Jacob in Padan-Aram,[6] he would no sooner humbly limit himself to the ringstraked-and-spotted exceptions of trade than the ringstraked-and-spotted would multiply and prevail.

---

5. Way of living or proceeding (from the Latin).
6. Genesis 30.25–43 tells how Jacob outwitted his father-in-law Laban and acquired from him the best of his flock ("ringstraked-and-spotted" refers to the type of sheep).

But most probably luck had little to do with it. Character is Fate, said Novalis,[7] and Farfrae's character was just the reverse of Henchard's, who might not inaptly be described as Faust[8] has been described—as a vehement gloomy being who had quitted the ways of vulgar men without light to guide him on a better way.

Farfrae duly received the request to discontinue attentions to Elizabeth-Jane. His acts of that kind had been so slight that the request was almost superfluous. Yet he had felt a considerable interest in her, and after some cogitation he decided that it would be as well to enact no Romeo[9] part just then—for the young girl's sake no less than his own. Thus the incipient attachment was stifled down.

A time came when, avoid collision with his former friend as he might, Farfrae was compelled, in sheer self-defence, to close with Henchard in mortal commercial combat. He could no longer parry the fierce attacks of the latter by simple avoidance. As soon as their war of prices began everybody was interested, and some few guessed the end. It was, in some degree, Northern insight matched against Southron doggedness—the dirk against the cudgel—and Henchard's weapon was one which, if it did not deal ruin at the first or second stroke, left him afterwards well-nigh at his antagonist's mercy.

Almost every Saturday they encountered each other amid the crowd of farmers which thronged about the market-place in the weekly course of their business. Donald was always ready, and even anxious, to say a few friendly words; but the Mayor invariably gazed stormfully past him, like one who had endured and lost on his account, and could in no sense forgive the wrong; nor did Farfrae's snubbed manner of perplexity at all appease him. The large farmers, corn-merchants, millers, auctioneers, and others had each an official stall in the corn-market room, with their names painted thereon; and when to the familiar series of 'Henchard,' 'Everdene,' 'Shiner,' 'Darton,'[1] and so on, was added one inscribed 'Farfrae,' in staring new letters, Henchard was stung into bitterness; like Bellerophon,[2] he wandered away from the crowd, cankered in soul.

From that day Donald Farfrae's name was seldom mentioned in Henchard's house. If at breakfast or dinner Elizabeth-Jane's mother inadvertently alluded to her favourite's movements, the girl would implore her by a look to be silent; and her husband would say, 'What—are you, too, my enemy?'

7. Baron von Hardenberg (1772–1801), German poet and novelist. Hardy probably knew the quotation from George Eliot's use of it (in the form "Character is destiny") in *The Mill on the Floss* (1860), Book 6, chapter 6.
8. Faust is so described in Thomas Carlyle's essay "Goethe's Helena" (1828).
9. In Shakespeare's play, Romeo courts Juliet despite the feud between their families.
1. Farmers Everdene, Shiner, and Darton all appear in other of Hardy's novels and stories.
2. Greek hero who incurred the hatred of the gods, and who thereafter entered into a bitter and self-imposed exile. See *Iliad*, VI, lines 201–2.

XVIII

There came a shock which had been foreseen for some time by Elizabeth, as the box passenger[1] foresees the approaching jerk from some channel across the highway.

Her mother was ill—too unwell to leave her room. Henchard, who treated her kindly, except in moments of irritation, sent at once for the richest, busiest doctor, whom he supposed to be the best. Bedtime came, and they burnt a light all night. In a day or two she rallied.

Elizabeth, who had been staying up, did not appear at breakfast on the second morning, and Henchard sat down alone. He was startled to see a letter for him from Jersey in a writing he knew too well, and had expected least to behold again. He took it up in his hands and looked at it as at a picture, a vision, a vista of past enactments; and then he read it as an unimportant finale to conjecture.

The writer said that she at length perceived how impossible it would be for any further communications to proceed between them now that his re-marriage had taken place. That such re-union had been the only straightforward course open to him she was bound to admit.

'On calm reflection, therefore,' she went on, 'I quite forgive you for landing me in such a dilemma, remembering that you concealed nothing before our ill-advised acquaintance; and that you really did set before me in your grim way the fact of there being a certain risk in intimacy with you, slight as it seemed to be after fifteen or sixteen years of silence on your wife's part. I thus look upon the whole as a misfortune of mine, and not a fault of yours.

'So that, Michael, I must ask you to overlook those letters with which I pestered you day after day in the heat of my feelings. They were written whilst I thought your conduct to me cruel; but now I know more particulars of the position you were in I see how inconsiderate my reproaches were.

'Now you will, I am sure, perceive that the one condition which will make any future happiness possible for me is that the past connection between our lives be kept secret outside this isle. Speak of it I know you will not; and I can trust you not to write of it. One safeguard more remains to be mentioned—that no writings of mine, or trifling articles belonging to me, should be left in your possession through neglect or forgetfulness. To this end may I request you to return to me any such you may have, particularly the letters written in the first abandonment of feeling.

'For the handsome sum you forwarded to me as a plaster to the wound I heartily thank you.

'I am now on my way to Bristol, to see my only relative. She is rich, and I hope will do something for me. I shall return through

1. The box passenger sat outside the coach next to the driver.

Casterbridge and Budmouth, where I shall take the packet-boat.[2] Can you meet me with the letters and other trifles? I shall be in the coach which changes horses at the Antelope Hotel at half-past five Wednesday evening; I shall be wearing a Paisley shawl with a red centre, and thus may easily be found. I should prefer this plan of receiving them to having them sent. —I remain still, yours ever,

'LUCETTA.'

Henchard breathed heavily. 'Poor thing—better you had not known me! Upon my heart and soul, if ever I should be left in a position to carry out that marriage with thee, I *ought* to do it—I ought to do it, indeed!'

The contingency that he had in his mind was, of course, the death of Mrs. Henchard.

As requested, he sealed up Lucetta's letters, and put the parcel aside till the day she had appointed; this plan of returning them by hand being apparently a little *ruse* of the young lady for exchanging a word or two with him on past times. He would have preferred not to see her; but deeming that there could be no great harm in acquiescing thus far, he went at dusk and stood opposite the coach-office.

The evening was chilly, and the coach was late. Henchard crossed over to it while the horses were being changed; but there was no Lucetta inside or out. Concluding that something had happened to modify her arrangements he gave the matter up and went home, not without a sense of relief.

Meanwhile Mrs. Henchard was weakening visibly. She could not go out of doors any more. One day, after much thinking which seemed to distress her, she said she wanted to write something. A desk was put upon her bed with pen and paper, and at her request she was left alone. She remained writing for a short time, folded her paper carefully, called Elizabeth-Jane to bring a taper and wax, and then, still refusing assistance, sealed up the sheet, directed it, and locked it in her desk. She had directed it in these words: —

'Mr. *Michael Henchard. Not to be opened till Elizabeth-Jane's wedding-day.*'

The latter sat up with her mother to the utmost of her strength night after night. To learn to take the universe seriously there is no quicker way than to watch—to be a 'waker,' as the country-people call it. Between the hours at which the last toss-pot went by and the first sparrow shook himself, the silence in Casterbridge—barring the rare sound of the watchman—was broken in Elizabeth's ear only by the time-piece in the bedroom ticking frantically against the clock on the stairs; ticking harder and harder till it seemed to clang like a gong; and all this while the subtle-souled girl asking herself why she was born, why sitting in a room, and blinking at the candle; why things around her had taken the shape

2. Boat used to carry mail as well as passengers.

they wore in preference to every other possible shape. Why they stared at her so helplessly, as if waiting for the touch of some wand that should release them from terrestrial constraint; what that chaos called consciousness, which spun in her at this moment like a top, tended to, and began in. Her eyes fell together; she was awake, yet she was asleep.

A word from her mother roused her. Without preface, and as the continuation of a scene already progressing in her mind, Mrs. Henchard said: 'You remember the note sent to you and Mr. Farfrae—asking you to meet some one in Durnover Barton—and that you thought it was a trick to make fools of you?'

'Yes.'

'It was not to make fools of you—it was done to bring you together. 'Twas I did it.'

'Why?' said Elizabeth, with a start.

'I—wanted you to marry Mr. Farfrae.'

'O mother!' Elizabeth-Jane bent down her head so much that she looked quite into her own lap. But as her mother did not go on, she said, 'What reason?'

'Well, I had a reason. 'Twill out one day. I wish it could have been in my time! But there—nothing is as you wish it! Henchard hates him.'

'Perhaps they'll be friends again,' murmured the girl.

'I don't know—I don't know.' After this her mother was silent, and dozed; and she spoke on the subject no more.

Some little time later on Farfrae was passing Henchard's house on a Sunday morning, when he observed that the blinds were all down. He rang the bell so softly that it only sounded a single full note and a small one; and then he was informed that Mrs. Henchard was dead—just dead—that very hour.

At the town-pump there were gathered when he passed a few old inhabitants, who came there for water whenever they had, as at present, spare time to fetch it, because it was purer from that original fount than from their own wells. Mrs. Cuxsom, who had been standing there for an indefinite time with her pitcher, was describing the incidents of Mrs. Henchard's death, as she had learnt them from the nurse.

'And she was as white as marble-stone,' said Mrs. Cuxsom. 'And likewise such a thoughtful woman, too—ah, poor soul—that a' minded every little thing that wanted tending. "Yes," says she, "when I'm gone, and my last breath's blowed, look in the top drawer o' the chest in the back room by the window, and you'll find all my coffin clothes; a piece of flannel—that's to put under me, and the little piece is to put under my head; and my new stockings for my feet—they are folded alongside, and all my other things. And there's four ounce pennies,[3] the heaviest I

---

3. Coins minted for private use, and heavier than standard pennies. According to popular belief, if the eyes were not held closed in this way, there would soon be another death in the family.

could find, a-tied up in bits of linen, for weights—two for my right eye and two for my left," she said. "And when you've used 'em, and my eyes don't open no more, bury the pennies, good souls, and don't ye go spending 'em, for I shouldn't like it. And open the windows as soon as I am carried out, and make it as cheerful as you can for Elizabeth-Jane.'"

'Ah, poor heart!'

'Well, and Martha did it, and buried the ounce pennies in the garden. But if ye'll believe words, that man, Christopher Coney, went and dug 'em up, and spent 'em at the Three Mariners. "Faith," he said, "why should death rob life o' fourpence? Death's not of such good report that we should respect 'en to that extent," says he.'

'"Twas a cannibal deed!' deprecated her listeners.

'Gad, then, I won't quite ha'e it,' said Solomon Longways. 'I say it to-day, and 'tis a Sunday morning, and I wouldn't speak wrongfully for a zilver zixpence at such a time. I don't see noo harm in it. To respect the dead is sound doxology;[4] and I wouldn't sell skellintons—leastwise respectable skellintons—to be varnished for 'natomies,[5] except I were out o' work. But money is scarce, and throats get dry. Why *should* death rob life o' fourpence? I say there was no treason in it.'

'Well, poor soul; she's helpless to hinder that or anything now,' answered Mother Cuxsom. 'And all her shining keys will be took from her, and her cupboards opened; and little things a' didn't wish seen, anybody will see; and her wishes and ways will all be as nothing!'

XIX

Henchard and Elizabeth sat conversing by the fire. It was three weeks after Mrs. Henchard's funeral; the candles were not lighted, and a restless, acrobatic flame, poised on a coal, called from the shady walls the smiles of all shapes that could respond—the old pier-glass,[1] with gilt columns and huge entablature,[2] the picture-frames, sundry knobs and handles, and the brass rosette at the bottom of each riband bell-pull on either side of the chimney-piece.

'Elizabeth, do you think much of old times?' said Henchard.

'Yes, sir; often,' said she.

'Who do you put in your pictures of 'em?'

'Mother and father—nobody else hardly.'

Henchard always looked like one bent on resisting pain when Elizabeth-Jane spoke of Richard Newson as 'father.' 'Ah! I am out of all that, am I not?' he said. . . . 'Was Newson a kind father?'

'Yes, sir; very.'

4. A formulaic hymn of praise; Longways means "theology."
5. Refers to the practice of robbing fresh graves in order to sell the bodies for medical research.
1. Tall mirror, fitted above a fireplace or between windows.
2. Ornamented upper part of the mirror frame, above the side columns.

Henchard's face settled into an expression of stolid loneliness which gradually modulated into something softer. 'Suppose I had been your real father?' he said. 'Would you have cared for me as much as you cared for Richard Newson?'

'I can't think it,' she said quickly. 'I can think of no other as my father, except my father.'

Henchard's wife was dissevered from him by death; his friend and helper Farfrae by estrangement; Elizabeth-Jane by ignorance. It seemed to him that only one of them could possibly be recalled, and that was the girl. His mind began vibrating between the wish to reveal himself to her and the policy of leaving well alone, till he could no longer sit still. He walked up and down, and then he came and stood behind her chair, looking down upon the top of her head. He could no longer restrain his impulse. 'What did your mother tell you about me—my history?' he asked.

'That you were related by marriage.'

'She should have told more—before you knew me! Then my task would not have been such a hard one. . . . Elizabeth, it is I who am your father, and not Richard Newson. Shame alone prevented your wretched parents from owning this to you while both of 'em were alive.'

The back of Elizabeth's head remained still, and her shoulders did not denote even the movements of breathing. Henchard went on: 'I'd rather have your scorn, your fear, anything than your ignorance; 'tis that I hate! Your mother and I were man and wife when we were young. What you saw was our second marriage. Your mother was too honest. We had thought each other dead—and—Newson became her husband.'

This was the nearest approach Henchard could make to the full truth. As far as he personally was concerned he would have screened nothing; but he showed a respect for the young girl's sex and years worthy of a better man.

When he had gone on to give details which a whole series of slight and unregarded incidents in her past life strangely corroborated; when, in short, she believed his story to be true, she became greatly agitated, and turning round to the table flung her face upon it weeping.

'Don't cry—don't cry!' said Henchard, with vehement pathos, 'I can't bear it, I won't bear it. I am your father; why should you cry? Am I so dreadful, so hateful to 'ee? Don't take against me, Elizabeth-Jane!' he cried, grasping her wet hand. 'Don't take against me—though I was a drinking man once, and used your mother roughly—I'll be kinder to you than *he* was! I'll do anything, if you will only look upon me as your father!'

She tried to stand up and confront him trustfully; but she could not; she was troubled at his presence, like the brethren at the avowal of Joseph.[3]

---

3. Genesis 45.1–4 tells how Joseph made himself known to his brothers, who years before had sold him into slavery.

'I don't want you to come to me all of a sudden,' said Henchard in jerks, and moving like a great tree in a wind. 'No, Elizabeth, I don't. I'll go away and not see you till to-morrow, or when you like; and then I'll show 'ee papers to prove my words. There, I am gone, and won't disturb you any more. . . . 'Twas I that chose your name, my daughter; your mother wanted it Susan. There, don't forget 'twas I gave you your name!' He went out at the door and shut her softly in, and she heard him go away into the garden. But he had not done. Before she had moved, or in any way recovered from the effect of his disclosure, he reappeared.

'One word more, Elizabeth,' he said. 'You'll take my surname now—hey? Your mother was against it; but it will be much more pleasant to me. 'Tis legally yours, you know. But nobody need know that. You shall take it as if by choice. I'll talk to my lawyer—I don't know the law of it exactly; but will you do this—let me put a few lines into the newspaper that such is to be your name?'

'If it is my name I must have it, mustn't I?' she asked.

'Well, well; usage is everything in these matters.'

'I wonder why mother didn't wish it?'

'Oh, some whim of the poor soul's. Now get a bit of paper and draw up a paragraph as I shall tell you. But let's have a light.'

'I can see by the firelight,' she answered. 'Yes—I'd rather.'

'Very well.'

She got a piece of paper, and bending over the fender wrote at his dictation words which he had evidently got by heart from some advertisement or other—words to the effect that she, the writer, hitherto known as Elizabeth-Jane Newson, was going to call herself Elizabeth-Jane Henchard forthwith. It was done, and fastened up, and directed to the office of the *Casterbridge Chronicle*.

'Now,' said Henchard, with the blaze of satisfaction that he always emitted when he had carried his point—though tenderness softened it this time—'I'll go upstairs and hunt for some documents that will prove it all to you. But I won't trouble you with them till to-morrow. Good-night, my Elizabeth-Jane!'

He was gone before the bewildered girl could realize what it all meant, or adjust her filial sense to the new centre of gravity. She was thankful that he had left her to herself for the evening, and sat down over the fire. Here she remained in silence, and wept—not for her mother now, but for the genial sailor Richard Newson, to whom she seemed doing a wrong.

Henchard in the meantime had gone upstairs. Papers of a domestic nature he kept in a drawer in his bedroom, and this he unlocked. Before turning them over he leant back and indulged in reposeful thought. Elizabeth was his at last, and she was a girl of such good sense and kind heart that she would be sure to like him. He was the kind of man to whom some human object for pouring out his heat upon—were it emotive or were it choleric—was almost a necessity. The craving of his heart for the re-establishment of this tenderest human tie had been great during his wife's lifetime, and now he had submitted to its mastery without reluctance and without fear. He bent over the drawer again, and proceeded in his search.

Among the other papers had been placed the contents of his wife's little desk, the keys of which had been handed to him at her request. Here was the letter addressed to him with the restriction, 'Not to be opened till Elizabeth-Jane's wedding-day.'

Mrs. Henchard, though more patient than her husband, had been no practical hand at anything. In sealing up the sheet, which was folded and tucked in without an envelope, in the old-fashioned way, she had overlaid the junction with a large mass of wax without the requisite under-touch of the same. The seal had cracked, and the letter was open. Henchard had no reason to suppose the restriction one of serious weight, and his feeling for his late wife had not been of the nature of deep respect. 'Some trifling fancy or other of poor Susan's, I suppose,' he said; and without curiosity he allowed his eyes to scan the letter:—

> MY DEAR MICHAEL,—For the good of all three of us I have kept one thing a secret from you till now. I hope you will understand why; I think you will; though perhaps you may not forgive me. But, dear Michael, I have done it for the best. I shall be in my grave when you read this, and Elizabeth-Jane will have a home. Don't curse me, Mike—think of how I was situated. I can hardly write it, but here it is. Elizabeth-Jane is not your Elizabeth-Jane—the child who was in my arms when you sold me. No; she died three months after that, and this living one is my other husband's. I christened her by the same name we had given to the first, and she filled up the ache I felt at the other's loss. Michael, I am dying, and I might have held my tongue; but I could not. Tell her husband of this or not, as you may judge; and forgive, if you can, a woman you once deeply wronged, as she forgives you.
>
> SUSAN HENCHARD.

Her husband regarded the paper as if it were a window-pane through which he saw for miles. His lip twitched, and he seemed to compress his frame, as if to bear better. His usual habit was not to consider whether destiny were hard upon him or not—the shape of his ideas in cases of affliction being simply a moody 'I am to suffer, I perceive.' 'This much scourging, then, is it for me.' But now through his passionate head there stormed this thought—that the blasting disclosure was what he had deserved.

His wife's extreme reluctance to have the girl's name altered from Newson to Henchard was now accounted for fully. It furnished another illustration of that honesty in dishonesty which had characterized her in other things.

He remained unnerved and purposeless for near a couple of hours; till he suddenly said, 'Ah—I wonder if it is true!'

He jumped up in an impulse, kicked off his slippers, and went with a candle to the door of Elizabeth-Jane's room, where he put his ear to the keyhole and listened. She was breathing profoundly. Henchard softly turned the handle, entered, and shading the light, approached the bed-side. Gradually bringing the light from behind a screening curtain he held it in such a manner that it fell slantwise on her face without shining on her eyes. He steadfastly regarded her features.

They were fair: his were dark. But this was an unimportant preliminary. In sleep there come to the surface buried genealogical facts, ancestral curves, dead men's traits, which the mobility of daytime animation screens and overwhelms. In the present statuesque repose of the young girl's countenance Richard Newson's was unmistakably reflected. He could not endure the sight of her, and hastened away.

Misery taught him nothing more than defiant endurance of it. His wife was dead, and the first impulse for revenge died with the thought that she was beyond him. He looked out at the night as at a fiend. Henchard, like all his kind, was superstitious, and he could not help thinking that the concatenation of events this evening had produced was the scheme of some sinister intelligence bent on punishing him. Yet they had developed naturally. If he had not revealed his past history to Elizabeth he would not have searched the drawer for papers, and so on. The mockery was, that he should have no sooner taught a girl to claim the shelter of his paternity than he discovered her to have no kinship with him.

This ironical sequence of things angered him like an impish trick from a fellow-creature. Like Prester John's, his table had been spread, and infernal harpies had snatched up the food.[4] He went out of the house, and moved sullenly onward down the pavement till he came to the bridge at the bottom of the High Street. Here he turned in upon a bypath on the river bank, skirting the north-eastern limits of the town.

These precincts embodied the mournful phases of Casterbridge life, as the south avenues embodied its cheerful moods. The whole way along here was sunless, even in summer time; in spring, white frosts lingered here when other places were steaming with warmth; while in winter it was the seed-field of all the aches, rheumatisms, and torturing cramps of the year. The Casterbridge doctors must have pined away for want of sufficient nourishment but for the configuration of the landscape on the north-eastern side.

4. Canto XXXIII of Ariosto's *Orlando Furioso* (1532) tells how Prester John was punished by God with blindness and starvation after he attempted to add Paradise to his kingdom; food was set before him, then snatched away before he could eat by harpies (creatures with the head of a woman and body of a vulture).

The river—slow, noiseless, and dark—the Schwarzwasser[5] of Casterbridge—ran beneath a low cliff, the two together forming a defence which had rendered walls and artificial earthworks on this side unnecessary. Here were ruins of a Franciscan priory, and a mill attached to the same, the water of which roared down a back-hatch like the voice of desolation. Above the cliff, and behind the river, rose a pile of buildings, and in the front of the pile a square mass cut into the sky. It was like a pedestal lacking its statue. This missing feature, without which the design remained incomplete, was, in truth, the corpse of a man; for the square mass formed the base of the gallows, the extensive buildings at the back being the county gaol. In the meadow where Henchard now walked the mob were wont to gather whenever an execution took place, and there to the tune of the roaring weir they stood and watched the spectacle.

The exaggeration which darkness imparted to the glooms of this region impressed Henchard more than he had expected. The lugubrious harmony of the spot with his domestic situation was too perfect for him, impatient of effects, scenes, and adumbrations. It reduced his heartburning to melancholy, and he exclaimed, 'Why the deuce did I come here!' He went on past the cottage in which the old local hangman had lived and died, in times before that calling was monopolized over all England by a single gentleman; and climbed up by a steep back lane into the town.

For the sufferings of that night, engendered by his bitter disappointment, he might well have been pitied. He was like one who had half fainted, and could neither recover nor complete the swoon. In words he could blame his wife, but not in his heart; and had he obeyed the wise directions outside her letter this pain would have been spared him for long—possibly for ever, Elizabeth-Jane seeming to show no ambition to quit her safe and secluded maiden courses for the speculative path of matrimony.

The morning came after this night of unrest, and with it the necessity for a plan. He was far too self-willed to recede from a position, especially as it would involve humiliation. His daughter he had asserted her to be, and his daughter she should always think herself, no matter what hypocrisy it involved.

But he was ill-prepared for the first step in this new situation. The moment he came into the breakfast-room Elizabeth advanced with open confidence to him and took him by the arm.

'I have thought and thought all night of it,' she said frankly. 'And I see that everything must be as you say. And I am going to look upon you as

---

5. Black water (from the German). In chapters 32 and 41, Hardy uses the name Blackwater for a pool or stream further upriver, perhaps recalling that the name Dorchester derives from "Dwyr," meaning dark.

the father that you are, and not to call you Mr. Henchard any more. It is so plain to me now. Indeed, father, it is. For, of course, you would not have done half the things you have done for me, and let me have my own way so entirely, and bought me presents, if I had only been your stepdaughter! He—Mr. Newson—whom my poor mother married by such a strange mistake' (Henchard was glad that he had disguised matters here), 'was very kind—O so kind!' (she spoke with tears in her eyes); 'but that is not the same thing as being one's real father after all. Now, father, breakfast is ready!' said she cheerfully.

Henchard bent and kissed her cheek. The moment and the act he had prefigured for weeks with a thrill of pleasure; yet it was no less than a miserable insipidity to him now that it had come. His reinstation of her mother had been chiefly for the girl's sake, and the fruition of the whole scheme was such dust and ashes[6] as this.

XX

Of all the enigmas which ever confronted a girl there can have been seldom one like that which followed Henchard's announcement of himself to Elizabeth as her father. He had done it in an ardour and an agitation which had half carried the point of affection with her; yet, behold, from the next morning onwards his manner was constrained as she had never seen it before.

The coldness soon broke out into open chiding. One grievous failing of Elizabeth's was her occasional pretty and picturesque use of dialect words—those terrible marks of the beast[1] to the truly genteel.

It was dinner-time—they never met except at meals—and she happened to say when he was rising from table, wishing to show him something, 'If you'll bide where you be a minute, father, I'll get it.'

'"Bide where you be,"' he echoed sharply. 'Good God, are you only fit to carry wash to a pig-trough, that ye use such words as those?'

She reddened with shame and sadness.

'I meant "Stay where you are," father,' she said, in a low, humble voice. 'I ought to have been more careful.'

He made no reply, and went out of the room.

The sharp reprimand was not lost upon her, and in time it came to pass that for 'fay' she said 'succeed'; that she no longer spoke of 'dumbledores' but of 'humble bees'; no longer said of young men and women that they 'walked together,' but that they were 'engaged'; that she grew to talk of 'greggles' as 'wild hyacinths'; that when she had not slept she did not quaintly tell the servants next morning that she had been 'hagrid,' but that she had 'suffered from indigestion.'

---

6. Disappointing or worthless materials. See Job 30.19.
1. Signs of unworthiness. Those marked with the sign of the beast are idolaters, in contrast with those marked by the seal of God's approval. See Revelation 13.15–17.

These improvements, however, are somewhat in advance of the story. Henchard, being uncultivated himself, was the bitterest critic the fair girl could possibly have had of her own lapses—really slight now, for she read omnivorously. A gratuitous ordeal was in store for her in the matter of her handwriting. She was passing the dining-room door one evening, and had occasion to go in for something. It was not till she had opened the door that she knew the Mayor was there in the company of a man with whom he transacted business.

'Here, Elizabeth-Jane,' he said, looking round at her, 'just write down what I tell you—a few words of an agreement for me and this gentleman to sign. I am a poor tool with a pen.'

'Be jowned,[2] and so be I,' said the gentleman.

She brought forward blotting-book, paper, and ink, and sat down.

'Now then—"An agreement entered into this sixteenth day of October"—write that first.'

She started the pen in an elephantine march across the sheet. It was a splendid round, bold hand of her own conception, a style that would have stamped a woman as Minerva's own[3] in more recent days. But other ideas reigned then: Henchard's creed was that proper young girls wrote ladies'-hand[4]—nay, he believed that bristling characters were as innate and inseparable a part of refined womanhood as sex itself. Hence when, instead of scribbling, like the Princess Ida,[5]

'In such a hand as when a field of corn
Bows all its ears before the roaring East,'

Elizabeth-Jane produced a line of chain-shot[6] and sand-bags, he reddened in angry shame for her, and, peremptorily saying, 'Never mind—I'll finish it,' dismissed her there and then.

Her considerate disposition became a pitfall to her now. She was, it must be admitted, sometimes provokingly and unnecessarily willing to saddle herself with manual labours. She would go to the kitchen instead of ringing, 'Not to make Phœbe come up twice.' She went down on her knees, shovel in hand, when the cat overturned the coal-scuttle; moreover, she would persistently thank the parlourmaid for everything, till one day, as soon as the girl was gone from the room, Henchard broke out with, 'Good God, why dostn't leave off thanking that girl as if she were a goddess-born! Don't I pay her a dozen pound a year to do things for 'ee?' Elizabeth shrank so visibly at the exclamation that he became sorry a few minutes after, and said that he did not mean to be rough.

2. Be damned (dialect).
3. Like that of Minerva, Roman goddess of wisdom and war.
4. The style of handwriting taught in private girls' schools: small, neat, and sloping.
5. Quoting lines 233–34 of Tennyson's *The Princess* (1847), in which the writer is in fact the Prince disguised as a woman.
6. Cannon shot formed of two balls linked by a short chain.

These domestic exhibitions were the small protruding needle-rocks which suggested rather than revealed what was underneath. But his passion had less terror for her than his coldness. The increasing frequency of the latter mood told her the sad news that he disliked her with a growing dislike. The more interesting that her appearance and manners became under the softening influences which she could now command, and in her wisdom did command, the more she seemed to estrange him. Sometimes she caught him looking at her with a louring invidiousness that she could hardly bear. Not knowing his secret it was a cruel mockery that she should for the first time excite his animosity when she had taken his surname.

But the most terrible ordeal was to come. Elizabeth had latterly been accustomed of an afternoon to present a cup of cider or ale and bread-and-cheese to Nance Mockridge, who worked in the yard wimbling hay-bonds. Nance accepted this offering thankfully at first; afterwards as a matter of course. On a day when Henchard was on the premises he saw his stepdaughter enter the hay-barn on this errand; and, as there was no clear spot on which to deposit the provisions, she at once set to work arranging two trusses of hay as a table, Mockridge meanwhile standing with her hands on her hips, easefully looking at the preparations on her behalf.

'Elizabeth, come here!' said Henchard; and she obeyed.

'Why do you lower yourself so confoundedly?' he said with suppressed passion. 'Haven't I told you o't fifty times? Hey? Making yourself a drudge for a common workwoman of such a character as hers! Why, ye'll disgrace me to the dust!'

Now these words were uttered loud enough to reach Nance inside the barn door, who fired up immediately at the slur upon her personal character. Coming to the door she cried, regardless of consequences, 'Come to that, Mr. Michael Henchard, I can let 'ee know she've waited on worse!'

'Then she must have had more charity than sense,' said Henchard.

'O no, she hadn't. 'Twere not for charity but for hire; and at a public-house in this town!'

'It is not true!' cried Henchard indignantly.

'Just ask her,' said Nance, folding her naked arms in such a manner that she could comfortably scratch her elbows.

Henchard glanced at Elizabeth-Jane, whose complexion, now pink and white from confinement, lost nearly all of the former colour. 'What does this mean?' he said to her. 'Anything or nothing?'

'It is true,' said Elizabeth-Jane. 'But it was only——'

'Did you do it, or didn't you? Where was it?'

'At the Three Mariners; one evening for a little while, when we were staying there.'

Nance glanced triumphantly at Henchard, and sailed into the barn;

for assuming that she was to be discharged on the instant she had resolved to make the most of her victory. Henchard, however, said nothing about discharging her. Unduly sensitive on such points by reason of his own past, he had the look of one completely ground down to the last indignity. Elizabeth followed him to the house like a culprit; but when she got inside she could not see him. Nor did she see him again that day.

Convinced of the scathing damage to his local repute and position that must have been caused by such a fact, though it had never before reached his own ears, Henchard showed a positive distaste for the presence of this girl not his own, whenever he encountered her. He mostly dined with the farmers at the market-room of one of the two chief hotels, leaving her in utter solitude. Could he have seen how she made use of those silent hours he might have found reason to reverse his judgment on her quality. She read and took notes incessantly, mastering facts with painful laboriousness, but never flinching from her self-imposed task. She began the study of Latin, incited by the Roman characteristics of the town she lived in. 'If I am not well-informed it shall be by no fault of my own,' she would say to herself through the tears that would occasionally glide down her peachy cheeks when she was fairly baffled by the portentous obscurity of many of these educational works.

Thus she lived on, a dumb, deep-feeling, great-eyed creature, construed by not a single contiguous being; quenching with patient fortitude her incipient interest in Farfrae, because it seemed to be one-sided, unmaidenly, and unwise. True, that for reasons best known to herself, she had, since Farfrae's dismissal, shifted her quarters from the back room affording a view of the yard (which she had occupied with such zest) to a front chamber overlooking the street; but as for the young man, whenever he passed the house he seldom or never turned his head.

Winter had almost come, and unsettled weather made her still more dependent upon indoor resources. But there were certain early winter days in Casterbridge—days of firmamental exhaustion which followed angry south-westerly tempests—when, if the sun shone, the air was like velvet. She seized on these days for her periodical visits to the spot where her mother lay buried—the still-used burial-ground of the old Roman-British[7] city, whose curious feature was this, its continuity as a place of sepulture. Mrs. Henchard's dust mingled with the dust of women who lay ornamented with glass hair-pins and amber necklaces, and men who held in their mouths coins of Hadrian, Posthumus, and the Constantines.[8]

Half-past ten in the morning was about her hour for seeking this spot—a time when the town avenues were deserted as the avenues of

7. Dorchester stands on the site of Durnovaria, built by the Romans around 70 C.E.
8. Roman emperors during the Roman occupation of Britain. The dead were buried with coins to pay the boatman Charon, whose task it was to ferry them over the river Styx into the underworld.

Karnac.[9] Business had long since passed down them into its daily cells, and Leisure had not arrived there. So Elizabeth-Jane walked and read, or looked over the edge of the book to think, and thus reached the churchyard.

There, approaching her mother's grave, she saw a solitary dark figure in the middle of the gravel-walk. This figure, too, was reading; but not from a book: the words which engrossed it being the inscription on Mrs. Henchard's tombstone. The personage was in mourning like herself, was about her age and size, and might have been her wraith or double, but for the fact that it was a lady much more beautifully dressed than she. Indeed, comparatively indifferent as Elizabeth-Jane was to dress, unless for some temporary whim or purpose, her eyes were arrested by the artistic perfection of the lady's appearance. Her gait, too, had a flexuousness about it, which seemed to avoid angularity of movement less from choice than from predisposition. It was a revelation to Elizabeth that human beings could reach this stage of external development—she had never suspected it. She felt all the freshness and grace to be stolen from herself on the instant by the neighbourhood of such a stranger. And this was in face of the fact that Elizabeth could now have been writ handsome, while the young lady was simply pretty.

Had she been envious she might have hated the woman; but she did not do that—she allowed herself the pleasure of feeling fascinated. She wondered where the lady had come from. The stumpy and practical walk of honest homeliness which mostly prevailed there, the two styles of dress thereabout, the simple and the mistaken, equally avouched that this figure was no Casterbridge woman's, even if a book in her hand resembling a guide-book had not also suggested it.

The stranger presently moved from the tombstone of Mrs. Henchard, and vanished behind the corner of the wall. Elizabeth went to the tomb herself; beside it were two footprints distinct in the soil, signifying that the lady had stood there a long time. She returned homeward, musing on what she had seen, as she might have mused on a rainbow or the Northern Lights,[1] a rare butterfly or a cameo.[2]

Interesting as things had been out of doors, at home it turned out to be one of her bad days. Henchard, whose two years' mayoralty was ending, had been made aware that he was not to be chosen to fill a vacancy in the list of aldermen; and that Farfrae was likely to become one of the Council. This caused the unfortunate discovery that she had played the waiting-maid in the town of which he was Mayor to rankle in his mind yet more poisonously. He had learnt by personal inquiry at the time that it was to Donald Farfrae—that treacherous upstart—that she had thus

9. Part of the ancient city of Thebes, in the Upper Nile region of Egypt.
1. Aurora Borealis, an atmospheric phenomenon in the region of the North Pole, very rarely seen as far south as Dorchester.
2. Small sculpture cut in relief into a stone or shell composed of several layers.

humiliated herself. And though Mrs. Stannidge seemed to attach no great importance to the incident—the cheerful souls at the Three Mariners having exhausted its aspects long ago—such was Henchard's haughty spirit that the simple thrifty deed was regarded as little less than a social catastrophe by him.

Ever since the evening of his wife's arrival with her daughter there had been something in the air which had changed his luck. That dinner at the King's Arms with his friends had been Henchard's Austerlitz;[3] he had had his successes since, but his course had not been upward. He was not to be numbered among the aldermen—that Peerage of burghers—as he had expected to be, and the consciousness of this soured him to-day.

'Well, where have you been?' he said to her with off-hand laconism.

'I've been strolling in the Walks and churchyard, father, till I feel quite leery.'[4] She clapped her hand to her mouth, but too late.

This was just enough to incense Henchard after the other crosses of the day. 'I *won't* have you talk like that!' he thundered. '"Leery," indeed. One would think you worked upon a farm! One day I learn that you lend a hand in public-houses. Then I hear you talk like a clodhopper. I'm burned, if it goes on, this house can't hold us two.'

The only way of getting a single pleasant thought to go to sleep upon after this was by recalling the lady she had seen that day, and hoping she might see her again.

Meanwhile Henchard was sitting up, thinking over his jealous folly in forbidding Farfrae to pay his addresses to this girl who did not belong to him, when if he had allowed them to go on he might not have been encumbered with her. At last he said to himself with satisfaction as he jumped up and went to the writing-table: 'Ah! he'll think it means peace, and a marriage portion—not that I don't want my house to be troubled with her, and no portion at all!' He wrote as follows:—

> Sir,—On consideration, I don't wish to interfere with your courtship of Elizabeth-Jane, if you care for her. I therefore withdraw my objection; excepting in this—that the business be not carried on in my house.—Yours,
>
> M. HENCHARD.
>
> Mr. Farfrae.

The morrow, being fairly fine, found Elizabeth-Jane again in the churchyard; but while looking for the lady she was startled by the apparition of Farfrae, who passed outside the gate. He glanced up for a moment from a pocket-book in which he appeared to be making figures as he went; whether or not he saw her he took no notice, and disappeared.

---

3. Napoleon's great victory at the battle of Austerlitz in 1805 proved to be the high point of his career.
4. Empty or hungry.

Unduly depressed by a sense of her own superfluity she thought he probably scorned her; and quite broken in spirit sat down on a bench. She fell into painful thought on her position, which ended with her saying quite loud, 'O, I wish I was dead with dear mother!'

Behind the bench was a little promenade under the wall where people sometimes walked instead of on the gravel. The bench seemed to be touched by something; she looked round, and a face was bending over her, veiled, but still distinct, the face of the young woman she had seen yesterday.

Elizabeth-Jane looked confounded for a moment, knowing she had been overheard, though there was pleasure in her confusion. 'Yes, I heard you,' said the lady, in a vivacious voice, answering her look. 'What can have happened?'

'I don't—I can't tell you,' said Elizabeth, putting her hand to her face to hide a quick flush that had come.

There was no movement or word for a few seconds; then the girl felt that the young lady was sitting down beside her.

'I guess how it is with you,' said the latter. 'That was your mother.' She waved her hand towards the tombstone. Elizabeth looked up at her as if inquiring of herself whether there should be confidence. The lady's manner was so desirous, so anxious, that the girl decided there should be confidence. 'It was my mother,' she said, 'my only friend.'

'But your father, Mr. Henchard. He is living?'

'Yes, he is living,' said Elizabeth-Jane.

'Is he not kind to you?'

'I've no wish to complain of him.'

'There has been a disagreement?'

'A little.'

'Perhaps you were to blame,' suggested the stranger.

'I was—in many ways,' sighed the meek Elizabeth. 'I swept up the coals when the servant ought to have done it; and I said I was leery;—and he was angry with me.'

The lady seemed to warm towards her for that reply. 'Do you know the impression your words give me?' she said ingenuously. 'That he is a hot-tempered man—a little proud—perhaps ambitious; but not a bad man.' Her anxiety not to condemn Henchard while siding with Elizabeth was curious.

'O no; certainly not *bad*,' agreed the honest girl. 'And he has not even been unkind to me till lately—since mother died. But it has been very much to bear while it has lasted. All is owing to my defects, I daresay; and my defects are owing to my history.'

'What is your history?'

Elizabeth-Jane looked wistfully at her questioner. She found that her questioner was looking at her; turned her eyes down; and then seemed compelled to look back again. 'My history is not gay or attractive,' she said. 'And yet I can tell it, if you really want to know.'

The lady assured her that she did want to know; whereupon Elizabeth-Jane told the tale of her life as she understood it, which was in general the true one, except that the sale at the fair had no part therein.

Contrary to the girl's expectation her new friend was not shocked. This cheered her; and it was not till she thought of returning to that home in which she had been treated so roughly of late that her spirits fell.

'I don't know how to return,' she murmured. 'I think of going away. But what can I do? Where can I go?'

'Perhaps it will be better soon,' said her friend gently. 'So I would not go far. Now what do you think of this: I shall soon want somebody to live in my house, partly as housekeeper, partly as companion; would you mind coming to me? But perhaps——'

'O yes,' cried Elizabeth, with tears in her eyes. 'I would, indeed—I would do anything to be independent; for then perhaps my father might get to love me. But, ah!'

'What?'

'I am no accomplished person. And a companion to *you* must be that.'

'O, not necessarily.'

'Not? But I can't help using rural words sometimes, when I don't mean to.'

'Never mind, I shall like to know them.'

'And—O, I know I shan't do!'—she cried with a distressful laugh. 'I accidentally learned to write round hand[5] instead of ladies'-hand. And, of course, you want some one who can write that?'

'Well, no.'

'What, not necessary to write ladies'-hand?' cried the joyous Elizabeth.

'Not at all.'

'But where do you live?'

'In Casterbridge, or rather I shall be living here after twelve o'clock to-day.'

Elizabeth expressed her astonishment.

'I have been staying at Budmouth for a few days while my house was getting ready. The house I am going into is that one they call High-Place Hall—the old stone one looking down the lane to the Market. Two or three rooms are fit for occupation, though not all: I sleep there to-night for the first time. Now will you think over my proposal, and meet me here the first fine day next week, and say if you are still in the same mind?'

Elizabeth, her eyes shining at this prospect of a change from an unbearable position, joyfully assented; and the two parted at the gate of the churchyard.

5. A bold, firm style of writing, as opposed to ladies'-hand.

XXI

As a maxim glibly repeated from childhood remains practically unmarked till some mature experience enforces it, so did this High-Place Hall now for the first time really show itself to Elizabeth-Jane, though her ears had heard its name on a hundred occasions.

Her mind dwelt upon nothing else but the stranger, and the house, and her own chance of living there, all the rest of the day. In the afternoon she had occasion to pay a few bills in the town and do a little shopping, when she learnt that what was a new discovery to herself had become a common topic about the streets. High-Place Hall was undergoing repair; a lady was coming there to live shortly; all the shop-people knew it, and had already discounted the chance of her being a customer.

Elizabeth-Jane could, however, add a capping touch to information so new to her in the bulk. The lady, she said, had arrived that day.

When the lamps were lighted, and it was yet not so dark as to render chimneys, attics, and roofs invisible, Elizabeth, almost with a lover's feeling, thought she would like to look at the outside of High-Place Hall. She went up the street in that direction.

The Hall, with its grey *façade* and parapet, was the only residence of its sort so near the centre of the town. It had, in the first place, the characteristics of a country mansion—bird's nests in its chimneys, damp nooks where fungi grew, and irregularities of surface direct from Nature's trowel. At night the forms of passengers were patterned by the lamps in black shadows upon the pale walls.

This evening motes of straw lay around, and other signs of the premises having been in that lawless condition which accompanies the entry of a new tenant. The house was entirely of stone, and formed an example of dignity without great size. It was not altogether aristocratic, still less consequential, yet the old-fashioned stranger instinctively said, 'Blood built it, and Wealth enjoys it,' however vague his opinions of those accessories might be.

Yet as regards the enjoying it the stranger would have been wrong, for until this very evening, when the new lady had arrived, the house had been empty for a year or two, while before that interval its occupancy had been irregular. The reason of its unpopularity was soon made manifest. Some of its rooms overlooked the market-place; and such a prospect from such a house was not considered desirable or seemly by its would-be occupiers.

Elizabeth's eyes sought the upper rooms, and saw lights there. The lady had obviously arrived. The impression that this woman of comparatively practised manner had made upon the studious girl's mind was so deep that she enjoyed standing under an opposite archway merely to think that the charming lady was inside the confronting walls, and to wonder what she was doing. Her admiration for the architecture of that front was entirely on account of the inmate it screened. Though for that matter the architecture deserved admiration, or at least study, on its own account. It was Palladian,[1] and like most architecture erected since the Gothic age was a compilation rather than a design. But its reasonableness made it impressive. It was not rich, but rich enough. A timely consciousness of the ultimate vanity of human architecture, no less than of other human things, had prevented artistic superfluity.

Men had till quite recently been going in and out with parcels and packing-cases, rendering the door and hall within like a public thoroughfare. Elizabeth trotted through the open door in the dusk, but becoming alarmed at her own temerity she went quickly out again by another which stood open in the lofty wall of the back court. To her surprise she found herself in one of the little-used alleys of the town. Looking round at the door which had given her egress, by the light of the solitary lamp fixed in the alley, she saw that it was arched and old—older even than the house itself. The door was studded, and the keystone of the arch was a mask. Originally the mask had exhibited a comic leer, as could still be discerned; but generations of Casterbridge boys had thrown stones at the mask, aiming at its open mouth; and the blows thereon had chipped off the lips and jaws as if they had been eaten away by disease. The appearance was so ghastly by the weakly lamp-glimmer that she could not bear to look at it—the first unpleasant feature of her visit.

The position of the queer old door and the odd presence of the leering mask suggested one thing above all others as appertaining to the mansion's past history—intrigue. By the alley it had been possible to come unseen from all sorts of quarters in the town—the old play-house, the old bull-stake, the old cock-pit,[2] the pool wherein nameless infants had been used to disappear. High-Place Hall could boast of its conveniences undoubtedly.

She turned to come away in the nearest direction homeward, which was down the alley, but hearing footsteps approaching in that quarter, and having no great wish to be found in such a place at such a time she quickly retreated. There being no other way out she stood behind a brick pier till the intruder should have gone his ways.

Had she watched she would have been surprised. She would have seen that the pedestrian on coming up made straight for the arched doorway: that as he paused with his hand upon the latch the lamplight fell upon the face of Henchard.

But Elizabeth-Jane clung so closely to her nook that she discerned nothing of this. Henchard passed in, as ignorant of her presence as she was ignorant of his identity, and disappeared in the darkness. Elizabeth came out a second time into the alley, and made the best of her way home.

---

1. In the classical style of architecture advocated by Andrea Palladio (1508–1580) and dominant in England for most of the eighteenth century.
2. Referring to the (generally lower-class) sports of bull-baiting and cock-fighting.

Henchard's chiding, by begetting in her a nervous fear of doing any-thing definable as unlady-like, had operated thus curiously in keeping them unknown to each other at a critical moment. Much might have resulted from recognition—at the least a query on either side in one and the self-same form: What could he or she possibly be doing there?

Henchard, whatever his business at the lady's house, reached his own home only a few minutes later than Elizabeth-Jane. Her plan was to broach the question of leaving his roof this evening; the events of the day had urged her to the course. But its execution depended upon his mood, and she anxiously awaited his manner towards her. She found that it had changed. He showed no further tendency to be angry; he showed some-thing worse. Absolute indifference had taken the place of irritability; and his coldness was such that it encouraged her to departure, even more than hot temper could have done.

'Father, have you any objection to my going away?' she asked.

'Going away! No—none whatever. Where are you going?'

She thought it undesirable and unnecessary to say anything at present about her destination to one who took so little interest in her. He would know that soon enough. 'I have heard of an opportunity of getting more cultivated and finished, and being less idle,' she answered, with hesita-tion. 'A chance of a place in a household where I can have advantages of study, and seeing refined life.'

'Then make the best of it, in Heaven's name—if you can't get culti-vated where you are.'

'You don't object?'

'Object—I? Ho—no! Not at all.' After a pause he said, 'But you won't have enough money for this lively scheme without help, you know? If you like I should be willing to make you an allowance, so that you be not bound to live upon the starvation wages refined folk are likely to pay 'ee.'

She thanked him for this offer.

'It had better be done properly,' he added after a pause. 'A small annu-ity is what I should like you to have—so as to be independent of me—and so that I may be independent of you. Would that please ye?'

'Certainly.'

'Then I'll see about it this very day.' He seemed relieved to get her off his hands by this arrangement, and as far as they were concerned the matter was settled. She now simply waited to see the lady again.

The day and the hour came; but a drizzling rain fell. Elizabeth-Jane, having now changed her orbit from one of gay independence to labori-ous self-help, thought the weather good enough for such declined glory as hers, if her friend would only face it—a matter of doubt. She went to the boot-room where her pattens had hung ever since her apotheosis;[3] took them down, had their mildewed leathers blacked, and put them on

3. Transformation (literally, into a divinity).

as she had done in old times. Thus mounted, and with cloak and umbrella, she went off to the place of appointment—intending, if the lady were not there, to call at the house.

One side of the churchyard—the side towards the weather—was sheltered by an ancient thatched mud wall whose eaves overhung as much as one or two feet. At the back of the wall was a corn-yard with its granary and barns—the place wherein she had met Farfrae many months earlier. Under the projection of the thatch she saw a figure. The young lady had come.

Her presence so exceptionally substantiated the girl's utmost hopes that she almost feared her good fortune. Fancies find room in the strongest minds. Here, in a churchyard old as civilization, in the worst of weathers, was a strange woman of curious fascinations never seen elsewhere: there might be some devilry about her presence. However, Elizabeth went on to the church tower, on whose summit the rope of a flag-staff rattled in the wind; and thus she came to the wall.

The lady had such a cheerful aspect in the drizzle that Elizabeth forgot her fancy. 'Well,' said the lady, a little of the whiteness of her teeth appearing with the word through the black fleece that protected her face, 'have you decided?'

'Yes, quite,' said the other eagerly.

'Your father is willing?'

'Yes.'

'Then come along.'

'When?'

'Now—as soon as you like. I had a good mind to send to you to come to my house, thinking you might not venture up here in the wind. But as I like getting out of doors, I thought I would come and see first.'

'It was my own thought.'

'That shows we shall agree. Then can you come to-day? My house is so hollow and dismal that I want some living thing there.'

'I think I might be able to,' said the girl, reflecting

Voices were borne over to them at that instant on the wind and raindrops from the other side of the wall. There came such words as 'sacks,' 'quarters,' 'threshing,' 'tailing,'[4] 'next Saturday's market,' each sentence being disorganized by the gusts like a face in a cracked mirror. Both the women listened.

'Who are those?' said the lady.

'One is my father. He rents that yard and barn.'

The lady seemed to forget the immediate business in listening to the technicalities of the corn trade. At last she said suddenly, 'Did you tell him where you were going to?'

'No.'

4. Grain of inferior quality.

'O—how was that?'

'I thought it safer to get away first—as he is so uncertain in his temper.'

'Perhaps you are right. . . . Besides, I have never told you my name. It is Miss Templeman. . . . Are they gone—on the other side?'

'No. They have only gone up into the granary.'

'Well, it is getting damp here. I shall expect you to-day—this evening, say, at six.'

'Which way shall I come, ma'am?'

'The front way—round by the gate. There is no other that I have noticed.'

Elizabeth-Jane had been thinking of the door in the alley.

'Perhaps, as you have not mentioned your destination, you may as well keep silent upon it till you are clear off. Who knows but that he may alter his mind?'

Elizabeth-Jane shook her head. 'On consideration I don't fear it,' she said sadly. 'He has grown quite cold to me.'

'Very well. Six o'clock then.'

When they had emerged upon the open road and parted, they found enough to do in holding their bowed umbrellas to the wind. Nevertheless the lady looked in at the corn-yard gates as she passed them, and paused on one foot for a moment. But nothing was visible there save the ricks, and the humpbacked barn cushioned with moss, and the granary rising against the church-tower behind, where the smacking of the rope against the flag-staff still went on.

Now Henchard had not the slightest suspicion that Elizabeth-Jane's movement was to be so prompt. Hence when, just before six, he reached home and saw a fly[5] at the door from the King's Arms, and his step-daughter, with all her little bags and boxes, getting into it, he was taken by surprise.

'But you said I might go, father?' she explained through the carriage window.

'Said!—yes. But I thought you meant next month, or next year. 'Od, seize it—you take time by the forelock![6] This, then, is how you be going to treat me for all my trouble about ye?'

'O father! how can you speak like that? It is unjust of you!' she said with spirit.

'Well, well, have your own way,' he replied. He entered the house, and, seeing that all her things had not yet been brought down, went up to her room to look on. He had never been there since she had occupied it. Evidences of her care, of her endeavours for improvement, were visible all around, in the form of books, sketches, maps, and little arrange-

5. One-horsed covered carriage available for hire.
6. Act promptly.

ments for tasteful effects. Henchard had known nothing of these efforts.
He gazed at them, turned suddenly about, and came down to the door.

'Look here,' he said, in an altered voice—he never called her by name
now—'don't 'ee go away from me. It may be I've spoke roughly to you—
but I've been grieved beyond everything by you—there's something that
caused it.'

'By me?' she said, with deep concern. 'What have I done?'

'I can't tell you now. But if you'll stop, and go on living as my daughter, I'll tell you all in time.'

But the proposal had come ten minutes too late. She was in the fly—
was already, in imagination, at the house of the lady whose manner had
such charms for her. 'Father,' she said, as considerately as she could, 'I
think it best for us that I go on now. I need not stay long; I shall not be
far away; and if you want me badly I can soon come back again.'

He nodded ever so slightly, as a receipt of her decision and no more.
'You are not going far, you say. What will be your address, in case I wish
to write to you? Or am I not to know?'

'Oh yes—certainly. It is only in the town—High-Place Hall.'

'Where?' said Henchard, his face stilling.

She repeated the words. He neither moved nor spoke, and waving her
hand to him in utmost friendliness she signified to the flyman to drive
up the street.

XXII

We go back for a moment to the preceding night, to account for
Henchard's attitude.

At the hour when Elizabeth-Jane was contemplating her stealthy
reconnoitring excursion to the abode of the lady of her fancy, he had
been not a little amazed at receiving a letter by hand in Lucetta's well-
known characters. The self-repression, the resignation of her previous
communication had vanished from her mood; she wrote with some of
the natural lightness which had marked her in their early acquaintance.

HIGH-PLACE HALL.

MY DEAR MR. HENCHARD,—Don't be surprised. It is for your
good and mine, as I hope, that I have come to live at
Casterbridge—for how long I cannot tell. That depends upon
another; and he is a man, and a merchant, and a Mayor, and one
who has the first right to my affections.

Seriously, *mon ami*, I am not so light-hearted as I may seem to be
from this. I have come here in consequence of hearing of the death
of your wife—whom you used to think of as dead so many years
before! Poor woman, she seems to have been a sufferer, though
uncomplaining, and though weak in intellect not an imbecile. I am
glad you acted fairly by her. As soon as I knew she was no more, it

was brought home to me very forcibly by my conscience that I ought to endeavour to disperse the shade which my *étourderie*[1] flung over my name, by asking you to carry out your promise to me. I hope you are of the same mind, and that you will take steps to this end. As, however, I did not know how you were situated, or what had happened since our separation, I decided to come and establish myself here before communicating with you.

You probably feel as I do about this. I shall be able to see you in a day or two. Till then, farewell. — Yours,

LUCETTA.

P.S. — I was unable to keep my appointment to meet you for a moment or two in passing through Casterbridge the other day. My plans were altered by a family event, which it will surprise you to hear of.

Henchard had already heard that High-Place Hall was being prepared for a tenant. He said with a puzzled air to the first person he encountered, 'Who is coming to live at the Hall?'

'A lady of the name of Templeman, I believe, sir,' said his informant.

Henchard thought it over. 'Lucetta is related to her, I suppose,' he said to himself. 'Yes, I must put her in her proper position, undoubtedly.'

It was by no means with the oppression that would once have accompanied the thought that he regarded the moral necessity now; it was, indeed, with interest, if not warmth. His bitter disappointment at finding Elizabeth-Jane to be none of his, and himself a childless man, had left an emotional void in Henchard that he unconsciously craved to fill. In this frame of mind, though without strong feeling, he had strolled up the alley and into High-Place Hall by the postern[2] at which Elizabeth had so nearly encountered him. He had gone on thence into the court, and inquired of a man whom he saw unpacking china from a crate if Miss Le Sueur was living there. Miss Le Sueur had been the name under which he had known Lucetta — or 'Lucette,' as she had called herself at that time.

The man replied in the negative; that Miss Templeman only had come. Henchard went away, concluding that Lucetta had not as yet settled in.

He was in this interested stage of the inquiry when he witnessed Elizabeth-Jane's departure the next day. On hearing her announce the address there suddenly took possession of him the strange thought that Lucetta and Miss Templeman were one and the same person, for he could recall that in her season of intimacy with him the name of the rich relative whom he had deemed somewhat a mythical personage had been given as Templeman. Though he was not a fortune-hunter, the

---

1. Thoughtlessness (French).
2. Back door.

possibility that Lucetta had been sublimed into a lady of means by some munificent testament on the part of this relative lent a charm to her image which it might not otherwise have acquired. He was getting on towards the dead level of middle age, when material things increasingly possess the mind.

But Henchard was not left long in suspense. Lucetta was rather addicted to scribbling, as had been shown by the torrent of letters after the *fiasco* in their marriage arrangements, and hardly had Elizabeth gone away when another note came to the Mayor's house from High-Place Hall.

'I am in residence,' she said, 'and comfortable, though getting here has been a wearisome undertaking. You probably know what I am going to tell you, or do you not? My good Aunt Templeman, the banker's widow, whose very existence you used to doubt, much more her affluence, has lately died, and bequeathed some of her property to me. I will not enter into details except to say that I have taken her name—as a means of escape from mine, and its wrongs.

'I am now my own mistress, and have chosen to reside in Casterbridge—to be tenant of High-Place Hall, that at least you may be put to no trouble if you wish to see me. My first intention was to keep you in ignorance of the changes in my life till you should meet me in the street; but I have thought better of this.

'You probably are aware of my arrangement with your daughter, and have doubtless laughed at the—what shall I call it?—practical joke (in all affection) of my getting her to live with me. But my first meeting with her was purely an accident. Do you see, Michael, partly why I have done it?—why, to give you an excuse for coming here as if to visit *her*, and thus to form my acquaintance naturally. She is a dear, good girl, and she thinks you have treated her with undue severity. You may have done so in your haste, but not deliberately, I am sure. As the result has been to bring her to me I am not disposed to upbraid you.—In haste, yours always,

LUCETTA.'

The excitement which these announcements produced in Henchard's gloomy soul was to him most pleasurable. He sat over his dining-table long and dreamily, and by an almost mechanical transfer the sentiments which had run to waste since his estrangement from Elizabeth-Jane and Donald Farfrae gathered around Lucetta before they had grown dry. She was plainly in a very coming-on disposition for marriage. But what else could a poor woman be who had given her time and heart to him so thoughtlessly, at that former time, as to lose her credit by it? Probably conscience no less than affection had brought her here. On the whole he did not blame her.

'The artful little woman!' he said, smiling (with reference to Lucetta's adroit and pleasant manœuvre with Elizabeth-Jane).

To feel that he would like to see Lucetta was with Henchard to start for her house. He put on his hat and went. It was between eight and nine o'clock when he reached her door. The answer brought him was that Miss Templeman was engaged for that evening; but that she would be happy to see him the next day.

'That's rather like giving herself airs!' he thought. 'And considering what we——' But after all, she plainly had not expected him, and he took the refusal quietly. Nevertheless he resolved not to go next day. 'These cursed women—there's not an inch of straight grain in 'em!' he said.

Let us follow the track of Mr. Henchard's thought as if it were a clue line,[3] and view the interior of High-Place Hall on this particular evening.

On Elizabeth-Jane's arrival she had been phlegmatically asked by an elderly woman to go upstairs and take off her things. She had replied with great earnestness that she would not think of giving that trouble, and on the instant divested herself of her bonnet and cloak in the passage. She was then conducted to the first door on the landing, and left to find her way further alone.

The room disclosed was prettily furnished as a boudoir or small drawing-room, and on a sofa with two cylindrical pillows reclined a dark-haired, large-eyed, pretty woman, of unmistakably French extraction on one side or the other. She was probably some years older than Elizabeth, and had a sparkling light in her eye. In front of the sofa was a small table, with a pack of cards scattered upon it faces upward.

The attitude had been so full of abandonment that she bounded up like a spring on hearing the door open.

Perceiving that it was Elizabeth she lapsed into ease, and came across to her with a reckless skip that innate grace only prevented from being boisterous.

'Why, you are late,' she said, taking hold of Elizabeth-Jane's hands.

'There were so many little things to put up.'

'And you seem dead-alive and tired. Let me try to enliven you by some wonderful tricks I have learnt, to kill time. Sit there and don't move.' She gathered up the pack of cards, pulled the table in front of her, and began to deal them rapidly, telling Elizabeth to choose some.

'Well, have you chosen?' she asked, flinging down the last card.

'No,' stammered Elizabeth, arousing herself from a reverie. 'I quite forgot, I was thinking of—you, and me—and how strange it is that I am here.'

Miss Templeman looked at Elizabeth-Jane with interest, and laid down the cards. 'Ah! never mind,' she said. 'I'll lie here while you sit by me; and we'll talk.'

Elizabeth drew up silently to the head of the sofa, but with obvious pleasure. It could be seen that though in years she was younger than her entertainer in manner and general vision she seemed more of the sage.

3. Thread used to trace a path through a maze or labyrinth.

Miss Templeman deposited herself on the sofa in her former flexuous position, and throwing her arm above her brow—somewhat in the pose of a well-known conception of Titian's[4]—talked up at Elizabeth-Jane invertedly across her forehead and arm.

'I must tell you something,' she said. 'I wonder if you have suspected it. I have only been mistress of a large house and fortune a little while.'

'Oh—only a little while?' murmured Elizabeth-Jane, her countenance slightly falling.

'As a girl I lived about in garrison towns and elsewhere with my father, till I was quite flighty and unsettled. He was an officer in the army. I should not have mentioned this had I not thought it best you should know the truth.'

'Yes, yes.' She looked thoughtfully round the room—at the little square piano with brass inlayings, at the window-curtains, at the lamp, at the fair and dark kings and queens on the card-table, and finally at the inverted face of Lucetta Templeman, whose large lustrous eyes had such an odd effect upside down.

Elizabeth's mind ran on acquirements to an almost morbid degree. 'You speak French and Italian fluently, no doubt,' she said. 'I have not been able to get beyond a wretched bit of Latin yet.'

'Well, for that matter, in my native isle speaking French does not go for much. It is rather the other way.'

'Where is your native isle?'

It was with rather more reluctance that Miss Templeman said, 'Jersey.[5] There they speak French on one side of the street and English on the other, and a mixed tongue in the middle of the road. But it is a long time since I was there. Bath is where my people really belong to, though my ancestors in Jersey were as good as anybody in England. They were the Le Sueurs, an old family who have done great things in their time. I went back and lived there after my father's death. But I don't value such past matters, and am quite an English person in my feelings and tastes.'

Lucetta's tongue had for a moment outrun her discretion. She had arrived at Casterbridge as a Bath lady, and there were obvious reasons why Jersey should drop out of her life. But Elizabeth had tempted her to make free, and a deliberately formed resolve had been broken.

It could not, however, have been broken in safer company. Lucetta's words went no further, and after this day she was so much upon her guard that there appeared no chance of her identification with the young Jersey woman who had been Henchard's dear comrade at a critical time. Not the least amusing of her safeguards was her resolute avoid-

---

4. The Venetian artist Tiziano Vecellio (c. 1485–1576), known as Titian, painted a number of sensuous portraits of reclining women.

5. The largest and most southerly of the Channel Islands, 30 miles from the northwest coast of France.

ance of a French word if one by accident came to her tongue more readily than its English equivalent. She shirked it with the suddenness of the
weak Apostle[6] at the accusation, 'Thy speech bewrayeth thee!'

Expectancy sat visibly upon Lucetta the next morning. She dressed
herself for Mr. Henchard, and restlessly awaited his call before mid-day;
as he did not come she waited on through the afternoon. But she did not
tell Elizabeth that the person expected was the girl's stepfather.

They sat in adjoining windows of the same room in Lucetta's great
stone mansion, netting,[7] and looking out upon the market, which formed
an animated scene. Elizabeth could see the crown of her stepfather's hat
among the rest beneath, and was not aware that Lucetta watched the same
object with yet intenser interest. He moved about amid the throng, at this
point lively as an ant-hill; elsewhere more reposeful, and broken up by
stalls of fruit and vegetables. The farmers as a rule preferred the open *carrefour*[8] for their transactions, despite its inconvenient jostlings and the
danger from crossing vehicles, to the gloomy sheltered market-room provided for them. Here they surged on this one day of the week, forming a
little world of leggings, switches, and sample-bags; men of extensive stomachs, sloping like mountain sides; men whose heads in walking swayed as
the trees in November gales; who in conversing varied their attitudes
much, lowering themselves by spreading their knees, and thrusting their
hands into the pockets of remote inner jackets. Their faces radiated tropi-
cal warmth; for though when at home their countenances varied with the
seasons, their market-faces all the year round were glowing little fires.

All over-clothes here were worn as if they were an inconvenience, a
hampering necessity. Some men were well-dressed; but the majority
were careless in that respect, appearing in suits which were historical
records of their wearer's deeds, sun-scorchings, and daily struggles for
many years past. Yet many carried ruffled cheque-books in their pockets
which regulated at the bank hard by a balance of never less than four figures. In fact, what these gibbous[9] human shapes specially represented
was ready money—money insistently ready—not ready next year like a
nobleman's—often not merely ready at the bank like a professional
man's, but ready in their large plump hands.

It happened that to-day there rose in the midst of them all two or three
tall apple-trees standing as if they grew on the spot; till it was perceived
that they were held by men from the cider-districts who came here to sell
them, bringing the clay of their county on their boots. Elizabeth-Jane,
who had often observed them, said, 'I wonder if the same trees come
every week?'

6. After Christ's arrest, Peter denied being one of his followers, but he was identified by his
   Galilean accent. See Matthew 26.73.
7. Engaged in needlework.
8. Square or open space where several roads meet (from the French).
9. Rotund or pot-bellied.

'What trees?' said Lucetta, absorbed in watching for Henchard.

Elizabeth replied vaguely, for an incident checked her. Behind one of the trees stood Farfrae, briskly discussing a sample-bag with a farmer. Henchard had come up, accidentally encountering the young man, whose face seemed to inquire, 'Do we speak to each other?'

She saw her stepfather throw a shine into his eye which answered 'No!' Elizabeth-Jane sighed.

'Are you particularly interested in anybody out there?' said Lucetta.

'O no,' said her companion, a quick red shooting over her face.

Luckily Farfrae's figure was immediately covered by the apple-tree.

Lucetta looked hard at her. 'Quite sure?' she said.

'O yes,' said Elizabeth-Jane.

Again Lucetta looked out. 'They are all farmers, I suppose?' she said.

'No. There's Mr. Bulge—he's a wine merchant; there's Benjamin Brownlet—a horse dealer; and Kitson, the pig breeder; and Yopper, the auctioneer; besides maltsters, and millers—and so on.' Farfrae stood out quite distinctly now; but she did not mention him.

The Saturday afternoon slipped on thus desultorily. The market changed from the sample-showing hour to the idle hour before starting homewards, when tales were told. Henchard had not called on Lucetta though he had stood so near. He must have been too busy, she thought. He would come on Sunday or Monday.

The days came but not the visitor, though Lucetta repeated her dressing with scrupulous care. She was disheartened. It may at once be declared that Lucetta no longer bore towards Henchard all that warm allegiance which had characterized her in their first acquaintance; the then unfortunate issue of things had chilled pure love considerably. But there remained a conscientious wish to bring about her union with him, now that there was nothing to hinder it—to right her position—which in itself was a happiness to sigh for. With strong social reasons on her side why their marriage should take place there had ceased to be any worldly reason on his why it should be postponed, since she had succeeded to fortune.

Tuesday was the great Candlemas fair.[1] At breakfast she said to Elizabeth-Jane quite coolly: 'I imagine your father may call to see you to-day. I suppose he stands close by in the market-place with the rest of the corn-dealers?'

She shook her head. 'He won't come.'

'Why?'

'He has taken against me,' she said in a husky voice.

'You have quarrelled more deeply than I know of.'

1. The feast of thanksgiving for the Purification of the Virgin, now February 2. The hiring fair in Dorchester, at which agricultural workers were taken on for the coming year, took place on Old Candlemas Day, February 14 (which is also St. Valentine's Day).

Elizabeth, wishing to shield the man she believed to be her father from any charge of unnatural dislike, said 'Yes.'

'Then where you are is, of all places, the one he will avoid?'

Elizabeth nodded sadly.

Lucetta looked blank, twitched up her lovely eyebrows and lip, and burst into hysterical sobs. Here was a disaster—her ingenious scheme completely stultified.

'O, my dear Miss Templeman—what's the matter?' cried her companion.

'I like your company much!' said Lucetta, as soon as she could speak.

'Yes, yes—and so do I yours!' Elizabeth chimed in soothingly.

'But—but—' She could not finish the sentence, which was, naturally, that if Henchard had such a rooted dislike for the girl as now seemed to be the case, Elizabeth-Jane would have to be got rid of—a disagreeable necessity.

A provisional resource suggested itself. 'Miss Henchard—will you go on an errand for me as soon as breakfast is over?—Ah, that's very good of you. Will you go and order——' Here she enumerated several commissions at sundry shops, which would occupy Elizabeth's time for the next hour or two, at least.

'And have you ever seen the Museum?'

Elizabeth-Jane had not.

'Then you should do so at once. You can finish the morning by going there. It is an old house in a back street—I forget where—but you'll find out—and there are crowds of interesting things—skeletons, teeth, old pots and pans, ancient boots and shoes, birds' eggs—all charmingly instructive. You'll be sure to stay till you get quite hungry.'

Elizabeth hastily put on her things and departed. 'I wonder why she wants to get rid of me to-day!' she said sorrowfully as she went. That her absence, rather than her services or instruction, was in request, had been readily apparent to Elizabeth-Jane, simple as she seemed, and difficult as it was to attribute a motive for the desire.

She had not been gone ten minutes when one of Lucetta's servants was sent to Henchard's with a note. The contents were briefly:—

DEAR MICHAEL,—You will be standing in view of my house to-day for two or three hours in the course of your business, so do please call and see me. I am sadly disappointed that you have not come before, for can I help anxiety about my own equivocal relation to you?—especially now my aunt's fortune has brought me more prominently before society? Your daughter's presence here may be the cause of your neglect; and I have therefore sent her away for the morning. Say you come on business—I shall be quite alone.

LUCETTA.

When the messenger returned her mistress gave directions that if a gentleman called he was to be admitted at once, and sat down to await results.

Sentimentally she did not much care to see him—his delays had wearied her; but it was necessary; and with a sigh she arranged herself picturesquely in the chair; first this way, then that; next so that the light fell over her head. Next she flung herself on the couch in the cyma-recta curve[2] which so became her, and with her arm over her brow looked towards the door. This, she decided, was the best position after all; and thus she remained till a man's step was heard on the stairs. Whereupon Lucetta, forgetting her curve (for Nature was too strong for Art as yet), jumped up and ran and hid herself behind one of the window-curtains in a freak of timidity. In spite of the waning of passion the situation was an agitating one—she had not seen Henchard since his (supposed) temporary parting from her in Jersey.

She could hear the servant showing the visitor into the room, shutting the door upon him, and leaving as if to go and look for her mistress. Lucetta flung back the curtain with a nervous greeting. The man before her was not Henchard.

XXIII

A conjecture that her visitor might be some other person had, indeed, flashed through Lucetta's mind when she was on the point of bursting out; but it was just too late to recede.

He was years younger than the Mayor of Casterbridge; fair, fresh, and slenderly handsome. He wore genteel cloth leggings with white buttons, polished boots with infinite lace holes, light cord breeches under a black velveteen coat and waistcoat; and he had a silver-topped switch in his hand. Lucetta blushed, and said with a curious mixture of pout and laugh on her face—'O, I've made a mistake!'

The visitor, on the contrary, did not laugh half a wrinkle.

'But I'm very sorry!' he said, in deprecating tones. 'I came and I inquired for Miss Henchard, and they showed me up heere, and in no case would I have caught ye so unmannerly if I had known!'

'I was the unmannerly one,' said she.

'But is it that I have come to the wrong house, madam?' said Mr. Farfrae, blinking a little in his bewilderment and nervously tapping his legging with his switch.

'O no, sir,—sit down. You must come and sit down now you are here,' replied Lucetta kindly, to relieve his embarrassment. 'Miss Henchard will be here directly.'

Now this was not strictly true; but that something about the young man—that hyperborean[1] crispness, stringency, and charm, as of a well-

2. An architectural term for the meeting of two curves, the upper one concave and the lower convex.
1. Far northern.

braced musical instrument, which had awakened the interest of Henchard, and of Elizabeth-Jane, and of the Three Mariners' jovial crew, at sight, made his unexpected presence here attractive to Lucetta. He hesitated, looked at the chair, thought there was no danger in it (though there was), and sat down.

Farfrae's sudden entry was simply the result of Henchard's permission to him to see Elizabeth if he were minded to woo her. At first he had taken no notice of Henchard's brusque letter; but an exceptionally fortunate business transaction put him on good terms with everybody, and revealed to him that he could undeniably marry if he chose. Then who so pleasing, thrifty, and satisfactory in every way as Elizabeth-Jane? Apart from her personal recommendations a reconciliation with his former friend Henchard would, in the natural course of things, flow from such a union. He therefore forgave the Mayor his curtness; and this morning on his way to the fair he had called at her house, where he learnt that she was staying at Miss Templeman's. A little stimulated at not finding her ready and waiting—so fanciful are men!—he hastened on to High-Place Hall to encounter no Elizabeth but its mistress herself.

'The fair to-day seems a large one,' she said when, by a natural deviation, their eyes sought the busy scene without. 'Your numerous fairs and markets keep me interested. How many things I think of while I watch from here!'

He seemed in doubt how to answer, and the babble without reached them as they sat—voices as of wavelets on a lopping sea, one ever and anon rising above the rest. 'Do you look out often?' he asked.

'Yes—very often.'

'Do you look for any one you know?'

Why should she have answered as she did?

'I look as at a picture merely. But,' she went on, turning pleasantly to him, 'I may do so now—I may look for you. You are always there, are you not? Ah—I don't mean it seriously! But it is amusing to look for somebody one knows in a crowd, even if one does not want him. It takes off the terrible oppressiveness of being surrounded by a throng, and having no point of junction with it through a single individual.'

'Ay! Maybe you'll be very lonely, ma'am?'

'Nobody knows how lonely.'

'But you are rich, they say?'

'If so, I don't know how to enjoy my riches. I came to Casterbridge thinking I should like to live here. But I wonder if I shall.'

'Where did ye come from, ma'am?'

'The neighbourhood of Bath.'

'And I from near Edinboro',' he murmured. 'It's better to stay at home, and that's true; but a man must live where his money is made. It is a great pity, but it's always so! Yet I've done very well this year. O yes,' he went on with ingenuous enthusiasm. 'You see that man with the drab kerseymere[2] coat? I bought largely of him in the autumn when wheat was down, and then afterwards when it rose a little I sold off all I had! It brought only a small profit to me; while the farmers kept theirs, expecting higher figures—yes, though the rats were gnawing the ricks hollow. Just when I sold the markets went lower, and I bought up the corn of those who had been holding back at less price than my first purchases. And then,' cried Farfrae impetuously, his face alight, 'I sold it a few weeks after, when it happened to go up again! And so, by contenting mysel' with small profits frequently repeated, I soon made five hundred pounds—yes!'—(bringing down his hand upon the table, and quite forgetting where he was)—'while the others by keeping theirs in hand made nothing at all!'

Lucetta regarded him with a critical interest. He was quite a new type of person to her. At last his eye fell upon the lady's and their glances met.

'Ay, now, I'm wearying you!' he exclaimed.

She said, 'No, indeed,' colouring a shade.

'What then?'

'Quite otherwise. You are most interesting.'

It was now Farfrae who showed the modest pink.

'I mean all you Scotchmen,' she added in hasty correction. 'So free from Southern extremes. We common people are all one way or the other—warm or cold, passionate or frigid. You have both temperatures going on in you at the same time.'

'But how do you mean that? Ye were best to explain clearly, ma'am.'

'You are animated—then you are thinking of getting on. You are sad the next moment—then you are thinking of Scotland and friends.'

'Yes. I think of home sometimes!' he said simply.

'So do I—as far as I can. But it was an old house where I was born, and they pulled it down for improvements, so I seem hardly to have any home to think of now.'

Lucetta did not add, as she might have done, that the house was in St. Helier, and not in Bath.

'But the mountains, and the mists and the rocks, they are there! And don't they seem like home?'

She shook her head.

'They do to me—they do to me,' he murmured. And his mind could be seen flying away northwards. Whether its origin were national or personal, it was quite true what Lucetta had said, that the curious double strands in Farfrae's thread of life—the commercial and the romantic—were very distinct at times. Like the colours in a variegated cord those contrasts could be seen intertwisted, yet not mingling.

'You are wishing you were back again,' said she.

'Ah, no, ma'am,' said Farfrae, suddenly recalling himself.

2. Fine woollen cloth.

The fair without the windows was now raging thick and loud. It was the chief hiring fair of the year, and differed quite from the market of a few days earlier. In substance it was a whitey-brown crowd flecked with white—this being the body of labourers waiting for places. The long bonnets of the women, like waggon-tilts,[3] their cotton gowns and checked shawls, mixed with the carters' smockfrocks;[4] for they, too, entered into the hiring. Among the rest, at the corner of the pavement, stood an old shepherd, who attracted the eyes of Lucetta and Farfrae by his stillness. He was evidently a chastened man. The battle of life had been a sharp one with him, for, to begin with, he was a man of small frame. He was now so bowed by hard work and years that, approaching from behind, a person could hardly see his head. He had planted the stem of his crook in the gutter and was resting upon the bow, which was polished to silver brightness by the long friction of his hands. He had quite forgotten where he was, and what he had come for, his eyes being bent on the ground. A little way off negotiations were proceeding which had reference to him; but he did not hear them, and there seemed to be passing through his mind pleasant visions of the hiring successes of his prime, when his skill laid open to him any farm for the asking.

The negotiations were between a farmer from a distant county and the old man's son. In these there was a difficulty. The farmer would not take the crust without the crumb of the bargain, in other words, the old man without the younger; and the son had a sweetheart on his present farm, who stood by, waiting the issue with pale lips.

'I'm sorry to leave ye, Nelly,' said the young man with emotion. 'But, you see, I can't starve father, and he's out o' work at Lady-day.[5] 'Tis only thirty-five mile.'

The girl's lips quivered. 'Thirty-five mile!' she murmured. 'Ah! 'tis enough! I shall never see 'ee again!' It was, indeed, a hopeless length of traction for Dan Cupid's magnet;[6] for young men were young men at Casterbridge as elsewhere.

'O! no, no—I never shall,' she insisted, when he pressed her hand; and she turned her face to Lucetta's wall to hide her weeping. The farmer said he would give the young man half-an-hour for his answer, and went away, leaving the group sorrowing.

Lucetta's eyes, full of tears, met Farfrae's. His, too, to her surprise, were moist at the scene.

'It is very hard,' she said with strong feelings. 'Lovers ought not to be parted like that! O, if I had my wish, I'd let people live and love at their pleasure!'

3. Canvas coverings over wagons.
4. Loose-fitting linen overgarments, worn in place of a coat by farm-laborers.
5. The Feast of the Annunciation, now March 25, but April 6 in the Old Style calendar used here. Lady Day was the start date for all year-long agricultural employments.
6. Cupid is the Roman god of love; Dan is an archaic term meaning "Master."

'Maybe I can manage that they'll not be parted,' said Farfrae. 'I want a young carter; and perhaps I'll take the old man too—yes; he'll not be very expensive, and doubtless he will answer my pairrpose somehow.'

'O, you are so good!' she cried, delighted. 'Go and tell them, and let me know if you have succeeded!'

Farfrae went out, and she saw him speak to the group. The eyes of all brightened; the bargain was soon struck. Farfrae returned to her immediately it was concluded.

'It is kind-hearted of you, indeed,' said Lucetta. 'For my part, I have resolved that all my servants shall have lovers if they want them! Do make the same resolve!'

Farfrae looked more serious, waving his head a half turn. 'I must be a little stricter than that,' he said.

'Why?'

'You are a—a thriving woman; and I am a struggling hay-and-corn merchant.'

'I am a very ambitious woman.'

'Ah, well, I cannet explain. I don't know how to talk to ladies, ambitious or no; and that's true,' said Donald with grave regret. 'I try to be civil to a' folk—no more!'

'I see you are as you say,' replied she, sensibly getting the upper hand in these exchanges of sentiment. Under this revelation of insight Farfrae again looked out of the window into the thick of the fair.

Two farmers met and shook hands, and being quite near the window their remarks could be heard as others' had been.

'Have you seen young Mr. Farfrae this morning?' asked one. 'He promised to meet me here at the stroke of twelve; but I've gone athwart and about the fair half-a-dozen times, and never a sign of him: though he's mostly a man to his word.'

'I quite forgot the engagement,' murmured Farfrae.

'Now you must go,' said she; 'must you not?'

'Yes,' he replied. But he still remained.

'You had better go,' she urged. 'You will lose a customer.'

'Now, Miss Templeman, you will make me angry,' exclaimed Farfrae.

'Then suppose you don't go; but stay a little longer?'

He looked anxiously at the farmer who was seeking him, and who just then ominously walked across to where Henchard was standing, and he looked into the room and at her. 'I like staying; but I fear I must go!' he said. 'Business ought not to be neglected, ought it?'

'Not for a single minute.'

'It's true. I'll come another time—if I may, ma'am?'

'Certainly,' she said. 'What has happened to us to-day is very curious.'

'Something to think over when we are alone, it's like to be?'

'Oh, I don't know that. It is commonplace after all.'

'No, I'll not say that. O no!'

'Well, whatever it has been, it is now over; and the market calls you to be gone.'

'Yes, yes. Market—business! I wish there were no business in the warrld.'

Lucetta almost laughed—she would quite have laughed—but that there was a little emotion going in her at the time. 'How you change!' she said. 'You should not change like this.'

'I have never wished such things before,' said the Scotchman, with a simple, shamed, apologetic look for his weakness. 'It is only since coming heere and seeing you!'

'If that's the case, you had better not look at me any longer. Dear me, I feel I have quite demoralized you!'

'But look or look not, I will see you in my thoughts. Well, I'll go— thank you for the pleasure of this visit.'

'Thank you for staying.'

'Maybe I'll get into my market-mind when I've been out a few minutes,' he murmured. 'But I don't know—I don't know!'

As he went she said eagerly, 'You may hear them speak of me in Casterbridge as time goes on. If they tell you I'm a coquette, which some may, because of the incidents of my life, don't believe it, for I am not.'

'I swear I will not!' he said fervidly.

Thus the two. She had enkindled the young man's enthusiasm till he was quite brimming with sentiment; while he, from merely affording her a new form of idleness had gone on to wake her serious solicitude. Why was this? They could not have told.

Lucetta as a young girl would hardly have looked at a tradesman. But her ups and downs, capped by her indiscretions with Henchard, had made her uncritical as to station. In her poverty she had met with repulse from the society to which she had belonged, and she had no great zest for renewing an attempt upon it now. Her heart longed for some ark[7] into which it could fly and be at rest. Rough or smooth she did not care so long as it was warm.

Farfrae was shown out, it having entirely escaped him that he had called to see Elizabeth. Lucetta at the window watched him threading the maze of farmers and farmers' men. She could see by his gait that he was conscious of her eyes, and her heart went out to him for his modesty—pleaded with her sense of his unfitness that he might be allowed to come again. He entered the market-house, and she could see him no more.

Three minutes later, when she had left the window, knocks, not of multitude but of strength, sounded through the house, and the waiting-maid tripped up.

'The Mayor,' she said.

7. In Genesis 8.9 the dove returns to Noah's ark when it cannot find dry land.

Lucetta had reclined herself, and was looking dreamily through her fingers. She did not answer at once, and the maid repeated the information with the addition, 'And he's afraid he hasn't much time to spare, he says.'

'Oh! Then tell him that as I have a headache I won't detain him to-day.' The message was taken down, and she heard the door close.

Lucetta had come to Casterbridge to quicken Henchard's feelings with regard to her. She had quickened them, and now she was indifferent to the achievement.

Her morning view of Elizabeth-Jane as a disturbing element changed, and she no longer felt strongly the necessity of getting rid of the girl for her stepfather's sake. When the young woman came in, sweetly unconscious of the turn in the tide, Lucetta went up to her, and said quite sincerely—

'I'm so glad you've come. You'll live with me a long time, won't you?'

Elizabeth as a watch-dog to keep her father off—what a new idea. Yet it was not unpleasing. Henchard had neglected her all these days, after compromising her indescribably in the past. The least he could have done when he found himself free, and herself affluent, would have been to respond heartily and promptly to her invitation.

Her emotions rose, fell, undulated, filled her with wild surmise[8] at their suddenness; and so passed Lucetta's experiences of that day.

XXIV

Poor Elizabeth-Jane, little thinking what her malignant star had done to blast[1] the budding attentions she had won from Donald Farfrae, was glad to hear Lucetta's words about remaining.

For in addition to Lucetta's house being a home, that raking view of the market-place which it afforded had as much attraction for her as for Lucetta. The *carrefour* was like the regulation Open Place[2] in spectacular dramas, where the incidents that occur always happen to bear on the lives of the adjoining residents. Farmers, merchants, dairymen, quacks, hawkers, appeared there from week to week, and disappeared as the afternoon wasted away. It was the node of all orbits.

From Saturday to Saturday was as from day to day with the two young women now. In an emotional sense they did not live at all during the intervals. Wherever they might go wandering on other days, on market-day they were sure to be at home. Both stole sly glances out of the window at Farfrae's shoulders and poll. His face they seldom saw, for, either through shyness, or not to disturb his mercantile mood, he avoided looking towards their quarters.

8. The phrase "wild surmise" is from Keats's sonnet "On First Looking into Chapman's Homer" (1816), line 13.
1. Strike, as by lightning, or cause to wither, as a young plant. Both senses are relevant here.
2. The action of classical Greek drama usually takes place out of doors in a public area.

Thus things went on, till a certain market-morning brought a new sensation. Elizabeth and Lucetta were sitting at breakfast when a parcel containing two dresses arrived for the latter from London. She called Elizabeth from her breakfast, and entering her friend's bedroom Elizabeth saw the gowns spread out on the bed, one of a deep cherry colour, the other lighter—a glove lying at the end of each sleeve, a bonnet at the top of each neck, and parasols across the gloves, Lucetta standing beside the suggested human figure in an attitude of contemplation.

'I wouldn't think so hard about it,' said Elizabeth, marking the intensity with which Lucetta was alternating the question whether this or that would suit best.

'But settling upon new clothes is so trying,' said Lucetta. 'You are that person' (pointing to one of the arrangements), 'or you are *that* totally different person' (pointing to the other), 'for the whole of the coming spring: and one of the two, you don't know which, may turn out to be very objectionable.'

It was finally decided by Miss Templeman that she would be the cherry-coloured person at all hazards. The dress was pronounced to be a fit, and Lucetta walked with it into the front room, Elizabeth following her.

The morning was exceptionally bright for the time of year. The sun fell so flat on the houses and pavement opposite Lucetta's residence that they poured their brightness into her rooms. Suddenly, after a rumbling of wheels, there were added to this steady light a fantastic series of circling irradiations upon the ceiling, and the companions turned to the window. Immediately opposite a vehicle of strange description had come to standstill, as if it had been placed there for exhibition.

It was the new-fashioned agricultural implement called a horse-drill,[3] till then unknown, in its modern shape, in this part of the country, where the venerable seed-lip was still used for sowing as in the days of the Heptarchy.[4] Its arrival created about as much sensation in the corn-market as a flying machine would create at Charing Cross.[5] The farmers crowded round it, women drew near it, children crept under and into it. The machine was painted in bright hues of green, yellow, and red, and it resembled as a whole a compound of hornet, grasshopper, and shrimp, magnified enormously. Or it might have been likened to an upright musical instrument with the front gone. That was how it struck Lucetta. 'Why, it is a sort of agricultural piano,' she said.

'It has something to do with corn,' said Elizabeth.

'I wonder who thought of introducing it here?'

---

3. Horse-drawn machine for planting seeds, replacing the older system of scattering them by hand.
4. The seven kingdoms, including Wessex, into which England was divided from about the sixth to the ninth centuries C.E.
5. Intersection in central London.

Donald Farfrae was in the minds of both as the innovator, for though not a farmer he was closely leagued with farming operations. And as if in response to their thought he came up at that moment, looked at the machine, walked round it, and handled it as if he knew something about its make. The two watchers had inwardly started at his coming, and Elizabeth left the window, went to the back of the room, and stood as if absorbed in the panelling of the wall. She hardly knew that she had done this till Lucetta, animated by the conjunction of her new attire with the sight of Farfrae, spoke out: 'Let us go and look at the instrument, whatever it is.'

Elizabeth-Jane's bonnet and shawl were pitchforked on in a moment, and they went out. Among all the agriculturists gathering round the only appropriate possessor of the new machine seemed to be Lucetta, because she alone rivalled it in colour.

They examined it curiously; observing the rows of trumpet-shaped tubes one within the other, the little scoops, like revolving salt-spoons, which tossed the seed into the upper ends of the tubes that conducted it to the ground; till somebody said, 'Good morning, Elizabeth-Jane.' She looked up, and there was her stepfather.

His greeting had been somewhat dry and thunderous, and Elizabeth-Jane, embarrassed out of her equanimity, stammered at random, 'This is the lady I live with, father—Miss Templeman.'

Henchard put his hand to his hat, which he brought down with a great wave till it met his body at the knee. Miss Templeman bowed. 'I am happy to become acquainted with you, Mr. Henchard,' she said. 'This is a curious machine.'

'Yes,' Henchard replied; and he proceeded to explain it, and still more forcibly to ridicule it.

'Who brought it here?' said Lucetta.

'Oh, don't ask me, ma'am!' said Henchard. 'The thing—why 'tis impossible it should act. 'Twas brought here by one of our machinists[6] on the recommendation of a jumped-up jackanapes of a fellow who thinks——' His eye caught Elizabeth-Jane's imploring face, and he stopped, probably thinking that the suit might be progressing.

He turned to go away. Then something seemed to occur which his stepdaughter fancied must really be a hallucination of hers. A murmur apparently came from Henchard's lips in which she detected the words, 'You refused to see me!' reproachfully addressed to Lucetta. She could not believe that they had been uttered by her stepfather; unless, indeed, they might have been spoken to one of the yellow-gaitered farmers near them. Yet Lucetta seemed silent; and then all thought of the incident was dissipated by the humming of a song, which sounded as though from the interior of the machine. Henchard had by this time vanished

---

6. Repairers or (as here) makers of machines.

into the market-house, and both the women glanced towards the corn-drill. They could see behind it the bent back of a man who was pushing his head into the internal works to master their simple secrets. The hummed song went on—

[handwritten margin note: Lucetta w/ goes w/ Whatford is popular]

> "Tw—s on a s—m—r aftern—n,
> A wee be—re the s—n w—nt d—n,
> When Kitty wi' a braw n—w g—wn
> C—me ow're the h—lls to Gowrie.'[7]

Elizabeth-Jane had apprehended the singer in a moment, and looked guilty of she did not know what. Lucetta next recognized him, and more mistress of herself said archly, 'The "Lass of Gowrie" from the inside of a seed-drill—what a phenomenon!'

Satisfied at last with his investigation the young man stood upright, and met their eyes across the summit.

'We are looking at the wonderful new drill,' Miss Templeman said. 'But practically it is a stupid thing—is it not?' she added, on the strength of Henchard's information.

[handwritten margin note: garners seed]

'Stupid? O no!' said Farfrae gravely. 'It will revolutionize sowing heer-about! No more sowers flinging their seed about broadcast, so that some falls by the wayside and some among thorns,[8] and all that. Each grain will go straight to its intended place, and nowhere else whatever!'

'Then the romance of the sower is gone for good,' observed Elizabeth-Jane, who felt herself at one with Farfrae in Bible-reading at least. '"He that observeth the wind shall not sow," so the Preacher said;[9] but his words will not be to the point any more. How things change!'

'Ay; ay. . . . It must be so!' Donald admitted, his gaze fixing itself on a blank point far away. 'But the machines are already very common in the East and North of England,' he added apologetically.

Lucetta seemed to be outside this train of sentiment, her acquaintance with the Scriptures being somewhat limited. 'Is the machine yours?' she asked of Farfrae.

'O no, madam,' said he, becoming embarrassed and deferential at the sound of her voice, though with Elizabeth-Jane he was quite at his ease. 'No, no—I merely recommended that it should be got.'

In the silence which followed Farfrae appeared only conscious of her; to have passed from perception of Elizabeth into a brighter sphere of existence than she appertained to. Lucetta, discerning that he was much mixed that day, partly in his mercantile mood and partly in his romantic one, said gaily to him—

[handwritten note: Elizabeth understands Farfrae]

---

7. Song with words by Lady Nairne (1766–1845), set to a traditional Scots melody.
8. Referring to Christ's parable of the sower. See Matthew 13.38.
9. First clause of Ecclesiastes 11.4.

[handwritten note: Lucetta vs Elizabeth]

'Well, don't forsake the machine for us,' and went indoors with her companion.

The latter felt that she had been in the way, though why was unaccountable to her. Lucetta explained the matter somewhat by saying when they were again in the sitting-room—

'I had occasion to speak to Mr. Farfrae the other day, and so I knew him this morning.'

Lucetta was very kind towards Elizabeth that day. Together they saw the market thicken, and in course of time thin away with the slow decline of the sun towards the upper end of the town, its rays taking the street endways and enfilading[1] the long thoroughfare from top to bottom. The gigs[2] and vans disappeared one by one till there was not a vehicle in the street. The time of the riding world was over; the pedestrian world held sway. Field labourers and their wives and children trooped in from the villages for their weekly shopping, and instead of a rattle of wheels and a tramp of horses ruling the sound as earlier, there was nothing but the shuffle of many feet. All the implements were gone; all the farmers; all the moneyed class. The character of the town's trading had changed from bulk to multiplicity, and pence were handled now as pounds had been handled earlier in the day.

Lucetta and Elizabeth looked out upon this, for though it was night and the street lamps were lighted, they had kept their shutters unclosed. In the faint blink of the fire they spoke more freely.

'Your father was distant with you,' said Lucetta.

'Yes.' And having forgotten the momentary mystery of Henchard's seeming speech to Lucetta she continued, 'It is because he does not think I am respectable. I have tried to be so more than you can imagine, but in vain! My mother's separation from my father was unfortunate for me. You don't know what it is to have shadows like that upon your life.'

Lucetta seemed to wince. 'I do not—of that kind precisely,' she said, 'but you may feel a—sense of disgrace—shame—in other ways.'

'Have you ever had any such feeling?' said the younger innocently.

'O no,' said Lucetta quickly. 'I was thinking of—what happens sometimes when women get themselves in strange positions in the eyes of the world from no fault of their own.'

'It must make them very unhappy afterwards.'

'It makes them anxious; for might not other women despise them?'

'Not altogether despise them. Yet not quite like or respect them.'

Lucetta winced again. Her past was by no means secure from investigation, even in Casterbridge. For one thing Henchard had never returned to her the cloud of letters she had written and sent him in her

---

1. Sweeping from end to end.
2. Two-wheeled open carriages.

first excitement. Possibly they were destroyed; but she could have wished that they had never been written.

The rencounter with Farfrae and his bearing towards Lucetta had made the reflective Elizabeth more observant of her brilliant and amiable companion. A few days afterwards, when her eyes met Lucetta's as the latter was going out, she somehow knew that Miss Templeman was nourishing a hope of seeing the attractive Scotchman. The fact was printed large all over Lucetta's cheeks and eyes to any one who could read her as Elizabeth-Jane was beginning to do. Lucetta passed on and closed the street door.

A seer's spirit took possession of Elizabeth, impelling her to sit down by the fire and divine events so surely from data already her own that they could be held as witnessed. She followed Lucetta thus mentally— saw her encounter Donald somewhere as if by chance—saw him wear his special look when meeting women, with an added intensity because this one was Lucetta. She depicted his impassioned manner; beheld the indecision of both between their lothness to separate and their desire not to be observed; depicted their shaking of hands; how they probably parted with frigidity in their general contour and movements, only in the smaller features showing the spark of passion, thus invisible to all but themselves. This discerning silent witch had not done thinking of these things when Lucetta came noiselessly behind her and made her start.

It was all true as she had pictured—she could have sworn it. Lucetta had a heightened luminousness in her eye over and above the advanced colour of her cheeks.

'You've seen Mr. Farfrae,' said Elizabeth demurely.

'Yes,' said Lucetta. 'How did you know?'

She knelt down on the hearth and took her friend's hands excitedly in her own. But after all she did not say when or how she had seen him or what he had said.

That night she became restless; in the morning she was feverish; and at breakfast-time she told her companion that she had something on her mind—something which concerned a person in whom she was interested much. Elizabeth was earnest to listen and sympathize.

'This person—a lady—once admired a man much—very much,' she said tentatively.

'Ah,' said Elizabeth-Jane.

'They were intimate—rather. He did not think so deeply of her as she did of him. But in an impulsive moment, purely out of reparation, he proposed to make her his wife. She agreed. But there was an unexpected hitch in the proceedings; though she had been so far compromised with him that she felt she could never belong to another man, as a pure matter of conscience, even if she should wish to. After that they were much apart, heard nothing of each other for a long time, and she felt her life quite closed up for her.'

'Ah—poor girl!'

'She suffered much on account of him; though I should add that he
could not altogether be blamed for what had happened. At last the obstacle which separated them was providentially removed; and he came to
marry her.'

'How delightful!'

'But in the interval she—my poor friend—had seen a man she liked
better than him. Now comes the point: Could she in honour dismiss the
first?'

'A new man she liked better—that's bad!'

'Yes,' said Lucetta, looking pained at a boy who was swinging the town
pump-handle. 'It is bad! Though you must remember that she was
forced into an equivocal position with the first man by an accident—that
he was not so well educated or refined as the second, and that she had
discovered some qualities in the first that rendered him less desirable as
a husband than she had at first thought him to be.'

'I cannot answer,' said Elizabeth-Jane thoughtfully. 'It is so difficult. It
wants a Pope to settle that!'

'You prefer not to, perhaps?' Lucetta showed in her appealing tone
how much she leant on Elizabeth's judgment.

'Yes, Miss Templeman,' admitted Elizabeth. 'I would rather not say.'

Nevertheless, Lucetta seemed relieved by the simple fact of having
opened out the situation a little, and was slowly convalescent of her
headache. 'Bring me a looking-glass. How do I appear to people?' she
said languidly.

'Well—a little worn,' answered Elizabeth, eyeing her as a critic eyes a
doubtful painting; fetching the glass she enabled Lucetta to survey herself in it, which Lucetta anxiously did.

'I wonder if I wear well, as times go!' she observed after a while.

'Yes—fairly.'

'Where am I worst?'

'Under your eyes—I notice a little brownness there.'

'Yes. That is my worst place, I know. How many years more do you
think I shall last before I get hopelessly plain?'

There was something curious in the way in which Elizabeth, though
the younger, had come to play the part of experienced sage in these discussions. 'It may be five years,' she said judicially. 'Or, with a quiet life,
as many as ten. With no love you might calculate on ten.'

Lucetta seemed to reflect on this as on an unalterable, impartial verdict. She told Elizabeth-Jane no more of the past attachment she had
roughly adumbrated as the experiences of a third person; and Elizabeth,
who in spite of her philosophy was very tender-hearted, sighed that night
in bed at the thought that her pretty, rich Lucetta did not treat her to the
full confidence of names and dates in her confessions. For by the 'she'
of Lucetta's story Elizabeth had not been beguiled.

XXV

The next phase of the supersession of Henchard in Lucetta's heart was an experiment in calling on her performed by Farfrae with some apparent trepidation. Conventionally speaking he conversed with both Miss Templeman and her companion; but in fact it was rather that Elizabeth sat invisible in the room. Donald appeared not to see her at all, and answered her wise little remarks with curtly indifferent monosyllables, his looks and faculties hanging on the woman who could boast of a more Protean[1] variety in her phases, moods, opinions, and also principles, than could Elizabeth. Lucetta had persisted in dragging her into the circle; but she had remained like an awkward third point which that circle would not touch.

Susan Henchard's daughter bore up against the frosty ache of the treatment, as she had borne up under worse things, and contrived as soon as possible to get out of the inharmonious room without being missed. The Scotchman seemed hardly the same Farfrae who had danced with her and walked with her in a delicate poise between love and friendship—that period in the history of a love when alone it can be said to be unalloyed with pain.

She stoically looked from her bedroom window, and contemplated her fate as if it were written on the top of the church-tower hard by. 'Yes,' she said at last, bringing down her palm upon the sill with a pat: '*He* is the second man of that story she told me!'

All this time Henchard's smouldering sentiments towards Lucetta had been fanned into higher and higher inflammation by the circumstances of the case. He was discovering that the young woman for whom he once felt a pitying warmth which had been almost chilled out of him by reflection, was, when now qualified with a slight inaccessibility and a more matured beauty, the very being to make him satisfied with life. Day after day proved to him, by her silence, that it was no use to think of bringing her round by holding aloof; so he gave in, and called upon her again, Elizabeth-Jane being absent.

He crossed the room to her with a heavy tread of some awkwardness, his strong, warm gaze upon her—like the sun beside the moon in comparison with Farfrae's modest look—and with something of a hail-fellow bearing, as, indeed, was not unnatural. But she seemed so transubstantiated by her change of position, and held out her hand to him in such cool friendship, that he became deferential, and sat down with a perceptible loss of power. He understood but little of fashion in dress, yet enough to feel himself inadequate in appearance beside her whom he had hitherto been dreaming of as almost his property. She said some-

---

1. The sea-god Proteus could change shape at will.

thing very polite about his being good enough to call. This caused him to recover balance. He looked her oddly in the face, losing his awe.

'Why, of course I have called, Lucetta,' he said. 'What does that non-sense mean? You know I couldn't have helped myself if I had wished—that is, if I had any kindness at all. I've called to say that I am ready, as soon as custom will permit, to give you my name in return for your devo-tion, and what you lost by it in thinking too little of yourself and too much of me; to say that you can fix the day or month, with my full con-sent, whenever in your opinion it would be seemly: you know more of these things than I.'

'It is full early yet,' she said evasively.

'Yes, yes; I suppose it is. But you know, Lucetta, I felt directly my poor ill-used Susan died, and when I could not bear the idea of marrying again, that after what had happened between us it was my duty not to let any unnecessary delay occur before putting things to rights. Still, I wouldn't call in a hurry, because—well, you can guess how this money you've come into made me feel.' His voice slowly fell; he was conscious that in this room his accents and manner wore a roughness not observ-able in the street. He looked about the room at the novel hangings and ingenious furniture with which she had surrounded herself.

'Upon my life I didn't know such furniture as this could be bought in Casterbridge,' he said.

'Nor can it be,' said she. 'Nor will it till fifty years more of civilization have passed over the town. It took a waggon and four horses to get it here.'

'H'm. It looks as if you were living on capital.'

'O no, I am not.'

'So much the better. But the fact is, your setting up like this makes my bearing towards you rather awkward.'

'Why?'

An answer was not really needed, and he did not furnish one. 'Well,' he went on, 'there's nobody in the world I would have wished to see enter into this wealth before you, Lucetta, and nobody, I am sure, who will become it more.' He turned to her with congratulatory admiration so fervid that she shrank somewhat, notwithstanding that she knew him so well.

'I am greatly obliged to you for all that,' said she, rather with an air of speaking ritual. The stint of reciprocal feeling was perceived, and Henchard showed chagrin at once—nobody was more quick to show that than he.

'You may be obliged or not for't. Though the things I say may not have the polish of what you've lately learnt to expect for the first time in your life, they are real, my lady Lucetta.'

'That's rather a rude way of speaking to me,' pouted Lucetta, with stormy eyes.

'Not at all!' replied Henchard hotly. 'But there, there, I don't wish to quarrel with 'ee. I come with an honest proposal for silencing your Jersey enemies, and you ought to be thankful.'

'How can you speak so!' she answered, firing quickly. 'Knowing that my only crime was the indulging in a foolish girl's passion for you with too little regard for correctness, and that I was what *I* call innocent all the time they called me guilty, you ought not to be so cutting! I suffered enough at that worrying time, when you wrote to tell me of your wife's return and my consequent dismissal, and if I am a little independent now, surely the privilege is due to me!'

'Yes, it is,' he said. 'But it is not by what is, in this life, but by what appears, that you are judged; and I therefore think you ought to accept me—for your own good name's sake. What is known in your native Jersey may get known here.'

'How you keep on about Jersey! I am English!'

'Yes, yes. Well, what do you say to my proposal?'

For the first time in their acquaintance Lucetta had the move; and yet she was backward. 'For the present let things be,' she said with some embarrassment. 'Treat me as an acquaintance; and I'll treat you as one. Time will——' she stopped; and he said nothing to fill the gap for awhile, there being no pressure of half acquaintance to drive them into speech if they were not minded for it.

'That's the way the wind blows, is it?' he said at last grimly, nodding an affirmative to his own thoughts.

A yellow flood of reflected sunlight filled the room for a few instants. It was produced by the passing of a load of newly trussed hay from the country, in a waggon marked with Farfrae's name. Beside it rode Farfrae himself on horseback. Lucetta's face became—as a woman's face becomes when the man she loves rises upon her gaze like an apparition.

A turn of the eye by Henchard, a glance from the window, and the secret of her inaccessibility would have been revealed. But Henchard in estimating her tone was looking down so plumb-straight that he did not note the warm consciousness upon Lucetta's face.

'I shouldn't have thought it—I shouldn't have thought it of women!' he said emphatically by-and-by, rising and shaking himself into activity; while Lucetta was so anxious to divert him from any suspicion of the truth that she asked him to be in no hurry. Bringing him some apples she insisted upon paring one for him.

He would not take it. 'No, no; such is not for me,' he said drily, and moved to the door. At going out he turned his eye upon her.

'You came to live in Casterbridge entirely on my account,' he said. 'Yet now you are here you won't have anything to say to my offer!'

He had hardly gone down the staircase when she dropped upon the sofa and jumped up again in a fit of desperation. 'I *will* love him!' she cried passionately; 'as for *him*—he's hot-tempered and stern, and it would be madness to bind myself to him knowing that. I won't be a slave to the past—I'll love where I choose!'

Yet having decided to break away from Henchard one might have supposed her capable of aiming higher than Farfrae. But Lucetta reasoned nothing: she feared hard words from the people with whom she had been earlier associated; she had no relatives left; and with native lightness of heart took kindly to what fate offered.

Elizabeth-Jane, surveying the position of Lucetta between her two lovers from the crystalline sphere of a straightforward mind, did not fail to perceive that her father, as she called him, and Donald Farfrae became more desperately enamoured of her friend every day. On Farfrae's side it was the unforced passion of youth. On Henchard's the artificially stimulated coveting of maturer age.

The pain she experienced from the almost absolute obliviousness to her existence that was shown by the pair of them became at times half dissipated by her sense of its humorousness. When Lucetta had pricked her finger they were as deeply concerned as if she were dying; when she herself had been seriously sick or in danger they uttered a conventional word of sympathy at the news, and forgot all about it immediately. But, as regarded Henchard, this perception of hers also caused her some filial grief; she could not help asking what she had done to be neglected so, after the professions of solicitude he had made. As regarded Farfrae, she thought, after honest reflection, that it was quite natural. What was she beside Lucetta?—as one of the 'meaner beauties of the night,'[2] when the moon had risen in the skies.

She had learnt the lesson of renunciation, and was as familiar with the wreck of each day's wishes as with the diurnal setting of the sun. If her earthly career had taught her few book philosophies it had at least well practised her in this. Yet her experience had consisted less in a series of pure disappointments than in a series of substitutions. Continually it had happened that what she had desired had not been granted her, and that what had been granted her she had not desired. So she viewed with an approach to equanimity the now cancelled days when Donald had been her undeclared lover, and wondered what unwished-for thing Heaven might send her in place of him.

XXVI

It chanced that on a fine spring morning Henchard and Farfrae met in the chestnut-walk which ran along the south wall of the town. Each had just come out from his early breakfast, and there was not another soul near. Henchard was reading a letter from Lucetta, sent in answer to a

---

2. Lesser beauties. In his poem "On His Mistress, the Queen of Bohemia," Sir Henry Wotton (1568–1639) asks the stars ("the meaner beauties of the night"), "What are you when the moon shall rise?"

note from him, in which she made some excuse for not immediately granting him a second interview that he had desired.

Donald had no wish to enter into conversation with his former friend on their present constrained terms; neither would he pass him in scowling silence. He nodded, and Henchard did the same. They had receded from each other several paces when a voice cried 'Farfrae!' It was Henchard's, who stood regarding him.

'Do you remember,' said Henchard, as if it were the presence of the thought and not of the man which made him speak, 'do you remember my story of that second woman—who suffered for her thoughtless intimacy with me?'

'I do,' said Farfrae.

'Do you remember my telling 'ee how it all began and how it ended?'

'Yes.'

'Well, I have offered to marry her now that I can; but she won't marry me. Now what would you think of her—I put it to you?'

'Well, ye owe her nothing more now,' said Farfrae heartily.

'It is true,' said Henchard, and went on.

That he had looked up from a letter to ask his questions completely shut out from Farfrae's mind all vision of Lucetta as the culprit. Indeed, her present position was so different from that of the young woman of Henchard's story as of itself to be sufficient to blind him absolutely to her identity. As for Henchard, he was reassured by Farfrae's words and manner against a suspicion which had crossed his mind. They were not those of a conscious rival.

Yet that there was rivalry by some one he was firmly persuaded. He could feel it in the air around Lucetta, see it in the turn of her pen. There was an antagonistic force in exercise, so that when he had tried to hang near her he seemed standing in a refluent current. That it was not innate caprice he was more and more certain. Her windows gleamed as if they did not want him; her curtains seemed to hang slily, as if they screened an ousting presence. To discover whose presence that was— whether really Farfrae's after all, or another's—he exerted himself to the utmost to see her again; and at length succeeded.

At the interview, when she offered him tea, he made it a point to launch a cautious inquiry if she knew Mr. Farfrae.

O yes, she knew him, she declared; she could not help knowing almost everybody in Casterbridge, living in such a gazebo[1] over the centre and arena of the town.

'Pleasant young fellow,' said Henchard.

'Yes,' said Lucetta.

'We both know him,' said kind Elizabeth-Jane, to relieve her companion's divined embarrassment.

1. Building or structure (typically a turret) commanding an extensive view.

There was a knock at the door; literally, three full knocks and a little one at the end.

'That kind of knock means half-and-half—somebody between gentle and simple,'[2] said the corn-merchant to himself. 'I shouldn't wonder therefore if it is he.' In a few seconds surely enough Donald walked in.

Lucetta was full of little fidgets and flutters, which increased Henchard's suspicions without affording any special proof of their correctness. He was well-nigh ferocious at the sense of the queer situation in which he stood towards this woman. One who had reproached him for deserting her when calumniated, who had urged claims upon his consideration on that account, who had lived waiting for him, who at the first decent moment had come to ask him to rectify, by making her his, the false position into which she had placed herself for his sake; such she had been. And now he sat at her tea-table eager to gain her attention, and in his amatory rage feeling the other man present to be a villain, just as any young fool of a lover might feel.

They sat stiffly side by side at the darkening table, like some Tuscan painting of the two disciples supping at Emmaus.[3] Lucetta, forming the third and haloed figure, was opposite them; Elizabeth-Jane, being out of the game, and out of the group, could observe all from afar, like the evangelist[4] who had to write it down: that there were long spaces of taciturnity, when all exterior circumstance was subdued to the touch of spoons and china, the click of a heel on the pavement under the window, the passing of a wheel-barrow or cart, the whistling of the carter, the gush of water into householders' buckets at the town-pump opposite; the exchange of greetings among their neighbours, and the rattle of the yokes by which they carried off their evening supply.

'More bread-and-butter?' said Lucetta to Henchard and Farfrae equally, holding out between them a plateful of long slices. Henchard took a slice by one end and Donald by the other; each feeling certain he was the man meant; neither let go, and the slice came in two.

'Oh—I am so sorry!' cried Lucetta, with a nervous titter. Farfrae tried to laugh; but he was too much in love to see the incident in any but a tragic light.

'How ridiculous of all three of them!' said Elizabeth to herself.

Henchard left the house with a ton of conjecture, though without a grain of proof, that the counter-attraction was Farfrae; and therefore he would not make up his mind. Yet to Elizabeth-Jane it was plain as the town-pump that Donald and Lucetta were incipient lovers. More than once, in spite of her care, Lucetta had been unable to restrain her

2. Below the rank of gentleman but above that of worker.
3. After the Resurrection Christ appeared to two of his disciples at Emmaus (see Luke 24.13–35). It is not clear which painting Hardy has in mind; Caravaggio's "The Supper at Emmaus" has been suggested, but Caravaggio (1571–1610) worked in Rome, not Tuscany.
4. Luke, who recorded the meeting at Emmaus.

glance from flitting across into Farfrae's eyes like a bird to its nest. But Henchard was constructed upon too large a scale to discern such minutiæ as these by an evening light, which to him were as the notes of an insect that lie above the compass of the human ear.

But he was disturbed. And the sense of occult rivalry in suitorship was so much superadded to the palpable rivalry of their business lives. To the coarse materiality of that rivalry it added an inflaming soul.

The thus vitalized antagonism took the form of action by Henchard sending for Jopp, the manager originally displaced by Farfrae's arrival. Henchard had frequently met this man about the streets, observed that his clothing spoke of neediness, heard that he lived in Mixen Lane—a back slum of the town, the *pis aller*[5] of Casterbridge domiciliation— itself almost a proof that a man had reached a stage when he would not stick at trifles.

Jopp came after dark, by the gates of the storeyard, and felt his way through the hay and straw to the office where Henchard sat in solitude awaiting him.

'I am again out of a foreman,' said the corn-factor. 'Are you in a place?'

'Not so much as a beggar's, sir.'

'How much do you ask?'

Jopp named his price, which was very moderate.

'When can you come?'

'At this hour and moment, sir,' said Jopp, who, standing hands-pocketed at the street corner till the sun had faded the shoulders of his coat to scarecrow green, had regularly watched Henchard in the market-place, measured him, and learnt him, by virtue of the power which the still man has in his stillness of knowing the busy one better than he knows himself. Jopp, too, had had a convenient experience; he was the only one in Casterbridge besides Henchard and the close-lipped Elizabeth who knew that Lucetta came truly from Jersey, and but proximately from Bath. 'I know Jersey, too, sir,' he said. 'Was living there when you used to do business that way. O yes—have often seen ye there.'

'Indeed! Very good. Then the thing is settled. The testimonials you showed me when you first tried for't are sufficient.'

That characters deteriorate in time of need possibly did not occur to Henchard. Jopp said, 'Thank you,' and stood more firmly, in the consciousness that at last he officially belonged to that spot.

'Now,' said Henchard, digging his strong eyes into Jopp's face, 'one thing is necessary to me, as the biggest corn-and-hay-dealer in these parts. The Scotchman, who's taking the town trade so bold into his hands, must be cut out. D'ye hear? We two can't live side by side—that's clear and certain.'

'I've seen it all,' said Jopp.

5. Last resort (from the French). A mixen is literally a place to lay dung.

'By fair competition I mean, of course,' Henchard continued. 'But as hard, keen, and unflinching as fair—rather more so. By such a desperate bid against him for the farmers' custom as will grind him into the ground—starve him out. I've capital, mind ye, and I can do it.'

'I'm all that way of thinking,' said the new foreman. Jopp's dislike of Farfrae as the man who had once usurped his place, while it made him a willing tool, made him, at the same time, commercially as unsafe a colleague as Henchard could have chosen.

'I sometimes think,' he added, 'that he must have some glass that he sees next year in. He has such a knack of making everything bring him fortune.'

'He's deep beyond all honest men's discerning; but we must make him shallower. We'll under-sell him, and over-buy him, and so snuff him out.'

They then entered into specific details of the process by which this would be accomplished, and parted at a late hour.

Elizabeth-Jane heard by accident that Jopp had been engaged by her stepfather. She was so fully convinced that he was not the right man for the place that, at the risk of making Henchard angry, she expressed her apprehension to him when they met. But it was done to no purpose. Henchard shut up her argument with a sharp rebuff.

The season's weather seemed to favour their scheme. The time was in the years immediately before foreign competition had revolutionized the trade in grain; when still, as from the earliest ages, the wheat quotations from month to month depended entirely upon the home harvest. A bad harvest, or the prospect of one, would double the price of corn in a few weeks; and the promise of a good yield would lower it as rapidly. Prices were like the roads of the period, steep in gradient, reflecting in their phases the local conditions, without engineering, levellings, or averages.

The farmer's income was ruled by the wheat-crop within his own horizon, and the wheat-crop by the weather. Thus, in person, he became a sort of flesh-barometer, with feelers always directed to the sky and wind around him. The local atmosphere was everything to him; the atmospheres of other countries a matter of indifference. The people, too, who were not farmers, the rural multitude, saw in the god of the weather a more important personage than they do now. Indeed, the feeling of the peasantry in this matter was so intense as to be almost unrealizable in these equable days. Their impulse was well-nigh to prostrate themselves in lamentation before untimely rains and tempests, which came as the Alastor[6] of those households whose crime it was to be poor.

After midsummer they watched the weather-cocks as men waiting in antechambers watch the lackey. Sun elated them; quiet rain sobered

6. Avenging spirit.

them; weeks of watery tempest stupefied them. That aspect of the sky which they now regard as disagreeable they then beheld as maleficent.

It was June, and the weather was very unfavourable. Casterbridge, being as it were the bell-board on which all the adjacent hamlets and villages sounded their notes, was decidedly dull. Instead of new articles in the shop-windows those that had been rejected in the foregoing summer were brought out again; superseded reap-hooks, badly-shaped rakes, shop-worn leggings, and time-stiffened water-tights[7] reappeared, furbished up as near to new as possible.

Henchard, backed by Jopp, read a disastrous garnering, and resolved to base his strategy against Farfrae upon that reading. But before acting he wished—what so many have wished—that he could know for certain what was at present only strong probability. He was superstitious—as such headstrong natures often are—and he nourished in his mind an idea bearing on the matter; an idea he shrank from disclosing even to Jopp.

In a lonely hamlet a few miles from the town—so lonely that what are called lonely villages were teeming by comparison—there lived a man of curious repute as a forecaster or weather-prophet. The way to his house was crooked and miry—even difficult in the present unpropitious season. One evening when it was raining so heavily that ivy and laurel resounded like distant musketry, and an out-door man could be excused for shrouding himself to his ears and eyes, such a shrouded figure on foot might have been perceived travelling in the direction of the hazel-copse which dripped over the prophet's cot. The turnpike-road became a lane, the lane a cart-track, the cart-track a bridle-path, the bridle-path a foot-way, the foot-way overgrown. The solitary walker slipped here and there, and stumbled over the natural springes[8] formed by the brambles, till at length he reached the house, which, with its garden, was surrounded with a high, dense hedge. The cottage, comparatively a large one, had been built of mud by the occupier's own hands, and thatched also by himself. Here he had always lived, and here it was assumed he would die.

He existed on unseen supplies; for it was an anomalous thing that while there was hardly a soul in the neighbourhood but affected to laugh at this man's assertions, uttering the formula, 'There's nothing in 'em,' with full assurance on the surface of their faces, very few of them were unbelievers in their secret hearts. Whenever they consulted him they did it 'for a fancy.' When they paid him they said, 'Just a trifle for Christmas,' or 'Candlemas,' as the case might be.

He would have preferred more honesty in his clients, and less sham ridicule; but fundamental belief consoled him for superficial irony. As

---

7. Waterproof boots.
8. Traps for birds or small animals.

stated, he was enabled to live; people supported him with their backs turned. He was sometimes astonished that men could profess so little and believe so much at his house, when at church they professed so much and believed so little.

Behind his back he was called 'Wide-oh,' on account of his reputation; to his face 'Mr.' Fall.

The hedge of his garden formed an arch over the entrance, and a door was inserted as in a wall. Outside the door the tall traveller stopped, bandaged his face with a handkerchief as if he were suffering from toothache, and went up the path. The window shutters were not closed, and he could see the prophet within, preparing his supper.

In answer to the knock Fall came to the door, candle in hand. The visitor stepped back a little from the light, and said, 'Can I speak to 'ee?' in significant tones. The other's invitation to come in was responded to by the country formula, 'This will do, thank 'ee,' after which the householder has no alternative but to come out. He placed the candle on the corner of the dresser, took his hat from a nail, and joined the stranger in the porch, shutting the door behind him.

'I've long heard that you can—do things of a sort?' began the other, repressing his individuality as much as he could.

'Maybe so, Mr. Henchard,' said the weather-caster.

'Ah—why do you call me that?' asked the visitor with a start.

'Because it's your name. Feeling you'd come I've waited for 'ee; and thinking you might be leery from your walk I laid two supper plates— look ye here.' He threw open the door and disclosed the supper-table, at which appeared a second chair, knife and fork, plate and mug, as he had declared.

Henchard felt like Saul at his reception by Samuel;[9] he remained in silence for a few moments, then throwing off the disguise of frigidity which he had hitherto preserved he said, 'Then I have not come in vain. . . . Now, for instance, can ye charm away warts?'

'Without trouble.'

'Cure the evil?'[1]

'That I've done—with consideration—if they will wear the toad-bag[2] by night as well as by day.'

'Forecast the weather?'

'With labour and time.'

'Then take this,' said Henchard. ''Tis a crown-piece. Now, what is the harvest fortnight to be? When can I know?'

'I've worked it out already, and you can know at once.' (The fact was

9. 1 Samuel 9.15–24 tells how the holy man Samuel surprises Saul by making him his chief guest at a dinner. In 1 Samuel 28 Saul asks the Witch of Endor to conjure up the spirit of Samuel, who correctly foretells Saul's coming death. Hardy here draws on both episodes.
1. Scrofula, a disease affecting the lymph glands.
2. Bag containing live toads, or toads' legs, whose twitchings were thought to cause a change in the wearer's constitution.

that five farmers had already been there on the same errand from different parts of the country.) 'By the sun, moon, and stars, by the clouds, the winds, the trees, and grass, the candle-flame and swallows, the smell of the herbs; likewise by the cats' eyes, the ravens, the leeches, the spiders, and the dungmixen, the last fortnight in August will be — rain and tempest.'

'You are not certain, of course?'

'As one can be in a world where all's unsure. 'Twill be more like living in Revelations[3] this autumn than in England. Shall I sketch it out for 'ee in a scheme?'

'O no, no,' said Henchard. 'I don't altogether believe in forecasts, come to second thoughts on such. But I ——.'

'You don't — you don't — 'tis quite understood,' said Wide-oh, without a sound of scorn. 'You have given me a crown because you've one too many. But won't you join me at supper, now 'tis waiting and all?'

Henchard would gladly have joined; for the savour of the stew had floated from the cottage into the porch with such appetizing distinctness that the meat, the onions, the pepper, and the herbs could be severally recognized by his nose. But as sitting down to hob-and-nob[4] there would have seemed to mark him too implicitly as the weather-caster's apostle, he declined, and went his way.

The next Saturday Henchard bought grain to such an enormous extent that there was quite a talk about his purchases among his neighbours the lawyer, the wine merchant, and the doctor; also on the next, and on all available days. When his granaries were full to choking, all the weather-cocks of Casterbridge creaked and set their faces in another direction, as if tired of the south-west. The weather changed; the sunlight, which had been like tin for weeks, assumed the hues of topaz. The temperament of the welkin[5] passed from the phlegmatic to the sanguine; an excellent harvest was almost a certainty; and as a consequence prices rushed down.

All these transformations, lovely to the outsider, to the wrong-headed corn-dealer were terrible. He was reminded of what he had well known before, that a man might gamble upon the square green areas of fields as readily as upon those of a card-room.

Henchard had backed bad weather, and apparently lost. He had mistaken the turn of the flood for the turn of the ebb. His dealings had been so extensive that settlement could not long be postponed, and to settle he was obliged to sell off corn that he had bought only a few weeks before at figures higher by many shillings a quarter. Much of the corn he had never seen; it had not even been moved from the ricks in which it lay stacked miles away. Thus he lost heavily.

3. The Revelation of St. John, the last book in the New Testament, foresees the end of the world.
4. Meet on friendly terms (dialect).
5. Sky (archaic or poetic).

In the blaze of an early August day he met Farfrae in the market-place. Farfrae knew of his dealings (though he did not guess their intended bearing on himself) and commiserated him; for since their exchange of words in the South Walk they had been on stiffly speaking terms. Henchard for the moment appeared to resent the sympathy; but he suddenly took a careless turn.

'Ho, no, no!—nothing serious, man!' he cried with fierce gaiety. 'These things always happen, don't they? I know it has been said that figures have touched me tight lately; but is that anything rare? The case is not so bad as folk make out perhaps. And dammy, a man must be a fool to mind the common hazards of trade!'

But he had to enter the Casterbridge Bank that day for reasons which had never before sent him there—and to sit a long time in the partners' room with a constrained bearing. It was rumoured soon after that much real property[6] as well as vast stores of produce, which had stood in Henchard's name in the town and neighbourhood, was actually the possession of his bankers.

Coming down the steps of the bank he encountered Jopp. The gloomy transactions just completed within had added fever to the original sting of Farfrae's sympathy that morning, which Henchard fancied might be satire disguised, so that Jopp met with anything but a bland reception. The latter was in the act of taking off his hat to wipe his forehead, and saying, 'A fine hot day,' to an acquaintance.

'You can wipe and wipe, and say, "A fine hot day," can ye!' cried Henchard in a savage undertone, imprisoning Jopp between himself and the bank wall. 'If it hadn't been for your blasted advice it might have been a fine day enough! Why did ye let me go on, hey?—when a word of doubt from you or anybody would have made me think twice! For you can never be sure of weather till 'tis past.'

'My advice, sir, was to do what you thought best.'

'A useful fellow! And the sooner you help somebody else in that way the better!' Henchard continued his address to Jopp in similar terms till it ended in Jopp's dismissal there and then, Henchard turning upon his heel and leaving him.

'You shall be sorry for this, sir; sorry as a man can be!' said Jopp, standing pale, and looking after the corn-merchant as he disappeared in the crowd of market-men hard by.

XXVII

It was the eve of harvest. Prices being low Farfrae was buying. As was usual, after reckoning too surely on famine weather the local farmers had flown to the other extreme, and (in Farfrae's opinion) were selling

---

6. Property in the form of freehold land.

off too recklessly—calculating with just a trifle too much certainty upon an abundant yield. So he went on buying old corn at its comparatively ridiculous price: for the produce of the previous year, though not large, had been of excellent quality.

When Henchard had squared his affairs in a disastrous way, and got rid of his burdensome purchases at a monstrous loss, the harvest began. There were three days of excellent weather, and then—'What if that curst conjuror should be right after all!' said Henchard.

The fact was, that no sooner had the sickles begun to play than the atmosphere suddenly felt as if cress would grow in it without other nourishment. It rubbed people's cheeks like damp flannel when they walked abroad. There was a gusty, high, warm wind; isolated raindrops starred the window-panes at remote distances: the sunlight would flap out like a quickly opened fan, throw the pattern of the window upon the floor of the room in a milky, colourless shine, and withdraw as suddenly as it had appeared.

From that day and hour it was clear that there was not to be so successful an ingathering after all. If Henchard had only waited long enough he might at least have avoided loss though he had not made a profit. But the momentum of his character knew no patience. At this turn of the scales he remained silent. The movements of his mind seemed to tend to the thought that some power was working against him.

'I wonder,' he asked himself with eerie misgiving; 'I wonder if it can be that somebody has been roasting a waxen image[1] of me, or stirring an unholy brew to confound me! I don't believe in such power; and yet—what if they should ha' been doing it!' Even he could not admit that the perpetrator, if any, might be Farfrae. These isolated hours of superstition came to Henchard in time of moody depression, when all his practical largeness of view had oozed out of him.

Meanwhile Donald Farfrae prospered. He had purchased in so depressed a market that the present moderate stiffness of prices was sufficient to pile for him a large heap of gold where a little one had been.

'Why, he'll soon be Mayor!' said Henchard. It was indeed hard that the speaker should, of all others, have to follow the triumphal chariot of this man to the Capitol.[2]

The rivalry of the masters was taken up by the men.

September-night shades had fallen upon Casterbridge; the clocks had struck half-past eight, and the moon had risen. The streets of the town were curiously silent for such a comparatively early hour. A sound of jangling horse-bells and heavy wheels passed up the street. These were followed by angry voices outside Lucetta's house, which led her and Elizabeth-Jane to run to the windows, and pull up the blinds.

1. According to popular belief, a means of harming one's enemy.
2. The temple of Jupiter in Rome, where successful generals marched in procession to give thanks, followed by their defeated enemies.

The neighbouring Market House and Town Hall abutted against its next neighbour the Church except in the lower storey, where an arched thoroughfare gave admittance to a large square called Bull Stake. A stone post rose in the midst, to which the oxen had formerly been tied for baiting with dogs to make them tender before they were killed in the adjoining shambles. In a corner stood the stocks.

The thoroughfare leading to this spot was now blocked by two four-horse waggons and horses, one laden with hay-trusses, the leaders having already passed each other, and become entangled head to tail. The passage of the vehicles might have been practicable if empty; but built up with hay to the bedroom windows as one was, it was impossible.

'You must have done it a' purpose!' said Farfrae's waggoner. 'You can hear my horses' bells half-a-mile such a night as this!'

'If ye'd been minding your business instead of zwailing[3] along in such a gawk-hammer[4] way, you would have zeed me!' retorted the wroth representative of Henchard.

However, according to the strict rule of the road it appeared that Henchard's man was most in the wrong; he therefore attempted to back into the High Street. In doing this the near hind-wheel rose against the churchyard wall, and the whole mountainous load went over, two of the four wheels rising in the air, and the legs of the thill horse.[5]

Instead of considering how to gather up the load the two men closed in a fight with their fists. Before the first round was quite over Henchard came upon the spot, somebody having run for him.

Henchard sent the two men staggering in contrary directions by collaring one with each hand, turned to the horse that was down, and extricated him after some trouble. He then inquired into the circumstances; and seeing the state of his waggon and its load began hotly rating Farfrae's man.

Lucetta and Elizabeth-Jane had by this time run down to the street corner, whence they watched the bright heap of new hay lying in the moon's rays, and passed and re-passed by the forms of Henchard and the waggoners. The women had witnessed what nobody else had seen — the origin of the mishap; and Lucetta spoke.

'I saw it all, Mr. Henchard,' she cried; 'and your man was most in the wrong!'

Henchard paused in his harangue and turned. 'Oh, I didn't notice you, Miss Templeman,' said he. 'My man in the wrong? Ah, to be sure; to be sure! But I beg your pardon notwithstanding. The other's is the empty waggon, and he must have been most to blame for coming on.'

'No; I saw it, too,' said Elizabeth-Jane. 'And I can assure you he couldn't help it.'

3. Swaying (dialect).
4. Idiotic (dialect).
5. Horse placed between the shafts of a wagon.

'You can't trust *their* senses!' murmured Henchard's man.

'Why not?' asked Henchard sharply.

'Why, you see, sir, all the women side with Farfrae—being a damn young dand—of the sort that he is—one that creeps into a maid's heart like the giddying worm[6] into a sheep's brain—making crooked seem straight to their eyes!'

'But do you know who that lady is you talk about in such a fashion? Do you know that I pay my attentions to her, and have for some time? Just be careful!'

'Not I. I know nothing, sir, outside eight shillings a week.'

'And that Mr. Farfrae is well aware of it? He's sharp in trade, but he wouldn't do anything so underhand as what you hint at.'

Whether because Lucetta heard this low dialogue, or not, her white figure disappeared from her doorway inward, and the door was shut before Henchard could reach it to converse with her further. This disappointed him, for he had been sufficiently disturbed by what the man had said to wish to speak to her more closely. While pausing the old constable came up.

'Just see that nobody drives against that hay and waggon to-night, Stubberd,' said the corn-merchant. 'It must bide[7] till the morning, for all hands are in the fields still. And if any coach or road-waggon wants to come along, tell 'em they must go round by the back street, and be hanged to 'em. . . . Any case tomorrow up in Hall?'

'Yes, sir. One in number, sir.'

'Oh, what's that?'

'An old flagrant[8] female, sir, swearing and committing a nuisance in a horrible profane manner against the church wall, sir, as if 'twere no more than a pot-house![9] That's all, sir.'

'Oh. The Mayor's out o' town, isn't he?'

'He is, sir.'

'Very well, then I'll be there. Don't forget to keep an eye on that hay. Good night t' 'ee.'

During those moments Henchard had determined to follow up Lucetta notwithstanding her elusiveness, and he knocked for admission.

The answer he received was an expression of Miss Templeman's sorrow at being unable to see him again that evening because she had an engagement to go out.

Henchard walked away from the door to the opposite side of the street, and stood by his hay in a lonely reverie, the constable having strolled elsewhere, and the horses being removed. Though the moon

---

6. Referring to a sheep disease known as "gid," in which tapeworms in the animal's brain cause it to grow giddy and then die.
7. Wait.
8. Stubberd's mistaken attempt at the word vagrant.
9. Ale-house, tavern.

was not bright as yet there were no lamps lighted, and he entered the shadow of one of the projecting jambs which formed the thoroughfare to Bull Stake; here he watched Lucetta's door.

Candle-lights were flitting in and out of her bedroom, and it was obvious that she was dressing for the appointment, whatever the nature of that might be at such an hour. The lights disappeared, the clock struck nine, and almost at the moment Farfrae came round the opposite corner and knocked. That she had been waiting just inside for him was certain, for she instantly opened the door herself. They went together by the way of a back lane westward, avoiding the front street; guessing where they were going he determined to follow.

The harvest had been so delayed by the capricious weather that whenever a fine day occurred all sinews were strained to save what could be saved of the damaged crops. On account of the rapid shortening of the days the harvesters worked by moonlight. Hence to-night the wheatfields abutting on the two sides of the square formed by Casterbridge town were animated by the gathering hands. Their shouts and laughter had reached Henchard at the Market House, while he stood there waiting, and he had little doubt from the turn which Farfrae and Lucetta had taken that they were bound for the spot.

Nearly the whole town had gone into the fields. The Casterbridge populace still retained the primitive habit of helping one another in time of need; and thus, though the corn belonged to the farming section of the little community—that inhabiting the Durnover quarter—the remainder was no less interested in the labour of getting it home.

Reaching the top of the lane Henchard crossed the shaded avenue on the walls, slid down the green rampart, and stood amongst the stubble. The 'stitches'[1] or shocks rose like tents about the yellow expanse, those in the distance becoming lost in the moonlit hazes.

He had entered at a point removed from the scene of immediate operations; but two others had entered at that place, and he could see them winding among the shocks. They were paying no regard to the direction of their walk, whose vague serpentining soon began to bear down towards Henchard. A meeting promised to be awkward, and he therefore stepped into the hollow of the nearest shock, and sat down.

'You have my leave,' Lucetta was saying gaily. 'Speak what you like.'

'Well, then,' replied Farfrae, with the unmistakable inflection of the lover pure, which Henchard had never heard in full resonance on his lips before, 'you are sure to be much sought after for your position, wealth, talents, and beauty. But will ye resist the temptation to be one of those ladies with lots of admirers—ay—and be content to have only a homely one?'

'And he the speaker?' said she, laughing. 'Very well, sir, what next?'

---

1. Dialect term for shocks; that is, sheaves of cut grain stacked in the fields to dry.

'Ah! I'm afraid that what I feel will make me forget my manners!'

'Then I hope you'll never have any, if you lack them only for that cause.' After some broken words which Henchard lost she added, 'Are you sure you won't be jealous?'

Farfrae seemed to assure her that he would not, by taking her hand.

'You are convinced, Donald, that I love nobody else,' she presently said. 'But I should wish to have my own way in some things.'

'In everything! What special thing did you mean?'

'If I wished not to live always in Casterbridge, for instance, upon finding that I should not be happy here?'

Henchard did not hear the reply; he might have done so and much more, but he did not care to play the eavesdropper. They went on towards the scene of activity, where the sheaves were being handed, a dozen a minute, upon the carts and waggons which carried them away.

Lucetta insisted on parting from Farfrae when they drew near the workpeople. He had some business with them and, though he entreated her to wait a few minutes, she was inexorable, and tripped off homeward alone.

Henchard thereupon left the field and followed her. His state of mind was such that on reaching Lucetta's door he did not knock but opened it, and walked straight up to her sitting-room, expecting to find her there. But the room was empty, and he perceived that in his haste he had somehow passed her on the way hither. He had not to wait many minutes, however, for he soon heard her dress rustling in the hall, followed by a soft closing of the door. In a moment she appeared.

The light was so low that she did not notice Henchard at first. As soon as she saw him she uttered a little cry, almost of terror.

'How can you frighten me so?' she exclaimed, with a flushed face. 'It is past ten o'clock, and you have no right to surprise me here at such a time.'

'I don't know that I've not the right. At any rate I have the excuse. Is it so necessary that I should stop to think of manners and customs?'

'It is too late for propriety, and might injure me.'

'I called an hour ago, and you would not see me, and I thought you were in when I called now. It is you, Lucetta, who are doing wrong. It is not proper in 'ee to throw me over like this. I have a little matter to remind you of, which you seem to forget.'

She sank into a chair, and turned pale.

'I don't want to hear it—I don't want to hear it!' she said through her hands, as he, standing close to the edge of her gown, began to allude to the Jersey days.

'But you ought to hear it,' said he.

'It came to nothing; and through you. Then why not leave me the freedom that I gained with such sorrow! Had I found that you proposed to marry me for pure love I might have felt bound now. But I soon learnt that you had planned it out of mere charity—almost as an unpleasant duty—because I had nursed you, and compromised myself, and you thought you must repay me. After that I did not care for you so deeply as before.'

'Why did you come here to find me, then?'

'I thought I ought to marry you for conscience' sake, since you were free, even though I—did not like you so well.'

'And why then don't you think so now?'

She was silent. It was only too obvious that conscience had ruled well enough till new love had intervened and usurped that rule. In feeling this she herself forgot for the moment her partially justifying argument—that having discovered Henchard's infirmities of temper, she had some excuse for not risking her happiness in his hands after once escaping them. The only thing she could say was, 'I was a poor girl then; and now my circumstances have altered, so I am hardly the same person.'

'That's true. And it makes the case awkward for me. But I don't want to touch your money. I am quite willing that every penny of your property shall remain to your personal use.[2] Besides, that argument has nothing in it. The man you are thinking of is no better than I.'

'If you were as good as he you would leave me!' she cried passionately.

This unluckily aroused Henchard. 'You cannot in honour refuse me,' he said. 'And unless you give me your promise this very night to be my wife, before a witness, I'll reveal our intimacy—in common fairness to other men!'

A look of resignation settled upon her. Henchard saw its bitterness; and had Lucetta's heart been given to any other man in the world than Farfrae he would probably have had pity upon her at that moment. But the supplanter was the upstart (as Henchard called him) who had mounted into prominence upon his shoulders, and he could bring himself to show no mercy.

Without another word she rang the bell, and directed that Elizabeth-Jane should be fetched from her room. The latter appeared, surprised in the midst of her lucubrations.[3] As soon as she saw Henchard she went across to him dutifully.

'Elizabeth-Jane,' he said, taking her hand, 'I want you to hear this.' And turning to Lucetta: 'Will you, or will you not, marry me?'

'If you—wish it, I must agree!'

'You say yes?'

'I do.'

No sooner had she given the promise than she fell back in a fainting state.

---

2. Prior to legislation of 1870 and 1882, the property of a married woman passed into the ownership or control of her husband, except when it had been protected by a marriage settlement. This seems to be what Henchard is proposing.

3. Studies.

'What dreadful thing drives her to say this, father, when it is such a pain to her?' asked Elizabeth, kneeling down by Lucetta. 'Don't compel her to do anything against her will! I have lived with her, and know that she cannot bear much.'

'Don't be a no'thern[4] simpleton!' said Henchard. drily. 'This promise will leave him free for you, if you want him, won't it?'

At this Lucetta seemed to wake from her swoon with a start.

'Him? Who are you talking about?' she said wildly.

'Nobody, as far as I am concerned,' said Elizabeth firmly.

'Oh—well. Then it is my mistake,' said Henchard. 'But the business is between me and Miss Templeman. She agrees to be my wife.'

'But don't dwell on it just now,' entreated Elizabeth, holding Lucetta's hand.

'I don't wish to, if she promises,' said Henchard.

'I have, I have,' groaned Lucetta, her limbs hanging like flails, from very misery and faintness. 'Michael, please don't argue it any more!'

'I will not,' he said. And taking up his hat he went away.

Elizabeth-Jane continued to kneel by Lucetta. 'What is this?' she said. 'You called my father "Michael" as if you knew him well? And how is it he has got this power over you, that you promise to marry him against your will? Ah—you have many many secrets from me!'

'Perhaps you have some from me,' Lucetta murmured with closed eyes, little thinking, however, so unsuspicious was she, that the secret of Elizabeth's heart concerned the young man who had caused this damage to her own.

'I would not—do anything against you at all!' stammered Elizabeth, keeping in all signs of emotion till she was ready to burst. 'I cannot understand how my father can command you so; I don't sympathize with him in it at all. I'll go to him and ask him to release you.'

'No, no,' said Lucetta. 'Let it all be.'

XXVIII

The next morning Henchard went to the Town Hall below Lucetta's house, to attend Petty Sessions,[1] being still a magistrate for the year by virtue of his late position as Mayor. In passing he looked up at her windows, but nothing of her was to be seen.

Henchard as a Justice of the Peace may at first seem to be an even greater incongruity than Shallow and Silence[2] themselves. But his rough and ready perceptions, his sledge-hammer directness, had often served him better than nice legal knowledge in despatching such simple business as fell to his hands in this Court. To-day Dr. Chalkfield, the

4. Northern. Proverbially, fools and cold weather come from the north.
1. Local courts dealing with minor offences.
2. Foolish country judges in Shakespeare's *Henry IV, Part II.*

Mayor for the year, being absent, the corn-merchant took the big chair, his eyes still abstractedly stretching out of the window to the ashlar[3] front of High-Place Hall.

There was one case only, and the offender stood before him. She was an old woman of mottled countenance, attired in a shawl of that name-less tertiary hue which comes, but cannot be made—a hue neither tawny, russet, hazel, nor ash; a sticky black bonnet that seemed to have been worn in the country of the Psalmist[4] where the clouds drop fatness; and an apron that had been white in times so comparatively recent as still to contrast visibly with the rest of her clothes. The steeped[5] aspect of the woman as a whole showed her to be no native of the country-side or even of a country-town.

She looked cursorily at Henchard and the second magistrate, and Henchard looked at her, with a momentary pause, as if she had remind-ed him indistinctly of somebody or something which passed from his mind as quickly as it had come. 'Well, and what has she been doing?' he said, looking down at the charge-sheet.

'She is charged, sir, with the offence of disorderly female and nui-sance,' whispered Stubberd.

'Where did she do that?' said the other magistrate.

'By the church, sir, of all the horrible places in the world!—I caught her in the act, your worship.'

'Stand back then,' said Henchard, 'and let's hear what you've got to say.'

Stubberd was sworn, the magistrate's clerk dipped his pen, Henchard being no note-taker himself, and the constable began—

'Hearing a' illegal noise I went down the street at twenty-five minutes past eleven P.M. on the night of the fifth instinct, Hannah Dominy.[6] When I had——'

'Don't go on so fast, Stubberd,' said the clerk.

The constable waited, with his eyes on the clerk's pen, till the latter stopped scratching and said, 'yes.' Stubberd continued: 'When I had pro-ceeded to the spot I saw defendant at another spot, namely, the gutter.' He paused, watching the point of the clerk's pen again.

'Gutter, yes, Stubberd.'

'Spot measuring twelve feet nine inches or thereabouts, from where I——' Still careful not to outrun the clerk's penmanship Stubberd pulled up again; for having got his evidence by heart it was immaterial to him whereabouts he broke off.

---

3. Faced with thin slabs of hewn stone.
4. Alluding to Psalm 65.11, "Thou crownest the year with thy goodness, and thy paths drop fat-ness." Her bonnet is greasy.
5. Stained.
6. Malapropisms for "instant," meaning "this month," and "Anno Domini," meaning "in the year of the Lord" (i.e., after the birth of Jesus).

'I object to that,' spoke up the old woman, "'spot measuring twelve feet nine or thereabouts from where I," is not sound testimony!'

The magistrates consulted, and the second one said that the bench was of opinion that twelve feet nine inches from a man on his oath was admissible.

Stubberd, with a suppressed gaze of victorious rectitude at the old woman, continued: 'Was standing myself. She was wambling[7] about quite dangerous to the thoroughfare, and when I approached to draw near she committed the nuisance, and insulted me.'

"'Insulted me." . . . Yes, what did she say?'

'She said, "Put away that dee[8] lantern," she says.'

'Yes.'

'Says she, "Dost hear, old turmit-head?[9] Put away that dee lantern. I have floored fellows a dee sight finer-looking than a dee fool like thee, you son of a bee,[1] dee me if I haint," she says.'

'I object to that conversation!' interposed the old woman. 'I was not capable enough to hear what I said, and what is said out of my hearing is not evidence.'

There was another stoppage for consultation, a book was referred to, and finally Stubberd was allowed to go on again. The truth was that the old woman had appeared in court so many more times than the magistrates themselves, that they were obliged to keep a sharp look-out upon their procedure. However, when Stubberd had rambled on a little further Henchard broke out impatiently, 'Come—we don't want to hear any more of them cust dees and bees! Say the words out like a man, and don't be so modest, Stubberd; or else leave it alone!' Turning to the woman, 'Now then, have you any questions to ask him, or anything to say?'

'Yes,' she replied with a twinkle in her eye; and the clerk dipped his pen.

'Twenty years ago or thereabout I was selling of furmity in a tent at Weydon Fair——'

"'Twenty years ago"—well, that's beginning at the beginning; suppose you go back to the Creation!' said the clerk, not without satire.

But Henchard stared, and quite forgot what was evidence and what was not.

'A man and a woman with a little child came into my tent,' the woman continued. 'They sat down and had a basin apiece. Ah, Lord's my life! I was of a more respectable station in the world then than I am now, being a land smuggler[2] in a large way of business; and I used to sea-

---

7. Walking unsteadily.
8. Euphemism for "damn."
9. Turnip-head, fool.
1. Euphemism for "bitch."
2. Distributor of smuggled rum.

son my furmity with rum for them who asked for't. I did it for the man; and then he had more and more; till at last he quarrelled with his wife, and offered to sell her to the highest bidder. A sailor came in and bid five guineas, and paid the money, and led her away. And the man who sold his wife in that fashion is the man sitting there in the great big chair.' The speaker concluded by nodding her head at Henchard and folding her arms.

Everybody looked at Henchard. His face seemed strange, and in tint as if it had been powdered over with ashes. 'We don't want to hear you life and adventures,' said the second magistrate sharply, filling the pause which followed. 'You've been asked if you've anything to say bearing on the case.'

'That bears on the case. It proves that he's no better than I, and has no right to sit there in judgment upon me.'

''Tis a concocted story,' said the clerk. 'So hold your tongue!'

'No—'tis true.' The words came from Henchard. ''Tis as true as the light,' he said slowly. 'And upon my soul it does prove that I'm no better than she! And to keep out of any temptation to treat her hard for her revenge, I'll leave her to you.'

The sensation in the court was indescribably great. Henchard left the chair, and came out, passing through a group of people on the steps and outside that was much larger than usual; for it seemed that the old furmity dealer had mysteriously hinted to the denizens of the lane in which she had been lodging since her arrival, that she knew a queer thing or two about their great local man Mr. Henchard, if she chose to tell it. This had brought them hither.

'Why are there so many idlers round the Town Hall to-day?' said Lucetta to her servant when the case was over. She had risen late, and had just looked out of the window.

'Oh, please, ma'am, 'tis this larry[3] about Mr. Henchard. A woman has proved that before he became a gentleman he sold his wife for five guineas in a booth at a fair.'

In all the accounts which Henchard had given her of the separation from his wife Susan for so many years, of his belief in her death, and so on, he had never clearly explained the actual and immediate cause of that separation. The story she now heard for the first time.

A gradual misery overspread Lucetta's face as she dwelt upon the promise wrung from her the night before. At bottom, then, Henchard was this. How terrible a contingency for a woman who should commit herself to his care.

During the day she went out to the Ring and to other places, not coming in till nearly dusk. As soon as she saw Elizabeth-Jane after her return

3. Commotion.

indoors she told her that she had resolved to go away from home to the seaside for a few days—to Port-Bredy; Casterbridge was so gloomy.

Elizabeth, seeing that she looked wan and disturbed, encouraged her in the idea, thinking a change would afford her relief. She could not help suspecting that the gloom which seemed to have come over Casterbridge in Lucetta's eyes might be partially owing to the fact that Farfrae was away from home.

Elizabeth saw her friend depart for Port-Bredy, and took charge of High-Place Hall till her return. After two or three days of solitude and incessant rain Henchard called at the house. He seemed disappointed to hear of Lucetta's absence, and though he nodded with outward indifference he went away handling his beard with a nettled mien.

The next day he called again. 'Is she come now?' he asked.

'Yes. She returned this morning,' replied his step-daughter. 'But she is not indoors. She has gone for a walk along the turnpike-road to Port-Bredy. She will be home by dusk.'

After a few words, which only served to reveal his restless impatience, he left the house again.

XXIX

At this hour Lucetta was bounding along the road to Port-Bredy just as Elizabeth had announced. That she had chosen for her afternoon walk the road along which she had returned to Casterbridge three hours earlier in a carriage was curious—if anything should be called curious in concatenations of phenomena wherein each is known to have its accounting cause. It was the day of the chief market—Saturday—and Farfrae for once had been missed from his corn-stand in the dealers' room. Nevertheless, it was known that he would be home that night— 'for Sunday,' as Casterbridge expressed it.

Lucetta, in continuing her walk, had at length reached the end of the ranked trees which bordered the highway in this and other directions out of the town. This end marked a mile; and here she stopped.

The spot was a vale between two gentle acclivities, and the road, still adhering to its Roman foundation, stretched onward straight as a surveyor's line till lost to sight on the most distant ridge. There was neither hedge nor tree in the prospect now, the road clinging to the stubbly expanse of corn-land like a stripe to an undulating garment. Near her was a barn—the single building of any kind within her horizon.

She strained her eyes up the lessening road, but nothing appeared thereon—not so much as a speck. She sighed one word—'Donald!' and turned her face to the town for retreat.

Here the case was different. A single figure was approaching her— Elizabeth-Jane's.

Lucetta, in spite of her loneliness, seemed a little vexed. Elizabeth's face, as soon as she recognized her friend, shaped itself into affectionate lines while yet beyond speaking distance. 'I suddenly thought I would come and meet you,' she said, smiling.

Lucetta's reply was taken from her lips by an unexpected diversion. A by-road on her right hand descended from the fields into the highway at the point where she stood, and down the track a bull was rambling uncertainly towards her and Elizabeth, who, facing the other way, did not observe him.

In the latter quarter of each year cattle were at once the mainstay and the terror of families about Casterbridge and its neighbourhood, where breeding was carried on with Abrahamic success.[1] The head of stock driven into and out of the town at this season to be sold by the local auctioneer was very large; and all these horned beasts, in travelling to and fro, sent women and children to shelter as nothing else could do. In the main the animals would have walked along quietly enough; but the Casterbridge tradition was that to drive stock it was indispensable that hideous cries, coupled with Yahoo[2] antics and gestures, should be used, large sticks flourished, stray dogs called in, and in general everything done that was likely to infuriate the viciously disposed and terrify the mild. Nothing was commoner than for a householder on going out of his parlour to find his hall or passage full of little children, nursemaids, aged women, or a ladies' school, who apologized for their presence by saying, 'A bull passing down street from the sale.'

Lucetta and Elizabeth regarded the animal in doubt, he meanwhile drawing vaguely towards them. It was a large specimen of the breed, in colour rich dun, though disfigured at present by splotches of mud about his seamy[3] sides. His horns were thick and tipped with brass; his two nostrils like the Thames Tunnel as seen in the perspective toys[4] of yore. Between them, through the gristle of his nose, was a stout copper ring, welded on, and irremovable as Gurth's collar of brass.[5] To the ring was attached an ash staff about a yard long, which the bull with the motions of his head flung about like a flail.

It was not till they observed this dangling stick that the young women were really alarmed; for it revealed to them that the bull was an old one, too savage to be driven, which had in some way escaped, the staff being the means by which the drover controlled him and kept his horns at arms' length.

1. Great success. God promised the patriarch Abraham that he would have many descendants. See Genesis 17.2–6.
2. Uncouth. In Book IV of *Gulliver's Travels* (1726), Jonathan Swift represents human beings at their most hideous and depraved by the name of Yahoos.
3. Wrinkled.
4. Toys in which a three-dimensional view of scenes or buildings, such as the Thames Tunnel (opened in 1843), could be seen by looking through a peep-hole into a box.
5. Gurth, a swineherd in Sir Walter Scott's novel *Ivanhoe* (1820), and serf to Cedric, wears a collar bearing the name of his owner.

They looked round for some shelter or hiding-place, and thought of the barn hard by. As long as they had kept their eyes on the bull he had shown some deference in his manner of approach; but no sooner did they turn their backs to seek the barn than he tossed his head and decided to thoroughly terrify them. This caused the two helpless girls to run wildly, whereupon the bull advanced in a deliberate charge.

The barn stood behind a green slimy pond, and it was closed save as to one of the usual pair of doors facing them, which had been propped open by a hurdle-stake,[6] and for this opening they made. The interior had been cleared by a recent bout of threshing except at one end, where there was a stack of dry clover. Elizabeth-Jane took in the situation. 'We must climb up there,' she said.

But before they had even approached it they heard the bull scampering through the pond without, and in a second he dashed into the barn, knocking down the hurdle-stake in passing; the heavy door slammed behind him; and all three were imprisoned in the barn together. The mistaken creature saw them, and stalked towards the end of the barn into which they had fled. The girls doubled so adroitly that their pursuer was against the wall when the fugitives were already half way to the other end. By the time that his length would allow him to turn and follow them thither they had crossed over; thus the pursuit went on, the hot air from his nostrils blowing over them like a sirocco,[7] and not a moment being attainable by Elizabeth or Lucetta in which to open the door. What might have happened had their situation continued cannot be said; but in a few moments a rattling of the door distracted their adversary's attention, and a man appeared. He ran forward towards the leading-staff, seized it, and wrenched the animal's head as if he would snap it off. The wrench was in reality so violent that the thick neck seemed to have lost its stiffness and to become half-paralysed, whilst the nose dropped blood. The premeditated human contrivance of the nose-ring was too cunning for impulsive brute force, and the creature flinched.

The man was seen in the partial gloom to be large-framed and unhesitating. He led the bull to the door, and the light revealed Henchard. He made the bull fast without, and re-entered to the succour of Lucetta; for he had not perceived Elizabeth, who had climbed on to the clover-heap. Lucetta was hysterical, and Henchard took her in his arms and carried her to the door.

'You—have saved me!' she cried, as soon as she could speak.

'I have returned your kindness,' he responded tenderly. 'You once saved me.'

'How—comes it to be you—you?' she asked, not heeding his reply.

6. Short wooden post.
7. Hot dry wind blowing from North Africa across the Mediterranean.

'I came out here to look for you. I have been wanting to tell you some-thing these two or three days; but you have been away, and I could not. Perhaps you cannot talk now?'

'Oh—no! Where is Elizabeth?'

'Here am I!' cried the missing one cheerfully; and without waiting for the ladder to be placed she slid down the face of the clover-stack to the floor.

Henchard supporting Lucetta on one side, and Elizabeth-Jane on the other, they went slowly along the rising road. They had reached the top and were descending again when Lucetta, now much recovered, recol-lected that she had dropped her muff in the barn.

'I'll run back,' said Elizabeth-Jane. 'I don't mind it at all, as I am not tired as you are.' She thereupon hastened down again to the barn, the others pursuing their way.

Elizabeth soon found the muff, such an article being by no means small at that time. Coming out she paused to look for a moment at the bull, now rather to be pitied with his bleeding nose, having perhaps rather intended a practical joke than a murder. Henchard had secured him by jamming the staff into the hinge of the barn-door, and wedging it there with a stake. At length she turned to hasten onward after her con-templation, when she saw a green-and-black gig approaching from the contrary direction, the vehicle being driven by Farfrae.

His presence here seemed to explain Lucetta's walk that way. Donald saw her, drew up, and was hastily made acquainted with what had occurred. At Elizabeth-Jane mentioning how greatly Lucetta had been jeopardized, he exhibited an agitation different in kind no less than in intensity from any she had seen in him before. He became so absorbed in the circumstance that he scarcely had sufficient knowledge of what he was doing to think of helping her up beside him.

'She has gone on with Mr. Henchard, you say?' he inquired at last.

'Yes. He is taking her home. They are almost there by this time."

'And you are sure she can get home?'

Elizabeth-Jane was quite sure.

'Your stepfather saved her?'

'Entirely.'

Farfrae checked his horse's pace; she guessed why. He was thinking that it would be best not to intrude on the other two just now. Henchard had saved Lucetta, and to provoke a possible exhibition of her deeper affection for himself was as ungenerous as it was unwise.

The immediate subject of their talk being exhausted she felt more embarrassed at sitting thus beside her past lover; but soon the two figures of the others were visible at the entrance to the town. The face of the woman was frequently turned back, but Farfrae did not whip on the horse. When these reached the town walls Henchard and his compan-ion had disappeared down the street; Farfrae set down Elizabeth-Jane on her expressing a particular wish to alight there, and drove round to the stables at the back of his lodgings.

On this account he entered the house through his garden, and going up to his apartments found them in a particularly disturbed state, his boxes being hauled out upon the landing, and his bookcase standing in three pieces. These phenomena, however, seemed to cause him not the least surprise. 'When will everything be sent up?' he said to the mistress of the house, who was superintending.

'I am afraid not before eight, sir,' said she. 'You see we wasn't aware till this morning that you were going to move, or we could have been forwarder.'[8]

'A—well, never mind, never mind!' said Farfrae cheerily. 'Eight o'clock will do well enough if it be not later. Now, don't ye be standing here talking, or it will be twelve, I doubt.' Thus speaking he went out by the front door and up the street.

During this interval Henchard and Lucetta had had experiences of a different kind. After Elizabeth's departure for the muff the corn-merchant opened himself frankly, holding her hand within his arm, though she would fain have withdrawn it. 'Dear Lucetta, I have been very, very anxious to see you these two or three days,' he said; 'ever since I saw you last! I have thought over the way I got your promise that night. You said to me, "If I were a man I should not insist." That cut me deep. I felt that there was some truth in it. I don't want to make you wretched; and to marry me just now would do that as nothing else could—it is but too plain. Therefore I agree to an indefinite engagement—to put off all thought of marriage for a year or two.'

'But—but—can I do nothing of a different kind?' said Lucetta. 'I am full of gratitude to you—you have saved my life. And your care of me is like coals of fire[9] on my head! I am a monied person now. Surely I can do something in return for your goodness—something practical?'

Henchard remained in thought. He had evidently not expected this. 'There is one thing you might do, Lucetta,' he said. 'But not exactly of that kind.'

'Then of what kind is it?' she asked with renewed misgiving.

'I must tell you a secret to ask it.——You may have heard that I have been unlucky this year? I did what I have never done before—speculated rashly; and I lost. That's just put me in a strait.'

'And you would wish me to advance some money?'

'No, no!' said Henchard, almost in anger. 'I'm not the man to sponge on a woman, even though she may be so nearly my own as you. No, Lucetta; what you can do is this; and it would save me. My great creditor is Grower, and it is at his hands I shall suffer if at anybody's; while a

8. Quicker, further on in the task.
9. According to Proverbs 25.22, to show kindness to an enemy is to "heap coals of fire upon his head."

fortnight's forbearance on his part would be enough to allow me to pull through. This may be got out of him in one way—that you would let it be known to him that you are my intended—that we are to be quietly married in the next fortnight.——Now stop, you haven't heard all! Let him have this story, without, of course, any prejudice to the fact that the actual engagement between us is to be a long one. Nobody else need know: you could go with me to Mr. Grower and just let me speak to 'ee before him as if we were on such terms. We'll ask him to keep it secret. He will willingly wait then. At the fortnight's end I shall be able to face him; and I can coolly tell him all is postponed between us for a year or two. Not a soul in the town need know how you've helped me. Since you wish to be of use, there's your way.'

It being now what the people called the 'pinking in' of the day, that is, the quarter-hour just before dusk, he did not at first observe the result of his own words upon her.

'If it were anything else,' she began, and the dryness of her lips was represented in her voice.

'But it is such a little thing!' he said, with a deep reproach. 'Less than you have offered—just the beginning of what you have so lately promised! I could have told him as much myself, but he would not have believed me.'

'It is not because I won't—it is because I absolutely can't,' she said, with rising distress.

'You are provoking!' he burst out. 'It is enough to make me force you to carry out at once what you have promised.'

'I cannot!' she insisted desperately.

'Why? When I have only within these few minutes released you from your promise to do the thing off-hand.'

'Because——he was a witness!'

'Witness? Of what?'

'If I must tell you——. Don't, don't upbraid me!'

'Well! Let's hear what you mean?'

'Witness of my marriage—Mr. Grower was!'

'Marriage?'

'Yes. With Mr. Farfrae. O Michael! I am already his wife. We were married this week at Port-Bredy. There were reasons against our doing it here. Mr. Grower was a witness because he happened to be at Port-Bredy at the time.'

Henchard stood as if idiotized. She was so alarmed at his silence that she murmured something about lending him sufficient money to tide over the perilous fortnight.

'Married him?' said Henchard at length. 'My good—what, married him whilst—bound to marry me?'

'It was like this,' she explained, with tears in her eyes and quavers in her voice; 'don't—don't be cruel! I loved him so much, and I thought you might tell him of the past—and that grieved me! And then, when I had promised you, I learnt of the rumour that you had—sold your first wife at a fair like a horse or cow! How could I keep my promise after hearing that? I could not risk myself in your hands; it would have been letting myself down to take your name after such a scandal. But I knew I should lose Donald if I did not secure him at once—for you would carry out your threat of telling him of our former acquaintance, as long as there was a chance of keeping me for yourself by doing so. But you will not do so now, will you, Michael? for it is too late to separate us.'

The notes of St. Peter's bells in full peal had been wafted to them while he spoke; and now the genial thumping of the town band, renowned for its unstinted use of the drum-stick, throbbed down the street.

'Then this racket they are making is on account of it, I suppose?' said he.

'Yes—I think he has told them, or else Mr. Grower has. . . . May I leave you now? My—he was detained at Port-Bredy to-day, and sent me on a few hours before him.'

'Then it is *his wife's* life I have saved this afternoon.'

'Yes—and he will be for ever grateful to you.'

'I am much obliged to him. . . . O you false woman!' burst from Henchard. 'You promised me!'

'Yes, yes! But it was under compulsion, and I did not know all your past——'

'And now I've a mind to punish you as you deserve! One word to this bran-new husband of how you courted me, and your precious happiness is blown to atoms!'

'Michael—pity me, and be generous!'

'You don't deserve pity! You did; but you don't now.'

'I'll help you to pay off your debt.'

'A pensioner of Farfrae's wife—not I! Don't stay with me longer—I shall say something worse. Go home!'

She disappeared under the trees of the south walk as the band came round the corner, awaking the echoes of every stock and stone in cele-bration of her happiness. Lucetta took no heed, but ran up the back street and reached her own home unperceived.

XXX

Farfrae's words to his landlady had referred to the removal of his boxes and other effects from his late lodgings to Lucetta's house. The work was not heavy, but it had been much hindered on account of the fre-quent pauses necessitated by exclamations of surprise at the event, of which the good woman had been briefly informed by letter a few hours earlier.

At the last moment of leaving Port-Bredy, Farfrae, like John Gilpin,[1] had been detained by important customers, whom, even in the exceptional circumstances, he was not the man to neglect. Moreover, there was a convenience in Lucetta arriving first at her house. Nobody there as yet knew what had happened; and she was best in a position to break the news to the inmates, and give directions for her husband's accommodation. He had, therefore, sent on his two-days' bride in a hired brougham, whilst he went across the country to a certain group of wheat and barley ricks a few miles off, telling her the hour at which he might be expected the same evening. This accounted for her trotting out to meet him after their separation of four hours.

By a strenuous effort, after leaving Henchard she calmed herself in readiness to receive Donald at High-Place Hall when he came on from his lodgings. One supreme fact empowered her to this, the sense that, come what would, she had secured him. Half-an-hour after her arrival he walked in, and she met him with a relieved gladness, which a month's perilous absence could not have intensified.

'There is one thing I have not done; and yet it is important,' she said earnestly, when she had finished talking about the adventure with the bull. 'That is, broken the news of our marriage to my dear Elizabeth-Jane.'

'Ah, and you have not?' he said thoughtfully. 'I gave her a lift from the barn homewards; but I did not tell her either; for I thought she might have heard of it in the town, and was keeping back her congratulations from shyness, and all that.'

'She can hardly have heard of it. But I'll find out; I'll go to her now. And, Donald, you don't mind her living on with me just the same as before? She is so quiet and unassuming.'

'O no, indeed I don't,' Farfrae answered with, perhaps, a faint awkwardness. 'But I wonder if she would care to?'

'O yes!' said Lucetta eagerly. 'I am sure she would like to. Besides, poor thing, she has no other home.'

Farfrae looked at her and saw that she did not suspect the secret of her more reserved friend. He liked her all the better for the blindness. 'Arrange as you like with her by all means,' he said. 'It is I who have come to your house, not you to mine.'

'I'll run and speak to her,' said Lucetta.

When she got upstairs to Elizabeth-Jane's room the latter had taken off her out-door things, and was resting over a book. Lucetta found in a moment that she had not yet learnt the news.

'I did not come down to you, Miss Templeman,' she said simply. 'I was coming to ask if you had quite recovered from your fright, but I found

---

1. In William Cowper's poem "The Diverting History of John Gilpin," Gilpin delays joining his wife to celebrate their anniversary in order to attend to his customers.

you had a visitor. What are the bells ringing for, I wonder? And the band, too, is playing. Somebody must be married; or else they are practising for Christmas.'

Lucetta uttered a vague 'Yes,' and seating herself by the other young woman looked musingly at her. 'What a lonely creature you are,' she presently said; 'never knowing what's going on, or what people are talking about everywhere with keen interest. You should get out, and gossip about as other women do, and then you wouldn't be obliged to ask me a question of that kind. Well, now, I have something to tell you.'

Elizabeth-Jane said she was so glad, and made herself receptive.

'I must go rather a long way back,' said Lucetta, the difficulty of explaining herself satisfactorily to the pondering one beside her growing more apparent at each syllable. 'You remember that trying case of conscience I told you of some time ago—about the first lover and the second lover?' She let out in jerky phrases a leading word or two of the story she had told.

'O yes—I remember; the story of *your friend*,' said Elizabeth drily, regarding the irises of Lucetta's eyes as though to catch their exact shade. 'The two lovers—the old and the new: how she wanted to marry the second, but felt she ought to marry the first; so that she neglected the better course to follow the evil, like the poet Ovid I've just been construing: "Video meliora proboque, deteriora sequor."'[2]

'O no; she didn't follow evil exactly!' said Lucetta hastily.

'But you said that she—or as I may say *you*'—answered Elizabeth, dropping the mask, 'were in honour and conscience bound to marry the first?'

Lucetta's blush at being seen through came and went again before she replied anxiously, 'You will never breathe this, will you, Elizabeth-Jane?'

'Certainly not, if you say not.'

'Then I will tell you that the case is more complicated—worse, in fact—than it seemed in my story. I and the first man were thrown together in a strange way, and felt that we ought to be united, as the world had talked of us. He was a widower, as he supposed. He had not heard of his first wife for many years. But the wife returned, and we parted. She is now dead; and the husband comes paying me addresses again, saying, "Now we'll complete our purpose." But, Elizabeth-Jane, all this amounts to a new courtship of me by him; I was absolved from all vows by the return of the other woman.'

'Have you not lately renewed your promise?' said the younger with quiet surmise. She had divined Man Number One.

'That was wrung from me by a threat.'

'Yes, it was. But I think when any one gets coupled up with a man in

---

2. Quoting from the Roman poet Ovid (43 B.C.E.–17 C.E.): "I see and approve the better course; I follow the worse" (*Metamorphoses*, VII.20–21). In earlier versions of the text, Elizabeth-Jane quoted a similar sentiment from St. Paul; see Romans 7.19.

the past so unfortunately as you have done, she ought to become his wife if she can, even if she were not the sinning party.'

Lucetta's countenance lost its sparkle. 'He turned out to be a man I should be afraid to marry,' she pleaded. 'Really afraid! And it was not till after my renewed promise that I knew it.'

'Then there is only one course left to honesty. You must remain a single woman.'

'But think again! Do consider——'

'I am certain,' interrupted her companion hardily. 'I have guessed very well who the man is. My father; and I say it is him or nobody for you.'

Any suspicion of impropriety was to Elizabeth-Jane like a red rag to a bull. Her craving for correctness of procedure was, indeed, almost vicious. Owing to her early troubles with regard to her mother a semblance of irregularity had terrors for her which those whose names are safeguarded from suspicion know nothing of. 'You ought to marry Mr. Henchard or nobody—certainly not another man!' she went on with a quivering lip in whose movement two passions shared.

'I don't admit that!' said Lucetta passionately.

'Admit it or not, it is true!'

Lucetta covered her eyes with her right hand, as if she could plead no more, holding out her left to Elizabeth-Jane.

'Why, you *have* married him!' cried the latter, jumping up with pleasure after a glance at Lucetta's fingers. 'When did you do it? Why did you not tell me, instead of teasing me like this? How very honourable of you! He did treat my mother badly once, it seems, in a moment of intoxication. And it is true that he is stern sometimes. But you will rule him entirely, I am sure, with your beauty and wealth and accomplishments. You are the woman he will adore, and we shall all three be happy together now!'

'O, my Elizabeth-Jane!' cried Lucetta distressfully. ''Tis somebody else that I have married! I was so desperate—so afraid of being forced to anything else—so afraid of revelations that would quench his love for me, that I resolved to do it off-hand, come what might, and purchase a week of happiness at any cost!'

'You—have—married Mr. Farfrae!' cried Elizabeth-Jane, in Nathan tones.[3]

Lucetta bowed. She had recovered herself.

'The bells are ringing on that account,' she said. 'My husband is downstairs. He will live here till a more suitable house is ready for us; and I have told him that I want you to stay with me just as before.'

'Let me think of it alone,' the girl quickly replied, corking up the turmoil of her feeling with grand control.

'You shall. I am sure we shall be happy together.'

---

3. Reprovingly. The prophet Nathan reproached David for his adultery with Bathsheba, and for causing the death of her husband Uriah. See 2 Samuel 12.1–15.

Lucetta departed to join Donald below, a vague uneasiness floating over her joy at seeing him quite at home there. Not on account of her friend Elizabeth did she feel it: for of the bearings of Elizabeth-Jane's emotions she had not the least suspicion; but on Henchard's alone.

Now the instant decision of Susan Henchard's daughter was to dwell in that house no more. Apart from her estimate of the propriety of Lucetta's conduct, Farfrae had been so nearly her avowed lover that she felt she could not abide there.

It was still early in the evening when she hastily put on her things and went out. In a few minutes, knowing the ground, she had found a suitable lodging, and arranged to enter it that night. Returning and entering noiselessly she took off her pretty dress and arrayed herself in a plain one, packing up the other to keep as her best; for she would have to be very economical now. She wrote a note to leave for Lucetta, who was closely shut up in the drawing-room with Farfrae; and then Elizabeth-Jane called a man with a wheelbarrow; and seeing her boxes put into it she trotted off down the street to her rooms. They were in the street in which Henchard lived, and almost opposite his door.

Here she sat down and considered the means of subsistence. The little annual sum settled on her by her stepfather would keep body and soul together. A wonderful skill in netting of all sorts—acquired in childhood by making seines in Newson's home—might serve her in good stead; and her studies, which were pursued unremittingly, might serve her in still better.

By this time the marriage that had taken place was known throughout Casterbridge; had been discussed noisily on kerbstones, confidentially behind counters, and jovially at the Three Mariners. Whether Farfrae would sell his business and set up for a gentleman on his wife's money, or whether he would show independence enough to stick to his trade in spite of his brilliant alliance, was a great point of interest.

XXXI

The retort of the furmity-woman before the magistrates had spread; and in four-and-twenty hours there was not a person in Casterbridge who remained unacquainted with the story of Henchard's mad freak at Weydon-Priors Fair, long years before. The amends he had made in after life were lost sight of in the dramatic glare of the original act. Had the incident been well known of old and always, it might by this time have grown to be lightly regarded as the rather tall wild oat, but well-nigh the single one, of a young man with whom the steady and mature (if somewhat headstrong) burgher of to-day had scarcely a point in common. But the act having lain as dead and buried ever since, the interspace of years was unperceived; and the black spot of his youth wore the aspect of a recent crime.

Small as the police-court incident had been in itself, it formed the edge or turn in the incline of Henchard's fortunes. On that day—almost at that minute—he passed the ridge of prosperity and honour, and began to descend rapidly on the other side. It was strange how soon he sank in esteem. Socially he had received a startling fillip[1] downwards; and, having already lost commercial buoyancy from rash transactions, the velocity of his descent in both aspects became accelerated every hour.

He now gazed more at the pavements and less at the house-fronts when he walked about; more at the feet and leggings of men, and less into the pupils of their eyes with the blazing regard which formerly had made them blink.

New events combined to undo him. It had been a bad year for others besides himself, and the heavy failure of a debtor whom he had trusted generously completed the overthrow of his tottering credit. And now, in his desperation, he failed to preserve that strict correspondence between bulk and sample which is the soul of commerce in grain. For this, one of his men was mainly to blame; that worthy, in his great unwisdom, having picked over the sample of an enormous quantity of second-rate corn which Henchard had in hand, and removed the pinched, blasted, and smutted grains[2] in great numbers. The produce if honestly offered would have created no scandal; but the blunder of misrepresentation, coming at such a moment, dragged Henchard's name into the ditch.

The details of his failure were of the ordinary kind. One day Elizabeth-Jane was passing the King's Arms, when she saw people bustling in and out more than usual when there was no market. A bystander informed her, with some surprise at her ignorance, that it was a meeting of the Commissioners under Mr. Henchard's bankruptcy. She felt quite tearful, and when she heard that he was present in the hotel she wished to go in and see him, but was advised not to intrude that day.

The room in which debtor and creditors had assembled was a front one, and Henchard, looking out of the window, had caught sight of Elizabeth-Jane through the wire blind. His examination had closed, and the creditors were leaving. The appearance of Elizabeth threw him into a reverie; till, turning his face from the window, and towering above all the rest, he called their attention for a moment more. His countenance had somewhat changed from its flush of prosperity; the black hair and whiskers were the same as ever, but a film of ash was over the rest.

'Gentlemen,' he said, 'over and above the assets that we've been talking about, and that appear on the balance-sheet, there be these. It all belongs to ye, as much as everything else I've got, and I don't wish to keep it from you, not I.' Saying this, he took his gold watch[3] from his pocket and laid it on the table; then his purse—the yellow canvas

1. Smart flick or blow, like that made by snapping the fingers.
2. Withered, blighted, or infected with a fungus disease known as "smut."
3. Based on a real-life bankruptcy in 1826, recorded in the *Dorset County Chronicle*.

money-bag, such as was carried by all farmers and dealers—untying it, and shaking the money out upon the table beside the watch. The latter he drew back quickly for an instant, to remove the hair-guard[4] made and given him by Lucetta. 'There, now you have all I've got in the world,' he said. 'And I wish for your sakes 'twas more.'

The creditors, farmers almost to a man, looked at the watch, and at the money, and into the street; when Farmer James Everdene[5] of Weatherbury spoke.

'No, no, Henchard,' he said warmly. 'We don't want that. 'Tis honourable in ye; but keep it. What do you say, neighbours—do ye agree?'

'Ay, sure: we don't wish it at all,' said Grower, another creditor.

'Let him keep it, of course,' murmured another in the background—a silent, reserved young man named Boldwood; and the rest responded unanimously.

'Well,' said the senior Commissioner, addressing Henchard, 'though the case is a desperate one, I am bound to admit that I have never met a debtor who behaved more fairly. I've proved the balance-sheet to be as honestly made out as it could possibly be; we have had no trouble; there have been no evasions and no concealments. The rashness of dealing which led to this unhappy situation is obvious enough; but as far as I can see every attempt has been made to avoid wronging anybody.'

Henchard was more affected by this than he cared to let them perceive, and he turned aside to the window again. A general murmur of agreement followed the Commissioner's words; and the meeting dispersed. When they were gone Henchard regarded the watch they had returned to him. ''Tisn't mine by rights,' he said to himself. 'Why the devil didn't they take it?—I don't want what don't belong to me!' Moved by a recollection he took the watch to the maker's just opposite, sold it there and then for what the tradesman offered, and went with the proceeds to one among the smaller of his creditors, a cottager of Durnover in straitened circumstances, to whom he handed the money.

When everything was ticketed that Henchard had owned, and the auctions were in progress, there was quite a sympathetic reaction in the town, which till then for some time past had done nothing but condemn him. Now that Henchard's whole career was pictured distinctly to his neighbours, and they could see how admirably he had used his one talent of energy to create a position of affluence out of absolutely nothing —which was really all he could show when he came to the town as a journeyman hay-trusser, with his wimble and knife in his basket—they wondered and regretted his fall.

Try as she might, Elizabeth could never meet with him. She believed in him still, though nobody else did; and she wanted to be

---

4. Guard chain for a watch made from woven hair.
5. Both Everdene and Boldwood are characters in Hardy's *Far from the Madding Crowd* (1874).

allowed to forgive him for his roughness to her, and to help him in his trouble.

She wrote to him; he did not reply. She then went to his house—the great house she had lived in so happily for a time—with its front of dun brick, vitrified[6] here and there, and its heavy sash-bars—but Henchard was to be found there no more. The ex-Mayor had left the home of his prosperity, and gone into Jopp's cottage by the Priory Mill—the sad purlieu[7] to which he had wandered on the night of his discovery that she was not his daughter. Thither she went.

Elizabeth thought it odd that he had fixed on this spot to retire to, but assumed that necessity had no choice. Trees which seemed old enough to have been planted by the friars still stood around, and the back hatch of the original mill yet formed a cascade which had raised its terrific roar for centuries. The cottage itself was built of old stones from the long dismantled Priory, scraps of tracery, moulded window-jambs, and archlabels,[8] being mixed in with the rubble of the walls.

In this cottage he occupied a couple of rooms, Jopp, whom Henchard had employed, abused, cajoled, and dismissed by turns, being the householder. But even here her stepfather could not be seen.

'Not by his daughter?' pleaded Elizabeth.

'By nobody—at present: that's his order,' she was informed.

Afterwards she was passing by the corn-stores and hay-barns which had been the headquarters of his business. She knew that he ruled there no longer; but it was with amazement that she regarded the familiar gateway. A smear of decisive lead-coloured paint had been laid on to obliterate Henchard's name, though its letters dimly loomed through like ships in a fog. Over these, in fresh white, spread the name of Farfrae.

Abel Whittle was edging his skeleton in at the wicket, and she said, 'Mr. Farfrae is master here?'

'Yaas, Miss Henchet,' he said, 'Mr. Farfrae have bought the concern and all of we work-folk with it; and 'tis better for us than 'twas—though I shouldn't say that to you as a daughter-law.[9] We work harder, but we bain't made afeard now. It was fear made my few poor hairs so thin! No busting out, no slamming of doors, no meddling with yer eternal soul and all that; and though 'tis a shilling a week less I'm the richer man; for what's all the world if yer mind is always in a larry, Miss Henchet?'

The intelligence was in a general sense true; and Henchard's stores, which had remained in a paralyzed condition during the settlement of his bankruptcy, were stirred into activity again when the new tenant had possession. Thenceforward the full sacks, looped with the shining chain,

6. Glazed by exposure to heat.
7. District.
8. Stone moldings above windows.
9. Stepdaughter.

went scurrying up and down under the cat-head,[1] hairy arms were thrust out from the different door-ways, and the grain was hauled in; trusses of hay were tossed anew in and out of the barns, and the wimbles[2] creaked; while the scales and steelyards[3] began to be busy where guess-work had formerly been the rule.

XXXII

Two bridges[1] stood near the lower part of Casterbridge town. The first, of weather-stained brick, was immediately at the end of High Street, where a diverging branch from that thoroughfare ran round to the low-lying Durnover lanes; so that the precincts of the bridge formed the merging point of respectability and indigence. The second bridge, of stone, was further out on the highway—in fact, fairly in the meadows, though still within the town boundary.

These bridges had speaking countenances. Every projection in each was worn down to obtuseness, partly by weather, more by friction from generations of loungers, whose toes and heels had from year to year made restless movements against these parapets, as they had stood there meditating on the aspect of affairs. In the case of the more friable bricks and stones even the flat faces were worn into hollows by the same mixed mechanism. The masonry of the top was clamped with iron at each joint; since it had been no uncommon thing for desperate men to wrench the coping off and throw it down the river, in reckless defiance of the magistrates.

For to this pair of bridges gravitated all the failures of the town; those who had failed in business, in love, in sobriety, in crime. Why the unhappy hereabout usually chose the bridges for their meditations in preference to a railing, a gate, or a stile, was not so clear.

There was a marked difference of quality between the personages who haunted the near bridge of brick, and the personages who haunted the far one of stone. Those of lowest character preferred the former, adjoining the town; they did not mind the glare of the public eye. They had been of comparatively no account during their successes; and, though they might feel dispirited, they had no particular sense of shame in their ruin. Their hands were mostly kept in their pockets; they wore a leather strap round their hips or knees, and boots that required a great deal of lacing, but seemed never to get any. Instead of sighing at their adversities they spat, and instead of saying the iron had entered into their souls[2] they said they were down on their luck. Jopp in his times of distress had

---

1. Projecting beam, bearing a pulley and tackle used to lift heavy objects.
2. Instruments used in trussing bundles of hay.
3. Portable weighing machines.
1. Swan Bridge (brick) over the Frome, and Grey's Bridge (stone) over the Cerne.
2. Proverbial expression denoting grief or disappointment. The phrase comes from the Book of Common Prayer, mistranslating Psalm 105.18, "he was laid in iron."

often stood here; so had Mother Cuxsom, Christopher Coney, and poor
Abel Whittle.

The *misérables*[3] who would pause on the remoter bridge were of a
politer stamp. They included bankrupts, hypochondriacs, persons who
were what is called 'out of a situation' from fault or lucklessness, the
inefficient of the professional class—shabby-genteel men, who did not
know how to get rid of the weary time between breakfast and dinner,
and the yet more weary time between dinner and dark. The eyes of
this species were mostly directed over the parapet upon the running
water below. A man seen there looking thus fixedly into the river was
pretty sure to be one whom the world did not treat kindly for some reason or other. While one in straits on the townward bridge did not mind
who saw him so, and kept his back to the parapet to survey the passers-
by, one in straits on this never faced the road, never turned his head
at coming footsteps, but, sensitive to his own condition, watched the
current whenever a stranger approached, as if some strange fish interested him, though every finned thing had been poached out of the
river years before.

There and thus they would muse; if their grief were the grief of
oppression they would wish themselves kings; if their grief were poverty,
wish themselves millionaires; if sin, they would wish they were saints or
angels; if despised love, that they were some much-courted Adonis[4] of
county fame. Some had been known to stand and think so long with this
fixed gaze downward that eventually they had allowed their poor carcas-
es to follow that gaze; and they were discovered the next morning out of
reach of their troubles, either here or in the deep pool called Blackwater,
a little higher up the river.

To this bridge came Henchard, as other unfortunates had come
before him, his way thither being by the riverside path on the chilly edge
of the town. Here he was standing one windy afternoon when Durnover
church clock struck five. While the gusts were bringing the notes to his
ears across the damp intervening flat a man passed behind him and
greeted Henchard by name. Henchard turned slightly and saw that the
comer was Jopp, his old foreman, now employed elsewhere, to whom,
though he hated him, he had gone for lodgings because Jopp was the
one man in Casterbridge whose observation and opinion the fallen corn-
merchant despised to the point of indifference.

Henchard returned him a scarcely perceptible nod, and Jopp stopped.

'He and she are gone into their new house to-day,' said Jopp.

'Oh,' said Henchard absently. 'Which house is that?'

'Your old one.'

---

3. Unhappy wretches (French). *Les Misérables*, the novel by Victor Hugo (1802–1885), was published in 1862.
4. In classical mythology, a beautiful youth, loved by Venus.

'Gone into my house?' And starting up Henchard added, 'My house of all others in the town!'

'Well, as somebody was sure to live there, and you couldn't, it can do 'ee no harm that he's the man.'

It was quite true: he felt that it was doing him no harm. Farfrae, who had already taken the yards and stores, had acquired possession of the house for the obvious convenience of its contiguity. And yet this act of his taking up residence within those roomy chambers while he, their former tenant, lived in a cottage, galled Henchard indescribably.

Jopp continued: 'And you heard of that fellow who bought all the best furniture at your sale? He was bidding for no other than Farfrae all the while! It has never been moved out of the house, as he'd already got the lease.'

'My furniture too! Surely he'll buy my body and soul likewise!'

'There's no saying he won't, if you be willing to sell.' And having planted these wounds in the heart of his once imperious master Jopp went on his way; while Henchard stared and stared into the racing river till the bridge seemed moving backward with him.

The low land grew blacker, and the sky a deeper grey. When the landscape looked like a picture blotted in with ink, another traveller approached the great stone bridge. He was driving a gig, his direction being also townwards. On the round of the middle of the arch the gig stopped. 'Mr. Henchard?' came from it in the voice of Farfrae. Henchard turned his face.

Finding that he had guessed rightly Farfrae told the man who accompanied him to drive home; while he alighted and went up to his former friend.

'I have heard that you think of emigrating, Mr. Henchard,' he said. 'Is it true? I have a real reason for asking.'

Henchard withheld his answer for several instants, and then said, 'Yes; it is true. I am going where you were going to a few years ago, when I prevented you and got you to bide here. 'Tis turn and turn about, isn't it! Do ye mind how we stood like this in the Chalk Walk when I persuaded 'ee to stay? You then stood without a chattel[5] to your name, and I was the master of the house in Corn Street. But now I stand without a stick or a rag, and the master of that house is you.'

'Yes, yes; that's so! It's the way o' the warrld,' said Farfrae.

'Ha, ha, true!' cried Henchard, throwing himself into a mood of jocularity. 'Up and down! I'm used to it. What's the odds after all!'

'Now listen to me, if it's no taking up your time,' said Farfrae, 'just as I listened to you. Don't go. Stay at home.'

'But I can do nothing else, man!' said Henchard scornfully. 'The little money I have will just keep body and soul together for a few weeks,

5. Possession.

and no more. I have not felt inclined to go back to journey-work[6] yet; but I can't stay doing nothing, and my best chance is elsewhere.'

'No; but what I propose is this—if ye will listen. Come and live in your old house. We can spare some rooms very well—I am sure my wife would not mind it at all—until there's an opening for ye.'

Henchard started. Probably the picture drawn by the unsuspecting Donald of himself under the same roof with Lucetta was too striking to be received with equanimity. 'No, no,' he said gruffly; 'we should quarrel.'

'You should hae a part to yourself,' said Farfrae; 'and nobody to inter-fere wi' you. It will be a deal healthier than down there by the river where you live now.'

Still Henchard refused. 'You don't know what you ask,' he said. 'However, I can do no less than thank 'ee.'

They walked into the town together side by side, as they had done when Henchard persuaded the young Scotchman to remain. 'Will you come in and have some supper?' said Farfrae when they reached the middle of the town, where their paths diverged right and left.

'No, no.'

'By-the-bye, I had nearly forgot. I bought a good deal of your furniture.'

'So I have heard.'

'Well, it was no that I wanted it so very much for myself; but I wish ye to pick out all that you care to have—such things as may be endeared to ye by associations, or particularly suited to your use. And take them to your own house—it will not be depriving me; we can do with less very well, and I will have plenty of opportunities of getting more.'

'What—give it to me for nothing?' said Henchard. 'But you paid the creditors for it!'

'Ah, yes; but maybe it's worth more to you than it is to me.'

Henchard was a little moved. 'I—sometimes think I've wronged 'ee!' he said, in tones which showed the disquietude that the night shades hid in his face. He shook Farfrae abruptly by the hand, and hastened away as if unwilling to betray himself further. Farfrae saw him turn through the thoroughfare into Bull Stake and vanish down towards the Priory Mill.

Meanwhile Elizabeth-Jane, in an upper room no larger than the Prophet's chamber,[7] and with the silk attire of her palmy days packed away in a box, was netting with great industry between the hours which she devoted to studying such books as she could get hold of.

Her lodgings being nearly opposite her stepfather's former residence, now Farfrae's, she could see Donald and Lucetta speeding in and out of

---

6. Work done for day-wages.
7. Room prepared for the prophet Elisha by a woman and her husband in Shunem. See 2 Kings 4.10.

their door with all the bounding enthusiasm of their situation. She avoided looking that way as much as possible, but it was hardly in human nature to keep the eyes averted when the door slammed.

While living on thus quietly she heard the news that Henchard had caught cold and was confined to his room—possibly a result of standing about the meads in damp weather. She went off to his house at once. This time she was determined not to be denied admittance, and made her way upstairs. He was sitting up in the bed with a greatcoat round him, and at first resented her intrusion. 'Go away—go away,' he said. 'I don't like to see 'ee!'

'But, father—'

'I don't like to see 'ee,' he repeated.

However, the ice was broken, and she remained. She made the room more comfortable, gave directions to the people below, and by the time she went away had reconciled her stepfather to her visiting him.

The effect, either of her ministrations or of her mere presence, was a rapid recovery. He soon was well enough to go out; and now things seemed to wear a new colour in his eyes. He no longer thought of emigration, and thought more of Elizabeth. The having nothing to do made him more dreary than any other circumstance; and one day, with better views of Farfrae than he had held for some time, and a sense that honest work was not a thing to be ashamed of, he stoically went down to Farfrae's yard and asked to be taken on as a journeyman hay-trusser. He was engaged at once. This hiring of Henchard was done through a foreman, Farfrae feeling that it was undesirable to come personally in contact with the ex-cornfactor more than was absolutely necessary. While anxious to help him he was well aware by this time of his uncertain temper, and thought reserved relations best. For the same reason his orders to Henchard to proceed to this and that country farm trussing in the usual way were always given through a third person.

For a time these arrangements worked well, it being the custom to truss in the respective stack-yards, before bringing it away, the hay bought at the different farms about the neighbourhood; so that Henchard was often absent at such places the whole week long. When this was all done, and Henchard had become in a measure broken in, he came to work daily on the home premises like the rest. And thus the once flourishing merchant and Mayor and what not stood as a day-labourer in the barns and granaries he formerly had owned.

'I have worked as a journeyman before now, ha'n't I?' he would say in his defiant way; 'and why shouldn't I do it again?' But he looked a far different journeyman from the one he had been in his earlier days. Then he had worn clean, suitable clothes, light and cheerful in hue; leggings yellow as marigolds, corduroys immaculate as new flax, and a neckerchief like a flower-garden. Now he wore the remains of an old blue cloth suit of his gentlemanly times, a rusty silk hat, and a once black satin

stock,[8] soiled and shabby. Clad thus he went to and fro, still comparatively an active man—for he was not much over forty—and saw with the
other men in the yard Donald Farfrae going in and out the green door
that led to the garden, and the big house, and Lucetta.

At the beginning of the winter it was rumoured about Casterbridge
that Mr. Farfrae, already in the Town Council, was to be proposed for
Mayor in a year or two.

'Yes; she was wise, she was wise in her generation!'[9] said Henchard to
himself when he heard of this one day on his way to Farfrae's hay-barn.
He thought it over as he wimbled his bonds, and the piece of news acted
as a reviviscent[1] breath to that old view of his—of Donald Farfrae as his
triumphant rival who rode rough-shod over him.

'A fellow of his age going to be Mayor, indeed!' he murmured with a
corner-drawn smile on his mouth. 'But 'tis her money that floats en
upward. Ha-ha—how cust odd it is! Here be I, his former master, working for him as man, and he the man standing as master, with my house
and my furniture and my what-you-may-call wife all his own.'

He repeated these things a hundred times a day. During the whole
period of his acquaintance with Lucetta he had never wished to claim
her as his own so desperately as he now regretted her loss. It was no mer-
cenary hankering after her fortune that moved him; though that fortune
had been the means of making her so much the more desired by giving
her the air of independence and sauciness which attracts men of his
composition. It had given her servants, house, and fine clothing—a setting that invested Lucetta with a startling novelty in the eyes of him who
had known her in her narrow days.

He accordingly lapsed into moodiness, and at every allusion to the
possibility of Farfrae's near election to the municipal chair his former
hatred of the Scotchman returned. Concurrently with this he underwent a moral change. It resulted in his significantly saying every now
and then, in tones of recklessness, 'Only a fortnight more!'—'Only a
dozen days!' and so forth, lessening his figures day by day.

'Why d'ye say only a dozen days?' asked Solomon Longways as he
worked beside Henchard in the granary weighing oats.

'Because in twelve days I shall be released from my oath.'

'What oath?'

'The oath to drink no spirituous liquid. In twelve days it will be twenty-one years since I swore it, and then I mean to enjoy myself, please
God!'

Elizabeth-Jane sat at her window one Sunday, and while there she
heard in the street below a conversation which introduced Henchard's

8. Stiff neckcloth.
9. Quoting Luke 16.8: "for the children of this world are in their generation wiser than the children of light."
1. Restoring to life.

name. She was wondering what was the matter, when a third person who was passing by asked the question in her mind.

'Michael Henchard have busted out drinking after taking nothing for twenty-one years!'

Elizabeth-Jane jumped up, put on her things, and went out.

XXXIII

At this date there prevailed in Casterbridge a convivial custom—scarcely recognized as such, yet none the less established. On the afternoon of every Sunday a large contingent of the Casterbridge journeymen—steady church-goers and sedate characters—having attended service, filed from the church doors across the way to the Three Mariners Inn. The rear was usually brought up by the choir,[1] with their bass-viols, fiddles, and flutes under their arms.

The great point, the point of honour, on these sacred occasions was for each man to strictly limit himself to half-a-pint of liquor. This scrupulosity was so well understood by the landlord that the whole company was served in cups of that measure. They were all exactly alike—straight-sided, with two leafless lime-trees done in eel-brown on the sides—one towards the drinker's lips, the other confronting his comrade. To wonder how many of these cups the landlord possessed altogether was a favourite exercise of children in the marvellous. Forty at least might have been seen at these times in the large room, forming a ring round the margin of the great sixteen-legged oak table, like the monolithic circle at Stonehenge[2] in its pristine days. Outside and above the forty cups came a circle of forty smoke-jets from forty clay pipes; outside the pipes the countenances of the forty church-goers, supported at the back by a circle of forty chairs.

The conversation was not the conversation of weekdays, but a thing altogether finer in point and higher in tone. They invariably discussed the sermon, dissecting it, weighing it, as above or below the average—the general tendency being to regard it as a scientific feat or performance which had no relation to their own lives, except as between critics and the thing criticized. The bass-viol player and the clerk usually spoke with more authority than the rest on account of their official connection with the preacher.

Now the Three Mariners was the inn chosen by Henchard as the place for closing his long term of dramless years. He had so timed his entry as to be well established in the large room by the time the forty church-goers entered to their customary cups. The flush upon his face proclaimed at once that the vow of twenty-one years had lapsed, and the

---

1. Not singers, but church musicians, playing various instruments. Both Hardy's father and grandfather had played in similar church bands.
2. Circle of standing stones on Salisbury Plain in Wiltshire, probably begun around 2800 B.C.E.

era of recklessness begun anew. He was seated on a small table, drawn
up to the side of the massive oak board reserved for the churchmen, a
few of whom nodded to him as they took their places and said, 'How be
ye, Mr. Henchard? Quite a stranger here.'

Henchard did not take the trouble to reply for a few moments, and his
eyes rested on his stretched-out legs and boots. 'Yes,' he said at length;
'that's true. I've been down in spirit for weeks; some of ye know the
cause. I am better now; but not quite serene. I want you fellows of the
choir to strike up a tune; and what with that and this brew of Stannidge's,
I am in hopes of getting altogether out of my minor key.'

'With all my heart,' said the first fiddle. 'We've let back our strings,
that's true; but we can soon pull 'em up again. Sound A, neighbours, and
give the man a stave.'[3]

'I don't care a curse what the words be,' said Henchard. 'Hymns, bal-
lets, or rantipole[4] rubbish; the Rogue's March or the cherubim's war-
ble[5]—'tis all the same to me if 'tis good harmony, and well put out.'

'Well—heh, heh—it may be we can do that, and not a man among us
that have sat in the gallery less than twenty year,' said the leader of the
band. 'As 'tis Sunday, neighbours, suppose we raise the Fourth Psa'am,
to Samuel Wakely's tune,[6] as improved by me?'

'Hang Samuel Wakely's tune, as improved by thee!' said Henchard.
'Chuck across one of your psalters[7]—old Wiltshire[8] is the only tune
worth singing—the psalm-tune that would make my blood ebb and flow
like the sea when I was a steady chap. I'll find some words to fit en.' He
took one of the psalters and began turning over the leaves.

Chancing to look out of the window at that moment he saw a flock of
people passing by, and perceived them to be the congregation of the
upper church, now just dismissed, their sermon having been a longer
one than that the lower parish was favoured with. Among the rest of the
leading inhabitants walked Mr. Councillor Farfrae with Lucetta upon
his arm, the observed and imitated of all the smaller tradesmen's womankind. Henchard's mouth changed a little, and he continued to turn
over the leaves.

'Now then,' he said, 'Psalm the Hundred-and-Ninth, to the tune of
Wiltshire: verses ten to fifteen. I gi'e ye the words:

> His seed shall orphans be, his wife
> A widow plunged in grief;

3. Strictly, the five lines on which notes of music are written, but here used for a piece of music.
4. Riotous. A "ballet" may be a ballad or (more probably) a madrigal.
5. Secular or sacred music. The Rogue's March is played while a soldier is being discharged from
   service in disgrace; cherubim are angels, often represented in art with innocent or childlike
   faces.
6. Victorian composer of hymn-tunes.
7. Books containing metrical versions of the Psalms, often with tunes.
8. Name given to a tune by George Smart (1776–1867), to which were sung a number of psalms,
   especially Psalm 34, which begins "I will bless the Lord at all times."

His vagrant children beg their bread
　　Where none can give relief.

His ill-got riches shall be made
　　To usurers a prey;
The fruit of all his toil shall be
　　By strangers borne away.

None shall be found that to his wants
　　Their mercy will extend,
Or to his helpless orphan seed
　　The least assistance lend.

A swift destruction soon shall seize
　　On his unhappy race;
And the next age his hated name
　　Shall utterly deface.'

'I know the Psa'am—I know the Psa'am!' said the leader hastily; 'but I would as lief not sing it. 'Twasn't made for singing. We chose it once when the gipsy stole the pa'son's mare, thinking to please him, but pa'-son were quite upset. Whatever Servant David[9] were thinking about when he made a Psalm that nobody can sing without disgracing himself, I can't fathom! Now then, the Fourth Psalm, to Samuel Wakely's tune, as improved by me.'

"Od seize your sauce—I tell ye to sing the Hundred-and-Ninth to Wiltshire, and sing it you shall!' roared Henchard. 'Not a single one of all the droning crew of ye goes out of this room till that Psalm is sung!' He slipped off the table, seized the poker, and going to the door placed his back against it. 'Now then, go ahead, if you don't wish to have your cust pates broke!'

'Don't 'ee, don't 'ee take on so!—As 'tis the Sabbath-day, and 'tis Servant David's words and not ours, perhaps we don't mind for once, hey?' said one of the terrified choir, looking round upon the rest. So the instruments were tuned and the comminatory verses[1] sung.

'Thank ye, thank ye,' said Henchard in a softened voice, his eyes grow-ing downcast, and his manner that of a man much moved by the strains. 'Don't you blame David,' he went on in low tones, shaking his head without raising his eyes. 'He knew what he was about when he wrote that! . . . If I could afford it, be hanged if I wouldn't keep a church choir at my own expense to play and sing to me at these low, dark times

9. David is traditionally regarded as the author of many of the Psalms.
1. Verses of condemnation. The Commination, denouncing sinners, forms part of the Anglican liturgy.

of my life. But the bitter thing is, that when I was rich I didn't need what I could have, and now I be poor I can't have what I need!'

While they paused, Lucetta and Farfrae passed again, this time homeward, it being their custom to take, like others, a short walk out on the highway and back, between church and tea-time. 'There's the man we've been singing about,' said Henchard.

The players and singers turned their heads and saw his meaning. 'Heaven forbid!' said the bass-player.

''Tis the man,' repeated Henchard doggedly.

'Then if I'd known,' said the performer on the clarionet solemnly, 'that 'twas meant for a living man, nothing should have drawn out of my wynd-pipe the breath for that Psalm, so help me!'

'Nor from mine,' said the first singer. 'But, thought I, as it was made so long ago perhaps there isn't much in it, so I'll oblige a neighbour; for there's nothing to be said against the tune.'

'Ah, my boys, you've sung it,' said Henchard triumphantly. 'As for him, it was partly by his songs that he got over me, and heaved me out. . . . I could double him up like that—and yet I don't.' He laid the poker across his knee, bent it as if it were a twig, flung it down, and came away from the door.

It was at this time that Elizabeth-Jane, having heard where her stepfather was, entered the room with a pale and agonized countenance. The choir and the rest of the company moved off, in accordance with their half-pint regulation. Elizabeth-Jane went up to Henchard, and entreated him to accompany her home.

By this hour the volcanic fires of his nature had burnt down, and having drunk no great quantity as yet he was inclined to acquiesce. She took his arm, and together they went on. Henchard walked blankly, like a blind man, repeating to himself the last words of the singers—

'And the next age his hated name
Shall utterly deface.'

At length he said to her, 'I am a man to my word. I have kept my oath for twenty-one years; and now I can drink with a good conscience. . . . If I don't do for him—well, I am a fearful practical joker when I choose! He has taken away everything from me, and by heavens, if I meet him I won't answer for my deeds!'

These half-uttered words alarmed Elizabeth—all the more by reason of the still determination of Henchard's mien.

'What will you do?' she asked cautiously, while trembling with disquietude, and guessing Henchard's allusion only too well.

Henchard did not answer, and they went on till they had reached his cottage. 'May I come in?' she said.

'No, no; not to-day,' said Henchard; and she went away; feeling that to caution Farfrae was almost her duty, as it was certainly her strong desire.

As on the Sunday, so on the week-days, Farfrae and Lucetta might have been seen flitting about the town like two butterflies—or rather like a bee and a butterfly in league for life. She seemed to take no pleasure in going anywhere except in her husband's company; and hence when business would not permit him to waste an afternoon she remained indoors waiting for the time to pass till his return, her face being visible to Elizabeth-Jane from her window aloft. The latter, however, did not say to herself that Farfrae should be thankful for such devotion, but, full of her reading, she cited Rosalind's exclamation: 'Mistress, know yourself; down on your knees and thank Heaven fasting for a good man's love.'[2]

She kept her eye upon Henchard also. One day he answered her inquiry for his health by saying that he could not endure Abel Whittle's pitying eyes upon him while they worked together in the yard. 'He is such a fool,' said Henchard, 'that he can never get out of his mind the time when I was master there.'

'I'll come and wimble[3] for you instead of him, if you will allow me,' said she. Her motive on going to the yard was to get an opportunity of observing the general position of affairs on Farfrae's premises now that her stepfather was a workman there. Henchard's threats had alarmed her so much that she wished to see his behaviour when the two were face to face.

For two or three days after her arrival Donald did not make any appearance. Then one afternoon the green door opened, and through came, first Farfrae, and at his heels Lucetta. Donald brought his wife forward without hesitation, it being obvious that he had no suspicion whatever of any antecedents in common between her and the now journeyman hay-trusser.

Henchard did not turn his eyes toward either of the pair, keeping them fixed on the bond he twisted, as if that alone absorbed him. A feeling of delicacy, which ever prompted Farfrae to avoid anything that might seem like triumphing over a fallen rival, led him to keep away from the hay-barn where Henchard and his daughter were working, and to go on to the corn department. Meanwhile Lucetta, never having been informed that Henchard had entered her husband's service, rambled straight on to the barn, where she came suddenly upon Henchard, and gave vent to a little 'Oh!' which the happy and busy Donald was too far off to hear. Henchard, with withering humility of demeanour, touched the brim of his hat to her as Whittle and the rest had done, to which she breathed a dead-alive 'Good afternoon.'

2. Rosalind, the heroine of Shakespeare's *As You Like It*, speaks these words to Phoebe, III.5.57–58.
3. Bind the trusses of hay.

'I beg your pardon, ma'am?' said Henchard, as if he had not heard.

'I said good afternoon,' she faltered.

'O yes, good afternoon, ma'am,' he replied, touching his hat again. 'I am glad to see you, ma'am.' Lucetta looked embarrassed, and Henchard continued: 'For we humble workmen here feel it a great honour that a lady should look in and take an interest in us.'

She glanced at him entreatingly; the sarcasm was too bitter, too unendurable.

'Can you tell me the time, ma'am?' he asked.

'Yes,' she said hastily; 'half-past four.'

'Thank 'ee. An hour and a half longer before we are released from work. Ah, ma'am, we of the lower classes know nothing of the gay leisure that such as you enjoy!'

As soon as she could do so Lucetta left him, nodded and smiled to Elizabeth-Jane, and joined her husband at the other end of the enclosure, where she could be seen leading him away by the outer gates, so as to avoid passing Henchard again. That she had been taken by surprise was obvious. The result of this casual rencounter was that the next morning a note was put into Henchard's hand by the postman.

'Will you,' said Lucetta, with as much bitterness as she could put into a small communication, 'will you kindly undertake not to speak to me in the biting undertones you used to-day, if I walk through the yard at any time? I bear you no ill-will, and I am only too glad that you should have employment of my dear husband; but in common fairness treat me as his wife, and do not try to make me wretched by covert sneers. I have committed no crime, and done you no injury.'

'Poor fool!' said Henchard with fond savagery, holding out the note. 'To know no better than commit herself in writing like this! Why, if I were to show that to her dear husband—pooh!' He threw the letter into the fire.

Lucetta took care not to come again among the hay and corn. She would rather have died than run the risk of encountering Henchard at such close quarters a second time. The gulf between them was growing wider every day. Farfrae was always considerate to his fallen acquaintance; but it was impossible that he should not, by degrees, cease to regard the ex-corn-merchant as more than one of his other workmen. Henchard saw this, and concealed his feelings under a cover of stolidity, fortifying his heart by drinking more freely at the Three Mariners every evening.

Often did Elizabeth-Jane, in her endeavours to prevent his taking other liquor, carry tea to him in a little basket at five o'clock. Arriving one day on this errand she found her stepfather was measuring up clover-seed and rape-seed in the corn-stores on the top floor, and she ascended to him. Each floor had a door opening into the air under a cat-head, from which a chain dangled for hoisting the sacks.

When Elizabeth's head rose through the trap she perceived that the upper door was open, and that her stepfather and Farfrae stood just within it in conversation, Farfrae being nearest the dizzy edge, and Henchard a little way behind. Not to interrupt them she remained on the steps without raising her head any higher. While waiting thus she saw—or fancied she saw, for she had a terror of feeling certain—her stepfather slowly raise his hand to a level behind Farfrae's shoulders, a curious expression taking possession of his face. The young man was quite unconscious of the action, which was so indirect that, if Farfrae had observed it, he might almost have regarded it as an idle outstretching of the arm. But it would have been possible, by a comparatively light touch, to push Farfrae off his balance, and send him head over heels into the air.

Elizabeth felt quite sick at heart on thinking of what this *might* have meant. As soon as they turned she mechanically took the tea to Henchard, left it, and went away. Reflecting, she endeavoured to assure herself that the movement was an idle eccentricity, and no more. Yet, on the other hand, his subordinate position in an establishment where he once had been master might be acting on him like an irritant poison; and she finally resolved to caution Donald.

XXXIV

Next morning, accordingly, she rose at five o'clock and went into the street. It was not yet light; a dense fog prevailed, and the town was as silent as it was dark, except that from the rectangular avenues which framed in the borough there came a chorus of tiny rappings, caused by the fall of water-drops condensed on the boughs; now it was wafted from the West Walk, now from the South Walk; and then from both quarters simultaneously. She moved on to the bottom of Corn Street, and, knowing his time well, waited only a few minutes before she heard the familiar bang of his door, and then his quick walk towards her. She met him at the point where the last tree of the engirding avenue flanked the last house in the street.

He could hardly discern her till, glancing inquiringly, he said, 'What—Miss Henchard—and are ye up so airly?'

She asked him to pardon her for waylaying him at such an unseemly time. 'But I am anxious to mention something,' she said. 'And I wished not to alarm Mrs. Farfrae by calling.'

'Yes?' said he, with the cheeriness of a superior. 'And what may it be? It's very kind of ye, I'm sure.'

She now felt the difficulty of conveying to his mind the exact aspect of possibilities in her own. But she somehow began, and introduced Henchard's name. 'I sometimes fear,' she said with an effort, 'that he may be betrayed into some attempt to—insult you, sir.'

'But we are the best of friends?'

'Or to play some practical joke upon you, sir. Remember that he has been hardly used.'

'But we are quite friendly?'

'Or to do something—that would injure you—hurt you—wound you.' Every word cost her twice its length of pain. And she could see that Farfrae was still incredulous. Henchard, a poor man in his employ, was not to Farfrae's view the Henchard who had ruled him. Yet he was not only the same man, but that man with his sinister qualities, formerly latent, quickened into life by his buffetings.

Farfrae, happy, and thinking no evil, persisted in making light of her fears. Thus they parted, and she went homeward, journeymen now being in the street, waggoners going to the harness-makers for articles left to be repaired, farm-horses going to the shoeing-smiths, and the sons of labour showing themselves generally on the move. Elizabeth entered her lodging unhappily, thinking she had done no good, and only made herself appear foolish by her weak note of warning.

But Donald Farfrae was one of those men upon whom an incident is never absolutely lost. He revised impressions from a subsequent point of view, and the impulsive judgment of the moment was not always his permanent one. The vision of Elizabeth's earnest face in the rimy[1] dawn came back to him several times during the day. Knowing the solidity of her character he did not treat her hints altogether as idle sounds.

But he did not desist from a kindly scheme on Henchard's account that engaged him just then; and when he met Lawyer Joyce, the town-clerk, later in the day, he spoke of it as if nothing had occurred to damp it.

'About that little seedsman's shop,' he said; 'the shop overlooking the churchyard, which is to let. It is not for myself I want it, but for our unlucky fellow-townsman Henchard. It would be a new beginning for him, if a small one; and I have told the Council that I would head a private subscription among them to set him up in it—that I would be fifty pounds, if they would make up the other fifty among them.'

'Yes, yes; so I've heard; and there's nothing to say against it for that matter,' the town-clerk replied, in his plain, frank way. 'But, Farfrae, others see what you don't. Henchard hates 'ee—ay, hates 'ee; and 'tis right that you should know it. To my knowlege he was at the Three Mariners last night, saying in public that about you which a man ought not to say about another.'

'Is that so—ah, is that so?' said Farfrae, looking down. 'Why should he do it?' added the young man bitterly; 'what harm have I done him that he should try to wrong me?'

'God only knows,' said Joyce, lifting his eyebrows. 'It shows much long-suffering in you to put up with him, and keep him in your employ.'

1. Frosty.

'But I cannet discharge a man who was once a good friend to me? How can I forget that when I came here 'twas he enabled me to make a footing for mysel'? No, no. As long as I've a day's wark to offer he shall do it if he chooses. 'Tis not I who will deny him such a little as that. But I'll drop the idea of establishing him in a shop till I can think more about it.'

It grieved Farfrae much to give up this scheme. But a damp having been thrown over it by these and other voices in the air, he went and countermanded his orders. The then occupier of the shop was in it when Farfrae spoke to him, and feeling it necessary to give some explanation of his withdrawal from the negotiation Donald mentioned Henchard's name, and stated that the intentions of the Council had been changed.

The occupier was much disappointed, and straightway informed Henchard, as soon as he saw him, that a scheme of the Council for setting him up in a shop had been knocked on the head by Farfrae. And thus out of error enmity grew.

When Farfrae got indoors that evening the tea-kettle was singing on the high hob of the semi-egg-shaped grate. Lucetta, light as a sylph, ran forward and seized his hands, whereupon Farfrae duly kissed her.

'Oh!' she cried playfully, turning to the window. 'See—the blinds are not drawn down, and the people can look in—what a scandal!'

When the candles were lighted, the curtains drawn, and the twain sat at tea, she noticed that he looked serious. Without directly inquiring why she let her eyes linger solicitously on his face.

'Who has called?' he absently asked. 'Any folk for me?'

'No,' said Lucetta. 'What's the matter, Donald?'

'Well—nothing worth talking of,' he responded sadly.

'Then, never mind it. You will get through it. Scotchmen are always lucky.'

'No—not always!' he said, shaking his head gloomily as he contemplated a crumb on the table. 'I know many who have not been so! There was Sandy Macfarlane, who started to America to try his fortune, and he was drowned; and Archibald Leith, he was murdered! And poor Willie Dunbleeze and Maitland Macfreeze—they fell into bad courses, and went the way of all such!'

'Why—you old goosey—I was only speaking in a general sense, of course! You are always so literal. Now when we have finished tea, sing me that funny song about high-heeled shoon and siller tags, and the one-and-forty wooers.'[2]

'No, no. I couldna sing to-night! It's Henchard—he hates me; so that I may not be his friend if I would. I would understand why there should be a wee bit envy; but I cannet see a reason for the whole intensity of what he feels. Now, can you, Lucetta? It is more like old-fashioned rivalry in love than just a bit of rivalry in trade.'

---

2. The song remains unidentified; possibly Lucetta has confused several songs.

Lucetta had grown somewhat wan. 'No,' she replied.

'I give him employment—I cannet refuse it. But neither can I blind myself to the fact that with a man of passions such as his, there is no safe-guard for conduct!'

'What have you heard—O Donald, dearest?' said Lucetta in alarm. The words on her lips were 'anything about me?'—but she did not utter them. She could not, however, suppress her agitation, and her eyes filled with tears.

'No, no—it is not so serious as ye fancy,' declared Farfrae soothingly; though he did not know its seriousness so well as she.

'I wish you would do what we have talked of,' mournfully remarked Lucetta. 'Give up business, and go away from here. We have plenty of money, and why should we stay?'

Farfrae seemed seriously disposed to discuss this move, and they talked thereon till a visitor was announced. Their neighbour Alderman Vatt came in.

'You've heard, I suppose, of poor Doctor Chalkfield's death? Yes—died this afternoon at five,' said Mr. Vatt. Chalkfield was the Councilman who had succeeded to the Mayoralty in the preceding November.

Farfrae was sorry at the intelligence, and Mr. Vatt continued: 'Well, we know he's been going some days, and as his family is well provided for we must take it all as it is. Now I have called to ask 'ee this—quite privately. If I should nominate 'ee to succeed him, and there should be no particular opposition, will 'ee accept the chair?'

'But there are folk whose turn is before mine; and I'm over young, and may be thought pushing!' said Farfrae after a pause.

'Not at all. I don't speak for myself only, several have named it. You won't refuse?'

'We thought of going away,' interposed Lucetta, looking at Farfrae anxiously.

'It was only a fancy,' Farfrae murmured. 'I wouldna refuse if it is the wish of a respectable majority in the Council.'

'Very well, then, look upon yourself as elected. We have had older men long enough.'

When he was gone Farfrae said musingly, 'See now how it's ourselves that are ruled by the Powers above us! We plan this, but we do that. If they want to make me Mayor I will stay, and Henchard must rave as he will.'

From this evening onward Lucetta was very uneasy. If she had not been imprudence incarnate she would not have acted as she did when she met Henchard by accident a day or two later. It was in the bustle of the market, when no one could readily notice their discourse.

'Michael,' said she, 'I must again ask you what I asked you months ago—to return me any letters or papers of mine that you may have—unless you have destroyed them? You must see how desirable it is that the time at Jersey should be blotted out, for the good of all parties.'

'Why, bless the woman!—I packed up every scrap of your handwriting to give you in the coach—but you never appeared.'

She explained how the death of her aunt had prevented her taking the journey on that day. 'And what became of the parcel then?' she asked.

He could not say—he would consider. When she was gone he recollected that he had left a heap of useless papers in his former dining-room safe—built up in the wall of his old house—now occupied by Farfrae. The letters might have been amongst them.

A grotesque grin shaped itself on Henchard's face. Had that safe been opened?

On the very evening which followed this there was a great ringing of bells in Casterbridge, and the combined brass, wood, catgut, and leather bands played round the town with more prodigality of percussion-notes than ever. Farfrae was Mayor—the two-hundredth odd of a series forming an elective dynasty dating back to the days of Charles I.—and the fair Lucetta was the courted of the town. . . . But, ah! that worm i' the bud[3]—Henchard; what he could tell!

He, in the meantime, festering with indignation at some erroneous intelligence of Farfrae's opposition to the scheme for installing him in the little seed-shop, was greeted with the news of the municipal election (which, by reason of Farfrae's comparative youth and his Scottish nativity—a thing unprecedented in the case—had an interest far beyond the ordinary). The bell-ringing and the band-playing, loud as Tamerlane's trumpet,[4] goaded the downfallen Henchard indescribably: the ousting now seemed to him to be complete.

The next morning he went to the corn-yard as usual, and about eleven o'clock Donald entered through the green door, with no trace of the worshipful about him. The yet more emphatic change of places between him and Henchard which this election had established renewed a slight embarrassment in the manner of the modest younger man; but Henchard showed the front of one who had overlooked all this; and Farfrae met his amenities half-way at once.

'I was going to ask you,' said Henchard, 'about a packet that I may possibly have left in my old safe in the dining-room.' He added particulars.

'If so, it is there now,' said Farfrae. 'I have never opened the safe at all as yet; for I keep ma papers at the bank, to sleep easy o' nights.'

'It was not of much consequence—to me,' said Henchard. 'But I'll call for it this evening, if you don't mind?'

It was quite late when he fulfilled his promise. He had primed himself with grog, as he did very frequently now, and a curl of sardonic

---

3. Concealment, with the power to destroy. The phrase is from Shakespeare's *Twelfth Night*, II.4.110–12: "She never told her love, / But let concealment like a worm i' the bud / Feed on her damask cheek."

4. The Tartar warrior Timur Lenk (1336–1405) conquered the area from Mongolia to the Mediterranean. His army carried huge trumpets, which feature prominently in Handel's opera *Tamerlane* (1724).

humour hung on his lip as he approached the house, as though he were contemplating some terrible form of amusement. Whatever it was, the incident of his entry did not diminish its force, this being his first visit to the house since he had lived there as owner. The ring of the bell spoke to him like the voice of a familiar drudge who had been bribed to forsake him; the movements of the doors were revivals of dead days.

Farfrae invited him into the dining-room, where he at once unlocked the iron safe built into the wall, his, Henchard's safe, made by an ingenious locksmith under his direction. Farfrae drew thence the parcel, and other papers, with apologies for not having returned them.

'Never mind,' said Henchard drily. 'The fact is they are letters mostly. . . . Yes,' he went on, sitting down and unfolding Lucetta's passionate bundle, 'here they be. That ever I should see 'em again! I hope Mrs. Farfrae is well after her exertions of yesterday?'

'She has felt a bit weary; and has gone to bed airly on that account.'

Henchard returned to the letters, sorting them over with interest, Farfrae being seated at the other end of the dining-table. 'You don't forget, of course,' he resumed, 'that curious chapter in the history of my past which I told you of, and that you gave me some assistance in? These letters are, in fact, related to that unhappy business. Though, thank God, it is all over now.'

'What became of the poor woman? 'asked Farfrae.

'Luckily she married, and married well,' said Henchard. 'So that these reproaches she poured out on me do not now cause me any twinges, as they might otherwise have done. . . . Just listen to what an angry woman will say!'

Farfrae, willing to humour Henchard, though quite uninterested, and bursting with yawns, gave well-mannered attention.

'"For me,"' Henchard read, '"there is practically no future. A creature too unconventionally devoted to you—who feels it impossible that she can be wife of any other man; and who is yet no more to you than the first woman you meet in the street—such am I. I quite acquit you of any intention to wrong me, yet you are the door through which wrong has come to me. That in the event of your present wife's death you will place me in her position is a consolation so far as it goes—but how far does it go? Thus I sit here, forsaken by my few acquaintance, and forsaken by you!"'

'That's how she went on to me,' said Henchard, 'acres of words like that, when what had happened was what I could not cure.'

'Yes,' said Farfrae absently, 'it is the way wi' women.' But the fact was that he knew very little of the sex; yet detecting a sort of resemblance in style between the effusions of the woman he worshipped and those of the supposed stranger, he concluded that Aphrodite[5] ever spoke thus, whosesoever the personality she assumed.

---

5. In Greek mythology, the goddess of sexual love.

Henchard unfolded another letter, and read it through likewise, stopping at the subscription as before. 'Her name I don't give,' he said blandly. 'As I didn't marry her, and another man did, I can scarcely do that in fairness to her.'

'Tr-rue, tr-rue,' said Farfrae. 'But why didn't you marry her when your wife Susan died?' Farfrae asked this and the other questions in the comfortably indifferent tone of one whom the matter very remotely concerned.

'Ah—well you may ask that!' said Henchard, the new-moon-shaped grin adumbrating itself again upon his mouth. 'In spite of all her protestations, when I came forward to do so, as in generosity bound, she was not the woman for me.'

'She had already married another—maybe?'

Henchard seemed to think it would be sailing too near the wind to descend further into particulars, and he answered 'Yes.'

'The young lady must have had a heart that bore transplanting very readily!'

'She had, she had,' said Henchard emphatically.

He opened a third and fourth letter, and read. This time he approached the conclusion as if the signature were indeed coming with the rest. But again he stopped short. The truth was that, as may be divined, he had quite intended to effect a grand catastrophe at the end of this drama by reading out the name; he had come to the house with no other thought. But sitting here in cold blood he could not do it. Such a wrecking of hearts appalled even him. His quality was such that he could have annihilated them both in the heat of action; but to accomplish the deed by oral poison was beyond the nerve of his enmity.

XXXV

As Donald stated, Lucetta had retired early to her room because of fatigue. She had, however, not gone to rest, but sat in the bedside chair reading and thinking over the events of the day. At the ringing of the door-bell by Henchard she wondered who it should be that would call at that comparatively late hour. The dining-room was almost under her bedroom; she could hear that somebody was admitted there, and presently the indistinct murmur of a person reading became audible.

The usual time for Donald's arrival upstairs came and passed, yet still the reading and conversation went on. This was very singular. She could think of nothing but that some extraordinary crime had been committed, and that the visitor, whoever he might be, was reading an account of it from a special edition of the *Casterbridge Chronicle*. At last she left the room, and descended the stairs. The dining-room door was ajar, and in the silence of the resting household the voice and the words were recognizable before she reached the lower flight. She stood transfixed. Her own words greeted her in Henchard's voice, like spirits from the grave.

Lucetta leant upon the banister with her cheek against the smooth hand-rail, as if she would make a friend of it in her misery. Rigid in this position, more and more words fell successively upon her ear. But what amazed her most was the tone of her husband. He spoke merely in the accents of a man who made a present of his time.

'One word,' he was saying, as the crackling of paper denoted that Henchard was unfolding yet another sheet. 'Is it quite fair to this young woman's memory to read at such length to a stranger what was intended for your eye alone?'

'Well, yes,' said Henchard. 'By not giving her name I make it an example of all womankind, and not a scandal to one.'

'If I were you I would destroy them,' said Farfrae, giving more thought to the letters than he had hitherto done. 'As another man's wife it would injure the woman if it were known.'

'No, I shall not destroy them,' murmured Henchard, putting the letters away. Then he arose, and Lucetta heard no more.

She went back to her bedroom in a semi-paralyzed state. For very fear she could not undress, but sat on the edge of the bed, waiting. Would Henchard let out the secret in his parting words? Her suspense was terrible. Had she confessed all to Donald in their early acquaintance he might possibly have got over it, and married her just the same—unlikely as it had once seemed; but for her or any one else to tell him now would be fatal.

The door slammed; she could hear her husband bolting it. After looking round in his customary way he came leisurely up the stairs. The spark in her eyes well-nigh went out when he appeared round the bedroom door. Her gaze hung doubtful for a moment, then to her joyous amazement she saw that he looked at her with the rallying smile of one who had just been relieved of a scene that was irksome. She could hold out no longer, and sobbed hysterically.

When he had restored her Farfrae naturally enough spoke of Henchard. 'Of all men he was the least desirable as a visitor,' he said; 'but it is my belief that he's just a bit crazed. He has been reading to me a long lot of letters relating to his past life; and I could do no less than indulge him by listening.'

This was sufficient. Henchard, then, had not told. Henchard's last words to Farfrae, in short, as he stood on the door-step, had been these: 'Well—I'm much obliged to 'ee for listening. I may tell more about her some day.'

Finding this, she was much perplexed as to Henchard's motives in opening the matter at all; for in such cases we attribute to an enemy a power of consistent action which we never find in ourselves or in our friends; and forget that abortive efforts from want of heart are as possible to revenge as to generosity.

Next morning Lucetta remained in bed, meditating how to parry this incipient attack. The bold stroke of telling Donald the truth, dimly conceived, was yet too bold; for she dreaded lest in doing so he, like the rest of the world, should believe that the episode was rather her fault than her misfortune. She decided to employ persuasion—not with Donald, but with the enemy himself. It seemed the only practicable weapon left her as a woman. Having laid her plan she rose, and wrote to him who kept her on these tenterhooks:—

'I overheard your interview with my husband last night, and saw the drift of your revenge. The very thought of it crushes me! Have pity on a distressed woman! If you could see me you would relent. You do not know how anxiety has told upon me lately. I will be at the Ring at the time you leave work—just before the sun goes down. Please come that way. I cannot rest till I have seen you face to face, and heard from your mouth that you will carry this horse-play no further.'

To herself she said, on closing up his appeal: 'If ever tears and pleadings have served the weak to fight the strong, let them do so now!'

With this view she made a toilette which differed from all she had ever attempted before. To heighten her natural attractions had hitherto been the unvarying endeavour of her adult life, and one in which she was no novice. But now she neglected this, and even proceeded to impair the natural presentation. Beyond a natural reason for her slightly drawn look, she had not slept all the previous night, and this had produced upon her pretty though slightly worn features the aspect of a countenance ageing prematurely from extreme sorrow. She selected—as much from want of spirit as design—her poorest, plainest, and longest discarded attire.

To avoid the contingency of being recognized she veiled herself, and slipped out of the house quickly, The sun was resting on the hill like a drop of blood on an eyelid by the time she had got up the road opposite the amphitheatre, which she speedily entered. The interior was shadowy, and emphatic of the absence of every living thing.

She was not disappointed in the fearful hope with which she awaited him. Henchard came over the top, descended, and Lucetta waited breathlessly. But having reached the arena she saw a change in his bearing: he stood still at a little distance from her; she could not think why.

Nor could any one else have known. The truth was that in appointing this spot, and this hour, for the rendezvous, Lucetta had unwittingly backed up her entreaty by the strongest argument she could have used outside words, with this man of moods, glooms, and superstitions. Her figure in the midst of the huge enclosure, the unusual plainness of her dress, her attitude of hope and appeal, so strongly revived in his soul the memory of another ill-used woman who had stood there and thus in bygone days, and had now passed away into her rest, that he was unmanned, and his heart smote him for having attempted reprisals on one of a sex so weak. When he approached her, and before she had spoken a word, her point was half gained.

His manner as he had come down had been one of cynical carelessness; but he now put away his grim half-smile, and said in a kindly subdued tone, 'Good night t'ye. Of course I'm glad to come if you want me.'

'O, thank you,' she said apprehensively.

'I am sorry to see 'ee looking so ill,' he stammered with unconcealed compunction.

She shook her head. 'How can you be sorry,' she asked, 'when you deliberately cause it?'

'What!' said Henchard uneasily. 'Is it anything I have done that has pulled you down like that?'

'It is all your doing,' said she. 'I have no other grief. My happiness would be secure enough but for your threats. O Michael! don't wreck me like this! You might think that you have done enough! When I came here I was a young woman; now I am rapidly becoming an old one. Neither my husband nor any other man will regard me with interest long.'

Henchard was disarmed. His old feeling of supercilious pity for womankind in general was intensified by this suppliant appearing here as the double of the first. Moreover, that thoughtless want of foresight which had led to all her trouble remained with poor Lucetta still; she had come to meet him here in this compromising way without perceiving the risk. Such a woman was very small deer to hunt; he felt ashamed, lost all zest and desire to humiliate Lucetta there and then, and no longer envied Farfrae his bargain. He had married money, but nothing more. Henchard was anxious to wash his hands of the game.

'Well, what do you want me to do?' he said gently. 'I am sure I shall be very willing. My reading of those letters was only a sort of practical joke, and I revealed nothing.'

'To give me back the letters and any papers you may have that breathe of matrimony or worse.'

'So be it. Every scrap shall be yours. . . . But, between you and me, Lucetta, he is sure to find out something of the matter, sooner or later.'

'Ah!' she said with eager tremulousness; 'but not till I have proved myself a faithful and deserving wife to him, and then he may forgive me everything!'

Henchard silently looked at her: he almost envied Farfrae such love as that, even now. 'H'm—I hope so,' he said. 'But you shall have the letters without fail. And your secret shall be kept. I swear it.'

'How good you are!—how shall I get them?'

He reflected, and said he would send them the next morning. 'Now don't doubt me,' he added. 'I can keep my word.'[1]

---

1. In the serial versions, this chapter concluded with a scene in which Farfrae met Henchard with Lucetta, but without recognizing her.

XXXVI

Returning from her appointment Lucetta saw a man waiting by the lamp nearest to her own door. When she stopped to go in he came and spoke to her. It was Jopp.

He begged her pardon for addressing her. But he had heard that Mr. Farfrae had been applied to by a neighbouring corn-merchant to recommend a working partner; if so, he wished to offer himself. He could give good security, and had stated as much to Mr. Farfrae in a letter; but he would feel much obliged if Lucetta would say a word in his favour to her husband.

'It is a thing I know nothing about,' said Lucetta coldly.

'But you can testify to my trustworthiness better than anybody, ma'am,' said Jopp. 'I was in Jersey several years, and knew you there by sight.'

'Indeed,' she replied. 'But I knew nothing of you.'

'I think, ma'am, that a word or two from you would secure for me what I covet very much,' he persisted.

She steadily refused to have anything to do with the affair, and cutting him short, because of her anxiety to get indoors before her husband should miss her, left him on the pavement.

He watched her till she had vanished, and then went home. When he got there he sat down in the fireless chimney corner looking at the iron dogs,[1] and the wood laid across them for heating the morning kettle. A movement upstairs disturbed him, and Henchard came down from his bedroom, where he seemed to have been rummaging boxes.

'I wish,' said Henchard, 'you would do me a service, Jopp, now — to-night, I mean, if you can. Leave this at Mrs. Farfrae's for her. I should take it myself, of course, but I don't wish to be seen there.'

He handed a package in brown paper, sealed. Henchard had been as good as his word. Immediately on coming indoors he had searched over his few belongings; and every scrap of Lucetta's writing that he possessed was here. Jopp indifferently expressed his willingness.

'Well, how have ye got on to-day?' his lodger asked. 'Any prospect of an opening?'

'I am afraid not,' said Jopp, who had not told the other of his application to Farfrae.

'There never will be in Casterbridge,' declared Henchard decisively. 'You must roam further afield.' He said good-night to Jopp, and returned to his own part of the house.

Jopp sat on till his eyes were attracted by the shadow of the candle-snuff[2] on the wall, and looking at the original he found that it had

---

1. Andirons: iron bars used to support burning wood in a fireplace.
2. The burned wick of a candle.

formed itself into a head like a red-hot cauliflower. Henchard's packet next met his gaze. He knew there had been something of the nature of wooing between Henchard and the now Mrs. Farfrae; and his vague ideas on the subject narrowed themselves down to these: Henchard had a parcel belonging to Mrs. Farfrae, and he had reasons for not returning that parcel to her in person. What could be inside it? So he went on and on till, animated by resentment at Lucetta's haughtiness, as he thought it, and curiosity to learn if there were any weak sides to this transaction with Henchard, he examined the package. The pen and all its relations being awkward tools in Henchard's hands, he said affixed the seals without an impression, it never occurring to him that the efficacy of such a fastening depended on this. Jopp was far less of a tyro;[3] he lifted one of the seals with his penknife, peeped in at the end thus opened, saw that the bundle consisted of letters; and, having satisfied himself thus far, sealed up the end again by simply softening the wax with the candle, and went off with the parcel as requested.

His path was by the river-side at the foot of the town. Coming into the light at the bridge which stood at the end of High Street he beheld lounging thereon Mother Cuxsom and Nance Mockridge.

'We be just going down Mixen Lane way, to look into Peter's Finger[4] afore creeping to bed,' said Mrs. Cuxsom. 'There's a fiddle and tambourine going on there. Lord, what's all the world—do ye come along too, Jopp—'twon't hinder ye five minutes.'

Jopp had mostly kept himself out of this company, but present circumstances made him somewhat more reckless than usual, and without many words he decided to go to his destination that way.

Though the upper part of Durnover was mainly composed of a curious congeries[5] of barns and farmsteads, there was a less picturesque side to the parish. This was Mixen Lane, now in great part pulled down.

Mixen Lane was the Adullam[6] of all the surrounding villages. It was the hiding-place of those who were in distress, and in debt, and trouble of every kind. Farm-labourers and other peasants, who combined a little poaching with their farming, and a little brawling and bibbing[7] with their poaching, found themselves sooner or later in Mixen Lane. Rural mechanics too idle to mechanize, rural servants too rebellious to serve, drifted or were forced into Mixen Lane.

The lane and its surrounding thicket of thatched cottages stretched out like a spit into the moist and misty lowland. Much that was sad,

---

3. Novice.
4. The name is a corruption of the name of a church, St Peter-ad-Vincula (St. Peter in Chains).
5. Collection.
6. Town near which David hid in a cave to escape Saul's anger: "And every one that was in distress, and every one that was in debt, and every one that was discontented, gathered themselves unto him." See 1 Samuel 22.1–2.
7. Drinking.

much that was low, some things that were baneful, could be seen in Mixen Lane. Vice ran freely in and out certain of the doors of the neighbourhood; recklessness dwelt under the roof with the crooked chimney; shame in some bow-windows; theft (in times of privation) in the thatched and mud-walled houses by the sallows.[8] Even slaughter had not been altogether unknown here. In a block of cottages up an alley there might have been erected an altar to disease in years gone by. Such was Mixen Lane in the times when Henchard and Farfrae were Mayors.

Yet this mildewed leaf in the sturdy and flourishing Casterbridge plant lay close to the open country; not a hundred yards from a row of noble elms, and commanding a view across the moor of airy uplands and corn-fields, and mansions of the great. A brook divided the moor from the tenements, and to outward view there was no way across it—no way to the houses but round about by the road. But under every householder's stairs there was kept a mysterious plank nine inches wide; which plank was a secret bridge.

If you, as one of those refugee householders, came in from business after dark—and this was the business time here—you stealthily crossed the moor, approached the border of the aforesaid brook, and whistled opposite the house to which you belonged. A shape thereupon made its appearance on the other side bearing the bridge on end against the sky; it was lowered; you crossed, and a hand helped you to land yourself, together with the pheasants and hares gathered from neighbouring manors. You sold them slily the next morning, and the day after you stood before the magistrates with the eyes of all your sympathizing neighbours concentrated on your back. You disappeared for a time; then you were again found quietly living in Mixen Lane.

Walking along the lane at dusk the stranger was struck by two or three peculiar features therein. One was an intermittent rumbling from the back premises of the inn half-way up; this meant a skittle alley. Another was the extensive prevalence of whistling in the various domiciles—a piped note of some kind coming from nearly every open door. Another was the frequency of white aprons over dingy gowns among the women around the doorways. A white apron is a suspicious vesture in situations where spotlessness is difficult; moreover, the industry and cleanliness which the white apron expressed were belied by the postures and gaits of the women who wore it—their knuckles being mostly on their hips (an attitude which lent them the aspect of two-handled mugs), and their shoulders against door-posts; while there was a curious alacrity in the turn of each honest woman's head upon her neck and in the twirl of her honest eyes, at any noise resembling a masculine footfall along the lane.

Yet amid so much that was bad needy respectability also found a home. Under some of the roofs abode pure and virtuous souls whose

8. Willows.

presence there was due to the iron hand of necessity, and to that alone. Families from decayed villages—families of that once bulky, but now nearly extinct, section of village society called 'liviers,' or lifeholders[9]— copyholders[1] and others, whose roof-trees[2] had fallen for some reason or other, compelling them to quit the rural spot that had been their home for generations—came here, unless they chose to lie under a hedge by the wayside.

The inn called Peter's Finger was the church of Mixen Lane.

It was centrally situate, as such places should be, and bore about the same social relation to the Three Mariners as the latter bore to the King's Arms. At first sight the inn was so respectable as to be puzzling. The front door was kept shut, and the step was so clean that evidently but few persons entered over its sanded surface. But at the corner of the public-house was an alley, a mere slit, dividing it from the next building. Half-way up the alley was a narrow door, shiny and paintless from the rub of infinite hands and shoulders. This was the actual entrance to the inn.

A pedestrian would be seen abstractedly passing along Mixen Lane; and then, in a moment, he would vanish, causing the gazer to blink like Ashton at the disappearance of Ravenswood.[3] That abstracted pedestrian had edged into the slit by the adroit fillip of his person sideways; from the slit he edged into the tavern by a similar exercise of skill.

The company at the Three Mariners were persons of quality in comparison with the company which gathered here; though it must be admitted that the lowest fringe of the Mariner's party touched the crest of Peter's at points. Waifs and strays of all sorts loitered about here. The landlady was a virtuous woman who years ago had been unjustly sent to gaol as an accessory to something or other after the fact. She underwent her twelvemonth, and had worn a martyr's countenance ever since, except at times of meeting the constable who apprehended her, when she winked her eye.

To this house Jopp and his acquaintances had arrived. The settles on which they sat down were thin and tall, their tops being guyed by pieces of twine to hooks in the ceiling; for when the guests grew boisterous the settles would rock and overturn without some such security. The thunder of bowls echoed from the backyard; swingels[4] hung behind the blower of the chimney;[5] and ex-poachers and ex-gamekeepers, whom squires had persecuted without a cause, sat elbowing each other—men who in

---

9. Tenants whose leases were held for the duration of the lives of specified persons, usually three generations of a family.
1. Tenants whose tenure was held according to a copy of the court-roll, the record of rents on a manor. Their tenancy was technically at the will of the lord of the manor, but in practice it was relatively secure.
2. Main beams in the ridge of a roof.
3. In Walter Scott's *The Bride of Lammermoor* (1819), Ashton sees his rival, Ravenswood, disappear suddenly into quicksand (chapter 35).
4. Cudgels or flails.
5. Sheet of metal or cloth to control the draught of a fire.

past times had met in fights under the moon, till lapse of sentences on the one part, and loss of favour and expulsion from service on the other, brought them here together to a common level, where they sat calmly discussing old times.

'Dos't mind how you could jerk a trout ashore with a bramble, and not ruffle the stream, Charl?' a deposed keeper was saying. ''Twas at that I caught 'ee once, if you can mind?'

'That can I. But the worst larry for me was that pheasant business at Yalbury Wood. Your wife swore false that time, Joe—O, by Gad, she did—there's no denying it.'

'How was that?' asked Jopp.

'Why—Joe closed wi' me, and we rolled down together, close to his garden hedge. Hearing the noise, out ran his wife with the oven pyle,[6] and it being dark under the trees she couldn't see which was uppermost. "Where beest thee, Joe, under or top?" she screeched. "O—under, by Gad!" says he. She then began to rap down upon my skull, back, and ribs with the pyle till we'd roll over again. "Where beest now, dear Joe, under or top?" she'd scream again. By George, 'twas through her I was took! And then when we got up in hall she sware that the cock pheasant was one of her rearing, when 'twas not your bird at all, Joe; 'twas Squire Brown's bird—that's whose 'twas—one that we'd picked off as we passed his wood, an hour afore. It did hurt my feelings to be so wronged! . . . Ah well—'tis over now.'

'I might have had 'ee days afore that,' said the keeper. 'I was within a few yards of 'ee dozens of times, with a sight more of birds than that poor one.'

'Yes—'tis not our greatest doings that the world gets wind of,' said the furmity-woman, who, lately settled in this purlieu, sat among the rest. Having travelled a great deal in her time she spoke with cosmopolitan largeness of idea. It was she who presently asked Jopp what was the parcel he kept so snugly under his arm.

'Ah, therein lies a grand secret,' said Jopp. 'It is the passion of love. To think that a woman should love one man so well, and hate another so unmercifully.'

'Who's the object of your meditation, sir?'

'One that stands high in this town. I'd like to shame her! Upon my life, 'twould be as good as a play to read her love-letters, the proud piece of silk and wax-work! For 'tis her love-letters that I've got here.'

'Love-letters? then let's hear 'em, good soul,' said Mother Cuxsom. 'Lord, do ye mind, Richard, what fools we used to be when we were younger? Getting a schoolboy to write ours for us; and giving him a penny, do ye mind, not to tell other folks what he'd put inside, do ye mind?'

By this time Jopp had pushed his finger under the seals, and unfastened the letters, tumbling them over and picking up one here and there

---

6. Long wooden pole with a flat piece at one end, used to place loaves or pies into the oven.

at random, which he read aloud. These passages soon began to uncover the secret which Lucetta had so earnestly hoped to keep buried, though the epistles, being allusive only, did not make it altogether plain.

'Mrs. Farfrae wrote that!' said Nance Mockridge. ''Tis a humbling thing for us, as respectable women, that one of the same sex could do it. And now she's vowed herself to another man!'

'So much the better for her,' said the aged furmity-woman. 'Ah, I saved her from a real bad marriage, and she's never been the one to thank me.'

'I say, what a good foundation for a skimmity-ride,'[7] said Nance.

'True,' said Mrs. Cuxsom, reflecting. ''Tis as good a ground for a skimmity-ride as ever I knowed; and it ought not to be wasted. The last one seen in Casterbridge must have been ten years ago, if a day.'

At this moment there was a shrill whistle, and the landlady said to the man who had been called Charl, ''Tis Jim coming in. Would ye go and let down the bridge for me?'

Without replying Charl and his comrade Joe rose, and receiving a lantern from her went out at the back door and down the garden-path, which ended abruptly at the edge of the stream already mentioned. Beyond the stream was the open moor, from which a clammy breeze smote upon their faces as they advanced. Taking up the board that had lain in readiness one of them lowered it across the water, and the instant its further end touched the ground footsteps entered upon it, and there appeared from the shade a stalwart man with straps round his knees, a double-barrelled gun under his arm and some birds slung up behind him. They asked him if he had had much luck.

'Not much,' he said indifferently. 'All safe inside?'

Receiving a reply in the affirmative he went on inwards, the others withdrawing the bridge and beginning to retreat in his rear. Before, however, they had entered the house a cry of 'Ahoy' from the moor led them to pause.

The cry was repeated. They pushed the lantern into an outhouse, and went back to the brink of the stream.

'Ahoy—is this the way to Casterbridge?' said some one from the other side.

'Not in particular,' said Charl. 'There's a river afore 'ee.'

'I don't care—here's for through it!' said the man in the moor. 'I've had travelling enough for to-day.'

'Stop a minute, then,' said Charl, finding that the man was no enemy. 'Joe, bring the plank and lantern; here's somebody that's lost his way. You should have kept along the turnpike road, friend, and not have strook across here.'

<hr>

7. A skimmington-ride: a procession with effigies and rough music, used to express disapproval at adultery or at the ill-treatment by a husband or wife of the partner. The custom was made illegal in 1882 but continued for some time after.

'I should—as I see now. But I saw a light here, and says I to myself, that's an outlying house, depend on't.'

The plank was now lowered; and the stranger's form shaped itself from the darkness. He was a middle-aged man, with hair and whiskers prematurely grey, and a broad and genial face. He had crossed on the plank without hesitation, and seemed to see nothing odd in the transit. He thanked them, and walked between them up the garden. 'What place is this?' he asked, when they reached the door.

'A public-house.'

'Ah. Perhaps it will suit me to put up at. Now then, come in and wet your whistle at my expense for the lift over you have given me.'

They followed him into the inn, where the increased light exhibited him as one who would stand higher in an estimate by the eye than in one by the ear. He was dressed with a certain clumsy richness—his coat being furred, and his head covered by a cap of seal-skin, which, though the nights were chilly, must have been warm for the daytime, spring being somewhat advanced. In his hand he carried a small mahogany case, strapped, and clamped with brass.

Apparently surprised at the kind of company which confronted him through the kitchen door, he at once abandoned his idea of putting up at the house; but taking the situation lightly, he called for glasses of the best, paid for them as he stood in the passage, and turned to proceed on his way by the front door. This was barred, and while the landlady was unfastening it the conversation about the skimmington was continued in the sitting-room, and reached his ears.

'What do they mean by a "skimmity-ride"?' he asked.

'O, sir!' said the landlady, swinging her long earrings with deprecating modesty; ''tis a' old foolish thing they do in these parts when a man's wife is—well, not too particularly his own. But as a respectable householder I don't encourage it.'

'Still, are they going to do it shortly? It is a good sight to see, I suppose?'

'Well, sir!' she simpered. And then, bursting into naturalness, and glancing from the corner of her eye, ''Tis the funniest thing under the sun! And it costs money.'

'Ah! I remember hearing of some such thing. Now I shall be in Casterbridge for two or three weeks to come, and should not mind seeing the performance. Wait a moment.' He turned back, entered the sitting-room, and said, 'Here, good folks; I should like to see the old custom you are talking of, and I don't mind being something towards it—take that.' He threw a sovereign on the table and returned to the landlady at the door, of whom, having inquired the way into the town, he took his leave.

'There were more where that one came from,' said Charl, when the sovereign had been taken up and handed to the landlady for safe keeping. 'By George! we ought to have got a few more while we had him here.'

'No no,' answered the landlady. 'This is a respectable house, thank God! And I'll have nothing done but what's honourable.'

'Well,' said Jopp; 'now we'll consider the business begun, and will soon get it in train.'

'We will!' said Nance. 'A good laugh warms my heart more than a cordial, and that's the truth on't.'

Jopp gathered up the letters, and it being now somewhat late he did not attempt to call at Farfrae's with them that night. He reached home, sealed them up as before, and delivered the parcel at its address next morning. Within an hour its contents were reduced to ashes by Lucetta, who, poor soul! was inclined to fall down on her knees in thankfulness that at last no evidence remained of the unlucky episode with Henchard in her past. For though hers had been rather the laxity of inadvertence than of intention, that episode, if known, was not the less likely to operate fatally between herself and her husband.

XXXVII

Such was the state of things when the current affairs of Casterbridge were interrupted by an event of such magnitude that its influence reached to the lowest social stratum there, stirring the depths of its society simultaneously with the preparations for the skimmington. It was one of those excitements which, when they move a country town, leave a permanent mark upon its chronicles, as a warm summer permanently marks the ring in the tree-trunk corresponding to its date.

A Royal Personage[1] was about to pass through the borough on his course further west, to inaugurate an immense engineering work out that way. He had consented to halt half-an-hour or so in the town, and to receive an address from the corporation of Casterbridge, which, as a representative centre of husbandry, wished thus to express its sense of the great services he had rendered to agricultural science and economics, by his zealous promotion of designs for placing the art of farming on a more scientific footing.

Royalty had not been seen in Casterbridge since the days of the third King George,[2] and then only by candlelight for a few minutes, when that monarch, on a night-journey, had stopped to change horses at the King's Arms. The inhabitants therefore decided to make a thorough *fête carillonnée*[3] of the unwonted occasion. Half-an-hour's pause was not long, it is true; but much might be done in it by a judicious grouping of incidents, above all, if the weather were fine.

The address was prepared on parchment by an artist who was handy

---

1. Prince Albert visited Dorchester in July 1849, shortly after the period in which the novel is set.
2. King George III (reigned 1760–1820) often passed through Dorchester on his way to spend the summer months in Weymouth.
3. Solemn festival, marked by bell-ringing (from the French).

at ornamental lettering, and was laid on with the best gold-leaf and colours that the sign-painter had in his shop. The Council met on the Tuesday before the appointed day, to arrange the details of the procedure. While they were sitting, the door of the Council Chamber standing open, they heard a heavy footstep coming up the stairs. It advanced along the passage, and Henchard entered the room, in clothes of frayed and threadbare shabbiness, the very clothes which he had used to wear in the primal days when he had sat among them.

'I have a feeling,' he said, advancing to the table and laying his hand upon the green cloth, 'that I should like to join ye in this reception of our illustrious visitor. I suppose I could walk with the rest?'

Embarrassed glances were exchanged by the Council, and Grower nearly ate the end of his quill-pen off, so gnawed he it during the silence. Farfrae the young Mayor, who by virtue of his office sat in the large chair, intuitively caught the sense of the meeting, and as spokesman was obliged to utter it, glad as he would have been that the duty should have fallen to another tongue.

'I hardly see that it would be proper, Mr. Henchard,' said he. 'The Council are the Council, and as ye are no longer one of the body, there would be an irregularity in the proceeding. If ye were included, why not others?'

'I have a particular reason for wishing to assist at the ceremony.'

Farfrae looked round. 'I think I have expressed the feeling of the Council,' he said.

'Yes, yes,' from Dr. Bath, Lawyer Long, Alderman Tubber, and several more.

'Then I am not to be allowed to have anything to do with it officially?'

'I am afraid so; it is out of the question, indeed. But of course you can see the doings full well, such as they are to be, like the rest of the spectators.'

Henchard did not reply to that very obvious suggestion, and, turning on his heel, went away.

It had been only a passing fancy of his, but opposition crystallized it into a determination. 'I'll welcome his Royal Highness, or nobody shall!' he went about saying. 'I am not going to be sat upon by Farfrae, or any of the rest of the paltry crew! You shall see.'

The eventful morning was bright, a full-faced sun confronting early window-gazers eastward, and all perceived (for they were practised in weather-lore) that there was permanence in the glow. Visitors soon began to flock in from county houses, village, remote copses, and lonely uplands, the latter in oiled boots and tilt bonnets,[4] to see the reception, or if not to see it, at any rate to be near it. There was hardly a workman in the town who did not put a clean shirt on. Solomon Longways,

---

4. Bonnets shaped like the covering of a wagon.

Christopher Coney, Buzzford, and the rest of that fraternity, showed their sense of the occasion by advancing their customary eleven o'clock pint to half-past ten; from which they found a difficulty in getting back to the proper hour for several days.

Henchard had determined to do no work that day. He primed himself in the morning with a glass of rum, and walking down the street met Elizabeth-Jane, whom he had not seen for a week. 'It was lucky,' he said to her, 'my twenty-one years had expired before this came on, or I should never have had the nerve to carry it out.'

'Carry out what?' said she, alarmed.

'This welcome I am going to give our Royal visitor.'

She was perplexed. 'Shall we go and see it together?' she said.

'See it! I have other fish to fry. You see it. It will be worth seeing!'

She could do nothing to elucidate this, and decked herself out with a heavy heart. As the appointed time drew near she got sight again of her stepfather. She thought he was going to the Three Mariners; but no, he elbowed his way through the gay throng to the shop of Woolfrey, the draper. She waited in the crowd without.

In a few minutes he emerged, wearing, to her surprise, a brilliant rosette, while more surprising still, in his hand he carried a flag of somewhat homely construction, formed by tacking one of the small Union Jacks, which abounded in the town to-day, to the end of a deal wand— probably the roller from a piece of calico. Henchard rolled up his flag on the doorstep, put it under his arm, and went down the street.

Suddenly the taller members of the crowd turned their heads, and the shorter stood on tiptoe. It was said that the Royal *cortège*[5] approached. The railway[6] had stretched out an arm towards Casterbridge at this time, but had not reached it by several miles as yet; so that the intervening distance, as well as the remainder of the journey, was to be traversed by road in the old fashion. People thus waited—the county families in their carriages, the masses on foot—and watched the far-stretching London highway to the ringing of bells and chatter of tongues.

From the background Elizabeth-Jane watched the scene. Some seats had been arranged from which ladies could witness the spectacle, and the front seat was occupied by Lucetta, the Mayor's wife, just at present. In the road under her eyes stood Henchard. She appeared so bright and pretty that, as it seemed, he was experiencing the momentary weakness of wishing for her notice. But he was far from attractive to a woman's eye, ruled as that is so largely by the superficies of things. He was not only a journeyman, unable to appear as he formerly had appeared, but he disdained to appear as well as he might. Everybody else, from the

---

5. Procession (from the French).
6. The railway reached Dorchester in 1847; Hardy has backdated the visit to fit the time-scheme of the novel.

Mayor to the washerwoman, shone in new vesture according to means; but Henchard had doggedly retained the fretted and weather-beaten garments of bygone years.

Hence, alas, this occurred: Lucetta's eyes slid over him to this side and to that without anchoring on his features—as gaily dressed women's eyes will too often do on such occasions. Her manner signified quite plainly that she meant to know him in public no more.

But she was never tired of watching Donald, as he stood in animated converse with his friends a few yards off, wearing round his young neck the official gold chain with great square links, like that round the Royal unicorn.[7] Every trifling emotion that her husband showed as he talked had its reflex on her face and lips, which moved in little duplicates to his. She was living his part rather than her own, and cared for no one's situation but Farfrae's that day.

At length a man stationed at the furthest turn of the high road, namely, on the second bridge of which mention has been made, gave a signal; and the Corporation in their robes proceeded from the front of the Town Hall to the archway erected at the entrance to the town. The carriages containing the Royal visitor and his suite arrived at the spot in a cloud of dust, a procession was formed, and the whole came on to the Town Hall at a walking pace.

This spot was the centre of interest. There were a few clear yards in front of the Royal carriage, sanded; and into this space a man stepped before any one could prevent him. It was Henchard. He had unrolled his private flag, and removing his hat he staggered to the side of the slowing vehicle, waving the Union Jack to and fro with his left hand, while he blandly held out his right to the Illustrious Personage.

All the ladies said with bated breath, 'O, look there!' and Lucetta was ready to faint. Elizabeth-Jane peeped through the shoulders of those in front, saw what it was, and was terrified; and then her interest in the spectacle as a strange phenomenon got the better of her fear.

Farfrae, with Mayoral authority, immediately rose to the occasion. He seized Henchard by the shoulder, dragged him back, and told him roughly to be off. Henchard's eyes met his, and Farfrae observed the fierce light in them despite his excitement and irritation. For a moment Henchard stood his ground rigidly; then by an unaccountable impulse gave way and retired. Farfrae glanced to the ladies' gallery, and saw that his Calphurnia's cheek was pale.[8]

'Why—it is your husband's old patron!' said Mrs. Blowbody, a lady of the neighbourhood who sat beside Lucetta.

'Patron!' said Donald's wife with quick indignation.

'Do you say the man is an acquaintance of Mr. Farfrae's?' observed

---

7. The unicorn in the Royal coat of arms wears a chain.
8. So Brutus observes of Calphurnia, the wife of Julius Caesar, after her husband has refused to accept the crown offered to him. See Shakespeare's *Julius Caesar*, I.2.186.

Mrs. Bath, the physician's wife, a new-comer to the town through her recent marriage with the doctor.

'He works for my husband,' said Lucetta.

'Oh—is that all? They have been saying to me that it was through him your husband first got a footing in Casterbridge. What stories people will tell!'

'They will indeed. It was not so at all. Donald's genius would have enabled him to get a footing anywhere, without anybody's help! He would have been just the same if there had been no Henchard in the world!'

It was partly Lucetta's ignorance of the circumstances of Donald's arrival which led her to speak thus; partly the sensation that everybody seemed bent on snubbing her at this triumphant time. The incident had occupied but a few moments, but it was necessarily witnessed by the Royal Personage, who, however, with practised tact, affected not to have noticed anything unusual. He alighted, the Mayor advanced, the address was read; the Illustrious Personage replied, then said a few words to Farfrae, and shook hands with Lucetta as the Mayor's wife. The ceremony occupied but a few minutes, and the carriages rattled heavily as Pharaoh's chariots[9] down Corn Street and out upon the Budmouth Road, in continuation of the journey coastward.

In the crowd stood Coney, Buzzford, and Longways. 'Some difference between him now and when he zung at the Dree Mariners,' said the first. ''Tis wonderful how he could get a lady of her quality to go snacks[1] wi' en in such quick time.'

'True. Yet how folk do worship fine clothes! Now there's a better-looking woman than she that nobody notices at all, because she's akin to that hontish[2] fellow Henchard.' Elizabeth

'I could worship ye, Buzz, for saying that,' remarked Nance Mockridge. 'I do like to see the trimming pulled off such Christmas candles. I am quite unequal to the part of villain myself, or I'd gi'e all my small silver to see that lady toppered.[3] . . . And perhaps I shall soon,' she added significantly.

'That's not a noble passiont for a 'oman to keep up,' said Longways.

Nance did not reply, but every one knew what she meant. The ideas diffused by the reading of Lucetta's letters at Peter's Finger had condensed into a scandal, which was spreading like a miasmatic fog through Mixen Lane, and thence up the back streets of Casterbridge.

This mixed assemblage of idlers known to each other presently fell apart into two bands by a process of natural selection, the frequenters of

9. When the Egyptians pursued the Israelites through the Red Sea, the Lord disabled their chariot wheels, so that "they drave them heavily." See Exodus 14.25.
1. Share, or get married.
2. Arrogant (dialect).
3. Brought down.

Peter's Finger going off Mixen Lane-wards, where most of them lived, while Coney, Buzzford, Longways, and that connection remained in the street.

'You know what's brewing down there, I suppose?' said Buzzford mysteriously to the others.

Coney looked at him. 'Not the skimmity-ride?'

Buzzford nodded.

'I have my doubts if it will be carried out,' said Longways. 'If they are getting it up they are keeping it mighty close.'

'I heard they were thinking of it a fortnight ago, at all events.'

'If I were sure o't I'd lay information,' said Longways emphatically. "Tis too rough a joke, and apt to wake riots in towns. We know that the Scotchman is a right enough man, and that his lady has been a right enough 'oman since she came here, and if there was anything wrong about her afore, that's their business, not ours.'

Coney reflected. Farfrae was still liked in the community; but it must be owned that, as the Mayor and man of money, engrossed with affairs and ambitions, he had lost in the eyes of the poorer inhabitants something of that wondrous charm which he had had for them as a light-hearted penniless young man, who sang ditties as readily as the birds in the trees. Hence the anxiety to keep him from annoyance showed not quite the ardour that would have animated it in former days.

'Suppose we make inquiration into it, Christopher,' continued Longways; 'and if we find there's really anything in it, drop a letter to them most concerned, and advise 'em to keep out of the way?'

This course was decided on, and the group separated, Buzzford saying to Coney, 'Come, my ancient friend; let's move on. There's nothing more to see here.'

These well-intentioned ones would have been surprised had they known how ripe the great jocular plot really was. 'Yes, to-night,' Jopp had said to the Peter's party at the corner of Mixen Lane. 'As a wind-up to the Royal visit the hit will be all the more pat by reason of their great elevation to-day.'

To him, at least, it was not a joke, but a retaliation.

XXXVIII

The proceedings had been brief—too brief—to Lucetta, whom an intoxicating *Weltlust*[1] had fairly mastered; but they had brought her a great triumph nevertheless. The shake of the Royal hand still lingered in her fingers; and the chit-chat she had overheard, that her husband might possibly receive the honour of knighthood, though idle to a degree,

---

1. Pleasure in worldy things (from the German).

seemed not the wildest vision; stranger things had occurred to men so good and captivating as her Scotchman was.

After the collision with the Mayor, Henchard had withdrawn behind the ladies' stand; and there he stood, regarding with a stare of abstraction the spot on the lapel of his coat where Farfrae's hand had seized it. He put his own hand there, as if he could hardly realize such an outrage from one whom it had once been his wont to treat with ardent generosity. While pausing in this half-stupefied state the conversation of Lucetta with the other ladies reached his ears; and he distinctly heard her deny him—deny that he had assisted Donald, that he was anything more than a common journeyman.

He moved on homeward, and met Jopp in the archway to the Bull Stake. 'So you've had a snub,' said Jopp.

'And what if I have?' answered Henchard sternly.

'Why, I've had one too, so we are both under the same cold shade.' He briefly related his attempt to win Lucetta's intercession.

Henchard merely heard his story, without taking it deeply in. His own relation to Farfrae and Lucetta overshadowed all kindred ones. He went on saying brokenly to himself, 'She has supplicated to me in her time; and now her tongue won't own me nor her eyes see me! . . . And he—how angry he looked. He drove me back as if I were a bull breaking fence. . . . I took it like a lamb, for I saw it could not be settled there. He can rub brine on a green wound![2] . . . But he shall pay for it, and she shall be sorry. It must come to a tussle—face to face; and then we'll see how a coxcomb[3] can front a man!'

Without further reflection the fallen merchant, bent on some wild purpose, ate a hasty dinner and went forth to find Farfrae. After being injured by him as a rival, and snubbed by him as a journeyman, the crowning degradation had been reserved for this day—that he should be shaken at the collar by him as a vagabond in the face of the whole town.

The crowds had dispersed. But for the green arches which still stood as they were erected Casterbridge life had resumed its ordinary shape. Henchard went down Corn Street till he came to Farfrae's house, where he knocked, and left a message that he would be glad to see his employer at the granaries as soon as he conveniently could come there. Having done this he proceeded round to the back and entered the yard.

Nobody was present, for, as he had been aware, the labourers and carters were enjoying a half-holiday on account of the events of the morning—though the carters would have to return for a short time later on, to feed and litter down the horses. He had reached the granary steps

---

2. Fresh wound. Salt water was used to prevent infection, but Henchard is thinking of the pain of the treatment rather than of its effectiveness.
3. Foolish or conceited person.

and was about to ascend, when he said to himself aloud, 'I'm stronger than he.'

Henchard returned to a shed, where he selected a short piece of rope from several pieces that were lying about; hitching one end of this to a nail, he took the other in his right hand and turned himself bodily round, while keeping his arm against his side; by this contrivance he pinioned the arm effectively. He now went up the ladders to the top floor of the corn-stores.

It was empty except of a few sacks, and at the further end was the door often mentioned, opening under the cathead and chain that hoisted the sacks. He fixed the door open and looked over the sill. There was a depth of thirty or forty feet to the ground; here was the spot on which he had been standing with Farfrae when Elizabeth-Jane had seen him lift his arm, with many misgivings as to what the movement portended.

He retired a few steps into the loft and waited. From this elevated perch his eye could sweep the roofs round about, the upper parts of the luxurious chestnut trees, now delicate in leaves of a week's age, and the drooping boughs of the limes; Farfrae's garden and the green door leading therefrom. In course of time—he could not say how long—that green door opened and Farfrae came through. He was dressed as if for a journey. The low light of the nearing evening caught his head and face when he emerged from the shadow of the wall, warming them to a complexion of flame-colour. Henchard watched him with his mouth firmly set, the squareness of his jaw and the verticality of his profile being unduly marked.

Farfrae came on with one hand in his pocket, and humming a tune in a way which told that the words were most in his mind. They were those of the song he had sung when he arrived years before at the Three Mariners, a poor young man, adventuring for life and fortune, and scarcely knowing whitherward:—

> 'And here's a hand, my trusty fiere,
> And gie's a hand o' thine.'[4]

Nothing moved Henchard like an old melody. He sank back. 'No; I can't do it!' he gasped. 'Why does the infernal fool begin that now!'

At length Farfrae was silent, and Henchard looked out of the loft door. 'Will ye come up here?' he said.

'Ay, man,' said Farfrae. 'I couldn't see ye. What's wrang?'

A minute later Henchard heard his feet on the lowest ladder. He heard him land on the first floor, ascend and land on the second, begin the ascent to the third. And then his head rose through the trap behind.

4. Slightly misquoted from the final verse of Robert Burns's song of friendship, "Auld Lang Syne." A "fiere" is a friend.

'What are you doing up here at this time?' he asked, coming forward. 'Why didn't ye take your holiday like the rest of the men?' He spoke in a tone which had just severity enough in it to show that he remembered the untoward event of the forenoon, and his conviction that Henchard had been drinking.

Henchard said nothing; but going back he closed the stair hatchway, and stamped upon it so that it went tight into its frame; he next turned to the wondering young man, who by this time observed that one of Henchard's arms was bound to his side.

'Now,' said Henchard quietly, 'we stand face to face—man and man. Your money and your fine wife no longer lift 'ee above me as they did but now, and my poverty does not press me down.'

'What does it all mean?' asked Farfrae simply.

'Wait a bit, my lad. You should ha' thought twice before you affront-ed to extremes a man who had nothing to lose. I've stood your rivalry, which ruined me, and your snubbing, which humbled me; but your hustling, that disgraced me, I won't stand!'

Farfrae warmed a little at this. 'Ye'd no business there,' he said.

'As much as any one among ye! What, you forward stripling, tell a man of my age he'd no business there!' The anger-vein swelled in his forehead as he spoke.

'You insulted Royalty, Henchard; and 'twas my duty, as the chief mag-istrate, to stop you.'

'Royalty be damned,' said Henchard. 'I am as loyal as you, come to that!'

'I am not here to argue. Wait till you cool doon, wait till you cool; and you will see things the same way as I do.'

'You may be the one to cool first,' said Henchard grimly. 'Now this is the case. Here be we, in this four-square loft, to finish out that little wres-tle you began this morning. There's the door, forty foot above ground. One of us two puts the other out by that door—the master stays inside. If he likes he may go down afterwards and give the alarm that the other has fallen out by accident—or he may tell the truth—that's his business. As the strongest man I've tied one arm to take no advantage of 'ee. D'ye understand? Then here's at 'ee!'

There was no time for Farfrae to do aught but one thing, to close with Henchard, for the latter had come on at once. It was a wrestling match, the object of each being to give his antagonist a back fall;[5] and on Henchard's part, unquestionably, that it should be through the door.

At the outset Henchard's hold by his only free hand, the right, was on the left side of Farfrae's collar, which he firmly grappled, the latter hold-ing Henchard by his collar with the contrary hand. With his right he

5. Hardy draws here on the report on a wrestling match in an 1829 issue of the *Dorset County Chronicle*.

endeavoured to get hold of his antagonist's left arm, which, however, he could not do, so adroitly did Henchard keep it in the rear as he gazed upon the lowered eyes of his fair and slim antagonist.

Henchard planted the first toe forward, Farfrae crossing him with his; and thus far the struggle had very much the appearance of the ordinary wrestling of those parts. Several minutes were passed by them in this attitude, the pair rocking and writhing like trees in a gale, both preserving an absolute silence. By this time their breathing could be heard. Then Farfrae tried to get hold of the other side of Henchard's collar, which was resisted by the larger man exerting all his force in a wrenching movement, and this part of the struggle ended by his forcing Farfrae down on his knees by sheer pressure of one of his muscular arms. Hampered as he was, however, he could not keep him there, and Farfrae finding his feet again the struggle proceeded as before.

By a whirl Henchard brought Donald dangerously near the precipice; seeing his position the Scotchman for the first time locked himself to his adversary, and all the efforts of that infuriated Prince of Darkness[6]—as he might have been called from his appearance just now—were inadequate to lift or loosen Farfrae for a time. By an extraordinary effort he succeeded at last, though not until they had got far back again from the fatal door. In doing so Henchard contrived to turn Farfrae a complete somersault. Had Henchard's other arm been free it would have been all over with Farfrae then. But again he regained his feet, wrenching Henchard's arm considerably, and causing him sharp pain, as could be seen from the twitching of his face. He instantly delivered the younger man an annihilating turn by the left fore-hip, as it used to be expressed, and following up his advantage thrust him towards the door, never loosening his hold till Farfrae's fair head was hanging over the window-sill, and his arm dangling down outside the wall.

'Now,' said Henchard between his gasps, 'this is the end of what you began this morning. Your life is in my hands.'

'Then take it, take it!' said Farfrae. 'Ye've wished to long enough!'

Henchard looked down upon him in silence, and their eyes met. 'O Farfrae!—that's not true!' he said bitterly. 'God is my witness that no man ever loved another as I did thee at one time. . . . And now—though I came here to kill 'ee, I cannot hurt thee! Go and give me in charge—do what you will—I care nothing for what comes of me!'

He withdrew to the back part of the loft, loosened his arm, and flung himself into a corner upon some sacks, in the abandonment of remorse. Farfrae regarded him in silence; then went to the hatch and descended through it. Henchard would fain have recalled him; but his tongue failed in its task, and the young man's steps died on his ear.

Henchard took his full measure of shame and self-reproach. The

6. Satan.

scenes of his first acquaintance with Farfrae rushed back upon him—
that time when the curious mixture of romance and thrift in the young
man's composition so commanded his heart that Farfrae could play
upon him as on an instrument. So thoroughly subdued was he that he
remained on the sacks in a crouching attitude, unusual for a man, and
for such a man. Its womanliness sat tragically on the figure of so stern a
piece of virility. He heard a conversation below, the opening of the
coach-house door, and the putting in of a horse, but took no notice.

Here he stayed till the thin shades thickened to opaque obscurity, and
the loft-door became an oblong of gray light—the only visible shape
around. At length he arose, shook the dust from his clothes wearily, felt
his way to the hatch, and gropingly descended the steps till he stood in
the yard.

'He thought highly of me once,' he murmured. 'Now he'll hate me
and despise me for ever!'

He became possessed by an overpowering wish to see Farfrae again
that night, and by some desperate pleading to attempt the well-nigh
impossible task of winning pardon for his late mad attack. But as he
walked towards Farfrae's door he recalled the unheeded doings in the
yard while he had lain above in a sort of stupor. Farfrae he remembered
had gone to the stable and put the horse into the gig; while doing so
Whittle had brought him a letter; Farfrae had then said that he would
not go towards Budmouth as he had intended—that he was unexpectedly summoned to Weatherbury, and meant to call at Mellstock on his
way thither, that place lying but one or two miles out of his course.

He must have come prepared for a journey when he first arrived in
the yard, unsuspecting enmity; and he must have driven off (though in
a changed direction) without saying a word to any one on what had
occurred between themselves.

It would therefore be useless to call at Farfrae's house till very late.

There was no help for it but to wait till his return, though waiting was
almost torture to his restless and self-accusing soul. He walked about the
streets and outskirts of the town, lingering here and there till he reached
the stone bridge of which mention has been made, an accustomed halt-
ing-place with him now. Here he spent a long time, the purl[7] of waters
through the weirs meeting his ear, and the Casterbridge lights glimmer-
ing at no great distance off.

While leaning thus upon the parapet his listless attention was awakened by sounds of an unaccustomed kind from the town quarter. They
were a confusion of rhythmical noises, to which the streets added yet
more confusion by encumbering them with echoes. His first incurious
thought that the clangour arose from the town band, engaged in an
attempt to round off a memorable day by a burst of evening harmony,

7. Murmur.

was contradicted by certain peculiarities of reverberation. But inexplic-ability did not rouse him to more than a cursory heed; his sense of degra-dation was too strong for the admission of foreign ideas; and he leant against the parapet as before.

XXXIX

When Farfrae descended out of the loft breathless from his encounter with Henchard, he paused at the bottom to recover himself. He arrived at the yard with the intention of putting the horse into the gig himself (all the men having a holiday), and driving to a village on the Budmouth Road. Despite the fearful struggle he decided still to persevere in his journey, so as to recover himself before going indoors and meeting the eyes of Lucetta. He wished to consider his course in a case so serious.

When he was just on the point of driving off Whittle arrived with a note badly addressed, and bearing the word 'immediate' upon the out-side. On opening it he was surprised to see that it was unsigned. It con-tained a brief request that he would go to Weatherbury that evening about some business which he was conducting there. Farfrae knew noth-ing that could make it pressing; but as he was bent upon going out he yielded to the anonymous request, particularly as he had a call to make at Mellstock which could be included in the same tour. Thereupon he told Whittle of his change of direction, in words which Henchard had overheard; and set out on his way. Farfrae had not directed his man to take the message indoors, and Whittle had not been supposed to do so on his own responsibility.

Now the anonymous letter was a well-intentioned but clumsy con-trivance of Longways and other of Farfrae's men to get him out of the way for the evening, in order that the satirical mummery[1] should fall flat, if it were attempted. By giving open information they would have brought down upon their heads the vengeance of those among their comrades who enjoyed these boisterous old games; and therefore the plan of sending a letter recommended itself by its indirectness.

For poor Lucetta they took no protective measure, believing with the majority there was some truth in the scandal, which she would have to bear as she best might.

It was about eight o'clock, and Lucetta was sitting in the drawing-room alone. Night had set in for more than half an hour, but she had not had the candles lighted, for when Farfrae was away she preferred waiting for him by the firelight, and, if it were not too cold, keeping one of the window-sashes a little way open that the sound of his wheels might reach her ears early. She was leaning back in her chair, in a more hope-ful mood than she had enjoyed since her marriage. The day had been

1. Pantomime.

such a success; and the temporary uneasiness which Henchard's show of effrontery had wrought in her disappeared with the quiet disappearance of Henchard himself under her husband's reproof. The floating evidences of her absurd passion for him, and its consequences, had been destroyed, and she really seemed to have no cause for fear.

The reverie in which these and other subjects mingled was disturbed by a hubbub in the distance, that increased moment by moment. It did not greatly surprise her, the afternoon having been given up to recreation by a majority of the populace since the passage of the Royal equipages. But her attention was at once riveted to the matter by the voice of a maid-servant next door, who spoke from an upper window across the street to some other maid even more elevated than she.

'Which way be they going now?' inquired the first with interest.

'I can't be sure for a moment,' said the second, 'because of the malter's chimbley.[2] O yes—I can see 'em. Well, I declare, I declare!'

'What, what?' from the first, more enthusiastically.

'They are coming up Corn Street after all! They sit back to back!'

'What—two of 'em—are there two figures?'

'Yes. Two images on a donkey, back to back, their elbows tied to one another's! She's facing the head, and he's facing the tail.'

'Is it meant for anybody particular?'

'Well—it mid be. The man has got on a blue coat and kerseymere leggings; he has black whiskers, and a reddish face. 'Tis a stuffed figure, with a falseface.'

The din was increasing now—then it lessened a little.

'There—I shan't see, after all!' cried the disappointed first maid.

'They have gone into a back street—that's all,' said the one who occupied the enviable position in the attic. 'There—now I have got 'em all endways nicely!'

'What's the woman like? Just say, and I can tell in a moment if 'tis meant for one I've in mind.'

'My—why—'tis dressed just as *she* was dressed when she sat in the front seat at the time the play-actors came to the Town Hall!'

Lucetta started to her feet; and almost at the instant the door of the room was quickly and softly opened. Elizabeth-Jane advanced into the firelight.

'I have come to see you,' she said breathlessly. 'I did not stop to knock—forgive me! I see you have not shut your shutters, and the window is open.'

Without waiting for Lucetta's reply she crossed quickly to the window and pulled out one of the shutters. Lucetta glided to her side. 'Let it be—hush!' she said peremptorily, in a dry voice, while she seized Elizabeth-Jane by the hand, and held up her finger. Their intercourse

2. Chimney; a malter or maltster made malt, used in the process of brewing from barley.

had been so low and hurried that not a word had been lost of the conversation without; which had thus proceeded:—

'Her neck is uncovered, and her hair in bands, and her back-comb in place; she's got on a puce silk, and white stockings, and coloured shoes.'

Again Elizabeth-Jane attempted to close the window, but Lucetta held her by main force.

"Tis me!' she said, with a face pale as death. 'A procession—a scandal—an effigy of me, and him!'

The look of Elizabeth betrayed that the latter knew it already.

'Let us shut it out,' coaxed Elizabeth-Jane, noting that the rigid wildness of Lucetta's features were growing yet more rigid and wild with the nearing of the noise and laughter. 'Let us shut it out!'

'It is of no use!' she shrieked out. 'He will see it, won't he? Donald will see it! He is just coming home—and it will break his heart—he will never love me any more—and O, it will kill me—kill me!'

Elizabeth-Jane was frantic now. 'O, can't something be done to stop it?' she cried. 'Is there nobody to do it—not one?'

She relinquished Lucetta's hands, and ran to the door. Lucetta herself, saying recklessly 'I will see it!' turned to the window, threw up the sash, and went out upon the balcony. Elizabeth immediately followed her, and put her arm round her to pull her in. Lucetta's eyes were straight upon the spectacle of the uncanny revel, now advancing rapidly. The numerous lights around the two effigies threw them up into lurid distinctness; it was impossible to mistake the pair for other than the intended victims.

'Come in, come in,' implored Elizabeth; 'and let me shut the window!'

'She's me—she's me—even to the parasol—my green parasol!' cried Lucetta with a wild laugh as she stepped in. She stood motionless for one second—then fell heavily to the floor.

Almost at the instant of her fall the rude music of the skimmington ceased. The roars of sarcastic laughter went off in ripples, and the trampling died out like the rustle of a spent wind. Elizabeth was only indirectly conscious of this; she had rung the bell, and was bending over Lucetta, who remained convulsed on the carpet in the paroxysms of an epileptic seizure. She rang again and again, in vain; the probability being that the servants had all run out of the house to see more of the Dæmonic Sabbath than they could see within.

At last Farfrae's man, who had been agape on the door-step, came up; then the cook. The shutters, hastily pushed to by Elizabeth, were quite closed, a light was obtained, Lucetta carried to her room, and the man sent off for a doctor. While Elizabeth was undressing her she recovered consciousness; but as soon as she remembered what had passed the fit returned.

The doctor arrived with unhoped-for promptitude; he had been standing at his door, like others, wondering what the uproar meant. As soon as he saw the unhappy sufferer he said, in answer to Elizabeth's mute appeal, 'This is serious.'

'It is a fit,' Elizabeth said.

'Yes. But a fit in the present state of her health means mischief. You must send at once for Mr. Farfrae. Where is he?'

'He has driven into the country, sir,' said the parlour-maid; 'to some place on the Budmouth Road. He's likely to be back soon.'

'Never mind; he must be sent for, in case he should not hurry.' The doctor returned to the bedside again. The man was despatched, and they soon heard him clattering out of the yard at the back.

Meanwhile Mr. Benjamin Grower, that prominent burgess of whom mention has been already made, hearing the din of cleavers, tongs, tambourines, kits, crouds, humstrums, serpents,[3] rams'-horns, and other historical kinds of music as he sat indoors in the High Street, had put on his hat and gone out to learn the cause. He came to the corner above Farfrae's, and soon guessed the nature of the proceedings; for being a native of the town he had witnessed such rough jests before. His first move was to search hither and thither for the constables; there were two in the town, shrivelled men whom he ultimately found in hiding up an alley yet more shrivelled than usual, having some not ungrounded fears that they might be roughly handled if seen.

'What can we two poor lammigers do against such a multitude!' expostulated Stubberd, in answer to Mr. Grower's chiding. ''Tis tempting 'em to commit *felo de se*[4] upon us, and that would be the death of the perpetrator; and we wouldn't be the cause of a fellow-creature's death on no account, not we!'

'Get some help, then! Here, I'll come with you. We'll see what a few words of authority can do. Quick now; have you got your staves?'[5]

'We didn't want the folk to notice us as law officers, being so short-handed, sir; so we pushed our Gover'ment staves up this water-pipe.'

'Out with 'em, and come along, for Heaven's sake! Ah, here's Mr. Blowbody; that's lucky.' (Blowbody was the third of the three borough magistrates.)

'Well, what's the row?' said Blowbody. 'Got their names—hey?'

'No. Now,' said Grower to one of the constables, 'you go with Mr. Blowbody round by the Old Walk and come up the street; and I'll go with Stubberd straight forward. By this plan we shall have 'em between us. Get their names only: no attack or interruption.'

---

3. *Tongs*: kitchen tongs; *kits*: small three-stringed fiddles; *crouds*: ancient stringed instruments, combining elements of violin and lyre; *humstrums*: hurdy-gurdies, crude stringed instruments played by turning a handle; *serpents*: bass wind instruments made of wood and formed into a coil shape.
4. Suicide (Anglo-Latin); Stubberd means to say "murder."
5. Sticks with official markings issued to local constables.

Thus they started. But as Stubberd with Mr. Grower advanced into Corn Street, whence the sounds had proceeded, they were surprised that no procession could be seen. They passed Farfrae's, and looked to the end of the street. The lamp flames waved, the Walk trees soughed, a few loungers stood about with their hands in their pockets. Everything was as usual.

'Have you seen a motley crowd making a disturbance?' Grower said magisterially to one of these in a fustian jacket, who smoked a short pipe and wore straps round his knees.

'Beg yer pardon, sir?' blandly said the person addressed, who was no other than Charl, of Peter's Finger. Mr. Grower repeated the words.

Charl shook his head to the zero of childlike ignorance. 'No; we haven't seen anything; have we, Joe? And you was here afore I.'

Joseph was quite as blank as the other in his reply.

'H'm—that's odd,' said Mr. Grower. 'Ah—here's a respectable man coming that I know by sight. Have you,' he inquired, addressing the nearing shape of Jopp, 'have you seen any gang of fellows making a devil of a noise—skimmington riding, or something of the sort?'

'O no—nothing, sir,' Jopp replied, as if receiving the most singular news. 'But I've not been far tonight, so perhaps——'

'Oh, 'twas here—just here,' said the magistrate.

'Now I've noticed, come to think o't, that the wind in the Walk trees makes a peculiar poetical-like murmur to-night, sir; more than common; so perhaps 'twas that?' Jopp suggested, as he rearranged his hand in his greatcoat pocket (where it ingeniously supported a pair of kitchen tongs and a cow's horn, thrust up under his waistcoat).

'No, no, no,—d'ye think I'm a fool? Constable, come this way. They must have gone into the back street.'

Neither in back street nor in front street, however, could the disturbers be perceived; and Blowbody and the second constable, who came up at this time, brought similar intelligence. Effigies, donkey, lanterns, band, all had disappeared like the crew of *Comus*.[6]

'Now' said Mr. Grower, 'there's only one thing more we can do. Get ye half-a-dozen helpers, and go in a body to Mixen Lane, and into Peter's Finger. I'm much mistaken if you don't find a clue to the perpetrators there.'

The rusty-jointed executors of the law mustered assistance as soon as they could, and the whole party marched off to the lane of notoriety. It was no rapid matter to get there at night, not a lamp or glimmer of any sort offering itself to light the way, except an occasional pale radiance through some window-curtain, or through the chink of some door which could not be closed because of the smoky chimney within. At last

---

6. In John Milton's masque (1637), the revellers gathered around the pagan god Comus are ordered to break off their "riotous and unruly noise" when the Lady approaches (lines 145–48).

they entered the inn boldly, by the till then bolted front-door, after a prolonged knocking of loudness commensurate with the importance of
their standing.

In the settles of the large room, guyed to the ceiling by cords as usual
for stability, an ordinary group sat drinking and smoking with statuesque
quiet of demeanour. The landlady looked mildly at the invaders, saying
in honest accents, 'Good evening, gentlemen; there's plenty of room. I
hope there's nothing amiss?'

They looked round the room. 'Surely,' said Stubberd to one of the
men, 'I saw you by now in Corn Street—Mr. Grower spoke to 'ee?'

The man, who was Charl, shook his head absently. 'I've been here this
last hour, hain't I, Nance?' he said to the woman who meditatively
sipped her ale near him.

'Faith, that you have. I came in for my quiet supper-time half-pint,
and you was here then, as was all the rest.'

The other constable was facing the clock-case, where he saw reflected in the glass a quick motion by the landlady. Turning sharply, he
caught her closing the oven-door.

'Something curious about that oven, ma'am!' he observed advancing,
opening it, and drawing out a tambourine.

'Ah,' she said apologetically, 'that's what we keep here to use when
there's a little quiet dancing. You see damp weather spoils it, so I put it
there to keep it dry.'

The constable nodded knowingly; but what he knew was nothing.
Nohow could anything be elicited from this mute and inoffensive assembly. In a few minutes the investigators went out, and joining those of
their auxiliaries who had been left at the door they pursued their way
elsewhither.

XL

Long before this time Henchard, weary of his ruminations on the bridge,
had repaired towards the town. When he stood at the bottom of the street
a procession burst upon his view, in the act of turning out of an alley just
above him. The lanterns, horns, and multitude startled him; he saw the
mounted images, and knew what it all meant.

They crossed the way, entered another street, and disappeared. He
turned back a few steps and was lost in grave reflection, finally wending
his way homeward by the obscure river-side path. Unable to rest there
he went to his stepdaughter's lodging, and was told that Elizabeth-Jane
had gone to Mrs. Farfrae's. Like one acting in obedience to a charm, and
with a nameless apprehension, he followed in the same direction in the
hope of meeting her, the roysterers having vanished. Disappointed in
this he gave the gentlest of pulls to the door-bell, and then learnt particulars of what had occurred, together with the doctor's imperative orders

that Farfrae should be brought home, and how they had set out to meet him on the Budmouth Road.

'But he has gone to Mellstock and Weatherbury!' exclaimed Henchard, now unspeakably grieved. 'Not Budmouth way at all.'

But, alas! for Henchard; he had lost his good name. They would not believe him, taking his words but as the frothy utterances of recklessness. Though Lucetta's life seemed at that moment to depend upon her husband's return (she being in great mental agony lest he should never know the unexaggerated truth of her past relations with Henchard), no messenger was despatched towards Weatherbury. Henchard, in a state of bitter anxiety and contrition, determined to seek Farfrae himself.

To this end he hastened down the town, ran along the eastern road over Durnover moor, up the hill beyond, and thus onward in the moderate darkness of this spring night till he had reached a second and almost a third hill about three miles distant. In Yalbury Bottom, or Plain, at the foot of the hill, he listened. At first nothing, beyond his own heart-throbs, was to be heard but the slow wind making its moan among the masses of spruce and larch of Yalbury Wood which clothed the heights on either hand; but presently there came the sound of light wheels whetting their felloes against the newly stoned patches of road, accompanied by the distant glimmer of lights.

He knew it was Farfrae's gig descending the hill from an indescribable personality in its noise, the vehicle having been his own till bought by the Scotchman at the sale of his effects. Henchard thereupon retraced his steps along Yalbury Plain, the gig coming up with him as its driver slackened speed between two plantations.

It was a point in the highway near which the road to Mellstock branched off from the homeward direction. By diverging to that village, as he had intended to do, Farfrae might probably delay his return by a couple of hours. It soon appeared that his intention was to do so still, the light swerving towards Cuckoo Lane, the by-road aforesaid. Farfrae's off gig-lamp[1] flashed in Henchard's face. At the same time, Farfrae discerned his late antagonist.

'Farfrae—Mr. Farfrae!' cried the breathless Henchard, holding up his hand.

Farfrae allowed the horse to turn several steps into the branch lane before he pulled up. He then drew rein, and said 'Yes?' over his shoulder, as one would towards a pronounced enemy.

'Come back to Casterbridge at once!' Henchard said. 'There's something wrong at your house—requiring your return. I've run all the way here on purpose to tell ye.'

Farfrae was silent, and at his silence Henchard's soul sank within him. Why had he not, before this, thought of what was only too obvious? He

---

1. Lamp on the right-hand side of the vehicle.

who, four hours earlier, had enticed Farfrae into a deadly wrestle stood now in the darkness of late night-time on a lonely road, inviting him to come a particular way, where an assailant might have confederates, instead of going his purposed way, where there might be a better opportunity of guarding himself from attack. Henchard could almost feel this view of things in course of passage through Farfrae's mind.

'I have to go to Mellstock,' said Farfrae coldly, as he loosened his rein to move on.

'But,' implored Henchard, 'the matter is more serious than your business at Mellstock. It is—your wife! She is ill. I can tell you particulars as we go along.'

The very agitation and abruptness of Henchard increased Farfrae's suspicion that this was a *ruse* to decoy him on to the next wood, where might be effectually compassed what, from policy or want of nerve, Henchard had failed to do earlier in the day. He started the horse.

'I know what you think,' deprecated Henchard, running after, almost bowed down with despair as he perceived the image of unscrupulous villainy that he assumed in his former friend's eyes. 'But I am not what you think!' he cried hoarsely. 'Believe me, Farfrae; I have come entirely on your own and your wife's account. She is in danger. I know no more; and they want you to come. Your man has gone the other way in a mistake. O Farfrae! don't mistrust me—I am a wretched man; but my heart is true to you still!'

Farfrae, however, did distrust him utterly. He knew his wife was with child, but he had left her not long ago in perfect health; and Henchard's treachery was more credible than his story. He had in his time heard bitter ironies from Henchard's lips, and there might be ironies now. He quickened the horse's pace, and had soon risen into the high country lying between there and Mellstock, Henchard's spasmodic run after him lending yet more substance to his thought of evil purposes.

The gig and its driver lessened against the sky in Henchard's eyes; his exertions for Farfrae's good had been in vain. Over this repentant sinner,[2] at least, there was to be no joy in heaven. He cursed himself like a less scrupulous Job,[3] as a vehement man will do when he loses self-respect, the last mental prop under poverty. To this he had come after a time of emotional darkness of which the adjoining woodland shade afforded inadequate illustration. Presently he began to walk back again along the way by which he had arrived. Farfrae should at all events have no reason for delay upon the road by seeing him there when he took his journey homeward later on.

Arriving at Casterbridge Henchard went again to Farfrae's house to

---

2. Jesus said that heaven rejoices more over one repentant sinner than over ninety-nine just persons who have no need to repent. See Luke 15.7.
3. Job remains silent for seven days under his sufferings, only then cursing his existence. See Job 2.9–10 and 3.1–10.

make inquiries. As soon as the door opened anxious faces confronted his from the staircase, hall, and landing; and they all said in grievous disappointment, 'O—it is not he!' The manservant, finding his mistake, had long since returned, and all hopes had been centred upon Henchard.

'But haven't you found him?' said the doctor.

'Yes. . . . I cannot tell 'ee!' Henchard replied as he sank down on a chair within the entrance. 'He can't be home for two hours.'

'H'm,' said the surgeon, returning upstairs.

'How is she?' asked Henchard of Elizabeth, who formed one of the group.

'In great danger, father. Her anxiety to see her husband makes her fearfully restless. Poor woman—I fear they have killed her!'

Henchard regarded the sympathetic speaker for a few instants as if she struck him in a new light; then, without further remark, went out of the door and onward to his lonely cottage. So much for man's rivalry, he thought. Death was to have the oyster, and Farfrae and himself the shells. But about Elizabeth-Jane; in the midst of his gloom she seemed to him as a pin-point of light. He had liked the look of her face as she answered him from the stairs. There had been affection in it, and above all things what he desired now was affection from anything that was good and pure. She was not his own; yet, for the first time, he had a faint dream that he might get to like her as his own,—if she would only continue to love him.

Jopp was just going to bed when Henchard got home. As the latter entered the door Jopp said, 'This is rather bad about Mrs. Farfrae's illness.'

'Yes,' said Henchard shortly, though little dreaming of Jopp's complicity in the night's harlequinade, and raising his eyes just sufficiently to observe that Jopp's face was lined with anxiety.

'Somebody has called for you,' continued Jopp, when Henchard was shutting himself into his own apartment. 'A kind of traveller, or sea-captain of some sort.'

'Oh?—who could he be?'

'He seemed a well-be-doing man—had grey hair and a broadish face; but he gave no name, and no message.'

'Nor do I gi'e him any attention.' And, saying this, Henchard closed his door.

The divergence to Mellstock delayed Farfrae's return very nearly the two hours of Henchard's estimate. Among the other urgent reasons for his presence had been the need of his authority to send to Budmouth for a second physician; and when at length Farfrae did come back he was in a state bordering on distraction at his misconception of Henchard's motives.

A messenger was despatched to Budmouth, late as it had grown; the night wore on, and the other doctor came in the small hours. Lucetta had been much soothed by Donald's arrival; he seldom or never left her side; and when, immediately after his entry, she had tried to lisp out to him the secret which so oppressed her, he checked her feeble words, lest talking should be dangerous, assuring her there was plenty of time to tell him everything.

Up to this time he knew nothing of the skimmington-ride. The dangerous illness and miscarriage of Mrs. Farfrae was soon rumoured through the town, and an apprehensive guess having been given as to its cause by the leaders in the exploit, compunction and fear threw a dead silence over all particulars of their orgie; while those immediately around Lucetta would not venture to add to her husband's distress by alluding to the subject.

What, and how much, Farfrae's wife ultimately explained to him of her past entanglement with Henchard, when they were alone in the solitude of that sad night, cannot be told. That she informed him of the bare facts of her peculiar intimacy with the corn-merchant became plain from Farfrae's own statements. But in respect of her subsequent conduct—her motive in coming to Casterbridge to unite herself with Henchard—her assumed justification in abandoning him when she discovered reasons for fearing him (though in truth her inconsequent passion for another man at first sight had most to do with that abandonment)—her method of reconciling to her conscience a marriage with the second when she was in a measure committed to the first: to what extent she spoke of these things remained Farfrae's secret alone.

Besides the watchman who called the hours and weather in Casterbridge that night there walked a figure up and down Corn Street hardly less frequently. It was Henchard's, whose retiring to rest had proved itself a futility as soon as attempted; and he gave it up to go hither and thither, and make inquiries about the patient every now and then. He called as much on Farfrae's account as on Lucetta's, and on Elizabeth-Jane's even more than on either's. Shorn one by one of all other interests, his life seemed centring on the personality of the step-daughter whose presence but recently he could not endure. To see her on each occasion of his inquiry at Lucetta's was a comfort to him.

The last of his calls was made about four o'clock in the morning, in the steely light of dawn. Lucifer[4] was fading into day across Durnover Moor, the sparrows were just alighting into the street, and the hens had begun to cackle from the outhouses. When within a few yards of Farfrae's he saw the door gently opened, and a servant raise her hand to the knocker, to untie the piece of cloth which had muffled it. He went across, the sparrows in his way scarcely flying up from the road-litter, so little did they believe in human aggression at so early a time.

'Why do you take off that?' said Henchard.

4. The planet Venus, known as the morning star.

She turned in some surprise at his presence, and did not answer for an instant or two. Recognizing him, she said, 'Because they may knock as loud as they will; she will never hear it any more.'

XLI

Henchard went home. The morning having now fully broke he lit his fire, and sat abstractedly beside it. He had not sat there long when a gentle footstep approached the house and entered the passage, a finger tapping lightly at the door. Henchard's face brightened, for he knew the motions to be Elizabeth's. She came into his room, looking wan and sad.

'Have you heard?' she asked. 'Mrs. Farfrae! She is—dead! Yes, indeed—about an hour ago!'

'I know it,' said Henchard. 'I have but lately come in from there. It is so very good of 'ee, Elizabeth, to come and tell me. You must be so tired out, too, with sitting up. Now do you bide here with me this morning. You can go and rest in the other room; and I will call 'ee when breakfast is ready.'

To please him, and herself—for his recent kindliness was winning a surprised gratitude from the lonely girl—she did as he bade her, and lay down on a sort of couch which Henchard had rigged up out of a settle in the adjoining room. She could hear him moving about in his preparations; but her mind ran most strongly on Lucetta, whose death in such fulness of life and amid such cheerful hopes of maternity was appallingly unexpected. Presently she fell asleep.

Meanwhile her stepfather in the outer room had set the breakfast in readiness; but finding that she dozed he would not call her; he waited on, looking into the fire and keeping the kettle boiling with housewifely care, as if it were an honour to have her in his house. In truth, a great change had come over him with regard to her, and he was developing the dream of a future lit by her filial presence, as though that way alone could happiness lie.

He was disturbed by another knock at the door, and rose to open it, rather deprecating a call from anybody just then. A stoutly built man stood on the doorstep, with an alien, unfamiliar air about his figure and bearing—an air which might have been called colonial by people of cosmopolitan experience. It was the man who had asked the way at Peter's Finger. Henchard nodded, and looked inquiry.

'Good morning, good morning,' said the stranger with profuse heartiness. 'Is it Mr. Henchard I am talking to?'

'My name is Henchard.'

'Then I've caught 'ee at home—that's right. Morning's the time for business, says I. Can I have a few words with you?'

'By all means,' Henchard answered, showing the way in.

'You may remember me?' said his visitor, seating himself.

Henchard observed him indifferently, and shook his head.

'Well—perhaps you may not. My name is Newson.'

Henchard's face and eyes seemed to die. The other did not notice it. 'I know the name well,' Henchard said at last, looking on the floor.

'I make no doubt of that. Well, the fact is, I've been looking for 'ee this fortnight past. I landed at Havenpool and went through Casterbridge on my way to Falmouth, and when I got there, they told me you had some years before been living at Casterbridge. Back came I again, and by long and by late I got here by coach, ten minutes ago. "He lives down by the mill," says they. So here I am. Now—that transaction between us some twenty years agone—'tis that I've called about. 'Twas a curious business. I was younger then than I am now, and perhaps the less said about it, in one sense, the better.'

'Curious business! 'Twas worse than curious. I cannot even allow that I'm the man you met then. I was not in my senses, and a man's senses are himself.'

'We were young and thoughtless,' said Newson. 'However, I've come to mend matters rather than open arguments. Poor Susan—hers was a strange experience.'

'It was.'

'She was a warm-hearted, home-spun woman. She was not what they call shrewd or sharp at all—better she had been.'

'She was not.'

'As you in all likelihood know, she was simpleminded enough to think that the sale was in a way binding. She was as guiltless o' wrong-doing in that particular as a saint in the clouds.'

'I know it, I know it. I found it out directly,' said Henchard, still with averted eyes. 'There lay the sting o't to me. If she had seen it as what it was she would never have left me. Never! But how should she be expected to know? What advantages had she? None. She could write her own name, and no more.'[1]

'Well, it was not in my heart to undeceive her when the deed was done,' said the sailor of former days. 'I thought, and there was not much vanity in thinking it, that she would be happier with me. She was fairly happy, and I never would have undeceived her till the day of her death. Your child died; she had another, and all went well. But a time came— mind me, a time always does come. A time came—it was some while after she and I and the child returned from America—when somebody she had confided her history to, told her my claim to her was a mockery, and made a jest of her belief in my right. After that she was never happy with me. She pined and pined, and socked[2] and sighed. She said she must leave me, and then came the question of our child. Then a man

---

1. Possibly a slip, since Susan left the letter for Henchard; but it may mean only that she learned to write after their separation.
2. Sighed or moaned (dialect).

advised me how to act, and I did it, for I thought it was best. I left her at Falmouth, and went off to sea. When I got to the other side of the Atlantic there was a storm, and it was supposed that a lot of us, including myself, had been washed overboard. I got ashore at Newfoundland, and then I asked myself what I should do. "Since I'm here, here I'll bide," I thought to myself; "'twill be most kindness to her, now she's taken against me, to let her believe me lost; for," I thought, "while she supposes us both alive she'll be miserable; but if she thinks me dead she'll go back to him, and the child will have a home." I've never returned to this country till a month ago, and I found that, as I had supposed, she went to you, and my daughter with her. They told me in Falmouth that Susan was dead. But my Elizabeth-Jane—where is she?'

'Dead likewise,' said Henchard doggedly. 'Surely you learnt that too?'

The sailor started up, and took an enervated pace or two down the room. 'Dead!' he said, in a low voice. 'Then what's the use of my money to me?'

Henchard, without answering, shook his head as if that were rather a question for Newson himself than for him.

'Where is she buried?' the traveller inquired.

'Beside her mother,' said Henchard, in the same stolid tones.

'When did she die?'

'A year ago and more,' replied the other without hesitation.

The sailor continued standing. Henchard never looked up from the floor. At last Newson said: 'My journey hither has been for nothing! I may as well go as I came! It has served me right. I'll trouble you no longer.'

Henchard heard the retreating footsteps of Newson upon the sanded floor, the mechanical lifting of the latch, the slow opening and closing of the door that was natural to a baulked or dejected man; but he did not turn his head. Newson's shadow passed the window. He was gone.

Then Henchard, scarcely believing the evidence of his senses, rose from his seat amazed at what he had done. It had been the impulse of a moment. The regard he had lately acquired for Elizabeth, the newsprung hope of his loneliness that she would be to him a daughter of whom he could feel as proud as of the actual daughter she still believed herself to be, had been stimulated by the unexpected coming of Newson to a greedy exclusiveness in relation to her; so that the sudden prospect of her loss had caused him to speak mad lies like a child, in pure mockery of consequences. He had expected questions to close in round him, and unmask his fabrication in five minutes; yet such questioning had not come. But surely they would come; Newson's departure could be but momentary; he would learn all by inquiries in the town; and return to curse him, and carry his last treasure away!

He hastily put on his hat, and went out in the direction that Newson had taken. Newson's back was soon visible up the road, crossing Bull-stake. Henchard followed; and saw his visitor stop at the King's Arms, where the morning coach which had brought him waited half-an-hour for another coach which crossed there. The coach Newson had come by was now about to move again. Newson mounted; his luggage was put in, and in a few minutes the vehicle disappeared with him.

He had not so much as turned his head. It was an act of simple faith in Henchard's words—faith so simple as to be almost sublime. The young sailor who had taken Susan Henchard on the spur of the moment and on the faith of a glance at her face, more than twenty years before, was still living and acting under the form of the grizzled traveller who had taken Henchard's words on trust so absolute as to shame him as he stood.

Was Elizabeth-Jane to remain his by virtue of this hardy invention of a moment? 'Perhaps not for long,' said he. Newson might converse with his fellow-travellers, some of whom might be Casterbridge people; and the trick would be discovered.

This probability threw Henchard into a defensive attitude, and instead of considering how best to right the wrong, and acquaint Elizabeth's father with the truth at once, he bethought himself of ways to keep the position he had accidentally won. Towards the young woman herself his affection grew more jealously strong with each new hazard to which his claim to her was exposed.

He watched the distant highway expecting to see Newson return on foot, enlightened and indignant, to claim his child. But no figure appeared. Possibly he had spoken to nobody on the coach, but buried his grief in his own heart.

His grief!—what was it, after all, to that which he, Henchard, would feel at the loss of her? Newson's affection, cooled by years, could not equal his who had been constantly in her presence. And thus his jealous soul speciously argued to excuse the separation of father and child.

He returned to the house half expecting that she would have vanished. No; there she was—just coming out from the inner room, the marks of sleep upon her eyelids, and exhibiting a generally refreshed air.

'O father!' she said, smiling. 'I had no sooner lain down than I napped, though I did not mean to. I wonder I did not dream about poor Mrs. Farfrae, after thinking of her so; but I did not. How strange it is that we do not often dream of latest events, absorbing as they may be.'

'I am glad you have been able to sleep,' he said, taking her hand with anxious proprietorship—an act which gave her a pleasant surprise.

They sat down to breakfast, and Elizabeth-Jane's thoughts reverted to Lucetta. Their sadness added charm to a countenance whose beauty had ever lain in its meditative soberness.

'Father,' she said, as soon as she recalled herself to the outspread meal, 'it is so kind of you to get this nice breakfast with your own hands, and I idly asleep the while.'

'I do it every day,' he replied. 'You have left me; everybody has left me; how should I live but by my own hands.'

'You are very lonely, are you not?'

'Ay, child—to a degree that you know nothing of! It is my own fault. You are the only one who has been near me for weeks. And you will come no more.'

'Why do you say that? Indeed I will, if you would like to see me.'

Henchard signified dubiousness. Though he had so lately hoped that Elizabeth-Jane might again live in his house as daughter, he would not ask her to do so now. Newson might return at any moment, and what Elizabeth would think of him for his deception it were best to bear apart from her.

When they had breakfasted his stepdaughter still lingered, till the moment arrived at which Henchard was accustomed to go to his daily work. Then she arose, and with assurances of coming again soon went up the hill in the morning sunlight.

'At this moment her heart is as warm towards me as mine is towards her; she would live with me here in this humble cottage for the asking! Yet before the evening probably he will have come; and then she will scorn me!'

This reflection, constantly repeated by Henchard to himself, accompanied him everywhere through the day, His mood was no longer that of the rebellious, ironical, reckless misadventurer; but the leaden gloom of one who has lost all that can make life interesting, or even tolerable. There would remain nobody for him to be proud of, nobody to fortify him; for Elizabeth-Jane would soon be but as a stranger, and worse. Susan, Farfrae, Lucetta, Elizabeth—all had gone from him, one after one, either by his fault or by his misfortune.

In place of them he had no interest, hobby, or desire. If he could have summoned music to his aid his existence might even now have been borne; for with Henchard music was of regal power. The merest trumpet or organ tone was enough to move him, and high harmonies transubstantiated him.[3] But hard fate had ordained that he should be unable to call up this Divine spirit in his need.

The whole land ahead of him was as darkness itself; there was nothing to come, nothing to wait for. Yet in the natural course of life he might possibly have to linger on earth another thirty or forty years—scoffed at; at best pitied.

The thought of it was unendurable.

To the east of Casterbridge lay moors and meadows through which much water flowed. The wanderer in this direction who should stand still for a few moments on a quiet night, might hear singular symphonies from these waters, as from a lampless orchestra, all playing in their

3. Literally, changed his substance; here, perhaps, uplifted him.

sundry tones from near and far parts of the moor. At a hole in a rotten weir they executed a recitative; where a tributary brook fell over a stone breastwork they trilled cheerily; under an arch they performed a metallic cymballing; and at Durnover Hole they hissed. The spot at which their instrumentation rose loudest was a place called Ten Hatches, whence during high springs there proceeded a very fugue of sounds.

The river here was deep and strong at all times, and the hatches on this account were raised and lowered by cogs and a winch. A path led from the second bridge over the highway (so often mentioned) to these Hatches, crossing the stream at their head by a narrow plank-bridge. But after night-fall human beings were seldom found going that way, the path leading only to a deep reach of the stream called Blackwater, and the passage being dangerous.

Henchard, however, leaving the town by the east road, proceeded to the second, or stone bridge, and thence struck into this path of solitude, following its course beside the stream till the dark shapes of the Ten Hatches cut the sheen thrown upon the river by the weak lustre that still lingered in the west. In a second or two he stood beside the weir-hole where the water was at its deepest. He looked backwards and forwards, and no creature appeared in view. He then took off his coat and hat, and stood on the brink of the stream with his hands clasped in front of him.

While his eyes were bent on the water beneath there slowly became visible a something floating in the circular pool formed by the wash of centuries; the pool he was intending to make his death-bed. At first it was indistinct by reason of the shadow from the bank; but it emerged thence and took shape, which was that of a human body, lying stiff and stark upon the surface of the stream.

In the circular current imparted by the central flow the form was brought forward, till it passed under his eyes; and then he perceived with a sense of horror that it was *himself*. Not a man somewhat resembling him, but one in all respects his counterpart, his actual double, was floating as if dead in Ten Hatches Hole.

The sense of the supernatural was strong in this unhappy man, and he turned away as one might have done in the actual presence of an appalling miracle. He covered his eyes and bowed his head. Without looking again into the stream he took his coat and hat, and went slowly away.

Presently he found himself by the door of his own dwelling. To his surprise Elizabeth-Jane was standing there. She came forward, spoke, called him 'father' just as before. Newson, then, had not even yet returned.

'I thought you seemed very sad this morning,' she said, 'so I have come again to see you. Not that I am anything but sad myself. But everybody and everything seem against you so; and I know you must be suffering.'

How this woman divined things! Yet she had not divined their whole extremity.

He said to her, 'Are miracles still worked, do ye think, Elizabeth? I am not a read man. I don't know so much as I could wish. I have tried to peruse and learn all my life; but the more I try to know the more ignorant I seem.'

'I don't quite think there are any miracles nowadays,' she said.

'No interference in the case of desperate intentions, for instance? Well, perhaps not, in a direct way. Perhaps not. But will you come and walk with me, and I will show 'ee what I mean.'

She agreed willingly, and he took her over the highway, and by the lonely path to Ten Hatches. He walked restlessly, as if some haunting shade, unseen of her, hovered round him and troubled his glance. She would gladly have talked of Lucetta, but feared to disturb him. When they got near the weir he stood still, and asked her to go forward and look into the pool, and tell him what she saw.

She went, and soon returned to him. 'Nothing,' she said.

'Go again,' said Henchard, 'and look narrowly.'

She proceeded to the river brink a second time. On her return, after some delay, she told him that she saw something floating round and round there; but what it was she could not discern. It seemed to be a bundle of old clothes.

'Are they like mine?' asked Henchard.

'Well—they are. Dear me—I wonder if—— Father, let us go away!'

'Go and look once more; and then we will get home.'

She went back, and he could see her stoop till her head was close to the margin of the pool. She started up, and hastened back to his side.

'Well,' said Henchard; 'what do you say now?'

'Let us go home.'

'But tell me—do—what is it floating there?'

'The effigy,' she answered hastily. 'They must have thrown it into the river higher up amongst the willows at Blackwater, to get rid of it in their alarm at discovery by the magistrates; and it must have floated down here.'

'Ah—to be sure—the image o' me! But where is the other? Why that one only? That performance of theirs killed her, but kept me alive!'

Elizabeth-Jane thought and thought of these words 'kept me alive,' as they slowly retraced their way to the town, and at length guessed their meaning. 'Father!—I will not leave you alone like this!' she cried. 'May I live with you, and tend upon you as I used to do? I do not mind your being poor. I would have agreed to come this morning, but you did not ask me.'

'May you come to me?' he cried bitterly. 'Elizabeth, don't mock me! If you only would come!'

'I will,' said she.

'How will you forgive all my roughness in former days? You cannot!'
'I have forgotten it. Talk of that no more.'

Thus she assured him, and arranged their plans for reunion; and at length each went home. Then Henchard shaved for the first time during many days, and put on clean linen, and combed his hair; and was as a man resuscitated thenceforward.

The next morning the fact turned out to be as Elizabeth-Jane had stated; the effigy was discovered by a cowherd, and that of Lucetta a little higher up in the same stream. But as little as possible was said of the matter, and the figures were privately destroyed.

Despite this natural solution of the mystery Henchard no less regarded it as an intervention that the figure should have been floating there. Elizabeth-Jane heard him say, 'Who is such a reprobate as I! And yet it seems that even I be in Somebody's hand!'

XLII

But the emotional conviction that he was in Somebody's hand began to die out of Henchard's breast as time slowly removed into distance the event which had given that feeling birth. The apparition of Newson haunted him. He would surely return.

Yet Newson did not arrive. Lucetta had been borne along the churchyard path; Casterbridge had for the last time turned its regard upon her, before proceeding to its work as if she had never lived. But Elizabeth remained undisturbed in the belief of her relationship to Henchard, and now shared his home. Perhaps, after all, Newson was gone for ever.

In due time the bereaved Farfrae had learnt the, at least, proximate cause of Lucetta's illness and death; and his first impulse was naturally enough to wreak vengeance in the name of the law upon the perpetrators of the mischief. He resolved to wait till the funeral was over ere he moved in the matter. The time having come he reflected. Disastrous as the result had been, it was obviously in no way foreseen or intended by the thoughtless crew who arranged the motley procession. The tempting prospect of putting to the blush people who stand at the head of affairs — that supreme and piquant enjoyment of those who writhe under the heel of the same — had alone animated them, so far as he could see; for he knew nothing of Jopp's incitements. Other considerations were also involved. Lucetta had confessed everything[1] to him before her death, and it was not altogether desirable to make much ado about her history, alike for her sake, for Henchard's, and for his own. To regard the event as an untoward accident seemed, to Farfrae, truest consideration for the dead one's memory, as well as best philosophy.

Henchard and himself mutually forbore to meet. For Elizabeth's sake

---

1. This seems to contradict Chapter 40, in which what Lucetta revealed to Farfrae "cannot be told."

the former had fettered his pride sufficiently to accept the small seed and root business[2] which some of the Town Council, headed by Farfrae, had purchased to afford him a new opening. Had he been only personally concerned Henchard, without doubt, would have declined assistance even remotely brought about by the man whom he had so fiercely assailed. But the sympathy of the girl seemed necessary to his very existence; and on her account pride itself wore the garments of humility.

Here they settled themselves; and on each day of their lives Henchard anticipated her every wish with a watchfulness in which paternal regard was heightened by a burning jealous dread of rivalry. Yet that Newson would ever now return to Casterbridge to claim her as a daughter there was little reason to suppose. He was a wanderer and a stranger, almost an alien; he had not seen his daughter for several years; his affection for her could not in the nature of things be keen; other interests would probably soon obscure his recollections of her, and prevent any such renewal of inquiry into the past as would lead to a discovery that she was still a creature of the present. To satisfy his conscience somewhat Henchard repeated to himself that the lie which had retained for him the coveted treasure had not been deliberately told to that end, but had come from him as the last defiant word of a despair which took no thought of consequences. Furthermore he pleaded within himself that no Newson could love her as he loved her, or would tend her to his life's extremity as he was prepared to do cheerfully.

Thus they lived on in the shop overlooking the churchyard, and nothing occurred to mark their days during the remainder of the year. Going out but seldom, and never on a market-day, they saw Donald Farfrae only at rarest intervals, and then mostly as a transitory object in the distance of the street. Yet he was pursuing his ordinary avocations, smiling mechanically to fellow-tradesmen, and arguing with bargainers—as bereaved men do after a while.

Time, 'in his own grey style,'[3] taught Farfrae how to estimate his experience of Lucetta—all that it was, and all that it was not. There are men whose hearts insist upon a dogged fidelity to some image or cause thrown by chance into their keeping, long after their judgment has pronounced it no rarity—even the reverse, indeed; and without them the band of the worthy is incomplete. But Farfrae was not of those. It was inevitable that the insight, briskness, and rapidity of his nature should take him out of the dead blank which his loss threw about him. He could not but perceive that by the death of Lucetta he had exchanged a looming misery for a simple sorrow. After that reve-

2. In Chapter 34 Farfrae abandoned the idea of setting Henchard up in business; either this is a slip on Hardy's part, or Farfrae has had a change of heart.
3. In Shelley's poem "Epipsychidion," Young Love is called upon to teach Time, "in his own grey style," the nature of a transcendent love. Farfrae's love is not of this ideal kind. See lines 55–57.

lation of her history, which must have come sooner or later in any circumstances, it was hard to believe that life with her would have been productive of further happiness.

But as a memory, notwithstanding such conditions, Lucetta's image still lived on with him, her weaknesses provoking only the gentlest criticism, and her sufferings attenuating wrath at her concealments to a momentary spark now and then.

By the end of a year Henchard's little retail seed and grain shop, not much larger than a cupboard, had developed its trade considerably, and the stepfather and daughter enjoyed much serenity in the pleasant, sunny corner in which it stood. The quiet bearing of one who brimmed with an·inner activity characterized Elizabeth-Jane at this period. She took long walks into the country two or three times a week, mostly in the direction of Budmouth. Sometimes it occurred to him that when she sat with him in the evening after these invigorating walks she was civil rather than affectionate; and he was troubled; one more bitter regret being added to those he had already experienced at having, by his severe censorship, frozen up her precious affection when originally offered.

She had her own way in everything now. In going and coming, in buying and selling, her word was law.

'You have got a new muff, Elizabeth,' he said to her one day quite humbly.

'Yes; I bought it,' she said.

He looked at it again as it lay on an adjoining table. The fur was of a glossy brown, and, though he was no judge of such articles, he thought it seemed an unusually good one for her to possess.

'Rather costly, I suppose, my dear, was it not?' he hazarded.

'It was rather above my figure,' she said quietly. 'But it is not showy.'

'O no,' said the netted lion, anxious not to pique her in the least.

Some little time after, when the year had advanced into another spring, he paused opposite her empty bedroom in passing it. He thought of the time when she had cleared out of his then large and handsome house in Corn Street, in consequence of his dislike and harshness, and he had looked into her chamber in just the same way. The present room was much humbler, but what struck him about it was the abundance of books lying everywhere. Their number and quality made the meagre furniture that supported them seem absurdly disproportionate. Some, indeed many, must have been recently purchased; and though he encouraged her to buy in reason, he had no notion that she indulged her innate passion so extensively in proportion to the narrowness of their income. For the first time he felt a little hurt by what he thought her extravagance, and resolved to say a word to her about it. But, before he had found the courage to speak an event happened which set his thoughts flying in quite another direction.

The busy time of the seed trade was over; and the quiet weeks that pre-

ceded the hay-season had come—setting their special stamp upon
Casterbridge by thronging the market with wood rakes, new waggons in
yellow, green, and red, formidable scythes, and pitchforks of prong sufficient to skewer up a small family. Henchard, contrary to his wont, went
out one Saturday afternoon towards the market-place, from a curious
feeling that he would like to pass a few minutes on the spot of his former
triumphs. Farfrae, to whom he was still a comparative stranger, stood a
few steps below the Corn Exchange door—a usual position with him at
this hour—and he appeared lost in thought about something he was
looking at a little way off.

Henchard's eyes followed Farfrae's, and he saw that the object of his
gaze was no sample-showing farmer, but his own stepdaughter, who had
just come out of a shop over the way. She, on her part, was quite unconscious of his attention, and in this was less fortunate than those young
women whose very plumes, like those of Juno's bird, are set with Argus
eyes[4] whenever possible admirers are within ken.[5]

Henchard went away, thinking that perhaps there was nothing significant after all in Farfrae's look at Elizabeth-Jane at that juncture. Yet he
could not forget that the Scotchman had once shown a tender interest
in her, of a fleeting kind. Thereupon promptly came to the surface that
idiosyncrasy of Henchard's which had ruled his courses from the beginning and had mainly made him what he was. Instead of thinking that a
union between his cherished stepdaughter and the energetic thriving
Donald was a thing to be desired for her good and his own, he hated the
very possibility.

Time had been when such instinctive opposition would have taken
shape in action. But he was not now the Henchard of former days. He
schooled himself to accept her will, in this as in other matters, as
absolute and unquestionable. He dreaded lest an antagonistic word
should lose for him such regard as he had regained from her by his devo-
tion, feeling that to retain this under separation was better than to incur
her dislike by keeping her near.

But the mere thought of such separation fevered his spirit much, and
in the evening he said, with the stillness of suspense: 'Have you seen Mr.
Farfrae today, Elizabeth?'

Elizabeth-Jane started at the question; and it was with some confusion
that she replied 'No.'

'Oh—that's right—that's right. . . . It was only that I saw him in the
street when we both were there.' He was wondering if her embarrassment justified him in a new suspicion—that the long walks which she
had lately been taking, that the new books which had so surprised him,

4. Argus, in classical myth, had a hundred eyes, of which only two ever slept simultaneously. After
   Argus had been killed by Hermes, the goddess Juno set the eyes in the tail of her sacred bird,
   the peacock.
5. Range of perception.

had anything to do with the young man. She did not enlighten him, and lest silence should allow her to shape thoughts unfavourable to their present friendly relations, he diverted the discourse into another channel.

Henchard was, by original make, the last man to act stealthily, for good or for evil. But the *solicitus timor*[6] of his love—the dependence upon Elizabeth's regard into which he had declined (or, in another sense, to which he had advanced)—denaturalized him. He would often weigh and consider for hours together the meaning of such and such a deed or phrase of hers, when a blunt settling question would formerly have been his first instinct. And now, uneasy at the thought of a passion for Farfrae which should entirely displace her mild filial sympathy with himself, he observed her going and coming more narrowly.

There was nothing secret in Elizabeth-Jane's movements beyond what habitual reserve induced; and it may at once be owned on her account that she was guilty of occasional conversations with Donald when they chanced to meet. Whatever the origin of her walks on the Budmouth Road, her return from those walks was often coincident with Farfrae's emergence from Corn Street for a twenty minutes' blow on that rather windy highway—just to winnow the seeds and chaff out of him before sitting down to tea, as he said. Henchard became aware of this by going to the Ring, and, screened by its enclosure, keeping his eye upon the road till he saw them meet. His face assumed an expression of extreme anguish.

'Of her, too, he means to rob me!' he whispered. 'But he has the right. I do not wish to interfere.'

The meeting, in truth, was of a very innocent kind, and matters were by no means so far advanced between the young people as Henchard's jealous grief inferred. Could he have heard such conversation as passed he would have been enlightened thus much:—

He.—'You like walking this way, Miss Henchard—and is it not so?' (uttered in his undulatory accents, and with an appraising, pondering gaze at her).

She.—'O yes. I have chosen this road latterly. I have no great reason for it.'

He.—'But that may make a reason for others.'

She (reddening).—'I don't know that. My reason, however, such as it is, is that I wish to get a glimpse of the sea every day.'

He.—'Is it a secret why?'

She (reluctantly).—'Yes.'

He (with the pathos of one of his native ballads).—'Ah, I doubt there will be any good in secrets! A secret cast a deep shadow over my life. And well you know what it was.'

Elizabeth admitted that she did, but she refrained from confessing

6. Anxious fear (from the Latin).

why the sea attracted her. She could not herself account for it fully, not knowing the secret possibly to be that, in addition to early marine associations, her blood was a sailor's.

'Thank you for those new books, Mr. Farfrae,' she added shyly. 'I wonder if I ought to accept so many!'

'Ay! why not? It gives me more pleasure to get them for you, than you to have them!'

'It cannot!'

They proceeded along the road together till they reached the town, and their paths diverged.

Henchard vowed that he would leave them to their own devices, put nothing in the way of their courses, whatever they might mean. If he were doomed to be bereft of her, so it must be. In the situation which their marriage would create he could see no *locus standi*[7] for himself at all. Farfrae would never recognize him more than superciliously; his poverty ensured that, no less than his past conduct. And so Elizabeth would grow to be a stranger to him, and the end of his life would be friendless solitude.

With such a possibility impending he could not help watchfulness. Indeed, within certain lines, he had the right to keep an eye upon her as his charge. The meetings seemed to become matters of course with them on special days of the week.

At last full proof was given him. He was standing behind a wall close to the place at which Farfrae encountered her. He heard the young man address her as 'Dearest Elizabeth-Jane,' and then kiss her, the girl looking quickly round to assure herself that nobody was near.

When they were gone their way Henchard came out from the wall, and mournfully followed them to Casterbridge. The chief looming trouble in this engagement had not decreased. Both Farfrae and Elizabeth-Jane, unlike the rest of the people, must suppose Elizabeth to be his actual daughter, from his own assertion while he himself had the same belief; and though Farfrae must have so far forgiven him as to have no objection to own him as a father-in-law, intimate they could never be. Thus would the girl, who was his only friend, be withdrawn from him by degrees through her husband's influence, and learn to despise him.

Had she lost her heart to any other man in the world than the one he had rivalled, cursed, wrestled with for life in days before his spirit was broken, Henchard would have said, 'I am content.' But content with the prospect as now depicted was hard to acquire.

There is an outer chamber of the brain in which thoughts unowned, unsolicited, and of noxious kind, are sometimes allowed to wander for a moment prior to being sent off whence they came. One of these thoughts sailed into Henchard's ken now.

7. Recognized position (from the Latin).

Suppose he were to communicate to Farfrae the fact that his betrothed was not the child of Michael Henchard at all—legally, nobody's child; how would that correct and leading townsman receive the information? He might possibly forsake Elizabeth-Jane, and then she would be her stepsire's own again.

Henchard shuddered, and exclaimed, 'God forbid such a thing! Why should I still be subject to these visitations of the devil, when I try so hard to keep him away?'

XLIII

What Henchard saw thus early was, naturally enough, seen at a little later date by other people. That Mr. Farfrae 'walked with that bankrupt Henchard's stepdaughter, of all women,' became a common topic in the town, the simple perambulating term being used hereabout to signify a wooing; and the nineteen superior young ladies of Casterbridge, who had each looked upon herself as the only woman capable of making the merchant Councilman happy, indignantly left off going to the church Farfrae attended, left off conscious mannerisms, left off putting him in their prayers at night amongst their blood relations; in short, reverted to their natural courses.

Perhaps the only inhabitants of the town to whom this looming choice of the Scotchman's gave unmixed satisfaction were the members of the philosophic party, which included Longways, Christopher Coney, Billy Wills, Mr. Buzzford, and the like. The Three Mariners having been, years before, the house in which they had witnessed the young man and woman's first and humble appearance on the Casterbridge stage, they took a kindly interest in their career, not unconnected, perhaps, with visions of festive treatment at their hands hereafter. Mrs. Stannidge, having rolled into the large parlour one evening and said that it was a wonder such a man as Mr. Farfrae, 'a pillow[1] of the town,' who might have chosen one of the daughters of the professional men or private residents, should stoop so low, Coney ventured to disagree with her.

'No, ma'am, no wonder at all. 'Tis she that's a stooping to he—that's my opinion. A widow man—whose first wife was no credit to him—what is it for a young perusing woman that's her own mistress and well liked? But as a neat patching up of things I see much good in it. When a man have put up a tomb of best marble-stone to the other one, as he've done, and weeped his fill, and thought it all over, and said to hisself, "T'other took me in; I knowed this one first; she's a sensible piece for a partner, and there's no faithful woman in high life now;"—well, he may do worse than not to take her, if she's tender-inclined.'

Thus they talked at the Mariners. But we must guard against a too lib-

---

1. A malapropism; Mrs. Stannidge means "pillar."

eral use of the conventional declaration that a great sensation was
caused by the prospective event, that all the gossips' tongues were set
wagging thereby, and so on, even though such a declaration might lend
some *éclat*[2] to the career of our poor only heroine. When all has been
said about busy rumourers, a superficial and temporary thing is the interest of anybody in affairs which do not directly touch them. It would be
a truer representation to say that Casterbridge (ever excepting the nineteen young ladies) looked up for a moment at the news, and withdrawing its attention, went on labouring and victualling, bringing up its children, and burying its dead, without caring a tittle for Farfrae's domestic
plans.

Not a hint of the matter was thrown out to her stepfather by Elizabeth
herself or by Farfrae either. Reasoning on the cause of their reticence he
concluded that, estimating him by his past, the throbbing pair were
afraid to broach the subject, and looked upon him as an irksome obstacle whom they would be heartily glad to get out of the way. Embittered
as he was against society, this moody view of himself took deeper and
deeper hold of Henchard, till the daily necessity of facing mankind, and
of them particularly Elizabeth-Jane, became well-nigh more than he
could endure. His health declined; he became morbidly sensitive. He
wished he could escape those who did not want him, and hide his head
for ever.

But what if he were mistaken in his views, and there were no necessity that his own absolute separation from her should be involved in the
incident of her marriage?

He proceeded to draw a picture of the alternative — himself living like
a fangless lion about the back rooms of a house in which his stepdaughter was mistress; an inoffensive old man, tenderly smiled on by
Elizabeth, and good-naturedly tolerated by her husband. It was terrible
to his pride to think of descending so low; and yet, for the girl's sake he
might put up with anything; even from Farfrae; even snubbings and masterful tongue-scourgings. The privilege of being in the house she occupied would almost outweigh the personal humiliation.

Whether this were a dim possibility or the reverse, the courtship —
which it evidently now was — had an absorbing interest for him.

Elizabeth, as has been said, often took her walks on the Budmouth
Road, and Farfrae as often made it convenient to create an accidental
meeting with her there. Two miles out, a quarter of a mile from the highway, was the prehistoric fort called Mai Dun,[3] of huge dimensions and
many ramparts, within or upon whose enclosures a human being, as
seen from the road, was but an insignificant speck. Hitherward
Henchard often resorted, glass in hand, and scanned the hedgeless

2. Brilliance (from the French).
3. Maiden Castle, a prehistoric earthwork to the southwest of Dorchester.

Via^4—for it was the original track laid out by the legions of the Empire—to a distance of two or three miles, his object being to read the progress of affairs between Farfrae and his charmer.

One day Henchard was at this spot when a masculine figure came along the road from Budmouth, and lingered. Applying his telescope to his eye Henchard expected that Farfrae's features would be disclosed as usual. But the lenses revealed that to-day the man was not Elizabeth-Jane's lover.

It was one clothed as a merchant captain; and as he turned in his scrutiny of the road he revealed his face. Henchard lived a lifetime the moment he saw it. The face was Newson's.

Henchard dropped the glass, and for some seconds made no other movement. Newson waited, and Henchard waited—if that could be called a waiting which was a transfixture.[5] But Elizabeth-Jane did not come. Something or other had caused her to neglect her customary walk that day. Perhaps Farfrae and she had chosen another road for variety's sake. But what did that amount to? She might be here to-morrow, and in any case Newson, if bent on a private meeting and a revelation of the truth to her, would soon make his opportunity.

Then he would tell her not only of his paternity, but of the ruse by which he had been once sent away. Elizabeth's strict nature would cause her for the first time to despise her stepfather, would root out his image as that of an arch-deceiver, and Newson would reign in her heart in his stead.

But Newson did not see anything of her that morning. Having stood still awhile he at last retraced his steps, and Henchard felt like a condemned man who has a few hours' respite. When he reached his own house he found her there.

'O father!' she said innocently, 'I have had a letter—a strange one—not signed. Somebody has asked me to meet him, either on the Budmouth Road at noon to-day, or in the evening at Mr. Farfrae's. He says he came to see me some time ago, but a trick was played him, so that he did not see me. I don't understand it; but between you and me I think Donald is at the bottom of the mystery, and that it is a relation of his who wants to pass an opinion on his choice. But I did not like to go till I had seen you. Shall I go?'

Henchard replied heavily, 'Yes; go.'

The question of his remaining in Casterbridge was for ever disposed of by this closing in of Newson on the scene. Henchard was not the man to stand the certainty of condemnation on a matter so near his heart. And being an old hand at bearing anguish in silence, and haughty withal, he resolved to make as light as he could of his intention, while immediately taking his measures.

4. Road (from the Latin).
5. Condition of being fixed to the spot by strong feeling.

He surprised the young woman whom he had looked upon as his all in this world by saying to her, as if he did not care about her more: 'I am going to leave Casterbridge, Elizabeth-Jane.'

'Leave Casterbridge!' she cried, 'and leave—me?'

'Yes, this little shop can be managed by you alone as well as by us both; I don't care about shops and streets and folk—I would rather get into the country by myself, out of sight, and follow my own ways, and leave you to yours.'

She looked down and her tears fell silently. It seemed to her that this resolve of his had come on account of her attachment and its probable result. She showed her devotion to Farfrae, however, by mastering her emotion and speaking out.

'I am sorry you have decided on this,' she said with difficult firmness. 'For I thought it probable—possible—that I might marry Mr. Farfrae some little time hence, and I did not know that you disapproved of the step!'

'I approve of anything you desire to do, Izzy,' said Henchard huskily. 'If I did not approve it would be no matter! I wish to go away. My presence might make things awkward in the future; and, in short, it is best that I go.'

Nothing that her affection could urge would induce him to reconsider his determination; for she could not urge what she did not know—that when she should learn he was not related to her other than as a stepparent she would refrain from despising him, and that when she knew what he had done to keep her in ignorance she would refrain from hating him. It was his conviction that she would not so refrain; and there existed as yet neither word nor event which could argue it away.

'Then,' she said at last, 'you will not be able to come to my wedding; and that is not as it ought to be.'

'I don't want to see it—I don't want to see it!' he exclaimed; adding more softly, 'but think of me sometimes in your future life—you'll do that, Izzy?—think of me when you are living as the wife of the richest, the foremost man in the town, and don't let my sins, *when you know them all*, cause 'ee to quite forget that though I loved 'ee late I loved 'ee well.'

'It is because of Donald!' she sobbed.

'I don't forbid you to marry him,' said Henchard. 'Promise not to quite forget me when——' He meant when Newson should come.

She promised mechanically, in her agitation; and the same evening at dusk Henchard left the town, to whose development he had been one of the chief stimulants for many years. During the day he had bought a new tool-basket, cleaned up his old hay-knife and wimble, set himself up in fresh leggings, knee-naps[6] and corduroys, and in other ways gone back to the working clothes of his young manhood, discarding for ever the

6. Leather patches to protect the knees.

shabby-genteel suit of cloth and rusty silk hat that since his decline had characterized him in the Casterbridge street as a man who had seen better days.

He went secretly and alone, not a soul of the many who had known him being aware of his departure. Elizabeth-Jane accompanied him as far as the second bridge on the highway—for the hour of her appointment with the unguessed visitor at Farfrae's had not yet arrived—and parted from him with unfeigned wonder and sorrow, keeping him back a minute or two before finally letting him go. She watched his form diminish across the moor, the yellow rush-basket at his back moving up and down with each tread, and the creases behind his knees coming and going alternately till she could no longer see them. Though she did not know it Henchard formed at this moment much the same picture as he had presented when entering Casterbridge for the first time nearly a quarter of a century before; except, to be sure, that the serious addition to his years had considerably lessened the spring of his stride, that his state of hopelessness had weakened him, and imparted to his shoulders, as weighted by the basket, a perceptible bend.

He went on till he came to the first milestone, which stood in the bank, half way up a steep hill. He rested his basket on the top of the stone, placed his elbows on it, and gave way to a convulsive twitch, which was worse than a sob, because it was so hard and so dry.

'If I had only got her with me—if I only had!' he said. 'Hard work would be nothing to me then! But that was not to be. I—Cain—go alone as I deserve—an outcast and a vagabond. But my punishment is *not* greater than I can bear!'[7]

He sternly subdued his anguish, shouldered his basket, and went on.

Elizabeth, in the meantime, had breathed him a sigh, recovered her equanimity, and turned her face to Casterbridge. Before she had reached the first house she was met in her walk by Donald Farfrae. This was evidently not their first meeting that day; they joined hands without ceremony, and Farfrae anxiously asked, 'And is he gone—and did you tell him?—I mean of the other matter—not of ours.'

'He is gone; and I told him all I knew of your friend. Donald, who is he?'

'Well, well, dearie; you will know soon about that. And Mr. Henchard will hear of it if he does not go far.'

'He will go far—he's bent upon getting out of sight and sound!'

She walked beside her lover, and when they reached the Crossways, or Bow, turned with him into Corn Street instead of going straight on to her own door. At Farfrae's house they stopped and went in.

Farfrae flung open the door of the ground-floor sitting-room, saying,

7. See Genesis 4.12–13, in which Cain, condemned to live as an outcast after murdering his brother, Abel, says, "My punishment is greater than I can bear."

'There he is waiting for you,' and Elizabeth entered. In the arm-chair sat the broad-faced genial man who had called on Henchard on a memorable morning between one and two years before this time, and whom the latter had seen mount the coach and depart within half-an-hour of his arrival. It was Richard Newson. The meeting with the light-hearted father from whom she had been separated half-a-dozen years, as if by death, need hardly be detailed. It was an affecting one, apart from the question of paternity. Henchard's departure was in a moment explained. When the true facts came to be handled the difficulty of restoring her to her old belief in Newson was not so great as might have seemed likely, for Henchard's conduct itself was a proof that those facts were true. Moreover, she had grown up under Newson's paternal care; and even had Henchard been her father in nature, this father in early domiciliation might almost have carried the point against him, when the incidents of her parting with Henchard had a little worn off.

Newson's pride in what she had grown up to be was more than he could express. He kissed her again and again.

'I've saved you the trouble to come and meet me—ha-ha!' said Newson. 'The fact is that Mr. Farfrae here, he said, "Come up and stop with me for a day or two, Captain Newson, and I'll bring her round." "Faith," says I, "so I will;" and here I am.'

'Well, Henchard is gone,' said Farfrae, shutting the door. 'He has done it all voluntarily, and, as I gather from Elizabeth, he has been very nice with her. I was got rather uneasy; but all is as it should be, and we will have no more deefficulties at all.'

'Now, that's very much as I thought,' said Newson, looking into the face of each by turns. 'I said to myself, ay, a hundred times, when I tried to get a peep at her unknown to herself—"Depend upon it, 'tis best that I should live on quiet for a few days like this till something turns up for the better." I now know you are all right, and what can I wish for more?'

'Well, Captain Newson, I will be glad to see ye here every day now, since it can do no harm,' said Farfrae. 'And what I've been thinking is that the wedding may as well be kept under my own roof, the house being large, and you being in lodgings by yourself—so that a great deal of trouble and expense would be saved ye?—and 'tis a convenience when a couple's married not to hae far to go to get home!'

'With all my heart,' said Captain Newson; 'since, as ye say, it can do no harm, now poor Henchard's gone; though I wouldn't have done it otherwise, or put myself in his way at all; for I've already in my lifetime been an intruder into his family quite as far as politeness can be expected to put up with. But what do the young woman say herself about it? Elizabeth, my child, come and hearken to what we be talking about, and not bide staring out o' the window as if ye didn't hear.'

'Donald and you must settle it,' murmured Elizabeth, still keeping up a scrutinizing gaze at some small object in the street.

'Well, then,' continued Newson, turning anew to Farfrae with a face expressing thorough entry into the subject, 'that's how we'll have it. And, Mr. Farfrae, as you provide so much, and houseroom, and all that, I'll do my part in the drinkables, and see to the rum and schiedam[8]—maybe a dozen jars will be sufficient?—as many of the folk will be ladies, and perhaps they won't drink hard enough to make a high average in the reckoning? But you know best. I've provided for men and shipmates times enough, but I'm as ignorant as a child how many glasses of grog a woman, that's not a drinking woman, is expected to consume at these ceremonies?'

'Oh, none—we'll no want much of that—O no!' said Farfrae, shaking his head with appalled gravity. 'Do you leave all to me.'

When they had gone a little further in these particulars Newson, leaning back in his chair and smiling reflectively at the ceiling, said, 'I've never told ye, or have I, Mr. Farfrae, how Henchard put me off the scent that time?'

He expressed ignorance of what the Captain alluded to .

'Ah, I thought I hadn't. I resolved that I would not, I remember, not to hurt the man's name. But now he's gone I can tell ye. Why, I came to Casterbridge nine or ten months before that day last week that I found ye out. I had been here twice before then. The first time I passed through the town on my way westward, not knowing Elizabeth lived here. Then hearing at some place—I forget where—that a man of the name of Henchard had been mayor here, I came back, and called at his house one morning. The old rascal!—he said Elizabeth-Jane had died years ago.'

Elizabeth now gave earnest heed to his story.

'Now, it never crossed my mind that the man was selling me a packet,' continued Newson. 'And, if you'll believe me, I was that upset, that I went back to the coach that had brought me, and took passage onward without lying in the town half-an-hour. Ha-ha!—'twas a good joke, and well carried out, and I give the man credit for't!'

Elizabeth-Jane was amazed at the intelligence. 'A joke?—O no!' she cried. 'Then he kept you from me, father, all those months, when you might have been here?'

The father admitted that such was the case.

'He ought not to have done it!' said Farfrae.

Elizabeth sighed. 'I said I would never forget him. But O! I think I ought to forget him now!'

Newson, like a good many rovers and sojourners among strange men and strange moralities, failed to perceive the enormity of Henchard's crime, notwithstanding that he himself had been the chief sufferer

---

8. Dutch gin, named after the town where it was made.

therefrom. Indeed, the attack upon the absent culprit waxing serious, he began to take Henchard's part.

'Well, 'twas not ten words that he said, after all,' Newson pleaded. 'And how could he know that I should be such a simpleton as to believe him? 'Twas as much my fault as his, poor fellow!'

'No,' said Elizabeth-Jane firmly, in her revulsion of feeling. 'He knew your disposition—you always were so trusting, father; I've heard my mother say so hundreds of times—and he did it to wrong you. After weaning me from you these five years by saying he was my father, he should not have done this.'

Thus they conversed; and there was nobody to set before Elizabeth any extenuation of the absent one's deceit. Even had he been present Henchard might scarce have pleaded it, so little did he value himself or his good name.

'Well, well—never mind—it is all over and past,' said Newson good-naturedly. 'Now, about this wedding again.'

XLIV

Meanwhile, the man of their talk had pursued his solitary way eastward till weariness overtook him, and he looked about for a place of rest. His heart was so exacerbated at parting from the girl that he could not face an inn, or even a household of the most humble kind; and entering a field he lay down under a wheatrick, feeling no want of food. The very heaviness of his soul caused him to sleep profoundly.

The bright autumn sun shining into his eyes across the stubble awoke him the next morning early. He opened his basket and ate for his breakfast what he had packed for his supper; and in doing so overhauled the remainder of his kit. Although everything he brought necessitated carriage at his own back, he had secreted among his tools a few of Elizabeth-Jane's cast-off belongings, in the shape of gloves, shoes, a scrap of her handwriting, and the like; and in his pocket he carried a curl of her hair. Having looked at these things he closed them up again, and went onward.

During five consecutive days Henchard's rush basket rode along upon his shoulder between the highway hedges, the new yellow of the rushes catching the eye of an occasional field-labourer as he glanced through the quickset,[1] together with the wayfarer's hat and head, and down-turned face, over which the twig shadows moved in endless procession. It now became apparent that the direction of his journey was Weydon Priors, which he reached on the afternoon of the sixth day.

The renowned hill whereon the annual fair had been held for so many generations was now bare of human beings, and almost of aught

1. Hedgerow.

besides. A few sheep grazed thereabout, but these ran off when Henchard halted upon the summit. He deposited his basket upon the turf, and looked about with sad curiosity; till he discovered the road by which his wife and himself had entered on the upland so memorable to both, five-and-twenty years before.

'Yes, we came up that way,' he said, after ascertaining his bearings. 'She was carrying the baby, and I was reading a ballet-sheet. Then we crossed about here—she so sad and weary, and I speaking to her hardly at all, because of my cursed pride and mortification at being poor. Then we saw the tent—that must have stood more this way.' He walked to another spot; it was not really where the tent had stood but it seemed so to him. 'Here we went in, and here we sat down. I faced this way. Then I drank, and committed my crime. It must have been just on that very pixy-ring[2] that she was standing when she said her last words to me before going off with him; I can hear their sound now, and the sound of her sobs: "O Mike! I've lived with thee all this while, and had nothing but temper. Now I'm no more to 'ee—I'll try my luck elsewhere."'

He experienced not only the bitterness of a man who finds, in looking back upon an ambitious course, that what he has sacrificed in sentiment was worth as much as what he has gained in substance; but the super-added bitterness of seeing his very recantation nullified. He had been sorry for all this long ago; but his attempts to replace ambition by love had been as fully foiled as his ambition itself. His wronged wife had foiled them by a fraud so grandly simple as to be almost a virtue. It was an odd sequence that out of all this tampering with social law came that flower of Nature, Elizabeth. Part of his wish to wash his hands of life arose from his perception of its contrarious inconsistencies—of Nature's jaunty readiness to support unorthodox social principles.

He intended to go on from this place—visited as an act of penance—into another part of the country altogether. But he could not help thinking of Elizabeth, and the quarter of the horizon in which she lived. Out of this it happened that the centrifugal tendency imparted by weariness of the world was counteracted by the centripetal influence of his love for his stepdaughter. As a consequence, instead of following a straight course yet further away from Casterbridge, Henchard gradually, almost unconsciously, deflected from that right line of his first intention; till, by degrees, his wandering, like that of the Canadian woodsman,[3] became part of a circle of which Casterbridge formed the centre. In ascending any particular hill he ascertained the bearings as nearly as he could by means of the sun, moon, or stars, and settled in his mind the exact direction in which Casterbridge and Elizabeth-Jane lay. Sneering at himself

---

2. Circle of grass of a different color from the grass around it, caused by fungi but popularly supposed to be caused by fairies dancing on it.
3. Annotating a book on *The Emigrant and Sportsman in Canada*, Hardy noted that without a compass even a skilled woodsman eventually begins to wander in circles.

for his weakness he yet every hour—nay, every few minutes—conjectured her actions for the time being—her sitting down and rising up, her goings and comings, till thought of Newson's and Farfrae's counter-influence would pass like a cold blast over a pool, and efface her image. And then he would say of himself. 'O you fool! All this about a daughter who is no daughter of thine!'

At length he obtained employment at his own occupation of hay-trusser, work of that sort being in demand at this autumn time. The scene of his hiring was a pastoral farm near the old western highway, whose course was the channel of all such communications as passed between the busy centres of novelty and the remote Wessex boroughs. He had chosen the neighbourhood of this artery from a sense that, situated here, though at a distance of fifty miles, he was virtually nearer to her whose welfare was so dear than he would be at a roadless spot only half as remote.

And thus Henchard found himself again on the precise standing which he had occupied a quarter of a century before. Externally there was nothing to hinder his making another start on the upward slope, and by his new lights achieving higher things than his soul in its half-formed state had been able to accomplish. But the ingenious machinery contrived by the Gods for reducing human possibilities of amelioration to a minimum—which arranges that wisdom to do shall come *pari passu*[4] with the departure of zest for doing—stood in the way of all that. He had no wish to make an arena a second time of a world that had become a mere painted scene to him.

Very often, as his hay-knife crunched down among the sweet-smelling grassy stems, he would survey mankind and say to himself: 'Here and everywhere be folk dying before their time like frosted leaves, though wanted by their families, the country, and the world; while I, an outcast, an encumberer of the ground, wanted by nobody, and despised by all, live on against my will!'

He often kept an eager ear upon the conversation of those who passed along the road—not from a general curiosity by any means—but in the hope that among these travellers between Casterbridge and London some would, sooner or later, speak of the former place. The distance, however, was too great to lend much probability to his desire; and the highest result of his attention to wayside words was that he did indeed hear the name 'Casterbridge' uttered one day by the driver of a road-waggon. Henchard ran to the gate of the field he worked in, and hailed the speaker, who was a stranger.

'Yes—I've come from there, maister,' he said, in answer to Henchard's inquiry. 'I trade up and down, ye know; though, what with this travelling without horses that's getting so common, my work will soon be done.'

4. At an equal pace, to an equal degree (from the Latin).

'Anything moving in the old place, mid I ask?'

'All the same as usual.'

'I've heard that Mr. Farfrae, the late mayor, is thinking of getting married. Now is that true or not?'

'I couldn't say for the life o' me. O no, I should think not.'

'But yes, John—you forget,' said a woman inside the waggon-tilt. 'What were them packages we carr'd there at the beginning o' the week? Surely they said a wedding was coming off soon—on Martin's Day?'[5]

The man declared he remembered nothing about it; and the waggon went on jangling over the hill.

Henchard was convinced that the woman's memory served her well. The date was an extremely probable one, there being no reason for delay on either side. He might, for that matter, write and inquire of Elizabeth; but his instinct for sequestration[6] had made the course difficult. Yet before he left her she had said that for him to be absent from her wedding was not as she wished it to be.

The remembrance would continually revive in him now that it was not Elizabeth and Farfrae who had driven him away from them, but his own haughty sense that his presence was no longer desired. He had assumed the return of Newson without absolute proof that the Captain meant to return; still less that Elizabeth-Jane would welcome him; and with no proof whatever that if he did return he would stay. What if he had been mistaken in his views; if there had been no necessity that his own absolute separation from her he loved should be involved in these untoward incidents? To make one more attempt to be near her: to go back; to see her, to plead his cause before her, to ask forgiveness for his fraud, to endeavour strenuously to hold his own in her love; it was worth the risk of repulse, ay, of life itself.

But how to initiate this reversal of all his former resolves without causing husband and wife to despise him for his inconsistency was a question which made him tremble and brood.

He cut and cut his trusses two days more, and then he concluded his hesitancies by a sudden reckless determination to go to the wedding festivity. Neither writing nor message would be expected of him. She had regretted his decision to be absent—his unanticipated presence would fill the little unsatisfied corner that would probably have place in her just heart without him.

To intrude as little of his personality as possible upon a gay event with which that personality could show nothing in keeping, he decided not to make his appearance till evening—when stiffness would have worn off, and a gentle wish to let bygones be bygones would exercise its sway in all hearts.

5. Martinmas, the feast of St. Martin of Tours, is on November 11.
6. (Here) isolation.

He started on foot, two mornings before St. Martin's-tide, allowing himself about sixteen miles to perform for each of the three days' journey, reckoning the wedding-day as one. There were only two towns, Melchester and Shottsford, of any importance along his course, and at the latter he stopped on the second night, not only to rest, but to prepare himself for the next evening.

Possessing no clothes but the working suit he stood in — now stained and distorted by their two months of hard usage, he entered a shop to make some purchases which should put him, externally at any rate, a little in harmony with the prevailing tone of the morrow. A rough yet respectable coat and hat, a new shirt and neck-cloth, were the chief of these; and having satisfied himself that in appearance at least he would not now offend her, he proceeded to the more interesting particular of buying her some present.

What should that present be? He walked up and down the street, regarding dubiously the display in the shop windows, from a gloomy sense that what he might most like to give her would be beyond his miserable pocket. At length a caged goldfinch met his eye. The cage was a plain and small one, the shop humble, and on inquiry he concluded he could afford the modest sum asked. A sheet of newspaper was tied round the little creature's wire prison, and with the wrapped up cage in his hand Henchard sought a lodging for the night.

Next day he set out upon the last stage, and was soon within the district which had been his dealing ground in bygone years. Part of the distance he travelled by carrier, seating himself in the darkest corner at the back of that trader's van; and as the other passengers, mainly women going short journeys, mounted and alighted in front of Henchard, they talked over much local news, not the least portion of this being the wedding then in course of celebration at the town they were nearing. It appeared from their accounts that the town band had been hired for the evening party, and, lest the convivial instincts of that body should get the better of their skill, the further step had been taken of engaging the string band from Budmouth, so that there would be a reserve of harmony to fall back upon in case of need.

He heard, however, but few particulars beyond those known to him already, the incident of the deepest interest on the journey being the soft pealing of the Casterbridge bells, which reached the travellers' ears while the van paused on the top of Yalbury Hill to have the drag[7] lowered. The time was just after twelve o'clock.

Those notes were a signal that all had gone well; that there had been no slip 'twixt cup and lip in this case; that Elizabeth-Jane and Donald Farfrae were man and wife.

Henchard did not care to ride any further with his chattering com-

7. Iron brake used to drag on or retard a wheel when descending a hill.

panions after hearing this sound. Indeed, it quite unmanned him; and in pursuance of his plan of not showing himself in Casterbridge street till evening, lest he should mortify Farfrae and his bride, he alighted here, with his bundle and bird-cage, and was soon left as a lonely figure on the broad white highway.

It was the hill near which he had waited to meet Farfrae, almost two years earlier, to tell him of the serious illness of his wife Lucetta. The place was unchanged; the same larches sighed the same notes; but Farfrae had another wife—and, as Henchard knew, a better one. He only hoped that Elizabeth-Jane had obtained a better home than had been hers at the former time.

He passed the remainder of the afternoon in a curious high-strung condition, unable to do much but think of the approaching meeting with her, and sadly satirize himself for his emotions thereon, as a Samson shorn.[8] Such an innovation on Casterbridge customs as a flitting of bridegroom and bride from the town immediately after the ceremony, was not likely, but if it should have taken place he would wait till their return. To assure himself on this point he asked a market-man when near the borough if the newly-married couple had gone away, and was promptly informed that they had not; they were at that hour, according to all accounts, entertaining a houseful of guests at their home in Corn Street.

Henchard dusted his boots, washed his hands at the river-side, and proceeded up the town under the feeble lamps. He need have made no inquiries beforehand, for on drawing near Farfrae's residence it was plain to the least observant that festivity prevailed within, and that Donald himself shared it, his voice being distinctly audible in the street, giving strong expression to a song of his dear native country that he loved so well as never to have revisited it. Idlers were standing on the pavement in front; and wishing to escape the notice of these Henchard passed quickly on to the door.

It was wide open; the hall was lighted extravagantly, and people were going up and down the stairs. His courage failed him; to enter footsore, laden, and poorly dressed into the midst of such resplendency was to bring needless humiliation upon her he loved, if not to court repulse from her husband. Accordingly he went round into the street at the back that he knew so well, entered the garden, and came quietly into the house through the kitchen, temporarily depositing the bird and cage under a bush outside, to lessen the awkwardness of his arrival.

Solitude and sadness had so emolliated[9] Henchard that he now feared circumstances he would formerly have scorned, and he began to wish that he had not taken upon himself to arrive at such a juncture.

8. See Judges 16.15–21. When Samson tells Delilah that his great strength depends on keeping his hair uncut, she has it shaved off while he is asleep, so that he becomes weak, "like any other man."
9. Softened, made weak.

However, his progress was made unexpectedly easy by his discovering alone in the kitchen an elderly woman who seemed to be acting as provisional housekeeper during the convulsions from which Farfrae's establishment was just then suffering. She was one of those people whom nothing surprises, and though to her, a total stranger, his request must have seemed odd, she willingly volunteered to go up and inform the master and mistress of the house that 'a humble old friend' had come.

On second thoughts she said that he had better not wait in the kitchen, but come up into the little back-parlour, which was empty. He thereupon followed her thither, and she left him. Just as she had got across the landing to the door of the best parlour a dance was struck up, and she returned to say that she would wait till that was over before announcing him — Mr. and Mrs. Farfrae having both joined in the figure.

The door of the front room had been taken off its hinges to give more space, and that of the room Henchard sat in being ajar, he could see fractional parts of the dancers whenever their gyrations brought them near the doorway, chiefly in the shape of the skirts of dresses and streaming curls of hair; together with about three-fifths of the band in profile, including the restless shadow of a fiddler's elbow, and the tip of the bass-viol bow.

The gaiety jarred upon Henchard's spirits; and he could not quite understand why Farfrae, a much-sobered man, and a widower, who had had his trials, should have cared for it all, notwithstanding the fact that he was quite a young man still, and quickly kindled to enthusiasm by dance and song. That the quiet Elizabeth, who had long ago appraised life at a moderate value, and who knew in spite of her maidenhood that marriage was as a rule no dancing matter, should have had zest for this revelry surprised him still more. However, young people could not be quite old people, he concluded, and custom was omnipotent.

With the progress of the dance the performers spread out somewhat, and then for the first time he caught a glimpse of the once despised daughter who had mastered him, and made his heart ache. She was in a dress of white silk or satin, he was not near enough to say which — snowy white, without a tinge of milk or cream; and the expression of her face was one of nervous pleasure rather than of gaiety. Presently Farfrae came round, his exuberant Scotch movement making him conspicuous in a moment. The pair were not dancing together, but Henchard could discern that whenever the changes of the figure made them the partners of a moment their emotions breathed a much subtler essence than at other times.

By degrees Henchard became aware that the measure was trod by some one who out-Farfraed Farfrae in saltatory[1] intenseness. This was

1. Dancing in leaps and bounds.

strange, and it was stranger to find that the eclipsing personage was Elizabeth-Jane's partner. The first time that Henchard saw him he was sweeping grandly round, his head quivering and low down, his legs in the form of an X and his back towards the door. The next time he came round in the other direction, his white waistcoat preceding his face, and his toes preceding his white waistcoat. That happy face—Henchard's complete discomfiture lay in it. It was Newson's, who had indeed come and supplanted him.

Henchard pushed to the door, and for some seconds made no other movement. He rose to his feet, and stood like a dark ruin, obscured by 'the shade from his own soul upthrown.'[2]

But he was no longer the man to stand these reverses unmoved. His agitation was great, and he would fain have been gone, but before he could leave the dance had ended, the housekeeper had informed Elizabeth-Jane of the stranger who awaited her, and she entered the room immediately.

'Oh—it is—Mr. Henchard!' she said, starting back.

'What; Elizabeth?' he cried, as he seized her hand. 'What do you say?—Mr. Henchard? Don't, don't scourge me like that! Call me worthless old Henchard—anything—but don't 'ee be so cold as this! O my maid—I see you have another—a real father in my place. Then you know all; but don't give all your thought to him! Do ye save a little room for me!'

She flushed up, and gently drew her hand away. 'I could have loved you always—I would have, gladly,' said she. 'But how can I when I know you have deceived me so—so bitterly deceived me! You persuaded me that my father was not my father—allowed me to live on in ignorance of the truth for years; and then when he, my warm-hearted real father, came to find me, cruelly sent him away with a wicked invention of my death, which nearly broke his heart. O how can I love as I once did a man who has served us like this!'

Henchard's lips half parted to begin an explanation. But he shut them up like a vice, and uttered not a sound. How should he, there and then, set before her with any effect the palliatives of his great faults—that he had himself been deceived in her identity at first, till informed by her mother's letter that his own child had died; that, in the second accusation, his lie had been the last desperate throw of a gamester who loved her affection better than his own honour? Among the many hindrances to such a pleading not the least was this, that he did not sufficiently value himself to lessen his sufferings by strenuous appeal or elaborate argument.

Waiving, therefore, his privilege of self-defence, he regarded only her discomposure. 'Don't ye distress yourself on my account,' he said, with

---

2. Quoted from Shelley's poem *The Revolt of Islam* (1818), Canto 8, stanza 6. The allusion suggests that Henchard is the victim of forces within himself, not of a hostile supernatural power.

proud superiority. 'I would not wish it—at such a time, too, as this. I have done wrong in coming to 'ee—I see my error. But it is only for once, so forgive it. I'll never trouble 'ee again, Elizabeth-Jane—no, not to my dying day! Good-night. Good-bye!'

Then, before she could collect her thoughts, Henchard went out from her rooms, and departed from the house by the back way as he had come; and she saw him no more.

XLV

It was about a month after the day which closed as in the last chapter. Elizabeth-Jane had grown accustomed to the novelty of her situation, and the only difference between Donald's movements now and former- ly was that he hastened indoors rather more quickly after business hours than he had been in the habit of doing for some time.

Newson had stayed in Casterbridge three days after the wedding party (whose gaiety, as might have been surmised, was of his making rather than of the married couple's), and was stared at and honoured as became the returned Crusoe[1] of the hour. But whether or not because Casterbridge was difficult to excite by dramatic returns and disappearances, through having been for centuries an assize town,[2] in which sensational exits[3] from the world, antipodean absences, and such like, were half-yearly occur- rences, the inhabitants did not altogether lose their equanimity on his account. On the fourth morning he was discovered disconsolately climb- ing a hill, in his craving to get a glimpse of the sea from somewhere or other. The contiguity of salt water proved to be such a necessity of his exis- tence that he preferred Budmouth as a place of residence, notwithstand- ing the society of his daughter in the other town. Thither he went, and set- tled in lodgings in a green-shuttered cottage which had a bow-window, jutting out sufficiently to afford glimpse of a vertical strip of blue sea to any one opening the sash, and leaning forward far enough to look through a narrow lane of tall intervening houses.

Elizabeth-Jane was standing in the middle of her upstairs parlour, crit- ically surveying some re-arrangement of articles with her head to one side, when the housemaid came in with the announcement, 'Oh, please ma'am, we know now how that bird-cage came there.'

In exploring her new domain during the first week or residence, gaz- ing with critical satisfaction on this cheerful room and that, penetrating cautiously into dark cellars, sallying forth with gingerly tread to the gar- den, now leaf-strewn by autumn winds, and thus, like a wise field-mar- shal, estimating the capabilities of the site whereon she was about to

---

1. The shipwrecked sailor of Daniel Defoe's novel *Robinson Crusoe* (1718), who returns after an absence of many years.
2. Town where civil and criminal cases were tried before judge and jury.
3. Executions, carried out in public until the 1860s.

open her housekeeping campaign—Mrs. Donald Farfrae had discovered
in a screened corner a new bird-cage, shrouded in newspaper, and at the
bottom of the cage a little ball of feathers—the dead body of a goldfinch.
Nobody could tell her how the bird and cage had come there; though
that the poor little songster had been starved to death was evident. The
sadness of the incident had made an impression on her. She had not
been able to forget it for days, despite Farfrae's tender banter; and now
when the matter had been nearly forgotten it was again revived.

'Oh, please ma'am, we know how that bird-cage came there. That
farmer's man who called on the evening of the wedding—he was seen
wi' it in his hand as he came up the street; and 'tis thoughted that he put
it down while he came in with his message, and then went away forgetting where he had left it.'

This was enough to set Elizabeth thinking, and in thinking she seized
hold of the idea, at one feminine bound, that the caged bird had been
brought by Henchard for her as a wedding gift and token of repentance.
He had not expressed to her any regrets or excuses for what he had done
in the past; but it was a part of his nature to extenuate nothing,[4] and live
on as one of his own worst accusers. She went out, looked at the cage,
buried the starved little singer, and from that hour her heart softened
towards the self-alienated man.

When her husband came in she told him her solution of the bird-cage
mystery; and begged Donald to help her in finding out, as soon as possible, whither Henchard had banished himself, that she might make her
peace with him; try to do something to render his life less that of an outcast, and more tolerable to him. Although Farfrae had never so passionately liked Henchard as Henchard had liked him, he had, on the other
hand, never so passionately hated in the same direction as his former
friend had done; and he was therefore not the least indisposed to assist
Elizabeth-Jane in her laudable plan.

But it was by no means easy to set about discovering Henchard. He
had apparently sunk into the earth on leaving Mr. and Mrs. Farfrae's
door. Elizabeth-Jane remembered what he had once attempted; and
trembled.

But though she did not know it Henchard had become a changed
man since then—as far, that is, as change of emotional basis can justify
such a radical phrase; and she needed not to fear. In a few days Farfrae's
inquiries elicited that Henchard had been seen by one who knew him
walking steadily along the Melchester highway eastward, at twelve
o'clock at night—in other words, retracing his steps on the road by
which he had come.

This was enough; and the next morning Farfrae might have been dis-

---

4. In Shakespeare's play, Othello asks that those who tell his story should "Nothing extenuate,"
   i.e., make no excuse for him. See *Othello*, V.2.342.

covered driving his gig out of Casterbridge in that direction, Elizabeth-Jane sitting beside him, wrapped in a thick flat fur—the victorine of the period—her complexion somewhat richer than formerly, and an incipient matronly dignity, which the serene Minerva-eyes of one 'whose gestures beamed with mind'[5] made becoming, settling on her face. Having herself arrived at a promising haven from at least the grosser troubles of her life, her object was to place Henchard in some similar quietude before he should sink into that lower stage of existence which was only too possible to him now.

After driving along the highway for a few miles they made further inquiries, and learnt of a road-mender, who had been working thereabouts for weeks, that he had observed such a man at the time mentioned; he had left the Melchester coach-road at Weatherbury by a forking highway which skirted the north of Egdon Heath. Into this road they directed the horse's head, and soon were bowling across that ancient country whose surface never had been stirred to a finger's depth, save by the scratchings of rabbits, since brushed by the feet of the earliest tribes. The tumuli these had left behind, dun and shagged with heather, jutted roundly into the sky from the uplands, as though they were the full breasts of Diana Multimammia[6] supinely extended there.

They searched Egdon, but found no Henchard. Farfrae drove onward, and by the afternoon reached the neighbourhood of some extension of the heath to the north of Anglebury, a prominent feature of which, in the form of a blasted clump of firs on the summit of a hill, they soon passed under. That the road they were following had, up to this point, been Henchard's track on foot they were pretty certain; but the ramifications which now began to reveal themselves in the route made further progress in the right direction a matter of pure guess-work, and Donald strongly advised his wife to give up the search in person, and trust to other means for obtaining news of her stepfather. They were now a score of miles at least from home, but, by resting the horse for a couple of hours at a village they had just traversed, it would be possible to get back to Casterbridge that same day; while to go much further afield would reduce them to the necessity of camping out for the night; 'and that will make a hole in a sovereign,' said Farfrae. She pondered the position, and agreed with him.

He accordingly drew rein, but before reversing their direction paused a moment and looked vaguely round upon the wide country which the elevated position disclosed. While they looked a solitary human form came from under the clump of trees, and crossed ahead of them. The person was some labourer; his gait was shambling, his regard fixed in

5. Quoting from Shelley's *The Revolt of Islam*, Canto 1, stanza 54, on female forms "whose gestures beamed with mind."
6. Diana the Many-Breasted, who as goddess of fruitfulness was depicted with many breasts in her temple at Ephesus.

front of him as absolutely as if he wore blinkers; and in his hand he carried a few sticks. Having crossed the road he descended into a ravine, where a cottage revealed itself, which he entered.

'If it were not so far away from Casterbridge I should say that must be poor Whittle. 'Tis just like him,' observed Elizabeth-Jane.

'And it may be Whittle, for he's never been to the yard these three weeks, going away without saying any word at all; and I owing him for two days' work, without knowing who to pay it to.'

The possibility led them to alight, and at least make an inquiry at the cottage. Farfrae hitched the reins to the gate-post, and they approached what was of humble dwellings surely the humblest. The walls, built of kneaded clay originally faced with a trowel, had been worn by years of rain-washings to a lumpy crumbling surface, channelled and sunken from its plane, its gray rents held together here and there by a leafy strap of ivy which could scarcely find substance enough for the purpose. The rafters were sunken, and the thatch of the roof in ragged holes. Leaves from the fence had been blown into the corners of the doorway, and lay there undisturbed. The door was ajar; Farfrae knocked; and he who stood before them was Whittle, as they had conjectured.

His face showed marks of deep sadness, his eyes lighting on them with an unfocused gaze; and he still held in his hand the few sticks he had been out to gather. As soon as he recognized them he started.

'What, Abel Whittle; is it that ye are heere?' said Farfrae.

'Ay, yes, sir! You see he was kind-like to mother when she wer here below, though 'a was rough to me.'

'Who are you talking of?'

'O sir—Mr. Henchet! Didn't ye know it? He's just gone—about half-an-hour ago, by the sun; for I've got no watch to my name.'

'Not—dead?' faltered Elizabeth-Jane.

'Yes, ma'am, he's gone! He was kind-like to mother when she wer here below, sending her the best ship-coal,[7] and hardly any ashes from it at all; and taties, and such-like that were very needful to her. I seed en go down street on the night of your worshipful's wedding to the lady at yer side, and I thought he looked low and faltering. And I followed en over Grey's Bridge, and he turned and zeed me, and said, "You go back!" But I followed, and he turned again, and said, "Do you hear, sir? Go back!" But I zeed that he was low, and I followed on still. Then 'a said, "Whittle, what do ye follow me for when I've told ye to go back all these times?" And I said, "Because, sir, I see things be bad with 'ee, and ye wer kind-like to mother if ye were rough to me, and I would fain be kind-like to you." Then he walked on, and I followed; and he never complained at me no more. We walked on like that all night; and in the blue o' the morning, when 'twas hardly day, I looked ahead o' me, and I zeed that

7. Imported coal, of high quality.

he wambled, and could hardly drag along. By that time we had got past
here, but I had seen that this house was empty as I went by, and I got
him to come back; and I took down the boards from the windows, and
helped him inside. "What, Whittle," he said, "and can ye really be such
a poor fond fool as to care for such a wretch as I!" Then I went on further, and some neighbourly woodmen lent me a bed, and a chair, and a
few other traps,[8] and we brought 'em here, and made him as comfortable as we could. But he didn't gain strength, for you see, ma'am, he
couldn't eat—no, no appetite at all—and he got weaker; and to-day he
died. One of the neighbours have gone to get a man to measure him.'[9]

'Dear me—is that so!' said Farfrae.

As for Elizabeth, she said nothing.

'Upon the head of his bed he pinned a piece of paper, with some writing upon it,' continued Abel Whittle. 'But not being a man o' letters, I
can't read writing; so I don't know what it is. I can get it and show ye.'

They stood in silence while he ran into the cottage; returning in a
moment with a crumpled scrap of paper. On it there was pencilled as
follows:—

'MICHAEL HENCHARD'S WILL

'That Elizabeth-Jane Farfrae be not told of my death, or made to
grieve on account of me.

'& that I be not bury'd in consecrated ground.

'& that no sexton be asked to toll the bell.

'& that nobody is wished to see my dead body.

'& that no murners walk behind me at my funeral.

'& that no flours be planted on my grave.

'& that no man remember me.

'To this I put my name.

'Michael Henchard.'

'What are we to do?' said Donald, when he had handed the paper to
her.

She could not answer distinctly. 'O Donald!' she said at last through
her tears, 'what bitterness lies there! O I would not have minded so
much if it had not been for my unkindness at that last parting! . . . But
there's no altering—so it must be.'

What Henchard had written in the anguish of his dying was respected as far as practicable by Elizabeth-Jane, though less from a sense of the
sacredness of last words, as such, than from her independent knowledge
that the man who wrote them meant what he said. She knew the directions to be a piece of the same stuff that his whole life was made of, and

8. Pieces of furniture.
9. For his coffin.

hence were not to be tampered with to give herself a mournful pleasure, or her husband credit for large-heartedness.

All was over at last, even her regrets for having misunderstood him on his last visit, for not having searched him out sooner, though these were deep and sharp for a good while. From this time forward Elizabeth-Jane found herself in a latitude of calm weather, kindly and grateful in itself, and doubly so after the Capharnaum[1] in which some of her preceding years had been spent. As the lively and sparkling emotions of her early married life cohered into an equable serenity, the finer movements of her nature found scope in discovering to the narrow-lived ones around her the secret (as she had once learnt it) of making limited opportunities endurable; which she deemed to consist in the cunning enlargement, by a species of microscopic treatment, of those minute forms of satisfaction that offer themselves to everybody not in positive pain; which, thus handled, have much of the same inspiriting effect upon life as wider interests cursorily embraced.

Her teaching had a reflex action upon herself, insomuch that she thought she could perceive no great personal difference between being respected in the nether parts of Casterbridge and glorified at the uppermost end of the social world. Her position was, indeed, to a marked degree one that, in the common phrase, afforded much to be thankful for. That she was not demonstratively thankful was no fault of hers. Her experience had been of a kind to teach her, rightly or wrongly, that the doubtful honour of a brief transit through a sorry world hardly called for effusiveness, even when the path was suddenly irradiated at some halfway point by daybeams rich as hers. But her strong sense that neither she nor any human being deserved less than was given, did not blind her to the fact that there were others receiving less who had deserved much more. And in being forced to class herself among the fortunate she did not cease to wonder at the persistence of the unforeseen, when the one to whom such unbroken tranquillity had been accorded in the adult stage was she whose youth had seemed to teach that happiness was but the occasional episode in a general drama of pain.

THE END

---

1. Capernaum, town in Galilee where Jesus preached, leading the people from darkness into "great light." See Matthew 4.13–16.

BACKGROUNDS AND CONTEXTS

Composition

CHRISTINE WINFIELD
The Manuscript of Hardy's *Mayor of Casterbridge*†

I

The manuscript of Thomas Hardy's novel *The Mayor of Casterbridge*, composed in 1884–85 and now in the possession of Dorset County Museum, Dorchester, is only partly complete. It is written on 374 sheets of ruled paper measuring 6 1/2" X 7 7/8". The sheets are numbered 1–479 in Hardy's hand, but five are fragmentary (ff. 97, 106, 215, 319, 396); 108 are missing altogether; and there are three supplementary sheets (ff. 116a–b, 133a) not included in the foliation. The missing leaves are generally in sequences of two to eight, though a number of scattered leaves are also absent. The missing leaves occur most frequently in the first twelve chapters of the novel. Only eleven lines of Chapter II survive, and Chapter VI is entirely absent. Of the novel's forty-five chapters, eighteen only are complete. If we exclude ff. 97 and 319 which have obviously been torn unintentionally, the presence of several fragmentary leaves is presumably explained by Hardy's practice of cutting away canceled material.[1]

Though offered as printers' copy,[2] the manuscript has many deletions, interlinear substitutions, and interpolations, and there are additions on the verso of thirty-eight leaves. There is moreover a marked disparity in the distribution of revisons throughout the text; for while a large area of the manuscript may be classed as fair copy, other portions present the text in various stages of development. With admitted simplification, these stages can be divided into three Sections: (1) ff. 1–225 (Chs. I–XXII), (2) ff. 226–418 (Chs. XXIII–XL), and (3) ff. 419–79 (Chs. XLI–XLV). The first and last sections generally contain the most heavi-

† From *Papers of the Bibliographical Society of America* 67 (1973): 37–58. Reprinted by permission of the Bibliographical Society of America and the author.

1. Richard Little Purdy, *Thomas Hardy: A Bibliographical Study* (London, 1954), p. 88, refers to this procedure in connection with the MS. of *Jude the Obscure*.
2. The *Mayor* was first published in twenty weekly installments (2 Jan.–15 May 1886) in *The Graphic: An Illustrated Weekly Newspaper*, and the use of the MS. by the *Graphic* printers is indicated by the presence of penciled square brackets and by the signatures "Alb," "Hickman," "Fred," and others (evidently those of compositors), which occur at regular intervals throughout the text. (See, e.g., ff. 4, 164, 182.)

ly revised areas of the text, while the intermediate section presents the least revised portion.

While the paper on which it is written is of the same type through-out—a ruled page of twenty-one lines—examination of the physical state of the leaves reveals that two quite separate stocks of the same type of paper were used during the course of composition. The paper in one stock (Stock A) is of poorer quality and condition than that in the other: the leaves are generally more soiled, and many are foxed and damp-stained. The paper is azure in color and the feint lines are pale blue and clearly defined. In the second stock (Stock B) the paper is of superior quality: the leaves are thicker in texture and whiter in color, with feint lines generally less conspicuous than those in the first stock. The paper is almost invariably in better condition, the leaves much less soiled and showing only occasional foxing and dampstaining.

Now a general correspondence is evident between the discrepancy in paper stock and the division of the manuscript text into areas distin-guished by their density of revision. The greater part of Sections I and III (the areas of heaviest revision) are written on leaves from Stock A, while that of Section II (the area of least revision) is written on leaves from Stock B. There are, however, notable exceptions in the first half of the manu-script which suggest a correlation not only between paper stock and stage of composition but also between paper stock and period of composition. For in Section I, Chapter XII (ff. 110–16a) contains paper from both stocks; and a inspection of the revisions here reveals that the chapter has been partly rewritten, and that the material on leaves belonging to Stock B (namely, ff. 110, 111, 113, 116, 116a) appears to have been written well after the first half of the story (that is, during the composition of Section II). In Section II itself, ff. 214–15 are written on paper from Stock A and appear from the revision they contain to be survivals from a previously dis-carded chapter. Further evidence for the correlation (in the first half of the text) between paper stock and period of composition is to be found in the surviving traces, through a minor portion of the text, of a canceled sys-tem of foliation—a feature discussed in Part II of this article.

One other preliminary factor to be considered in any textual study of Hardy's work is the similarity between Hardy's handwriting and that of his first wife Emma.[3] The differences between the two scripts are small enough almost to escape notice on a cursory reading. It is well known that Emma often acted as transcriber for the fair copies of her husband's manuscripts (large sections of *The Return of the Native* and *The Woodlanders*, for instance, appear in her hand), and it has been sug-gested that Emma, who herself entertained literary aspirations, may pos-

3. This problem is identified (with use of inadequate criteria for distinguishing the scripts) in Carl J. Weber's article "The Manuscript of Hardy's *Two on a Tower*," *PBSA*, 40 (1946), 1–21; and much more satisfactorily, by Dale Kramer in "A Query Concerning Handwriting in Hardy's Manuscripts," *PBSA*, 57 (1963), 357–60.

sibly have entered on her husband's manuscripts not only his revisions but her own as well.[4] While this conjecture is of course impossible to prove, the extent of Emma's contribution at least deserves consideration.

Fortunately the manuscript of the *Mayor* appears to be almost entirely in Hardy's hand.[5] The script of the interlinear elements of the text is slightly more difficult to identify, since Hardy's style of writing in this area tends to differ somewhat from his usual hand. Assuming however that Emma was simply transcribing and not creating revisions, the identification of the handwriting is not of great importance.

The absence of material earlier than the present manuscript of the *Mayor* makes it impossible to establish with any confidence the closeness of the roughest drafts in the manuscript to the period of inception. Unlike Dickens, George Eliot, and Joyce, who left in note form tentative plans of the structure of certain of their novels and so offered valuable information on their methods of composition, Hardy almost invariably destroyed the first experimental plans of his work, and hence the earliest surviving drafts of his novels are usually the manuscripts offered to the printers. Yet the limited evidence that *is* available of Hardy's earliest working plans suggests that the apparently tentative nature of many of the heavily altered or canceled passages must undoubtedly have been preceded by much preparatory work.

The source of this evidence is twofold: first, the manuscript of the sketches "A Few Crusted Characters,"[6] which Hardy entitled "Wessex Folk" and described as a "First Rough Draft"; and second, two surviving fragments of the "First Draft" of *Far from the Madding Crowd* (now in the Dorset County Museum). According to Purdy, the "Wessex Folk" manuscript is "a very rough hurried first draft (in places hardly more than notes)" and it has "notes and alterations on the verso of many leaves and at the end a good many trial names."[7] The surviving leaves of the first draft of *Far from the Madding Crowd*, while showing Hardy's work at a more advanced stage of composition than the "Wessex Folk" manuscript, nevertheless displays the same features of experiment and denotation suggested in Purdy's description. The second of the two fragments forms part of an unnumbered chapter[8] to which Hardy later supplied the

---

4. Kramer, "A Query Concerning Handwriting," p. 358.
5. The only exceptions I have noted are those found in the canceled writing on the verso of ff. 112, 116a, 172, 335, 413 (first one and a half lines); in the surviving fragment of the first line of f. 319, and the folio number and first line of ff. 94 and 331, all of which appear to be in Emma Hardy's hand.
6. The sketches form one of a collection of nine stories first published in book form by Osgood, McIlvaine in 1894, under the title *Life's Little Ironies*. The MS. is now in the Bliss collection.
7. Purdy, *Thomas Hardy*, p. 84.
8. Although the chapter was later canceled, elements of a descriptive passage on f. 106f were incorporated into the description of the Hollow in Ch. XLIV of the familiar text of *Far from the Madding Crowd*. The fragment is headed simply "Chapter," a factor which together with the surviving lines of material (later canceled) on ff. 106 and 155ᵛ of the *Mayor* MS., headed by a similarly unspecified "Chapter," suggests that Hardy's practice was to number his chapters some considerable time after composition.

note "Details of sheep-rot—omitted from MS. when revised." This fragment is composed of eleven leaves (numbered 106a–k) of heavily
revised material. The tentative nature of the writing, evident throughout, is seen in his placing of queries after words: "The <fatting> wethers
(?) about to be fatted had no bell." (f. 106h);[9] and in the offer of several
alternatives for a descriptive adjective:

>   steaming
>   the fulsome firmament above
>   noxious
>   vapoury   (f.106e)

Of greater interest still is the fragmentary sentence on f. 106f, completion of which is indicated by suspension points and a brief note (simply
a phrase from *Hamlet*) incorporating the idea to be expanded:

> the presence, of the fiery mist was caused by the effect of the hot
> sun's rays upon the swamp that afternoon . . . "god kissing car-
> rion" etc.
> its colour, of course, by the reflection and refraction of the sun's
> rays +   (f. 106f)

The addendum to this note (indicated at the end of the sentence by the
mark +) appears on the verso of f. 106e, and consists of a partially constructed sentence comprising only those aspects of the description
salient in the author's mind; namely, the unpleasing anthropomorphic
features of the objects described—an element characteristic of Hardy's
handling of natural scenery. Blanks are left for material as yet unformu-
lated: "desc. these fungi thus. Then there was the——with its bloody skin
and——spots. . . . There was also" (f. 106e). Immediately above this
note further details of the fungi (written in pencil and later erased) have
been added: "clammy tops, crowns, oozing gills—splotches red as arter-
ial blood." The fragment contains many similar pencilings, a method of
composition which Hardy confined not only to early draft, for there are
frequent traces throughout the *Mayor* manuscript of interlinear pencilings, usually comprising words or phrases later overwritten in ink.
Indeed the remaining traces of a now erased penciled note in Chapter
XII present the single instance of revision in the *Mayor* to show the
incompleteness of the working draft. This occurs between lines 12 and
13 on f. 114, where Hardy has added a summary of material to be

---

9. In all quotation from the Hardy MSS. discussed here the following method will be used: deletions will be placed within angular brackets (< >), and where the reading of a cancellation is
   doubtful the word in question will be followed by a query enclosed in square brackets ([?]);
   where illegible, it will be replaced by a blank (—); interlinear additions which represent the
   final form of the MS. text will be placed in italics. All wording, spelling, and interior punctuation will correspond with the original, even where unconventional (e.g., Hardy frequently
   omitted quotation marks enclosing dialogue).

expanded: Henchard has just told the young Scotsman Farfrae of his recent involvement with Lucetta Le Sueur, and the note suggests that he is to set the seal on the episode with an emphatic, if melodramatic, gesture, for the erasure reads as follows: "there's an end of her and here goes her picture. Burns it flame creeps up face etc." The incident however does not appear in the final form of the manuscript, either because Hardy may not after all have expanded the note, or because he omitted it when reworking the chapter, most of which was rewritten before the completion of the manuscript. With this one exception virtually no material in the *Mayor* manuscript presents Hardy's work at so preliminary a stage as that of the first draft of *Far from the Madding Crowd*.

While the manuscript of the *Mayor* presents a far from homogeneous text—that is to say, a study of its revisions reveals several different phases in the composition of the novel—Hardy's particular methods of revision frequently make it difficult to distinguish between fair copy and earlier draft. There are of course numerous leaves on which fair copy is readily detected: the relative absence of revision on ff. 212, 261, and 269, for instance, together with factors of line-spacing (as on ff. 42 and 120) and foliation (f. 116a) suggests that rewriting had taken place. Yet if absence of revision implies fair copy, the very frequency with which Hardy reviewed his material makes density of revision an unreliable criterion for assessing the stage of composition. There are numerous leaves in the manuscript which, if intended as fair copy, are yet difficult to detect as such, from the extent of later emendation, as well as from changes made during the act of copying.

This point is of particular relevance to those areas of the text which generally receive the greatest amount of revision; namely, dialogue (that of rustic characters in particular) and passages of description. The text of many such passages, while sufficiently polished to have originally represented fair copy (prior, that is, to revision), nevertheless contain several layers of emendation, as for example, ff. 49, 73, 174,[1] 371, 445, and 473. Hardy appears then to have rewritten pages of fair copy only when the extent of subsequent revision made this imperative.

Evidence that Hardy subjected his work to revision immediately after and sometimes during the act of composition (or perhaps more accurately, during the act of copying) is provided by the canceled material on the verso of a number of sheets which contain the discarded beginnings of several leaves.[2] Hardy's practice seems to have been to invert and use as fair copy the verso of a previously discarded leaf if the canceled material did not extend beyond nine or ten lines. Several of these pages contain corrections even when the material extends to no more

---

1. A facsimile of f. 174 is reproduced on the following page [*Editor*].
2. Viz. the verso of ff. 112, 116a, 128, 155, 172, 244, 261, 327, 335, 384, 413, and 454.

XVIII OF THE MAYOR MANUSCRIPT
A typical example of Hardy's careful revision of passages of rustic dialogue.

than a sentence in length. Three illustrations of this practice may be cited:

243

"Then the romance of the sower is gone for ever," sd
                    Donald returned
"Yes—Yes. . . . It must be so!" <Farfrae murmured>, his gaze
fixing itself
<going> far away, and his mind following as usual.   (f. 244ᵛ)

260

They sat *stiffly* in a <stiff> row, like the people in certain early
devotional paintings, Lucetta *being* opposite them.   (f. 261ᵛ)

283

People thus *waited and* watched the far-off London highway, to
the ringing of bells, till a man stationed at the turn of the road
was seen to give a signal.   (f. 384ᵛ)

While it would be a gross simplification to suggest that the corrections in a heavily revised manuscript like the *Mayor* could be divided into discrete chronological units, the interlinear position, style of writing, pen thickness, and ink color in which many of the changes are made do make it possible to detect what appear to be specific groups of revision. In particular two separate groupings may be distinguished: first, those revisions written with a very fine-nibbed pen and in black ink (the color used throughout the manuscript); second, those revisions written in a greyish purple ink and with a pen thickness similar to that used throughout the manuscript.

These revision groupings are worth noting, not only for the information they yield on the probable stage of composition at which certain amendments were made, but also for the illustration they afford of the frequency and thoroughness of Hardy's revision; for their distribution in the text suggests that Hardy reviewed his material after completing about two thirds of the novel, as well as subjecting it to a more extensive revision after completion of the entire work.

The fine-pen revisions register numerous kinds of change, both stylistic and substantive, as well as a number of name changes, in particular, the amendment of the Scotsman's surname from the earlier "Stansbie" to the final form "Farfrae." Moreover, several additions on leaf verso are written in fine-pen.[3] The revisions in grey ink in Section I most frequently register the name changes "Alan" to "Donald" (for the Scotsman), and "Giles" to "James" (earlier forms of Henchard's first name), whereas in Section II they register various kinds of change. Both groups of revision represent a

---

3. Viz. the verso of ff. 46, 81, 456.

fairly late stage in the novel's composition, since many from each group
are in fact corrections of already revised material:

He's   homespun
A *simple* <old> *man* . . .
'Tis barren ignorance that leads to such words.
A never was fit for good company . . .   (f. 76)

(fine-pen revision in italics)

<tables>
the square <cloth> of hedged fields   (f. 269)
surfaces   )   (grey-ink revision in italics)

When a number of revisions from one or other of these groups appear
regularly over a stretch of text, it would seem reasonable to assume that
they form a series of revisions entered over one specific period. Yet there
is evidence to suggest that these revision groupings can be subdivided:
while certain of the revisions in fine-pen have clearly been made before
Chapter XLII at the latest, other revisions in a similar pen have obviously
been entered after completion of the novel. Evidence for this appears in
the series of changes made for the names of Michael Henchard and
Donald Farfrae. Henchard's first name is recorded as "Giles" until
Chapter XLII where it then appears as "James," remaining in that form
for the rest of the manuscript. Thus all fine-pen revisions in the final section amending "James" to "Michael" must have been entered after completion of the text. The Scotsman's surname appears as "Stansbie" until
Chapter XXIII[4] where it is then recorded as "Farfrae." Now in an addition on the verso of f. 160 the unrevised "Farfrae" appears with "G.
Henchard," a concurrence which indicates, then, that a further group of
fine-pen revision (namely those including the alteration "Farfrae") must
have been entered during the period of the earliest phase of Henchard's
first name: that is, before Chapter XLII.

When supported by factors of foliation and revision, evidence of
name change can prove a valuable criterion in identifying different
phases of the manuscript's history, and in this connection one series of
changes in particular may be mentioned. These concern the revisions
made in the naming of Donald Farfrae.

It would appear that the Scotsman was first called "Alan Stansbie,"
later "Alan Farfrae," and finally "Donald Farfrae." This order of change
is suggested, though not exclusively so, on the one hand by the presence
on several leaves of the unrevised "Alan" with the amendment "Farfrae,"
and on the other hand by the appearance of the revision "Donald" in an
ink coloring used for the series of alterations which seem to postdate
those of the "Farfrae" group. With the exception of six leaves, the name
"Alan Stansbie" together with the interlinear substitutions "Donald" and

---

"Farfrae" appears throughout the text until Chapter XXIII (f. 233) where for the first time the name "Donald Farfrae" appears unrevised, and is maintained in that form for the rest of the text.

Exceptions to the appearance of the Scotsman's name as "Alan Stansbie" in leaves prior to Chapter XXIII are to be found on three scattered leaves between Chapters VIII and IX and on three leaves in Chapter XII, where the name appears unrevised in its final form. Its presence on ff. 110, 113, and 116 in Chapter XII is easily explained since the foliation, paper stock, and series of alterations suggest that the leaves in question were written at a later date than the rest of the chapter.[5] The appearance, unrevised, of the final form of the surname between Chapters VIII and IX presents a greater difficulty. Chapter VI, in which the Scotsman is first introduced into the novel, is entirely absent from the manuscript; mention of him simply as "the Scotch gentleman" (f. 61), or as "the young Scotchman" (f. 64), occurs in Chapter VII; and he makes his first appearance in Chapter VIII, where his name is recorded as "Alan" (f. 72). His surname first occurs on f. 73, then on ff. 77 and 81, and on all three occasions the name appears *unrevised* as "Farfrae." These represent the only occurrences of the surname until f. 95 where it is recorded as "Stansbie," remaining in that form (Ch. XII excepted) until Chapter XXIII.

The appearance of the surname in its final form at this stage in the text would seem initially to suggest either that "Farfrae" was the name that Hardy first thought of, later discarded, and finally returned to halfway through the manuscript, or that the pages on which the name appears were written at a later date than the surrounding leaves. Yet nothing in the foliation, paper stock, or other revisions indicates later composition; and while the possibility of a return to a previously discarded name presents a more likely alternative, the very physical appearance of the name on ff. 73, 77, and 81 makes this doubtful. On all three leaves the name has been written with a fine-nibbed pen, conspicuously different from the surrounding writing, and corresponding to the series of revisions in a similar fine writing made at a later stage of the novel's composition.

There seem to be two possible explanations: either that Hardy was unable to decide on a suitable surname at this stage of composition and simply left a blank space which he filled in on subsequent revision, or alternatively, that a surname was entered tentatively in pencil and later erased when the name "Farfrae" had been finally established. The suggestion of tentative penciling is strengthened by the presence, mentioned earlier, of occasional traces throughout the manuscript of portions of the text which first appear in pencil and are later overwritten in ink. Erasure of a previous entry in ink is not likely, since there is no indication that the surface of the paper has been disturbed—a feature pre-

5. Evidence for this assumption is discussed below.

sent elsewhere in the manuscript where erasure of writing in ink has been made.[6]

II

Section I. Chapters I–X

The first ten chapters of the manuscript contain leaves from the earliest traceable phase of the novel's history. None of these chapters is complete, most are fragmentary, and one is missing altogether. The surviving leaves of Chapter I contain some of the heaviest revision in the manuscript, and an inspection of the cancellations on these sheets reveals not only the existence of an earlier text embedded in the first twenty leaves of the manuscript but also a marked discrepancy between the system of the foliation of the leaves and the order of their composition. While the plot was subjected to a major reorganization before the first leaves of the present manuscript were written, sheets from an earlier phase of the novel's history have been retained and adapted to fit the later conception. While the existence of this earliest text is most apparent in Chapter I, the salvaging and subsequent adaptation of leaves from an earlier text results in the presence, until well into the twenty-second chapter of the manuscript, of traces of an earlier draft of the novel.

The surviving traces of the earlier text suggest that a fundamental reappraisal of the relationships between the major characters occurred shortly after composition began, while the remnants of the earlier plot suggest a development divergent from that of the definitive version. The main features of the earlier text however are not in evidence until f. 14 of the manuscript. The first five leaves present the Henchard family situation as it appears in the definitive form—that of a young couple with their only child. The most significant revisions in these opening leaves concern the husband's trade, for deletions indicate that Henchard was first depicted not as the haytrusser of the familiar version but as a mechanic:

> At his back he carried by a looped strap a rush basket
> *from which protruded at one end the crutch of a hay-knife,*
> \<of tools, and from a little side pocket down his thigh\>
> *a wimble for hay bonds being also visible in the aperture*
> \<gleamed the brass joint of a two-foot rule\>.	(f. 2)

---

6. E.g., the following words, which have been written over a previous erasure: "trusser," "hay truss-er" (f. 17), "browsing" (f. 130), "a very fugue of sounds" (f. 428). It seems worth mentioning here that the original name of the Scotsman ("Stansbie") and that of the Mayor himself ("Giles Henchard") both appear to have been drawn from John Hutchins' *The History and Antiquities of the County of Dorset*, 3rd edn., 4 vols. (London 1861–73)—a work with which Hardy was thoroughly acquainted, and a copy of which he kept in his library. * * *

His . . . walk was the walk of the <mechanic> . . .   (f. 2)

skilled countryman

"Any trade doing here?" he asked. . . . "Anything in the
hay trussing
<building> line?"

Not until ff. 14–20 do the cancellations reveal that the "mechanic" of the opening leaves is itself a replacement of earlier attempts at representing the protagonist's craft. Inspection of the revisions here indicates that ff. 14–20 antedate ff. 1–5 and are survivals from an earlier phase of the novel's composition. Originally numbered 12–18, the figures have been altered to read 14–20 to fit the reorganized opening of the chapter. Deletions made over Henchard's trade are much heavier than before and reveal that he was first visualized as a woodman, and then more specifically, as a sawyer. "Woodman" has in several places been altered to "workman," but there are other instances of more elaborate revision:

<stone mason>
"Set it higher, auctioneer," said the <woodman> <sawyer>,
trusser   (f. 15)

trusser
". . . the bargain's complete," said the <woodman>
<stone mason>   (f. 17)

Traces of the earlier plot are now apparent, and they reveal that the Henchard family was originally composed not of one daughter but of two; while Susan, on being sold to the sailor Richard Newson, was to take one child with her, the second remaining with the husband:

if she wants to,
". . . She shall take <one of> the girl<s, her favourite one,> and
my tools
go her ways. I'll take <mine> and go my ways. . . ."   (f. 14)

". . . 'Twill be better for me and the child both.
<Take care of the girl. I'll take care of this one>   (f. 17)[7]

with her right hand, and
Seizing the sailor's arm <and dragging on the smaller girl>
mounting the little girl on her left she went out.   (f. 17)

Moreover, Henchard and his wife were originally conceived as older than they appear in the present text. They had been married for five years, with one daughter at least old enough to offer her mother advice:

7. A facsimile of f. 17 appears on page 267 [*Editor*].

<"Don't mother!" whispered the girl who sat on the woman's side. "Father don't know what he's saying."> (f. 14)

while Susan tells her husband:

a couple of
"I've lived with thee <five> years . . ." (f. 17)

While all references to a single child on ff. 14–20 form interlinear additions which frequently replace previous references to two children:

". . . she is willing [to go] *provided she can have the child*."
(f. 17)

"Very well—<then> *she shall have the child and* the bargain's complete." said the trusser. (f. 17)

The sailor looked at the woman, and smiled. "Come along!" he said *kindly.* "*The little one too—the more the merrier!*" She paused for an instant, with a close glance at him. Then dropping her eyes again . . . she *took up the child and* followed him. . . .
(f. 17)

". . . *'Twill be better for me and the child both*
<Take care of the girl. I'll take care of this one>. (f. 17)

no such replacement is necessary in the opening leaves of the manuscript:

. . . a young man and woman, the latter carrying a child, were approaching the large village of Weydon-Priors on foot. (f. 1)

. . . [the woman] walked the highway alone, save for the child she bore. (f. 3)

If any word at all was uttered by the little group it was an occasional whisper of the woman to the child—a little girl in short clothes and blue boots of knitted yarn . . . (f. 3)

All but the first eleven lines of Chapter II are missing, and the surviving fragment breaks off at a critical point in the development of the plot. Henchard has just woken the morning after selling his wife, and the leaf ends with the now canceled lines:

. . . a rustling on his left hand caused him to turn. The girl on the bench was just opening her eyes. He rose (f. 20)

At this point in the manuscript further revelation of the course of the original plot is precluded by the sequence of missing leaves (ff. 21–28), and with the next grouping of leaves the plot appears to have reached the stage of development apparent in the opening leaves. The instability of the author's notion of Henchard's craft is now less evident, for Elizabeth Jane asks her mother:

The fairly heavy revision reveals traces of an earlier phase of the plot, including evidence of the two children originally ascribed to the Henchard family (lines 20, 21), and the alteration of the husband's trade from "woodman," "sawyer," and "stonemason," to "hay trusser" (lines 10, 17). The canceled number in the top right-hand corner indicates an earlier system of foliation.

hay trusser
"He was a \<stone mason\>, wasn't he, when you last heard of him?
(f. 29)

In the absence of appropriate reference within the text, however, one cannot assert with complete confidence that Hardy had at this stage dispensed with the idea of two daughters, since it is quite possible that "woodman" may have been replaced by "stone mason" (ff. 15, 17, 19) before the cancellation of the opening of Chapter I of the earlier text. That is to say, it is not possible to state conclusively whether ff. 29–32 was written before or after ff. 1–5 of the present manuscript.

Futher deletions in Chapter IV, V, and X indicate that the role of Richard Newson in the earlier text was not meant to extend beyond the first chapter. The sailor's death, which, in anticipation of his reappearance later in the novel, is described rather vaguely in the final form of the manuscript, was originally made quite explicit:

lost to them
The sailor was now \<dead and buried\>. . . .   (f. 35)

was lost
Father \<died\> last spring.   (f. 96)

This assumption is confirmed by further deletions which reveal that until f. 96 at least, the Henchard of the earlier text was the real father of the now adult Elizabeth Jane:

Susan Henchard's
\<Elizabeth Jane's father, and the elder woman's\> husband, in law at least, sat there. . . .   (f. 45)

encumbered with no recollections as her mother was
Elizabeth\<s last view of him having been been before her recollection\> . . .   (f. 45)

the master of the premises
Elizabeth Jane now entered, and stood before \<her father\>

(f. 94)
twelve
"I was \<thirteen\> when we came here from Canada."   (f. 96)

By such conversation he discovered the circumstances which had enveloped his wife and *her* child in . . . total obscurity . . .
(f. 96)

In the evolution of Henchard's trade from woodman, through mechanic, and finally to hay-trusser, the resemblance between the earliest and the last trade makes it tempting to see in the final choice of hay-trusser a reversion to a craft which, in identifying the protagonist more closely with physical nature, provides a more fitting complement to the character of a man of elementary passions.[8] It is also tempting to see the changes made over Elizabeth Jane's parentage and the expansion of the role of Richard Newson serving the function not only of gratifying the reader's "love of the uncommon in human experience"[9] but also of reinforcing the persistence of an ironic fate, or perhaps more accurately, of reinforcing the expression of character in terms of that fate, since it is largely through Henchard's manipulation of the truth of Elizabeth Jane's parentage—one more instance of his playing with chance—that the tragic outcome of Newson's reappearance is determined.

However, since all surviving traces of the earliest phase of the plot are confined to the opening chapters of the manuscript, and since the information offered on the likely direction of the plot is insufficient to establish with any certainty an affinity between the character and fate intended for the Henchard of the earlier version with that of the protagonist in the final manuscript text, any attempt to assess the author's motives for reorganizing the plot must in the end be unprofitable.

Section II. Chapters XII, XVIII, and XXII

Further traces of an earlier text appear with the introduction and development of the Henchard-Lucetta theme in Chapters XII, XVIII, and XXII. Since these chapters present material drawn from different phases of the novel's history they are, not unexpectedly, written on sheets from two different paper stocks, with material from the earlier text heavily revised to comply with that of the later version.

The Henchard-Lucetta theme is first introduced in Chapter XII. In the final form of the manuscript text this chapter contains a conversation between Henchard and Farfrae, in which the Mayor discloses past incidents in his life—the sale of his first wife and child more than twenty years ago, and his recent marriage to Lucetta Le Sueur, undertaken in gratitude to her for having saved his life in an accident in Jersey. Lucetta is expected to arrive in Casterbridge the following evening; an event which Farfrae agrees to forestall by meeting her boat at Budmouth Harbour with a letter from Henchard explaining the unexpected return of the wife he had believed dead, and the consequent annulment of his more recent marriage.[1]

---

8. Hardy used both earlier versions of Henchard's trade for the occupations of central figures in two later novels: in *The Woodlanders*, published in 1887 (though according to Florence Emily Hardy, *The Life of Thomas Hardy, 1840–1928* [London, 1962], p. 102, originally conceived as early as 1874), George Melbury is a timber merchant, and Giles Winterbourne, though actually in the "apple and cider trade," is closely connected with the timber business through his association with Melbury; while the eponymous hero of *Jude* (1896) is a stonemason.
9. "The real, if unavowed, purpose of fiction is to give pleasure by gratifying the love of the uncommon in human experience, mental or corporeal." (Note made in July 1881 and included in *The Life of Thomas Hardy*, p. 150.)
1. In the version submitted to the *Graphic*, both the history and the outcome of Henchard's affair with Lucetta, it may be noted, differ markedly from that of the familiar version of the text, the main lines of which were introduced in the reworking of the serial for the first book-form edition in 1886.

The chapter presents a fairly complex synthesis of material. Alterations reveal that the leaves in their final form were revised on no fewer than three different occasions, and hence the surviving pages, several of which have been renumbered, present a patchwork from two different paper stocks.

The opening leaves of the chapter are missing, and the last page (f. 106) before the sequence of missing leaves (ff. 107–09) has been cut just above the opening lines of what would have been Chapter XII (such cutting being indicative of the removal of canceled material). The final numbering of the surviving leaves in this chapter is 110–16a, with 115 missing. All leaves before Chapter XII, and with three exceptions the seventy-six leaves following, are written on paper from Stock A. Of the leaves in Chapter XII two (112, 114) are from Stock A and the remainder (110, 111, 113, 116, 116a) from Stock B. Deletions and additions on the surviving leaves reveal several stages of composition, and the suggested order of their composition is: 112, 114, 110, 111, 113, 116, 116a. The evidence for assuming this order is offered as an illustration of the different layers of revision within the manuscript, and the consequent difficulty in assessing fair copy.

Folios 112 and 114 are survivals from an earlier phase of writing. These were originally consecutive leaves: 112 was previously numbered 113, and the now canceled line at the end of the leaf is completed on 114:

> . . . it turns out she is not your wife, the first   (f. 112)

> being alive; so ye cannot see her . . .   (f. 114)

Further, Farfrae's name appears as "Alan" on f. 112, which assigns it to the earlier period of composition, as the appearance of "Farfrae" unrevised on ff. 110, 113, and 116 assigns them to a later period.

At the second stage of composition the remaining leaves—110, 111, 113, 116, and 116a—were written. All occurrences of Farfrae's name appear on these leaves unrevised in its final form. Folio 110 has obviously been written after the leaves assigned to stage one, since it includes, or rather reiterates, Henchard's disclosure of his first wife's return, information which also appears on (the chronologically earlier) f. 112:

> No wife or daughter could I hear of . . . till this very day. And now—they have come back.   (f. 110)

> This morning—this very morning . . . my first wife, my real wife, returned to me.   (f. 112)

Folio 112 must by this time have been discarded, for ff. 111 and 113 were originally consecutive: 113 was previously numbered 112, and the now canceled sentence at the foot of one leaf is completed at the top of the next:

> No: somebody must meet her, and let her know all: so that she goes
> back by   (f. 111)

> the same packet which returns at once.   (f. 113)

The last five lines of f. 113 are left blank, the leaf having been written to precede the already composed 114.

The third stage of composition includes the reintroduction of the presumably discarded f. 112, and the deletions and substitutions made on f. 111 to adapt the later written leaf to the earlier. The reason for resurrecting this leaf may well have been the author's wish to maintain the strict tone of propriety in Henchard's attitude towards his relationship with Lucetta, for the leaf contains a speech by Henchard in which full acceptance of his responsibility for the outcome of events, and a concern with the ethical aspects of his position, strike the predominant note:

> Now see what misery a man may lay up for himself! Even after that
> wrongdoing at the fair . . . if I had never taken the second false step
> at Jersey, all might now be well. For don't you suppose I complain of
> losing the younger . . . woman I last married: I do no such thing: I
> willingly bear all that . . . but I complain of the trickery of things,
> whereby a perfectly fair course is made impossible. I must injure one
> of them, and it is the second. Honour where honour is due — my first
> duty is to Susan — there's no doubt about that.   (f. 112)

and farther on:

> But these two women — I feel I should like to treat them as honest-
> ly as a man can in such a case.   (f. 112)

The mark × at the beginning of the sentence "That account of my escape at Jersey I didn't quite complete," on f. 111 denotes a textual addition which has been written in pencil on the verso of f. 110. This recounts Henchard's accident in Jersey and subsequent rescue by Lucetta, and was presumably added when Hardy, on revising the amalgamated version, realized that the account of Henchard's escape existed by this time only on sheets either destroyed or containing inadaptable material.

While the deletions on the leaves in Chapter XII appear to be remnants of an earlier phase of the introduction of the Henchard-Lucetta *motif*, there are cancellations on sheets incorporated in two later chapters (namely, XVIII and XXII) which appear to antedate the earliest traceable stages of composition present in Chapter XII. Like the earlier chapter Chapters XVIII and XXII show evidence of the adaptation of material from different phases of the novel's composition.

A canceled system of foliation at the top left-hand corner of the leaf, beginning at f. 125 and, with several exceptions, extending through to f. 215, offers valuable evidence for identifying within this area of the manuscript a still earlier phase of the Henchard-Lucetta theme. Of equal importance, the canceled foliation confirms the assumption made earlier, that leaves from Stock A (up to f. 215 at least) differ in date from those in Stock B; for the leaves from which the canceled foliation is absent are *without exception* those drawn from Stock B. The correlation between the earlier system of foliation and that of the final manuscript form is represented in the table below.

The Henchard-Lucetta theme, introduced in the largely rewritten Chapter XII, is resumed in Chapter XVIII (which begins on f. 165). Marks

LEAVES MISSING numbers refer to present foliation	EARLIER FOLIATIONS top left hand corner	PRESENT FOLIATION top right hand corner	PAPER STOCK 'A' unless otherwise stated	COMMENTS
	125–161	same		
162–163				
	164–165	same		
	—	166	'B'	written at a later date, hence no l.h. foliation
	166–170	167–171		
	170a	172		added later, but before l.h. foliation abandoned
	171–172	173–174		
175–180				
	179	181		
	—	182	'B'	written at a later date, hence no l.h. foliation
	180–181	183–184		
185				
	183	186		
187–188				
	186–187	189–190		
191–192				
	· 190–191	193–194		
195–197				
	195–197	198–200		
201–204				
	202–207	205–210		
	—	211–212	'B'	written at a later date, hence no l.h. foliation
213	211–212	214–215		

of alteration and adaptation are evident in the opening leaves of the chapter, and the suggested order of composition is: 165 (lines 1–15), 167, 165 (lines 16–20), 166.

Folio 165 is composed of portions of two separate leaves joined together. This is obviously not a once complete leaf torn and then mended, since the feint lines of the lower half (the last five lines of the leaf) differ in color from those of the top half, though both are of the same paper stock. Moreover the canceled system of foliation reveals that the following leaf (166) has been inserted at a later date, and that f. 167 originally followed f. 165 (top portion). Folio 165 has been cut shortly after the beginning of the reported content of Lucetta's first recorded letter to Henchard:

> She said that she perceived full well how impossible it would be for any further communications to proceed between them, now that his remarriage had taken place.
> <"But Giles," she> [cut]   (f. 165)

In the affixed lines and in the leaf following, which present the text of Lucetta's letter, the writer refers to "our ill-advised marriage" (165) and requests the return of letters written to Henchard "immediately after being sent back to Jersey when I had come to join you" (166). This accords with the text presented in Chapter XII where even the earliest composed sheets of the chapter refer to Henchard's marriage with the woman from Jersey. Yet f. 167, which has many deletions and alterations, contains traces of a still earlier phase of the plot, revealing that the relationship between the two was originally conceived in terms conspicuously different from those in the final form of the manuscript. Whereas the strictest propriety in the relations between the pair is observed in the text offered to the *Graphic*, the survival of the earlier text on f. 167 suggests that the relationship was originally a predominantly sexual one and that no marriage had taken place:

> Poor thing—six years of shilly-shallying with me—engagement as she calls it! Upon my heart and life, if ever I were left in a position to take another wife she *ought* in justice to be you—she *ought* to be you!   (f. 167)

while further correction in the same paragraph—

>   you   saved   's life than mine!
> better <she> had <seen> the devil <than me>   (f. 167)

—suggests that the life-saving episode which eventually leads to Henchard's marriage to Lucetta belongs to a later stage in the reorganization of the subplot.

Further traces of the earlier text appear in Chapter XXII. Opening on f. 211, the chapter is included in that area of the manuscript written on leaves from Stock B. Survivals from the earlier text are evident on ff. 214–15, both of which are drawn from Stock A, the latter half of f. 215 having been cut, presumably because the material it contained was no longer adaptable to the later text. Further traces of the sexual nature of Henchard's relationship with Lucetta are apparent:

> She was in a very coming-on disposition *for marriage*; of that there could be no doubt. But what else could a poor woman be
> *herself to him so unluckily at first*
> who had given <the freshest years of her life to him?>   (f. 214)

The original tone of their relationship, which the rewriting noticeably suppresses, is nicely illustrated in the following alteration:

> *woman*
> "The artful little <wench>!" he said smiling. . . .   (f. 214)

The rearrangement of material in chapters of the manuscript dealing with the introduction and development of the Henchard-Lucetta theme points to a fundamental reorganization of this aspect of the plot sometime after its original composition. It is not possible to decide at what stage in the manuscript's history this occurred, but cancellations on several scattered leaves suggest that the major revision of Chapter XII, where the Henchard-Lucetta theme is first introduced, was probably not undertaken until well over half the novel was completed. The evidence for this assumption may be summarized as follows. In Chapter XII, it will be remembered, Farfrae agrees to meet Lucetta at Budmouth with the explanatory letter from Henchard:

> No—somebody must meet her, and let her know all; so that she may go back by the packet which returns as soon as the other arrives. . . . will you do me the good turn of going for me? "Yes—I will," said Farfrae . . .   (ff. 112–113)

Now the verso of f. 112 carries several heavily canceled lines which comprise material from the earliest traceable phase of the subplot, and suggests that the extent of Farfrae's participation in forestalling Lucetta's arrival was originally much smaller than it appears in the final manuscript form. The deletions, which are in Emma Hardy's hand, are practically illegible; but the leaf seems originally to have been numbered 121 [?] and reads as follows:

> In about forty minutes they were on the Quay in Budmouth Harbour. There was but a lamp or two here or there and the man who took down Miss Le Sueur's personal luggage neither —— suspected who had brought her, Henchard leaving her there. Henchard drove away and stabled his horse, after which he returned on foot to the Quay.

While the evidence here, as in the opening leaves of the manuscript, is too slight to make conjecture on the possible course of the earlier form of the plot a profitable task, these lines seem to indicate that at one stage in the narrative Lucetta had in fact arrived from Jersey and was escorted from Casterbridge not by Farfrae, but by Henchard himself. The assumption is confirmed still further by deletions in Chapter XVIII which suggest that Farfrae's assistance in the original form of Chapter XII corresponded fairly closely with the text of the first edition. For the canceled fragment of Lucetta's letter on f. 167—

> which I poured out to you the sentiments of a soul as warm as ever lodged in woman's heart! Especially send the one in which I wrote what I regret—if it is not destroyed."

—is followed by a parenthetical explanation:

> (This referred to the letter on which he [Henchard] had consulted Stansbie.)   (f. 167)

while the following deletion appears later in the chapter:

>   *the letters*
> Farfrae took the bundle [of Lucetta's letters]. . . . guessed <they>
>   *property of the lady*   *become involved with*
> were the <letters> Henchard had <spoken of> <in their friendly
> days> . . .   (f. 170)

The original conception of the Henchard-Lucetta relationship revealed in the fragments of the earlier text thus bears a marked similarity to the version of their relationship "rewritten" for the first edition in 1886, in which Hardy simplified the plot by removing, among other elements designed expressly for the household reader, the ramifications of Henchard's marriage with Lucetta. Nevertheless one feature of the original conception—the sexual element in the relationship—remained suppressed until the publication of the first uniform edition of 1895.

The absence of any historical evidence either from letters between Hardy and the editor of the *Graphic* or from information included in the *Life of Thomas Hardy* makes it impossible to identify with complete assurance the immediate cause of the changes in this area of the plot; the inducement however was undoubtedly deference to the prudery of the magazine-reading public. In the light of previous objections from family magazine editors to his candid treatment of relations between the sexes,[2] Hardy may have subjected his original story to close scrutiny and,

---

2. In 1874 when Hardy was writing *Far from the Madding Crowd* for serialization in the *Cornhill*, Leslie Stephen wrote to him that the seduction of Fanny Robin would "require to be treated in a gingerly fashion," and asked Hardy to "excuse this wretched shred of concession to popular stupidity. . . ." Three years later when Hardy submitted a portion of the MS. of *The Return of the Native*, Stephen refused to accept the story for the *Cornhill* without first seeing the entire novel, because "though he liked the opening, he feared that the relations between Eustacia,

in anticipation of difficulties ahead, have doctored the sexual element, on his own initiative. A more likely possibility is that the changes were made as a direct result of editorial pressure from the *Graphic*. The general appearance of the revisions on several leaves in Chapter XII suggests a hasty and at times rather perfunctory rearrangement of material. In particular, the penciled addition on the verso of f. 110, though apparently a fairly rough draft,[3] nevertheless presents with very little alteration the text as it appeared in the *Graphic*. Certainly the general quality of the changes made here suggests the motive to have been one of expediency rather than of critical reappraisal.

Wildeve, and Thomasin might develop into something 'dangerous' for a family magazine. . . ."
Both letters are quoted in F. W. Maitland, *Life and Letters of Leslie Stephen* (London 1906)—a work to which Hardy contributed material on Stephen as editor (pp. 270–78).
3. Cancellations within the line indicating changes made during the act of copying, viz.:

"For many years <I've been in the> it has been my custom
to go to Jersey <every now and then> in the way of business." (f 110ᵛ)

Hardy's Nonfictional Writings

From The Life and Work of Thomas Hardy[†]

[1874] However, that he did not care much for a reputation as a novel-ist in lieu of being able to follow the pursuit of poetry—now for ever hin-dered, as it seemed—becomes obvious from a remark written to Mr Stephen[1] about this time:

> The truth is that I am willing, and indeed anxious, to give up any points which may be desirable in a story when read as a whole, for the sake of others which shall please those who read it in numbers. Perhaps I may have higher aims some day, and be a great stickler for the proper artistic balance of the completed work, but for the present circumstances lead me to wish merely to be considered a good hand at a serial.

* * *

[1875] One reflection about himself at this date sometimes made Hardy uneasy. He perceived that he was "up against" the position of having to carry on his life not as an emotion, but as a scientific game; that he was committed to novel-writing as a regular trade, as much as he had for-merly been to architecture; and that hence he would, he deemed, have to look for material in manners—in ordinary social and fashionable life as other novelists did. Yet he took no interest in manners, but in the sub-stance of life only. So far what he had written had not been novels at all,

† Much of the last decade or so of Hardy's life was taken up with preparation of two volumes that appeared after his death as The Early Life of Thomas Hardy 1840–91 (1928) and The Later Years of Thomas Hardy (1930), reissued in a one-volume edition in 1962 as The Life of Thomas Hardy 1840–1928. The title page states that the work was "compiled largely from contempo-rary notes, letters, diaries, and biographical memoranda, as well as from oral information in conversations extending over many years by Florence Emily Hardy," but although Florence continued to be listed as the author, it has long been known that the work was essentially a dic-tated autobiography, crafted and written by Hardy himself, then typed up by Florence. The edi-tion now commonly used is that edited by Michael Millgate as The Life and Work of Thomas Hardy, by Thomas Hardy (London: Macmillan, 1984), from which the following passages have been taken. At first glance the Life seems to be a relatively casual compilation, but Hardy clear-ly took pains to include a number of key statements about his work both as novelist and poet. The most significant of these are included here, along with the few direct references to The Mayor of Casterbridge. Dates in square brackets have been added by the editor of this edition.
1. Leslie Stephen (1832–1904), editor of the Cornhill Magazine, for which at this time Hardy was writing Far from the Madding Crowd.

as usually understood—that is pictures of modern customs and obser-
vances—and might not long sustain the interest of the circulating-library
subscriber who cared mainly for those things. On the other hand, to go
about to dinners and clubs and crushes as a business was not much to
his mind. Yet that was necessary meat and drink to the popular author.
Not that he was unsociable, but events and long habit had accustomed
him to solitary living. * * * He mentioned this doubt of himself one
day to Miss Thackeray,[2] who confirmed his gloomy misgivings by saying
with surprise: "Certainly; a novelist must necessarily like society!"

* * *

[1875] [F]inding himself committed to prose, he renewed his consideration of a prose style, as is evident from the following note:
    "Read again Addison, Macaulay, Newman, Sterne, De Foe, Lamb,
Gibbon, Burke, Times Leaders, &c. in a study of style. Am more and
more confirmed in an idea I have long held, as a matter of commonsense, long before I thought of any old aphorism bearing on the subject:
'Ars est celare artem'.[3] The whole secret of a living style and the difference between it and a dead style, lies in not having too much style—
being—in fact, a little careless, or rather seeming to be, here and there.
* * * Otherwise your style is like worn half-pence—all the fresh
images rounded off by rubbing, and no crispness or movement at all.
    "It is, of course, simply a carrying into prose of the knowledge I have
acquired in poetry—that inexact rhymes and rhythms now and then are
more pleasing than correct ones."

* * *

[1877] "So, then, if nature's defects must be looked in the face and tran-
scribed, whence arises the *art* in poetry and novel-writing? which must
certainly show art, or it becomes merely mechanical reporting. I think
the art lies in making these defects the basis of a hitherto unperceived
beauty, by irradiating them with 'the light that never was'[4] on their surface, but is seen to be latent in them by the spiritual eye."

* * *

[1878] "April—Note. A Plot, or Tragedy, should arise from the gradual
closing in of a situation that comes of ordinary human passions, preju-

2. Anne Thackeray (1837–1919), novelist and essayist; daughter of the novelist William
   Makepeace Thackeray.
3. "The art lies in concealing the art" (from the Latin).
4. Quoting William Wordsworth's (1770–1850) "Elegiac Stanzas, Suggested by a Picture of Peele
   Castle": "The light that never was, on sea or land, / The consecration, and the Poet's dream"
   (lines 15–16).

dices, and ambitions, by reason of the characters taking no trouble to ward off the disastrous events produced by the said passions, prejudices, and ambitions."

* * *

[1882] "June 3rd. . . . As, in looking at a carpet, by following one colour a certain pattern is suggested, by following another colour, another; so in life the seer should watch that pattern among general things which his idiosyncrasy moves him to observe, and describe that alone. This is, quite accurately, a going to Nature; yet the result is no mere photograph, but purely the product of the writer's own mind."

* * *

[1884] Off and on he was now writing *The Mayor of Casterbridge*; but before leaving London he agreed with the Macmillans to take in hand a story of twelve numbers for their magazine, no time being fixed. It came out two years later under the title of *The Woodlanders*.

* * *

[1885] "Easter Sunday. Evidences of art in Bible narratives. They are written with a watchful attention (though disguised) as to their effect on their reader. Their so-called simplicity is, in fact, the simplicity of the highest cunning. And one is led to inquire, when even in these latter days artistic development and arrangement are the qualities least appreciated by readers, who was there likely to appreciate the art in these chronicles at that day?

"Looking round on a well-selected shelf of fiction or history, how few stories of any length does one recognize as well told from beginning to end! The first half of this story, the last half of that, the middle of another. . . . The modern art of narration is yet in its infancy."

* * *

[1885] "Friday, April 17. Wrote the last page of 'The Mayor of Casterbridge', begun at least a year ago, and frequently interrupted in the writing of each part."

"April 19th. The business of the poet and novelist is to show the sorriness underlying the grandest things, and the grandeur underlying the sorriest things."

* * *

[1885] "Tragedy. It may be put thus in brief: a tragedy exhibits a state of things in the life of an individual which unavoidably causes some natural aim or desire of his to end in a catastrophe when carried out."

* * *

[1886] "1886.—January 2nd. 'The Mayor of Casterbridge' begins today in the *Graphic* newspaper, and *Harper's Weekly*. I fear it will not be so good as I meant, but after all it is not improbabilities of incident but improbabilities of character that matter."

* * *

[1886] *The Mayor of Casterbridge* was issued complete about the end of May. It was a story which Hardy fancied he had damaged more recklessly as an artistic whole, in the interest of the newspaper in which it appeared serially, than perhaps any other of his novels, his aiming to get an incident into almost every week's part causing him in his own judgment to add events into the narrative somewhat too freely. However as at this time he called his novel-writing "mere journeywork", he cared little about it as art, though it must be said in favour of the plot, as he admitted later, that it was quite coherent and organic, in spite of its complications. And others thought better of it than he did himself, as is shown by the letter R. L. Stevenson[5] writes thereon:

Skerryvore, Bournemouth
[1886]

My dear Hardy:
    I have read the Mayor of Casterbridge with sincere admiration: Henchard is a great fellow, and Dorchester is touched in with the hand of a master.
    Do you think you would let me try to dramatize it? I keep unusually well, and am

Yours very sincerely,
Robert Louis Stevenson.

What became of this dramatic project there is no evidence to show in the *Life of Stevenson*, so far as is remembered by the present writer. The story in long after years became highly popular; but it is curious to find that Hardy had some difficulty in getting it issued in volume-form, Mr James Payn the publishers' reader having reported to Mr Smith[6] that the

---

5. Hardy met Robert Louis Stevenson in 1885. Despite his admiration for *The Mayor*, Stevenson loathed *Tess of the d'Urbervilles*, and Hardy was deeply wounded by the publication after Stevenson's death in 1894 of letters he had exchanged with Henry James attacking the novel.
6. Of Smith, Elder & Co., who did eventually publish *The Mayor* in book form.

lack of gentry among the characters made it uninteresting—a typical estimate of what was, or was supposed to be, mid-Victorian taste.

* * *

[1887] "The 'simply natural' is interesting no longer. The much decried, mad, late-Turner[7] rendering is now necessary to create my interest. The exact truth as to material fact ceases to be of importance in art—it is a student's style—the style of a period when the mind is serene and unawakened to the tragical mysteries of life; when it does not bring anything to the object that coalesces with and translates the qualities that are already there,—half hidden, it may be—and the two united are depicted as the All."

* * *

[1890] "August 5.—Reflections on Art. Art is a changing of the actual proportions and order of things, so as to bring out more forcibly than might otherwise be done that feature in them which appeals most strongly to the idiosyncrasy of the artist. The changing, or distortion, may be of two kinds: (1) The kind which increases the sense of vraisemblance:[8] (2) That which diminishes it. (1) is high art: (2) is low art.

"High art may choose to depict evil as well as good, without losing its quality. Its choice of evil, however, must be limited by the sense of its worthiness." A continuation of the same note was made a little later, and can be given here:

"Art is a disproportioning—(i.e., distorting, throwing out of proportion)—of realities, to show more clearly the features that matter in those realities, which, if merely copied or reported inventorially, might possibly be observed, but would more probably be overlooked. Hence 'realism' is not Art."

* * *

[1892] "Oct. 24. The best tragedy—highest tragedy in short—is that of the WORTHY encompassed by the INEVITABLE. The tragedies of immoral and worthless people are not of the best."

* * *

7. The later paintings of J. M. W. Turner (1775–1851) are now among his most admired works, but at the time they attracted a good deal of abuse for the extreme freedom with which they rendered the effects of light and color.
8. Closeness to reality.

[1893] "Feb. 23. A story must be exceptional enough to justify its telling. We tale-tellers are all Ancient Mariners, and none of us is warranted in stopping Wedding Guests (in other words, the hurrying public) unless he has something more unusual to relate than the ordinary experience of every average man and woman.

"The whole secret of fiction and the drama—in the constructional part—lies in the adjustment of things unusual to things eternal and universal. The writer who knows exactly how exceptional, and how nonexceptional, his events should be made, possesses the key to the art."

* * *

[1895] "Tragedy may be created by an opposing environment either of things inherent in the universe, or of human institutions. If the former be the means exhibited and deplored, the writer is regarded as impious; if the latter, as subversive and dangerous; when all the while he may never have questioned the necessity or urged the non-necessity of either."[9]

* * *

[1896] "Poetry. Perhaps I can express more fully in verse ideas and emotions which run counter to the inert crystallized opinion—hard as a rock—which the vast body of men have vested interests in supporting. To cry out in a passionate poem that (for instance) the Supreme Mover or Mover, the Prime Force or Forces, must be either limited in power, unknowing, or cruel—which is obvious enough, and has been for centuries—will cause them merely a shake of the head; but to put it in argumentative prose will make them sneer, or foam, and set all the literary contortionists upon me, a harmless agnostic, as if I were a clamorous atheist, which in their crass illiteracy they seem to think is the same thing. . . . If Galileo had said in verse that the world moved, the Inquisition might have left him alone."

* * *

[1897] The change,[1] after all, was not so great as it seemed. It was not as if he had been a writer of novels proper, and as more specifically understood, that is, stories of modern artificial life and manners showing a certain smartness of treatment. He had mostly aimed, and mostly succeeded, to keep his narratives close to natural life, and as near to poetry in

9. The comment reflects Hardy's anger at the hostile reception given to both *Tess* (1891) and *Jude the Obscure* (1895).
1. From prose to verse: Hardy published *The Well-Beloved*, his last completed novel, in 1897, and *Wessex Poems*, his first volume of verse, in 1898.

their subject as conditions would allow, and had often regretted that those conditions would not let him keep them nearer still.

* * *

The curator of the Dorset County Museum having expressed a wish for a MS. of Hardy's, he sent this month the holograph of *The Mayor of Casterbridge*.

* * *

[1921] Early in July a company of film actors arrived in Dorchester for the purpose of preparing a film of *The Mayor of Casterbridge*. Hardy met them outside The King's Arms, the hotel associated with the novel. Although the actors had their faces coloured yellow and were dressed in the fashion of some eighty years earlier, Hardy observed, to his surprise, that the townsfolk passed by on their ordinary affairs and seemed not to notice the strange spectacle, nor did any interest seem aroused when Hardy drove through the town with the actors to Maiden Castle, that ancient earthwork which formed the backdrop to one part of the film.

[Dialect in the Novel]†

SIR,—In your last week's article on the "Papers of the Manchester Literary Club," there seems a slight error, which, though possibly accidental, calls for a word of correction from myself. In treating of dialect in novels, I am instanced by the writer as one of two popular novelists "whose thorough knowledge of the dialectical peculiarities of certain districts has tempted them to write whole conversations which are, to the ordinary reader, nothing but a series of linguistic puzzles." So much has my practice been the reverse of this (as a glance at my novels will show), that I have been reproved for too freely translating dialect-English into readable English, by those of your contemporaries who attach more importance to the publication of local niceties of speech than I do. The rule of scrupulously preserving the local idiom, together with the words which have no synonym among those in general use, while printing in the ordinary way most of those local expressions which are but a modified articulation of words in use elsewhere, is the rule I usually follow; and it is, I believe, generally recognised as the best, where every such rule must of necessity be a compromise, more or less unsatisfactory to lovers of form. It must, of course, be always a matter for regret that, in

---

† Hardy's letter to the *Spectator* (15 October 1881), in response to a slighting comment on his handling of dialect in his novels.

order to be understood, writers should be obliged thus slightingly to treat varieties of English which are intrinsically as genuine, grammatical, and worthy of the royal title as is the all-prevailing competitor which bears it; whose only fault was that they happened not to be central, and therefore were worsted in the struggle for existence, when a uniform tongue became a necessity among the advanced classes of the population. —I am, Sir, &c.,   THOMAS HARDY.

From The Dorsetshire Labourer[†]

It seldom happens that a nickname which affects to portray a class is honestly indicative of the individuals composing that class. The few features distinguishing them from other bodies of men have been seized on and exaggerated, while the incomparably more numerous features common to all humanity have been ignored. In the great world this wild colouring of so-called typical portraits is clearly enough recognised. Nationalities, the aristocracy, the plutocracy, the citizen class, and many others have their allegorical representatives, which are received with due allowance for flights of imagination in the direction of burlesque.

But when the class lies somewhat out of the ken of ordinary society the caricature begins to be taken as truth. Moreover, the original is held to be an actual unit of the multitude signified. He ceases to be an abstract figure and becomes a sample. Thus when we arrive at the farm-labouring community we find it to be seriously personified by the pitiable picture known as Hodge;[1] not only so, but the community is assumed to be a uniform collection of concrete Hodges.

This supposed real but highly conventional Hodge is a degraded being of uncouth manner and aspect, stolid understanding, and snail-like movement. His speech is such a chaotic corruption of regular language that few persons of progressive aims consider it worth while to enquire what views, if any, of life, of nature, or of society are conveyed in these utterances. Hodge hangs his head or looks sheepish when spoken to, and thinks Lunnon[2] a place paved with gold. Misery and fever lurk in his cottage, while, to paraphrase the words of a recent writer on the labouring classes, in his future there are only the workhouse and the

---

[†] "The Dorsetshire Labourer" was first published in *Longman's Magazine* (July 1883, pp. 252–69), as one of a series of articles by different authors on the conditions and way of life of rural workers across the nation. As he does in *The Mayor of Casterbridge*, Hardy scrupulously notes both losses and gains in his account of the changes that had taken place in his lifetime. The full text of the essay is given in *Thomas Hardy's Personal Writings*, edited by Harold Orel (London: Macmillan, 1967), pp. 168–91.

1. A familiar form of the name Roger, used as a generic term for a farm-laborer from the late fourteenth century.

2. London.

grave. He hardly dares to think at all. He has few thoughts of joy, and little hope of rest. His life slopes into a darkness not "quieted by hope."[3]

If one of the many thoughtful persons who hold this view were to go
by rail to Dorset, where Hodge in his most unmitigated form is supposed
to reside, and seek out a retired district, he might by and by certainly
meet a man who, at first contact with an intelligence fresh from the contrasting world of London, would seem to exhibit some of the above-
mentioned qualities. The latter items in the list, the mental miseries, the
visitor might hardly look for in their fulness, since it would have become
perceptible to him as an explorer, and to any but the chamber theorist,
that no uneducated community, rich or poor, bond or free, possessing
average health and personal liberty, could exist in an unchangeable
slough of despond,[4] or that it would for many months if it could. Its
members, like the accursed swine, would rush down a steep place and
be choked in the waters.[5] He would have learnt that wherever a mode of
supporting life is neither noxious nor absolutely inadequate, there
springs up happiness, and will spring up happiness, of some sort or other.
Indeed, it is among such communities as these that happiness will find
her last refuge on earth, since it is among them that a perfect insight into
the conditions of existence will be longest postponed.

That in their future there are only the workhouse and the grave is no
more and no less true than that in the future of the average well-to-do
householder there are only the invalid chair and the brick vault.

Waiving these points, however, the investigator would insist that the
man he had encountered exhibited a suspicious blankness of gaze, a
great uncouthness and inactivity; and he might truly approach the unin-
telligible if addressed by a stranger on any but the commonest subject.
But suppose that, by some accident, the visitor were obliged to go home
with this man, take pot-luck with him and his, as one of the family. For
the nonce[6] the very sitting down would seem an undignified performance, and at first, the ideas, the modes, and the surroundings generally, would be puzzling—even impenetrable; or if in a measurable pene-
trable, would seem to have but little meaning. But living on there for a
few days the sojourner would become conscious of a new aspect in the
life around him. He would find that, without any objective change whatever, variety had taken the place of monotony; that the man who had
brought him home—the typical Hodge, as he conjectured—was somehow not typical of anyone but himself. His host's brothers, uncles, and
neighbours, as they became personally known, would appear as different

---

3. In Robert Browning's book-length poem *Sordello* (1840), Dante looks "Into a darkness quieted
   by hope" while pacing the shore of Hell (Book I, line 370).
4. Swamp of misery. In John Bunyan's allegorical story *Pilgrim's Progress* (Part I, 1678) the hero
   Christian has to pass through the Slough of Despond.
5. Mark 5.11–13 tells how a herd of swine were possessed by devils and rushed into the sea.
6. For a time.

from his host himself as one member of a club, or inhabitant of a city street, from another. As, to the eye of a diver, contrasting colours shine out by degrees from what has originally painted itself of an unrelieved earthy hue, so would shine out the characters, capacities, and interests of these people to him. He would, for one thing, find that the language, instead of being a vile corruption of cultivated speech, was a tongue with grammatical inflection rarely disregarded by his entertainer, though his entertainer's children would occasionally make a sad hash of their talk. Having attended the National School[7] they would mix the printed tongue as taught therein with the unwritten, dying, Wessex English that they had learnt of their parents, the result of this transitional state of theirs being a composite language without rule or harmony.

Six months pass, and our gentleman leaves the cottage, bidding his friends good-bye with genuine regret. The great change in his perception is that Hodge, the dull, unvarying, joyless one, has ceased to exist for him. He has become disintegrated into a number of dissimilar fellow-creatures, men of many minds, infinite in difference; some happy, many serene, a few depressed; some clever, even to genius, some stupid, some wanton, some austere; some mutely Miltonic, some Cromwellian;[8] into men who have private views of each other, as he has of his friends; who applaud or condemn each other; amuse or sadden themselves by the contemplation of each other's foibles or vices; and each of whom walks in his own way the road to dusty death.[9] Dick the carter, Bob the shepherd, and Sam the ploughman, are, it is true, alike in the narrowness of their means and their general open-air life; but they cannot be rolled together again into such a Hodge as he dreamt of, by any possible enchantment. And should time and distance render an abstract being, representing the field labourer, possible again to the mind of the inquirer (a questionable possibility) he will find that the Hodge of current conception no longer sums up the capacities of the class so defined.

The pleasures enjoyed by the Dorset labourer may be far from pleasures of the highest kind desirable for him. They may be pleasures of the wrong shade. And the inevitable glooms of a straitened hard-working life occasionally enwrap him from such pleasures as he has; and in times of special storm and stress the "Complaint of Piers the Ploughman"[1] is still echoed in his heart. But even Piers had his flights of merriment and humour; and ploughmen as a rule do not give sufficient thought to the

---

7. One of the schools founded by the National Society for Promoting the Education of the Poor in the Principles of the Established Church. Hardy entered the Stinsford National School in 1848.
8. Possessing the qualities of a poet or leader. Hardy is alluding to Thomas Gray's "Elegy Written in a Country Churchyard" (1751): "Some mute inglorious Milton here may rest, / Some Cromwell guiltless of his country's blood" (lines 59–60).
9. Quoting *Macbeth*, V.5.22.
1. *The Vision of Piers Plowman* is the title of a long poem by William Langland (c. 1330–c. 1386).

morrow[2] to be miserable when not in physical pain. Drudgery in the slums and alleys of a city, too long pursued, and accompanied as it too often is by indifferent health, may induce a mood of despondency which is well-nigh permanent; but the same degree of drudgery in the fields results at worst in a mood of painless passivity. A pure atmosphere and a pastoral environment are a very appreciable portion of the sustenance which tends to produce the sound mind and body, and thus much sustenance is, at least, the labourer's birthright.

If it were possible to gauge the average sufferings of classes, the probability is that in Dorsetshire the figure would be lower with the regular farmer's labourers—"workfolk" as they call themselves—than with the adjoining class, the unattached labourers, approximating to the free labourers of the middle ages, who are to be found in the larger villages and small towns of the county—many of them, no doubt, descendants of the old copyholders[3] who were ousted from their little plots when the system of leasing large farms grew general. They are, what the regular labourer is not, out of sight of patronage; and to be out of sight is to be out of mind when misfortune arises, and pride or sensitiveness leads them to conceal their privations.

* * *

To see the Dorset labourer at his worst and saddest time, he should be viewed when attending a wet hiring-fair at Candlemas,[4] in search of a new master. His natural cheerfulness bravely struggles against the weather and the incertitude; but as the day passes on, and his clothes get wet through, and he is still unhired, there does appear a factitiousness in the smile which, with a self-repressing mannerliness hardly to be found among any other class, he yet has ready when he encounters and talks with friends who have been more fortunate. In youth and manhood, this disappointment occurs but seldom; but at threescore and over, it is frequently the lot of those who have no sons and daughters to fall back upon, or whose children are ingrates, or far away.

Here, at the corner of the street, in this aforesaid wet hiring-fair, stands an old shepherd. He is evidently a lonely man. The battle of life has always been a sharp one with him, for, to begin with, he is a man of small frame. He is now so bowed by hard work and years that, approaching from behind, you can scarcely see his head. He has planted the stem of his crook in the gutter, and rests upon the bow, which is polished to silver brightness by the long friction of his hands. He has quite forgotten

2. Referring to Christ's Sermon on the Mount: "Take therefore no thought for the morrow: for the morrow shall take thought for the things of itself." See Matthew 6.34.
3. Tenants whose tenure was held according to a copy of the court-roll (the record of rents on a manor), to be continued or terminated according to the will of the lord of the manor).
4. At the Candlemas fair on February 2, workers would seek new employment for the coming year, to be entered into on April 6 (Lady Day, Old Style).

where he is and what he has come for, his eyes being bent on the ground. "There's work in en," says one farmer to another, as they look dubiously across; "there's work left in en still; but not so much as I want for my acreage." "You'd get en cheap," says the other. The shepherd does not hear them, and there seem to be passing through his mind pleasant visions of the hiring successes of his prime—when his skill in ovine surgery laid open any farm to him for the asking, and his employer would say uneasily in the early days of February, "You don't mean to leave us this year?"

But the hale and strong have not to wait thus, and having secured places in the morning, the day passes merrily enough with them.

* * * Dorset labourers now look upon an annual removal as the most natural thing in the world, and it becomes with the younger families a pleasant excitement. Change is also a certain sort of education. Many advantages accrue to the labourers from the varied experience it brings, apart from the discovery of the best market for their abilities. They have become shrewder and sharper men of the world, and have learnt how to hold their own with firmness and judgment. Whenever the habitually-removing man comes into contact with one of the old-fashioned stationary sort, who are still to be found, it is impossible not to perceive that the former is much more wide awake than his fellow-worker, astonishing him with stories of the wide world comprised in a twenty-mile radius from their homes.

They are also losing their peculiarities as a class; hence the humorous simplicity which formerly characterised the men and the unsophisticated modesty of the women are rapidly disappearing or lessening, under the constant attrition of lives mildly approximating to those of workers in a manufacturing town. It is the common remark of villagers above the labouring class, who know the latter well as personal acquaintances, that "there are no nice homely workfolk now as there used to be." There may be, and is, some exaggeration in this, but it is only natural that, now different districts of them are shaken together once a year and redistributed, like a shuffled pack of cards, they have ceased to be so local in feeling or manner as formerly, and have entered on the condition of inter-social citizens, "whose city stretches the whole county over." Their brains are less frequently than they once were "as dry as the remainder biscuit after a voyage,"[5] and they vent less often the result of their own observations than what they have heard to be the current ideas of smart chaps in towns. The women have, in many districts, acquired the rollicking air of factory hands. That seclusion and immutability, which was so bad for their pockets, was an unrivalled fosterer of their personal charm in the eyes of those whose experiences had been less limited. But the artistic merit of their old condition is scarcely a reason why they should have

5. Quoting Shakespeare's *As You Like It*, II.7.39–40.

continued in it when other communities were marching on so vigorously towards uniformity and mental equality. It is only the old story that
progress and picturesqueness do not harmonise. They are losing their
individuality, but they are widening the range of their ideas, and gaining
in freedom. It is too much to expect them to remain stagnant and old-
fashioned for the pleasure of romantic spectators.

But, picturesqueness apart, a result of this increasing nomadic habit
of the labourer is naturally a less intimate and kindly relation with the
land he tills than existed before enlightenment enabled him to rise
above the condition of a serf who lived and died on a particular plot, like
a tree. During the centuries of serfdom, of copyholding tenants, and
down to twenty or thirty years ago, before the power of unlimited migra-
tion had been clearly realised, the husbandman of either class had the
interest of long personal association with his farm. The fields were those
he had ploughed and sown from boyhood, and it was impossible for
him, in such circumstances, to sink altogether the character of natural
guardian in that of hireling. Not so very many years ago, the landowner,
if he were good for anything, stood as a court of final appeal in cases of
the harsh dismissal of a man by the farmer. "I'll go to my lord" was a
threat which overbearing farmers respected, for "my lord" had often personally known the labourer long before he knew the labourer's master.
But such arbitrament is rarely practicable now. The landlord does not
know by sight, if even by name, half the men who preserve his acres
from the curse of Eden.[6] They come and go yearly, like birds of passage,
nobody thinks whence or whither. This dissociation is favoured by the
customary system of letting the cottages with the land, so that, far from
having a guarantee of a holding to keep him fixed, the labourer has not
even the stability of a landlord's tenant; he is only tenant of a tenant, the
latter possibly a new comer, who takes strictly commercial views of his
man and cannot afford to waste a penny on sentimental considerations.

Thus, while their pecuniary condition in the prime of life is bettered,
and their freedom enlarged, they have lost touch with their environment,
and that sense of long local participancy which is one of the pleasures of
age. The old *casus conscientiae*[7] of those in power—whether the weak
tillage of an enfeebled hand ought not to be put up with in fields which
have had the benefit of that hand's strength—arises less frequently now
that the strength has often been expended elsewhere. The sojourning
existence of the town masses is more and more the existence of the rural
masses, with its corresponding benefits and disadvantages. With uncertainty of residence often comes a laxer morality, and more cynical views
of the duties of life. Domestic stability is a factor in conduct which noth-

6. After the Fall of Adam and Eve, God curses the ground: "thorns also and thistles shall it bring
   forth to thee." See Genesis 3.17–18.
7. Matter of conscience (from the Latin): a reference to the moral rule that one should act according to the dictates of one's conscience, even when not legally bound to do so.

ing else can equal. On the other hand, new varieties of happiness evolve themselves like new varieties of plants, and new charms may have arisen among the classes who have been driven to adopt the remedy of locomotion for the evils of oppression and poverty—charms which compensate in some measure for the lost sense of home.

* * *

The changes which are so increasingly discernible in village life by no means originate entirely with the agricultural unrest. A depopulation is going on which in some quarters is truly alarming. Villages used to contain, in addition to the agricultural inhabitants, an interesting and better-informed class, ranking distinctly above those—the blacksmith, the carpenter, the shoemaker, the small higgler,[8] the shopkeeper (whose stock-in-trade consisted of a couple of loaves, a pound of candles, a bottle of brandy-balls and lumps of delight,[9] three or four scrubbing-brushes, and a frying-pan), together with nondescript-workers other than farm-labourers, who had remained in the houses where they were born for no especial reason beyond an instinct of association with the spot. Many of these families had been life-holders,[1] who built at their own expense the cottages they occupied, and as the lives dropped, and the property fell in they would have been glad to remain as weekly or monthly tenants of the owner. But the policy of all but some few philanthropic landowners is to disapprove of these petty tenants who are not in the estate's employ, and to pull down each cottage as it falls in, leaving standing a sufficient number for the use of the farmer's men and no more. The occupants who formed the backbone of the village life have to seek refuge in the boroughs. This process, which is designated by statisticians as "the tendency of the rural population towards the large towns," is really the tendency of water to flow uphill when forced. The poignant regret of those who are thus obliged to forsake the old nest can only be realised by people who have witnessed it—concealed as it often is under a mask of indifference. It is anomalous that landowners who are showing unprecedented activity in the erection of comfortable cottages for their farm labourers, should see no reason for benefiting in the same way these unattached natives of the village who are nobody's care. They might often expostulate in the words addressed to King Henry the Fourth by his fallen subject:—

> Our house, my sovereign liege, little deserves
> The scourge of greatness to be used on it;

8. Door-to-door salesman or dealer.
9. Brandy-balls are sweets flavored with brandy; lumps of delight are sweets made of jelly coated with powdered sugar.
1. Persons holding rights of tenancy for a specified number of lives or generations within one family (usually three): also known as liviers.

> And that same greatness, too, which our own hands
> Have holp to make so portly.[2]

The system is much to be deplored, for every one of these banished people imbibes a sworn enmity to the existing order of things, and not a few
of them, far from becoming merely honest Radicals, degenerate into
Anarchists, waiters on chance, to whom danger to the State, the town—
nay, the street they live in, is a welcomed opportunity.

A reason frequently advanced for dismissing these families from the
villages where they have lived for centuries is that it is done in the interests of morality; and it is quite true that some of the "liviers" (as these
half-independent villagers used to be called) were not always shining
examples of churchgoing, temperance, and quiet walking. But a natural
tendency to evil, which develops to unlawful action when excited by
contact with others like-minded, would often have remained latent amid
the simple isolated experiences of a village life. The cause of morality
cannot be served by compelling a population hitherto evenly distributed
over the country to concentrate in a few towns, with the inevitable
results of overcrowding and want of regular employment. But the question of the Dorset cottager here merges in that of all the houseless and
landless poor, and the vast topic of the Rights of Man, to consider which
is beyond the scope of a merely descriptive article.

From The Profitable Reading of Fiction[†]

* * *

It may seem something of a paradox to assert that the novels which
most conduce to moral profit are likely to be among those written without a moral purpose. But the truth of the statement may be realized if
we consider that the didactic novel is so generally devoid of *vraisemblance* as to teach nothing but the impossibility of tampering with natural truth to advance dogmatic opinions. Those, on the other hand,
which impress the reader with the inevitableness of character and environment in working out destiny, whether that destiny be just or unjust,
enviable or cruel, must have a sound effect, if not what is called a good
effect, upon a healthy mind.

Of the effects of such sincere presentation on weak minds, when the
courses of the characters are not exemplary, and the rewards and punishments ill adjusted to deserts, it is not our duty to consider too closely.

---

2. Spoken by the Earl of Worcester in Shakespeare's *Henry IV, Part I*, I.3.10–13.
† From Hardy's essay on "The Profitable Reading of Fiction," first published in *Forum* (March
1888, pp. 57–70); reprinted in *Thomas Hardy's Personal Writings*, edited by Harold Orel
(London: Macmillan, 1967), pp. 110–25.

A novel which does moral injury to a dozen imbeciles, and has bracing results upon a thousand intellects of normal vigor, can justify its existence; and probably a novel was never written by the purest-minded author for which there could not be found some moral invalid or other whom it was capable of harming.

* * *

From Candour in English Fiction[†]

* * *

By a sincere school of Fiction we may understand a Fiction that expresses truly the views of life prevalent in its time, by means of a selected chain of action best suited for their exhibition. What are the prevalent views of life just now is a question upon which it is not necessary to enter further than to suggest that the most natural method of presenting them, the method most in accordance with the views themselves, seems to be by a procedure mainly impassive in its tone and tragic in its developments.

Things move in cycles; dormant principles renew themselves, and exhausted principles are thrust by. There is a revival of the artistic instincts towards great dramatic motives—setting forth that "collision between the individual and the general"—formerly worked out with such force by the Periclean and Elizabethan dramatists, to name no other. More than this, the periodicity which marks the course of taste in civilised countries does not take the form of a true cycle of repetition, but what Comte, in speaking of general progress, happily characterises as "a looped orbit":[1] not a movement of revolution but—to use the current word—evolution. Hence, in perceiving that taste is arriving anew at the point of high tragedy, writers are conscious that its revived presentation demands enrichment by further truths—in other words, original treatment: treatment which seeks to show Nature's unconsciousness not of essential laws, but of those laws framed merely as social expedients by humanity, without a basis in the heart of things; treatment which expresses the triumph of the crowd over the hero, of the commonplace majority over the exceptional few.

But originality makes scores of failures for one final success, precisely

---

[†] From Hardy's contribution to a symposium on "Candour in English Fiction" in the *New Review* (January 1890, pp. 15–21), written before the hostile reception given to *Tess of the d'Urbervilles* (1891) but while Hardy was having difficulty shaping that work into a form acceptable to the publishers. The full text of the essay is given in *Thomas Hardy's Personal Writings*, edited by Harold Orel (London: Macmillan, 1967), pp. 125–33.

1. Auguste Comte argued in his *Cours de philosophie positive* (1830–42) that society had developed in three stages: theological, metaphysical, and positive. His belief that the positive stage made possible a new, scientifically based "religion of humanity" was widely influential.

because its essence is to acknowledge no immediate precursor or guide. It is probably to these inevitable conditions of further acquisition that may be attributed some developments of naturalism in French novelists of the present day, and certain crude results from meritorious attempts in the same direction by intellectual adventurers here and there among our own authors.

Anyhow, conscientious fiction alone it is which can excite a reflective and abiding interest in the minds of thoughtful readers of mature age, who are weary of puerile inventions and famishing for accuracy; who consider that, in representations of the world, the passions ought to be proportioned as in the world itself. This is the interest which was excited in the minds of the Athenians by their immortal tragedies, and in the minds of Londoners at the first performance of the finer plays of three hundred years ago. They reflected life, revealed life, criticised life. Life being a physiological fact, its honest portrayal must be largely concerned with, for one thing, the relations of the sexes, and the substitution for such catastrophes as favour the false colouring best expressed by the regulation finish that "they married and were happy ever after," of catastrophes based upon sexual relations as it is. To this expansion English society opposes a well-nigh insuperable bar.

The popular vehicles for the introduction of a novel to the public have grown to be, from one cause and another, the magazine and the circulating library; and the object of the magazine and circulating library is not upward advance but lateral advance; to suit themselves to what is called household reading, which means, or is made to mean, the reading either of the majority in a household or of the household collectively. The number of adults, even in a large household, being normally two, and these being the members which, as a rule, have least time on their hands to bestow on current literature, the taste of the majority can hardly be, and seldom is, tempered by the ripe judgment which desires fidelity. However, the immature members of a household often keep an open mind, and they might, and no doubt would, take sincere fiction with the rest but for another condition, almost generally coexistent: which is that adults who would desire true views for their own reading insist, for a plausible but questionable reason, upon false views for the reading of their young people.

As a consequence, the magazine in particular and the circulating library in general do not foster the growth of the novel which reflects and reveals life. They directly tend to exterminate it by monopolising all literary space. * * * That the magazine and library have arrogated to themselves the dispensation of fiction is not the fault of the authors, but of circumstances over which they, as representatives of Grub Street, have no control.

* * *

From General Preface to the Novels and Poems[†]

* * *

It has sometimes been conceived of novels that evolve their action on a circumscribed scene—as do many (though not all) of these—that they cannot be so inclusive in their exhibition of human nature as novels wherein the scenes cover large extents of country, in which events figure amid towns and cities, even wander over the four quarters of the globe. I am not concerned to argue this point further than to suggest that the conception is an untrue one in respect of the elementary passions. But I would state that the geographical limits of the stage here trodden were not absolutely forced upon the writer by circumstances; he forced them upon himself from judgment. I considered that our magnificent heritage from the Greeks in dramatic literature found sufficient room for a large proportion of its action in an extent of their country not much larger than the half-dozen counties here reunited under the old name of Wessex, that the domestic emotions have throbbed in Wessex nooks with as much intensity as in the palaces of Europe, and that, anyhow, there was quite enough human nature in Wessex for one man's literary purpose. So far was I possessed by this idea that I kept within the frontiers when it would have been easier to overleap them and give more cosmopolitan features to the narrative.

Thus, though the people in most of the novels (and in much of the shorter verse) are dwellers in a province bounded on the north by the Thames, on the south by the English Channel, on the east by a line running from Hayling Island to Windsor Forest, and on the west by the Cornish coast, they were meant to be typically and essentially those of any and every place where

Thought's the slave of life, and life time's fool,[1]

—beings in whose hearts and minds that which is apparently local should be really universal.

But whatever the success of this intention, and the value of these novels as delineations of humanity, they have at least a humble supplementary quality of which I may be justified in reminding the reader, though it is one that was quite unintentional and unforeseen. At the dates represented in the various narrations things were like that in Wessex: the inhabitants lived in certain ways, engaged in certain occupations, kept

---

[†] This preface, dated October 1911, was written for the Wessex Edition of 1912, where it appeared in Volume I. It begins by distinguishing the novels as "Novels of Character and Environment," "Romances and Fantasies," and "Novels of Ingenuity." *The Mayor of Casterbridge* is assigned to the first group.

1. Hotspur's dying words; see Shakespeare's *Henry IV, Part I*, V.4.81.

alive certain customs, just as they are shown doing in these pages. And in particularizing such I have often been reminded of Boswell's remarks on the trouble to which he was put and the pilgrimages he was obliged to make to authenticate some detail, though the labour was one which would bring him no praise. Unlike his achievement, however, on which an error would as he says have brought discredit, if these country customs and vocations, obsolete and obsolescent, had been detailed wrongly, nobody would have discovered such errors to the end of Time. Yet I have instituted inquiries to correct tricks of memory, and striven against temptations to exaggerate, in order to preserve for my own satisfaction a fairly true record of a vanishing life.

It is advisable also to state here, in response to inquiries from readers interested in landscape, prehistoric antiquities, and especially old English architecture, that the description of these backgrounds has been done from the real — that is to say, has something real for its basis, however illusively treated. Many features of the first two kinds have been given under their existing names; for instance, the Vale of Blackmoor or Blakemore, Hambledon Hill, Bulbarrow, Nettlecombe Tout, Dogbury Hill, High-Stoy, Bubb-Down Hill, The Devil's Kitchen, Cross-in-Hand, Long-Ash Lane, Benvill Lane, Giant's Hill, Crimmercrock Lane, and Stonehenge. The rivers Froom, or Frome, and Stour, are, of course, well known as such. And the further idea was that large towns and points tending to mark the outline of Wessex — such as Bath, Plymouth, The Start, Portland Bill, Southampton, etc. — should be named clearly. The scheme was not greatly elaborated, but, whatever its value, the names remain still.

In respect of places described under fictitious or ancient names in the novels — for reasons that seemed good at the time of writing them — and kept up in the poems — discerning people have affirmed in print that they clearly recognize the originals: such as Shaftesbury in "Shaston," Sturminster Newton in "Stourcastle," Dorchester in "Casterbridge," Salisbury Plain in "The Great Plain," Cranborne Chase in "The Chase," Beaminster in "Emminster," Bere Regis in "Kingsbere," Woodbury Hill in "Greenhill," Wool Bridge in "Wellbridge," Harfoot or Harput Lane in "Stagfoot Lane," Hazlebury in "Nuttlebury," Bridport in "Port Bredy," Maiden Newton in "Chalk Newton," a farm near Nettlecombe Tout in "Flintcomb Ash," Sherborne in "Sherton Abbas," Milton Abbey in "Middleton Abbey," Cerne Abbas in "Abbot's Cernel," Evershot in "Evershed," Taunton in "Toneborough," Bournemouth in "Sandbourne," Winchester in "Wintoncester," Oxford in "Christminster," Reading in "Aldbrickham," Newbury in "Kennetbridge," Wantage in "Alfredston," Basingstoke in "Stoke Barehills," and so on. Subject to the qualifications above given, that no detail is guaranteed, — that the portraiture of fictitiously named towns and villages was only suggested by certain real places, and wantonly wanders from inventorial descriptions of them — I do not contradict these keen hunters for the real; I am satisfied with their statements as as least an indication of their interest in the scenes.

* * *

One word on what has been called the present writer's philosophy of life. * * * Positive views on the Whence and the Wherefore of things have never been advanced by this pen as a consistent philosophy. Nor is it likely, indeed, that imaginative writings extending over more than forty years would exhibit a coherent scientific theory of the universe even if it had been attempted—of that universe concerning which Spencer owns to the "paralyzing thought" that possibly there exists no comprehension of it anywhere.[2] But such objectless consistency never has been attempted, and the sentiments in the following pages have been stated truly to be mere impressions of the moment, and not convictions or arguments.

That these impressions have been condemned as "pessimistic"—as if that were a very wicked adjective—shows a curious muddle-mindedness. It must be obvious that there is a higher characteristic of philosophy than pessimism, or than meliorism, or even than the optimism of these critics—which is truth. Existence is either ordered in a certain way, or it is not so ordered, and conjectures which harmonize best with experience are removed above all comparison with other conjectures which do not so harmonize. So that to say one view is worse than other views without proving it erroneous implies the possibility of a false view being better or more expedient than a true view; and no pragmatic proppings can make that *idolum specus*[3] stand on its feet, for it postulates a prescience denied to humanity.

And there is another consideration. Differing natures find their tongue in the presence of differing spectacles. Some natures become vocal at tragedy, some are made vocal by comedy, and it seems to me that to whichever of these aspects of life a writer's instinct for expression the more readily responds, to that he should allow it to respond. That before a contrasting side of things he remains undemonstrative need not be assumed to mean that he remains unperceiving.

* * *

2. The idea appears in a section on "The Unknowable" in Herbert Spencer's *First Principles* (1862).
3. Referring to Francis Bacon's *Novum Organum* (1620); literally, "an idol of the cave," it suggests the confusion of a mere image of reality with reality itself.

Hardy's Wessex

Fictitious names as
Exonbury
Real names as
Portsmouth

From *The Life and Death of the Mayor of Casterbridge*, by Thomas Hardy (London: The Macmillan Co. Ltd., 1912), pp. 388–89. Reprinted by permission of the Trustees of the Hardy Estate and Macmillan London and Basingstoke and the Macmillan Company of Canada Ltd.

Map of the
WESSEX
of the
Novels and Poems

Scale of Miles

Septentrio

Occidens

Oriens

Meridies

Lumsdon
Christminster

R Thames

NORTH

The Brown House
Alfredston
Cresscombe
Marygreen

River Thames

MID
WESSEX

Marlbury
Downs

Gaymead

Kennetbridge

Castle
Royal
Aldbrickham

ESSEX

Inkpen Beacon

e Great
lain
Stonehenge

Weydon
Priors

Stoke Barehills

Icenway
House

Quartershot

UPPER

Wintoncester

Melchester

Wingreen
Chase
The Slopes
e Cross
Chaseborough
Knollingwood Hall
sford
Trantorn Inn
um
Warborne
h
Chene
Manor
and
EX
Havenpool
Sandbourne
egbury
riesgate
Knollsea

Fernel Hall

Deansleigh
Park

WESSEX

Southampton

Portsmouth

Solentsea

Bramshurst
The Great
Forest

The
Island

he Channel

Emery Walker, sc.

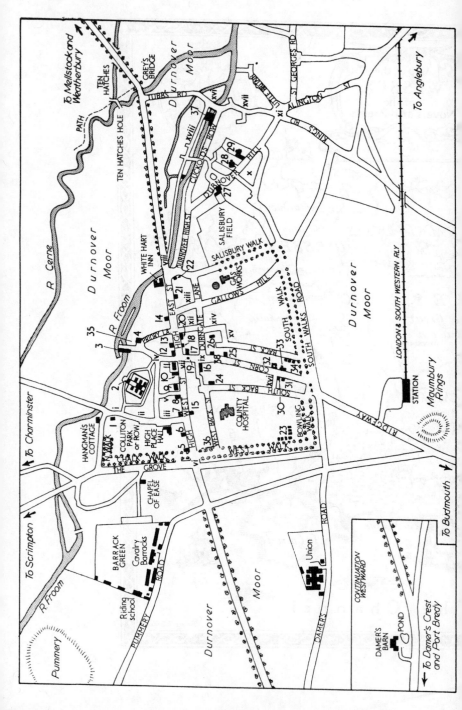

Map of Casterbridge and Durnover (circa 1848)†

KEY

1 House referred to in *The Burghers*(?)
2 Gaol entrance arch and gallows site
3 Water mill
4 Theatre ('the old playhouse')
5 Laura Maumbry's uncle's house
6 No 51 (the house with the oriel)
7 Shire Hall
8 Seedman's shop (?)
9 Holy Trinity church
10 The George Inn
11 St Peter's church
12 Town Hall
13 King's Arms Hotel
14 The Three Mariners Inn
15 The Ship Inn
16 The Antelope Inn
17 Hardy's site for High Place Hall
18 Waggon Office (?) (No 21)
19 Town Pump
20 All Saints church
21 The Phoenix Inn
22 Dorford chapel
23 Cottages probably including Susan Henchard's
24 Museum 'in a back street'
25 Henchard's house
26 Henchard's corn-store
27 Durnover old vicarage and garden
28 Church of St George, Durnover
29 Durnover Barton
30 William Barnes's house
31 John Hicks's house
32 Napper's Mite almshouses
33 Hardy's Grammar School
34 Cottages probably including Abe [sic] Whittle's

35 Site of priory or friary
36 Section of Roman wall
37 Durnover Mill
38 Old Greyhound Inn (site)

i Glyde Path Hill
ii Colliton Row
iii Shire Hall Lane
iv Bull Stake (North Square)
v Grey's School Passage
vi Top o' Town
vii The Bow or Crossways
viii Town or Swan Bridge
ix Cornhill
x Durnover Green
xi Durnover Cross
xii Church Lane
xiii Old Gaol Lane
xiv Charles Street
xv Bowling Green Lane
xvi Standfast or Prince's Bridge
xvii Standfast Road
xviii Mixen (Mill) Lane

Key to Hardy Names

'High Place Hall' = Colliton House
'Chalk Walk' = Colliton Walks
'Chapel of Ease' = Christ Church
'Durnover Moor' = Fordington Field
'Durnover Green, Cross' = Fordington Green, Cross
'Pummery' = Poundbury
'Corn Street' = South Street and Cornhill
'Bowling Walk' = Bowling Alley Walks

† From Denys Kay-Robinson, *Hardy's Wessex Reappraised*, pp. 16–17. Map and accompanying key reprinted by kind permission of the publisher, David and Charles (London, 1972).

Place-Names in *The Mayor of Casterbridge*

In his 1895 Preface to *Far from the Madding Crowd*, Hardy explained that he had "disinterred" the name Wessex—used for the first time in Chapter 50 of that novel—because he thought some such "territorial definition" would lend unity to a series of novels with a mainly local character. This account must owe something to hindsight, since in 1874, while at work on *Far from the Madding Crowd*, it had not been at all clear to Hardy that he was going to restrict himself to novels dealing with the southern and southwestern counties of England. But he was soon identified in the public mind as a Wessex novelist, and it was a title he was ready to accept. "Wessex" is the name for the territory that he knew best and felt most loyal to, but it was also, as Hardy was shrewd enough to recognize, a reminder to his readers of what he had to offer them—in effect, a brand name. Many of the revisions he made for the Osgood, McIlvaine edition of 1895 were intended to make place names, directions, and distances more consistent, not least because by this time some who read the novels had begun to hunt out the original locations. It was for this edition that he made the map of Wessex reproduced on pp. 298–99.

At the same time, however, Hardy was careful to point out that Wessex was "a partly real, partly dream-country." As well as its own topography, it has its own fictional laws—for example, those who leave Wessex almost always return, as first Susan and then Newson do in this novel—and when it suited Hardy's purpose to change the geography or to conflate elements of different buildings into one, he did so. But in *The Mayor of Casterbridge* in particular there is a high degree of correspondence between fiction and actuality. The *Saturday Review* pretended to be baffled, but Richard Hutton, writing in the *Spectator*, had no difficulty in recognizing Casterbridge as Dorchester, and neither did most other readers. The following list identifies the names used in the novel with the places that can plausibly be seen as their nonfictional prototypes.

Wessex Name	*Actual Name*
Anglebury	Wareham
Budmouth	Weymouth
Casterbridge	Dorchester
Durnover	Fordington
Egdon Heath	area of wild land between Dorchester and Bournemouth
Haverpoole	Poole
The Hintocks	
Great Hintock	Minterne Magna

King's Hintock	Melbury Sampford
Little Hintock	Melbury Osmond
Kingsbere	Bere Regis
Mai Dun	Maiden Castle
Melchester	Salisbury
Mellstock	Stinsford, together with Lower and Higher Bockhampton
Overcombe	Sutton Poyntz
Port-Bredy	Bridport
Sherton-Abbas	Sherborne
Shottsford	Blandford Forum
Upper Wessex	Hampshire
Weatherbury	Puddletown
Weydon-Priors	Weyhill
Yalbury Hill	Yellowham Hill

A Note on the Corn Laws

Hardy's Preface refers to three historical events that helped suggest the action of *The Mayor of Casterbridge*, including "the uncertain harvests which immediately preceded the repeal of the Corn Laws." Laws regulating the import of cereal grains had long been a feature of Britain's commercial policy. They were suspended during the Napoleonic Wars, but legislation introduced in 1815 prohibited the import of corn into Britain when the average price at home fell below eighty shillings a quarter (eight bushels). Only when the price was above this figure could corn be brought into the country without attracting import duties. The price of corn was thus kept artificially high, benefiting the producers at the expense of the consumers. The original aim was to protect the landowning classes—to all intents and purposes, the aristocracy—from the effects of variable harvests on prices, but as the century wore on the Corn Laws were increasingly important in restricting the impact of foreign competition, especially from America.

The campaign to repeal the Corn Laws was long, bitter, and sometimes violent, including what became known as the "Peterloo Massacre" of 1819, when a crowd that had gathered in St. Peter's Fields in Manchester to protest against the laws was charged by the militia, leaving eleven people dead and four hundred wounded. In the following decade the operation of the laws was modified several times, with the introduction of a sliding scale of import duties, but they remained deeply unpopular, and the campaign for their abolition continued. In March 1839 the Anti-Corn Law League was founded in Manchester and quickly became the center of a movement for free trade and an end to protectionism. The campaign was strongest in the north of the country, but it extended into Dorset, and Hardy, born in 1840, included anti-Corn Law agitation among his childhood memories. In 1845 a bad harvest and the threat of famine in Ireland gave new urgency to the League's arguments. Prime Minister Robert Peel was persuaded of the need for change, and at last, in May 1846, the Corn Laws were repealed.

This was not, however, the end of the matter. The leaders of the Anti-Corn Law League had already begun to extend their campaign into a wider movement intended to shift power in the country away from the aristocracy and the landed interest, and toward the manufacturing middle classes. As one historian has written, the debate about the Corn Laws raised "fundamental questions" about "the place of agriculture in society, the relationship between consumers and producers, the composition of Parliament, the competing claims of landlords and industrialists, and the proper role of government" (Asa Briggs, *The Age of Improvement, 1783–1867* [London, 1959], p. 201). By the time Hardy came to write *The Mayor of Casterbridge*, these questions had taken a different form, but they had lost none of their urgency.

MICHAEL MILLGATE

The Evolution of Wessex[†]

The manuscript of *Under the Greenwood Tree* already contains some of the disguised place names which Hardy was to employ throughout his later work, and it was in this novel that he established the basic topographical framework of Mellstock (with Yalbury Wood), Casterbridge, and Budmouth. *Far from the Madding Crowd* developed the presentation of Casterbridge and Budmouth, introduced a number of minor settings, created the village of Weatherbury in all the rich variety of its agricultural life, and introduced the name Wessex into Hardy's fiction for the first time. In his 1895 Preface to *Far from the Madding Crowd* Hardy recalled: "The series of novels I projected being mainly of the kind called local, they seemed to require a territorial definition of some sort to lend unity to their scene. Finding that the area of a single county did not afford a canvas large enough for this purpose, and that there were objections to an invented name, I disinterred the old one." It is hard to believe that Hardy, by the autumn of 1874, had in fact gone much beyond a rather general recognition of the attractions and advantages of choosing the settings of future novels from a fairly limited geographical area. Despite *The Trumpet-Major* and the sketch-map of Egdon Heath drawn for the first edition of *The Return of the Native*, he seems to have retained throughout the 1870s a fairly limited conception of Wessex and of its potentialities for development, and the publication of *A Laodicean* and *Two on a Tower* in the early 1880s suggests that he remained fundamentally uncertain as to the kind of novel, of setting, and of period most appropriate to his talents.

It was only with *The Mayor of Casterbridge* that Hardy achieved a full realisation of the Wessex concept, a realisation which depended on the establishment of Casterbridge itself (significantly insisted upon in the novel's title) as the central point, the economic, administrative, and social capital, of a whole region. Critics have long noticed the allusions in *The Mayor of Casterbridge* to the world of *Far from the Madding Crowd*,[1] and W. J. Keith has more recently pointed to the way in which the novel incorporates other references which seem deliberately designed to draw into its orbit places which provide the setting for other novels and stories: Hardy describes, for example, the carriers' vans which travelled to Casterbridge "from Mellstock, Weatherbury, The Hintocks, Sherton-Abbas, Kingsbere, Overcombe, and many other towns and vil-

† From Michael Millgate, *Thomas Hardy: His Career as a Novelist* (London: The Bodley Head, 1971), pp. 235–43. Copyright © 1971 by Michael Millgate. Reprinted by permission of Macmillan. Page references have been changed to correspond to this Norton Critical Edition.
1. Certainly as early as Bertram C. A. Windle, *The Wessex of Thomas Hardy* (London, 1902), p. 4.

lages round" [48].[2] Budmouth, Shottsford, and Melchester are all mentioned; the appearance of a church choir, with "bass-viols, fiddles, and flutes under their arms" [175], provides a specific reminiscence of the Mellstock world; Mixen Lane is not simply an appendage to Casterbridge itself but "the Adullam of all the surrounding villages" [192]. The whole structure of the novel, with its emphasis on arrivals and departures—Susan Henchard's, Farfrae's, Lucetta's, Newson's, Henchard's—serves to strengthen the impression of Casterbridge as a focal point, and the role played in the central action by the hay and corn trade and by the market-place itself, the town's physical and symbolic heart, works consistently to reinforce the importance of Casterbridge as what the novel itself calls "the pole, focus, or nerve-knot of the surrounding country life" [49].

It seems reasonable to suggest that this reassertion of the Wessex pattern was directly related to Hardy's desire, after wandering to and fro between various parts of Dorset and various sections of London, to settle down permanently in Dorchester—the original of Casterbridge, the actual nerve-knot of his own native countryside—and build himself a house. From the moment of thus firming his roots back into his native soil Hardy's handling of Wessex settings became both more frequent and more confident. He wrote to his publishers to recommend a more consistent use of the terms Wessex and Wessex Novels in their advertisements of his books, and when in 1895–96 he was preparing the first collected edition of his novels he took the opportunity of revising the place-names, distances, and descriptions in the various volumes in order to bring them into line with each other and with his developed conception of the Wessex world.[3]

It was apparently in March 1884, some nine months after his return to Dorchester, that Hardy began reading systematically through back files of the local weekly newspaper, the Dorset County Chronicle and Somersetshire Gazette. He seems to have begun with the issues of January 1826, and the memoranda in his "Facts" notebook suggest that by the summer of 1884 he had read through to the issues for late 1829 or early 1830. During this long and peculiarly intimate exposure to a particular period in the past of the county town and the surrounding countryside he came across several items which he was able to incorporate, more or less directly, into the novel on which he was then beginning work.

In the early decades of the nineteenth century the Dorset County

---

2. W. J. Keith, "Critical Approaches to Hardy's Wessex", *Association of Canadian University Teachers of English: Report*, 1963, pp. 22–3. * * *
3. Hardy to Marston (of Sampson Low, Marston, Searle & Rivington), [1885?] (Purdy coll.); for the revisions to the Osgood, McIlvaine edn., see Richard Little Purdy, *Thomas Hardy: A Bibliographical Study* (London, 1954, 1968), p. 281, and W. J. Keith, "Thomas Hardy and the Literary Pilgrims", *Nineteenth-Century Fiction*, 24 (1969), pp. 84–8.

Chronicle, like most other newspapers in London and the provinces, was largely filled with reports of crimes, accidents, and sensational legal proceedings. Hardy duly summarised a number of such reports, including one of the murder of Maria Marten. The contemporary conception of "human interest" also extended to extraordinary events of the "believe it or not" variety, including inexplicable suicides and disappearances, astounding reappearances by people long presumed dead, and coincidences far more bizarre than anything to be found in Hardy's own fiction. As might have been expected, Hardy noted down a good many items of the kind: the young man, for instance, who tapped at night on his fiancée's window and was stabbed and killed through the glass by the girl's father, who thought he was a burglar; the man who returned to his native village after twenty-seven years of absence, found his wife married to a second husband, and simply settled down again to live by himself in the same village.[4]

But Hardy was no less interested in items which spoke directly and unsensationally of their period: descriptions of current fashions in dress; the names and times of the stage-coaches leaving the King's Arms, Dorchester, in late 1827; stories of injuries and deaths caused by spring-guns; an account of the Yeovil glove trade and the opportunities it provided for the wives and children of farm labourers to supplement the family income; a report, copied out by Hardy at some length, of speeches made at an election meeting in Ilchester in 1826.[5] In the issue of December 4, 1828, Hardy found a long account of the Dorchester Tradesmen's Dinner for that year, held in the King's Arms. The report mentions the special tribute paid to Major Garland, a native of the town who had fought at Waterloo, describes the actual dinner (including "a noble baron of beef"), disclaims completeness for its list of twenty-three toasts drunk during the dinner, and concludes:

> Several excellent songs were sung in very superior style in the course of the evening, and on the Chairman's quitting the Chair, about nine o'clock, it was taken by Major Garland, and the festivities of the day were continued to a late hour, when the company departed highly delighted with the enjoyment of the convivial and harmonious meeting of which they had partaken.[6]

Hardy may originally have noted and summarised this report simply for its reference to Waterloo and for its general "period" flavour. But at some point, clearly, he drew upon it for the description of the dinner at the King's Arms over which Henchard presides in *The Mayor of Casterbridge*.

4. "Facts" Notebook, pp. 32, 48.
5. "Facts", pp. 42, 71, 32, 27, 34–5.
6. *Dorset County Chronicle*, December 4 1828, p. [4]; cf. "Facts", p. [94].

In the issue of April 27, 1826, Hardy discovered, and summarised in
his notebook, the following item:

> On Wednesday se'nnight a meeting of the Commissioners under
> the bankruptcy of Mr. Harvey of Launceston, banker, took place at
> the White Hart Inn there, for the purpose of his final examination.
> At the close of the proceedings Mr. Harvey laid his gold watch and
> pocket-money on the table; but they were immediately returned by
> the unanimous vote of the creditors present. The senior
> Commissioner, Mr. Tonkin, addressed Mr. Harvey, and said he had
> been a commissioner for a number of years, but in all his experi-
> ence he had never yet found a bankrupt who had acted more hon-
> orably and honestly; his balance sheet was the most satisfactory that
> he had seen on any similar occasion, and his creditors—a great
> number of whom were present—ought to feel perfectly well satis-
> fied with his conduct. The other commissioners, Mr. Bird and Mr.
> R. K. Frost, perfectly coincided in the opinion expressed by Mr.
> Tonkin, and only one feeling appeared to pervade the meeting—
> that of sympathy with Mr. Harvey.[7]

Bankruptcies are of course common enough, and in a letter of January
1903 Hardy was to recall that not long after the publication of *The
Mayor of Casterbridge* a "leading member of the Town Council here, in
the *same business* as the Mayor, became bankrupt just as he did".[8] But
there can be little doubt of Hardy's indebtedness to this passage for the
scene in which Henchard produced his gold watch and purse in precisely similar circumstances:

> 'Well,' said the senior Commissioner, addressing Henchard,
> 'though the case is a desperate one, I am bound to admit that I have
> never met a debtor who behaved more fairly. I've proved the bal-
> ance-sheet to be as honestly made out as it could possibly be; we
> have had no trouble; there have been no evasions and no conceal-
> ments. The rashness of dealing which led to this unhappy situation
> is obvious enough; but as far as I can see every attempt has been
> made to avoid wronging anybody.' [167]

If this item provided an opportunity for showing Henchard at his best,
the scene in which he bullies Abel Whittle was perhaps suggested by a
story (in the issue of September 14, 1826) about a soldier who shot himself after having been marched through the streets of Kilkenny without
shirt, stockings, or shoes.[9] From the *Dorset County Chronicle* of July 9,
1829, Hardy noted an item, headed "Sobriety and its beneficial consequences", about a man who had raised himself from a "common nui-

7. *Dorset County Chronicle*, April 27 1826, p. [4]; cf. "Facts", p. 30.
8. Hardy to Douglas, January 28 1903, in W. M. Parker, "Hardy's Letters to Sir George Douglas",
   English, 14 (1963), p. 222.
9. Cf. "Facts", p. 52.

sance" to a "respectable tradesman" by deciding "to *swear* that for *seven years* he would not taste of any liquid stronger than tea. This oath he kept most inviolably, and by his regularity obtained a friend who put him into business. In November last the term of his oath expired, and he anxiously looked forward to the day, that he might enjoy himself without infringing upon his conscience. In fact he did get as much intoxicated as he ever had been, but on the next day renewed his oath for *twelve years*, since which he has gone on in the steady money-getting way in which he had passed the last seven years."[1]

Once again, the relevance to the story of Henchard seems plain, and it is perhaps of some significance that an attempt has been made, presumably by Hardy himself, to render the notebook entry illegible. Other notes have been more effectively scored through or scraped away, and some have been removed altogether. It is, of course, impossible to make a positive identification of material excised in this way, but in some instances it is at least possible to determine the issue of the *Dorset County Chronicle* from which the note must originally have been taken. In one such issue, that of August 17, 1826, appears the following report:

> *Phoebe Hooper*, aged about 50, and apparently a respectable woman, was indicted for feloniously marrying Jonathan Puxtone, her former husband, Wm. Hooper, being living.
>
> The object of the prosecution did not appear, nor was it suggested that any injury had been sustained by any person in consequence of the alleged offence of the prisoner.
>
> It was proved that a marriage had taken place in 1810, between a man named Hooper, and a female supposed to be the prisoner, by her maiden name of Holloway; but the witness, the parish clerk, who was called to prove this fact, said he was not certain of the prisoner's identity. She appeared to be the the same woman; but she was, if the same, very much altered in appearance. The second marriage with one Puxtone, a farmer, in the present year, (as well as the prisoner's identity with regard to this marriage,) was clearly proved. This took place in April in the present year. To clear up the fact as to the identity of the prisoner on the first marriage, the constable who apprehended her was called. She was living with her second husband, farmer Puxtone, at the time. When told there was a warrant against her for bigamy, she said it was impossible, as there had been an agreement between "them" — an agreement prepared by a lawyer; and therefore she, at first, could not be made to believe that there could be any legal charge against her. The meaning of the expression "them" would be clearly made out as referring to the two husbands, if the conversation on the same subject, at the same time, but occurring while the prisoner was dressing herself, in order

to go to prison, could be made legal evidence against her; but as it took place in her absence, it was not admitted in evidence. Upon this defect in the case on the part of the prosecution, the learned Judge directed an acquittal, because, although it had been proved that there had been a marriage between two persons in the year 1819, it was not proved, either by evidence, or by the prisoner's confession, that she was one of them.

The Jury accordingly acquitted her. The prisoner, from her appearance and manner, as well as from her deportment through the trial, excited the sympathy of every person in court. Nothing was alleged against her character in any respect whatever.[2]

It is tempting to see in this passage the basis not only of important plot elements in *The Mayor of Casterbridge* but of much of the actual characterisation of Susan Henchard. The legal nicety about a conversation which took place in the prisoner's "absence"—apparently because she was dressing herself out of sight of the officers arresting her—may also have suggested to Hardy the furmity-woman's courtroom quibble: "I was not capable enough to hear what I said, and what is said out of my hearing is not evidence" [153].

For the story of wife-selling Hardy had no need to go to the files of the *Dorset County Chronicle*. The existence of such practices was well known, and a long entry on the subject appears in John Timbs's *Things Not Generally Known, Faithfully Explained* (1856), a book of miscellaneous information which Hardy owned, probably from childhood. He did, however, jot down at least three instances of wife-selling from the pages of the *Dorset County Chronicle*, and one such note, attributed to the issue of December 6, 1827, is of particular interest:

> *Selling wife.* At Buckland, nr. Frome, a labring [sic] man named Charles Pearce sold wife to shoemaker named Elton for £5, & delivered her in a halter in the public street. She seemed very willing. Bells rang.[3]

The sum mentioned here closely corresponds to the five guineas which Newson pays in *The Mayor of Casterbridge*; in other reports the payment is sometimes no more than the price of a few drinks. What seems more important is that the scene of the transaction, though outside Dorset, is well within the boundaries of "Wessex". Both the Somersetshire setting of the Buckland wife-selling and its date in the late 1820s—"before the nineteenth century had reached one-third of its span" [5]—suggest, in fact, that this may have been the specific incident to which Hardy referred in his 1895 Preface to *The Mayor of Casterbridge*:

2. *Dorset County Chronicle*, August 17 1826, p. [4]; cf "Facts", p. 47.
3. "Facts", p. [74]; see also pp. 32–3, 116. * * *

The incidents narrated arise mainly out of three events, which chanced to range themselves in the order and at or about the intervals of time here given, in the real history of the town called Casterbridge and the neighbouring country. They were the sale of a wife by her husband, the uncertain harvests which immediately preceded the repeal of the Corn Laws, and the visit of a Royal personage to the aforesaid part of England.

It is clear from chapter 37 that the "Royal personage" must have been Prince Albert, who passed through Dorchester in July 1849 on his way to Weymouth, "for the purpose", as the *Dorset County Chronicle* put it, "of laying the foundation stone of that highly important national work, the Portland Breakwater". In the novel the royal visitor leaves Casterbridge by "the Budmouth Road" [202] to "inaugurate an immense engineering work out that way" [198]. The newspaper report continued:

His Royal Highness's condescending goodness in undertaking the journey to Portland for this purpose was fully appreciated by the loyal inhabitants of Portland, Weymouth, and Dorchester. Every possible means of demonstrating the loyal and excellent feelings of the public in this county was had recourse to. On the auspicious day the bells of St. Peter's, Dorchester, rang merry peals, and a band of music was untiring in its efforts to give expression to the lively pleasure with which all persons seemed to be animated. The railway terminus was very tastefully decorated, and a pretty triumphal arch was erected between the trees at the entrance to the drive up to the station. Further on the Weymouth road was a remarkably handsome arch of boughs and flowers erected opposite the toll gate at Monckton, being surrounded with a crown, and having the inscription in the arch "Welcome, Prince Albert".[4]

The reference to the Dorchester railway station, opened two years before the Prince Consort's visit, points to at least one way in which the novel diverges from strict historical accuracy: "The railway had stretched out an arm towards Casterbridge at this time, but had not reached it by several miles as yet; so that the intervening distance, as well as the remainder of the journey, was to be traversed by road in the old fashion" [200]. But if Hardy deliberately kept Casterbridge, however tenuously, beyond the reach of the invading railway, the report in the *Dorchester County Chronicle* provides ample evidence for the authenticity of his allusions to the ringing of bells, the presentation of an illuminated address, and the erection of "green arches" [204] over the royal route.[5] Hardy no doubt turned to such reports before writing chapter 37 of *The*

---

4. *Dorset County Chronicle*, July 26 1849, p. [4].
5. According to the *Yeovil Times*, July 31 1849, p. 4, the arch at Monckton Gate "was tastefully decorated with Union Jacks, and had a beautiful and tasty [sic] appearance".

Mayor of Casterbridge. He may also have witnessed the Dorchester ceremonies himself, as a child of nine, and drawn directly, thirty-five years later, upon his own memories of the Prince's visit, while his source for the episode of Henchard's ludicrous and pathetic gesture of welcome may well have been the Reverend Henry Moule's story, preserved by Handley C. G. Moule in *Memories of a Vicarage*, of how the Mayor of Dorchester "was so much moved by the royal presence that he dropped on *both* knees to read his address".[6]

* * *

6. Handley C. G. Moule, *Memories of a Vicarage* (London, 1913), pp. 31–2. The Rev. Henry Moule was one of the local committee responsible for arranging the Dorchester ceremony.

CRITICISM

Contemporary Reception

From The Athenaeum

May 29, 1886

Mr. Hardy, though in some respects probably the best of our existing novelists, has not reached the degree of absolute merit which we once hoped he might do. He has a wonderful knowledge of the minds of men and women, particularly those belonging to a class which better-educated people are often disposed to imagine has no mind, chiefly because it cannot express itself with much fluency or "lucidity." Also he knows the ways and humours of country-folk, and can depict them vividly and in few strokes. Also he is most ingenious in devising problems, and bringing his people into situations of a complicated nature, which, nevertheless, the reader cannot pronounce to be wholly improbable. And, most of all, he has the gift of so telling his story that it sticks by the reader for days afterwards, mixing itself with his impressions and recollections of real scenes and people just as a very vivid dream will sometimes do, till he is not quite sure whether it also does not belong to them. Perhaps he has never shown these qualities better than in his latest novel. It will not be so popular as 'The Trumpet-Major,' nor does it deserve to be, recounting as it does the tragedy (if it may be so called) of a self-willed instead of an unselfish hero. But it displays as much as any of his books the characteristics which we have indicated briefly, and which, combined as they are with an almost Olympian ruthlessness towards his own creations, might under other conditions have made of Mr. Hardy a great dramatist. At the same time it must be said that his old faults, chiefly of style, are as prominent as ever. The worst of these is a tendency to far-fetched and unpleasant similes and epithets, *e.g.*, "the sun was resting on the hill *like a drop of blood on an eyelid*," or "the espaliers . . . had pulled their stakes out of the ground, and stood distorted and writhing *in vegetable agony, like leafy Laocoöns*." The language of the peasants again is a point on which we have an old quarrel with Mr. Hardy. It is neither one thing nor the other—neither dialect exactly reproduced nor a thorough rendering into educated English. If a man says, "I have been working within sound o't all day," he would not say, "The real business is done earlier than this," but surely "be done earlier nor this." But this is perhaps too long a question to enter into here; only Mr. Hardy may take our word for it that his method diminishes the reader's satisfaction.

[GEORGE SAINTSBURY][†]

From The Saturday Review

May 29, 1886

It is small dispraise of Mr. Hardy's novel *The Mayor of Casterbridge* to say that it is not equal to the author's great and most picturesque romance of rural life, *Far From the Madding Crowd*. Nevertheless, *The Mayor of Casterbridge* is a disappointment. The story, which is very slight and singularly devoid of interest, is, at the same time, too improbable. It is fiction stranger than truth; for, even at the comparatively distant date—some fifty years ago—and in the remote region— which we are unable to localize—when and where the scenes are laid, it is impossible to believe that the public sale by a husband of his wife and child to a sailor, in a crowded booth at a village fair, could have attracted such slight attention from the many onlookers, that the newly-assorted couple should have been able to walk off and disappear so entirely within a few hours, and that the vendor on coming to his senses the following morning, repenting him of the evil, and perhaps thinking that 5*l*. was too small a price for a good-looking young woman, was unable to trace them, though he appears to have attempted the task in earnest. Again, is it possible that Michael Henchard, thoroughly selfish and unprincipled when young, could have been refined by a temperance vow, and a hard-handed money-getting life, into a man of considerable delicacy, honour, and generosity? Mrs. Henchard, alias Newson, is so colourless as to be almost imperceptible. Elizabeth-Jane is excellent, but rather more than a trifle dull; and unless corn-factors have hitherto been a grossly maligned race, surely Farfrae has more scruples than any corn-factor that ever lived. Are flourishing businesses established in small country towns by refusal to deal with a rival's old customers; or rather, we should say, were they *ever* thus established? No one nowadays is in the least likely to try the experiment. It is matter for regret that the author omits to publish "Donald Farfrae's" secret

---

[†] Unsigned, but probably written by George Saintsbury. In a letter to C. Kegan Paul (1 July 1886), Hardy commented: "I am not disposed to think the review entirely the product of stupidity. That there should be no mistake about the locality I told the editor the real name of the town: so the paragraph about not recognising it is meant as a civil snub, I suppose." See *The Collected Letters of Thomas Hardy*, edited by Richard Little Purdy and Michael Millgate, 7 vols. (Oxford: Clarendon Press, 1978–88), 1:145.

recipe for turning "grown" wheat into good wholesome bread stuff, "restored quite enough to make good seconds out of it," though he frankly admits that "to fetch it back entirely is impossible. Nature won't stand so much as that." We are inclined to think that Nature will not.

But if Mr. Hardy's narrative is not thrilling, his descriptive powers are as great as ever. Nothing can be better than his sketches of Casterbridge, the old Roman garrison town, overgrown rather than obliterated by an English *urbs in rure*. His strongest point, however, is his capacity for portraying the average peasant, more especially the peasant who has passed middle age. The dialect of the agricultural labourer, his ways of thought, and his mode of speech are alike admirably given. The rustic dialogue, indeed, forms the most, if not the only, amusing portion of the book. One of the best specimens which, if space permitted, we should be tempted to quote at length is the conversation between Mrs. Cuxsom and Solomon Longways, wherein village views on funeral rites are frankly set forth. With his keen insight into the character of the rural poor Mr. Hardy has not failed to notice that with them custom breeds, if not contempt of gifts and the giver, at any rate a lack of the courtesy of acknowledgment. "Nance Mockridge," standing with her hands on her hips, "easefully looking at the preparations on her behalf" made by her young mistress, is drawn from the life. Equally characteristic of the country mayor who has risen from the ranks is Henchard's intolerance of his stepdaughter's natural good breeding, which prompts her to go to the kitchen instead of ringing, and persistently to thank the parlour-maid for everything she does; but for a man who cannot talk English even decently his anger at Elizabeth Jane's provincialisms is not quite so intelligible.

Another proof of how thoroughly Mr. Hardy has studied the workings of the rustic mind is given in the short account of Henchard's visit to "Fall" or "Wide-oh," as he was called behind his back, a sort of mild professor of the black art, whose simple magic was secretly invoked by yokels of all classes, who nevertheless always comported themselves during the séance as it were under protest. Whenever they consulted him they did it "for a fancy." When they paid him they said, "Just a trifle for 'Xmas or Candlemas," as the case might be. The "skimmington" or "skimmity" ride will, we fancy, be a novelty to most readers, though the author has doubtless witnessed, or has excellent warranty for describing, this burlesque but forcible protest against what villagers regard as unseemly pre-nuptial conduct on the part of a bride. The worst feature of the book is, that it does not contain a single character capable of arousing a passing interest in his or her welfare. Even the *dramatis personæ*, with the exception of Lucetta, who conceives so sudden and violent a passion for Farfrae, are in doubt almost up to the last moment whether they really care about anybody.

318

[RICHARD HOLT HUTTON]

From The Spectator[†]

June 5, 1886

Mr. Hardy has not given us any more powerful study than that of Michael Henchard. Why he should especially term his hero in his title-page a "man of character," we do not clearly understand. Properly speaking, character is the stamp graven on a man, and character therefore, like anything which can be graven, and which, when graven, remains, is a word much more applicable to that which has fixity and permanence, than to that which is fitful and changeful, and which impresses a totally different image of itself on the wax of plastic circumstance at one time, from that which it impresses on a similarly plastic surface at another time. To keep strictly to the associations from which the word 'character' is derived, a man of character ought to suggest a man of steady and unvarying character, a man who conveys very much the same conception of his own qualities under one set of circumstances, which he conveys under another. This is true of many men, and they might be called men of character *par excellence*. But the essence of Michael Henchard is that he is a man of large nature and depth of passion, who is yet subject to the most fitful influences, who can do in one mood acts of which he will never cease to repent in almost all his other moods, whose temper of heart changes many times even during the execution of the same purpose, though the same ardour, the same pride, the same wrathful magnanimity, the same inability to carry out in cool blood the angry resolve of the mood of revenge or scorn, the same hasty unreasonableness, and the same disposition to swing back to an equally hasty reasonableness, distinguish him throughout. In one very good sense, the great deficiency of Michael Henchard might be said to be in 'character.' It might well be said that with a little *more* character, with a little more fixity of mind, with a little more power of recovering *himself* when he was losing his balance, his would have been a nature of gigantic mould; whereas, as Mr. Hardy's novel is meant to show, it was a nature which ran mostly to waste. But, of course, in the larger and wider sense of the word 'character,' that sense which has less reference to the permanent definition of the stamp, and more reference to the confidence with which the varying moods may be anticipated, it is not inadmissible to call Michael Henchard a "man of character." Still, the words on the title-page rather mislead. One looks for the picture of a man of much more constancy of purpose, and much less tragic mobility of mood, than Michael Henchard. None the less, the picture is a very

† Unsigned, but written by Richard Holt Hutton. For the identification, see *Thomas Hardy: An Annotated Bibliography of Writings about Him*, compiled by W. Eugene Davis and Helmut E. Gerber (De Kalb, Ill.: Northern Illinois University Press, 1973).

vivid one, and almost magnificent in its fullness of expression. The largeness of his nature, the unreasonable generosity and suddenness of his friendships, the depth of his self-humiliation for what was evil in him, the eagerness of his craving for sympathy, the vehemence of his impulses both for good and evil, the curious dash of stoicism in a nature so eager for sympathy, and of fortitude in one so moody and restless, — all these are lineaments which, mingled together as Mr. Hardy has mingled them, produce a curiously strong impression of reality, as well as of homely grandeur.

Our only quarrel with Mr. Hardy is that while he draws a figure which, in spite of the melancholy nature of its career and the tragic close of that career, is certainly a noble one, and one, on the whole, *more* noble in its end than in its beginning, he intersperses throughout his story hints of the fashionable pessimism, a philosophy which seems to us to have little appropriateness to the homely scenery and characters which he portrays. For example, as Mr. Hardy approaches the end of his story, he says of his hero: —

> "Externally there was nothing to hinder his making another start on the upward slope, and by his new lights achieving higher things than his soul in its half-formed state had been able to accomplish. But the ingenious machinery contrived by the gods for reducing human possibilities of amelioration to a minimum—which arranges that wisdom to do shall come *pari passu* with the departure of zest for doing—stood in the way of all that. He had no wish to make an arena a second time of a world that had become a mere painted scene to him."

To our minds, these very pagan reflections are as much out of place as they are intrinsically false. The natural and true reflection would have been that Michael Henchard, after his tragic career of passionate sin, bitter penitence, and rude reparation, having been brought to a better and humbler mind than that which had for the most part pervaded his life, the chief end of that life had been achieved, and that it mattered little in comparison whether he should or should not turn the wisdom he had acquired to the purpose of hewing out for himself a wiser and soberer career. Those who believe that the only "human possibilities of amelioration" of any intrinsic worth, are ameliorations of the spirit of human character, cannot for a moment admit that when that has been achieved, it can add much to such an amelioration, that it should receive the sanction of a little earthly success. If life be the school of character, and if the character, once fairly schooled into a nobler type, passes from this school to another and higher school, we have no reason to complain. What Mr. Hardy calls "the ingenious machinery contrived by the gods for reducing human possibilities of amelioration to a minimum," appears to us to be the means taken by the moral wisdom which overrules our fate for showing us that the use of character is not to mould circumstance, but rather that it is the use of circumstance to chasten and purify character. Michael

Henchard's proud and lonely death shows, indeed, that he had but half learned his lesson; but it certainly does not in any way show that the half-learned lesson had been wasted. There is a grandeur of conception about this shrewd, proud, illiterate, primitive nature, which, so far as we remember, surpasses anything which even Mr. Hardy has yet painted for us in that strong and nervous school of delineation in which he excels so much. Michael Henchard's figure should live with us as Scott's picture of Steenie Mucklebackit or David Deans lives with us. Indeed, Scott never gave to a figure of that kind so much study and such painstaking portraiture as Mr. Hardy has given to his Mayor of Casterbridge.

He has succeeded quite as well, — though the figure is not so interesting, — with the Mayor's step-daughter, Elizabeth Jane, a reticent and self-contained nature of singular gentleness and wisdom, cast in an altogether lower tone of vitality, though in a higher plane of self-restraint. There is much beauty and charm in the picture, though the carefully subdued tone of the character makes it seem a little tame, and we are not at all scandalised at the easy victory gained by the lively Jersey beauty over her sober-minded, un-self-asserting rival. This Jersey beauty is also admirably touched off; but as for the all-conquering Scotchman who fascinates everybody (except the reader) so easily, there must, we think, be some failure of art there. Mr. Hardy makes Farfrae vivid enough. We cannot complain of not seeing him exactly as he is represented. But we have, perhaps, a right to complain that he seems so very cold-blooded to us, so very inferior to the master whom he supplants, though to all Mr. Hardy's *dramatis personæ*, Farfrae seemed so greatly the superior of Michael Henchard. Part of the reason is that Mr. Hardy paints the Scotchman from the outside, and the Southron from the inside, and that while we see the Southron as no one in the story sees him, unless it be himself, we only see the Scotchman as all the others see him. But though that explains why we like the Southron so much *better*, it hardly explains why we like the canny Scotchman, with all his imaginative sentiment, so little, though he wins so easy a victory over the hearts of the people of Casterbridge.

[WILLIAM DEAN HOWELLS][†]

From Harper's New Monthly Magazine

November 1886

In *The Mayor of Casterbridge* Mr. Hardy seems to have started with an intention of merely adventurous fiction, and to have found himself in

---

† Unsigned, but written by William Dean Howells. In a letter of 9 November 1886, Hardy wrote to Howells: "Accept my best thanks for your kindly notice of 'The Mayor of Casterbridge' in

possession of something so much more important that we could fancy him almost regretting the appeal first made to the reader's wonder. Henchard' sale of his wife is not without possibility, or even precedent; Mr. Hardy sufficiently establishes that; and yet when the grave, every-day problems resulting from that wild act began to grow under his hand, so fine an artist might well have wished them derived from some fact more commonly within the range of experience. After you have said this, however, you can have very little else to say against the story; and we are not strenuous that this is much against it. We suppose it is a condition of a novelist's acceptance by the criticism of a country now so notably behind the rest of Europe in fiction as England that he must seize the attention in an old-fashioned way; and we willingly concede to Mr. Hardy the use of the wife-sale for this purpose, though we are not sure that the non-professional readers of his book, even in England, would have exacted so much of him. The tangled web woven from Henchard's error is of the true modern design and honesty of material; and one forgets that he sold his wife in following all the consequences to his innocent and beneficent after-life, and to the good and guiltless lives of others. The wrong he has done cannot be repaired, because it cannot, to his mistaken thinking, be owned; and in the tragedy of its expiation your pity is more for him than for all the others. That wrong pursues him, it hunts him to death, with what natural reliefs and pauses the reader knows. Mr. Hardy has never achieved anything more skilful or valuable in its way than the recognition and development of these in his last story; we are not sure that he has not placed himself abreast of Tolstoï and the greatest of the Continental realists in their management.

Then the book is full of his proper and peculiar charm, which is for us always very great. It is a quality which, if he had no other great quality, would give him a claim upon his generation hardly less than that of any other contemporary novelist. It seems to exist apart from any beauty of style or felicity of phrase, and is like the grace of his women, which remains in your thought when you have ceased to think of their different pretty faces and variously alluring figures. It would be as hard to say what it is as to say what that grace is, and we can only suggest that it is a very frank and simple way of dealing with every kind of life, and of approaching men and women as directly as if they had never been written about before. In fact, thanks no doubt to his early training in another profession (Mr. Hardy was an architect), his first sense of people is apparently not a literary sense, but something very much more natural. He studies their exterior graphically, and deals with their souls as we do

---

Harper's—It is what the book would probably have deserved if the story had been written as it existed in my mind, but, alas, was never put on paper." See *The Collected Letters of Thomas Hardy*, edited by Richard Little Purdy and Michael Millgate, 7 vols. (Oxford: Clarendon Press, 1978–88), 1:156.

with those of our neighbors, only perhaps a little more mercifully. This absence of literosity, if we may coin a word as offensive as the thing, accounts for an occasional bluntness of phrase, which we have sometimes felt in Mr. Hardy's work, and for here and there an uncouthness of diction—or call it awkwardness; but we gain infinitely more than we lose by it. His natural method gives us in this story country folks as veritable as those in *Far from the Madding Crowd*, or *Under the Greenwood Tree*, never ironically or sentimentally handled, but left to make their own impression, among scenes and in surroundings portrayed as sympathetically and unconventionally as themselves. In fact, his landscapes are no more composed than his figures, and share evenly with them the charm of his treatment; no one except Tourguénief gives a fact or trait of nature with a more living freshness.

We should say that *The Mayor of Casterbridge* was not inferior to any other story of Mr. Hardy's in its grasp of character; and his humanity is so very pervasive that each of the leading personages has almost to the same degree that charm of his which we have not been very successful in defining. Henchard is brutal only in our first moments of him; his life, after these, is a willingness, if not an effort, to repair his wrong to his wife; and the heart aches with him through all his necessary ruin to the pitiable end of the old, broken, friendless man. Then that young Scot, Farfrae, gay, thrifty, and good, who supplants his benefactor in business, in love, and in public honors, without intending harm to Henchard is one of the freshest and most clean-cut figures in recent fiction; if you have known any bright young Scotchman, this one will make you think of him. Henchard's wife is one of those women, single-minded, unknowing, upright, which Mr. Hardy has the secret of divining and presenting to us in all their probability; there is not much of her, but every word of that little seems true. There is not very much of Lucetta either, but she too is every word true; she is perhaps only too captivating in that combination of shrewdness and blind imprudence, of fickleness and tenderheartedness, of fascinating grace and helplessness. She is of the order of women whom Mr. Hardy is rather fond of drawing, like Bathsheba in *Far from the Madding Crowd*, like Fancy in *Under the Greenwood Tree*, like Elfride in *A Pair of Blue Eyes*, and some delicious young person in nearly every one of his books; the sort who guiltlessly compromise themselves by some love impulse, and then more or less amusingly, more or less distressingly, pay for it, but remain in the reader's mind an appealing, a distracting presence. Nothing is better in the book than Lucetta's dropping Henchard, and her conquest of the young Scotchman, whom she wins away from Henchard's putative daughter, Elizabeth Jane, such being the fond and foolish heart of man in the thriftiest and best of all. But Elizabeth Jane, with her unswerving right-mindedness and her never-failing self-discipline, is a very beautiful and noble figure; and Mr. Hardy has made her supremely interesting merely by letting us see into her pure soul. Hers is the final triumph, unmixed with remorse, because nothing but goodness like hers could come unscathed out of all that sorrow and trouble. The author who can discover such a type, on whom the reader's liking may wholesomely rest, has done his public a real favor. It is a very great thing to show goodness and justice and mercy like hers in their actual relation to other lives, and lovable; and it is all the more useful to know Elizabeth Jane because her limitations are more than suggested, and she is not made St. Elizabeth Jane.

Modern Criticism

VIRGINIA WOOLF
[Hardy's Impression of Life]†

* * * If we are to place Hardy among his fellows, we must call him the greatest tragic writer among English novelists.

But let us, as we approach the danger-zone of Hardy's philosophy, be on our guard. Nothing is more necessary, in reading an imaginative writer, than to keep at the right distance above his page. Nothing is easier, especially with a writer of marked idiosyncrasy, than to fasten on opinions, convict him of a creed, tether him to a consistent point of view. Nor was Hardy any exception to the rule that the mind which is most capable of receiving impressions is very often the least capable of drawing conclusions. It is for the reader, steeped in the impression, to supply the comment. It is his part to know when to put aside the writer's conscious intention in favour of some deeper intention of which perhaps he may be unconscious. Hardy himself was aware of this. A novel "is an impression, not an argument", he has warned us, and, again

> Unadjusted impressions have their value, and the road to a true philosophy of life seems to lie in humbly recording diverse readings of its phenomena as they are forced upon us by chance and change.

Certainly it is true to say of him that, at his greatest, he gives us impressions; at his weakest, arguments. In *The Woodlanders*, *The Return of the Native*, *Far from the Madding Crowd*, and, above all, in *The Mayor of Casterbridge*, we have Hardy's impression of life as it came to him without conscious ordering. Let him once begin to tamper with his direct intuitions and his power is gone. "Did you say the stars were worlds, Tess?" asks little Abraham as they drive to market with their bee-hives. Tess replies that they are like "the apples on our stubbard-tree,

† From "The Novels of Thomas Hardy," pp. 245–57, in *The Second Common Reader* by Virginia Woolf, copyright © 1932 by the Hogarth Press and Harcourt, Inc., and renewed 1960 by Leonard Woolf. Reprinted by permission of the publishers and the Executors of the Virginia Woolf Estate. This excerpt was written in January 1928, the month of Hardy's death.

most of them splendid and sound—a few blighted". "Which do we live on—a splendid or a blighted one?" "A blighted one", she replies, or rather the mournful thinker who has assumed her mask speaks for her. The words protrude, cold and raw, like the springs of a machine where we had seen only flesh and blood. We are crudely jolted out of that mood of sympathy which is renewed a moment later when the little cart is run down and we have a concrete instance of the ironical methods which rule our planet.

That is the reason why *Jude the Obscure* is the most painful of all Hardy's books, and the only one against which we can fairly bring the charge of pessimism. In *Jude the Obscure* argument is allowed to dominate impression, with the result that though the misery of the book is overwhelming it is not tragic. As calamity succeeds calamity we feel that the case against society is not being argued fairly or with profound understanding of the facts. Here is nothing of that width and force and knowledge of mankind which, when Tolstoy criticises society, makes his indictment formidable. Here we have revealed to us the petty cruelty of men, not the large injustice of the gods. It is only necessary to compare *Jude the Obscure* with *The Mayor of Casterbridge* to see where Hardy's true power lay. Jude carries on his miserable contest against the deans of colleges and the conventions of sophisticated society. Henchard is pitted, not against another man, but against something outside himself which is opposed to men of his ambition and power. No human being wishes him ill. Even Farfrae and Newson and Elizabeth Jane whom he has wronged all come to pity him, and even to admire his strength of character. He is standing up to fate, and in backing the old Mayor whose ruin has been largely his own fault, Hardy makes us feel that we are backing human nature in an unequal contest. There is no pessimism here. Throughout the book we are aware of the sublimity of the issue, and yet it is presented to us in the most concrete form. From the opening scene in which Henchard sells his wife to the sailor at the fair to his death on Egdon Heath the vigour of the story is superb, its humour rich and racy, its movement large-limbed and free. The skimmity ride, the fight between Farfrae and Henchard in the loft, Mrs. Cuxsom's speech upon the death of Mrs. Henchard, the talk of the ruffians at Peter's Finger with Nature present in the background or mysteriously dominating the foreground, are among the glories of English fiction. Brief and scanty, it may be, is the measure of happiness allowed to each, but so long as the struggle is, as Henchard's was, with the decrees of fate and not with the laws of man, so long as it is in the open air and calls for activity of the body rather than of the brain, there is greatness in the contest, there is pride and pleasure in it, and the death of the broken corn merchant in his cottage on Egdon Heath is comparable to the death of Ajax lord of Salamis. The true tragic emotion is ours.

ALBERT J. GUERARD

[Henchard's Self-Condemnation]†

Henchard, who is Hardy's Lord Jim, stands at the very summit of his creator's achievement; his only tragic hero and one of the greatest tragic heroes in all fiction. He takes his place at once with certain towering and possessed figures of Melville, Hawthorne, and Dostoevsky: a man of character obsessed by guilt and so committed to his own destruction. He anticipates not merely Lord Jim and the Razumov of *Under Western Eyes* but also the Michel of Andé Gide's *L'Immoraliste*. Fifty years before Karl Menninger, Hardy recognized—as Shakespeare did three centuries before him—that the guilty not merely flagellate themselves but also thrust themselves in the way of bad luck; *create* what appear to be unlucky accidents. Henchard's decline in Casterbridge was no more fortuitous than Lord Jim's in Patusan. These two "men of character" pursued strikingly similar destinies: forceful, conscientious, and proud, alike outcasts thanks to the unaccountable flarings of a moment's fear and anger, dedicating their lives to an impossible rehabilitation and a distant ideal of honor. They are isolated and obsessed by guilt even in their fat years of power and prestige; they are determined to bear yet face down the past. Both are men of character in a strangely double sense. They want to atone for the past through self-punishment; yet they resist, humanly, merely compulsive self-punishment. In the end both are paralyzed by "chance" reminders from the past (Brown and the furmity-woman)—reminders which, in fact, they had never ceased to carry about with them. They achieve death in solitude, each having one dull-witted uncomprehending native who remains faithful to the last. Of the two Henchard, whose will was a final self-condemnation, may have shown more courage than Lord Jim, who turned to his executioners and to the world with a last look of proud defiance. Henchard was a "man of character"; Lord Jim was "one of us."

There was nothing in Hardy's earlier novels to suggest that he would some day produce such a figure; there is no series of links and experiments leading from Springrove or Manston to Henchard. Gabriel Oak, Diggory Venn, and many others seem to act perversely against their own interest, but this is owing to meditative impotence and a lack of normal aggressiveness. They are spectators rather than actors against themselves. Unlike them Henchard is a man of great force and destructive energy, which he turns outward occasionally but inward far more often. He has thus nothing in common with the irresponsible Wildeve, but a great deal in common with both Jude and Sue. There is little justification for

† From *Thomas Hardy: The Novels and Stories* (Cambridge, Mass.: Harvard University Press, 1949). Reprinted by permission of the author.

the critic who sums up Henchard's tragic flaws as temper and addiction to drink; these were symptoms of the self-destructive impulse rather than its causes. Hardy himself was explicit enough:

> Thereupon promptly came to the surface that idiosyncrasy of Henchard's which had ruled his courses from the beginning, and had mainly made him what he was. Instead of thinking that a union between his cherished stepdaughter and the energetic thriving Donald was a thing to be desired for her good and his own, he hated the very possibility.

> Among the many hindrances to such a pleading, not the least was this, that he did not sufficiently value himself to lessen his sufferings by strenuous appeal or elaborate argument.

> He had not expressed to her any regrets or excuses for what he had done in the past; but it was a part of his nature to extenuate nothing and live on as one of his own worst accusers.

Henchard is simply incapable of acting consistently in his own interest. Captain Ahab, traveling the wide seas in pursuit of his own destruction, supposes cosmic hostilities in a whale. And so Henchard, earthbound in Casterbridge, comes at last to think "some sinister intelligence bent on punishing him." Had someone roasted a wax image of him? Was some power working against him? Unaware that the power was wholly inward, he "looked out at the night as at a fiend."

Thus Hardy, who had seldom troubled himself with crime and punishment, at last explored the great nineteenth-century myth of the isolated, damned, and self-destructive individualist—the more impressively because his Lara, Vautrin, Tito Melema, and Ahab was an ordinary Wessex farmer-merchant. The particular myth was conceived in terms as grand as the Wessex environment would allow—beginning with no less than the angry, drunken, and impulsive sale of a wife on the fairgrounds of Weydon Priors, to which Henchard would return a quarter of a century later in full circle. The tendency to paranoia and self-flagellation must have had its origin, like that of Sue Bridehead, in some part of an undisclosed childhood. At the very beginning Henchard has already the "instinct of a perverse character"; he drinks too much and thinks he has ruined his chances by marrying at eighteen. It is the crime of selling his wife which concentrates his energies, however; which both makes his character and destroys it. (Here too he is exactly like Lord Jim, who might have remained, in innocence, a fairly ordinary sea captain and trader.) Henchard looks in vain for his wife; swears an oath not to drink for twenty years; becomes mayor of Casterbridge, though equipped with little more than energy—becomes a man of character. When Susan finally reappears, he stolidly and conscientiously marries her; when Lucetta reappears, he acts honorably, though long tempted to revenge himself on Farfrae through her; when the furmity-woman reappears, he publicly acknowledges his guilt. He is fair in his savage fashion, and fights Farfrae with one hand tied behind his back. Ruined, he is the most conscientious of bankrupts.

The Mayor of Casterbridge is a novel of temperament in action, in minute action even; its distinction derives from a severe concentration on the self-destructive aspects of that temperament. The obligation to punish and degrade the self is at times fairly conscious. Thus Henchard marries Susan not merely to make amends to her and to provide Elizabeth-Jane with a home, but also "to castigate himself with the thorns which these restitutory acts brought in their train; among them the lowering of his dignity in public opinion by marrying so comparatively humble a woman." He licks his wounds by demanding that the journeymen sing the terrible One Hundred and Ninth Psalm; he goes to work for Farfrae wearing the rusty silk hat of his former dignity; he humbles himself unnecessarily before Lucetta; he lingers on the second stone bridge where the failures and drifters of the town gather. But Hardy recognized, intuitively at least, that the guilty may also punish themselves unconsciously and cause their own "bad luck." The man who repeatedly cuts and burns himself is no mere victim of absurd mischance; he is compelled to cut and burn himself, though he may not understand his compulsion. Freud has documented the hidden psychology of errors; Menninger the motives of chronic failures and of those who suffer repeated "accidents." Psychologists have proved that the unfortunate are more often than not the guilty, who must pay daily hostages to their fear.

Henchard is such a man, for whom everything "goes wrong" once he has begun to struggle with his guilt. So his elaborate public entertainment fails dismally while Farfrae's modest one succeeds. Rain does not fall at the beck of the accusing conscience, but Henchard's party is ruined by more than rain. "A man must be a headstrong stunpoll to think folk would go up to that bleak place today." Later he gambles on disastrous rains to drive up the price of corn and is confirmed in his prophecy by the mysterious Mr. Fall; he buys enormous quantities of corn and is ruined by the blazing August weather. But the adverse force was his own lack of Wessex prudence. "He was reminded of what he had well known before, that a man might gamble upon the square green areas of fields as readily as upon those of a card-room . . . 'For you can never be sure of weather till 'tis past.'" Henchard's subconscious self-destructiveness shows itself far less equivocally at the time of the Royal Progress. He has a "passing fancy" to join in welcoming the royal visitor, though no longer a member of the town council. But what might have appeared a last conscious effort to reassert his dignity was in fact a half-conscious effort to degrade himself before the collected townfolk in the most humiliating way. "He was not only a journeyman, unable to appear as he formerly had appeared, but he disdained to appear as well as he might. Everybody else, from the Mayor to the washerwoman, shone in new vesture according to means; but Henchard had doggedly retained the fretted and weather-beaten garments of bygone years." And he was drunk. When he resumed drinking after twenty years, a short time before this, he had committed himself to focal suicide and certain self-punishment. Character is fate; and Newson and the furmity-woman, those symbolic reminders, were part of his character and fate. Henchard would have destroyed himself even had they not returned. As a man of character he was morally obligated to do so. Yet he was also obligated to resist mere compulsive self-destructiveness. Here too, in fighting his suicidal destiny, he was a man of character.

Thus grandly and minutely conceived, Henchard might yet have remained as wooden as Farmer Boldwood. But he is very nearly the most personalized of Hardy's men: a voice and an unforgettable massive presence, with his twitching mouth and distant gaze, his "vehement" gloominess, his severe friendliness, and his businesslike bluntness even when proposing marriage. No doubt it is as a well-meaning man isolated by guilt that he makes his strongest appeal to our sympathy. Loneliness as well as guilt prompts him to hire Farfrae impulsively and to pour out his confession at once. And guilt as well as loneliness attaches him to Elizabeth-Jane: "He had liked the look of her face as she answered him from the stairs. There had been affection in it, and above all things what he desired now was affection from anything that was good and pure." Finally, though his history is highly selective, we have the impression that we know Henchard's life in its every significant detail. The measure of the characterization's success is our unquestioning acceptance in its context of Henchard's stylized and symbolic will. It does not seem to us a gratuitous or merely ornamental offering of Hardy's pessimism, as a few of Jude Fawley's philosophical speeches do. Michael Henchard's excommunication of self is a reasoned one, for his life has actually so added up:

> That Elizabeth-Jane Farfrae be not told of my death, or made to grieve on account of me.
> & that I be not bury'd in consecrated ground.
> & that no sexton be asked to toll the bell.
> & that nobody is wished to see my dead body.
> & that no murners walk behind me at my funeral.
> & that no flours be planted on my grave.
> & that no man remember me.
> To this I put my name.

JULIAN MOYNAHAN

The Mayor of Casterbridge and the Old Testament's First Book of Samuel[†]

I

From one standpoint, the major theme of Thomas Hardy's *The Mayor of Casterbridge* is not "character is fate" or "man against himself,"[1] but rather it is the conflict between generations. This is a very ancient subject matter, one of the archetypal themes noted by the Jungian literary psychologist Maud Bodkin, who traces it in classical Greek drama and in Shakespeare's *Hamlet* and *King Lear*.[2] In Hardy's novel the conflicting generations are represented by Michael Henchard, the middle-aged corn factor and mayor, and Donald Farfrae, the energetic young Scotchman whose two-fold abilities, "the commercial and the romantic," while exercised with the best of intentions, prove deadly to his patron. Because of the ineluctability of this theme, it is necessary that the affection between the two men should turn to hate and that Henchard, as the older, should go under. The special bitterness of Henchard's inevitable failure is perhaps Hardy's characteristically pessimistic contribution. But we might also relate this quality of bitterness to the lack—increasingly in Hardy's time and almost totally in ours—of a generally accepted religious outlook which could transform Henchard's sufferings into a mitigating ritual and his death into a sacrificial symbol. Whereas Lear dies in the bosom of his family, as it were, surrounded by both his living and dead relatives, in full view of an awed and edified audience, Henchard's death is hidden from the eyes of all men except the faithful "fool" Whittle, whose report is necessarily limited to a few concrete particulars. Under the circumstances, Elizabeth-Jane's "what bitterness lies there!" is, at least on one level of the narrative, a final comment which every reader must echo.

Nevertheless, there is another level of significance in the novel, a level on which Henchard assumes the august dimensions of a legendary king, while his opponent, Farfrae, undergoes a similar enlarging transformation. How does this happen? Through a strategy of association Henchard's career is connected with the career of Saul, the melancholy king of Old Testament narrative; Henchard's shift from affection and

[†] From "*The Mayor of Casterbridge* and the Old Testament's First Book of Samuel: A Study of Some Literary Relationships," *PMLA* 71 (1956): 118–30. Reprinted by permission of the Modern Language Association of America.

1. See A. J. Guerard, *Thomas Hardy: The Novels and Stories* (Cambridge, Mass.: Harvard University Press, 1949), pp. 146–53, for a psychiatrically oriented discussion of Henchard's self-destructive and masochistic traits.
2. *Archetypal Patterns in Poetry* (London, 1934), pp. 23–24.

trust to suspicion and finally hatred for Farfrae is connected to a corresponding shift in the relations between Saul and David; Farfrae, whose character combines the ingredients of shrewdness, musical sensitivity, and a strong capacity for romantic attachment, is connected to David, the brilliant, poetic, yet politic young Bethlehemite outlander who began his public career as Saul's armour bearer and beloved companion, later became his hated rival, and ended as king of all Israel.

Extended parallels between the Henchard-Farfrae conflict and the Saul-David conflict have never been noted before, so far as I am aware, although every careful reader of the novel notices Hardy's general indebtedness to biblical narrative for allusions and metaphors.[3] The novel's one direct statement of comparison between Henchard and Saul is "Henchard felt like Saul at his reception by Samuel" and is from the episode of the visit to the weather prophet. This disarmingly casual sentence does not encourage the reader to develop the stated resemblance beyond the narrowly circumscribed context in which it occurs. But the resemblance can be developed to a striking degree by anyone who attempts a close reading of those chapters in I Samuel which deal with the relationship of Saul and David along with an attentive rereading of *The Mayor of Casterbridge.*

The identification of characters and incidents with their biblical counterparts does not extend beyond the central dramatic situation of the novel, which I take to be the aggressive rivalry of the two men in their careers and in their personal affairs. Within this area the parallels are both detailed and illuminating. In fact, I would argue that the full meaning of certain scenes can be grasped only by having the reader make the appropriate connections between corresponding features of the Henchard *vs.* Farfrae action and its archaic prototype. But this is a critical question which can be settled only after the existence and scope of the extended parallelism have been established.

II

In *The Mayor of Casterbridge* the hazards of grain speculation seem roughly to correspond with the constant threat of Philistine invasion which haunts the reign of King Saul. When Farfrae arrives in Casterbridge, Henchard is at the height of his power as leading merchant and civil magistrate. But for the moment he is seriously embarrassed from having been forced to sell spoiled corn to the townspeople. Farfrae, appearing from out of the blue, saves Henchard from embarrassment and financial loss by showing him a method for restoring the corn. He asks no payment and wishes to continue his journey to the New World. But Henchard, with characteristic generosity and impulsiveness,

---

3. Arthur McDowall in his *Thomas Hardy* (London, 1931), p. 74, describes Farfrae as "the David to Henchard's Saul" but does not go on to develop the point.

offers Farfrae a position as general manager of his enterprises and is willing to give him a third share in the ownership if he will only stay in Casterbridge. It is immediately clear that on Henchard's side there is a good deal of personal attachment involved and that these personal elements in the relationship are bound up with Henchard's great loneliness and with his sensitivity to music. When the mayor overhears Farfrae's singing at the Three Mariners inn, he pauses in the street and after listening attentively comments "to be sure, to be sure, how that fellow does draw me! . . . I suppose 'tis because I'm lonely."

The part played by music in *The Mayor of Casterbridge* is extremely important and will be discussed in some detail below. Here it is sufficient that we recall the young David's musical accomplishments and the strong sensitivity to music shown by King Saul on many occasions in his career. David recommended himself to Saul by slaying Goliath and by his skill at music. Farfrae recommended himself to Henchard by his saving of the damaged corn and by his musical talent. Both David and Farfrae are not only strangers when they make their first appearances upon the public scene, but they are also "foreigners": Farfrae a Scot among Wessex men; David a member of the tribe of Judah at the court of a Benjamite king. Both make contact with their temporarily inaccessible future patrons when they proclaim confidently that they can settle the problem at hand. Word reaches Saul when the servants carry David's boast by word of mouth; Farfrae quietly sends in his own note.

As though to underline the parallelism which is being established, the language describing Farfrae when he makes his first appearance in the novel is taken, in large part, directly from the only two verses in the entire Bible which give a physical description of David: "He was ruddy and of a fair countenance, bright-eyed and slight in build" (*The Mayor of Casterbridge*).[4] "Now he was ruddy, and withal of a beautiful countenance, and goodly to look to" (I Samuel 16.12).[5] "And when the Philistine looked about, and saw David, he disdained him: for he was but a youth, and ruddy, and of a fair countenance" (I Samuel 17.42). The slight build is also traditionally ascribed to David on the grounds that Saul's failure to perform God's commands had convinced Him that the standard of enormous physical strength and great height by which Saul had been selected as first king of the Hebrews was no longer appropriate. Henceforth, the Lord will judge by other criteria and He advises the prophet Samuel to do likewise: "Look not on his countenance, or on the height of his stature; . . . for the Lord seeth not as man seeth; for man looketh on the outward appearance, but the Lord looketh on the heart" (I Samuel 16.7).

---

4. See p. 31 of this Norton Critical Edition [*Editor*].
5. I make use of the Authorized Version of the Bible for all scriptural citations and references in this essay.

Henchard's personal qualities, as they are exposed in the early action of the novel, are entirely congruous with those we usually attribute to Saul. Emphasis is placed on his strength, generosity, moodiness, and an impulsiveness which is intensified at times to an almost suicidal rashness. This last quality is particularly notable in Saul, who is perhaps one of the most famous examples in world literature of the depressive temperament. When we read that Henchard "threw himself back so that his elbow rested on the table, his forehead being shaded by his hand, which, however, did not hide the marks of introspective inflexibility on his features," it is not difficult to connect such an image of brooding with the Saul who was troubled by "an evil spirit from the Lord" (I Samuel 16.14). When Henchard tries to explaine to Farfrae how he became involved with Lucetta on the Isle of Jersey he says, "I fell quite ill, and in my illness I sank into one of those gloomy fits I sometimes suffer from, on account o' the loneliness of my domestic life, when the world seems to have the blackness of hell, and, like Job, I could curse the day that gave me birth." Henchard's gloom is traceable to the rash act which doomed him to loneliness, the sale of wife and child to the sailor, Newson. Saul's gloom is similarly traceable to a rash act which cost him God's favor, his disobedience to God's commands during his military campaign against the Amalekites. At the same time, gloom seems to be constitutional for both these figures. We are seldom privileged to see them in any other state of feeling.

The friendship between Henchard and Farfrae turns sour only gradually. Their relationship is spoiled by Henchard's jealousy of Farfrae's phenomenal popularity with the local farmers and townspeople. From the innocent mouth of a child the older man hears the answer to his query as to why people always want his manager instead of him: "'And he's better-tempered, and Henchard's a fool to him,' they say. And when some of the women were a-walking home they said, 'He's a diment— he's a chap 'o wax—he's the best—he's the horse for my money,' says they. And they said, 'He's the most understanding man o' them two by long chalks. I wish he was the master instead of Henchard,' they said." In very much the same way Saul grew envious of David, because the younger man's popularity as a military leader against the Philistines exceeded his own. And, as in the novel, the problem is dramatized in terms of the praise of women. When David returned from an expedition he was met by female musicians who improvised songs in praise of his exploits, "and the women answered one another as they played, and said, Saul hath slain his thousands and David his ten thousands" (I Samuel 18.7).

In each case jealousy is accompanied by a growth of gloomy suspicion. Saul suspects that David wants to usurp his throne. Henchard fears that he has put himself in Farfrae's power by telling him too many personal secrets. At the same time, Henchard does not actually dismiss Farfrae from his employment. His suspicions come in waves and "when his jealous temper had passed away, his heart sank within him at what he had said and done." His affection returns—until some new success of his young assistant sets him off again. Eventually, Farfrae must withdraw from Henchard's employment of his own decision, just as David must eventually flee Saul's court after enduring the monarch's murderous rages as long as he can. We sense in both cases that the older men are victims of their emotions rather than masters of them. They are trapped in a cyclic pattern of ambivalent feeling, oscillating between love and hate.

When Henchard has finally maneuvered Farfrae into a position where he can destroy him, when he has him down during the fight in the hayloft, he discovers that he cannot go through with it. He has tied one arm behind his back so that Farfrae may have a fair chance. But is not the tied arm also construable as a symbol of the conflict of feeling which partially paralyzes Henchard during this scene?: "God is my witness that no man ever loved another as I did thee at one time. . . . And now—though I came here to kill 'ee, I cannot hurt thee!" He is overwhelmed with shame and self-hate as he recalls with piercing intensity "that time when the curious mixture of romance and thrift in the young man's composition so commanded his heart that Farfrae could play upon him as on an instrument." As Farfrae departs, Henchard remains in a state of acute depression, huddled in a corner of the loft on a pile of sacks.

The appropriate scene from the biblical narrative to place with this incident is the highly dramatic encounter of David and Saul in the wilderness at En-Gedi. David has been a hunted man for some time when he comes upon his persecutor lying sound asleep. Instead of killing him, he respects the sacrosanct person of the monarch and merely cuts off the border of Saul's robe as a sign of his opportunity and forbearance. When Saul awakes and realizes what has happened he has a poignant moment of intense regret; the old love for David comes flooding back and with it the bitterness of shame. He hears David, who is in hiding near by, cry out for the Lord to judge the cause that is between Saul and himself: "And it came to pass, when David had made an end of speaking these words unto Saul, that Saul said, Is this thy voice, my son David? And Saul lifted up his voice, and wept. And he said to David, Thou art more righteous than I: for thou hast rewarded me good, whereas I have rewarded thee evil" (I Samuel 24.16–17).

In I Samuel the king falls into David's hands twice, and twice is permitted to go on his way unharmed. There are, of course, no regular parallels to these incidents in *The Mayor of Casterbridge*. Instead, it is Henchard who twice is on the verge of murdering Farfrae and who both times lets him go unharmed. On an earlier occasion in the same hayloft which supplied the setting for the fight, Henchard had raised his hand behind Farfrae's back as the latter stood dangerously close to the open

loft door. But after an inward struggle, his better impulses had conquered, and he had lowered his arm to his side. We may choose to see
in this pair of incidents a sort of transposed or inverted parallelism in
which events taken over from the older narrative are remade in order to
fit them into the dramatic structure of the novel.

The biblical place-name Adullam undergoes a curious shift as it is
taken over into the novel. In I Samuel Adullam is the great cave where
David hid from Saul's searching parties. It was apparently an inaccessible hideout in which thieves and smugglers, as well as political refugees
like David, might avoid the authorities. In *The Mayor of Casterbridge*
Mixen Lane, the thieves' quarter of Casterbridge, is called "the Adullam
of all the surrounding villages." This is an appropriate metaphor, but the
name plays no part in any system of correspondences between the locations of events in the biblical narrative and locations of similar events in
the novel. Farfrae, after all, has no connection with Mixen Lane.

III
The Motif of Music

The Saul-David parallels may serve as a key to an understanding of
the extraordinary, even magical, role played by music generally and by
Farfrae's musical talents in particular in the action of the novel. Here
David's great skill as singer, harpist, psalmist, and, as it happens, dancer
should be kept in mind.

Farfrae begins his career in Casterbridge by enchanting the topers at
the Three Mariners with his Scotch songs. The lonely mayor is drawn
by this music into a feeling of loving kinship with the younger man. The
townspeople admire Farfrae for his commercial abilities, but they are
attracted to him, at least equally, on account of his singing ability. A
turning point in the fortunes of both men is reached when they compete
at providing entertainment for the citizenry on the public holiday.
Henchard's spread is rained out—throughout the novel Henchard is victimized by inclement weather—while Farfrae's entertainment of music
and dance is a success. As the disappointed mayor watches the people
flock to Farfrae's ingeniously constructed tent where the Scot is dancing
briskly in the costume of a Highlander, he is struck by envy. And when
he perceives "the immense admiration for the Scotchman that revealed
itself in the women's faces," he is so stung that his surly remarks provoke
Farfrae to break openly with him, once and for all.

So intimately is Farfrae's charm bound up with the theme of music that
even Lucetta, when she has had no contact with him in his role as a
singer, succumbs to his "hyperborean crispness, stringency, and charm, as
of a well-braced musical instrument." Here it is not a matter of specific
abilities; rather, it is Farfrae's very nature that is being defined metaphorically in musical terms. Another form of this definition in musical terms is

given by some expressions already quoted in another connection: Henchard's heart is so "commanded" by Farfrae that the latter could "play upon him as on an instrument." It may be appropriate to recall here that at the beginning of the scene in which these expressions occur—the scene of the hayloft fight—Farfrae had entered the loft building humming the same tune of friendship ("And here's a hand, my trusty fiere,/And gie's a hand o' thine.") which he had sung at the Three Mariners several years previous, upon first arriving in Casterbridge. Henchard's reaction revealed once again the power of Farfrae's music over him: "Nothing moved Henchard like an old melody. He sank back. 'No; I can't do it!' he gasped. 'Why does the infernal fool begin that now!'"

Near the end of the novel, when Henchard has sunk into a fixed despair, we learn that "if he could have summoned music to his aid his existence might even now have been borne; for with Henchard music was of regal power. The merest trumpet or organ tone was enough to move him, and high harmonies transubstantiated him. But hard fate had ordained that he should be unable to call up this Divine spirit in his need." There is a complicated irony here which extends into both sides of our parallelism. Music has power over Saul and over Henchard. Both these inwardly tormented figures are able to escape their melancholy through music. But in both cases the power of music is in the control of their young rivals. In driving away David, Saul drove away the "divine spirit" of music itself. And Henchard in alienating Farfrae has done the same: in the literal sense he has lost Farfrae, the singer of old melodies; and in the sense of the music metaphor he has lost the beloved young friend whose benign control over his feelings was comparable to mastery of a musical instrument.

An even more penetrating irony (or series of ironies) is developed in the superb scene in which the drunken Henchard forces the Casterbridge church choir, who had retired to the Three Mariners for their regular Sunday morning ale, to sing the bloody and vindictive verses 10–15 of the Davidic Psalm CIX, as Farfrae and Lucetta pass by on their way from the church. These verses constitute an elaborate cursing prophecy and in the Tate and Brady metrical version used by Hardy end with these lines:

> A swift destruction soon shall seize
> On his unhappy race;
> And the next age his hated name
> Shall utterly deface.

Henchard intends the curse for Farfrae. He is, from one point of view, attempting to steal Farfrae's magic, the magic of the power of music, and turn it against its owner. He feels that he is only paying Farfrae off in kind, for "it was partly by his songs that he got over me, and heaved me out." The psalm lends itself beautifully to such a purpose, because it is an extremely primitive production, and whoever composed it doubtless assumed that this cursing poem would, of itself, magically confound the enemy upon recitation.

But there are two ironies here. First, as nearly every reader notices, the verses, instead of prescribing a terrible end for Farfrae, do, in fact, describe Henchard's own fate. The final provision of Henchard's bleakly worded will—"and that no man remember me"—echoes the last two lines of the quatrain I have just quoted. Henchard dies alone, and no child or other relative survives him. His line is at an end. The curse which he invoked against Farfrae comes to be enacted on his own miserable head.

A second irony emerges when we refer to the Saul-David parallelism. There is a certain grim humor, of the sort that we have learned to term Hardyesque, in the fact that Henchard should choose a Davidic hymn with which to insult the person who is, after all, the triumphant David of his own personal history. There is also a tremendous pathos as we sense the total blindness and confusion which afflict Henchard. When he points out Farfrae as the man at whom the singing of the psalm was aimed, and the shocked choristers gasp indignantly, we recognize how entirely and pitiably wrong Henchard is. For Farfrae is the "next age" in relation to Henchard, even as David was the next age for King Saul. "Don't you blame David. He knew what he was about when he wrote that," says Henchard to the choir members. It is Henchard's tragedy that he does not know, either in this scene or in the novel as a whole, what he is about.

IV
Encountering the Supernatural

Let us turn to another scene in *The Mayor of Casterbridge* where we can trace some detailed parallels to one of the most striking incidents in the career of King Saul. I am referring to the scene in which Henchard visits the weather prophet Fall. The corresponding biblical episode is, of course, Saul's visit to the witch of Endor (I Samuel 28.3–25).

Saul seeks out the witch on the eve of his great battle against the Philistine army at Mt. Gilboa. In this battle Saul and three of his sons will be slain, and one consequence of these deaths will be the transference of the royal line from the House of Kish to the House of Jesse. David will be king. Henchard seeks out the weather prophet on the eve of his great commercial battle with Farfrae. He will stake his fortunes on Fall's predictions of a rainy harvest by purchasing grain early in the harvest season at a relatively high price. If the weather turns fair, prices will fall, he will be caught with the high-priced grain in his granaries and forced to sell at a tremendous loss on a low market. Fall's prediction does turn out to be wrong, and Henchard's business suffers a blow from which it never recovers. Subsequent to this fatal speculation, Henchard becomes bankrupt and Farfrae, who has speculated more wisely, succeeds him as the leading merchant of the town. To make the revolution in the fortunes of the two men complete and symmetrical, he also succeeds Henchard as mayor. When Farfrae buys up his former employer's corn stores and hay barns he orders the name of Henchard obliterated from the gateway and his own painted in, so that all may know that Henchard "ruled there no longer." A new commercial dynasty has been established.

Henchard, unlike Saul, does not die immediately after his visit to the seer, but his way is all downhill after he has acted on the basis of Fall's prediction of bad weather. Saul, unlike Henchard, does not receive bad advice, but the knowledge which he receives from Samuel's ghost—that he and his sons must die on the morrow, "because thou obeyedst not the voice of the Lord, nor executedst his fierce wrath upon Amalek" (I Samuel 28.18)—cannot help him to change fate.

Supporting the general resemblance between the episodes are a few more detailed parallels. Both Saul and Henchard arrive for their respective appointments by night, and both attempt to remain anonymous by muffling their faces. Henchard would be embarrassed to have it known that he believes in the superstition of weather prophecy. And in a sense Saul also is embarrassed, because as king he has been carrying on a campaign to rid his territories of wizards and witches. Fall knows Henchard at once and addresses him by name. To show off his prophetic powers he has even set a place at his dinner table for him, although Henchard had sent no advance warning that he was coming for a consultation. There is an uncanniness about this which is not matched by anything in the biblical episode. The witch penetrates Saul's disguise, but only after she has conjured up the ghost of Samuel. There is no immediate recognition.

Nevertheless, this incident of the pre-set dinner table in Hardy's novel does have a parallel in the full narrative of Saul's life, and our attention is directed specifically to this parallel by the sentence Hardy uses to express Henchard's surprise: "Henchard felt like Saul at his reception by Samuel." To make sense out of this we have to go back to a very early event in the life of Saul before he had become king. The prophet Samuel in his foreknowledge of events had gone to meet Saul at Ramah in the land of Zuph, where the young man had arrived while searching for his father's lost asses. Saul was amazed when the prophet, whom he had never seen before, escorted him into a banquet room where thirty persons were waiting and where a choice cut of meat had already been set aside for him: "And Samuel said, Behold that which is left! set it before thee and eat: for unto this time hath it been kept for thee since I said, I have invited the people. So Saul did eat with Samuel that day" (I Samuel 9.24).

Henchard refuses to eat with Fall for fear that "sitting down to hob-and-nob there would have seemed to mark him too implicitly as the weather-caster's apostle." Saul, likewise, refuses to eat but his servants prevail upon him to partake of a fatted calf and some unleavened bread which the woman prepares for him. In both stories the issue of breaking bread with the soothsayers adds a contrasting touch of homely realism to these encounters with the supernatural.

V

I believe that thus far I have demonstrated the existence of extensive parallels between Hardy's account of the Henchard-Farfrae rivalry and the biblical account of the Saul-David conflict. Whether these parallels result from the fully conscious intention of the artist, or whether we are dealing here with a degree of unconscious influence from the older narrative, are extremely difficult questions to answer. We do know that Hardy's mind was saturated in the imagery and episodes of the Bible and that he constantly employed a wide range of biblical allusions in his novels. Without going any farther than *The Mayor of Casterbridge* itself, it is a simple matter to collect references to characters, incidents and settings of several other books of the Old Testament. For example, Henchard freely compares himself to Cain and to Job; Farfrae in his commercial success is like Jacob in Padan-Aran; Elizabeth-Jane questions Lucetta about her love life in "Nathan tones"; the enterprise of cattle raising in Casterbridge is carried on with "Abrahamic success." These frequent allusions, by themselves, tend to bring the world of early nineteenth-century Wessex and the world of the early Hebrews into significant relation with one another. They prepare us for the more detailed correspondences we have been tracing.

In the midst of an inevitable uncertainty as to Hardy's intentions, there is one matter on which we can be certain; that is, that Hardy read his Bible not as fact and not as foundation upon which to erect a system of religious belief or unbelief. Rather, he read the Bible narratives as fictional art, containing much to teach the modern novelist. On Friday, 17 April 1885, Hardy wrote in his diary that he had just completed the writing of *The Mayor of Casterbridge*. The entry immediately preceding is dated Easter Sunday of the same year and deals with "Evidences of art in Bible narratives":

> They are written with a watchful attention (though disguised) as to their effect on their reader. Their so-called simplicity is, in fact, the simplicity of the highest cunning. And one is led to inquire when even in these latter days artistic development and arrangement are

the qualities least appreciated by readers, who was there likely to appreciate the art in these chronicles at that day?

Looking round on a well-selected shelf of fiction or history, how few stories of any length does one recognize as well told from beginning to end! The first half of this story, the last half of that, the middle of another. . . . The modern art of narration is yet in its infancy.

But in these Bible lives and adventures there is the spherical completeness of perfect art. And our first, and second, feeling that they must be true because they are so impressive, becomes, as a third feeling, modified to 'Are they so very true, after all?' Is not the fact of their being so convincing an argument, not for their actuality, but for the actuality of a consummate artist who was no more content with what Nature offered than Sophocles and Pheidias were content?[6]

What is the relevance for literary criticism in these parallels? No relevance whatsoever if one decides that I Samuel is merely the source for a set of characters and incidents in Hardy's *The Mayor of Casterbridge*. I would suggest, however, that we are dealing here with something more than a source. It seems to me that the Saul-David conflict represents a kind of framing action for the main dramatic situation of the novel, and that this frame, as soon as it is recognized, becomes a part of the novel's total organization or form. The form of Hardy's novel in this respect deserves comparison with that tour de force of framed narrative, James Joyce's *Ulysses*, although obviously Joyce has exploited the parallels between Bloom's wanderings in early twentieth-century Dublin and Ulysses' adventures in the ancient world with a degree of system and of exhaustive detail that is quite unknown to Hardy's novel. We all accept the fact that an adequate response to *Ulysses* requires a reader constantly to make relations between the contemporary and the legendary levels of the action. I would suggest that *The Mayor of Casterbridge*, although a much less highly evolved example of the framed novel, requires a similar effort. In the end it is not simply that Henchard is like Saul, that his glooms and rages recall the glooms and rages of the Hebrew king, and that the pathos of his decline and death is reminiscent of the sad decline and death of the aging monarch. In another sense Henchard *is* Saul just as Farfrae is David, and the relationship of love and hate which exists between the older man and the younger is a permanently possible, endlessly recurrent relationship between successive generations. Through these identifications the unity of experience is stressed. We are back here to Miss Bodkin's archetype. In *The Mayor of Casterbridge* the evocation of the considerably more archaic version of essentially the same dra-

6. Florence Emily Hardy, *The Life of Thomas Hardy* (Macmillan: London, 1962), pp. 170–71 [*Editor*].

matic conflict fixes the significance of that conflict in unmistakable terms. It comes to be contemplated as a pattern or image of human action, of action which occurs in time but is not bound by the temporal limits of any historical epoch, since it may occur again and again. At the same time a situation which arises so naturally out of the local and narrowly restricted circumstances of a particular region has been universalized by its association with an ancient "Asiatic" prototype.

VI

If we turn our attention to the setting of the action in *The Mayor of Casterbridge* we may note a characteristic which suggests an analogy to the ancient-modern parallelism of person and incident in the dramatic situation. I am referring to the remarkable sense of continuity of the past with present times which is expressed through the archaeological features of the setting.

Roman soldiers lie buried in the fields and gardens of Casterbridge, and the city cemetery where Susan Henchard is interred has preserved its "continuity as a place of sepulture" since the days of Roman occupation: "Mrs. Henchard's dust mingled with the dust of women who lay ornamented with glass hair-pins and amber necklaces, and men who held in their mouths coins of Hadrian, Posthumus, and the Constantines." Although the townspeople "were quite unmoved by these hoary shapes" because "between them and the living there seemed to stretch a gulf too wide for even a spirit to pass," they avoided the great ruins of the Roman amphitheatre which stood near the town, "for some old people said that at certain moments in the summer time, in broad daylight, persons sitting with a book or dozing in the arena had, on lifting their eyes, beheld the slopes lined with a gazing legion of Hadrian's soldiery as if watching the gladiatorial combat; and had heard the roar of their excited voices; that the scene would remain but a moment, like a lightning flash, and then disappear." And there are monuments in the neighborhood of Casterbridge which date from before the period of Roman occupation, from a time perhaps as ancient as that recorded in I Samuel: "Two miles out, a quarter of a mile from the highway, was the prehistoric fort called Mai Dun, of huge dimensions and many ramparts, within or upon whose enclosures a human being, as seen from the road, was but an insignificant speck."

My point here is that the huge vistas of time opened up by these descriptions are quite in keeping with the discovery that the struggles of Henchard and Farfrae reflect the struggles of Saul and David. This distinctive feature of the setting works together with the framing narrative to supply a spacious context within which our response to the whole action may be ordered. And yet it would be a sentimental mistake to employ this larger context to obscure or scant the immediate, "contemporary" implications of that action. Henchard, after all, is remarkable not because of the scope and intensity of his sufferings as King Saul, but because he suffers in his own person as hay trusser Henchard and as Mayor Henchard, the petty Wessex magistrate. The final comment we can reach here is not that Henchard is a king but rather that kings are men and that men are destined to suffer and decline in an orderly succession of generations.

JOHN PATERSON

The Mayor of Casterbridge as Tragedy†

As a man of his time and place, Thomas Hardy was ill-equipped to meet the challenge of tragedy in its traditional form. Although the romantic and scientific humanisms to which his expatriation in London had exposed him did not exclude a tragic vision of human experience, they were incompetent, by their denial of moral and religious universals, to provide that framework of theme and form which could alone make peace with a tragic vision. Hence the maimed achievements of *The Return of the Native* and *Jude the Obscure*. In the absence of a justice, an ethical substance, which is beyond man's power to shape or control but to which, at the same time, he is necessarily responsible, the disasters in which these works culminate are deprived of a moral and hence fully tragic significance. Celebrating the human at the expense of the superhuman, they cannot justify the ways of God to man.

Hardy was not, however, exclusively or even primarily a man of his century. As the citizen of a provincial Dorset which had had no news of Swinburne and Darwin, he inherited a traditional moral wisdom not yet damaged by the romantic and scientific inspirations which were everywhere shaking the confidence of the modern imagination. In *Far From the Madding Crowd* and *The Woodlanders*, for example, he could magnify not the romantic agonies of those condemned, like the Eustacias and the Judes, to live in a world without justice or dignity but the modest pieties of the Oaks and the Winterbornes, their decent adoration of a Nature that was still a mystery and a miracle, still the earnest of a moral consciousness in the universe. Their diabolical antagonists, the Sergeant Troys and Dr. Fitzpiers, invite in fact not the fatuous indulgence of the romantic imagination but the horror and disgust of the medieval imagination in the presence of Dr. Faust. Even in *The Return of the Native*, the "tragic" apotheosis in death of the rebellious Eustacia Vye is criti-

† From "*The Mayor of Casterbridge* as Tragedy," *Victorian Studies* 3 (1959): 151–72. Reprinted by permission of the publisher, Indiana University Press.

cized retroactively by the comic apotheosis in marriage of Diggory Venn and Thomasin Yeobright[1] who have, like the Oaks and the Winterbornes, come to terms with central headquarters. As the beneficiary of a pre-nineteenth-century culture whose primitive decencies neither Swinburne nor Darwin had entirely confounded, Hardy's imagination could still be possessed, evidently, by what Keats has nostalgically called "our deep eternal theme," by "the fierce dispute,/Betwixt damnation and impassioned clay" that authorizes the form and substance of traditional tragedy.

Hence the lonely and peculiar significance in the literature of modern times of *The Mayor of Casterbridge*. Temporarily freed from the disabling humanistic biases of his age, exploiting a level of the mind to which his romantic sympathies and naturalistic assumptions could not penetrate, Hardy here assumes what the literature of tragedy after Shakespeare has not found it easy or possible to assume: the existence of a moral order, an ethical substance, a standard of justice and rectitude, in terms of which man's experience can be rendered as the drama of his salvation as well as the drama of his damnation. Reviving a body of beliefs about man and fate, nature and society, that were once the ordinary possession of the Western imagination, he exploits a wisdom that makes possible the achievement of tragedy in the heroical sense of a Sophocles or a Shakespeare.

I

The traditional basis of *The Mayor of Casterbridge* as tragedy emerges at once in the plainly fabulous or hyperbolical quality of its first episode. Discouraged by his failure to get on in the world and impatient of ordinary domestic restraints, Michael Henchard, the journeyman haytrusser, arrives at the fair at Weydon-Priors, steeps himself in the alcoholic brews of the furmity-woman, and in a drunken moment sells his wife to a sailor for five guineas. Clearly calculated to startle the imagination, to appeal to its sense for the grand and the heroic in human experience, Henchard's act of violence bears the same relation to the novel as the betrayal of Cordelia and the murder of Laius to *Lear* and *Oedipus*.[2] Arousing such forces of retribution as will not be satisfied with less than

---

1. As Hardy was himself to confess in a celebrated footnote on p. 473 of the British Wessex edition (1912), he was forced, by editorial pressure and the necessities of serial publication, to provide for a happy ending. The allegedly extraneous sixth book of *The Return of the Native* is less inapposite, however, than Hardy and some of his critics would lead one to believe. His attitude to Eustacia's romantic revolt, to the extraordinary and the tragic in human experience, is not after all wholly uncritical. Hence the celebration of the ordinary and the comic in human experience which is the domesticating effect of the sixth book is not altogether foreign to the novel as originally conceived. The implications of this footnote notwithstanding, in other words, Hardy in effect converted editorial necessity into artistic virtue.

2. D. A. Dike has explored some of the analogies between *The Mayor of Casterbridge* and *Oedipus Rex* in his "A Modern Oedipus: The Mayor of Casterbridge," *Essays in Criticism*, II (1952), 169–179.

the total humiliation of the offender and the ultimate restoration of the order offended, it will come to represent, like its counterpart in *Lear* and *Oedipus*, the violation of a moral scheme more than human in its implications.

That such is indeed its significance is underlined by its dramatic isolation in the structure of the novel, by the fact that twenty years intervene between the shocking event that commands the attention of the first two chapters and the events of the chapters that follow. For the primary effect of this structural peculiarity is to dramatize the causal relation between Henchard's crime and punishment. Recording the remorseless private and public deterioration of the protagonist, the novel enacts the indignation of the moral order whose serenity his act of impiety has violently affronted. Forsaken by Farfrae, blasted by the disclosure that Elizabeth-Jane is not his daughter, and deprived of the love and loyalty of Lucetta; humiliated by the revelations of the furmity-woman and ruined in a trade war with his Scottish antagonist; crushed by his public rebuke on the occasion of the Royal Visit, rejected by the "daughter" whose affection had consoled him in defeat, and reduced in the end to the starkest of deaths, Henchard will be forced, like Oedipus and Faust and Lear, to rediscover in suffering and sorrow the actuality of the moral power he had so recklessly flouted.

The actuality of this power is otherwise expressed in the inexorability with which the guilty past asserts, as in *Hamlet* and *Oedipus*, its claim to recognition and atonement. The series of fatal reappearances that challenges and undermines Henchard's illegitimate power—i.e., Lucetta's, the furmity-woman's, Newson's as well, of course, as Susan Henchard's ("Mrs. Henchard was so pale that the boys called her 'The Ghost'")—schematizes the determined revenge of a supernatural authority for which a wrong left uncorrected and unpunished is intolerable. This sinister theme is early adumbrated in the mayor's proud refusal to make restitution for the damaged wheat he has sold to the community. "But what are you going to do to repay us for the past?" an indignant townsman challenges him from the street. "If anybody will tell me how to turn grown wheat into wholesome wheat," the arrogant man replies with an irony of which he is, in the pride of his office, tragically unconscious, "I'll take it back with pleasure. But it can't be done." Henchard thus defines in allegorical terms the conditions of his crime and punishment, his answer pointing up not only the irrevocability of that other and profounder crime buried in his past but also the uncanny pertinacity with which it will return, as the agent of a wounded moral intelligence, to haunt and destroy his life.

The authenticity of a moral intelligence beyond man's power to control is verified in the heroic imagination of Henchard himself. For it is the measure of his grandeur, the measure of his dissociation from such mere victims of naturalistic or unconscious force as Tess and Jude and

Eustacia, that he should acknowledge from the very beginning the extra-human and specifically moral agency of the opposition that has set itself against him. On the morning after the sale of his wife, for example, he seeks as it were to propitiate the offended powers by presenting himself in the local church and swearing to give up drinking for twenty years. He will come to feel, as disaster overwhelms him, "that some power [is] working against him," that he has fully deserved the opposition of a "sinister intelligence bent on punishing him." His recognition of a justice beyond his power to control will be solemnized, finally, not only in the great words with which he leaves Casterbridge[3] but also in the heroic self-condemnation of his last will and testament.

The universality of Henchard's experience is guaranteed by its reenactment in the story of Lucetta La Sueur. For one thing, she has sought, in the wilful and impious fashion of the mayor himself, to dissociate herself from the past: "my ancestors in Jersey," she says defensively, "were as good as anybody in England. . . . I went back and lived there after my father's death. But I don't value such past matters . . ."[4] More to the point, however, in having lived in sin with Henchard in Jersey, she too has been guilty of a moral indiscretion in the past. Indeed, in rejecting her old lover and electing to marry Farfrae, she has refused, once again like her more heroic male counterpart, to recognize and make restitution for her crime. "I won't be a slave to the past—," she cries pathetically, when the demoniacal Henchard seeks forcibly to legalize their old association, "I'll love where I choose!" At the very moment, however, when her love-letters have been burned and she thinks herself free from the consequences of her delinquency, she hears the sounds of the skimmington ride which will publish her shame and eventually bring about her death. Her melodramatic and middle-class reenactment of Henchard's authentic moral drama bears witness, like Gloucester's prose reenactment of Lear's crime and punishment, to the reality of an order whose indignation, once provoked, can neither be appeased nor controlled.

Henchard's terrible retrogression obeys, certainly, a law so distinct and irrefutable in its logic as to suggest an origin more supernatural than natural. Reduced to the humble trade with which he began, discarding the shabby-genteel suit of cloth and the rusty silk hat which had been the emblems of his illegitimate power, taking again to the drink he had twenty years before repudiated, leaving Casterbridge exactly as he had

---

3. "I—Cain—go alone as I deserve—an outcast and a vagabond. But my punishment is *not* greater than I can bear!"

4. Her irreligious disrespect for the past is more indirectly suggested in her frivolous description of its trophies in the local museum: "there are crowds of interesting things," she tells Elizabeth without conviction, "skeleton, teeth, old pots and pans, ancient boots and shoes, birds' eggs— all charmingly instructive." Her careless impiety has in fact been underscored by the piety in death of her rival and foil, for Susan Henchard's dust has been said to mingle "with the dust of women who lay ornamented with glass hair-pins and amber necklaces, and men who held in their mouths the coins of Hadrian, Posthumus, and the Constantines."

entered it, revisiting Weydon-Priors, the scene of the original crime, and dying at last, broken in body and spirit, on the barren wastes of Egdon Heath, Henchard travels with every stage of his decline and fall the long road by which he had come, embraces with every step the past he had denied, and rediscovers, like Lear, in the conditions of his going out the conditions of his setting forth. Having, as Tess and Jude have not, exchanged his humanity for worldly power and prestige, he is systematically deprived of that for which he had exchanged his humanity. Guilty, in a sense that Tess and Jude are not, of pride offensive to the gods, his suffering and death acquire a value to which theirs cannot quite lay claim. The fate that presides over Henchard's destruction as the witness of a moral intention in the universe is hardly interchangeable, indeed, with the vulgar and even brutish fate that presides, either as crass casualty or as unwitting opposition, over the destruction of the Tesses and the Judes and the Eustacias.[5]

In its mysterious remoteness and refinement, fate in *The Mayor of Casterbridge* has much in common with Hegel's sublime and indestructible "ethical substance." The conflict upon which the novel is founded does not suggest, after all, the grotesquely unequal contest between good and evil in which a malevolent "superhumanity" triumphs, as in *Tess* and *Jude* and to a certain extent in *The Return of the Native*, over an innocent and helpless humanity. It suggests, rather, the more equal, the more ambiguous, conflict that occurs when, to the discomfiture of a supernatural wisdom within whose bounds all merely natural oppositions are absorbed and reconciled, one great good is asserted at the expense of another. In this context, the conditions of Henchard's heroic grandeur—his pride, his passion, his ambition—are exactly the conditions of his downfall and destruction. They invite the correction of that absolute wisdom for which the more modest humanity of Elizabeth-Jane and Donald Farfrae is equally sympathetic.

Thus while Henchard stands for the grandeur of the human passions,

---

5. The critical consensus would have it that fate for Hardy was always synonymous either with a perverse and even wilful Chance or with an exclusively social or natural Necessity. His weakness as a tragedian, Arthur Mizener believes, inheres in his naturalistic assumption "that there can be only one kind of reality . . ." ("*Jude the Obscure* as Tragedy," *Southern Review*, VI [1940], 202). Presupposing that "the nature of inanimate things is unconscious and undesigning," Hardy sees events, writes Jacques Barzun, as "chance collidings of willful and indifferent forces among themselves . . ." ("Truth and Poetry in Thomas Hardy," *Southern Review*, VI [1940], 184). Generalizations appropriate for *Tess* and *Jude*, however, meet in the case of *The Mayor of Casterbridge* with unexpectedly stiff resistance. Assuming as it does more than "one kind of reality," its events suggesting not so much "chance collidings of willful and indifferent forces" as a logic or pattern beyond man's power to control and even to understand, *The Mayor of Casterbridge* can fairly be called a *lusus naturae*. It may be objected that the novel is unique only insofar as the hero's character creates the events leading to his downfall. In the last analysis, however, these events follow a logic, a pattern, in which the hero as character may participate but for which he is not finally responsible. The logic or the pattern acquires a reality of its own independent of the hero's particular contribution. As in much Shakespearean tragedy, in other words, character itself becomes a part or instrument of that general fate which presides, on behalf of a supernature, over the course of affairs.

for the heroism of spirit that prefers the dangerous satisfactions of the superhuman to the mild comforts of the merely human, Farfrae and Elizabeth stand for the claims of reason and thought, for the spirit of moderation that is prepared to come to terms with merely human possibilities. Elizabeth-Jane's Cordelia is said to feel "none of those ups and downs of spirit which beset so many people without cause; . . . never a gloom in [her] soul but she well knew how it came there . . ." Her would-be father, on the other hand, his morale destroyed by his crime, is victimized by mysterious and rebellious depressions which he can neither understand nor control. With her "field-mouse fear of the coulter of destiny," Elizabeth declines to adorn herself in the pomp and pride of fine clothing: "I won't be too gay on any account. It would be tempting Providence to hurl mother and me down . . ." With his leonine pride and contempt of Fortune, on the other hand, Henchard makes love to his own destruction, affecting in his first appearance as chief magistrate "an old-fashioned evening suit, an expanse of frilled shirt . . . ; jewelled studs, and a heavy gold chain."

Again, if Henchard suggests the passionate extremities of King Oedipus, Farfrae suggests the less spectacular appeal to reason and compromise for which Creon stands. "In my business, 'tis true that strength and bustle build up a firm," says the mayor, unconsciously allegorizing the terms of their opposition as well as the basis of his own failure: "But judgment and knowledge are what keep it established. Unluckily, I am bad at science, Farfrae; bad at figures—a rule o' thumb sort of man. You are just the reverse . . ."[6] The conflict between the passion of the one and the reason of the other is thus dramatized as a conflict between the rugged individualist and the organization man, between primitive and modern ways of doing business. In his victory over Henchard's gallant but corrupt and self-defeating Mark Antony, Farfrae in fact recalls, as much in his narrowness as in his shrewdness, the not altogether attractive figure of Octavius Caesar. He brings to the firm an order and regularity of which the owner is rendered, by the very largeness of his nature, mentally incapable: "the old crude *viva voce* system of Henchard, in which everything depended upon his memory, and bargains were made by the tongue alone, was swept away. Letters and ledgers took the place of 'I'll do't,' and 'you shall hae't' . . ." Later, identifying himself with the new mechanization, Farfrae will be responsible for introducing a modern sowing machine while Henchard, identifying himself with custom and tradition, will remain true to "the venerable seed-lip [which] was still used for sowing as in the days of the Heptarchy." Indeed, for all the irregularity of his behavior, the mayor is moved by profound emo-

6. In his symbolic acknowledgment of his brotherhood with the Scotchman—"Your forehead, Farfrae, is something like my poor brother's—now dead and gone . . ."—Henchard appears to recognize, albeit momentarily, the interdependency between reason and passion which his behavior consistently and tragically refutes.

tions to which, in his rudimentary piety, he cannot or will not be unfaithful. As the Fortinbras, as the Octavius Caesar, of the drama, on the other hand, Farfrae is ready, not long after Lucetta's death, to dishonor the emotion to which he once had thrilled. "There are men," Hardy remarks, and he must have had Henchard in mind, "whose hearts insist upon a dogged fidelity to some image or cause . . . long after their judgment has pronounced it no rarity . . . and without them the band of the worthy is incomplete. But Farfrae was not of those. . . . He could not but perceive that by the death of Lucetta he had exchanged a looming misery for a simple sorrow."

The novel does not commemorate, then, as *Tess* and *Jude* commemorate, the total degradation of the good and the true. Henchard's defeat and Farfrae's accession to power simply reassert, however painfully, the necessary balance between two great values with equal claims to recognition and fulfilment: the grandeur that would transcend the limits of the human condition and the moderation that is satisfied to live within these limits. The fate that controls the world of *The Mayor of Casterbridge* resembles, to this extent, not the brutal and insentient force that presides over *Tess* and *Jude* but the ideal justice and wisdom that Hegel found presiding over the tragic drama of Sophocles and Shakespeare.

II

In the end, of course, Henchard carries within him, in the perverse instinct for betraying his own best interests, the seeds of his own downfall and disaster. *The Mayor of Casterbridge* is not, however, any more than *Lear* and *Oedipus*, a study in the impulse to self-destruction. Presupposing a concept of man as traditional as its concept of fate, the novel defines the disharmonies of Henchard's mind and imagination within an ethical and religious rather than a psychiatric or scientific frame of reference.

Founding itself upon an ancient psychology, *The Mayor of Casterbridge* celebrates, first of all, the subordination of the passions that link man with nature to the reason that unites him with God. It is Henchard's tragedy that, like Lear and Othello, he reverses and destroys this order. For when he sells his wife to a sailor for five guineas in violation of the profoundest moral tact, it is at a moment when, under the spell of the furmity-woman, he has allowed the passions to distort and deform the reason. Indeed, the surrender to passion responsible for the original crime will, in spite of his heroic resolution to give up drinking for twenty years, repeat itself in those sudden angers and indignations that alienate Farfrae, Elizabeth, and Lucetta, among others, and eventually deprive him of the ordinary consolations of love and friendship. The precarious balance between reason and passion will be reestablished only at the very end when, thoroughly scourged and chastised, all passion spent, Henchard is displaced by the Farfraes and Elizabeths in whose persons the claims of reason are piously acknowledged.[7]

The novel rests, however, not only on the hierarchic psychology that enjoins the subordination of passion to reason but also on the hierarchic cosmology that enjoins the subordination of the human to the superhuman. Henchard's tragedy is that he has, in repudiating his solidarity with the human community, subverted the order that has placed man in the middleground between God and nature. Hence his explicit identification with Dr. Faustus, the archetypal representative of human rebellion: Henchard could be described, Hardy writes, "as Faust has been described—as a vehement gloomy being who had quitted the ways of vulgar men without light to guide him on a better way." Indeed, in selling his wife to a sailor who will later return to claim his due, in joining with Farfrae to make his damaged wheat whole again (that is, to manipulate and defraud nature),[8] in approaching the conjuror Fall for illegitimate insights into the future course of the weather, Henchard is discovered in the attitude and situation made legendary in the story of the diabolical doctor.

Hence the traditional pattern of his decline and fall. In contriving to be more than human, Henchard inevitably becomes a great deal less than human. Arrogating powers and prerogatives that rightly belong to the gods, he forfeits, like Faust and Lear and Othello before him, his own humanity. This retrogression is first of all apparent in his brutal loneliness, in his increasing alienation from the human community. It is also apparent, however, though more indirectly, in the elemental or natural imagery with which he is persistently associated. Troubled by the presence of Elizabeth-Jane, he moves "like a great tree in a wind." After the cruel discovery that she is not after all his daughter, he greets her in a manner described as "dry and thunderous." His habit, after his estrangement from Farfrae, is to look "stormfully past him" and in their grim trial of strength in the loft, they rock and writhe "like trees in a gale."

At the very last, of course, the mayor is restored to the human community from which he has wilfully separated himself. In marching Abel Whittle off to work without his breeches and exposing him to public humiliation, Henchard had committed once more, at the level of the comic and pathetic, the startling crime at Weydon-Priors. Once again he had dishonored, as Cain to the Abel of his servant and factotum, the sacred bond that unites man with even the lowliest of his kind. For when

7. Thus in the last pages of the novel, Elizabeth is celebrated in having, unlike Henchard, discovered the secret "of making limited opportunities endurable," in having cultivated "those minute forms of satisfaction that offer themselves to everybody not in positive pain."
8. "To fetch it [the damaged wheat] back entirely is impossible," Farfrae tells him; "Nature won't stand so much as that, but heere you go a great way towards it."

the antiheroic terms of Abel's creation are granted, his nature is ironically revealed as essentially continuous with the mayor's: he is, in all but
the pomp and pride of office, Michael Henchard's own brother. "There
is sommit wrong in my make, your worshipful!" the poor man confesses
in terms that describe his master as well as himself, "especially in the
inside . . ." Indeed, Abel reacts to his public humiliation with a gloomy
and morbid sensitivity that recalls Henchard himself in the days of his
decline and fall: "Yes—I'll go to Blackmoor Vale half naked as I be, since
he do command; but I shall kill myself afterwards; I can't outlive the disgrace; for the women-folk will be looking out of their windows at my
mortification all the way along, and laughing me to scorn as a man
'ithout breeches! You know how I feel such things, Maister Farfrae, and
how forlorn thoughts get hold upon me. Yes—I shall do myself harm—
I feel it coming on!" Hence the significance of the novel's final episodes
in which Henchard dies abandoned by all but his simple and stubbornly-
loyal workman. He has rediscovered in the figure of a hapless and dim-
witted laborer, as Lear has rediscovered in a fool and a madman, that
brotherhood with all men to which he had in the pride of his nature and
his office been unfaithful. The novel invokes, in short, as *The Return of
the Native* and *Jude the Obscure* with their humanistic orientation do
not, the traditional notion that man has been confined not unjustly to a
fixed place in the hierarchy of being and is inspired to go his wilful way
only at the risk of the direst penalties.

III

As the particular terms of Henchard's deterioration may already have
suggested, the novel's concept of nature is in many respects as traditional as its concept of man and fate. Certainly, there is no equivalent in *The
Mayor of Casterbridge* for the grotesque image of an Egdon Heath that
dwarfs and ultimately overwhelms a helpless humankind. Where nature
does enter the novel, it enters as a force obedient and instrumental to a
moral order whose rights and claims take priority over man's. Like
Oedipus in murdering his father and like Lear in denying his daughter,
Henchard affronts, in casting off wife and child, a nature that antedates
both Wordsworth and Darwin.

The barbarous violence of his deed and the Babylonian character of
the fair that is appropriately its setting are opposed, for example, to a
piety in nature that is a reflex of a piety in the universe:

> The difference between the peacefulness of inferior nature and the
> wilful hostilities of mankind was very apparent at this place. In con-
> trast with the harshness of the act just ended within the tent was the
> sight of several horses crossing their necks and rubbing each other
> lovingly as they waited in patience to be harnessed for the home-
> ward journey. Outside the fair, in the valleys and woods, all was

quiet. The sun had recently set, and the west heaven was hung with rosy cloud . . .[9]

The specifically moral agency of this nature becomes most obvious, however, in the catastrophic weather that eventually insures the defeat and humiliation of the hero. For if the rains and tempests that control the world of *The Mayor of Casterbridge* do not perform in the violent and dramatic terms of the storm in *Lear*, they bear in the end the same significance. They reflect, as the symptom of a demoralization in nature, the demoralization of the order that Henchard's unnatural act has, much in the manner of Lear's, produced. Insofar, too, as they confound his designs at the same time that they cooperate with Farfrae's, they reveal the extent to which he has lost the power to "sympathize" with, to intuit, its mysteries. Finally and more especially, they enforce, as the agents of the superhuman, the powerful claims which Henchard's guilty humanity has flouted and abrogated.

The presidency of a rational power in the universe is apparent not alone, however, in the anthropomorphism of the novel's rains and tempests.[1] It is also apparent in the power of the conjuror Fall to divine the mysteries of the weather. More than a mere concession to local color, more than a symptom of the amateur anthropologist's interest in the folklore of his native region, the weird prophet to whom Henchard comes for help has a function in the novel not unlike that of the oracle in *Oedipus*. The authenticity of his wisdom, the accuracy of his prognostications, argues, as the Delphic oracle argues, the existence of an order beyond man's power to alter or control. Hence it is one aspect of the general armistice towards which the novel moves that the hero is restored in the end to that rudimentary natural order whose decencies he had flouted and over whose mysteries he had sought to prevail. Returned to the primitive world of Abel Whittle where time is told by the sun, he perishes in a mud hovel scarcely distinguishable in its dilapidation from the natural world surrounding it and in fact resembling Lear's humble refuge in the storm. The concept of nature upon which *The Mayor of Casterbridge* is founded antedates, then, the permissive nature invoked by nineteenth-century transcendentalism and the mech-

---

9. The sense in which the hero's crime has violated, and separated him from, a profound morality in nature is elsewhere suggested by the floral imagery with which he is identified in the days of his prelapsarian innocence: "he looked a far different journeyman from the one he had been in his earlier days. Then he had worn clean, suitable clothes, light and cheerful in hue; leggings yellow as marigolds, corduroys immaculate as new flax, and a neckerchief like a flower-garden."

1. The irritability of an intelligent and moral power confronted by the mayor's continuing perversity—he has virtually driven Elizabeth from his house—is intimated in the ominously-repeated "smacking of the rope against the flag-staff." Later, when the weather turns to accomplish his ruin, it performs as the agent of a virtually conscious design: "the sunlight would flap out like a quickly opened fan, throw the pattern of the window upon the floor of the room in a milky, colourless shine, as withdraw as suddenly as it had appeared."

anistic nature invented by nineteenth-century science. It operates, like man and fate, within a traditional moral frame of reference.

IV

The traditional basis of the novel is nowhere more distinct than in the anachronistic theory of society upon which it is predicated. Isolated and dissociated from a nineteenth century whose unity has been undermined by science, industry, and democracy, Casterbridge suggests, with its agrarian economy, with its merchant aristocracy and its rude population of mechanics, artisans, and laborers, a primitive hierarchic society. Thus Henchard resembles less the modern mayor than the tribal chieftain and is in fact displaced by Farfrae not in a democratic vote but, figuratively if not literally, in a rude trial of strength. His status and stature as a tragic hero are not affected, certainly, by his membership, at the novel's most superficial level, in the anti-heroic middle-class. He is not after all the mayor of Dorchester, the provincial town whose reality is continuous with London and Liverpool and Manchester, but the mayor of Casterbridge, the provincial capital whose historical associations are more Roman and Hebraic than English.[2] Hence, although he is greater in will and energy than the Christopher Coneys and Solomon Longways, he is at the same time, in his taciturnity, in his fatalism, in his grotesque and often brutal humor, their true apotheosis, their "hero" in the epic sense. In his physical resemblance to the town of Casterbridge itself—they are both described in terms of squares and rectangles, for example—he becomes the very symbol of the place, his leadership acquiring to this extent a supernaturalistic rather than a merely naturalistic sanction.

Hence the virtually religious interdependence of the man and the city. Participating, like nature, in a universal moral organization, society is demoralized, as Henchard himself has been demoralized, by the outrage for which no atonement has been made. In receiving and rewarding a man whose ancient crime has gone unacknowledged and uncorrected, Hardy's city has invited, like the Thebes of Sophocles and the Denmark of Shakespeare, the disapprobation of the gods—a plague, a profound social and political disturbance—from which it will not be released until the guilty party has been publicly identified and punished.

The pollution of the provincial capital is first of all suggested in the

---

2. The novel is literally saturated with allusions to Hebraic and, more notably, as the Latin root of "Casterbridge" would suggest, to Roman, life and literature. It is worth noting, in this connection, that the Saul-David legend was apparently employed by Hardy to frame, and give historical depth to, his "contemporary" narrative (see Julian Moynahan's demonstration in "*The Mayor of Casterbridge* and the Old Testament's First Book of Samuel: A Study of Some Literary Relationships," PMLA, LXXI [1956], 118–30) [see pp. 330–42]. Henchard's analogy with Saul as well as with Oedipus supports the notion developed in the following pages that the archetype of the diseased monarch is fundamental to the hero's conception.

imagery of damp and decay that conditions the atmosphere of the novel.[3] It is even more strongly suggested, however, by the frequent allusions to the corrupt and criminal past that evidently underlies—and the analogy with Henchard's own case is unmistakable—the apparently innocent appearance of the city. "Casterbridge is a old hoary place o' wickedness . . . ," one of its gloomier citizens acknowledges. "'Tis recorded in history that we rebelled against the King one or two hundred years ago, in the time of the Romans, and that lots of us was hanged on Gallows Hill, and quartered, and our different jints sent about the country like butcher's meat . . ." To bear out this depressed description, the violent history of the Roman amphitheater outside the town is developed in lugubrious detail:

> Apart from the sanguinary nature of the games originally played therein, such incidents attached to its past as these: that for scores of years the town-gallows had stood at one corner; that in 1705 a woman who had murdered her husband was half-strangled and then burnt there in the presence of ten thousand spectators. . . . In addition to these old tragedies, pugilistic encounters almost to the death had come off down to recent dates in that secluded arena . . . [4]

Later in the novel, depressed and embittered by the disclosure that he is not Elizabeth's father, Henchard encounters in a walk by the river a half-phantasmagorical scene emblematic not only of his own crime and guilt but also of the crime and guilt that attaches to Casterbridge itself:

> Here were the ruins of a Franciscan priory, and a mill attached to the same, the water of which roared down a back-hatch like the voice of desolation. Above the cliff, and behind the river, rose a pile of buildings, and in the front of the pile a square mass cut into the sky. It was like a pedestal lacking its statue. This missing feature . . . was, in truth, the corpse of a man; for the square mass formed the base of the gallows, the extensive buildings at the back being the county gaol. In the meadow where Henchard now walked the mob were wont to gather whenever an execution took place, and there to the tune of the roaring weir they stood and watched the spectacle.

3. In the early chapters, for example, the mayor has sold the bakers grown wheat, wheat damaged by damp, and debased the bread of an embittered population. Later, when the weather turns to defeat his speculations, the air itself feels "as if cress would grow in it without other nourishment." Imagined as "the mildewed leaf in the sturdy and flourishing Casterbridge plant," Mixen Lane, the haunt of criminals and the very sign and symptom of the town's moral disease, is described in nearly symbolic terms as stretching out "like a spit into the moist and misty lowland." Shortly thereafter, the secret of Lucetta's past will spread through the town "like a miasmatic fog."
4. "Persons sitting with a book or dozing in the arena," the novel goes on to report, "had, on lifting their eyes, beheld the slopes lined with a gazing legion of Hadrian's soldiery as if watching the gladiatorial combat; and had heard the roar of their excited voices. . . ."

Later still, an allusion is made to a large square called Bull Stake, hidden, significantly, between the Market House and the Church and stained, like the amphitheater and the priory, by a history of brutality and suffering: "a stone post rose in the midst, to which the oxen had formerly been tied for baiting with dogs to make them tender before they were killed in the adjoining shambles. In a corner stood the stocks."

The demoralization of the present by the corruption of the past is perhaps most vividly allegorized in the description of Lucetta's Casterbridge house and, specifically, in the description of its structural peculiarity. The front it offered to the world was "Palladian," the novel records, "and like most architecture erected since the Gothic age was a compilation rather than a design. But its reasonableness made it impressive." Like Henchard and Lucetta herself, however, the house has a guilty secret. Its reasonable exterior conceals ugly and grotesque passions, passions associated here with the Gothic. For one thing, the secret exit Elizabeth discovers in the rear, an ancient archway significantly described as "older even than the house itself," has for its keystone a sinister mask which evokes once again the theme of a hidden decay and disease: "Originally the mask had exhibited a comic leer . . . but generations of Casterbridge boys had thrown stones at the mask, aiming at its open mouth; and the blows thereon had chipped off the lips and jaws as if they had been eaten away by disease." More significantly, the door and the mask conjure up once again the imagery of the vile and violent crimes in the past: "The position of the queer old door and the odd presence of the leering mask suggested . . . intrigue. By the alley it had been possible to come unseen from all sorts of quarters in the town—the old play-house, the old bull-stake, the old cock-pit, the pool wherein nameless infants had been used to disappear."

Like its maimed and guilt-haunted ruler, then, Casterbridge is demoralized and disabled by a grisly past.[5] Infected, like Thebes and Denmark, by the strong stench of time and human evil, it suggests nothing so much, in fact, as a grim and unhallowed wasteland. For one thing, the local peasantry are plainly discovered in a harsher and more skeptical light than they were in Under the Greenwood Tree, Far From the Madding Crowd, and even The Return of the Native. This reinterpretation in part registers a developing realistic bias in Hardy already adumbrated in The Trumpet Major and eventually dominant in Tess and Jude. More exactly, however, it cooperates with the larger purposes of The

5. This is not to suggest that as a "cause" of the city's demoralization, the criminality of its past history operates on the same level as the criminality of its chief magistrate. It enters the novel only at the level of reference and allusion and not at the level of action and to this extent serves no more than a symbolic function. The city's gruesome history acts, in short, less as a direct cause of its discomposure than as an analogy with the history of Michael Henchard. Indeed, insofar as he is haunted by the same history of crime and passion as Casterbridge itself, the virtually religious basis of his rulership—the interdependence of the man and the city—is once again verified.

Mayor of Casterbridge, a brutalized populace bearing witness, like the pimps and whores of *Measure for Measure* and the gravediggers of *Hamlet*, to the moral delinquency of a society that has winked at crime and, in a metaphorical sense at least, offended the gods.

The demoralization of the folk, their disillusioned and even cynical way of looking at things, is emphasized in being juxtaposed with the romantic idealism of Donald Farfrae, the Fortinbras-like visitor from the brisker and more bracing climate of the Scottish world to the north. Celebrating in a sentimental song the loveliness of his homeland, he evokes in Casterbridge's hollow men a response at once comic and disenchanted. "Danged," says one, "if our country down here is worth singing about like that! When you take away from among us the fools and the rogues, and the lammigers, and the wanton hussies, and the slatterns, and such like, there's cust few left to ornament a song with in Casterbridge, or the country round." "We be bruckle folk here," adds Christopher Coney, defining at once the sterility of the landscape and the brutalization of its inhabitants, "the best o' us hardly honest sometimes, what with hard winters, and so many mouths to fill, and God a'mighty sending his little taties so terrible small to fill 'em with. We don't think about flowers and fair faces, not we—except in the shape o' cauliflowers and pigs' chaps."[6]

The local demoralization is perhaps rendered most dramatically in the sinister community of Mixen Lane. Without precedent in the novels that antedate *The Mayor of Casterbridge*, these polluted precincts harbor a peasantry no longer redeemed, as even Christopher Coney and Solomon Longways are redeemed, by their whimsicality and humor: "Vice ran freely in and out certain of the doors of the neighbourhood; recklessness dwelt under the roof with the crooked chimney; shame in some bow-windows; theft (in times of privation) in the thatched and mud-walled houses by the sallows. Even slaughter had not been altogether unknown here. In a block of cottages up an alley there might have been erected an altar to disease in years gone by." Far from celebrating its charm and picturesqueness, the novel contemplates the delinquent proletariat of Casterbridge with something resembling aristocratic irony and disdain. The inn called Peter's Finger is described as "the church of Mixen Lane." Satirically defined as "a virtuous woman who years ago had been unjustly sent to gaol as an accessory to something or other after the fact," the landlady has "worn a martyr's countenance ever since, except at times of meeting the constable who apprehended her, when she winked her eye." Her customers are described, meanwhile,

---

6. Indeed, for all his whimsy Christopher will later be guilty of a moral dereliction not significantly different from Henchard's. Acting from an ineluctable moral premise ("Why should death rob life o' fourpence?") and in violation of the profoundest moral tact ("And when you've used 'em, and my eyes don't open no more, bury the pennies, good souls, and don't ye go spending 'em . . ."), he will rifle the grave of Susan Henchard for the four ounce pennies that serve as weights for her eyes.

with a nearly bitter irony, as "ex-poachers and ex-gamekeepers whom squires had persecuted without a cause . . ." The monstrous rites of the skimmington ride will in fact expose on the level of action this deterioration of the folk. Having terrorized a helpless woman, they will slink "like the crew of Comus" back to the miasmal suburbs from which they have momentarily emerged; questioned by the constables, they will answer with a sinister and dishonorable evasiveness.

In the end, of course, the denizens of Mixen Lane are no more condemned for their moral dereliction than are Shakespeare's pimps and gravediggers. They are less the causes of the moral and social disorder than its victims. They express the bitterness and despair of a society whose magistrates, in having offended against justice, have forfeited their clear moral authority to rule. For the demoralization of the city is apparent not alone in the brutalization of the lower orders. It is also apparent in the brutalization of those proud merchant princes who, in having welcomed and celebrated a man offensive to the gods, in having become infected by the mayor's pride and arrogance, have submitted their humanity to base and ugly distortions.[7]

It is therefore one aspect of the city's ordeal that its safety and stability are threatened throughout by serious internal conflicts. As in *Hamlet* and *Lear*, the disturbance of the moral order expresses itself in the disturbance of the social order. The discontinuity between the moral order that Henchard has insulted and the social order that has received and rewarded him is made evident almost at once. Twenty years after the original crime, Susan enters the provincial capital expecting with good reason to find the culprit occupying the stocks: she finds him instead presiding arrogantly over a civic banquet as the wealthiest and most powerful man in the community. Hence, while the mayor and the members of the local oligarchy hold court in the King's Arms for all the world like depraved Roman emperors, a surly populace, alienated by the corruption of its bread, gathers in the outer darkness of the street on the point of revolt. "As we plainer fellows bain't invited," one citizen remarks in unconscious criticism of the insolence of high office, "they leave the winder-shutters open that we may get jist a sense o't out here." "They

---

7. At the banquet held in the mayor's honor, for example, they are described in terms that suggest a fallen, a bestialized, humanity: "the younger guests were talking and eating with animation; their elders were searching for tit-bits, and sniffing and grunting over their plates like sows nuzzling for acorns." Later unmanned, like Henchard himself twenty years earlier, by drink, they undergo Circean transformations: "square-built men showed a tendency to become hunchbacks; men with a dignified presence lost it in a curious obliquity of figure, in which their features grew disarranged and one-sided; whilst the heads of a few who had dined with extreme thoroughness were somehow sinking into their shoulders, the corners of their mouth and eyes being bent upwards by the subsidence." At the scene of the market, finally, these Bulges, Brownlets, Kitsons and Yoppers, whose gross and cacophonous names define the rudimentariness of their spiritual condition, are described in terms of an elemental imagery that suggests, as in Henchard's case, a less than complete humanity: they are described as "men of extensive stomachs, sloping like mountain sides; men whose heads in walking swayed as the trees in November gales."

can blare their trumpets and thump their drums, and have their roaring dinners," a local Madame Lafarge has declared in terms that point up the Roman character of the revels, "but we must needs be put-to for want of a wholesome crust."

The corruption of those in power will eventually be exposed, of course, with the re-appearance and trial of the furmity-woman, the agent of the mayor's original moral subversion. Charged with committing an outrage on the church wall, charged in effect with an irreligious act not different from that for which Henchard, her judge, has gone unpunished, she publicizes the crime he has concealed for twenty years and exposes therewith the discrepancy between the social order of which he is the head and the moral order to which he has done violence. She not only represents, then, the past's determined and inexorable reassertion of its rights and bears witness, in her own moral delinquency, to the brutalization of the lower classes already discoverable in Christopher Coney and the maimed citizens of Mixen Lane. She also expresses their revulsion against the social and political order whose mandate to rule and administer justice has, by the fact of its own moral disability, been rendered fraudulent. "It proves," says she, delivering the moral of the occasion, "that he's no better than I, and has no right to sit there in judgment upon me." The moral inadequacy of Henchard's society is in fact underlined by Hardy's farcical treatment of the whole episode. For if, in his tragic embarrassment, the mayor recalls the figure of Duke Angelo, the arresting constable Stubberd recalls, and indeed fulfills the same function as, Shakespeare's clownish constable Elbow. Regarding the furmity-woman "with a suppressed gaze of victorious rectitude," Stubberd reflects, in his physical decrepitude, in his ignorance and absurd self-righteousness, the moral impotence of the society whose law he has been hired to enforce.

The disharmony and confusion to which Henchard's original act of impiety has exposed the city becomes climacteric, finally, in the nearly-savage violence of the skimmington ride. For the hidden imposthume that silently undermines the moral stability of the town has not, in spite of Henchard's public degradation, been fully removed. In refusing like the mayor to acknowledge the crime in her past, in marrying the man who has supplanted him as the town's chief merchant and magistrate, Lucetta has in effect perpetuated the ancient wrong.[8] Furthermore, in publicly repudiating the sadly-deteriorated Henchard on the occasion of the Royal Visit, Farfrae as well as Lucetta becomes guilty of the same pride, of the same offense against human solidarity, of which the fallen mayor himself had been found guilty.

8. The Royal Visit over which she and her husband preside suggests in fact the same barbaric pride and arrogance as the civic banquet over which the guilty Henchard had presided earlier in the novel: Lucetta is defined as Farfrae's Calphurnia as the official carriages are described as rattling "heavily as Pharaoh's carriages down Corn Street."

In this light, the skimmington ride expresses the demoralization and confusion of a social order that has continued wilfully to dissociate itself from the moral order. If, as Farfrae not altogether wrongly suspects, the organizers of the barbaric rite have been inspired by "the tempting prospect of putting to the blush people who stand at the head of affairs," it is because their claims to rulership have been fraudulent and dishonest. Indeed, the moral incompetence of the society over which Farfrae and Lucetta prevail is dramatized, as in the episode of the furmity-woman's trial, by the comedy of its cowardly constabulary. Described as shrivelled men — "yet more shrivelled than usual, having some not ungrounded fears that they might be roughly handled if seen" — Stubberd and his crew conceal in a water-pipe the staves that are the instruments of their office and take refuge up an alley until the skimmington ride is over.

At the very last, of course, the agonies of this divided and demoralized society are permitted to subside. With the total eclipse of Henchard and Lucetta and the marriage of Farfrae and Elizabeth-Jane, the social order is brought once again into harmony with the moral order. In marrying Lucetta with her pride and her guilt and her fine clothing, Farfrae had compromised his right to rule, had aroused, like Henchard in his day, the animosity of his citizen-subjects.[9] However, in uniting himself with Elizabeth-Jane who has declined, unlike Lucetta, to antagonize the superintending powers, Farfrae restores himself to the good graces of the folk and brings to an end the civil division that had registered the resentment of an affronted moral order.[1] Hence, in the novel's final passages, the restoration of the society whose authority Henchard and Lucetta had jeopardized, the reconciliation of the classes whose mutual hostility had threatened its total collapse, can be celebrated in the mild dominion of an Elizabeth-Jane who perceives "no great personal difference between being respected in the nether parts of Casterbridge and glorified at the uppermost end of the social world."

In the context of this novel, then, the social order acquires a virtually religious sanction of which it is almost wholly deprived in the naturalistic contexts of *Tess* and *Jude*. Michael Henchard is not, like the protagonists of the later novels, crucified by a brutal and depraved society. Disabled, on the contrary by *his* crime and guilt, society emerges not as the victimizer but as the victim. Its corruption and demoralization register, as in *Oedipus* and *Hamlet*, the corruption and demoralization of its chief magistrate. They register the disapprobation of a universal order whose moral-

9. "How folk do worship fine clothes!" one good citizen had bitterly remarked at the time of Farfrae's marriage to Lucetta. "I do like to see the trimming pulled off such Christmas candles," another had ominously declared. Indeed, their preference for Elizabeth was made explicit on this same occasion: "now there's a better-looking woman than she that nobody notices at all. . . ."
1. "As a neat patching-up of things I see much good in it," says Christopher Coney, giving the assent of the folk to the new dispensation.

ity the defection of the hero has profoundly disturbed. Like fate and nature, society here operates within a traditional moral frame. The sociology of the novel is as archaic as its psychology and cosmology.

V

To argue that *The Mayor of Casterbridge* observes the traditional norms of tragedy is not of course to argue that it has no realistic basis whatsoever. It would hardly be a novel if it did not admit something of the life of its particular time and place. The presence of the conjuror Fall and the incident of the skimmington ride bear witness to the amateur anthropologist's authentic interest in the folkways of a dying culture. Indeed, Hardy was himself to acknowledge in his preface that the story was specifically inspired by three events in the real history of the Dorchester locality: the sale of a wife, the uncertain harvests which preceded the repeal of the Corn Laws, and the visit of a member of the royal house. To describe the dominating motive of the novel as therefore realistic, however, would be not only to underestimate, but also to leave largely unexplained, the great vitality that it ultimately generates. It would be to ignore the fact that its realistic data are in the end assimilated and controlled by the tragic form, and that it is this form and not the content, not its fidelity to the data of social history, that finally accounts for its perennial power. Wife-sale may well have been a virtual commonplace in the rural England of the nineteenth century,[2] and such magicians as the conjuror Fall may still have frequented the countryside of Wessex. But their appearance in *The Mayor of Casterbridge* as the *matériel* of two of its most crucial episodes is adequately explained less by their reference to aspects of contemporary reality than by their reference to the novel's artistic necessities, by their adaptation as stations in the tragic martyrdom of Michael Henchard. Again, Hardy may well have been concerned, as a social historian, with the new mechanization, with the decay of the primitive agriculture that had been practised since the days of the Heptarchy. Quite clearly, however, this conflict between the old method and the new is exploited not for the sake of history but for the sake of the novel: it defines and develops the tragic conflict between Henchard and Farfrae, between the old god and the new. The novel is not damaged as tragedy, in other words, as *Tess* and *Jude* were to be damaged by a preoccupation with social history or social issues.[3]

---

2. Miss Ruth Firor has suggested so much (*Folkways in Thomas Hardy* [Philadelphia, 1931], p. 237) as indeed has Hardy himself at the beginning of ch. iv.
3. Jacques Barzun has pointed out that "no reform of the divorce laws or the entrance requirements of Oxford would by itself alter the chances of Tess' and Jude's coming to happier ends" ("Truth and Poetry in Thomas Hardy," p. 188). This is another way of saying, however, that these issues have an interest in and for themselves that the conflict between the old and the new cannot claim. Certainly, these questions do dominate *Tess* and *Jude* as the agricultural question does not dominate *The Mayor of Casterbridge*.

Cut off from contemporary experience as the later novels are not, *The Mayor of Casterbridge* repudiates prose fiction's characteristic willingness to admit, more undiscriminatingly than is possible for epic and tragedy, the unblessed life of time and history.[4] This is so much the case that, as has already been pointed out, the atmosphere of the novel is more Roman and Hebraic than English: it evokes not so much the world of London, Liverpool, and Manchester as the world of Thebes, Padan-Aram, and ancient Rome.

To argue, finally, that *The Mayor of Casterbridge* satisfies the traditional norms of tragedy is not to argue that the celebrant of nineteenth-century romantic and scientific doctrines is altogether suppressed. If the novel assumes, in its concepts of man and fate, nature and society, a traditional frame of reference tolerant of tragedy, there are inevitably occasions when the Swinburnian and Darwinian Hardy reasserts himself with results that make for a reduction of the tragic temperature. After he has identified an order in nature as the delicate reflex of a moral order in the universe, he must pay his respects to the contemporary scientific doctrine that has taken nature out of its traditional frame: "in presence of this scene after the other, there was a natural instinct to abjure man as the blot on an otherwise kindly universe; till it was remembered that . . . mankind might some night be innocently sleeping when these quiet objects were raging aloud." And having decided that the ugly weathers of the novel expressed the reaction of a just and morally intelligent fate, he must temporarily reassert his humanistic allegiances and openly commiserate with a cruelly-persecuted humanity: the impulse of the peasantry, he remarks, "was well-nigh to prostate themselves in lamentation before untimely rains and tempests, which came as the Alastor of those households whose crime it was to be poor."[5]

Not even the traditional symbolism of Mixen Lane as the cancer that undermines the sanity and health of the Casterbridgean city-state is proof against an author tempted momentarily to humanistic apologetics: "yet amid so much that was bad needy respectability also found a home. Under some of the roofs abode pure and virtuous souls whose presence there was due to the iron hand of necessity, and to that alone." Most glaringly of all, perhaps, the balance between the heroic passion of Henchard, on the one hand, and the modesty of Farfrae and Elizabeth, on the other, is at times upset by the author's insurgent romantic sympathies. Rebelling against the traditional frame he has himself set up,

---

4. Which is to question Arthur Mizener's assertion that Hardy "never freed himself wholly from the naturalistic assumption that narrative must be significant historically rather than fabulously" ("*Jude the Obscure* as a Tragedy," p. 196).

5. Indeed, Henchard's heroic recognition of the moral authority that has humbled his pride, a recognition irrefutably validated in the narrative structure of the novel, is at one point repudiated as bearing witness to his fetishism: "Henchard, like all his kind, was superstitious, and he could not help thinking that the concatenation of events this evening had produced was the scheme of some sinister intelligence bent on punishing him. Yet they had developed naturally."

rebelling against the moral dispensation that Henchard himself has been great enough to accept as right and just, Hardy will bitterly revile the mediocrities who have supplanted his doomed and suffering protagonist. Elizabeth's "craving for correctness" he denounces as "almost vicious"; Farfrae he mocks as celebrating the "dear native country that he loved so well as never to have revisited it."

The outrage and indignation of the nineteenth-century humanist in the presence of a suffering mankind, common enough in Tess and Jude and indeed the primary condition of their creation, are not, however, the predominating motives of The Mayor of Casterbridge. These emotions may flare momentarily at the surface of the novel; but they do not penetrate to or issue from its vital center. They appear after all only at the superficial level of authorial commentary and are contradicted and ultimately overwhelmed by the novel's fundamental assumptions, by the traditional moral or religious values rendered at the crucial level of character and action, form and structure. Hence the novel's emergence as one of the truly remarkable anachronisms in the history of English literature. Rejecting the disabling doctrine of the nineteenth century and exploiting the enabling doctrine of a time still capable of vibrating to the vision of a just and ordered universe, The Mayor of Casterbridge approximates, as perhaps no novel before or since has approximated, the experience of tragedy in its olden, in its Sophoclean or Shakespearean, sense.

MICHAEL MILLGATE

[The Role of Elizabeth-Jane]†

* * * [The novel ends] not with Henchard but with Elizabeth-Jane—married, and with every appearance of contentment if not of ecstasy, to Farfrae. Quiet and unobtrusive though she is, Elizabeth-Jane's role is an extraordinarily interesting one, without a close parallel elsewhere in Hardy's work. In the early chapters there may seem something irritating in her insistence on respectability, in her primness, but as the novel progresses what is revealed is precisely the process of her self-education. If her conscious effort is towards the kind of education contained in and symbolised by books, her more substantial and more significant progress is towards the kind of education in the business of living which is usually called wisdom. Elizabeth-Jane sits quietly, suffers quietly, watches, and learns. Like the Fanny Price of Mansfield Park she

† From Michael Millgate, Thomas Hardy: His Career as a Novelist (London: The Bodley Head, 1971), pp. 228–34. Copyright © 1971 by Michael Millgate. Reprinted by permission of Macmillan. Page references have been changed to correspond to this Norton Critical Edition.

is, though not especially sympathetic, absolutely a person, essentially right-thinking, and very much to be taken seriously. Because of her position of onlooker, and because of her good sense, she gradually establishes herself for the reader as much the most acute and reliable intelligence within the novel, the one whose judgments are most to be trusted. In a real sense, she becomes the reader's representative within the novel's world, and it is perhaps significant that she should be so often on the scene when there is no absolute necessity for her presence. She stands at the point of intersection of all the social and emotional ties within the group of major characters—she is Henchard's step-daughter and long believes herself to be his actual daughter; she is Lucetta's chosen friend and confidante; she is early courted by Farfrae and later marries him—and the action revolves about her almost as its central pivot.

The role of Elizabeth-Jane prompts certain questions about Hardy's handling of point of view in *The Mayor of Casterbridge.* No more than in earlier novels is there any apparent awareness of the rich technical possibilities described and exploited by Henry James; nor does Hardy display any particular rigour in accepting, with whatever degree of deliberateness, the freedoms available to the omniscient narrator. What is noticeable is a recurrent, though by no means consistent, tendency to present action and description as seen by one of the participants or by an isolated observer, often an unseen witness or eavesdropper.[1] In *Far from the Madding Crowd* Gabriel Oak shows an almost voyeuristic talent for finding himself in positions from which he can observe Bathsheba unseen; in *The Hand of Ethelberta* polite society is viewed from the servants' hall; in *The Return of the Native* Diggory Venn becomes almost an ubiquitous seeing eye. In *The Mayor of Casterbridge,* particularly the first two-thirds, Hardy repeatedly uses Elizabeth-Jane as the point from which events are viewed. Wherever she happens to be living, she seems always to be in a position to overlook significant meetings and activities. It is she, technically speaking, who observes Henchard's dining-room [27], the grim back entrance of High Place Hall, and much of the detail of Casterbridge life [24–26]; she looks on at the Three Mariners when Farfrae first wins the hearts of the patrons with his sentimental songs; she is present, though often silent and ignored, at many encounters involving permutations of the Henchard-Lucetta-Farfrae triangle.

Elizabeth-Jane is thus kept constantly before the reader even during stretches of the action in which she has no substantial part to play. Sometimes, too, her presence as the observer—for example, in the scenes of Farfrae's courtship of Lucetta—lends poignancy to what might otherwise be a rather conventional or even ludicrous episode. When the viewpoint is temporarily shifted to another character it is often for a quite

---

1. For a comment on the role of "inquisitiveness" in *The Mayor of Casterbridge,* see Robert Kiely, "Vision and Viewpoint in *The Mayor of Casterbridge,*" *Nineteenth-Century Fiction,* 23 (1968), 189–200, esp. p. 197.

specific reason: Lucetta's first impression of Farfrae both dramatises his impact upon her and gives the reader a fresh view of Farfrae at a moment when his fortunes are on the rise; the implications which flow from the superiority of Farfrae's entertainment over Henchard's are emphasised as much by the presentation of Farfrae's "pavilion" through Henchard's eyes as by the explicit comments of bystanders. Yet it is not always possible to justify Hardy's manipulation of viewpoint in such positive terms. His approach to the problem is technically very limited, comparable to the interest of an artist in perspective, a theatrical producer in sight lines, a film director in camera angles. His need is apparently to visualise quite specifically, to think himself into, the precise point within the world of the novel from which each scene is being observed. His concern is not so much with the quality of the observer's response as with the visual and auditory possibilities of the vantage point he occupies.

Hardy's observers can thus scarcely be said to mediate between the author and his created world in the manner of such figures as Conrad's Marlow or even James's Strether. Characteristically, the observers perceive but rarely comment. What their eyes and ears report is absorbed directly into the narrative fabric, not filtered through a unique consciousness or isolated as "objective" dramatisation. They function not as surrogates for the author but rather as a distancing device. Even when no specific observer is introduced Hardy often writes as if one were present. At the beginning of chapter 5 [3], the progress of Susan Henchard and her daughter is described with a heavy use of the passive voice and the implication of watching eyes: "Change was only to be observed in details" [17]; "A glance was sufficient to inform the eye that this was Susan Henchard's grown-up daughter" [17]; "it could be perceived that this was the act of simple affection" [17]. It is almost as though Hardy shrank from the responsibilities of omniscience, from the necessity for moral judgments and firm intellectual commitments, and found a certain security in adopting—usually quite inconsistently and on a scene-to-scene basis—the limited but essentially human perspectives available to particular characters.

Both the tendency to delimitation and the urgent need for visualisation find their ideal correlative in the incorporation within the structure of the novel of patterns and techniques essentially theatrical. At the beginning of chapter 24 Hardy explains why Elizabeth-Jane—again it is her view that is primarily invoked—takes pleasure in the prospect of remaining at High Place Hall:

> For in addition to Lucetta's house being a home, that raking view of the market-place which it afforded had as much attraction for her as for Lucetta. The *carrefour* was like the regulation Open Place in spectacular dramas, where the incidents that occur always happen

to bear on the lives of the adjoining residents. Farmers, merchants, dairymen, quacks, hawkers appeared there from week to week, and disappeared as the afternoon wasted away. It was the node of all orbits. [126]

Lucetta and Elizabeth-Jane are so positioned as to be able to look down upon the market-place, chief setting for the rivalry of Henchard and Farfrae, as if from a pavilion overlooking a jousting field. Specifically, they are, at the window of High Place Hall, spectators of a weekly performance conducted as if for their benefit. From the same vantage point they observe the collision of the two waggons, as well as the final disastrous performance of the skimmity ride itself, which achieves despite its garishness a deadly realism:

'My—why—'tis dressed just as *she* was dressed when she sat in the front seat at the time the play-actors came to the Town Hall!' [210]

There is a momentary suggestion here of a receding perspective of plays-within-plays-within-plays. Hardy does not pursue, perhaps does not wholly recognise, this hint, yet he certainly exploits the grotesque and quasi-magical aspects of the primitive ritual which is being enacted, incorporating them very powerfully (and with touches reminiscent of Hawthorne's story "My Kinsman, Major Molineux") in the scene in which Henchard, the following day, is deterred from suicide by the appearance in the water of a figure which seems to be "*himself*. Not a man somewhat resembling him, but one in all respects his counterpart, his actual double" [224]. Several other episodes in the novel seem deliberately theatrical: the melting away of the crowd at the end of the first chapter until Henchard is left alone with his guilt; the scene in which Lucetta, expecting Henchard, suddenly finds Farfrae before her for the first time; Henchard's highly melodramatic rescue of Lucetta from the menacing bull. There are, too, the encounters in the Ring—in secret, yet oppressed and virtually overlooked by that sense of the long and dubious history of the spot which Hardy has earlier evoked in terms of the ghosts of Hadrian's "gazing" [57] soldiery and of the ten thousand spectators who watched the execution of a woman there—and the description of Farfrae drawing everyone at the Three Mariners inwards towards the sound of his voice.

In this last scene, as elsewhere in the novel, the rustics like Solomon Longways, Mother Cuxsom, and Christopher Coney perform a modest choral function, and if the members of this group are often reminiscent of the lively, disenchanted figures who populate the low-life world of Shakespeare's history plays, Hardy seems nonetheless to have precedents from Greek literature chiefly in mind. The novel as a whole resumes with more sophistication and less obtrusiveness the attempt earlier made in *The Return of the Native* to recapture certain aspects of the techniques and experience of tragic drama. Certainly the focus on Casterbridge provides a unified sense of place at least as consistent as the Egdon setting in *The Return of the Native*, and if there is no attempt to achieve technical unity of time—any more, indeed, than in *The Return of the Native* in its published from—time is to some extent shaped and vitalised by Henchard's vow in chapter 2 to "avoid all strong liquors for the space of twenty-one years to come, being a year for every year that I have lived" [16].

Although the action of *The Mayor of Casterbridge* is diversified by reversals and discoveries of the kind so richly strewn throughout the earlier novel, the controlling image is that of fortune's wheel: "Small as the police-court incident had been in itself, it formed the edge or turn in the incline of Henchard's fortunes. On that day—almost at that minute—he passed the ridge of prosperity and honour, and began to descend rapidly on the other side" [166]. This hint of a "morality" structure implicit in the sequence of Henchard's rise and fall is further stressed in the full title of the novel—*The Life and Death of the Mayor of Casterbridge: A Story of a Man of Character*[2]—with its deliberate echo of such allegorical works as Bunyan's *The Life and Death of Mr Badman*. But it is unnecessary to debate the precise ancestry of the dramatic patterns incorporated within *The Mayor of Casterbridge* in order to insist on the presence of unmistakably tragic elements in the story of Henchard's life or in the manner of his death, as he shares with Othello a determination to "extenuate nothing" [248] and echoes in his dying testament the bitter epitaph found on "the rude tomb" of Timon of Athens.

It is only at the very end of the novel that it becomes possible to appreciate the full importance of the central if unspectacular position occupied by Elizabeth-Jane. Henchard's retention of the reader's sympathy in the final chapters is largely dependent upon his now unequivocal love for Elizabeth-Jane, and upon the revival of her love and compassion for him. Equally, however, it is our now developed responsiveness to Elizabeth-Jane's good sense and good judgment which ensures that in our surrender to the power of Henchard we do not utterly reject the man who, next to Henchard himself, is most responsible for his downfall. Farfrae has real if limited virtues, and Elizabeth-Jane's acceptance of him in marriage ensures that we remember these. The ending of the novel is quiet, low-keyed, like the ending of a Shakespearean tragedy: the central figure has been removed by death and the lesser ones who formerly stood in his shadow are left to pick up the pieces and restore order

---

2. The title only received its final form in the 1912 Wessex edn. In the MS, f.1 ([Dorchester County Museum]), it is simply *The Mayor of Casterbridge*; the first edn. has *The Mayor of Casterbridge: The Life and Death of a Man of Character*; the Osgood, McIlvaine edn. of 1895 follows the Sampson Low edn. of 1887 in reading *The Mayor of Casterbridge: A Story of a Man of Character*.

as best they can. So Elizabeth-Jane is left with Donald Farfrae, accommodating herself patiently to his limitations and to the knowledge that she is his second choice. Because of her, because of what she has learned, because she is in a real sense Henchard's heir even if not his actual daughter, the book ends on a note of quiet hopefulness which we recognise as essentially hers, the impress of her character as we have come to know it. In her marriage with Farfrae we perhaps glimpse the possibility which E. M. Forster later pursued in *Howards End*, that efficiency *can* be combined with humanity, that the commercial life need not necessarily imply insensitivity to the natural affections or to the natural world itself. Henchard is dead, and something profoundly valuable—something which connected him with the land, the seasons, and with the rural way of life—seems to have died with him. But that death, Hardy seems to suggest, was perhaps necessary. Although Henchard experienced it as defeat it may be the part of wisdom to temper regret with realism and to recognise the inevitability of change as old ways, dating from the "days of the Heptarchy" [127], necessarily yield to more modern methods. And so the novel ends not on Henchard's bitter cry of despair but upon Elizabeth-Jane's note of quiet acceptance. Implicit in that acceptance, however, is the sense of having lived on into a world from which a kind of greatness has disappeared, and perhaps for ever.

IRVING HOWE

The Struggles of Men†

To shake loose from one's wife; to discard that drooping rag of a woman, with her mute complaints and maddening passivity; to escape not by a slinking abandonment but through the public sale of her body to a stranger, as horses are sold at a fair; and thus to wrest, through sheer amoral willfulness, a second chance out of life—it is with this stroke, so insidiously attractive to male fantasy, that *The Mayor of Casterbridge* begins. In the entire history of European fiction there are few more brilliant openings.

When some of the reviewers complained that Michael Henchard's sale of his wife is incredible, Hardy hastened to defend himself with his customary appeal to history. Cases of wife-selling, he noted, had been frequent in rural England and were still to be heard of during the mid-nineteenth century. Today this argument seems naive: we recognize that the historically possible or even the historically actual is not a sufficient

† Reprinted with permission of Macmillan Publishing Co. and Simon & Schuster from *Thomas Hardy* by Irving Howe. Copyright © 1966 by Irving Howe.

basis for the imaginatively plausible. Still, Hardy's defense is not quite so irrelevant as recent criticism has made out, for in ways more complicated than Hardy could say, history does form a matrix of the literary imagination. Had he lived a few decades later than he did, Hardy might have argued that the opening scene of the novel, partly because it does rest on a firm historical foundation, embodies a mythic kind of truth. Speaking to the depths of common fantasy, it summons blocked desires and transforms us into secret sharers. No matter what judgments one may make of Henchard's conduct, it is hard, after the first chapter, simply to abandon him; for through his boldness we have been drawn into complicity with the forbidden.

The detached composure with which this first chapter is written Hardy would seldom equal again. Nothing is rushed, nothing overstated. There is almost no effort to fill out the characters of Henchard and Susan, since for the moment they matter as representative figures in outline, a farm laborer and his wife plodding along a country road in search of work. Nor is there any effort to set off a quick emotional vibration. What Henchard feels we barely know, and Susan, carrying her baby and trying—the phrase is subtly evocative—to keep "as close to his side as possible without actual contact," remains impassive in her distress. Hardy's intention here is not to penetrate the deeper feelings of his characters, but to set up a bare situation that will serve as the premise of their fate. This is a novel in which plot—the shaping of an action toward a disciplined implication—is to be central. And accordingly, the prose displays few signs of portentousness, strain or ornament. At least in this book, Hardy trusts the tale.

We encounter at the very outset Hardy's characteristic mixture of realism and grotesque, with the realism in the characterization and the grotesque in the event. The place is the familiar countryside of Wessex, and the figures are the familiar agents of its traditional life; but the action seems startling, extreme, and with an aura of the legendary. Details of conduct establish a context of verisimilitude: a farm laborer with the "measured" and "springless" walk of "the skilled countryman as distinct from the desultory shamble of the general laborer"; and then the two of them, husband and wife, sullen in their "atmosphere of stale familiarity." Each feels trapped, neither quite knows why. Through a few broad descriptive strokes, these barely articulate people are sketched in. Henchard and his wife are approaching the town of Weydon-Priors, in Upper Wessex, and it is a fair day. First the stress is placed upon the economics of trading and hiring, but then, a few paragraphs later, Hardy turns to the fair as a communal activity, with its slackening of moral standards and its echoes of old custom. "A haggish creature," the furmity woman sits in her tent and mixes her brew—she looks like one of the witches in *Macbeth* and is clearly meant to be more than realistic in reverberation. Henchard, grown "brilliantly quarrelsome" on drink, sells his wife for five pounds. That he does this through a travesty of an auction heightens the terribleness of his deed. For, with the spitefulness to which guilt can drive a man, he forces himself to prolong and brutally measure out what had begun as a whim.

The terms of the drama are now set: a violation of human dignity, by which an intimate relationship is made subject to the cash nexus. Yet it should be stressed that Henchard does this not out of greed but because he is supremely dissatisfied with the drabness of life and driven toward a gesture that will proclaim his defiance and disgust. What Henchard does now will later become a curse settling upon his life—Hardy might, with Hawthorne, have said, there will be blood to drink! The intended stroke of liberation proves to be a seal of enslavement; the seller, sold. And much of what follows in the novel consists of a series of variations upon Henchard's initial crime, with each variation crowding him further into aloneness. As a realistic portrait of social life, *The Mayor of Casterbridge* is by no means always credible or well drawn; but as a chain of consequences in which Henchard is trapped and from which he keeps struggling to break loose, it is severely appropriate. Here, as often in Hardy, verisimilitude is subordinated to internal pressures of theme and vision. To the ordinary program of literary realism Hardy cannot long be faithful.

At the same time, the sale of Henchard's wife constitutes a kind of fortunate fall. From this deed there follows whatever suffering and consciousness Henchard can reach—and it is one of Hardy's most remarkable achievements that, through incident and gesture, we are steadily made aware of how deeply Henchard suffers at being unable to declare in language the consciousness he has won. A major reason for Henchard's recurrent fits of temper is a rage over the inadequacy of his own tongue.

In the opening chapter, then, the dynamics of Henchard's psychology are set into motion. He is a man with energy in excess of his capacity for release. He is a blundering overreacher confined to a petty locale, so that he must try to impart some grandeur to a life of smallness even while dimly sensing the futility of his effort. He thrashes out at whatever comes within reach, sometimes with open hostility, sometimes with clumsy affection—but soon enough, with exhausted regret and self-contempt. He can neither contain his aggressions nor keep them going in cold blood. Everything he does comes from inner heat and ends with the clammy despair of contrition. He cannot draw a clear boundary between self and other, what is his and what is not. Having sold his wife, he is foolishly indignant that she keeps their child: "She'd no business to take the maid—'tis my maid." There is an element in human character which consists of primitive thrusting will and fiercely refuses social adjustment; it is particularly strong in Henchard.

Once he realizes what he has done, Henchard searches for months to find his wife and child, for he is now convinced that he must "put up with the shame as best he could. It was of his own making, and he ought to bear it." There is, as Hardy remarks, "something fetichistic in this man's beliefs." To give this observation its proper weight, a cannier novelist would have postponed it until later in the book, but even here, awkwardly placed, it has a strong impact. For Henchard is one of those unfortunate people whose burden it is that he responds with excessive force to both the demands of ego and the claims of moral commandment. He is "fetichistic" in that he lives by the persuasion that meaning does inhabit the universe, but a meaning that, somehow, maliciously eludes him. Bewildered, he must fall back upon curses, superstition and self-lacerating vows (he swears he will not touch liquor for twenty years).

Meanwhile, another motif is introduced in these early pages. Throughout Hardy's novels there keep appearing figures who need to confront life as if it were a dramatic performance being acted out on a cramped stage. Seldom conscious rebels yet refusing to accept their lot, they choose, at whatever cost, the roles of assertion and power. Is the world indifferent, dry and listless? Then they will impose themselves upon it. Is the universe drained of purpose and faith? All the more reason to impress upon one's time, with a kind of clenched prometheanism, the conquest of personality which a chosen act of drama can signify.

The impulse to create a drama of self-assertion is one of the main sources of "character" in Hardy's world, "character" here indicating energy and pride of personal being. (Not accidentally, there is at work in the novels a counter-principle to which Hardy is still more strongly attached: a wisdom of passivity that consists in accepting traditional roles and bearing inherited burdens.) In a world where the trees and the waters no longer speak of meaning or spirit, certain powerful figures can still slash their way to a marred identity. Their probable end is failure and pain, but struggle remains the substance of their experience. "My punishment," says Henchard at the end, "is *not* greater than I can bear."

It is this contrast between a setting of dusty indifference and figures both fierce and zestful in their performance that provides much of the drama in *The Mayor of Casterbridge*. The two are kept in a balance of tension, as if to satisfy Coleridge's description of the poet as one who achieves a "reconciliation of opposite or discordant qualities." Once the cast of the book is brought fully on stage, there follow a number of contests structured as a series of intensifying crises, and through these contests Henchard realizes himself to the full—that is, completes his own destruction.

Strong anticipations of this clash between listlessness and desire, the inert universe and driven men, appear in the first few chapters. The road upon which Henchard walks is "neither straight nor crooked, neither level nor hilly," just another nondescript and wearisome road such as men have climbed for centuries. The only sound breaking the silence is "the voice of a weak bird singing a trite old evening song that might have

been heard on the hill at the same hour, with the self-same trills, quavers, and breves at any sunset of that season for centuries untold." And
then comes Henchard's gesture of perverse self-definition—the humiliation of the human being closest to him—by means of which he seeks
to release his grievance against the universe. Yet, no sooner does he leave
the furmity woman's tent than things lapse back into their accustomed
listlessness. The rural folk who have watched the sale of Susan now sink
into a drunken stupor, and the only creatures witnessing Henchard's
departure are a dog and a fly.

The irony here is both austere and wounding. Henchard's defiance of
customary standards and the moral law has no importance to anyone but
a handful of people; the world, barely noticing, continues with its customary drone. Henchard has strained past decorum and conscience to
assert himself, but Hardy, watching, as it were, from a distant height, sees
that in any larger scheme of things even the most extreme gesture is trivial and unavailing. Later—it is another superb touch—the furmity
woman, who is to be Henchard's Nemesis, will barely be able to remember what happened in her tent. Fate itself seems absentminded.

The prologue is now complete. A period of twenty years is skipped
over, years in which Henchard rises to mercantile prosperity and political prominence. This leap in time is strictly justifiable, once we have
been persuaded by the opening chapters that, if Henchard can but hold
his turbulence in check, he is a man vigorous and hard enough to succeed in the commerce of a country town. The way is thus open for the
main action of the novel: Henchard's steady downward course in both
personal life and social condition. And what sets this downward course
into motion is precisely the complex of character traits that has been at
work in his opening appearance. The spring of Henchard's decline is
personal in nature—the return of his wife Susan and her daughter
Elizabeth-Jane to Casterbridge, which makes impossible any further
evasion of his youthful sin. The occasion for Henchard's decline is social
in nature—a prolonged and doomed struggle with a new merchant,
Donald Farfrae, who brings to Casterbridge methods of economy
Henchard can neither understand nor compete with. And the plot of the
novel, as it moves from Henchard's vulgar triumph as mayor to his lonely unregenerate death, is structured with the intent of making the consequences of Henchard's past seem organically related to the social
struggle occupying the present.

As a maker of plots—I assume for a moment that this aspect of a novel
can be conveniently isolated from the total act of composition—Hardy
was never brilliantly successful. He came at a difficult moment in the
history of English fiction: he could neither fully accept nor quite break
away from the conventions of his Victorian predecessors. He felt obliged to use a variant of the overelaborate and synthetic plot that had
become fixed in the Victorian novel, the kind of superstructure that,

becoming an end in itself, could smother seriousness of thought and make impossible seriousness of characterization. And he kept using the Victorian plot not only because it satisfied the requirements of the serial form in which he first printed his fiction but also for a more important reason: he wanted plot to serve as a sign of philosophic intent and this seduced him into relying too heavily upon mechanical devices. Yet Hardy also came to look upon the Victorian plot as a rigid and repressive convention, from which in his final great novels he would slowly "liberate" himself. What he could not do, however, was either to employ a plot with the confidence of a Fielding that it would release his full vision, or work his way into a modern view of plot, according to which the action must be strictly adjusted to the psychological makeup of the characters. His novels are therefore likely to seem curiously uneven: the men and women he imagines are superbly vital, while the events he assigns to them are frequently beyond their bearing or our belief.

Hardy made excessive demands upon his plots. Just as certain writers of our day suppose that the color of a man's soul can be inferred from the way he holds a cigarette or bends the brim of his hat, so Hardy supposed that the motions of fate—which he declared to be ethically indifferent while often writing as if they were ethically malicious—could be revealed through the manipulation of plot. Whether operating as psychological claim or literary method, such assumptions are naive. They posit equations too neat for our sense of social reality or our sense of literary form.

Hardy hoped to endow the worn devices of Victorian plotting with nothing less than a metaphysical value: the plot of The Mayor is meant to serve as a kind of seismograph registering his vision of man's place in the universe. Where plot in Victorian fiction had often become little more than a means of providing a low order of suspense and complication, plot in Hardy's novels is supposed to signify, through its startling convolutions, a view of the human condition. But to succeed in such an aim, Hardy would have had to establish in his fiction an aura of the inevitable—and this was very difficult for a writer whose idea of fatality was itself pretty much of an improvisation. The aura of the inevitable was possible to classical tragedy, in which the gods were clearly apprehended and their desires, if not always their motives, were beyond question. It is also possible, I think, to modern fiction, in which the psychology of the characters controls the action. But it is virtually impossible for a novelist using the Victorian plot or something like it. Because Hardy remained enough of a Christian to believe that purpose courses through the universe but not enough of a Christian to believe that purpose is benevolent or the attribute of a particular Being, he had to make his plots convey the oppressiveness of fatality without positing an agency determining the course of fate. Why he should have boxed himself into this position is intellectually understandable but very hard to justify esthetically. The result was that he often seems to be coercing his plots, jostling them away from their own inner logic. And sometimes, in his passion to bend plot to purpose, he seems to be plotting against his own characters.

The plot of *The Mayor* suffers from most of Hardy's faults: coincidences which cannot be justified even in terms of his darkening view of life, transitions so awkwardly managed they cannot be excused by references to Hardy's kinship with the balladeers, improbabilities that threaten the suspension of disbelief he has himself induced. Yet the plot of *The Mayor* is probably the best that Hardy ever contrived, if only because its numerous flaws pertain to the things happening near and around Henchard but never seriously diminish his power at the center of the book. The thread of credence may be broken by certain turns of the action, such as the reappearance and withdrawal of the sailor who had bought Henchard's wife; such incidents are poorly managed, and it would be foolish to seek excuses, through vague invocations of Hardy's metaphysics, for what is mostly ineptitude and carelessness. But Henchard's own responses at such critical moments—his boiling self-incitements which start with a plunge into brutal aggression or oppressive affection and end with a dull and bewildered regret—are always credible. The accumulation of disasters with which he is afflicted must strike even the most indulgent reader as excessive; but the mixture of heroic force and sickening blindness with which he confronts these disasters is never in doubt. The plot may creak, but Henchard lives. And since he does emerge vivid and intact, it seems reasonable to conclude that the plot serves the rough but essential purpose of charting and enabling the curve of Henchard's fate. The plot fulfills the potential for dramatic gesture—or, if you prefer, self-destruction—which is Henchard's project in life. It does not do this smoothly, or without shocks of disbelief; it does not always persuade us that quite so overwhelming a concentration of troubles is really in the nature of things; but what it does succeed in doing is to persuade us that Henchard's personal struggle—the struggle of a splendid animal trying to escape a trap and thereby entangling itself all the more—is true. By the end of the story, there is nothing further for Henchard to do; he has exhausted himself as a man, he has exhausted himself as a character.

In its opening chapters *The Mayor of Casterbridge* reads like a fable, a story stripped to a line of essential happenings, but once Hardy leaps across two decades and shows Susan and Elizabeth-Jane returning to the town where Henchard is now a prosperous middle-aged merchant, the setting is thickened with social detail. Hardy portrays Casterbridge in its unsettled condition, which is somewhere between a small-scale market economy and the new impersonal commerce.

In these pages Hardy comes as close as he ever can to being a social

novelist. It would be idle to look for the subtleties of observation we asso-
ciate with a book like *Middlemarch*, that marvellous confrontation of
social status and spiritual being. What Hardy does offer is an authoritative portrait of a country town as it begins to experience a social change
it can neither control nor comprehend. He keeps observing the lag of
consciousness behind events, both as a factor in historical development
and a common fact of existence. Few people in Casterbridge try to grasp
any meaning in their lives, few even suppose there is a need to. Most
accept the lumpishness of daily routine. Henchard does not really care
to understand what is happening to him; he merely wants, through will
and magic, to coerce the direction of his personal fate and the turns of
the impersonal market, which in his case are almost indistinguishable.

Slowly the isolation of Casterbridge is coming to an end; that mystery
known as the market, beyond scrutiny or challenge, plays on every
nerve; and soon machinery will transform and replace labor. Yet it is crucial to Hardy's theme that Casterbridge remains a town dependent on
agriculture, "the complement of the rural life around, not its urban
opposite."

Signs of class division are frequent, but not yet fixed into a rigid hierarchy. Hardy contrasts the mayor and his half-drunken merchant cronies
at the banquet with the poor folk staring through the window; he quietly remarks upon the snobberies to which Susan and Elizabeth-Jane are
subject when they come to town; and he soon brings into play the shabby "rustics" of Mixen Lane, who form a kind of *lumpen* mixture during
the transition from country to town. Yet all of these people are bound
together in a community of sorts—which is not to say that they live in
harmonious bliss but that they do experience a sense of relationship with
both one another and their common past. When Henchard's doting
workman, Abel Whittle, cannot wake up early enough to begin a business journey, Henchard does not discharge him as an "enlightened"
employer might. He does something better and worse. He rushes to
Whittle's cottage, shakes him out of sleep and marches him through the
town without his breeches—in order to teach him a lesson and get him
on the job. It is an outrageous thing to do, but it is personal and direct.

Hardy is shrewd at juxtaposing old and new styles of economy:

> Here lived burgesses who daily walked the fallow; shepherds in an
> intra-mural squeeze. A street of farmers' homesteads—a street ruled
> by a mayor and corporation, yet echoing with the thump of the
> flail, the flutter of the winnowing fan, and the purr of milk into the
> pails . . .

The tone here, as throughout the book, is dispassionate and balanced.
Hardy is not so foolish as to yield himself to an unqualified nostalgia for
the agricultural past nor so heartless as simply to embrace the ways of the
future. The social biases at work in both his earlier and later novels

come together in *The Mayor* as an uneasy equilibrium, somewhat like that which forms the character of Henchard.

The portrait steadily built up of Casterbridge is never to be at the center of Hardy's concern, yet is essential to all that follows in the book. For without a full exposure to this social milieu, it would not be possible to register the significance of the struggle between Henchard and his young rival, the Scotchman Farfrae. First his friend and employee, then his competitor in business and love, and finally his employer and replacement as mayor, Farfrae comes—his name suggests it—as the stranger from afar.

At first their conflict is apprehended as a clash of temperaments, a contrast in kinds of character. So the absorbed reader is likely to regard the book, and so the scrutinizing critic ought finally to take it.

Henchard responds to his personal experience passionately, through volcanic upheavals; Farfrae sentimentally, through mild quaverings. Henchard wishes to wrench his environment; Farfrae to glide through it. Henchard can never adjust self to social role; Farfrae keeps self and social role harmonious, as partners in a busy enterprise. Henchard is rock; Farfrae smooth pebble. Their clash cannot be avoided, if only because Henchard keeps assaulting whatever equilibrium of personal and business relations they establish. Repeatedly Henchard provokes Farfrae to contests of manliness and guile, without realizing that the two are by no means the same. And the more Henchard emerges as a personal force, the less he survives as a social power.

Their conflict reflects, but is not reducible to, a shake-up within the dominant social class of Casterbridge, the merchants and traders. Men accustomed to a free-and-easy personal economy, in which arrangements are sealed by a word, will now be replaced by agents of an economy more precise and rational, in which social relationships must be mediated through paper. Henchard is "bad at figures," he keeps his money in an old safe, and

> His accounts were like bramblewood when Mr. Farfrae came. He used to reckon his sacks by chalk strokes all in a row like garden palings, measure his ricks by stretching with his arms, weigh his trusses by a lift, judge his hay by a chaw, and settle the price with a curse.

Henchard runs his affairs by hunches—which works well enough as long as he need only confront problems he can apprehend intuitively, as elements of an economy local and familiar. Toward the men who work for him Henchard is both generous and despotic, close and overbearing. He can be an autocrat, but never a hypocrite. He prepares the way for a triumph of bourgeois economy, but cannot live at ease with the style it brings. And he is not really able to distinguish between business and personal affairs, since for better or worse, he assumes that a man's life should be all of a piece. Will Farfrae be his manager? Then Farfrae must be his friend. And not only must Farfrae help with the books and the grain, he must eat heavy breakfasts with him and listen to the story of his life, as if to slake Henchard's thirst for relationship and impact.

Farfrae, says Hardy at one point, "is the reverse of Henchard." It is an important observation, and important, paradoxically, because of its generality. For what matters in the kind of social displacement Hardy is here portraying, is not so much the character of the newcomer, who must be something of a riddle precisely because he is new, as the ordeal of the old-timer, who forms part of a known and shared experience.

Farfrae bears the fruits of sciences; he introduces new machines to the farmers; he treats his men with "progressive" blandness, which at this point in history means neither to abuse nor pay them as much as Henchard. With Farfrae there comes to Casterbridge the rule of "functional rationality," what Karl Mannheim describes as "a series of actions . . . organized in such a way that it leads to a previously defined goal, every element in this series of actions receiving a functional position and role." This outlook is expressed by Farfrae with amusing precision when he explains the benefits of the new seed-drill:

> "It will revolutionize sowing hereabouts! No more sowers flinging their seed about broadcast, so that some falls by the wayside and some among thorns . . . Each grain will go straight to its intended place, and nowhere else whatever."

Who, comparing the ways of Henchard and Farfrae, will easily choose between them? Certainly not Hardy. He is too canny, too reflective for an unambiguous stand, and his first loyalty is neither to Henchard nor Farfrae but the larger community of Wessex. Hardy's feelings may go out to Henchard but his mind is partly with Farfrae. He knows that in important respects the Scotchman will help bring a better life to Casterbridge, even if a life less vivid and integral. Yet he also recognizes that the narrowing of opportunity for men like Henchard represents a loss in social strength. In his own intuitive and "poetic" way Hardy works toward an attitude of mature complexity, registering gains and losses, transcending the fixed positions of "progress" and "tradition." Because he is so entirely free of sentimental or ideological preconceptions in The Mayor, he achieves not only a more balanced view of the developments in Casterbridge than either Henchard or Farfrae can reach; his voice also emerges as that of a communal protector and spokesman.

Hardy's design requires that, to sharpen the contrast between looming protagonist and the secondary figures, Henchard be scaled as somewhat larger than life: that which is passing away seems larger than that which is yet to come. And in defeat men can grow into eloquence; they rant, they rave; sometimes they even discover their humanity. Farfrae, however, has no reason to cry out. He lives in modest harmony with the prevailing social trends, and need never call upon—need not even discover whether he has any—deeper emotional resources. Farfrae's feelings are always obedient to his will and are not, in any case, of a kind that could seriously interfere with his role as businessman. But Hardy also recognizes tacitly that a disagreeable role in society does not necessarily make for a disagreeable character, and he avoids the error of portraying Farfrae as a slick commercial schemer.

It has been customary among Hardy's critics and, I would guess, frequent among his readers to feel some dissatisfaction with Farfrae. He is said to be a figure too dim, never closely examined, more outline than substance. This kind of complaint rests, I think, upon a misunderstanding of both the book and the character. *The Mayor* is not a psychological novel in the sense that it provides, through a narrator's scrutiny, an intensive probing of psychic life. Henchard's psychology is, of course, extraordinarily interesting, but it is a psychology neither analyzed nor minutely examined: we must infer it from the unfolding of his behavior. Much the same, if on a smaller scale, holds true for Farfrae. And dramatically there is no reason why we should be allowed a fuller scrutiny of Farfrae's inner life. His function in this novel is to serve as "the reverse of Henchard," and if there is something a little shadowy about him, that is partly because he is a stranger bringing untested ways to a tested place.

In any case, Hardy maintains a finely balanced poise—it holds together wariness, irony and some respect—toward Farfrae. Clearly the Scotchman cannot engage Hardy as a Jude or even a Henchard can, yet he is conceived with clarity of outline and a modest quotient of sympathy. Farfrae wants no revenge upon Henchard and is quite ready to help him once everything has been lost; in fact, Farfrae wants nothing but quiet prosperity, domestic peace and modest preferment. As the victor, he is even ready to be tolerant toward Henchard's outbursts and provocations. That there must also be something intolerable in the tolerance of the victor, Hardy silently recognizes—it is the kind of recognition we expect from him. And it informs some of the most striking incidents in the novel, those showing Henchard, after his downfall, in the grip of a compulsive and self-lacerating pride. They are incidents that stay in one's memory as tokens of Hardy's intuitive craft: when Henchard comes to work as a day laborer for Farfrae, wearing the silk hat that is the single remnant of his lost prosperity; when he encounters Lucetta as the wife of his new employer and elaborately pretends to humble himself before her; and when he thrusts himself forward, as if from an inflamed will, during the visit of "the royal personage."

Shrewd as a Scotchman, Farfrae is sentimental as a Scotchman. At the Three Mariners tavern he delights the Casterbridge folk with his nostalgic song, *"It's hame, and it's hame, hame fain would I be."* Yet this is the same Farfrae whose first appearance in the novel comes as a man who has chosen to leave his old hame, like many Scotchmen of the nineteenth century who had drifted south in search of prosperity. As Hardy remarks in a quietly sardonic sentence, Farfrae is always "giving strong expression to a song of his dear native country that he loved so well as never to have revisited it." That anyone should manage as readily as Farfrae to compartmentalize his experience is a somewhat comic idea: the dry comedy of self-insulation.

Hardy marshals expertly the materials compelling us to see Henchard and Farfrae as representative men, each the agent for an embattled segment within the merchant class of Casterbridge; yet he also writes out of a fine realization that no human figure, unless meant as comic caricature, can be grasped entirely through his social function. Men like Henchard and Farfrae will release impulses and display characteristics that are not strictly harmonious—indeed, are likely to clash—with their social roles. Farfrae is indeed a new man of commerce, but also a stranger, a sentimentalist, a creature of milky mildness. Henchard does come out of the besieged old order, but also carries within himself some of the vices that will characterize the new. Among the most striking pages in *The Mayor* are those in which the private voice of one man is taken as public speech by another—as in the critical incident in which Henchard pleads with Farfrae to return to his sick wife and, because of the battle that has just occurred between the two men, is simply not believed.

I have spoken of Henchard's guilt and of his drive to impose significance upon his life through a dramatic overreaching of the will. Let us, for convenience, call these the personal themes of *The Mayor*. How then—the question must arise—do they relate to the social confrontation between Henchard and Farfrae, so clearly meant to have a large representative weight?

The first impulse of a critic facing this kind of question is usually to look for patterns of neat alignment, so that the different strands of action can be brought together and the novel declared to have a satisfactory structure. I wonder, however, at the value of such a procedure. Is it not a mistake to keep tidying up works of fiction, like compulsive housekeepers after a wild party? Is not one of the pleasures of the novel as a *genre*—and the novel more than any other *genre*—that within a structure of some comeliness and coherence there is likely to be a portion of that contingency, that vital disorder we know to be present in human existence? For a novel to emerge as a work of art, its materials must be shaped, selected, suppressed; for the form thereby achieved to persuade and move us, it must also create an illusion of the rich formlessness of reality.

Now what I have called the personal and the social themes of *The Mayor* do converge toward a significant interlocking. Henchard's personal qualities are distinctively his own, but they take on a resonance that would be quite impossible were they not rooted in a portion of Wessex history. The fortitude of character that renders him so notable a man is not merely an idiosyncratic trait; it has been nurtured and made possible by the society of old Wessex. A figure of potency and assurance in the Wessex that is dying, he is a mere foundering wreck in the Wessex that is coming to birth.

After the first few chapters we see that Hardy is weaving together an entanglement between the personal and public sides of Henchard's experience, the psychic turbulence that erupts within him and the social contests in which he finds himself caught up. This entanglement is tightened at a key point, when the old furmity woman comes before Henchard sitting as magistrate. She serves the plot as a kind of Nemesis, the voice of memory as it dredges up the mayor's shame. Thereby the theme first advanced in the opening chapter is brought to climax: Henchard cannot escape the consequences of his past. But reappearing at the moment she does, the furmity woman also hastens the collapse of Henchard as a social force in the world of Casterbridge.

That this connection is logically unassailable may surely be doubted. There is no necessary or sufficiently coercive reason why the consequences of a personal sin should coincide in time and impact with the climax of a socio-economic failure. Several things, to be sure, are working for Hardy which enable him to paper over the difficulty: first, that behind the two strands of action—Henchard's personal story and his social struggle—there operate the same turbulent elements of his character, so that we may thereby be induced to accept a similarity of effects; second, that we are emotionally persuaded to acquiesce in the notion that troubles run in packs, one kind precipitating another; and third, that by this point in the book Hardy is so involved in overplotting that the relentless accumulation of intrigue distracts us from the weakness of this major turning point in the plot. Yet, even if one makes all these allowances, it cannot be said that Hardy succeeds in establishing the aura of inexorability which both the logic of his story and the conception behind his protagonist require. The fault is a serious one, still another instance of the way Hardy's plots crumble beneath the thematic weight with which he burdens them.

Faults of this kind and magnitude can be found in all of Hardy's fiction, and it would be idle to deny that they are troublesome; yet they are not, either in The Mayor or Hardy's other major novels, finally decisive. They count for more in one's reflections upon Hardy's work than in one's actual experience of it. For the strongest impression created by a book like The Mayor is that of a unified tone, an integration of sensibility and effects. And if we do not claim for the book a tragic stature it neither invites nor requires,[1] the impression of unity is particularly strong. It is an impression that depends upon specific compositional achievements.

---

1. Apparently out of a wish to honor the novel, critics in recent years have spoken about The Mayor as a tragedy, with consequent comparisons between Henchard and Oedipus and Lear. I doubt that these help us in responding to the book Hardy actually wrote.

The Mayor is a novel packed with incident, and if we examine closely some of the devices Hardy used to keep his serial exciting, we can
charge him with overcrowding. Except, however, in the first few chapters, none of the incidents is developed at much length or with much
fullness. Hardy continues—rightly enough, since this is where his greatness lies—to depend upon a series of intensely wrought and symbolically charged bits of action, scattered through the book and so brief in
scope as to prevent us from thinking of them as dramatic scenes. These
bits of action form the intermittent points of climax, transition and accumulation in the movement of the plot.

Another reason for the integration of effects is the way Hardy handles
his "rustics." In his earlier novels these figures weave in and out of the
main action, serving mostly as comic relief or minor conveniences of
plot, at best as a low-keyed chorus expressing a traditional wisdom in
response to the deracination or defeat of the major characters. But in
The Mayor they form a significant part of the story. It is they who precipitate the skimmity-ride which throws Lucetta into a fever and then
death. The social transformation Hardy dramatizes through the clash
between Henchard and Farfrae is sharply reflected in the life of the "rustics," now ill at ease in the town, beginning to express a measure of social
ressentiment, and clearly losing their cohesion as a group. Some of the
usual tasks of the Hardyan chorus are still performed here, and very
beautifully, as when Mother Cuxsom muses on the death of Susan:

> Well, poor soul; she's helpless to hinder that or anything now . . .
> And all her shining keys will be took from her, and her cupboards
> opened; and little things 'a didn't wish seen, anybody will see; and
> her wishes and ways will all be as nothing!

or when Abel Whittle recalls Henchard's end:

> We walked on like that all night; and in the blue o' the morning,
> when 'twas hardly day, I looked ahead o' me, and I zeed that he
> wambled, and could hardly drag along. By that time we had got
> past here . . . and I took down the boards from the windows, and

---

Certain elements in *The Mayor* do bear a resemblance to tragic action, but then so do elements in any serious work of fiction. What seems lacking in the story and character of
Henchard, however, is that "proper magnitude" of which Aristotle speaks. By this admittedly
vague phrase I take Aristotle to mean a resonance of large philosophic and cultural issues: the
destiny of a race, the fate of a people, the ordeal of a hero who embodies the strivings of a
nation. Impressive as Henchard may be, he cannot be said to embody in his character or conduct issues of such magnitude. He is too clearly related to the particularities of a historical
moment and a social contest; he is too clearly a character with only the most limited grasp, or
growth, of consciousness; and he does not elicit, in my judgment, that blend of pity and awe
which is characteristic of the tragic hero.

My own sense of Henchard would place him not in the line of tragedy but in the tradition
of romanticism. He strikes me as a descendant of those stubborn figures in romantic poetry and
fiction who refuse to submit to their own limitations and demand more from the world than it
can give them.

helped him inside. "What, Whittle," he said, "and can ye really be such a poor fond fool as to care for such a wretch as I!"

But such passages, fewer here than in Hardy's earlier novels, are really no more than occasional grace notes. In the main, the rustics are viewed in a hard and realistic light; their moral seediness and decay reflect the social changes portrayed through the dominant line of plot. One could almost speak of the events at Mixen Lane as a sub-plot, the darkened reflection through plebeian grotesquerie of the main strand of action.

Yet it surely must be the common experience of Hardy's readers that in *The Mayor of Casterbridge* it is Henchard himself who is the unremittent center of interest. He is that rarity in modern fiction: an integral characterization, a figure shown not through a dimension of psychology or an aspect of conduct, but at a single stroke, in his full range of being. Henchard neither grows nor changes; and we do not really come to understand him any better as the novel progresses. We do not need to. For we know him immediately and completely, through an act of intuitive apprehension. He appears before us through those gestures of conduct and speech which realize his uniqueness: a man exemplifying the heroism and futility of the human will. For a novelist to have created this image of character is a very great achievement—it adds to the stock of archetypal possibilities that inhabit our minds.

J. HILLIS MILLER

[A Nightmare of Frustrated Desire][†]

* * *

Henchard in *The Mayor of Casterbridge* is Hardy's fullest portrait of the man who knows "no moderation in his requests and impulses." He is driven by a passionate desire for full possession of some other person. This means that his life is a sequence of relationships in which he focuses first on one person and then on another, desiring each with unlimited vehemence when she seems to promise what he wants, turning from her just as abruptly when she fails to provide it. From Susan, to Lucetta, to Farfrae, to Elizabeth-Jane, Henchard moves in exasperated desire, striving to fill the "emotional void" in himself, turning from Susan and Lucetta, one after the other, when they have yielded to him, desiring Lucetta anew when she becomes desirable to Farfrae, centering his whole life suddenly on Elizabeth-Jane after Susan's death only to dis-

† Reprinted by permission of the publisher from J. Hillis Miller, *Thomas Hardy: Distance and Desire* (Cambridge, Mass.: The Belknap Press of Harvard University Press, 1970), pp. 147–50.

cover at that very moment that she is not his daughter, so that a new barrier is created as if by magic between them, turning against Farfrae in an attempt to destroy the rival who is the mediator of his loving, determining for him without his awareness which women will be desirable to him, turning back again at last to Elizabeth-Jane and desiring her with burning possessive jealousy when Farfrae comes again between him and what he wants, to take her too from him.

The Mayor of Casterbridge is a nightmare of frustrated desire. It is structured around episodes which provide repeated opportunities for formulations of the law of love in Hardy's world. "[W]hen I was rich," says Henchard, "I didn't need what I could have, and now I be poor I can't have what I need." If he has something he does not want it. When it is unavailable his desire is inflamed. Elizabeth-Jane suffers the same incongruity of desire and possession: "Continually it had happened that what she had desired had not been granted her, and that what had been granted her she had not desired." When Lucetta was Henchard's mistress he felt nothing for her but "a pitying warmth" which "had been almost chilled out of him by reflection," but as soon as she begins turning toward Farfrae and so becomes "qualified with a slight inaccessibility" she becomes "the very being to make him satisfied with life." Her marriage to Farfrae makes him desire her all the more: "During the whole period of his acquaintance with Lucetta he had never wished to claim her as his own so desperately as he now regretted her loss." The same pattern is repeated later with Elizabeth-Jane. "Shorn one by one of all other interests," says the narrator of Henchard, "his life seemed centering on the personality of the stepdaughter whose presence but recently he could not endure." This new movement of desire, like the others, produces the circumstances which will frustrate it, in this case the return of Newson, Elizabeth-Jane's real father, and the courtship of Elizabeth-Jane by Farfrae after Lucetta's death. The "sudden prospect of [Elizabeth-Jane's] loss" causes him "to speak mad lies like a child," and his affection for her grows "more jealously strong with each new hazard to which his claim to her [is] exposed." The narrator speaks toward the end of the novel for Henchard's indistinct awareness of the pattern of his life: "Susan, Farfrae, Lucetta, Elizabeth—all had gone from him, one after one, either by his fault or by his misfortune."

It is both his fault and his misfortune, or rather it is neither. It is a law of life in Hardy's world that if someone by nature seeks complete possession of another person he is doomed to be disappointed over and over, either by his failure to obtain the woman he loves or by his discovery that he does not have what he wants when he possesses her. Character is indeed fate, and The Mayor of Casterbridge is the story of "the life and death of a man of character," as the subtitle says. Henchard is destroyed neither by an external fate nor by a malign deity, but by "the shade from his own soul upthrown," as the quotation from Shelley's The Revolt of

Islam specifies. The context of the phrase from Shelley sheds much light on Hardy's conception of Henchard. The passage comes in the eighth canto of *The Revolt of Islam*. The heroine, having been captured by some sailors, explains to them that the conception of God has arisen by projection from evil qualities in man:

> What is that Power? Some moon-struck sophist stood
> Watching the shade from his own soul upthrown
> Fill Heaven and darken Earth, and in such mood
>   The Form he saw and worshipped was his own,
>   His likeness in the world's vast mirror shown . . .
>
> (ll. 3244-3248)[1]

Just as in Shelley's view God is not an independently existing Power who governs heaven and earth, but is the reification of tyrannical tendencies in man's mind, so Henchard is not, as he sometimes thinks, the victim of a malign power imposing suffering on him: "The movements of his mind seemed to tend to the thought that some power was working against him." Henchard's fate is determined not by a "power" external to himself, but by his own character. This has projected itself on the world around him, creating necessarily the conditions which will produce repetitions of the same pattern of failure in his relations to other people. His fate-producing character is not a psychological mechanism, not some unconscious drive to self-punishment. He is rather one of Hardy's most dramatic demonstrations of a condition of existence in his universe. However vehemently Henchard approaches another person, the shadow cast between them by his own soul will remain as an impenetrable obstacle, his consciousness forbidding union with any of the people he loves.

IAN GREGOR

A Man and His History†

II

The function of the opening two chapters is to initiate the action and to serve as an overture to the novel as a whole. Their subject matter is the arrival of Henchard with his wife at the Fair in Weydon-Priors; the

1. Percy Bysshe Shelley, *The Complete Poetical Works*, ed. Thomas Hutchinson (London: Oxford University Press, 1960), p. 117.
† From Ian Gregor, *The Great Web: The Form of Hardy's Major Fiction* (London: Faber and Faber, 1974), pp. 117–29. Copyright © 1974 by Ian Gregor. Reprinted by permission of Faber and Faber.

selling of Susan to the sailor in a mood of drunken frustration; Henchard's recognition, the following day, of the terrible deed he has done; his solemn vow never to touch alcohol for twenty-one years, 'being a year for every year I have lived'; and his setting off alone to Casterbridge to look for work and to begin a new life.

> One evening of late summer, before the nineteenth century had reached one-third of its span, a young man and woman, the latter carrying a child, were approaching the large village of Weydon-Priors, in Upper Wessex, on foot. They were plainly but not ill clad, though the thick hoar of dust which had accumulated on their shoes and garments from an obviously long journey lent a disadvantageous shabbiness to their appearance just now.

The novel opens in these classical cadences of 'once upon a time'. At the centre, taking the attention, is Henchard, at first sour and indifferent, then made quarrelsome and pugnacious by drink, then bewildered but finally determined in his remorse. It is a kaleidoscope of moods all being lived out at the nerve's end, and fuelling them all, there is a deep and diffused sense of self-estrangement. Self-enclosed, his wife appears 'to walk the highway alone, save for the child she bore'. About the family there is an 'atmosphere of stale familiarity', and in Nature too, life has faded, the leaves are 'doomed' and 'blackened green', the 'grassy margins of the bank' are 'powdered by dust'. The mood is suggestive of that described by Donne in 'The Nocturnall upon St. Lucie's Day':

> The world's whole sap is sunke:
> The generall balm the hydroptique earth hath drunk,
> Whither, as to the bed's-feet, life is shrunke.

That is the general mood of these opening pages; Henchard's particular mood is more difficult to define. We feel in it bafflement, frustration, a sense that life has possibilities which have been denied him. It is interesting that the very first words which are spoken in the novel, the first gesture towards self-fulfilment, takes the form of the question 'Any trade doing here?' It is the sense of the centrality of work in finding fulfilment that is such a major preoccupation of this novel.

As soon as we put it that way we can see what a rare novel *The Mayor of Casterbridge* is in the history of English fiction, where the model of self-fulfilment is found, invariably, in personal relationships. If we think of Lawrence, a novelist who comes very close to Hardy in many ways, and think of the self-estrangement of Tom Brangwen and the self-estrangement of Henchard, the rarity of Hardy's position becomes plain. *The Mayor* is an intensely public novel in its drive; how public can be gauged from the fact that it must be one of the very few major novels — or for that matter, very few novels — where sexual relationships are not, in one way or another, the dominant element. That Hardy can write a novel which engages his full imaginative range without making us feel the relative absence of such relationships, suggests that it is not the individual human heart which beats at the centre of his fictional world.

The marriage that is broken at Weydon-Priors is not, so far as Hardy is concerned, an individual affair. In these opening chapters we move steadily away from the individual—we are never, at any point, taken 'inside' Henchard—to the world in which he is finding it difficult to make a living, the world of houses being pulled down and people having nowhere to go. There is the voice of the auctioneer selling off the last of the horses and gradually insinuating into Henchard's mind a wish to start again, to shake himself free from all encumbrance, to sell his wife. Susan is sold at a strange dream-like auction in which there are no bidders, but the price goes up and up. I think it is possible to make too much of the particulars of this vivid and bizarre scene, so that the whole emphasis falls on the act of selling itself, the reduction of a person to a commodity. But Hardy's interests are not those, say, of James in *The Spoils of Poynton*. His eye is not so much on money, as on the notion of 'freedom' it appears to offer, and which Henchard is so intent on grasping, 'if I were a free man again I'd be worth a thousand pound before I'd done o't'. That is the sentence which catches the undercurrent of meditation that runs persistently through the chapter, the keenly felt 'if I were'. It is that sentiment which is present in the visitation of the late swallow finding its way into the tent, like the men who watch it, 'absently', a migrant, but unlike them free in a way they can never be. This meditative note is struck most firmly at the end of the chapter when we are taken outside the tent, and the sight of the horses 'crossing their necks and rubbing each other lovingly' is set in contrast to the harsh act of humanity we have just witnessed. But, immediately, that note is played in a different key: we are asked to reflect on the occasions when humanity sleeps innocently while inanimate nature rages round him. And there at the end of the paragraph we find an unobtrusive phrase which gives us bearings on the whole scene—'all terrestrial conditions were intermittent'. In other words those who seek to impress themselves on the universe, to lay violent hands on time, to forget that man is the slave of limit—such men can only succeed in destroying themselves. They will be extinguished as surely as the last candle is, when the furmity seller goes out to leave Henchard alone in the tent sunk in a drunken sleep.

But for Hardy flux is always followed by reflux, an essential element in his narrative compulsion, no less than in his metaphysical outlook. Chapter I then tells for Hardy precisely half of the human story; Chapter 2 reverses the emphasis and, in so doing, tells the other half.

Henchard is again at the centre, Henchard now waking to find 'the morning sun' streaming through the crevices. Outside, 'the freshness of the September morning inspired and braced him as he stood.' He can see far across the valleys 'dotted with barrows, and trenched with . . . prehistoric forts'. *This* is a world upon which man has impressed himself, so that 'The whole scene lay under the rays of a newly risen sun, which had not as yet dried a single blade of the heavily dewed grass.' The voice of the weak bird of the previous night singing 'a trite old evening song' gives way to 'the yellow-hammers which flitted about the hedges with straws in their bills'. This vitality and purposiveness encompasses Henchard too.

The previous night he sought to set aside time, to disown his past; now he will bind himself to time, more, he will mortgage his future. He gave himself away in a drunken stupor in a furmity tent, now in re-collecting himself he swears his great vow on the clamped book which lies on the Communion table in a nearby village church. Instinctively, he seeks a ritual gesture, 'a fit place and imagery', which will release him from the thraldom of the moment. 'He shouldered his basket and moved on' — that is the driving sentiment of this second chapter. Purposeful and resilient, Henchard has now a full consciousness of his position. He tries, without success, to find his wife and family and then, learning of their emigration, 'he said he would search no longer . . . Next day he started, journeying south-westward, and did not pause, except for nights' lodgings, till he reached the town of Casterbridge, in a far distant part of Wessex.' In that closing sentence of the chapter we hear the classical cadences of the archetypal story, present in the opening paragraph, announce themselves again. And it is to be there, in Casterbridge, that the complementary tensions so explicitly set up in these two opening chapters will be developed and pursued.

'A series of seemings' — the opening of *The Mayor of Casterbridge* reveals, in a remarkably pure way, the characteristic Hardy stance towards experience. Within each chapter a set of reverberations is released from a single violent act — the sale of the wife, Henchard's vow. A perspective on the human deed is established. The act of an individual person cannot be contained by that individual life; it leads persistently outwards to the whole social context, a context both personal and social, as the full title of the novel we are considering makes plain: *The Life and Death of the Mayor of Casterbridge*. The 'seemings' are here, but in themselves they don't constitute the shape of a life. They are true to consciousness heightened in moments of vision; they fail to do justice to consciousness as continually present, continually altering. It is here that 'series' has its part to play, with its emphasis on process and continuity.

In the aesthetic structure of a Hardy novel the tension between the terms is expressed in the dynamic interplay between plot and image, and encompassing both is the compassionate presence of the narrator, whose mediating consciousness is an integral part of the drama he is concerned to reveal. In the very elements which go to make up his fiction—the narrative trajectory, the sudden moment of symbolic concentration, the oscillations between story and commentary—in all of these elements, Hardy is acting out his own impression of life as a series of seemings, and the novelist's art is here not simply to reveal but to enact it. In particular terms, this is communicated most frequently in that air of ambivalence which hangs over so many incidents in the novel, an ambivalence which creates in the reader not so much an awareness of complexity as a desire to suspend judgement and to sense a more inclusive view.

It is an air which is strongly present in the presentation of Casterbridge itself. Our first glimpse of the town is in lamplight 'through the engirdling trees, conveying a sense of great snugness and comfort inside'. But to the eyes of the travelled, if inexperienced, Elizabeth-Jane it already seems 'an old-fashioned place'. Hardy holds a delicate balance in his initial presentation of Casterbridge between the warm nostalgia prompted by his boyhood memories of Dorchester in the 1840s and the reflections of an adult already aware of its remoteness, its inability to adapt itself to a changing world. 'Country and town met at a mathematical line'—it is like a child's drawing, and like such a drawing exhibits its own charm, its own falsity. The town's band may be shaking the windows with 'The Roast Beef of Old England', Henchard may be re-introduced to us through his laughter, but outside in the streets, the newly arrived wayfarers hear that he has over-reached himself: he has sold 'blown wheat', and there has never been such 'unprincipled bread in Casterbridge before'. The adjective does more than catch the vivacity of dialect, it casts a sardonic eye on one aspect at least of the Mayor's rise to prosperity. To the wayfarers, Casterbridge offers 'a sense of great snugness and comfort', but to Buzzford, the local dealer, it is 'a old hoary place o' wickedness'.

From the outset of the novel the reader is made quietly aware of ambivalence, and aware of it as arising from 'the way things are' rather than through the artifice of the novelist. Consider the relatively unobtrusive, but significant, play which is made of Farfrae's songs of home. The tone is lightly ironical at the expense of a man who looks back fondly on a country he has certainly no wish to return to; but at the same time, his sentiments are expressed in song, indicative of his resilience, his desire to travel, the ease he feels in company, and the unfeigned pleasure he gives to others. As the rivalry between Farfrae and Henchard builds up, we feel the same duality of feeling present, so that when Abel Whittle is reprimanded for his lateness at work, we feel Henchard's treatment is concerned, but humiliating, Farfrae's impersonal but just. In the rival entertainments they set up for the town, Henchard is bountiful but patronising, Farfrae cannily prudent, but infectiously ingenious.

The oscillation of sympathy is not confined to the main action. It is present in that fine town-pump chat which followed the death of Susan

Henchard. 'She was as white as marble-stone,' says Mrs. Cuxsom with evident relish, as she proceeds to relay the details of Susan's preparations for her burial. 'Ah, poor heart!'—and a general sigh goes up. Then suddenly the tone changes from elegy to indignation. Christopher Coney has removed the pennies from the dead woman's eyes and spent them at The Three Mariners. '"Faith," he said, "why should death rob life o' fourpence . . . money is scarce and throats get dry."' Beneath the humour a genuine point is being made. Just as suddenly the tone shifts back again, not to the gossipy note of concern with which the conversation began, but to an impersonal note of elegy, which both pays tribute to Susan and also recognises the substance in Coney's remark, though without approving his action:

> 'Well, poor soul; she's helpless to hinder that or anything now,' answered Mother Cuxsom. 'And all her shining keys will be took from her, and her cupboards opened; and little things a' didn't wish seen, anybody will see; and her wishes and ways will all be as nothing.'

It is a small incident, existing in the margin of the main action, but like Abel Whittle's speech about the death of Henchard in the last chapter, making the grain of the novel suddenly glow—the cadence may point to the inevitable obliterations of time, but there, in the centre, taking the eye, hard and personal, are Susan's 'shining keys'.

All this indicates something of the distinctive rhythm of the novel; but before looking at the resolutions towards which it moves, I would like to examine a chapter which exists almost at the very centre of the novel. I emphasise the word 'chapter' here because it is the rhythm established by that aesthetic unit that I wish to draw attention to. It is Chapter 24 and the subject matter is simply told.

Lucetta, now a lady of means, and Elizabeth-Jane are regarding the affairs of the Casterbridge market-place. From Lucetta's window they can observe the varied activity, and one day they see the arrival of a new seed-drill. Going out into the market-place to satisfy their curiosity, they find its arrival due to Farfrae, who is busy examining and displaying it. Hesitantly, the two women meet Henchard, who is also looking at the machine, and there is a sardonic exchange about the latest innovation. Both women are made increasingly conscious of their emotional involvements. Elizabeth, isolated from her father, has a growing sense of Lucetta's fascination with Farfrae. Lucetta admits as much, and the episode closes with an oblique attempt on her part to seek Elizabeth's advice.

Even from such a summary as this it is clear that Hardy, in a sure and economical way, is securing the interpenetration of the public and private themes of the novel and bringing them into sharp focus, almost wittily, in Farfrae's singing his romantic song of exile from inside the new agricultural machine. As he sings about Kitty 'wi' a braw new gown', we remember that Lucetta is also wearing a new gown which alone rivalled the machine in colour. New machines, new London fashions: the complementary development is made. Lucetta looking at her gown spread out on the bed chooses 'to be the cherry-coloured person at all hazards' as surely as Mixen Lane will choose that particular gown to identify her in the skimmity-ride. These are ironies of a now familiar kind, but what ought to take our attention in this chapter is not the oscillation of feeling, but a point of growth, a decisive move forward in the articulation of the novel.

The chapter opens with the phrase 'Poor Elizabeth-Jane', and it closes with the sentence 'For by the "she" of Lucetta's story Elizabeth had not been beguiled.' The decisive move in this chapter lies not in the scene contemplated from the window or in the marketplace, sharp and vivacious as it is, but in Hardy's creation of 'a contemplative eye' for Elizabeth. He is in the delicate process in this chapter of merging the authorial consciousness of the veiled narrator with that of Elizabeth. Hinted parallels between the artist's eye and Elizabeth's begin to be made. We are told that the market-place offers itself to the House like a stage for a drama, and when Elizabeth reacts to the new seed-drill it is in a very literary manner. Responding to Farfrae's enthusiasm about its efficiency she says, 'Then the romance of the sower is gone . . .' and then, more characteristically, 'How things change!' It is worth observing the reactions of Farfrae and Lucetta to this. Farfrae says, 'But the machines are already very common in the East and North of England.' And Lucetta, whose acquaintance with Scripture is, as Hardy says, 'somewhat limited', remarks admiringly and practically, 'Is the machine yours?' It is a small exchange, but it neatly conveys a new authorial relationship to 'poor Elizabeth-Jane'. This, of course, is given a decisive orientation at the end of the chapter when Elizabeth is asked to respond to Lucetta's carefully contrived story of her past. She has no difficulty in interpreting its true meaning. Interpreting, but not condemning, this provides her initiation into sympathetic detachment, beginning paradoxically with her own increasing emotional involvement with Lucetta and with Farfrae. And in that paradox Elizabeth is revealing herself not simply as a companion for Lucetta, but as a companion for Hardy too. In Chapter 24 we have a decisive step in her education: she is to learn the distinction between the fictive world and the real one, Newson's daughter, not Henchard's.

The full importance of Elizabeth's role, which begins to appear in this chapter, becomes quite clear in the final chapters of the novel. Hardy is going to need her 'quiet eye' less in the dramatic unfolding of the tale — though she has her small part to play here too — than as a way of enabling us to understand its resolution. It is a resolution which will involve the most dramatic nuancing of 'the series of seemings', and which will incorporate the developed consciousness of Elizabeth-Jane as part of its meaning.

The last two chapters stand in the same dramatic relationship to the novel as the first two. The main action is completed and the centre of our attention is Henchard—once more a wayfarer and a hay-trusser. 'He could not help thinking of Elizabeth'—that is the dominant mood of the penultimate chapter, everything else takes its bearings from that. But first Henchard must encounter his past again. He returns to the hill at Weydon-Priors where the furmity tent had stood twenty-five years previously, 'Here we went in, and here we sat down'. With absorbed intentness he recreates the scene of his crime and the authorial voice lends him support: 'And thus Henchard found himself again on the precise standing which he had occupied a quarter of a century earlier. Externally there was nothing to hinder his making another start on the upward slope. . . .' But it is too late in the day for that. Haunted by thoughts of Elizabeth in Casterbridge, he hears that arrangements have been made for her wedding to Farfrae, and he resolves to return for the occasion. Delaying his arrival until the festivities are well under way, he makes himself known at the house, after unobtrusively leaving his gift in the garden—a caged goldfinch. It is the first time he has met Elizabeth since she discovered that Henchard had delayed Newson's return to her. Face to face now, he seeks forgiveness, but she rejects him, and without any further defence of his conduct he bids her a final farewell and goes out into the night.

It is interesting to recall that it was this chapter which Hardy decided to omit from the first edition of the novel, fearing that Henchard's return to Elizabeth would weaken the final effect of the tragedy. Hardy was prevailed upon to restore the chapter, and this was done for the 1895 edition. And rightly, because its inclusion gives the emphasis to two essential elements in the conclusion of the novel. The first is the force given to Henchard's isolation from the community, not simply by a kind of muted withdrawal, but by rejection. The second is the creation of a reverse effect. Elizabeth's life with Farfrae is, we must feel assured, to be one of happiness. Whatever happens to Henchard that relationship will prosper in its own quiet way. And so we find the chapter reaching out towards that balance of contraries so characteristic of the novel as a whole. And reaching out in a way that quite naturally will employ the rhetoric which conveys a classical ending to an archetypal story—the marriage and wedding feast on the one hand, the exclusion of the disruptive force on the other.

But Hardy distrusts this kind of finality, this confident distribution of sympathy. And so in his final chapter Hardy is concerned to de-individualise his novel, to distance its themes. There is a moment in the penultimate chapter where we can see the kind of temptation which hovered over the ending, a temptation to go for emotional 'bravura'. Henchard's wedding gift to Elizabeth, the caged goldfinch, remains an unfocused poignancy—the size of the gesture concealing its imprecision, so that if it is meant as some kind of symbolic expression about Henchard's fate, we remain uneasy as to whether the expression is Henchard's or Hardy's. I draw attention to the goldfinch only to show how sure Hardy's touch is in the remainder of the last chapter, where there is no forced symbolism of any kind, nothing mawkish in a situation where that tone is difficult to resist. And, when we consider that the chapter is written from the vantage point of a worried and remorseful daughter, the achievement becomes all the more remarkable.

It is the discovery of the bird-cage which sets Elizabeth and Farfrae off to look for Henchard. If it is Casterbridge and the wedding feast which set the mood for the preceding chapter, so now, in the last chapter, it is the heath and an isolated hut which 'of humble dwellings was surely the humblest'. Henchard has returned to a tract of land 'whose surface never had been stirred to a finger's depth, save by the scratching of rabbits, since brushed by the feet of the earliest tribes.' In this sense everything is to be stripped to essentials, the world which is to be seen by the travellers is a moral landscape as well as a natural one, and we are moved to see, in Wordsworth's phrase, into 'the life of things'. Characteristically, on this bedrock of human experience, Hardy continues his contraries.

The perspective the Heath offers is one of timeless change, the endless ebb and flow of human existence, stretching back to a limitless past, forward to a limitless future. At the centre, two wayfarers pursue a difficult search. The scene offers itself irresistibly as an image of our terrestrial condition. Then, suddenly, casually, a figure appears, Abel Whittle, whose only role in the novel so far has been to provide the first occasion when Henchard and Farfrae clashed. And now—like Mother Cuxsom on the death of Susan—it is this marginal figure who is chosen to express, in one of the most moving passages of the novel, the contrary perspective to that proffered by the Heath. Comparison has sometimes been made between Whittle's role here and that of the Fool in *King Lear*. Like the larger comparison, the smaller is wide of the mark. The Fool proffers 'wisdom', a self-conscious commentary on Lear's plight. Whittle offers the purest form of human gesture, the instinctual made sublime by its disinterestedness, 'ye wer kind-like to mother if ye were rough to me, and I would fain be kind-like to you.' It is 'love thy neighbour as thyself', presented with total dramatic simplicity and conviction. It is the felicity of 'kind-like' with all its overtures of kinship and kindred, that demands, in Hardy's eyes, no less recognition as part of our terrestrial condition than the humbling perspectives suggested by the Heath. In Henchard's Will we find the confluence of these views. There is the wish for annihilation in death, 'that no man remember me'; there is also the unshakable belief in the personal rightness of the testimony, 'To this I put my name—Michael Henchard', just as twenty-five years before, 'Dropping his head upon the clamped book which lay on the Communion-table, he said aloud—"I, Michael Henchard, . . ."'. It is a perspective which resists challenge and remains untouched by irony, Hardy's sense of 'a man of character'.

For Henchard life has been tragic, but never at any time has it lost dignity and it is this which Elizabeth responds to when she comes finally to mediate this experience for us. The Heath, Abel Whittle—the contraries caught here are too intense for the ebb and flow of ordinary lives. It is 'the ordinary' Elizabeth offers. When she responds to Henchard's Will it is not to the prescriptions, but to the knowledge that 'the man who wrote them meant what he said . . . (they) were not to be tampered with to give herself a mournful pleasure, or her husband credit for large-heartedness.' She disclaims 'mournful pleasures', and with Henchard's life now behind her she is given full liberty to reflect. It is a reflection which attempts to render continual justice to the contraries of existence, to the series of seemings, as these make themselves felt in the last, and much misunderstood, sentence of the novel:

> And in being forced to class herself among the fortunate she did not cease to wonder at the persistence of the unforeseen, when the one to whom such unbroken tranquillity had been accorded in the adult stage was she whose youth had seemed to teach that happiness was but the occasional episode in a general drama of pain.

How often the final phrase has been wrenched from its context and made to do duty for a view not only of this novel, but of the general tenor of Hardy's fiction. 'The persistence of the unforeseen', it is this phrase which mobilises the paragraph, keeps the contraries open, and is as resistant to a view of life as 'a general drama of pain' as it is to one of 'unbroken tranquillity'. Elizabeth's eye—and Hardy's too—is on the wonder of change here, on flux and reflux, putting her youth beside her 'adult stage', not intent on finding in those phases prescriptions for life in general. It is not simply the unseen that keeps us alert to such change, but its *persistence*: it is this which becomes part of the fabric of everyday living. At times, Henchard had tried to separate out the unseen from that fabric and to live by it, and the past and the future devoured his present; at times, Farfrae was so totally absorbed by the fabric that being out on the heath was being 'reduced', and staying overnight there a matter of making 'a hole in a sovereign'. Elizabeth, like Thomasin in *The Return of the Native*, accepts the Heath, and the drama it has witnessed, calmly, and for what it is, neither an implacable force nor a backdrop to man's desires.

ELAINE SHOWALTER

The Unmanning of the Mayor of Casterbridge†

To the feminist critic, Hardy presents an irresistible paradox. He is one of the few Victorian male novelists who wrote in what may be called a

† Elaine Showalter, "The Unmanning of the Mayor of Casterbridge," in *Critical Approaches to the Fiction of Thomas Hardy*, ed. Dale Kramer (London: Macmillan Press, 1979), pp. 99–115. Copyright © 1979 by Elaine Showalter. Reprinted by permission of the publisher. Page references have been changed to correspond to this Norton Critical Edition.

female tradition; at the beginning of his career, Hardy was greeted with the same uncertainty that had been engendered by the pseudonymous publication of *Jane Eyre* and *Adam Bede*: was the author man or woman? *Far from the Madding Crowd*, serialised in the *Cornhill* in 1874, was widely attributed to George Eliot, and Leslie Stephen wrote reassuringly to Hardy about the comparisons: 'As for the supposed affinity to George Eliot, it consists, I think, simply in this that you have both treated rustics of the farming class in a humorous manner—Mrs. Poyser would be home I think, in Weatherbury—but you need not be afraid of such criticisms. You are original and can stand on your own legs.'[1]

It hardly needs to be said that Stephen's assessment of Hardy's originality was correct; but on the other hand, the relationship to Eliot went beyond similarities in content to similarities in psychological portraits, especially of women. Hardy's remarkable heroines, even in the earlier novels, evoked comparisons with Charlotte Brontë, Jane Austen, and George Eliot, indicating a recognition (as Havelock Ellis pointed out in his 1883 review-essay) that 'the most serious work in modern English fiction . . . has been done by women.'[2] Later, Hardy's heroines spoke even more directly to women readers; after the publication of *Tess of the d'Urbervilles*, for example, Hardy received letters from wives who had not dared to tell their husbands about their premarital experience; sometimes these women requested meetings which he turned down on his barrister's advice.[3] Twentieth-century criticism has often focused on the heroines of the novels; judging from the annual *Dissertation Abstracts* (Ann Arbor, Michigan) this perennial favourite of dissertation topics has received new incentive from the women's movement. Recent feminist criticism, most notably the distinguished essays of Mary Jacobus on Tess and Sue, has done much to unfold the complexities of Hardy's imaginative response to the 'woman question' of the 1890s.[4] Hardy knew and respected many of the minor women novelists of his day: Katherine Macquoid, Rhoda Broughton, Mary Braddon, Sarah Grand, Mona Caird, Evelyn Sharp, Charlotte Mew. He actually collaborated on a short story with the novelist Florence Henniker, and possibly revised the work of other female protegées; his knowledge of the themes of feminist writing in the 1880s and 1890s was extensive.[5]

1. Letter of February 1874, given in Richard Little Purdy, *Thomas Hardy: A Bibliographical Study* (London: Oxford University Press, 1954), 338.
2. Havelock Ellis, 'Thomas Hardy's Novels', *Westminster Review*, LXIII n.s. (1883) 334.
3. See Florence Emily Hardy, *The Later Years of Thomas Hardy, 1892–1928* (London and New York: Macmillan, 1930), 5.
4. Mary Jacobus, 'Sue the Obscure', *Essays in Criticism*, XXV (1975) 304–28; and 'Tess's Purity', *Essays in Criticism*, XXVI (1976) 318–38.
5. For Hardy's personal need to have a 'literary lady—not his wife—whom he could mastermind, and who would appreciate him in return', see Robert Gittings, *The Older Hardy* (London: Heinemann; Boston: Little, Brown, 1978), 77–81. Hardy had recommended Mona Caird's essay on 'The Evolution of Marriage' (eventually published in her *The Morality of Marriage* [1897]) to the *Contemporary Review* in 1890; he wrote to Florence Henniker about Sarah Grand's best-selling feminist novel, *The Heavenly Twins* (1893).

Yet other aspects of Hardy's work reveal a much more distanced and divided attitude towards women, a sense of an irreconcilable split between male and female values and possibilities. If some Victorian women recognised themselves in his heroines, others were shocked and indignant. In 1890, Hardy's friend Edmund Gosse wrote: 'The unpopularity of Mr. Hardy's novels among women is a curious phenomenon. If he had no male admirers, he could almost cease to exist. . . . Even educated women approach him with hesitation and prejudice.'[6] Hardy hoped that *Tess of the d'Urbervilles* would redeem him; he wrote to Edmund Yates in 1891 that 'many of my novels have suffered so much from misrepresentation as being attacks on womankind.'[7] He took heart from letters from mothers who were 'putting "Tess" into their daughters' hands to safeguard their future', and from 'women of society' who said his courage had 'done the whole sex a service.'[8] Gosse, however, read the hostile and uncomprehending reviews of such women as Margaret Oliphant as evidence of a continuing division between feminist critics, who were 'shrivelled spinsters', and the 'serious male public.'[9] There were indeed real and important ideological differences between Hardy and even advanced women of the 1890s, differences which Gosse wished to reduce to questions of sexual prudery. Hardy's emphasis on the biological determinism of childbearing, rather than on the economic determinants of female dependency, put him more in the camp of Grant Allan than in the women's party. In 1892 he declined membership in the Women's Progressive Society because he had not 'as yet been converted to a belief in the desirability of the Society's first object' — women's suffrage.[1] By 1906 his conversion had taken place; but his support of the suffrage campaign was based on his hope (as he wrote to Millicent Garrett Fawcett) that 'the tendency of the women's vote will be to break up the present pernicious conventions in respect of manners, customs, religion, illegitimacy, the stereotyped household (that it must be the unit of society), the father of a woman's child (that it is anybody's business but the woman's own except in cases of disease or insanity)'.[2]

Looking at the novels of the 1890s, and at Hardy's treatment of his heroines as they encounter pernicious conventions, A. O. J. Cockshut has concluded that there were unbridgeable gaps between Hardy's position and that of *fin-de-siècle* feminism:

6. Edmund Gosse, 'Thomas Hardy', *The Speaker*, II (1890) 295. Gosse attributed this unpopularity to Hardy's unconventional conception of feminine character.
7. Letter of 31 December 1891, in *The Collected Letters of Thomas Hardy*, Vol. I: 1840–1892, ed. Richard Little Purdy and Michael Millgate (Oxford: Clarendon Press, 1978), 250.
8. Letter to Edmund Gosse, 20 January 1892, in *Collected Letters*, I. 255.
9. Letter to Hardy of 19 January 1892, in Evan Charteris, *The Life and Letters of Sir Edmund Gosse* (London: Heinemann, 1931), 225–26.
1. Letter to Alice Grenfell, 23 April 1892, in *Collected Letters*, I. 266.
2. Letter of November 1906, in the Fawcett Library (London), quoted in Elaine Showalter, *A Literature of Their Own: British Women Novelists from Brontë to Lessing* (Princeton: Princeton University Press, 1977), 185.

Hardy decisively rejects the whole feminist argument of the preceding generation, which was the soil for the growth of the idea of
the 'New Woman' à la Havelock Ellis and Grant Allen: and this is
his final word on the matter. The feminists saw the natural disabil-
ities as trivial compared with those caused by bad traditions and
false theories. Hardy reversed this, and he did so feelingly. The
phrase 'inexorable laws of nature' was no cliché for him. It represented the slowly-garnered fruits of his deepest meditations on life.
It was an epitome of what found full imaginative expression in
memorable descriptions, like that of Egdon Heath. The attempt to
turn Hardy into a feminist is altogether vain.[3]

But the traditional attention to Hardy's heroines has obscured other
themes of equal significance to a feminist critique. Through the heroes
of his novels and short stories, Hardy also investigated the Victorian
codes of manliness, the man's experience of marriage, the problem of
paternity. For the heroes of the tragic novels—Michael Henchard, Jude
Fawley, Angel Clare—maturity involves a kind of assimilation of female
suffering, an identification with a woman which is also an effort to come
to terms with their own deepest selves. In Hardy's career too there is a
consistent element of self-expression through women; he uses them as
narrators, as secretaries, as collaborators, and finally, in the (auto) biography he wrote in the persona of his second wife, as screens or ghosts of
himself. Hardy not only commented upon, and in a sense, infiltrated,
feminine fictions; he also understood the feminine self as the estranged
and essential complement of the male self. In The Mayor of Casterbridge
(1886), Hardy gives the fullest nineteenth-century portrait of a man's
inner life—his rebellion and his suffering, his loneliness and jealousy,
his paranoia and despair, his uncontrollable unconscious. Henchard's
efforts, first to deny and divorce his passional self, and ultimately to
accept and educate it, involve him in a pilgrimage of 'unmanning'
which is a movement towards both self-discovery and tragic vulnerability. It is in the analysis of this New Man, rather than in the evaluation of
Hardy's New Women, that the case for Hardy's feminist sympathies may
be argued.

The Mayor of Casterbridge begins with a scene that dramatises the
analysis of female subjugation as a function of capitalism which Engels
had recently set out in The Origins of the Family, Private Property and the
State (1884): the auction of Michael Henchard's wife Susan at the fair at
Weydon-Priors. Henchard's drunken declaration that Susan is his 'goods'
is matched by her simple acceptance of a new 'owner', and her belief that
in paying five guineas in cash for her Richard Newson has legitimised
their relationship. Hardy never intended the wife-sale to seem natural or

3. A. O. J. Cockshut, Man and Woman: A Study of Love and the Novel 1740–1940 (London:
   Collins, 1977; New York: Oxford University Press, 1978), 128–29.

even probable, although he assembled in his Commonplace Book factual accounts of such occurrences from the *Dorset County Chronicle* and
the *Brighton Gazette*.[4] The auction is clearly an extraordinary event,
which violates the moral sense of the Casterbridge community when it is
discovered twenty years later. But there is a sense in which Hardy recognised the psychological temptation of such a sale, the male longing to
exercise his property rights over women, to free himself from their burden
with virile decision, to simplify his own conflicts by reducing them to 'the
ruin of good men by bad views' [9].

This element in the novel could never have been articulated by
Hardy's Victorian readers, but it has been most spiritedly expressed in
our century by Irving Howe:

> To shake loose from one's wife; to discard that drooping rag of a
> woman, with her mute complaints and maddening passivity; to
> escape not by a slinking abandonment but through the public sale
> of her body to a stranger, as horses are sold at a fair; and thus to
> wrest, through sheer amoral willfulness, a second chance out of
> life—it is with this stroke, so insidiously attractive to male fantasy,
> that *The Mayor of Casterbridge* begins.[5]

The scene, Howe goes on, speaks to 'the depths of common fantasy, it
summons blocked desires and transforms us into secret sharers. No matter what judgments one may make of Henchard's conduct, it is hard,
after the first chapter, simply to abandon him; for through his boldness
we have been drawn into complicity with the forbidden.'

Howe brings an enthusiasm and an authority to his exposition of
Henchard's motives that sweeps us along, although we need to be aware
both that he invents a prehistory for the novel that Hardy withholds, and
that in speaking of 'our' common fantasies, he quietly transforms the
novel into a male document. A woman's experience of this scene must
be very different; indeed, there were many sensation novels of the 1870s
and 1880s which presented the sale of women into marriage from the
point of view of the bought wife. In Howe's reading, Hardy's novel
becomes a kind of sensation-fiction, playing on the suppressed longings
of its male audience, evoking sympathy for Henchard because of his
crime, and not in spite of it.

In this exclusive concentration on the sale of the wife, however,
Howe, like most of Hardy's critics, overlooks the simultaneous event
which more profoundly determines Henchard's fate: the sale of the
child. Paternity is a central subject of the book, far more important than
conjugal love. Perhaps one reason why the sale of the child has been so

---

4. See Christine Winfield, 'Factual Sources of Two Episodes in *The Mayor of Casterbridge*',
   Nineteenth-Century Fiction, XXV (1970) 224–31.
5. Irving Howe, *Thomas Hardy* (London: Weidenfeld and Nicolson, 1968; New York, Macmillan,
   1967), 84.

consistently ignored by generations of Hardy critics is that the child is female. For Henchard to sell his son would be so drastic a violation of patriarchal culture that it would wrench the entire novel out of shape; but the sale of a daughter—in this case only a 'tiny girl'—seems almost natural. There may even be a suggestion that this too is an act insidiously attractive to male fantasy, the rejection of the wife who has only borne female offspring.

It is the combined, premeditated sale of wife and child which launches Henchard into his second chance. Orphaned, divorced, without mother or sisters, wife or daughter, he has effectively severed all his bonds with the community of women, and re-enters society alone—the new Adam, reborn, self-created, unencumbered, journeying southward without pause until he reaches Casterbridge. Henchard commits his life entirely to the male community, defining his human relationships by the male codes of money, paternity, honour, and legal contract. By his act Henchard sells out or divorces his own 'feminine' self, his own need for passion, tenderness, and loyalty. The return of Susan and Elizabeth-Jane which precipitates the main phase of the novel is indeed a return of the repressed, which forces Henchard gradually to confront the tragic inadequacy of his codes, the arid limits of patriarchal power. The fantasy that women hold men back, drag them down, drain their energy, divert their strength, is nowhere so bleakly rebuked as in Hardy's tale of the 'man of character'. Stripped of his mayor's chain, his master's authority, his father's rights, Henchard is in a sense unmanned; but it is in moving from romantic male individualism to a more complete humanity that he becomes capable of tragic experience. Thus sex-role patterns and tragic patterns in the novel connect.

According to Christine Winfield's study of the manuscript of *The Mayor of Casterbridge*, Hardy made extensive revisions in Chapter I. The most striking detail of the early drafts was that the Henchard family was originally composed of two daughters, the elder of whom was old enough to try to dissuade Susan from going along with the sale: "'Don't mother!' whispered the girl who sat on the woman's side. "Father don't know what he's saying."' On being sold to the sailor Newson, however, Susan takes the younger girl ('her favourite one') with her; Henchard keeps the other. Hardy apparently took his detail from the notice of a wife-sale in the *Brighton Gazette* for 25 May 1826: 'We understand they were country people, and that the woman has had two children by her husband, one of whom he consents to keep, and the other he throws in as a makeweight to the bargain.'[6]

Hardy quickly discarded this cruel opening, and in the final text he emphasises the presence and the sale of a single infant daughter. From

6. Quoted by Winfield, p. 226.

the beginning, she and her mother form an intimate unit, as close to each other as Henchard and his wife are separate. Susan speaks not to her husband, but to her baby, who babbles in reply; her face becomes alive when she talks to the girl. In a psychoanalytic study of Hardy, Charles K. Hofling has taken this bond between mother and daughter as the source of Henchard's jealous estrangement,[7] but all the signs in the text point to Henchard's dissociation from the family as his own choice. The personalities of husband and wife are evidenced in all the nuances of this scene, one which they will both obsessively recall and relive. Hardy takes pains to show us Henchard's rigid unapproachability, his body-language eloquent of rejection. In Henchard's very footsteps there is a 'dogged and cynical indifference personal to himself' [5]; he avoids Susan's eyes and possible conversation by 'reading, or pretending to read' [5] a ballad sheet, which he must hold awkwardly with the hand thrust through the strap of his basket. The scene is in marked contrast to Mrs Gaskell's opening in *Mary Barton*, for example, where fathers and brothers help to carry the infants; Hardy plays consciously against the reader's expectation of affectionate closeness. When Susan and Elizabeth-Jane retrace the journey many years later, they are holding hands, 'the act of simple affection' [17].

Henchard's refusal of his family antedates the passionate declaration of the auction, and it is important to note that such a sale has been premeditated or at least discussed between husband and wife. There are several references to previous threats: 'On a previous occasion when he had declared during a fuddle that he would dispose of her as he had done, she had replied that she would not hear him say that many times more before it happened, in the resigned tones of a fatalist' [15]. When Newson asks whether Susan is willing to go with him, Henchard answers for her: 'She is willing, provided she can have the child. She said so only the other day when I talked o't!' [12]. After the sale, Henchard tries to evade the full responsibility for his act by blaming it on an evening's drunkenness, a temporary breakdown in reason and control; he even blames his lost wife's 'simplicity' for allowing him to go through with the act: 'Seize her, why didn't she know better than bring me into this disgrace! . . . She wasn't queer if I was. 'Tis like Susan to show such idiotic simplicity' [15–16]. His anger and humiliation, none the less, cannot undo the fact that the bargain that was struck, and the 'goods' that were divided (Susan takes the girl, Henchard the tools) had been long contemplated. When it is too late, Henchard chiefly regrets his over-hasty division of property: 'She'd no business to take the maid—'tis my maid; and if it were the doing again she shouldn't have her!' [13].

7. Charles K. Hofling, 'Thomas Hardy and the Mayor of Casterbridge', *Comprehensive Psychiatry*, IX, (1968) 431.

In later scenes, Hardy gives Henchard more elaborated motives for the sale: contempt for Susan's ignorance and naiveté; and, as Henchard recalls on his first pilgrimage to Weydon-Priors, twenty-five years after the fair, his 'cursed pride and mortification at being poor' [240]. Financial success, in the mythology of Victorian manliness, requires the subjugation of competing passions. If it is marriage that has threatened the youthful Henchard with 'the extinction of his energies' [9], a chaste life will rekindle them. Henchard's public auction and his private oath of temperance are thus consecutive stages of the same rite of passage. Henchard's oath is both an atonement for his drunken surrender to his fantasies, and a bargain with success. In Rudyard Kipling's *The Man Who Would Be King* (1899), a similar 'contrack' is made, whereby Peachey Carnehan and Daniel Dravot swear to abjure liquor and women. When Dravot breaks his promise, they are exiled from their kingdom; so too will Henchard be expelled from Casterbridge when he breaks his vows. Save for the romance with Lucetta, in which he appears to play a passive role, Henchard is chaste during his long separation from his wife; he enjoys the local legend he has created of himself as the 'celebrated abstaining worthy' [29]; the man whose 'haughty indifference to the society of womankind, his silent avoidance of converse with the sex' [64] is well known. His prominence in Casterbridge is produced by the commercialised energies of sexual sublimation, and he boasts to Farfrae that 'being by nature something of a woman-hater, I have found it no hardship to keep mostly at a distance from the sex' [61]. There is nothing in Henchard's consciousness which corresponds to the aching melancholy of Hardy's poem 'He abjures love' (1883):

> At last I put off love,
>   For twice ten years
> The daysman of my thought,
>   And hope, and doing.

Indeed, in marrying Susan for the second time, Henchard forfeits something of his personal magic, and begins to lose power in the eyes of the townspeople; it is whispered that he has been 'captured and enervated by the genteel widow' [64].

Henchard's emotional life is difficult to define; in the first half of the novel, Hardy gives us few direct glimpses of his psyche, and soberly refrains from the kind of romantic symbolism employed as psychological notation by the Brontës and by Dickens—dreams, doubles, hallucinatory illnesses. But the very absence of emotion, the 'void' which Hardy mentions, suggests that Henchard has divorced himself from feeling, and that it is feeling itself which obstinately retreats from him as he doggedly pursues it. When J. Hillis Miller describes Henchard as a man 'driven by a passionate desire for full possession of some other person' and calls the

novel 'a nightmare of frustrated desire',[8] he misleadingly sugge
nature and intensity of Henchard's need is sexual. It is an absen
ing which Henchard looks to others to supply, a craving unfoc
liness rather than a desire towards another person. Henchard uoes not
seek possession in the sense that he desires the confidences of others; such
reciprocity as he requires, he coerces. What he wants is a 'greedy exclusiveness' [221], a title; and this feeling is stimulated by male competition.

Given Henchard's misogyny, we cannot be surprised to see that his
deepest feelings are reserved for another man, a surrogate brother with
whom he quickly contracts a business relationship that has the emotional overtones of a marriage. Henchard thinks of giving Farfrae a third
share in his business to compel him to stay; he urges that they should
share a house and meals. Elizabeth-Jane is the frequent observer of the
manly friendship between Henchard and Farfrae, which she idealises:

> She looked from the window and saw Henchard and Farfrae in the
> hay-yard talking, with that impetuous cordiality on the Mayor's part,
> and genial modesty on the younger man's, that was now so generally
> observable in their intercourse. Friendship between man and man;
> what a rugged strength there was in it, as evinced by these two. [75]

Yet Elizabeth-Jane is also an 'accurate observer' who sees that
Henchard's 'tigerish affection . . . now and then resulted in a tendency to domineer' [71]. It is a tigerish affection that does not respect that
other's separateness, that sets its own terms of love and hate. Farfrae's
passivity in this relationship is feminine at first, when he is constrained
by his economic dependence on Henchard. There is nothing homosexual in their intimacy; but there is certainly on Henchard's side an open,
and, he later feels, incautious embrace of homosocial friendship, an
insistent male bonding.[9] Success, for Henchard, precludes relationships
with women; male cameraderie and, later, contests of manliness must
take their place. He precipitately confides in Farfrae, telling him all the
secrets of his past, at a point when he is determined to withhold this
information from Elizabeth-Jane: 'I am not going to let her know the
truth' [63]. Despite Henchard's sincerity, the one-sidedness of the
exchange, his indifference to Farfrae's feelings if he can have his company, leads the younger man to experience their closeness as artificial,
and to resist 'the pressure of mechanized friendship' [79].

The community of Casterbridge itself has affinities with its Mayor
when it is first infiltrated by Farfrae and the women. Like Henchard, it

---

8. J. Hillis Miller, *Thomas Hardy: Distance and Desire* (London: Oxford University Press;
   Cambridge, Mass.: Harvard University Press, 1970), 147–48.
9. For a discussion of the homosexual implications of the relationship, see Dale Kramer, *Thomas
   Hardy: The Forms of Tragedy* (London: Macmillan; Detroit: Wayne State University Press,
   1975), 86–87. Kramer concludes that 'to stress the potentially sensational aspect of Henchard's
   character in this manner is to misunderstand seriously the reasons for the success of the novel
   as tragedy.'

pulls itself in, refuses contact with its surroundings. 'It is huddled all together', remarks Elizabeth-Jane when she sees it for the first time. The narrator goes on: 'Its squareness was, indeed, the characteristic which most struck the eye in this antiquated borough . . . at that time, recent as it was, untouched by the faintest sprinkle of modernism. It was compact as a box of dominoes. It had no suburbs—in the ordinary sense. Country and town met at a mathematical line' [23]. The 'rectangular frame' of the town recalls Hardy's descriptions of the perpendicularity of Henchard's face; entering Casterbridge Susan and Elizabeth-Jane encounter the 'stockade of gnarled trees', the town wall, part of its 'ancient defences', the 'grizzled church' whose bell tolls the curfew with a 'peremptory clang' [25]. All these details suggest Henchard, who is barricaded, authoritarian, coercive. He has become, as Christopher Coney tells the women, 'a pillar of the town' [29].

Deeply defended against intimacy and converse with women, Henchard is vulnerable only when he has been symbolically unmanned by a fit of illness and depression; his susceptibility to these emotional cycles (the more integrated Farfrae is immune to them) is evidence of his divided consciousness. His romance with Lucetta takes place during such an episode: 'In my illness I sank into one of those gloomy fits I sometimes suffer from, on account o' the loneliness of my domestic life, when the world seems to have the blackness of hell, and, like Job, I could curse the day that gave me birth' [61]. Again, when Henchard is living with Jopp, and becomes ill, Elizabeth-Jane is able to penetrate his solitude, and reach his affections. At these moments, his proud independence is overwhelmed by the woman's warmth; he is forced into an emotionally receptive passivity. Yet affection given in such circumstances humiliates him; he needs to demand or even coerce affection in order to feel manly and esteemed.

In health, Henchard determines the conditions of his relationships to women with minimal attention to their feelings. His remarriage to Susan is the product of 'strict mechanical rightness' [64]; his effort to substantiate the union, to give it the appearance of some deeper emotion, is typical of his withholding of self:

> Lest she should pine for deeper affection than he could give he made a point of showing some semblance of it in external action. Among other things he had the iron railings, that had smiled sadly in dull rust for the last eighty years, painted a bright green, and the heavily-barred, small-paned Georgian sash windows enlivened with three coats of white. He was as kind to her as a man, mayor, and churchwarden could possibly be. [67]

To Susan, his kindness is an official function, and although he promises her that he will earn his forgiveness by his future works, Henchard's behaviour to women continues to be manipulative and proprietary. He deceives Elizabeth-Jane in the uncomfortable masquerade of the second courtship; he has not sufficient respect for Susan to follow her instructions on the letter about her daughter's true parentage. When he wants Lucetta to marry him, he threatens to blackmail her; when he wants to get rid of Elizabeth-Jane he makes her a small allowance. He trades in women, with dictatorial letters to Farfrae, and lies to Newson, with an ego that is alive only to its own excited claims.

Having established Henchard's character in this way, Hardy introduces an overlapping series of incidents in the second half of the novel which reverses and negates the pattern of manly power and self-possession. These incidents become inexorable stages in Henchard's unmanning, forcing him to acknowledge his own human dependency and to discover his own suppressed or estranged capacity to love. The first of these episodes is the reappearance of the furmity-woman at Petty Sessions, and her public denunciation of Henchard. Placed centrally in the novel (in Chapter XXVIII), this encounter seems at first reading to have the arbitrary and fatal timing of myth; the furmity-woman simply appears in Casterbridge to commit her 'nuisance' and to be arraigned. But the scene in fact follows Henchard's merciless coercion of Lucetta into a marriage she no longer desires. This violation, carried out from rivalry with Farfrae rather than disappointed love, repeats his older act of aggression against human feeling. Thus the declaration of the furmity-woman, the public humbling of Henchard by a woman, seems appropriate. It is for drunk and disorderly behaviour, for disrespect to the church and for profanity that she is accused; and her revelation of Henchard's greater disorder is an effective challenge to the authority of patriarchal law. Hardy's narrative underlines the scene explicitly as forming the 'edge or turn in the incline of Henchard's fortunes. On that day—almost at that minute—he passed the ridge of prosperity and honour, and began to descend rapidly on the other side. It was strange how soon he sank in esteem. Socially he had received a startling fillip downwards; and, having already lost commercial buoyancy from rash transactions, the velocity of his descent in both aspects became accelerated every hour' [166]. The emphasis at this point is very much on Henchard's fortunes and his bankruptcy; although the furmity-woman's story spreads so fast that within twenty-four hours everyone in Casterbridge knows what happened at Weydon-Priors fair, the one person from whom Henchard has most assiduously kept the secret—Elizabeth-Jane—unaccountably fails to confront him with it. Indeed, Hardy seems to have forgotten to show her reaction; when she seeks him out it is only to forgive his harshness to her. Retribution for the auction thus comes as a public rather than a private shaming; and Henchard responds publicly with his dignified withdrawal as magistrate, and later, his generous performance in bankruptcy.

The next phase of Henchard's unmanning moves into the private sphere. Hearing of Lucetta's marriage to Farfrae, he puts his former threat of blackmail into action, tormenting her by reading her letters to her husband. Henchard cannot actually bring himself to reveal her name, to cold-bloodedly destroy her happiness; but Lucetta, investing him with a more implacable will than he possesses, determines to dissuade him, and so arranges a secret morning meeting at the Roman amphitheatre, which is far more successful than even she had dared to hope:

> Her figure in the midst of the huge enclosure, the unusual plainness of her dress, her attitude of hope and appeal, so strongly revived in his soul the memory of another ill-used woman who had stood there and thus in bygone days, had now passed away into her rest, that he was unmanned, and his breast smote him for having attempted reprisals on one of a sex so weak. [189–90]

'Unmanning' here carries the significance of enervation, of a failure of nerve and resolve; and also the intimation of sympathy with the woman's position. The scene is carefully constructed to repeat the earlier meeting in the arena, when the wronged Susan came to Henchard in all her weakness; Henchard's old feeling of supercilious pity for womankind in general was intensified by this suppliant appearing here as the double of the first' [190]. But Hardy does not allow us such simple sentiments; he intensifies the ironic complexities that make this meeting different. There is certainly a sense in which Lucetta is both touchingly reckless of her reputation, and weak in her womanhood; these elements will come together in the fatal outcome of the skimmington-ride, when her wrecked honour and her miscarriage provide the emotional and physical shocks that kill her. While the Victorian belief in the delicacy of pregnant women, and also the statistical realities of the maternal death rate, are behind this incident (no contemporary reader of *The Mayor of Casterbridge* found it difficult to believe), Hardy obviously intends it symbolically as a demonstration of female vulnerability.

But, in another sense, Henchard is still deceiving himself about women's weakness, and flattering himself about men's strength; his 'supercilious pity' for womankind is obtuse and misplaced. Lucetta's pathetic appearance, her plea of loss of attractiveness, is deliberately and desperately calculated to win his pity and to pacify his competitiveness. She is employing 'the only practicable weapon left her as a woman' in this meeting with her enemy. She makes her toilette with the intention of making herself look plain; having missed a night's sleep, and being pregnant ('a natural reason for her slightly drawn look') she manages to look prematurely aged. Skilled at self-production and self-promotion, Lucetta thus turns her hand successfully to this negative strategy, with the result that Henchard ceases to find her desirable, and 'no longer envied Farfrae his bargain'. She has transformed herself into a drooping rag; and Henchard is again eager to get away. Lucetta's cleverest stroke is to remove the stimulus to Henchard's sense of rivalry by telling him

that 'neither my husband nor any other man will regard me with interest long' [190]. Although he is defeated by a woman, Henchard's understanding of women is still constituted by a kind of patriarchal innocence;
he is ashamed of himself but for all the wrong reasons.

It is out of this unmanning, out of his disturbed self-esteem which
has been deprived of an enemy, that Henchard tries to reassert his legitimate authority, and rebuild his diminished stature, by invading the
welcoming ceremonies for the Royal Personage. Defiantly clad in 'the
fretted and weather-beaten garments of bygone years', Henchard
indeed stands out upon the occasion, and makes himself as prominent
and distinctive as Farfrae, who wears 'the official gold chain with great
square links, like that round the Royal unicorn' [201]. The scene is the
necessary preamble to the fight between the two men; Henchard's flag-
waving salute to Royalty is really a challenge to Farfrae, the lion against
the unicorn. He puts himself in the young mayor's path precisely in
order to be snubbed and driven back, to be inflamed so that he can
take his revenge in 'the heat of action'. The wrestling-match with
Farfrae is the central male contest of the novel—rivalries over business
and women resolved by hand-to-hand combat. But in mastering
Farfrae, even with one hand tied behind his back, Henchard is again
paradoxically unmanned, shamed, and enervated. The sense of
Farfrae's indifference to him, the younger man's resistance to even this
ultimate and violent coercion of passion, robs Henchard of the thrill
of his victory. Again, it is the apparently weaker antagonist who pre-
vails; and in the emotional crisis, roles are reversed so that Farfrae is
the winner. As for Henchard,

> The scenes of his first acquaintance with Farfrae rushed back upon
> him—that time when the curious mixture of romance and thrift in
> the young man's composition so commanded his heart that Farfrae
> could play upon him as on an instrument. So thoroughly subdued
> was he that he remained on the sacks in a crouching attitude,
> unusual for a man, and for such a man. Its womanliness sat tragi-
> cally on the figure of so stern a piece of virility. [207–8]

The rugged friendship between man and man, so impressive when seen
from a distance by Elizabeth-Jane, comes down to this regressive, almost
foetal, scene in the loft. Henchard has finally crossed over psychically
and strategically to the long-repressed 'feminine' side of himself—has
declared love for the first time to another person, and accepted the
meaning of that victory of the weak over the strong. Thus, as Dale
Kramer points out, 'In relation to the pattern of tragedy, the "feminine"
Henchard is by his own definition a weakened man.'[1] But again,
Henchard's surrender opens him for the first time to an understanding

1. Kramer, p. 87.

of human need measured in terms of feeling rather than property. In his hasty and desperate lie to Newson, Henchard reveals finally how dependent he has become on ties of love.

Thus the effigy which Henchard sees floating in Ten Hatches Hole, whence he has fled in suicidal despair after the encounter with Newson, is in fact the symbolic shell of a discarded male self, like a chrysalis. It is the completion of his unmanning—a casting-off of the attitudes, the empty garments, the facades of dominance and authority, now perceived by the quiet eye of Elizabeth-Jane to be no more than 'a bundle of old clothes' [225]. Returning home, Henchard is at last able to give up the tattered and defiant garments of his 'primal days', to put on clean linen. Dedicating himself to the love and protection of Elizabeth-Jane, he is humanly reborn.

The final section of the novel fulfils the implications of Henchard's unmanning in a series of scenes which are reversals of scenes in the first part of the book. It is Elizabeth-Jane who assumes ascendancy: 'In going and coming, in buying and selling, her word was law' [228]. He makes her tea with 'housewifely care' [219]. As the 'netted lion' [228], Henchard is forced into psychological indirection, to feminine psychological manoeuvres, because he does not dare to risk a confrontation: 'He would often weigh and consider for hours together the meaning of such and such a deed or phrase of hers, when a blunt settling question would formerly have been his first instinct' [229]. It is a humbling, and yet educative and ennobling apprenticeship in human sensitivity, a dependence, Hardy writes, into which he had 'declined (or, in another sense, to which he had advanced)' [230].

In his final self-imposed exile, Henchard carries with him mementoes of Elizabeth-Jane: 'gloves, shoes, a scrap of her handwriting, . . . a curl of her hair' [239]. Retracing his past, he has chosen to burden himself with reminders of womanhood, and to plot his journey in relation to a female centre. Even the circle he traces around the 'centripetal influence' [240] of his stepdaughter contrasts with the defended squareness of the Casterbridge he has left behind, the straight grain of masculine direction. Henchard's final pilgrimage, to Elizabeth-Jane's wedding, is, detail by detail, a reliving of the journey made by the women at the beginning of the novel. He enters the town for the last time as they entered at the first: the poor relation, the suppliant, the outsider. 'As a Samson shorn' [244] he timidly presents himself at the kitchen-door, and from the empty back-parlour awaits Elizabeth-Jane's arrival. As Susan and Elizabeth-Jane watched him preside over the meeting of the Council, so he now must watch his stepdaughter preside over her wedding-party. As Susan was overpowered by the sight of her former husband's glory, and wished only 'to go—pass away—die' [28], so is Henchard shamed and overwhelmed by Elizabeth-Jane's moral ascendancy. What is threatened and forgotten in the first instance comes to pass in the second—the rejected guest departs, and neither Elizabeth-Jane nor the reader sees him more.

In a sense which Hardy fully allows, the moral as well as the temporal victory of the novel is Elizabeth-Jane's. It is she to whom the concluding paragraphs are given, with their message of domestic serenity, their Victorian feminine wisdom of 'making limited opportunities endurable', albeit in 'a general drama of pain' [252]. Casterbridge, under the combined leadership of Elizabeth-Jane and Farfrae, is a gentled community, its old rough ways made civil, its rough edges softened. We might read the story of Henchard as a tragic taming of the heroic will, the bending and breaking of his savage male defiance in contest with a stoic female endurance. In such a reading, Henchard becomes a second Heathcliff, who is also overcome by the domestic power of a daughter-figure; like Heathcliff, Henchard is subdued first to the placidities of the grange, then to the grave.[2]

Yet this romantic and nostalgic reading would underestimate Hardy's generosity of imagination. Virginia Woolf, one of Hardy's earliest feminist critics, attributed the 'tragic power' of his characters to 'a force within them which cannot be defined, a force of love or of hate, a force which in the men is the cause of rebellion against life, and in the women implies an illimitable capacity for suffering.'[3] In Henchard the forces of male rebellion and female suffering ultimately conjoin; and in this unmanning Hardy achieves a tragic power unequalled in Victorian fiction. It may indeed be true that Hardy could not be accounted a feminist in the political terms of the 1880s, or the 1970s; but in *The Mayor of Casterbridge* the feminist critic can see Hardy's swerving from the bluff virility of the Rabelais Club, and the misogyny of Gosse, towards his own insistent and original exploration of human motivation. The skills which Henchard struggles finally to learn, skills of observation, attention, sensitivity, and compassion, are also those of the novelist; and they are feminine perhaps, if one contrasts them to the skills of the architect or the statesman. But it is because Hardy dares so fully to acknowledge this side of his own art, to pursue the feminine spirit in his man of character, that his hero, like the great heroines he would create in the 1890s, is more Shakespearean than Victorian.

2. Frederick R. Karl has suggested that Henchard's domination of the novel is equivalent to the 'all-powerful Heathcliff' in *Wuthering Heights*; 'The Mayor of Casterbridge: A New Fiction Defined', *Modern Fiction Studies*, VI (1960) 211.
3. Virginia Woolf, 'The Novels of Thomas Hardy', *The Common Reader: Second Series* (London: The Hogarth Press, 1932), 253.

406

GEORGE LEVINE

[Reversing the Real]†

* * *

Critics have long recognized that Henchard, in one way or another, *is* the world of *The Mayor of Casterbridge*. Like Frankenstein before him, he absorbs all external reality into his dream of the self. Technically, this means not only that every character and event in the novel relates direct-ly to Henchard, but that the more intensely one examines the novel, the more evident it is that every character in it reflects aspects of his enor-mous selfhood. As Victor Frankenstein is his monster's double, but also Clerval's, his mother's, his brother's, Walton's,[1] so Henchard is the dou-ble of Farfrae and Elizabeth-Jane, Jopp and Abel Whittle, Newson and Lucetta. As Victor moves with erratic repetitiveness from act to reaction, from aspiration to repentance, so Henchard enacts his self-division and Hardy projects that division on the landscape of his narrative. It is all done with the recklessness of conventional plausibility that marks goth-ic conventions, and yet it achieves a new sort of plausibility. For the large techniques of romance are incorporated here into the texture of a real-ism that allows every monstrous quirk its credible place in a social, his-torical, and geographical context belonging importantly to the conven-tions of realism. The landscape of the self in this novel, almost displaces the landscape of that hard, unaccommodating actual to the representa-tion of which the realist has always been dedicated. But self and other exist here in a delicate balance, and it is probably more appropriate to say that in *The Mayor of Casterbridge* Hardy makes overt the continuing and inevitable presence of romance in all realistic fiction.

We may take the remarkable first scene, in which Henchard sells his wife, as a perfect example of the way Hardy's narrative embodies the ten-sions between the conventions of realism and that of romance in style and substance, and the way it daringly asserts the presence of the uncommon in the common. The whole sequence confronts directly the problem of inventing satisfying ways to cope with the limiting pressures of the realist's contingent world on large human energies and aspiration. Exploiting the conventions of realism to free itself from the convention-al real, and at the risk both of alienating its readers by claiming kinship with great tragedy or mere sensationalism and of disrupting the life of its

† From George Levine, *The Realistic Imagination: English Fiction from Frankenstein to Lady Chatterley* (Chicago and London: University of Chicago Press, 1981), pp. 243–51. Reprinted by permission of the University of Chicago Press and the author. Page references have been changed to correspond to this Norton Critical Edition.
1. See U. C. Knoepflmacher, "Thoughts on the Aggression of Daughters," in U. C. Knoepflmacher and George Levine, eds., *The Endurance of Frankenstein* (Berkeley, 1979), pp. 88–119.

protagonists, Hardy's narrative implies both a new freedom of imagination and a new conception of human dignity. The freedom and the dignity are precisely in the willingness to take the risk—of uncommon art, of large hopes for renewal.

Strikingly, the human action begins in more than disenchantment, in utter fatigue with the Victorian realist's happy ending—marriage. By the time we meet the still young Henchard, he has been married for some time, and there is no romance in it. The ideal of the hearth, of the limited but satisfying life to which Dickens led his protagonists, in which Adam Bede resolves his career, has turned bitter. The married couple are not at home and content, but on the road and wearily out of touch with each other. We are here beyond the point to which George Eliot takes us when she begins *Middlemarch* with the fated marriage of Dorothea and Casaubon. For Hardy is not engaged in exploring the process by which marital ideals dissolve into sullen separateness and bitter disappointment. That is part of the progress of realism, to be sure. But Hardy begins with the given—with the assumption that marriage is bitterly disappointing and imprisoning. And that assumption, one might note, casts a suspicious shadow over the happy marriage between Farfrae and Elizabeth-Jane, with which the novel concludes.

Yet the scene is narrated with a realist's tender care for precision, an almost awkward quest for authenticity, which seduces us into trusting the narrator. Henchard, for example, is described as a man of "fine figure, swarthy, and stern in aspect; and he showed in profile a facial angle so slightly inclined as to be almost perpendicular" [5]. The language struggles to place the characters and define them against recognizable nonliterary categories, and implies that the narrator has a wide familiarity with the ways of agrarian laborers. He notes a typical "sullen silence," apparently bred of familiarity, between man and the woman. He describes Henchard's "measured, springless walk," which distinguishes him as a "skilled country man" rather than as a "general laborer" [5]. Later, he describes the furmity tent with the particularity customary to the realist: "At the upper end stood a stove, containing a charcoal fire, over which hung a large three-legged crock, sufficiently polished round the rim to show that it was made of bell metal" [8]. The narrator's omniscience is restrained: without entering the minds of his characters he implies a wise familiarity with their ways of thought and feeling: "But there was more in that tent than met the cursory glance; and the man, with the instinct of a perverse character, scented it quickly" [8]. Later, we are told that the "conversation took a high turn, as it often does on such occasions" [9]. Everything implies a quiet, worldly-wise narration of a story growing out of and repeating a thousand such untold stories buried in history, and whose connections with life outside the fiction will be constantly suggested. Peasant wisdom and bluntness mix with the larger historically saddened intelligence of the narrator. Yet within moments we discover that these devices have been working to force our acceptance of Henchard's sale of Susan: "It has been done elsewhere," says Henchard, "and why not here?" [12].

Just as the scene begins to burst the limits of the conventions of realism, and daringly requires comparison to the abrupt beginning of *King Lear*, so Henchard attempts to free himself from the limiting conditions of his life. Everything noted in the densely particular style suggests that he has been diminished by his context; the sullenness of his relation to a wife who has herself been ground down by "civilization" [6]; the "stale familiarity" [6] of their relationship; the "dogged and cynical indifference" [5] manifest in every movement and feature of the man. As we meet him plodding beside his wife, Henchard is (significantly) reading a ballad sheet, turning from the reality of his intimacy with her to a poet's dream of the uncommon. As he drinks, this partly defeated man is transformed, rising to "serenity," then becoming "jovial," then "argumentative," and finally "the qualities signified by the shape of his face, the occasional clench of his mouth, and the fiery spark of his dark eye, begin to tell in his conduct; he was overbearing—even brilliantly quarrelsome" [9]. The latent Henchard, released from the restrictions of convention and responsibility, becomes realized. He asserts the sense of his own power and is longing to be free to exercise it: "I'd challenge England to beat me in the fodder business; and if I were a free man again, I'd be worth a thousand pound before I'd done o't" [9].

In George Eliot, this boast would be deflated immediately, but here the larger wish becomes father to the fact, and the realistically created scene slides into romance in which Henchard is hero. Within a few pages, by a process we are not allowed to observe, Henchard has become mayor of Casterbridge. But he is clearly a man who, however firmly his will keeps him under control (as it keeps him from drinking for twenty-one years), acts outside the limits that confine ordinary people. He seems able to withstand the pressures that impinge on other lives, yet all of his life in reality curls around the monstrous secret of the sale of his wife. As Frankenstein hides from his monster, attempts to rejoin the community and conceal his great dream and his great mistake, so Henchard hides from the reality so vividly and abruptly rendered in the first scene. All of the novel grows—as all of *Frankenstein* grows—from the narrative of the inevitable reemergence of that hidden fact, that illicit thrust at freedom, into the community in which Henchard seeks to find his peace. And as with Frankenstein, but more richly and complexly, we find that the protagonist in the community is ultimately only reenacting his forbidden scene. In Casterbridge Henchard seeks with respectability to assert the absolute power of his self over a constricting and contingent world. The pressures he denied at the start avenge themselves on him with a completeness far beyond what the logic of his situation would require. But once set in a world carefully defined in the language of social analysis and historical tradition, once seen in the context of delicate financial and human transactions, Henchard must be destroyed. The man of large feeling and deep need—the hero of romance—cannot survive in the context of a carefully particularized society. Henchard is incapable of compromise. Neither success nor failure can be ordinary for him. And since the conventions the novel adopts make failure the only possibility for the largely aspiring man, it must be an extraordinary failure. The novel concentrates on his losses, juxtaposes his large ambitions to the moderate ones of Farfrae, and conspires to keep him from the comforts of the real. Henchard is his fate; and the narrative line transcends the limits of realism by cooperating with Henchard's refusal to compromise. All coincidences conspire to make things worse than the compromising conditions of realism would demand.

In retrospect, one feels, they are not quite coincidences, but Henchard writ large. His domination of the book, uncharacteristic of Hardy's work as a whole, forces us to see his hand—or spirit—everywhere. He evokes all the characters whose coincidental appearances play so important a part in the novel; and with each of these, at some point, he reverses roles. In the third chapter, for example, we learn of Susan and Elizabeth-Jane's search for Henchard, which brings them to Casterbridge and reopens his past; not long before we heard of Henchard's search for them, itself significantly cut short by "a certain shyness of revealing his conduct" [17]. Again, Henchard is responsible for persuading Farfrae, who will end the novel as the new mayor of Casterbridge, to remain in the town. Later, Lucetta, who had nursed him in an illness, arrives in order to marry Henchard, and he must repay her kindness and reverse their early relationship. The furmity woman comes to town to expose him and, in the powerful scene in which she is brought to trial before him, she argues: "he's no better than I, and has no right to sit there in judgment upon me." Henchard agrees, "I'm no better than she" [154]. Even Jopp, who is responsible for the information leading to the skimmity ride, arrives in town just after Farfrae to take the job that Henchard has offered to Farfrae; by the end, Henchard is living where Jopp lives. Henchard creates the world which is to destroy him—even becomes that world.

The remarkable force of the idea that, as Hardy quotes Novalis, "character is fate" [89] is worked out with a minuteness that seems to translate the whole world of the novel into a psychic landscape. Farfrae's dramatic entrance into the novel, for example, corresponds precisely to the moment when Henchard, defending himself against the demand that he replace the bad wheat he has sold, says "If anybody will tell me how to turn grown wheat into wholesome wheat, I'll take it back with pleasure. But it can't be done" [31]. Farfrae arrives and does it; and he stays because of Henchard's overwhelming emotional demands on him: "It's providence!" Farfrae says, "should anyone go against it?" [51]. Henchard makes "providence."

More important for a full sense of the daring of Hardy's achievement in his challenge of realist conventions is the way he takes pains to call attention to the creaking mechanics of his novel. It is as though, if we had not noticed how remarkable, unlikely or chancy an event has been, Hardy wants to make sure that we do not find it plausible or common-place. When Farfrae turns up, the narrator remarks, "He might possibly have passed without stopping at all, or at most for half a minute to glance in at the scene, had not his advent coincided with the discussion on corn and bread; in which event this history had never been enacted" [31]. Here Hardy turns what might very well have been taken as a donnée of the plot into a coincidence upon which the whole plot must turn. As the story unfolds, Henchard's impulsive energy can be seen to be responsi-ble for every stage of his eventual self-obliteration. He too impulsively reveals his past to Farfrae; he too intensely punishes Abel Whittle; he too ambitiously tries to outdo Farfrae in setting up a fair for the holidays; he too hastily dismisses Farfrae and too angrily responds to Farfrae's deter-mination to set up his own business; he cuts off the courtship between Farfrae and Elizabeth-Jane though, as the narrator remarks, "one would almost have supposed Henchard to have had policy to see that no better *modus vivendi* could be arrived at with Farfrae than by encouraging him to become his son-in-law" [88]. Later he too hastily buys corn and then far too hastily sells it. He opens Susan's letter about Elizabeth-Jane at precisely that moment when being recognized as Elizabeth-Jane's father, "the act he had prefigured for weeks with a thrill of pleasure," was to become "no less than a miserable insipidity. . . . His reinstation of her mother had been chiefly for the girl's sake, and the fruition of the whole scheme was such dust and ashes as this" [99].

The novel even implies that it is Henchard's responsibility that Susan dies. After reading a letter from Lucetta, Henchard says, "Upon my heart and soul, if ever I should be left in a position to carry out that marriage with thee, I *ought* to do it—I *ought* to do it, indeed!" The narrator com-ments, "The contingency he had in mind was, of course, the death of Mrs. Henchard" [91]. And the narrative immediately records the death of Mrs. Henchard. It is this kind of thing—possibly to be described as simple coincidence, possibly to be explained in naturalistic terms—which finally gives to *The Mayor of Casterbridge* its distinctive shape and power. Every detail of the action seems to feed into Henchard's being, and every detail of the text requires that we accept it only if we are will-ing to accept the extravagant with the plausible, or as part of it.

George Eliot had tried, by subtle allusion and careful elaboration of plot, to make the ordinary reverberate with mythic force. But in Hardy, sometimes with, sometimes without mythic allusions, the plot itself makes the real mythic. Henchard, the tragic king, responsible both for his kingdom and the sin that blights its wheat and him, must move with ironic absoluteness to death. And the movement toward death is prefigured early. "Why the deuce did I come here!" Henchard asks himself as he finds himself in the place of public execution after he has discovered, because of his refusal to heed the instructions on the envelope, that Elizabeth-Jane is not his daughter [98]. "The momentum of his character knew no patience," the narrator later remarks [145]. That momentum moves him, past all possibility of compromise, to disaster. He is saved from suicide after the skimmity ride only by the magical appearance of his effigy in the water. When the furmity woman returns, Henchard has no instinct toward the deception which would keep his long-held secret quiet. By attempting to kill Farfrae he not only finally alienates the last man who can save him, but makes it impossible for Farfrae to believe him when he attempts to inform Farfrae of Lucetta's illness. Again, his relation to Farfrae is rather like Oedipus' relation to the careful Creon. Thus, since he carelessly gave Jopp Lucetta's letters he is responsible for Lucetta's death in two ways.

Finally, his last two self-assertive acts complete his self-annihilation. He breaks into the royal visit, demanding the recognition which he had lost and forcing another scuffle with Farfrae. And when Newson returns to claim Elizabeth-Jane, Henchard unhesitatingly (driven by those same impulses which led him to sell his wife) asserts that she is dead; his final act of deceit loses for him his last possibility of ordinary survival.

His last acts have about them the quality, not of a modern novel, but of a pagan, religious ritual of self-annihilation. He refuses to plead for himself to Elizabeth-Jane: "Among the many hindrances to such a pleading not the least was this, that he did not sufficiently value himself to lessen his sufferings by strenuous appeal or elaborate argument" [246]. Elizabeth-Jane discovers that "it was part of his nature to extenuate nothing, and to live on as one of his own worst accusers". She then goes out to look for Henchard. We find that, to the last, the power of his being draws people after him. Elizabeth-Jane and Farfrae seek him; Abel Whittle against Henchard's command, follows him, and aids him as he can. Henchard walks until he can walk no more and ends in a hovel (the whole scene deliberately and daringly constructed to recall King Lear and Edgar in the storm) by writing his will—and the will wills his total obliteration:

"MICHAEL HENCHARD'S WILL.
"That Elizabeth-Jane Farfrae be not told of my death, or made to
    grieve on account of me.
"& that I be not bury'd in consecrated ground.
"& that no sexton be asked to toll the bell.
"& that nobody is wished to see my dead body.
"& that no murners walk behind me at my funeral.
"& no flours be planted on my grave.

"& that no man remember me.
"to this I put my name. MICHAEL HENCHARD." [251]

The irony of "willing" his self-obliteration is powerful, complex, and inescapable. Even the putting of his name in upper-case letters becomes an important part of the effect. For Henchard's last written words are the name he is asking to obliterate—and boldly imprinted. The annihilation he asks is in excess of the possible, and so by a wonderful and moving irony, Henchard effects in death what he always fell short of in life—the dominance of his name. It is as though Henchard has stumbled onto the modernist criticism that reminds us of the peculiar status of language. It cannot quite name what it names; it speaks only of itself. It is a fact in the world, but not a representation of it. Henchard becomes here the absolute self of the fiction he created of his life and of the world. He ends, like the late-century writers who had, in effect, given up on the ideals of the Victorian writers speaking to their audiences and attempting to move the world. Since he cannot transform the ideal into the real, he transforms the real into the ideal.

In death, Henchard takes us as far as this novel can to the self-anni-hilating consequences of the contradictions and failures of the realist ideal. But in the last chapters, the narrator finally extends to Farfrae, that mixed sort of protagonist of realistic fiction, the kind of irony to which he could have been vulnerable throughout the novel. Everywhere, of course, Farfrae acts so as to represent a practical alternative to Henchard's egoist passion for the absolute. The final complex of alter-natives and doublings comes when Henchard arrives at the wedding feast, like the ancient mariner, an uninvited guest with a monstrous, Frankensteinian tale he might tell. But he is mute, and hears instead Donald's voice "giving strong expression to a song of his dear native country that he loved so well as never to have revisited" [244]. And yet here is Henchard, actually "revisiting" his home, although he had intended to flee it forever. It is Henchard, not Farfrae, who sentimental-ly leaves the canary; and it is at this point that Farfrae is described as "not the least indisposed" to try to find Henchard, but largely because he has never cared enough either to hate or to love him. For a moment, that is, we can almost say that romance is parodying realism, that it is, through Hardy, having its revenge on an art that has attempted to drain all excess from experience and to subject human nature to the rules of common sense and the inevitable contingencies of ordinary life.

But the last word in the novel belongs to Elizabeth-Jane, a figure who does not fit easily into any of the patterns I have been suggesting apply to the novel, and one who seems rather at home in the world of realistic conventions that Henchard's narrative implicitly mocks. Elizabeth-Jane provides the only other perspective from which we see a large part of the experience, and despite her obvious littleness in relation to Henchard, she is a character more impressively drawn and more important than she is generally given credit for. Although she never surrenders to her impulses or to her needs, she is not, as I have already suggested, simply a Farfrae. If Farfrae, in supplanting Henchard in every detail of his life, in fact continues the life of the Henchard who is excessively sensitive to the demands of respectability, Elizabeth-Jane, herself entangled in respectability, becomes the most authentic commentator on Henchard's experience. Her heart remains always in hiding. It stirs momentarily for Henchard's grand misguided attempts at mastery. But in her quiet submission to the movements of the novel's narrative, she becomes an expression of the way in which "happiness was but the occasional episode in a general drama of pain" [252]. By accepting this view, staying protected within the limits of respectability and not rejoicing too much when good fortune comes, she survives to find "tranquility" and to forget the Henchard whose death brought her vision. She is the best sort of realistic audience to a tragic drama.

Her preoccupation with respectability indicates her acceptance of the limits society imposes on action and on dreams, but with her, clearly, the acceptance is an act of self-protection. There is something in Elizabeth-Jane of Hardy's own tentativeness, for while, in Henchard, Hardy ambitiously projects the passions of a large ego beyond the limits of conventional fiction, as, one imagines, he himself would have liked to do, the narrative voice in which he tells the story has something of Elizabeth-Jane's own reserve, and of the wisdom Elizabeth-Jane has achieved by the end of the novel. Henchard is Hardy's monstrous fantasy: but he must, like the monster, be destroyed. Thus, it is through Elizabeth-Jane that Hardy allows us to return to the conventions of realism with a new understanding of their importance and of their tenuousness. Elizabeth-Jane makes us aware that it is not possible any longer to imagine the world as fundamentally accessible to the commonsense structures and language of earlier realists, that behind the veneer of society and quiet movement of ordinary life, there lies the "unforeseen," the continuing pain, the irrational intensities of nature and human nature.

Elizabeth-Jane's ultimate vision is a consequence of the experience of disaster. It embodies the wish in art that Hardy seems to have feared to enact in life. The only way to overcome the "worst" that lies beneath all human experience is to confront it intensely. Ironically, what Elizabeth-Jane arrives at is, in effect, the ideology of realism. She has learned and she teaches "the secret . . . of making limited opportunities endurable; which she deemed to consist in the cunning enlargement, by a species of microscopic treatment, of those minute forms of satisfaction that offer themselves to everybody not in positive pain" [252]. We emerge from the world of The Mayor of Casterbridge, in which the balances of fictional reality have all been reversed and in which, by the sheer force of narrative intensity, the conventions of realism are found wanting weighed against the monstrous energies of human nature, with a sense that the compromises of realism are after all essential. They do not, we see, adequately describe reality; they are modern disguises of realities that, ironically, belong to far more conventional literature; but they are conditions for our survival. Elizabeth-Jane does not allow herself to feel the pressure of Henchard's selfhood as we feel it in his bold concluding signature. Instead, she sensibly (and realistically) follows Henchard's literal instructions on the grounds "that the man who wrote them meant what he said" [251]. But in his life, he had rarely done what he "meant."

Realism survives in Hardy, not as a program for writing fiction, but as a discipline to be learned in the containment of the monstrous and the self-divided energies that make of mankind such an anomaly in a hostile universe.

WILLIAM GREENSLADE

Degenerate Spaces[†]

* * * In *The Mayor of Casterbridge* (1886) and the novels which followed it, a complex landscape, new to Victorian fiction, made the 'urbanising' of rural life show through.

It is a landscape shaped by a construction of difference; by a magnification of divisions between the normative and the 'other', marking out boundaries between the healthy and the polluted, the respectable and disreputable, between the 'official' and subversive class formations and social groups, and the prospect of these boundaries being transgressed. Such meanings shape Hardy's representation of the social space of 'Casterbridge', his *urbs in rure*.

Midway through the novel, Michael Henchard, the unemployed haytrusser who has risen to prosperous corn factor and town mayor, is descending a steep slope of economic decline. Declared bankrupt, he stands at the lower of the two bridges which Hardy precisely distinguishes as gravitation points of two very different groups of social and economic failures. Henchard falls into the category of *'misérables . . . of a politer stamp'*,[1]—the glance at Hugo is deliberate.[2] These include 'bankrupts, hypochondriacs, persons who were what is called "out of a situation" from fault or lucklessness, the inefficient of the professional

---

† From William Greenslade, *Degeneration, Culture and the Novel 1880–1940* (Cambridge: Cambridge University Press, 1994), pp. 54–64. Reprinted with the permission of Cambridge University Press. References to this Norton Critical Edition are given in brackets after the author's original citations.
1. Thomas Hardy, *The Mayor of Casterbridge* (2 vols. 1886; repr. London: Macmillan, 1974), p. 248 [170]. Subsequent references are incorporated in the text.
2. See John Goode, *Thomas Hardy: The Offensive Truth* (Oxford: Basil Blackwell, 1988), p. 91.

class . . . The eyes of this species were mostly directed over the parapet upon the running water below' (248)[170]. Farfrae, now in every way Henchard's vanquisher, drives up and Henchard takes the opportunity of reminding him of the social symbolism of the situation:

> I am going where you were going to a few years ago, when I prevented you and got you to bide here. Tis turn and turn about isn't it? Do ye mind how we stood like this in the Chalk Walk when I persuaded 'ee to stay? You then stood without a chattel to your name, and I was master of the house in Corn Street. But now I stand without a stick or a rag, and the master of that house is you. (250)[171]

That earlier Chalk Walk meeting at the top part of the town is recalled: 'The young man's hand remained steady in Henchard's for a moment or two. He looked over the fertile country that stretched beneath them, then backward along the shaded walk reaching to the top of the town' (94)[51]. As the men shake hands, the configuration of the landscape offers, in a moment of poise, the possibilities for both of them. Hardy's use of place resonates with personal and social significance. Henchard's descent, when mayor, back down into Casterbridge with Farfrae is proleptic of his passage from the prosperity of Corn Street down to the low-lying bridge. Excluded from the town houses higher up, he stands incongruously within the slum domain at Durnover, the parish which contains Mixen Lane, 'a back slum of the town', as Hardy puts it, 'the *pis aller* of Casterbridge domiciliation'.[3] And Henchard's re-employment of the morally bankrupt Jopp, who has gravitated to the Mixen Lane community, is itself a 'last resort' to wrest back from Farfrae his financial hegemony.

Mixen Lane constitutes a memorable and vividly realised social space in the novel.

> Mixen Lane was the Adullam of all the surrounding villages. It was the hiding-place of those who were in distress, and in debt, and in trouble of every kind. Farm-labourers and other peasants, who combined a little poaching with their farming, and a little brawling and bibbing with their poaching, found themselves sooner or later in Mixen Lane. Rural mechanics too idle to mechanize, rural servants too rebellious to serve, drifted or were forced into Mixen Lane.
>
> The lane and its surrounding thicket of thatched cottages stretched out like a spit into the moist and misty lowland. Much that was sad, much that was low, some things which were baneful, could be seen in Mixen Lane. Vice ran freely in and out certain of

---

3. There is an echo here of John Morley's essay "Of the Possible Utility of Error," in *On Compromise* (1866), where he considers the view that "the history of mankind is a huge *pis aller* just as our present society is; a prodigious wasteful experiment." *On Compromise* (Thinker's Library: London: Watts and Co., 1933), p. 46.

the doors in the neighbourhood; recklessness dwelt under the roof
with the crooked chimney; shame in some bow windows; theft (in
times of privation) in the thatched and mud-walled houses by the
sallows. Even slaughter had not been altogether unknown here.
(278)[192–93]

This is indeed where the 'refuse' of the community is consigned. A
'mixen' is a dungheap, and so this nomenclature enforces the identification between these down-and-outs with the nether regions of town, social
order, and human body—all that is rejected, disposable, repressed: it finds
a graphic synecdoche in Henry Mayhew's description of the inmates of an
'Asylum for the Houseless' in London, Labour and the London Poor where
the visitor 'is overcome with a sense of the vast heap of social refuse—the
mere human street-sweepings—the great living mixen—that is destined,
as soon as the spring returns, to be strewn far and near over the land, and
serve as manure to the future crime-crops of the country.'[4]

Yet Hardy gives us a more variegated and clear-sighted picture. His
dispossessed are not reducible merely to the waste matter of the social
order, we have rather a diversity of types and of their motivation. While
there is certainly degraded behaviour—'vice', 'shame', 'theft', 'slaughter'—there is also the diversity of circumstances which makes people
vulnerable to the social process—'debt', 'brawling and bibbing', a refusal
to conform to the disciplines of work and conduct. Hardy's allusion to
the cave of Adullam is surely meant to elicit sympathy for the plight of
those who like David (and those that sought his company in their trouble) have fled to the cave for solace from Saul's anger.[5]

Mixen Lane also harbours a more respectable class which has fallen
on hard times: 'families from decayed villages . . . of that once bulky,
but now nearly extinct, section of village society called 'liviers' or life-
holders—copyholders and others' (279)[194]. While both are consigned
to the same disreputable territory, Hardy distinguishes between the
respectable tradesmen, uprooted from a traditional and legally sanc-
tioned way of life, and the small-town proletariat with their deviant culture. If the respectable inhabitants wanted to move on and out, there is
little sign that the rest would wish to do so, since they have evolved their
alternative traditions, based on a cunning mutual aid. The 'rusty-jointed
executors of the law' (304)[213] prove to be no match for this efficiently organised sub-culture whose members can finely judge how far to step
outside the law without incurring its penalties. Mixen Lane is literally
lawless.

The idea of the 'no-go' area, with its long history, has considerable
imaginative appeal for Hardy. These areas were traditional sanctuaries

4. Henry Mayhew, London, Labour, and the London Poor, III. 429, cited by A. Susan Williams,
   The Rich Man and the Diseased Poor (London: Macmillan, 1987), p. 92.
5. See Ian Gregor's note to his edition of Hardy, The Mayor of Casterbridge (London: Macmillan,
   1974), p. 368.

for those perceived by the authorities to be a source of threat—the destitute poor, beggars and vagrants. But these 'no-go' areas were also means of containment—the only form of control where the rule of law was either unenforceable or tacitly suspended. Such areas—'suburbs' or 'rookeries'—were from mediaeval times beyond the reach of corporation authority. Indeed up to the eighteenth century the city 'fed harassed thieves into 'sanctuaries' which sometimes gave freedom from arrest'.[6] The early nineteenth-century city still had such sanctuaries, Angel Meadow, for one, 'the lowest, most filthy, most unhealthy and most wicked locality in Manchester', according to the *Morning Chronicle* of 1850,[7] or 'China' in Merthyr Tydfil, described in an 1847 report as 'a mere sink of thieves and prostitutes such as unhappily constitutes an appendage to every large town' and a 'Welsh Alsatia'.

The sanctuary of 'Alsatia' (like Alsace, debatable land) had originally been a precinct for law-breakers and debtors in Whitefriars in London. But as one observer recorded in 1860, 'the city of cadgers is not what it was . . . the introduction of a police station in the immediate vicinity' changed the lawless character of this once notorious district: 'formerly its boundaries were lawless like Alsatia . . . it was a refuge for the desperate, the thief, the cadger and the prostitute'.[8] Mayhew, in the 1860s, also noted St Giles and its decline over twenty years.[9] With a unified police force established in London by 1839, and county forces made obligatory in 1856, these areas of sanctuary were being steadily reduced.[1] As the metropolis developed so did its moral topography. According to Dyos and Reeder, the term 'slum', originally a room of low repute, was extended by Pierce Egan in 1821 to 'back slums' which now comprehended 'low, unfrequented parts of the town', and thence to 'everyday use'.[2] The massive schemes of slum clearance, involving elaborate road building programmes from the 1860s (many of them designed precisely to open up and destroy the rookeries) aggravated the slum problem, by driving the poor out to other areas of the city.[3]

But testimony from Charles Booth would suggest that in the London of the 1880s the 'sanctuary' was still a powerful, if more efficiently policed, presence. Among his class A (the lowest) there were those who resisted

6. Erving Goffman, *Asylums* (1961; repr. Harmondsworth: Penguin, 1968), p. 209.
7. Raphael Samuel, "Comers and Goers," in H. J. Dyos and Michael Wolff (eds.) *The Victorian City: Images and Realities* (2 vols. London: Routledge, 1973), I. 123–60 (p. 126).
8. *Ibid.*, p. 126.
9. See Renton Nicholas, *Autobiography* (1860), pp. 262–3, cited by Gareth Stedman Jones, "Working Class Culture and Working Class Politics in London 1870–1900: Notes on the Remaking of a Working Class," *Journal of Social History*, 7 (4) (1974), p. 470; see also J. J. Tobias, *Crime and Industrial Society in the Nineteenth Century* (London: Batsford, 1967), pp. 24–7, 13–5, 176–7.
1. Samuel, "Comers and Goers," p. 126.
2. See Tobias, *Crime and Industrial Society*, p. 232. The multitude of seasonal fairs were also frequented by the migratory and the deviant—from Ben Jonson's *Bartholomew Fair* to Hardy's seasonal fair at Weyhill and to Howard Brenton's *Epsom Downs*.
3. See H. J. Dyos and D. A. Reeder, "Slums and Suburbs," in *The Victorian City*, I. 362–3.

'the efforts of philanthropy or order'. Their 'instinct of self-preservation seeks some undisturbed sanctuary where they can still herd together, and, secured by the mutual protection of each other's character for evil, keep respectability at bay'.[4] Allowing such a class to colonise a territory was to be avoided at all costs: 'no sooner do they make a street their own', says Booth, 'than it is ripe for destruction and should be destroyed'.[5]

The emotive potential of the 'Alsatia' is mobilised in a novel by Lucas Malet (Mary Kingsley, 1852–1931), *Colonel Enderby's Wife* (1885), which explores the disruptive effects of inherited degeneracy on an established county family. One scene describes the philanthropic Mrs Farrel venturing into the dangerous slum:

> [She] took her way by back streets to a quarter of Tullingworth that lies across the river, along the low ground between the canal and a range of dreary brickfields. This region presented a marked contrast to the rest of the smart, pleasure-loving little town. It is a moral Alsatia, to which, by the law of social gravitation, all the human refuse of the place finds its melancholy way. Mean one-storied houses open on to narrow, black wharves and ugly cinder-paths, where bargemen and labourers loiter at dreary corners, and ragged shrill-voiced children angle for sluggish minnows in the slimy water, while the smoke and stench of the burning bricks fill the thick air. Dirty little shops maintain a feeble existence, with an attenuated show of attraction behind the panes of their dim windows. Only the public-house rises prosperous, cheerful, defiant above the dingy squalor of unpaved streets and lanes. Such places are altogether too common on the outskirts of even flourishing well-to-do places like Tullingworth for it to be incumbent on one to make much fuss over them.[6]

Here is a clearly demarcated setting out of social and moral space. It turns on a simple binary opposition, 'a marked contrast' between normative and 'other', between the 'smart pleasure-loving town', and a region of 'human refuse'. A standard figure of popular Darwinism, exploiting the language of fitness, informs the opposition. The 'dirty little shops' maintain a 'feeble existence', on the outskirts of the 'flourishing' town; only the morally questionable pub offers an ironic degenerate fitness. The promise of life and energy is everywhere foreshortened—the offerings of the shops 'attenuated', the minnows 'sluggish'.

4. Charles Booth, *Life and Labour of the People in London*, 17 vols. (London: Macmillan, 1902–03), I. 174.
5. *Ibid.*, I. 174.
6. Lucas Malet [Mary Kingsley], *Colonel Enderby's Wife* (3 vols. London: Kegan Paul Trench, 1885), II. 299–300. The symbolic passage of the female philanthropist through the slum appears in an earlier novel, but without degenerationist overtones. The heroine of Rhoda Broughton's *Not Wisely, but Too Well* (3 vols., 1867; repr. London: Cassell, 1967), Kate Chester, who nurses a "mortal fear of men of the lower orders" (178), carries "a philanthropic basket on her arm" (162), and enters "a narrow bricked passage . . . down into the region of back slums and alleys, where the sun has far too good taste to show its grand kingly face" (104).

But this vision of marked contrasts is equivocal, in that both the healthy and the diseased find their symbolic inversion. Just as the 'region' is degenerately fit, so the morally and socially normative Tullingworth is made sick by its organic relationship with its degenerate suburb. Moreover the spatial relationship between the two is uncertain. At the opening of the description the danger posed by the *terra incognita* is strongly marked (as it has to be in the standard rite of passage of the urban explorer), the slum appears distant and separate from the town out of which Mrs Farrel walks. Yet by the end of the passage this region's proximity is foregrounded with the admission that such a parasitical relationship with prosperity is 'altogether too common'.

Hardy, too, is caught up in the contradictions offered by the idea of urban degeneration when he invokes a truly Spencerian organic image to describe Mixen Lane's relationship to the body of Casterbridge. It is, he remarks, 'a mildewed leaf in the sturdy and flourishing Casterbridge plant' (278)[193]. The hold exerted by such organic tropes is tenacious indeed, and here rather leads Hardy astray, since the Casterbridge he actually renders offers a different way of seeing. Many of the denizens of Mixen Lane bear witness to the fact that Casterbridge does not flourish for everyone. This Spencerian Darwinism is caught napping by the clarity of his social vision, which pulls against the naturalistic determinism. For the passive, intransitive way in which the blighted are seen by this ideology is actually contested within the text itself: there is an alternative ethic available to Hardy, self-determining, anarchic and resistant to such naturalistic incorporation.

None the less the homologies between these descriptions from two novels, published within months of each other, are quite striking. In both we find the blighted leaf on the 'flourishing' town: an area morally tainted on the outskirts of a town on low ground, cut off here by a river. The river in *The Mayor* marks the dividing line (which the poacher has to cross between 'moor' and 'tenements') where the process of gravitation (we recall Hardy's river image in the 'Dorsetshire Labourer' essay) figures the economic and moral descent of 'human refuse', as if being swept down by, and further polluting, an already dirty stream.

As an image and repository of degeneracy, the polluted river has a central place in nineteenth-century writing about the city. In *The Condition of the Working Class* Engels had described the 'coal-black stinking' river Irk, 'full of filth and garbage' which it deposits on the 'lower-lying bank . . . out of whose depths bubbles of miasmatic gases constantly rise' to 'give forth a stench that is unbearable'. The river takes 'the total entirety of the liquid wastes from nearby tanneries, dye-works, bone mills and gasworks' together with contents of 'the adjacent sewers and privies'.[7]

7. Frederich Engels, *The Condition of the Working-Class in England* (1844; repr. Oxford: Basil Blackwell, 1958), cited by Steven Marcus, "Reading the Illegible," in *The Victorian City*, I. 257–76 (p. 267).

Rivers, notes Anthony Wohl, were an 'easy solution' to the mounting problem of 'human and industrial filth' of this kind, which reformers saw as the major cause of death.[8] In Gissing's *Demos* (1886) the stinking Regent's canal which runs through north London '*maladetta e sventura-ta fossa*—stagnating in utter foulness',[9] marks a boundary (so important for the post-Darwinian city) between areas of respectability and of ill-repute: it divides the 'mean and spirit-broken leisure of dwelling houses' to the north, from the 'region of malodorous market streets . . . facto-ries, timber yards' to the south. Here the pavements are trodden by 'working folk of the coarsest type, the corners and lurking-holes showing destitution at its ugliest'.[1] Gissing's previous novel *A Life's Morning*, writ-ten the previous year, 1885 (but not published until 1888), offers a stream derived from 'an impure source' as one index of a pervasive blighted landscape—which is the more striking because it is rural heath-land.[2] The dividing river cuts off the 'official' world of the authorial observer from the *terra incognita* in which the values of order, propriety and respectable morality are symbolically inverted, beyond the terms of civilisation, but not beyond its discourses of appropriation. The hideous fascination of the 'other' at the same time sustained the comfortable sense of civic virtue.

The threat from unofficial space in its symbolic configuration, imaged in terms of heights of a city terrorised by the depths, is recalled by the Victorian circus showman and celebrity 'Lord' George Sanger. As an old man he looked back to the 1840s to tell of a destructive raid on his father's circus troupe, camped on the heights of Lansdown outside the city of Bath, by a gang of roughs from 'Bull Paunch Alley, the lowest slum in the cathedral city, where no policeman ever dared to penetrate'. The gang is led by 'a red-headed virago, a dreadful giantess of a woman known as "Carroty Kate" . . . a big brutal animal, caring nothing for magistrates or gaol' and long 'the terror of every respectable person in Bath'.[3] Despite his itinerant status as a member of a travelling circus, Sanger's view is from social as well as topographical high ground, con-firmed by his encounter with low, 'outcast' Bath. In 'the lowest slum . . . where no policeman ever dared to penetrate' is the rhetoric of social panic, constructing both the spectacle of society's lamplight and the dark purlieus beyond its reach.

In the narratives of Malet and Gissing outcast London remains, in Mearns' epithet, 'abject'. But in *The Mayor* the inhabitants of Mixen

8. Anthony Wohl, *Endangered Lives*, p. 238.
9. George Gissing, *Demos* (3 vols., 1886; repr. Brighton: Harvester Press, 1972), p. 25.
1. *Ibid.*, p. 26.
2. George Gissing, *A Life's Morning* (3 vols., 1888; repr. London: Home and Van Thal, 1947), p. 85.
3. George Sanger, *Seventy Years a Showman* (1910; repr. London: J. M. Dent, 1927), p. 76.

Lane, in their sly way, fight back; there is rebellion as well as contagion as their disruptive influence works back up to the official, public, high ground of the town. In Casterbridge this is first given shape in the spread of 'scandal': 'The ideas diffused by the reading of Lucetta's letters at Peter's Finger had condensed into a scandal, which was spreading like a miasmatic fog through Mixen Lane, and thence up the back streets of Casterbridge' (290)[202]. Casterbridge's residuum will act like Victor Hugo's 'ditch of truth' in Les Misérables (1861) which 'at times flowed back into the town giving Paris a taste of bile . . . The town was angered by the audacity of its filth, and could not accept that its ordure should return.'[4] As Stallybrass and White suggest, 'Hugo imagines a social "return of the repressed" in terms of the city's topography.'[5] So does Hardy.

One of the things repressed in The Mayor is the past. It falls to the figure of the furmity woman, in court on a vagrancy charge, to reveal what Henchard has kept hidden, his participation in the illegal wife-sale. In helping to precipitate his fall from grace, she symbolically becomes a principal agent of retribution. And it is through active ret-ribution—in the form of the skimmington ride—that Mixen Lane, to which she gravitates, will assert itself. The root of Mixen Lane's grudge is economic, and in the experience of the furmity woman Hardy con-denses its causes.

Her decline is mirrored in the decline of the traditional fair, a reliable index of the economic health of the countryside. When Susan passes through Weydon-Priors with Elizabeth-Jane, eighteen years after she was sold there, she notices that it has lost its former vitality: 'The new peri-odical great markets of neighbouring towns were beginning to interfere seriously with the trade carried on here for centuries. The pens for sheep, the tie-ropes for horses, were about half as long as they had been' (53)[18]. The furmity woman now serves a markedly inferior brew to the 'nourishing' 'Good Furmity' which Susan and Henchard had gratefully consumed. When later Henchard revisits Weydon-Priors he finds that the fair has disappeared altogether.

Hardy's factual source for the decline of the fair which pauperises the furmity woman was a report from the Dorset County Chronicle of 15 October 1829, which he intended to stand as an index of deteriorating economic conditions in the Dorset of the late 1820s: 'Weyhill Fair—By 12 o'c only 40 wagons had passed through Andover gate—in former abundant years, 400 have passed it by same hour.'[6] Such 'facts' (which

4. Victor Hugo, Les Misérables (1862; repr. Harmondsworth: Penguin, 1980), II. 371, cited by P. Stallybrass and A. White, The Politics and Poetics of Transgression, pp. 141–2.
5. Ibid., p. 141.
6. Thomas Hardy, Facts from Newspapers, Histories, Biographies and other chronicles—mainly local (abbreviated to "Facts Notebook"), p. 117. See William Greenslade, "Thomas Hardy's 'Facts' Notebook: A Further Source for The Mayor of Casterbridge," Thomas Hardy Journal, 2 (January 1986), pp. 33–5.

include three wife-sales and countless examples of family tragedy, crime and 'rough justice') testify to a world penetrated by developments more usually associated with the growth of large cities: greater centralisation, more efficient law-enforcement and increasing accessibility (made possible in the late 1840s by the coming of the railway). Even when Hardy was a young man, the town of Dorchester was acquiring, in miniature, some of the characteristics of a large city. Merryn Williams points out that while the population of surrounding small towns and villages like Cerne Abbas fell in the period 1841–1901, the population of Dorchester rose steadily through the century, and especially in the parish of Fordington—the 'Durnover' of Casterbridge. After 1850 the town prospered, but it also attracted a growing population of paupers as did any city. Fordington was, Williams suggests, 'the nearest thing Dorset had to an industrial slum'.[7]

Hardy was driven to recreate the old, unregulated world, of which Henchard in *The Mayor* is the epitome. The years around the date of his birth, 1840, marked a watershed between this primitive culture and the world of his youth when social change was fast rendering that culture obsolete. This impoverished and disaffected underclass speaks directly to the 'outcast' London of the period of the novel's composition: Hardy's way of seeing Casterbridge is moulded both by this unassimilated, resistant culture and the language of contemporary commentators.

In a crucial sequence of chapters (36–9) official and unofficial Casterbridge intersect: the visit of a 'Royal Personage' to Casterbridge collides with the skimmington ride. It is a conjuncture which Laurence Lerner claims, quite unaccountably, 'sets off no ideological or class conflicts in Casterbridge'.[8] The reverse is true. Chapter 36 records how the love letters between Henchard and Lucetta, which Jopp has let fall into the hands of Mrs Cuxsom and the company of Peter's Finger, serve as the 'good foundation for a skimmity-ride' (264)[196]. In the next chapter Hardy describes the visit to Casterbridge by the 'Illustrious Personage', the unexpected climax of which is Henchard's Brechtian upstaging of the mayoral duty, which Farfrae, his vanquisher and rival, 'performs'. This precipitates their confrontation and physical struggle in the following chapter (38). Chapter 39 describes the skimmington ride itself, and its fatal consequences for Lucetta, its target.

The bizarre juxtaposition of the royal visit and the skimmington ride is seen by Mixen Lane as an opportunity for defiance not to be missed. Jopp voices the general feeling: 'as a wind-up to the Royal visit the hit will be all the more pat by reason of their great elevation today' (291)[203]. It is a piece of agitprop theatre which mimics the official

7. Merryn Williams, *Thomas Hardy and Rural England* (London: Macmillan, 1972), p. 201, and generally, pp. 201–5.
8. Laurence Lerner, *Thomas Hardy's "The Mayor of Casterbridge": Tragedy or Social History?* (London: Chatto and Windus, 1975), pp. 31–2.

play in which Lucetta, sitting at Farfrae's side as the mayor's wife, has a leading role, and to which Henchard's performance is the merest ironic counterpoint.[9] The ceremonious official 'play', with its echoes of the speeches at the *comices agricoles* in Flaubert's *Madame Bovary* (1857), attempts to involve the community of Casterbridge (not, though, the 'lowest social stratum', who hear of it by accident, rather than by design) in its ritualised display. The town Corporation thanks the 'Royal Personage' for his services to 'agricultural science and economics by his zealous designs for placing the art of farming on a more scientific footing' (285)[198]. What are those made jobless by such developments, we are encouraged to ask, to make of that?

The answer is the symbolic act of charivari.[1] Any pretended consent which the inhabitants of Mixen Lane might display, by their presence at the ceremony, is made laughable. The Corporation claim to speak for the whole community and are ridiculed for their pains, and the whole solemn show is reduced to farce. And the masque requires — and precipitates — its anti-masque. As law and order are reasserted, 'effigies, donkey, lanterns, band, all had disappeared like the crew of *Comus*' (304)[213].

Of course the denizens of Mixen Lane represent the 'undeserving', not 'deserving' poor, the distinction affirmed in Booth's sociology.[2] Hardy gives us an image of this distinction (so necessary to Victorian philanthropy) in his characterisation of the clientele of the two inns — Peter's Finger, and higher (symbolically) up the High Street, the more respectable Three Mariners where Farfrae made his first favourable impression in Casterbridge.[3] The dispossessed residuum — Nance Mockridge, Mother Cuxsom and Charl (later drawing in Jopp and the furmity woman) — gather in the lower; in the higher the 'philosophic party' of small tradesmen, Longways, Coney, Buzzford, Billy Wills. Hardy makes explicit both the difference and the possibility of slippage from one social category to the other: 'the company at the Three Mariners were persons of quality in comparison with the company which gathered here; though it must be admitted that the lowest fringe of the Mariner's party touched the crest of Peter's at points' (280)[194].

The morning of the royal visit finds the clientele of the Three Mariners displaying their respectable credentials: 'there was hardly a

---

9. Douglas Gray has also noticed the element of satiric performance in this act of charivari in "Rough Music: Some Early Invectives and Flytings," in Claude Rawson (ed.) *English Satire and the Satiric Tradition* (Oxford: Basil Blackwell, 1984), pp. 21–43 (pp. 24–5).
1. See E. P. Thompson, "Rough Music': Le Charivari anglais," *Annales*, 27 (2) (Mars–Avril 1972), pp. 285–312. An extended version of this article appears in *Customs in Common* (London: Merlin Press, 1991), pp. 467–538.
2. Designed to determine the effective distribution of charity, it was a distinction employed by individuals like Octavia Hill and the Charity Organisation Society — satirised by Gissing in the figure of the philanthropist, Miss Lant, in George Gissing, *The Nether World* (1889; repr. Brighton: Harvester Press, 1976), p. 189.
3. See also Nooral Hasan, *Thomas Hardy: The Sociological Imagination* (London: Macmillan, 1982), pp. 70–71.

workman in the town who did not put a clean shirt on' (286–7)[199];
these drinkers 'showed their sense of occasion by advancing their customary eleven o'clock pint to half-past ten' (287)[200]. Later that day,
once the full implications of the skimmington ride become clear, Hardy
calls on an explicitly Darwinian figure at the moment of gathering social
and moral crisis: 'this mixed assemblage of idlers . . . [including
Coney, Buzzford and Nance Mockridge] . . . fell apart into two bands
by a process of natural selection, the frequenters of Peter's Finger going
off Mixen-Lane-wards, where most of them lived, while Coney,
Buzzford, Longways and that connection remained in the street'
(290)[202–3]. And their next action, a worthy attempt to mitigate the
consequences for Lucetta of the skimmington ride by removing Farfrae
from the scene of humiliation, sets them even further apart from the
unsentimental subversives of Mixen Lane.

The clarity with which a social and cultural structure finds its symbolic landscape is, to my mind, a major achievement of Hardy's novel.
The topography of Casterbridge, with its keenly observed configura-
tions, encodes the polarisations which incessantly inflect writing about
the late nineteenth-century city. Family distress and degradation, class
antagonism, fear, censoriousness were inscribed in the demarcations of
the town's social space. In the real Dorchester's Top of Town and low-
lying Fordington there was a model to hand. But unlike other contemporary writers on the urban poor, Hardy cannot be relied upon to deliver these demarcations in strictly degenerationist terms. Slipping in and
out of contemporary discourse, he is able to offer his outcast types the
possibility of a subversive, if crude, resistance to the terms of incorporation and exile held out by the dominant social order. In this, as in all the
things that mattered to him, Hardy was his own man.

H. M. DALESKI

[The Paradoxes of Love]†

* * *

The opening of the novel is striking not only in itself but also in
respect of Hardy's previous work, for it starts with a failed marriage, not
working up to this through a woman's wrong choice as between two
opposed men, but confronting us at once with the brute fact of the bad

† From H. M. Daleski, *Thomas Hardy and the Paradoxes of Love* (Columbia and London:
University of Missouri Press, 1997), pp. 108–24. Reprinted by permission of University of
Missouri Press. Copyright © 1997 by the Curators of the University of Missouri. Page refer-
ences have been changed to correspond to this Norton Critical Edition.

marriage through the man's wish to escape from it. From the outset the wish is implicit in the "dogged and cynical indifference" the man shows to his wife and child, the group preserving a "perfect silence" as they move along the road together [5]. On his part the silence is an "ignoring silence," negating his wife, and reading, "or pretending to read," as he walks, he appears to want "to escape an intercourse that would have been irksome to him" [5]. What he wants to escape, in the light of what follows, is suggestive, the word "intercourse" reverberating in respect of his relations with the woman. But we are not told what has gone wrong with the marriage, the narrator merely implying sourly that this is the nature of the beast: "That the man and woman were husband and wife, and the parents of the girl in arms, there could be little doubt. No other such relationship would have accounted for the atmosphere of stale familiarity which the trio carried along with them like a nimbus as they moved down the road" [6].

In the tent of the furmity-woman, however, there is talk about marriage, and then it appears the man, married for three years, is convinced the woman has ruined him: "The conversation took a high turn, as it often does on such occasions. The ruin of good men by bad wives, and, more particularly, the frustration of many a promising youth's high aims and hopes and the extinction of his energies by an early imprudent marriage, was the theme"; and the trusser's contribution is to say, "I did for myself that way thoroughly" [9]. The trusser is out of work, but it is not evident in what way the woman is responsible for this, as he seems to believe. What does come through is his conviction that close contact with a woman is inimical to a man, not only "doing" for him in a worldly sense but undoing him, destroying his male self at its core, extinguishing his vital force. His conclusion is that "men who have got wives and don't want 'em [should] get rid of 'em as these gipsy fellows do their old horses" [9]. The man's not "wanting" a wife, we see, is not merely a matter of his preferring not to have one; more profoundly, it expresses his feeling that he does not need a wife, as the gipsies do not need their old horses. He is a man who does not need a wife because he is sure he is sufficient to himself—and would be far better off without one: "I haven't more than fifteen shillings in the world . . ." he says, but "if I were a free man again I'd be worth a thousand pound before I'd done o't" [9]. It is in this context that Michael Henchard's story begins with the sale of his wife.

In his readiness to dispense with women, Henchard is the culminating instance of a line of men in Hardy. He follows Henry Knight of *A Pair of Blue Eyes*, who is "a bachelor by nature," and Farmer Boldwood of *Far from the Madding Crowd*, who is "a confirmed bachelor." Whereas both Knight and Boldwood in the end fall in love with women and their prolonged bachelordom is exposed as a function of sexual inhibition, Henchard, more dramatically, is, as he himself puts it, "by nature something of a woman-hater" who finds it "no hardship to keep mostly at a distance from the sex" [61]. Since he has been, in Solomon Longways's words, a "widow man" [29] for nineteen years following the sale of his wife, and since (as remains to be discussed) he has lapsed into a relationship with a woman only once during this time, and that for a short period and only after sixteen years, Henchard takes the stage at the beginning of the narrative proper as a man who would seem "by nature to be sexually self-sufficient. Without a woman, seemingly enabled to husband his energies rather than have them extinguished, he appears to have found a viable alternative to a failed marriage and has become "the masterful, coercive Mayor of the town" [64]. His mastery, of himself and of all around him, is compensation for the long years of abstinence. In this respect, his abstinence from drink in accordance with his vow may be regarded as concretizing a more radical abstention. All his passion goes into his dominating mastery, for when he "[carries] his point" it is a "blaze of satisfaction that he always [emits]" [95]. Keeping himself to himself, it is thus that in a number of respects he holds his own.[1]

When Susan seeks out Henchard after the lapse of nineteen years, his response is interesting. Arranging to meet her in a note he sends with Elizabeth-Jane, he encloses five guineas, the amount Newson paid for her, as if "tacitly [saying] to her that he [buys] her back again" [55]. Henchard, that is, takes her back as a chattel, recovering what belongs to him. Neither in the note nor at the meeting with her does he express any love for her or is there any movement of feeling toward her. His "first words," the narrator stresses, are "I don't drink. . . . You hear, Susan?—I don't drink now—I haven't since that night" [57], a way of begging her forgiveness that rather leaves her out of account. What he proposes to her is a pro forma marriage in more than one sense, and he sets about courting her "with business-like determination," seeming to school himself "into a course of strict mechanical rightness" toward her to conceal his lack of "amatory fire" [64]. When Susan moves into his house, however, he does try to "[show] some semblance" of feeling for her by being "kind" to her, "lest she should pine for deeper affection than he [can] give" [67].

What is unclear at this stage is whether his inability to give affection is due to Susan's failure to arouse such feeling in him or whether it is an incapacity on his part that extends to all women. Certainly, the protracted period of his celibacy would seem to indicate a more general incapacity—

1. Henchard seems to be taken at his word in the criticism. Cf. Ian Gregor, who says "[Hardy's] eye is not so much on money, as on the notion of 'freedom' [the sale] appears to offer, and which Henchard is so intent on grasping" (The Great Web: The Form of Hardy's Major Fiction [London: Faber and Faber, 1974], 119); D. H. Fussell, who notes that "the family is seen by Henchard as a constraint to self-advancement" ("The Maladroit Delay: The Changing Times in Hardy's The Mayor of Casterbridge," Critical Quarterly 21 [1979]: 24); and Bruce Johnson, who maintains that "the [wife] auction signals the triumph of social and commercial significa- tion over the more primitive, even atavistic sources of Henchard's being" (True Correspondence: A Phenomenology of Thomas Hardy's Novels [Tallahassee: University of Florida Press, 1983], 78).

or lack of desire. We can perhaps profitably relate to this problem by recurring to his kinship with Boldwood and considering Boldwood's own kinship with Bathsheba. Boldwood, we saw, was said to be "nearly [Bathsheba's] own self rendered into another sex"; and Bathsheba is a woman who "[feels] herself sufficient to herself," Diana being "the goddess whom [she] instinctively adore[s]." I suggested that for Bathsheba sex entails the violation of her self-sufficiency and that she is unable to open herself sexually. It seems to me that we can best understand Henchard's varied relations in this novel by viewing him as a male exemplar of the Diana complex. He deceives himself into believing his actions are dictated by his pride in his self-sufficiency and his need for self-enclosure, but in fact he longs to break out of his isolation. The difficulty is that it is only rarely he can bring himself to admit this and that in his fierce manliness he cannot, until it is too late, open himself—to anyone.

When he does succumb sexually to a woman, this takes place in Jersey, where he has gone on business, and in special circumstances, as he tells Farfrae:

> "I fell quite ill, and in my illness I sank into one of those gloomy fits I sometimes suffer from, on account o' the loneliness of my domestic life, when the world seems to have the blackness of hell, and like Job, I could curse the day that gave me birth. . . . While in this state I was taken pity on by a woman . . . [who] was as lonely as I. This young creature was staying at the boarding-house where I happened to have my lodging; and when I was pulled down she took upon herself to nurse me. Heaven knows why, for I wasn't worth it. But being together in the same house, and her feelings warm, we got naturally intimate. I won't go into particulars of what our relations were. It is enough to say that we honestly meant to marry. There arose a scandal, which did me no harm, but was of course ruin to her. . . . At last I was well and came away." [61–62]

It is only when Henchard is really ill and so deprived of his habitual sense of independence that his isolation, the "loneliness of [his] domestic life," hits home and undermines him. It undermines him to such an extent that we are to understand it plunges him into a suicidal depression, for in the blackness of the "gloomy fit" he "sinks" into he wants, like Job, to end it all. He later acknowledges this even more directly when he rescues Lucetta from the bull and she cries out, "You—have saved me!"—"saved my life," as she adds; and he replies: "I have returned your kindness. . . . You once saved me" [157, 159]. It is thus with an instinctive grasping at life that he responds to Lucetta when she takes pity on him. And it is in the helplessness of his dependence that he allows her to nurse him, for when he is depressed, we are told, "all his practical largeness of view [oozes] out of him" [145]: drained and depleted then, his self-supporting sense of mastery falls in on itself. That they eventually become "intimate" would seem to be due more to her than to him, for it is her feelings that are "warm." What is notable is the manner in which he backs away from her when he is restored to himself: he implies that it is the scandal which breaks up the relationship, but this does him "no harm" and would rather be a reason for his standing by her, especially since they mean to marry. But he neither stays with her nor marries her, seeming incapable of moving toward her or of accepting moral responsibility for her "ruin." He tells Farfrae the story three years after his break with Lucetta and begins by indicating he now views his submission to her as a "blunder" [61].

Henchard's sexual entanglements, it emerges, are characterized by a repetition compulsion on his part. This is pointed, when he meets Lucetta in the Ring as he has previously met Susan, by her "appearing . . . as the double of the first" [190]. Initially, he seems driven to reject the woman with whom he has been intimate. This is more startling in the case of Susan, but Lucetta feels no less abandoned, "forsaken," as she says in one of her letters to him [186]. The rejection is followed by his attempt eventually to make up to the woman, formally to do right by her. Thus, when Susan appears in Casterbridge, he remarries her; and after three years of Lucetta's badgering, he offers to marry her, though his readiness to make her this "return" [62] is nullified by the advent of Susan.

When Susan dies, his sense of obligation to Lucetta is strong, and he reflects that he "must put her in her proper position": "It was by no means with the oppression that would once have accompanied the thought that he regarded the moral necessity now; it was, indeed, with interest, if not warmth. His bitter disappointment at finding Elizabeth-Jane to be none of his, and himself a childless man, had left an emotional void in Henchard that he unconsciously craved to fill" [113]. The passage throws light, first, on his previous abandonment of Lucetta. For him the mere thought of marriage has been an "oppression," so oppressive as to make him flee her and then resist her pleas. Now, however, he is doubly driven. He is driven morally by a need to make a required—and acknowledged—restitution to her; and he is driven emotionally by the need to fill an inner void. The propulsive force of such a void is Hardy's central metaphor for sexual impulsion, for a psychology of sex in which men and women are driven to one another. The idea of the void is definitively formulated in *Far from the Madding Crowd* when Gabriel Oak, "having for some time known the want of a satisfactory form to fill an increasing void within him," fills it with Bathsheba, whom he does not know at that stage but whom he loves steadily thereafter. The crucial difference between Oak and Henchard is that the former is aware of the void within him and consciously seeks to fill it, whereas the latter "unconsciously craves" to do so and is impelled by a need that, in his vaunted self-sufficiency, he would even deny exists.

Oak vs Henchard

Henchard's lack of awareness of the void within has several consequences. In his aversion to sexual relationship, he is driven to intense
emotional involvements of an apparently nonsexual nature, as remains
to be discussed in respect to his relationships with Farfrae and Elizabeth-
Jane. It is when these relationships fail him that Lucetta comes to
Casterbridge, and then "by an almost mechanical transfer the sentiments which [have] run to waste since his estrangement from Elizabeth-
Jane and Donald Farfrae [gather] around Lucetta before they [have]
grown dry" [114]. But if the idea of marriage to her now seems less
oppressive, he cannot muster any passion for her: there is no "warmth"
or "strong feeling" [113] in his mechanical approach to her.

A further difference between Oak and Henchard is highlighted by the
fact that Oak's need makes him not only fall in love with Bathsheba but
also "paint her a beauty," whereas the only "charm" Lucetta has for
Henchard is that she is "a lady of means," and that "[lends] a charm to
her image which it might not otherwise have acquired" [114]. Indeed, it
is because he has been "dreaming of [her] as almost his property," significantly to be added on to him, as it were, that he lets "his strong, warm
gaze [rest] upon her" [133] when he visits her. But by then she no longer
feels "that warm allegiance" which she previously bore toward him, and
her "pure love" has been "considerably chilled" [118]. By then, moreover, she has been drawn to Farfrae. Elizabeth-Jane registers the rivalry
of the two men, seeing how they become "more desperately enamoured
of her friend every day," but the outcome is not in doubt: "On Farfrae's
side it was the unforced passion of youth. On Henchard's the artificially
stimulated coveting of maturer age" [136].

The repeated pattern in Hardy of triangular relationship is manifested in
The Mayor of Casterbridge in the rivalry of Henchard and Farfrae for
Lucetta. The two men are strongly opposed physically and tempera-
mentally, may indeed be seen as opposites, but they do not conform to
Hardy's habitual male sexual typology. Nor is the narrative focus on
Lucetta's choice of one of them, or on her marriage to Farfrae when she
chooses him. Exceptionally in this novel, Hardy is more concerned with
the relationship of the men themselves since the fact that Henchard, the
central focus, is conceived as a "woman-hater" serves to subordinate sexual relationships.

The male relationship is inaugurated when Farfrae restores
Henchard's grown wheat and the latter offers him a position as manager
of the corn branch of his business. Henchard says to him:

> "Your forehead, Farfrae, is something like my poor brother's—now
> dead and gone; and the nose, too, isn't unlike his. You must be,
> what—five foot nine, I reckon? I am six foot one and a half out of
> my shoes. But what of that? In my business, 'tis true that strength

and bustle build up a firm. But judgement and knowledge are what
keep it established. Unluckily, I am bad at science, Farfrae; bad at
figures—a rule o' thumb sort of man. You are just the reverse—I
can see that. . . ." [39]

Henchard is drawn to Farfrae as a displacement of his dead brother,
seemingly stirred emotionally by his appearance. But in his isolation
he is also impelled to Farfrae as a substitution for the kind of close relation with a woman that he has forsworn: "[H]ow that fellow does draw
me," he says to himself. "I suppose 'tis because I'm so lonely" [45]. In
this respect it is significant that he should move so abruptly and apparently inconsequently from the supposed resemblance of Farfrae to his
brother to a reckoning of the differences between himself and Farfrae,
clearly being drawn to him as his complement, for all the world as if
he were relating to a woman. It is repeatedly insisted that "Farfrae's
character [is] just the reverse of Henchard's" [89]; and on Farfrae's part
too "the great difference in their characters" adds to his liking for
Henchard [60]. From the outset Henchard, who never expresses feeling for or to a woman (other than his stepdaughter), readily declares
himself to Farfrae: "[H]ang it, Farfrae," he says, "I like thee well"; and
when Farfrae agrees to work for him and be "[his] man," he at once
claims him, moving to a different plane of relationship: "'Now you are
my friend!' he exclaimed" [51]. And his "interest" in his "new friend"
is said to be "keenly excited" [54].

On the very day that Henchard takes Farfrae into his business, he is
informed by Elizabeth-Jane of Susan's return and arranges, when he
meets her that evening, to remarry her. But far from alleviating, this
serves only to intensify his sense of loneliness. Returning from the Ring,
he insists on Farfrae's having supper with him and, though they are still
strangers, unburdens himself of the story of his relations with both Susan
and Lucetta: "It is odd," says Henchard, "that two men should meet as
we have done on a purely business ground, and that at the end of the
first day I should wish to speak to 'ee on a family matter. But, damn it
all, I am a lonely man, Farfrae: I have nobody else to speak to; and why
shouldn't I tell it to 'ee?" [60]. If Henchard, as we have seen, in the
gloom of his loneliness and illness, becomes "naturally intimate" with
Lucetta, he now forces intimacy on Farfrae. In a parody of sexual intimacy, he bares himself, pouring out what he has for long years kept to
himself and finding "great relief" [63] in doing so. The narrator comments that he is "plainly under that strange influence which sometimes
prompts men to confide to the new-found friend what they will not tell
to the old" [61], but what seems to be decisive is not so much the new-
ness of the friend as his sex. From the start, though the narrator remarks
on this explicitly only at the end of the narrative, Henchard's liking for
Farfrae is "passionate" [248]. That he is driven by the void within him,

the sense of which is intensified, if anything, by his alienation on Susan's return, and that he unconsciously wishes to possess Farfrae, to take him into himself, so to speak, is suggested when Elizabeth-Jane's discerning eye detects his devouring feeling for him: though he puts his arm on the manager's shoulder "as if Farfrae were a younger brother," she recognizes "Henchard's tigerish affection for the younger man" [71]. Outwardly, however, they are merely friends, as the narrator pointedly remarks when Elizabeth-Jane observes them together on another occasion: "Friendship between man and man; what a rugged strength there was in it, as evinced by these two. And yet the seed that was to lift the foundation of this friendship was at that moment taking root in a chink of its structure" [75].

What makes the chink in this apparently rugged and strong friendship is Henchard's need for mastery. Farfrae has to be *his* man, rendered unto him, as Susan was his woman, even though discarded by him. Their relationship begins to crack when Farfrae countermands Henchard's humiliating punishment of Abel Whittle, ordering him to go home and get his breeches:

> "Hullo, hullo!" said Henchard, coming up behind. "Who's sending him back?"
> All the men looked towards Farfrae.
> "I am," said Donald. "I say this joke has been carried far enough."
> "And I say it hasn't! Get up in the waggon, Whittle."
> "Not if I am manager," said Farfrae. "He either goes home, or I march out of this yard for good." [77]

Instead of caving in, as Henchard anticipates, Farfrae stands his ground and directly challenges his employer. He insists that he is master in his own sphere, and it is Henchard who unexpectedly gives way. He knows he is in the wrong, and once he speaks to Farfrae "like a sullen boy" [77], the game is over. What rankles with Henchard as much as the challenge to his authority is his public humiliation: "Why did you speak to me before [the workmen] like that, Farfrae?" he says. "You might have stopped till we were alone" [77]. And when one of the men subsequently turns to him for directions, he says, "Ask Mr Farfrae. He's master here!" [78]. Henchard thus directly reveals what is at issue for him; at the same time he himself turns Farfrae into a rival, foisting the role on him.

Where he previously expressed his affection for Farfrae, Henchard now draws back: "The corn-factor seldom or never again put his arm upon the young man's shoulder so as to nearly weigh him down with the pressure of mechanized friendship" [79]. The narrator's reference to the "mechanized friendship" that Henchard has previously extended to Farfrae retrospectively complicates our view of the tigerish gesture noted above. It would seem that no intense relationship, whether

with man or woman, is natural to Henchard, that he cannot give himself to such closeness and has mechanically to force himself to maintain it. In reaction, he retreats, as always, into an entrenched self and
moves to reject the one he has favored. But first his passion goes into
the rivalry he has created: "fired with emulation," he sets out to better
Farfrae in the entertainment he is getting up "in celebration of a
national event" [80]. What follows is once again his public humiliation; and as a result he dismisses Farfrae, now in effect asserting he
does not need him and openly rejecting him, as he has previously
rejected Susan and Lucetta.

Far from putting an end to the rivalry, the practical consequence of
Henchard's dismissal of Farfrae is to intensify it, for once the younger
man sets up on his own in the same line of business, he is "compelled,
in sheer self-defence, to close with Henchard in mortal commercial
combat" [89]. The language in which this commercial struggle is
described points proleptically (and precisely) to the climactic physical
combat that Henchard finally forces on Farfrae. But first there also
develops their rivalry over Lucetta, and "the sense of occult rivalry in
suitorship" is "superadded to the palpable rivalry of their business lives"
[139]. Farfrae is victorious on all fronts and ends by moving with Lucetta
into Henchard's old house, while Henchard goes to work for him "as a
day-labourer in the barns and granaries he formerly had owned" [173].
If it is the reappearance of the furmity-woman and her public denunciation of Henchard that forms "the edge or turn in the incline of [his] fortunes" [166], and if it is he himself who seems to put all his weight into
his downward movement, it is surely Farfrae who ensures that the revolution of the wheel of fortune should be felt as so complete: "Here be I,
his former master," Henchard says to himself, "working for him as man,
and he the man standing as master, with my house and my furniture and
my what-you-may-call wife all his own" [174].

There remains one final public humiliation for Henchard, an event
that he thinks of as a "crowning degradation" [204]. With Farfrae
installed as mayor and a royal visit to Casterbridge pending, Henchard
asks to be included in the reception of the visitor but is turned down by
the mayor. On the day of the visit he drunkenly staggers to the side of
the royal vehicle, holding out a hand to "the Illustrious Personage":

> Farfrae, with Mayoral authority, immediately rose to the occa-
> sion. He seized Henchard by the shoulder, dragged him back, and
> told him roughly to be off. Henchard's eyes met his, and Farfrae
> observed the fierce light in them despite his excitement and irrita-
> tion. For a moment Henchard stood his ground rigidly; then by an
> unaccountable impulse gave way and retired. [201]

Since Henchard afterward says "brokenly to himself," "He drove me
back as if I were a bull breaking fence" [204], there is a suggestive par-

allel between this scene, in which Farfrae saves the day, and an earlier episode in which Henchard saves Lucetta and Elizabeth-Jane from a bull that is attacking them. On that occasion Henchard seizes the bull's leading-staff and wrenches its head "as if he would snap it off." The bull's "thick neck" seems to become "half-paralysed," and its nose drops blood. The "creature [flinches]," and Henchard leads it to the door and fastens it outside the barn [157]. The interesting point in the parallel is not Henchard's bullishness but the manner in which the bull flinches before him, just as he gives in to Farfrae. The parallel seems to lie in the way superior force carries the day, Henchard's courage and physical force in the first instance being matched by Farfrae's courage and force of will in the second. But the narrator says it is "by an unaccountable impulse" that Henchard gives way, suggesting he is unable or unwilling to explain this and at the same time implying that Henchard himself is unwilling or unable to acknowledge what it is that makes him back off. The crucial moment seems to come when Henchard's eyes meet Farfrae's, and this detail links the scene to one that follows it as well as to the one that precedes it, for a meeting of eyes is once again decisive in the physical fight to the death between the two men that ensues, as we shall see. I suggest that Henchard is overcome here not by Farfrae's willpower but by the force, despite the fierceness of his gaze, of his own deepest feeling for the younger man, the kind of feeling that makes him abjure his own superior physical strength, that leads him for once to master himself rather than the other.[2]

Afterward, however, Henchard's public humiliation rankles more and more deeply as he bitterly recalls how he was "shaken at the collar by him as a vagabond in the face of the whole town" [204]; and he forces Farfrae to "finish out [the] little wrestle" begun that morning [206] in a fight that gives body to their earlier "mortal commercial combat." Henchard, as "the strongest man," ties one arm to his side but soon has the advantage:

> "Now," said Henchard between his gasps, "this is the end of what you began this morning. Your life is in my hands."

2. Some critics relate Henchard directly to the bull. Cf. Howard O. Brogan, who says the bull is "the very image of Henchard's unruly passions" ("'Visible Essences' in *The Mayor of Casterbridge*," *English Literary History* 17 [1950]: 308); and Richard C. Carpenter, who calls the bull Henchard's "symbolic alter ego" and says he treats it "as cruelly as life treats him" (*Thomas Hardy* [New York: Twayne, 1964], 108). Other critics have commented on the parallel between the scene with the bull and that of the royal visit. See, for instance, Frederick R. Karl, who says "Henchard is recognizably the bull, or at least suggestive of the bull in its brazen fierceness and then in its flinching half-paralysis once a stronger force masters it" ("*The Mayor of Casterbridge*: A New Fiction Defined," *Modern Fiction Studies* 6 [1960]: 202); and Juliet Grindle, who comments that "images of bulls have, of course, a particular bearing on Henchard who is bull-like in respect of his largeness, slowness, clumsiness, strength, unpredictability, and—in the end, the manner in which he is susceptible to being tamed" ("Compulsion and Choice in *The Mayor of Casterbridge*," in Anne Smith, ed., *The Novels of Thomas Hardy*, [New York: Barnes and Noble, 1979] 103).

"Then take it, take it!" said Farfrae. "Ye've wished to long enough!"

Henchard looked down upon him in silence, and their eyes met. "O Farfrae!—that's not true!" he said bitterly. "God is my witness that no man ever loved another as I did thee at one time. . . . And now—though I came here to kill 'ee, I cannot hurt thee! Go and give me in charge—do what you will—I care nothing for what comes of me!"

He withdrew to the back part of the loft, loosened his arm, and flung himself into a corner upon some sacks, in the abandonment of remorse. Farfrae regarded him in silence; then went to the hatch and descended through it. . . .

Henchard took his full measure of shame and self-reproach. . . . So thoroughly subdued was he that he remained on the sacks in a crouching attitude, unusual for a man, and for such a man. Its womanliness sat tragically on the figure of so stern a piece of virility. [207–8]

If the fight ends unexpectedly in Henchard's unmanning as he crouches like a woman, Elaine Showalter, in a feminist account of the novel—arguably the best piece of criticism on it—maintains that at this point he "finally [crosses] over psychically and strategically to the long-repressed 'feminine' side of himself." She says that Hardy "understood the feminine self as the estranged and essential complement of the male self," that, in selling Susan, Henchard "sells out or divorces his own 'feminine' self" and that his efforts, "first to deny and divorce his passional self, and ultimately to accept and educate it, involve him in a pilgrimage of 'unmanning.'"[3] This is illuminating, but it seems to me that Showalter settles too lightly for the "finality" of the change in Henchard; he is made up a little too much of the same stuff for that. And there are perhaps additional dimensions to the crucial episode of the fight.

The scene, it seems to me, hinges on the issue of giving and taking. All his life Henchard has been habituated, especially in his personal relations, to taking, to taking to himself in acts of possession that have been the only mode of his masterfulness. Farfrae has been his man and has then been rejected by him in the only countermanding mode available to him. Now, on the verge of an ultimate kind of taking, he gives Farfrae's life back to him. This is not the same as giving himself to Farfrae, but it comes close to it. The turning point is their meeting of eyes when all Henchard's deep feeling for Farfrae wells up in him, as

3. Elaine Showalter, "The Unmanning of the Mayor of Casterbridge," 112, 101, 103, 101–2. Simon Gatrell cites Showalter, saying that she reaches "a similar conclusion [to him] by a different route," and he also remarks that "in erotic terms [Henchard is] a character subversive of the norms of the dominant culture" (*Thomas Hardy and the Proper Study of Mankind* [Charlottesville: University Press of Virginia, 1993], 188, 73).

earlier that day, and he gives himself to the emotion in the astonishing declaration, given the circumstances, that he has "loved" him. The love is defensively located in the past, but he asserts that it was supreme of its kind, no man ever having loved another as he did Farfrae.[4] It is at this point that his proud self-possession crumbles, and giving way altogether, he lets himself go "in the abandonment of remorse." This is followed by an "overpowering wish," though this is frustrated by Farfrae's departure from Casterbridge, to make it up with him; and this too breaks a habitual pattern, for he does not wish now to make restitution but "to attempt the well-nigh impossible task of winning pardon for his late mad attack" [208].

The first time Henchard says he loves anyone is when he admits to Farfrae that he has loved him. The fact that it is a man and not a woman who elicits this declaration and that he is a self-professed misogynist suggest that he is perhaps confessing to more than he consciously realizes. There is no overt homosexual tendency in his feeling for Farfrae, and the younger man is certainly quite unaware of such a possibility, but to view Henchard as a latent homosexual not only adds further depth to the powerful scene of their fight but also helps explain his relations with Susan and Lucetta. It throws a different light too on his supposed self-sufficiency and can perhaps be seen as his crowning self-deception. It is suggestive that a later writer and close reader of Hardy, D. H. Lawrence, would seem to have picked up such vibrations in the scene of the fight and then elaborated them in *Women in Love*, in which Birkin's latent homosexuality is more apparent. It is a moot point whether Lawrence was consciously following Hardy, but the parallels are notable.

In *Women in Love*, Birkin's desire for an "eternal union with a man too: another kind of love"[5] is depicted in his relationship with Gerald Crich. He proposes that they "swear a Blutbrüderschaft," that is, that they "swear to love each other" and to be "given to each other, organically" (206–7). The word takes on flesh, as it were, in the well-known wrestling encounter between the two men, in which they strip naked and seem "to drive their white flesh deeper and deeper against each other, as if they would break into a oneness" (270). Henchard may not propose a blood brotherhood to Farfrae, but he is clearly drawn to him,

4. Robert Kiely, seemingly ignoring the earlier episode, also stresses the importance of the meeting of eyes in this scene, though he attributes a different significance to it: "This is the first scene," he says, "in which Henchard looks into Farfrae's eyes and sees, if only for a moment, that he might not be what he [has] made him out to be. . . . For Henchard, this glimpse of Farfrae as another helpless mortal rather than a cunning viper signals the beginning of an internal disintegration analogous to the one he has already suffered socially and financially" ("Vision and Viewpoint in *The Mayor of Casterbridge*," *Nineteenth-Century Fiction* 23 [1968]: 193–94).
5. D. H. Lawrence, *Women in Love*, David Farmer et al. (eds.) (Cambridge: Cambridge University Press, 1987), 481. Further page references to *Women in Love* are incorporated parenthetically in the text.

as I have noted, as a displacement of his dead brother; and he is also drawn to him as if to a woman who might be his complement. His "tigerish affection for the younger man" may also be seen as an unconscious wish to take him into himself in a different sense from that previously suggested. When the two men wrestle, at any rate, the struggle knits them together, as it does Birkin and Gerald: they rock and writhe "like trees in a gale"; and Farfrae "[locks] himself to his adversary" [207]. And the wrestling, of course, is the occasion of Henchard's declaration of love for Farfrae.

Farfrae also correlates with Gerald Crich in a different connection, thus strengthening the overall parallel. Just as Gerald, the mining magnate, is responsible for the mechanization of his mines, so Farfrae recommends the introduction of a "new-fashioned agricultural implement called a horse-drill" not previously known in that part of the country [127]. When Elizabeth-Jane laments that "the romance of the sower is gone for good," Farfrae declares that it "will revolutionize sowing heerabout": "Each grain," he proudly says, "will go straight to its intended place, and nowhere else whatever!" [129]. Comparably, Gerald undertakes "the great reform" of his mines, bringing in new machinery from America, "great iron men" as they are called, and everything is run "on the most accurate and delicate scientific method" (230).

Hardy's critics, however, have tended to raise the question of a possible homosexual dimension to the relationship only to dismiss it. Elaine Showalter emphatically says "there is nothing homosexual in their intimacy; but there is certainly on Henchard's side an open, and, he later feels, incautious embrace of homosocial friendship, an insistent male bonding." She is echoed by Marjorie Garson, who insists that the nature of Henchard's feeling for Farfrae remains "undefined and unexaminable"; by contrast she maintains that it is Lawrence in *Women in Love* who has rewritten the wrestling match "to release its erotic potential." She does, however, grant that "it is possible to feel that there is an erotic dimension to Henchard's attraction for the younger man" but says that "Farfrae's failure to recognize the intensity of Henchard's emotion facilitates the repression of this dimension." Dale Kramer, on the other hand, in terms not altogether dissimilar to those I have proposed, grants the case for seeing a homosexual dimension in the relationship but then brusquely undercuts it when he says that "to turn Henchard into a latent homosexual whose downfall stems from an inability to maintain the latency may stimulate fresh readings of the novel, but it does not help us to understand either the formal or the emotional qualities of the novel." A recent account of this aspect of the novel continues to take back with one hand what it gives with the other: Robert Langbaum says that "Henchard's sudden passion for Farfrae, which is striking after his coolness toward women, suggests homosexuality on his side. . . . But their relationship does not develop in a way that bears out this hypothesis; for it quickly turns into male power rivalry once Farfrae breaks out of Henchard's proprietorship."[6]

It seems to me, however, that the parallels between *The Mayor of Casterbridge* and *Women in Love* are so striking that they cannot be ignored. It is true that the homoerotic dimension of the male relationship in the earlier novel is much more muted, but when we read back from Lawrence to Hardy, the relationship of Henchard and Farfrae is placed in a context that brings out its undertones. The fight between them, at all events, puts an end to the relationship, and Henchard is driven back on himself into customary self-enclosure.

SUZANNE KEEN

[Narrative Annexes: Mixen Lane][†]

This study of the Victorian novel identifies a technique employed across its various kinds—in social fictions, fictional autobiographies, *Bildungsromanen*, Condition of England novels, romances, and realistic novels—to renovate the nineteenth-century house of fiction. *Narrative annexes*, as I name them, allow unexpected characters, impermissible subjects, and plot-altering events to appear, in a bounded way, within fictional worlds that might be expected to exclude them. Like other Victorian renovations, narrative annexes may appear to disfigure the structure they alter, but they at the same time reveal Victorian novelists' creative responses to the capacities and limitations of their form. Annexes are initiated by a combined shift in genre and setting that changes the fictional world of the novel, and they work by interrupting the norms of a story's world, temporarily replacing those norms, and carrying the reader, the perceiving and reporting characters, and the plot-line across a boundary and through an altered, particular, and briefly realized zone of difference. In small spaces and few pages, narrative annexes challenge both cultural and literary norms to form imaginative worlds more variously, in sometimes distracting or dissonant interludes. Yet annexes never stop the plot, but serve the story by modifying the story-world. As alternatives to the techniques of fantasy or multiplied plot lines, Victorian annexes simultaneously anticipate the fragmentation

6. Showalter, "The Unmanning"; Marjorie Garson, *Hardy's Fables of Integrity: Woman, Body, Text* (Oxford: Clarendon Press, 1991) 110; Dale Kramer, *Thomas Hardy: The Forms of Tragedy* (Detroit: Wayne State University, Press, 1975), 86–87; Robert Langbaum, *Thomas Hardy in Our Time* (New York: St. Martin's Press, 1995), 129.

† From Suzanne Keen, *Victorian Renovations of the Novel: Narrative Annexes and the Boundaries of Representation* (Cambridge: Cambridge University Press, 1998), pp. 1–4, 130–44. Reprinted with the permission of Cambridge University Press. References to this Norton Critical Edition appear in brackets after the author's original citations.

associated with modern fiction, and resemble the flexible worldmaking of prose fiction before the novel. Extending and qualifying the boundaries of representation, narrative annexes draw attention and contribute to the generic diversity of the Victorian novel, complicating the traditional opposition of realism and romance. Narrative annexes are sites of Victorian novelists' negotiation with the conventional, and as such they reveal not only the effort to employ alternative representational strategies, but also the subjects that instigate that effort.

All narrative annexes possess a shift to a previously unrepresented place and a simultaneous alteration in narrative language that sends signals of adjusted genre. All narrative annexes make a change within the primary level of a fictional world without departing it entirely, as an embedded text or an interpolated story does. The connection of the setting and the consistency of the narrative situation permit the perceiving (and, in the case of the first person, narrating) character to journey through the annex, by crossing a boundary line or border region, marked with signs of generic and spatial difference.

A constitutive feature of annexes, these boundaries or border regions indicate the commitment of Victorian novelists to the representation of spatially coherent fictional worlds, and at the same time allude to the contemporary critical discourse on the proper "realm" of the novel. * * * Since boundaries, borders, and lines of demarcation evoke not only the long tradition of traversing an ever-altering imaginary terrain, but also the censorious language of the Victorian cultural watchdog, or the formal purist (often but not always the same person), they become a vital element of novelists' manipulation of spatial difference and dramatic generic admixture to challenge representational norms.

For instance, Thomas Hardy simultaneously alters the generic signals and the location of *The Mayor of Casterbridge* (1886) when he conveys Michael Henchard through a border-region that becomes a forbidding barrier around the abode of the weather prophet: "The turnpike became a lane, the lane a cart-track, the cart-track a bridle-path, the bridle-path a foot-way, the foot-way overgrown. The solitary walker slipped here and there, and stumbled over the natural springes formed by the brambles, till at length he reached the house, which, with its garden, was surrounded with a high, dense hedge."[1] This hedge marks the boundary between the ordinary world of Casterbridge and the weather-prophet's house, but the incantatory language and the difficult journey have already combined to suggest an annex, an alternative realm outside Casterbridge where magical forecasts rather than up-to-date technology and practical knowledge might work. Passing through the door in the hedge, Henchard pays for bad advice from Mr. Fall. This action, insu-

1. Thomas Hardy, *The Mayor of Casterbridge*, ed. Martin Seymour-Smith (Harmondsworth: Penguin Books, 1978), p. 258 [141].

lated from the main setting of the novel, makes an essential contribution to the plot, as it precipitates Henchard's financial ruin. The bounded realm of the annex serves the downward turning of Henchard's plot-line, contains the unprecedented action of Henchard's reliance on another's guesswork, and results in Jopp's alienation from his employer, which in turn leads to the work of the novel's later narrative annex (discussed [below]).

This brief example points to a fourth feature present, with changed genre, altered setting, and a crossed boundary, in all annexes (the four markers do vary in prominence). The events contained in narrative annexes, while insulated from the primary fictional world by the passage through the annexes' boundary, are always consequential for the plot. Here Seymour Chatman's distinction between "kernel" and "satellite" plot events helps us to see the tricky narrative work an annex performs. Unlike a satellite event, which can be omitted from a plot summary without misrepresentation of the story, a kernel event contributes in an indispensable way to the story's development and outcome.[2] The combination in narrative annexes of an appearance of digressiveness, difference, even marginality, and essential kernel plot events with real consequences for the temporarily departed primary fictional world results in odd deformations of mainly verisimilar Victorian fictional worlds. It is therefore not surprising to discover that the very episodes I call annexes were often singled out by critics and contemporary readers as especially unlikely or peculiar. * * *

* * *

The narrative annex in [*The Mayor of Casterbridge*] maps a marginal social space, the ancient environs known as Mixen Lane, within the town of Casterbridge. The work of the annex depends on Mixen Lane's hiddenness, and its accessibility; on its antiquity, and its presence in contemporary Casterbridge; on its forbidding borders, and their permeability; as well as on its capacity to hold and discharge characters into the outer plot. The events narrated in chapter 36 take place in a liminal location (Peter's Finger in Mixen Lane), and the small-scale social drama enacted there permits a critical, corrective solution to be forced onto the problems that have been generated in the main world of the novel—the public zones of Casterbridge, especially those arenas associated with spectacles of transaction.[3] Mixen Lane functions as the most porous boundary of the otherwise well-regulated town of Casterbridge. It provides a space where, paradoxically, sexual favors can be purchased

2. Seymour Chatman, *Story and Discourse: Narrative Structure in Fiction and Film* (Ithaca: Cornell University Press, 1978), pp. 53–6.
3. See Leonora Epstein, "Sale and Sacrament: The Wife Auction in *The Mayor of Casterbridge*," *English Language Notes* 24:4 (1987), p. 54.

and communal punishments for sexual transgressors can be planned. This combination of "turning a blind eye" and "pointing the finger" coexists in the annex, particularly in the carefully hidden public house, Peter's Finger.[4] If, as Hardy's narrator comments, "the inn called Peter's Finger was the church of Mixen Lane," we enter more than an alternative social center when we follow Jopp and Mother Cuxsom as they enter. The ritual of excommunication which takes place in Peter's Finger shifts generic and social registers so people brought "to a common level" (*Mayor* 331)[195], that is, to the lowest level, speak in a plural, choral voice. Here prostitutes and poachers invade Lucetta's privacy and choose the form of her punishment. This transgression of privacy is all the more remarkable because, other than letters, there are so few truly private places or things in the novel. (Even the originary crime of the plot, the wife-sale, takes place in full view of an almost entirely complicitous audience.) The old furmity woman in whose tent the wife-sale takes place shows up time and again in the novel to remind us of the public nature of that act and of the long memory of the witness, and this economy in the appearance and reappearance of characters gives the novel its texture of coincidence and inevitability.

The location of the action and the movements of characters through a sequence of different locales link placement and possibility in all of Hardy's novels. Although *The Life and Death of the Mayor of Casterbridge: A Story of a Man of Character* has been seen as primarily a character study,[5] Hardy's settings can take on agency more powerful and complicated even than individual characters. Few novelists so successfully convince readers that they have entered a fictional territory, a world with idiosyncratic places, landscapes, and geographical features (even as Hardy compromises the sense of actuality he evokes by employing intricate plots and coincidences). *The Mayor of Casterbridge* differs from *Jude the Obscure* and *Tess of the d'Urbervilles* in that the plot remains fixed on the stage of Casterbridge, while characters appear, disappear, and reappear within its boundaries. In *The Mayor of Casterbridge*, Hardy does not avail himself of the advantages of episodic shifts in setting. He compresses all of the symbolic and narrative functions of changed place and shifted genre into a single narrative annex.

One of the most important surprises of the novel comes when the reader realizes that Casterbridge has an area within it, Mixen Lane, where behavior impossible in any other public space not only occurs, but alters the outcome of the novel. Because Hardy demarcates the

---

4. I am indebted to Rosemarie Morgan for pointing out that a pub of this name still exists in Dorchester, and that tradition holds that Peter's Finger "wags" at heavy drinkers.
5. See, canonically, D. A. Dike, "A Modern Oedipus: *The Mayor of Casterbridge*," *Essays in Criticism* 2 (April 1952), pp. 167–79; John Paterson, "*The Mayor of Casterbridge* as Tragedy," in *Hardy: A Collection of Critical Essays*, ed. A. J. Guerard (Engelwood Cliffs, NJ: Prentice-Hall, 1963), pp. 91–112; and Robert Schweik, "Character and Fate in *The Mayor of Casterbridge*," in R. P. Draper (ed.), *Hardy: The Tragic Novels*, pp. 133–47.

annex from the main world of the text so explicitly, the alternative place Mixen Lane heightens the significance of spaces in a fictional world already rigorously organized by locations. Geographically isolated from the rest of Casterbridge, and yet very much a part of it, the annex unleashes events that bring the linked plots of Henchard, Lucetta, Farfrae, Elizabeth and Newson to their various ends. In a novel in which characters repeatedly start over—with new vows, names, husbands, fathers, lovers, clothing, houses, and jobs—the annex allows the work of ending to begin. The archaic practices of an ancient environ erupt out of the annex to put an end to the proliferating repetitions of the middle, which have been set in motion by a striking double beginning.

The opening sequence of the novel, in which Newson purchases Susan from her husband Henchard, establishes the sale of a wife in a public marketplace as possible, though outrageous.[6] This beginning contaminates every transaction between men that follows. Though the novel in fact focuses on a series of transactions between the two Mayors of Casterbridge, Henchard and Farfrae, business transactions at the lowest end of the social scale instigate and move the plot along. Business forms the basis of political power and prestige in the world of *The Mayor of Casterbridge*, and the witnesses to and participants in business transactions believe in their efficacy and binding nature—only when Susan Newson ceases to believe in the legality of her union with her buyer does the sailor absent himself from her life and the story. Newson's reentry into the novel (through the narrative annex) provides Elizabeth-Jane with a father she can believe in—a father who can give her away—and it also underlines the presence of an illicit economy and zone of commerce within the boundaries of Casterbridge.

The fundamental problems posed by *The Mayor of Casterbridge* operate through a structure of analogy that asks its readers to see that the buying, selling, and decision-making of the lowest social stratum not only resemble, but coexist with and intervene in, the commerce, marriage, and civic behavior of the prosperous and respectable classes. So, for instance, although Hardy presents the traffic in women as an archaic survival practiced outside of Casterbridge in country fairs, and as a sinful practice that decent people abhor, the more socially acceptable forms of that traffic in fact structure the novel.[7] When Henchard remar-

---

6. On Hardy's derivation of the wife-sale from his reading of 1820s editions of the local newspaper, and his transcription of items into his commonplace book, "Facts: From Newspapers, Histories, Biographies, and Other Chronicles—(Mainly Local)," see Christine Winfield, "Factual Sources of Two Episodes in *The Mayor of Casterbridge*," *Nineteenth-Century Fiction* 25:2 (1970), pp. 234–41. On other instances, see Michael Taft, "Hardy's Manipulation of Folklore and Literary Imagination: The Case of the Wife-Sale in *The Mayor of Casterbridge*," *Studies in the Novel* 13:4 (1981), pp. 399–407. For the most thorough interpretation of wife sales, see E. P. Thompson, "The Sale of Wives," *Customs in Common* (London: The Merlin Press, 1991), pp. 404–66.
7. Gayle Rubin, "The Traffic in Women: Notes on the 'Political Economy' of Sex," *Towards an Anthropology of Women*, ed. Rayna R. Reiter (New York: Monthly Review Press, 1975), p. 174.

ries his wife Susan he has already bought her back for the exact amount for which he sold her: "He said nothing about the enclosure of five guineas. The amount was significant; it may tacitly have said to her that he bought her back again."[8] (The marriage realigns the characters into a family, although a false one, for Elizabeth-Jane is not in fact Henchard's daughter.) Hardy deepens the novel's critique of marriage by pointing out its symmetry with commercial exchange, anticipating Lévi-Strauss' description of matrimony as the most powerful form of exchange enforcing exogamy: "For the woman herself is nothing other than . . . the supreme gift among those that can only be obtained in the form of reciprocal gifts."[9] Although men literally sell and buy Susan Newson, her daughter Elizabeth-Jane serves as a model gift-object, transacted from man to man according to the rules of exogamy—in Gayle Rubin's terms, "a conduit of a relationship rather than a partner to it."[1] Hardy devotes part of the work of the annex to solving his overlapping puzzles of triangulation, by reintroducing the one character who has the right to give Elizabeth-Jane away to Farfrae.

To this end, the sailor Newson, presumed drowned, reappears through Mixen Lane, where the marginal space of the narrative annex permits the "dead" husband and father to be reintegrated into the living world.[2] Newson's passage from the dark field over the plank bridge, into the public house, where he participates in the planning of the skimmington, and out of Mixen Lane into Casterbridge itself emphasizes the annex's liminality. Progressing from "some one from the other side," to "the man in the moor," to "no enemy," Newson passes the porous border:

> "Ahoy—is this the way to Casterbridge?" said some one from the other side.
> "Not in particular," said Charl. "There's a river afore 'ee."
> "I don't care—here's for through it!" said the man in the moor. "I've had enough for travelling today."
> "Stop a minute, then," said Charl, finding that the man was no enemy. "Joe, bring the plank and lantern; here's somebody that's lost his way. You should have kept along the turnpike road, friend, and not have strook across here." (333)[196]

8. Thomas Hardy, The Mayor of Casterbridge, ed. Martin Seymour-Smith, p. 138 [55]. Subsequent references to this edition appear within the text.
9. Claude Lévi-Strauss, The Elementary Structure of Kinship trans. James Bell et al. (Boston: Beacon Press, 1969), p. 65. For a contemporary source, see Edward Westermarck, The History of Human Marriage (1881) (New York: Macmillan and Co., n.d.), pp. 399–400, cited in Epstein, "Sale and Sacrament," p. 52n.
1. Elaine Showalter points out that the child with Susan Newson is also sold and purchased in the furmity woman's tent ("The Unmanning of the Mayor of Casterbridge," in Dale Kramer, ed., Critical Approaches to the Fiction of Thomas Hardy [London: Macmillan, 1979] p. 103) [see p. 404].
2. See Martin Seymour-Smith's "Introduction" to the Penguin Edition of The Mayor of Casterbridge, p. 52.

The very unsuitability of the entry-way, even from the point of view of those who open it, emphasizes the significance of Newson's reappearance and underlines the spatiality of Hardy's plotting. Merely a ghost, or a memory, before he shouts "Ahoy," Newson joins the furmity woman in embodying the return of the repressed. The annex provides the opportunity for Newson to take on flesh, as it were, and social connections. By the time he leaves Mixen Lane, Newson is a ghost no more; by purchasing a drink, he becomes a customer, resuming his most important role for the novel's plot. Further, he contributes a sovereign to the "performance," the skimmington ride planned by the people in Peter's Finger. Before he even makes his first attempt to find his daughter, he has linked himself with coins to the punishment that will make it possible for him to give Elizabeth-Jane away to Farfrae.

Symmetrically, the annex also eliminates a woman, Lucetta, who has attempted to give herself, sequentially, to two different men. Although Henchard, too, has relationships with two different women, his thwarted desire for Farfrae and the transformation of that love into hatred sets him up for his fall. Eliminating Lucetta, degrading and humiliating Henchard, and freeing Farfrae, the narrative annex sets up a "right" triangle that allows Elizabeth-Jane to be transacted from father to husband. The structures of these transactions call attention to the structures that bind the characters in social places, and connect social places to literal locations.

Modeled on Dorchester, Hardy's Casterbridge is remarkable for the clarity of its layout, especially for the strict border between town and country: "Casterbridge, as has been hinted, was a place deposited in the block upon a corn-field. There was no suburb in the modern sense, or transitional intermixture of town and down. It stood, with regard to the wide fertile land adjoining, clean-cut and distinct, like a chessboard on a green table-cloth" (162) [71]. The chessboard provides a particularly apt metaphor for the setting of the novel, for Hardy makes Casterbridge a remarkably public, exposed ground for action. Here observers mark every actor's every move. There is no need to imagine, as Dickens does, the removal of the rooftops in order to see into the private lives of individuals,[3] for people in Casterbridge transact their business in full view of the public.[4] Hardy makes the marketplace in the middle of the town the most important arena, where the rise of Farfrae and the decline of Henchard play out in front of and among the people whose personal and pragmatic estimations of worth make that chiasmic action possible.

This is not to imply that all the action, or even all the important action in the novel takes place outdoors, but to emphasize the impor-

3. Charles Dickens, *Dombey and Son* (1848), ed. Peter Fairclough with an introduction by Raymond Williams (Harmondsworth: Penguin Books, 1984), p. 738.
4. See Robert Kiely, "Vision and Viewpoint in *The Mayor of Casterbridge*," *Nineteenth-Century Fiction* 23:2 (1968), pp. 189–200.

tance of place in mapping social relations. Casterbridge's variety of public spaces mark characters' rises and falls in status and fortune. Farfrae
not only takes over Henchard's positions as most prominent corn broker
and Mayor, but he also takes the bankrupt's business place and house.
Farfrae literally makes a place for himself early in the novel, when the
rival entertainment Henchard plans fails because Farfrae has made one
of the walks marking the border of the town into an indoor place where
the fun can go on in a downpour, transforming with rickcloths in the
trees the familiar walk into an outdoor ballroom. Farfrae's tent includes:
everyone may come, just as everyone in Casterbridge may watch and
judge the actions of their fellow citizens. However, far from inviting an
eruption of carnivalesque celebration, both entertainments arise at the
prompting of national authority: "Thus their lives rolled on till a day of
public rejoicing was suggested to the country at large in celebration of a
national event that had recently taken place" (173)[79].

Like the tented celebration, the Ring (the second "alternate" space
built into the primary world of Casterbridge) has its roots in an official
past. The Roman amphitheatre has become the site for "secret" meetings, for its shape enables these encounters, technically, to take place in
public:

> Melancholy, impressive, lonely, yet accessible from every part of
> the town, the historic circle was the frequent spot for appointments
> of a furtive kind. Intrigues were arranged there; tentative meetings
> were there experimented after divisions and feuds . . . pugilistic
> encounters almost to the death had come off down to recent dates
> in that secluded arena, entirely invisible to the outside world save
> by climbing to the top of the enclosure, which few townspeople in
> the daily round of their lives ever took the trouble to do. (141)[56]

The very fact of potential visibility virtually guarantees invisibility. To
avoid surveillance inside a structure that was built for the mass observation of spectacles foretells the story of the function of Mixen Lane; originally a place where crowds come together to watch entertainments, the
social space has become one devoted to concealment.[5] Both the Ring
and Mixen Lane are associated, in their remote pasts, with contrasting
modes of entertainment, one arising from authority and the other arising from peoples' covert activities, and that association is maintained in
the present time of the novel. The narrator makes it clear that the association of blood sports and executions makes the Ring too sinister a place
for liaisons of happy lovers. In fact, happy love affairs and marriages have
hardly a place at all in Casterbridge: the union between Susan and her

---

5. See Lawrence Dessner's discussion of overhearing in "Space, Time, and Coincidence in
   Hardy," *Studies in the Novel* 24:2 (1992), p. 162. Cf. Ross Murfin, *Swinburne, Hardy, Lawrence
   and the Burden of Belief* (University of Chicago Press, 1978), p. 132.

"husband" Newson and Henchard's affair with Lucetta take place far away from Casterbridge and its observing inhabitants.

Long before any character enters into the place known as Mixen Lane, Hardy establishes Lucetta's bold entrance into the social world of *The Mayor of Casterbridge* in relation to it. Lucetta's apartment overlooks the central marketplace; she and Elizabeth-Jane spend hours scanning the crowd from their vantage point in the windows. High-Place Hall backs on "one of the little-used alleys of the town," Mixen Lane (210)[108]. Although the mansion (like Lucetta) puts up a fairly convincing from of respectability, Elizabeth-Jane discovers behind it the border between a world subject to surveillance and the concealed vice of Mixen Lane: "By the alley it had been possible to come unseen from all sorts of quarters in the town—the old play-house, the old bull-stake, the old cock-pit, the pool wherein nameless infants had been used to disappear" (212)[108]. This sequence draws attention to locations where people could watch performances, gamble at bloodsports, and practice infanticide without fear of censure.[6] Of course, the play-house, bull-stake, and cock-pit hold crowds who gather to watch the spectacle, crowds who have come from all parts of town. The disappearance of "nameless infants" taints the recreations in the sequence, marking Mixen Lane as a location where secrecy covers activities that would be considered sordid in the outer part of Casterbridge. In rewriting Dorchester's Mill Street, Fordington, and Colleton Row into Casterbridge's Mixen Lane, Hardy adopts their unsavory historical reputations. Historian David Underdown connects Hardy's Mixen Lane with its ill-governed counterparts, where poaching, underage drinking, and adulterous trysting were recorded in the seventeenth century.[7] In the novel, what has been a zone of carnivalesque celebration becomes a secret arena for activity that would be judged criminal were it to be drawn out into the open. Paradoxically, it is also the only place where the lowest characters, people who have fallen out of the legitimate commercial economy of Casterbridge, can exercise power as moral arbiters. Even the decrepit old furmity woman has a place in the marketplaces and courts of Casterbridge, but the people who inhabit Mixen Lane carry on commerce that official Casterbridge would not recognize. The events in Mixen Lane eventually permit a comic outcome to the novel's love plot (Farfrae will marry Elizabeth-Jane), but the resolution is achieved by the exposure and punishment of illicit sexual behavior by a mob that pours out of the annex, exercising its vengeful disapproval of Lucetta in a most old-fashioned manner.

6. John Paterson in *"The Mayor of Casterbridge* as Tragedy" sees these as signs of Casterbridge's demoralization by its unsavoury past, but attributes to the criminality no more than a symbolic function (p. 104n) [see p. 353n].
7. David Underdown, *Fire From Heaven: Life in an English Town in the Seventeenth Century* (New Haven: Yale University Press, 1992), p. 264.

But before Hardy allows this force to erupt out of the narrative annex, he establishes a boundary between respectable Casterbridge and disorderly Mixen Lane. The door between the mansion and the alley marks the border with a mask that forms the keystone of its arch- way: "Originally the mask had exhibited a comic leer, as could still be discerned; but generations of Casterbridge boys had thrown stones at the mask, aiming at its open mouth; and the blows thereon had chipped off the lips and jaws as if they had been eaten away by dis- ease" (211–12)[108] This gruesome syphilitic sentinel reiterates the connection of sexuality (the leer; disease), bloodsports (stoning), and acting (the comic mask) in the zone it guards. The mask indicates Mixen Lane's former use as a place where festive laughter governed action. It has become a grotesque, however, and its decay symbolises the decadence of Mixen Lane's social function. Although no character passes the mask to enter into Mixen Lane until late in the novel, the alley and its environs are established as a place that once fulfilled a role in providing certain "conveniences" to an otherwise well-regulated town. The narrator coyly reveals that this border region functions as a haven for the disreputable and down-and-out folk of Casterbridge, to provide a secret means of egress for poachers and thieves, and certain other services.

An attentive observer such as the narrator might discern the signs of these activities:

> One was an intermittent rumbling from the back premises of the inn half-way up; this meant a skittle alley. Another was the exten- sive prevalence of whistling in the various domiciles—a piped note of some kind coming from nearly every open door. Another was the frequency of white aprons over dingy gowns among the women around the doorways. A white apron is a suspicious vestment in sit- uations where spotlessness is difficult; moreover, the industry and cleanliness which the white apron expressed were belied by the postures and gaits of the women who wore it. (329)[193]

The white aprons advertise the practice of prostitution. The adoption of a sign of domestic, housewifely cleanliness, rather than the trade the women practice, draws suspicion. In "The Dorsetshire Labourer," Hardy satirizes the philanthropic ladies who are misled by the color of a cot- tage's interior and its inhabitants' dress:

> A cottage in which the walls, the furniture, and the dress of the inmates reflect the brighter rays of the solar spectrum is read by these amiable visitors as a cleanly, happy home while one whose prevailing hue happens to be dingy russet, or a quaint old leather tint, or any of the numerous varieties of mud colour is thought nec- essarily the abode of filth and Giant Despair. ("Dorsetshire Labourer" 255)

Yet the slovenly woman's manipulation of the sign of cleanliness anticipates the false advertising of the prostitutes of Mixen Lane. Hardy quotes
one such housewife:

> "I always kip a white apron behind the door to slip on when the
> gentlefolk knock, for if so be they see a white apron they think ye
> be clane," said an honest woman one day, whose bedroom floors
> could have been scraped with as much advantage as a pigeon-loft,
> but who, by a judicious use of high lights, shone as a pattern of
> neatness in her patrons' eyes. ("Dorsetshire Labourer" 255)

In the annex, however, signs that normally mean "spotlessness" and
"industry" have connotations that only "postures" and "gaits" can
express. The novel presents prostitution as a residual form, an economic practice that adopts and taints the sign of domestic industry.
Sequestered in the annex like nuns in a convent, the prostitutes' white
"vestments" mark them as women who have found a marginal location
within an economy that has no room for them otherwise.

In the outer world of Casterbridge, Lucetta chooses a spring outfit of
red that marks her less ambiguously as one of their kind. Prophetically,
Lucetta remarks on the importance of the choice of clothing: "'You are
that person' (pointing to one of the arrangements), 'or you are that totally different person' (pointing to the other), 'for the whole of the coming
spring: and one of the two, you don't know which, may turn out to be
very objectionable.'" With an uncharacteristic and inadvertent truthfulness Lucetta chooses to "be the cherry-coloured person at all hazards"
(*Mayor* 238)[127]. The cherry-colored outfit is a much more expensive
way of calling attention to her person than the white aprons of the prostitutes, and the new clothes are intended to remind her observers that
she is a wealthy lady, but the force of the reaction against Lucetta can be
explained, in part, by her self-advertisement. Ultimately, the spectacle of
the skimmity presents an unmistakable effigy of the "lady" Lucetta, to
convey her disgrace.

Hardy complicates the narrative annex's connection with female sexuality in several important ways. The shape of the entrance to the inn,
Peter's Finger (which serves as the social center of Mixen Lane), emphasizes the connections between that locale, commerce, and illicit sexuality: "at the corner of the public house was an alley, a mere slit, dividing
it from the next building. Half-way up the alley was a narrow door shiny
and paintless from the rub of infinite hands and shoulders. This was the
actual entrance to the inn" (330)[194]. Here is an entrance, buffed to a
shine through use, that suggests the secret that everyone knows, the customary estre or path through the neighborhood. It also serves as a second
synecdoche of the white-aproned women. The slit into which Jopp
edges leads to a barroom where the characters who have individually
served minor choral functions in the novel gather together: ex-poachers

and ex-gamekeepers, Nance Mockridge and Mother Cuxsom, the ubiquitous furmity woman, and the other regulars of Peter's Finger encourage Jopp to read the letters he possesses. Their voices have a profound effect on the community and on the plot when they make their judgment in the annex. Out of the zone marked by a corrupted mask of comedy, Hardy musters the force required to bring his tragedy to its climax and catastrophe.

Though Hardy's handling of tragedy in *The Mayor of Casterbridge* relies on scenes that could be blocked for stage performance, his plotting and character study requires the representation of interiority. Characteristically, he makes plot devices of the vehicles of characters' private expression. The public nature of domestic life in Casterbridge makes it difficult for characters to speak confidentially with one another, especially with those of the opposite sex. The one space that the novel provides for lovers, or anyone else, to make contact with any privacy at all is the "space" of the letter.[8] No fewer than sixteen notes or letters crisscross the novel. Though Hardy invariably reveals their contents to the reader, their privacy is respected within the fiction. Even when the sender remains anonymous, as Susan does when she brings Elizabeth-Jane and Farfrae together, the letters reach their intended readers. In one instance, another of Susan's letters reaches its recipient (Henchard) too soon, disrupting the relationship of "father" and daughter and indirectly undoing the courtship of Elizabeth-Jane and Farfrae. Though Henchard reads aloud from Lucetta's letters to Farfrae in an excruciating scene, Henchard does not reveal the identity of the writer. He comes close to breaking the rules of privacy that protect letters; indeed, Lucetta, who eavesdrops on part of the scene, thinks he has violated that trust. Yet technically he keeps it. In the primary world of Casterbridge, letters function as specially protected spaces where secrets, plans, and requests can be communicated in true privacy. Just as it seems that Henchard will keep his word and Lucetta's secret, Jopp carries the packet of letters into the annex, where the rules of communal knowledge and action override respect for individual privacy. In the annex, Jopp violates the norm established in the rest of the plot by reading Lucetta's incriminating letters aloud, exposing her (and Henchard) to a judgmental audience.

Though the folk are themselves of questionable character, they condemn Lucetta immediately: "'Tis a humbling thing for us, as respectable women, that one of the same sex could do it. And now she's vowed herself to another man!'" (332)[196]. Throughout the novel

---

8. For a fascinating and thorough treatment of written texts within the novel, see Earl Ingersoll, "Writing and Memory in *The Mayor of Casterbridge*," *English Literature in Transition (1880–1920)* 33:3 (1990), pp. 299–309. Ian Gregor, in *The Great Web: The Form of Hardy's Major Fiction* (London: Faber and Faber, 1974), pp. 116–7, sees the letters as symptoms of the author's troubled plotting, along with other incidents Hardy attributes to the exigencies of serial publication.

Hardy associates the lower-class characters with orality and memory. Yet it is Jopp's literacy that makes public the private, and rewrites the dive into the second court-room of the novel. In the liminal space of the narrative annex, the people arrive at a verdict and plan a punishment for a crime that outrages them, at least in part because they have failed to witness it. Common practice in the seventeenth century,[9] and known to have occurred within a few years of the composition of *The Mayor of Casterbridge*. the skimmington they plan is based on the communal right to judge other people's behavior. (According to Ruth A. Firor, skimmingtons commonly occurred in Dorset towns through 1884, despite the fact that after 1882 they were judged violations of the Highway Act.)[1] The skimmington ride itself takes place in the main world of the novel, in the public marketplace and streets. The impetus for the action, coming as it does from centuries-old tradition, takes place in the annex. That this secret part should turn out to rule over the outer Casterbridge refigures the social world with boundaries encompassing the underclass and its traditions.

Thus the annex provides an alternate story space where a solution that mingles the traditional rough justice of folk practice, the logic of a ballad's conclusion, and conventional Victorian morality can be unleashed into the fantastically regulated world that surrounds it. While Hardy's novel has contained many revelations, this one is unique in that it proves to be fatal; Lucetta will not survive the publicity that this old form of community regulation plans. (Henchard does not die immediately, but he faces the figure of his annihilation after the skimmington.) The malice of the punishment is in this case directed more cruelly against Lucetta than against Henchard (or Farfrae), and the spectacle kills the guilty woman by displaying her effigy in the unmistakable position of shame. Ultimately, though Henchard's effigy does come back to haunt him in a later scene, the skimmington's function in the plot is to get rid of the woman who has tried to give herself to two different men.

The folk of the annex remind us of the diversity of people who make up the social world of Casterbridge. That their residual practice comes from within the town suggests that the conflict in the novel has to do not only with rural values coming into conflict with cosmopolitan, modernized ways, but also with the impossibility of constructing Casterbridge as a mere backdrop to an individual's fate. Those who were safely "behind the scenes" of the tragedy erupt from the surprisingly capacious backstage, demonstrating that they were part of Casterbridge all along. Their enactment of the traditional punishment completes Henchard's and Lucetta's tragedies, but it also converts the afflicted individuals into the most recent set of figures to occupy positions in a ritual that has been

9. On Dorchester skimmingtons, see David Underdown, *Fire From Heaven*, pp. 264–5.
1. Ruth A. Firor, *Folkways in Thomas Hardy* (New York: Russell & Russell, 1931), p. 241.

repeated countless times in the past. Not as complicitous members of an audience, but as actors, the people assert their power to judge and punish, participating in the making of Henchard's tragedy, Lucetta's melodrama, and their own social drama.

When the nameless mob pours out of the dark corners of the town to stage the spectacle of the skimmington, it lasts no longer than the annex that generates it, and melts away when its work has been done: "The ideas diffused by the reading of Lucetta's letters at Peter's Finger had condensed into a scandal, which was spreading like a miasmatic fog through Mixen Lane, and thence up the back streets of Casterbridge" (341)[202]. The perpetrators of the skimmington are as difficult to lay hands on as the miasma that spreads rumor, like disease. When the tailor-poet Alton Locke falls into a fever-dream in Kingsley's novel, the entrance into the annex is precipitated by a miasma that carries cholera. According to contemporary theories of contagion, miasma was thought to induce delirium and death, as this excerpt from a poem appearing in *Household Words* suggests:

> Near a cotter's back door, in a murky lane,
> Beneath steaming dirt and stagnant rain,
> Miasma lay in a festering drain.
> . . .
> Then Miasma arose from his reeking bed,
> And around the children his mantle spread—
> "To save them from harm," Miasma said.
>
> But they sighed a last sigh. He had stolen their breath
> And had wrapped them in Cholera's cloak of death.[2]

The malevolent "Miasma" of the poem suggests the degree to which the word itself is associated with mortality. That the real-world "Mixen Lane" should have been the site of one of England's last outbreaks of cholera, in 1854, suggests the killing power of a miasma flowing from that locale.[3] The miasmatic rumor of Hardy's novel also resonates with the fog that covers and permeates the London of Dickens' *Bleak House* (1853), for both cloudy substances are derived from the deliberations in courts. Both also destabilize genre. The fog covers London and its surroundings horizontally and is swallowed into the interiors of throats and lungs. Yet it also permits a fanciful elevation: "Chance people on the bridges peeping over the parapets into a nether sky of fog, with fog all around them, as if they were up in a balloon, and hanging in the misty clouds" (*Bleak House* 5). Hawthorne's contrast between the romance

---

2. "Miasma," *Household Words* 8 (1854), p. 348.
3. Merryn Williams, *A Preface to Hardy*, 2nd edn. (London: Longman, 1993), p. 109.

realm of the clouds and the "actual soil of the County of Essex" (*The House of the Seven Gables* 2) is here melded into one transformed and combining zone by Dickens' fog. In the fog, the "romantic side of familiar things" can be descried (*Bleak House*, "Preface" 4), but the danger of infection is also risked. Hardy's miasma wafts into the streets of Casterbridge to infect, to transform, and to disguise. Within the annex, ideas are fixed and made visible by the transfer of coins; outside, in the back streets of Casterbridge, they form the fog that occludes vision even as it communicates scandal.

When the skimmington that is planned in the annex takes place, everyone sees it, but no one is apprehended except for its objects: "Neither in back street nor in front street, however, could the disturbers be perceived; . . . Effigies, donkey, lanterns, band, all had disappeared like the crew of Comus" (*Mayor* 356)[213]. This comparison reminds us that the business of Mixen Lane has been to combine the production of spectacle with concealment. The worlds of law and order and masque overlap but cannot communicate. When the blundering constables attempt to penetrate the annex, they discover nothing because of the way they enter Peter's Finger:

> The rusty-jointed executors of the law mustered assistance as soon as they could, and the whole party marched off to the lane of notoriety. It was no rapid matter to get there at night, not a lamp or a glimmer of any sort offering itself to light the way, except an occasional pale radiance through some window-curtain, or through the chink of some door which could not be closed because of the smoky chimney within. At last they entered the inn boldly, by the till then bolted front-door. (356)[213–14]

After the work of the annex has been accomplished, it leaves hardly a trace in the text. The place remains, but entered the right way, by the front-door, it looks like an ordinary barroom. "The constable nodded knowingly; but what he knew was nothing. Nohow could anything be elicited from this mute and inoffensive assembly" (357)[214]. This final glimpse of Mixen Lane is particularly revealing in its failure to reveal. The constables who police the main world of Casterbridge stare into the very place where alternative folkways have permitted a crime to be planned, a crime that puts an end to plots unloosed by the original wife-sale[4] but the constables cannot see a thing. The only thing to do is to carry on with a plot that has been shaped by the work of the annex, putting it behind them: "In a few minutes the investigators went out, and joining those of their auxiliaries who had been left at the door they pursued their way elsewither" (357)[214]. The reader follows, heading for

---

4. See Daniel R. Schwarz, "Beginnings and Endings in Hardy's Major Fiction," in Dale Kramer, *Critical Approaches to the Fiction of Thomas Hardy* (London: Macmillan), pp. 17–35.

the multiple resolutions unleashed into the plot by the peculiar commerce and community action headquartered in Mixen Lane.

Ironically, the women and men who punish Lucetta are themselves
people who find it convenient to live outside the reach of the law. They
continue to provide some of the services of the ancient quarter, yet they
also preserve a code of morality that would condemn those activities.[5]
The question of how Hardy means us to take this paradoxical situation
remains. Hardy's contemporaries, some of whom were to prove so
intractable when it came to his frank representation of sexuality, react
approvingly to the actions of the mob. For instance, although he finds
The Mayor of Casterbridge improbable, George Saintsbury seems to
concur with the judgement of this convention-upholding underclass. In
the *Saturday Review* (29 May 1886), he writes, "The 'skimmington' or
'skimmity' ride will, we fancy, be a novelty to most readers, though the
author has doubtless witnessed, or has excellent warranty for describing,
this burlesque but forcible protest against what villagers regard as
unseemly pre-nuptial conduct on the part of a bride" [317]. Does Hardy
anticipate the approval of his middle-class critics, and subversively represent them as sharing the opinions of a mob, or as John Kucich suggests, does Hardy's critique of honesty subvert the common novelistic
association of middle class and honest behavior ("Moral Authority"
223)? Which ever way we read the inhabitants of Mixen Lane, they are
surely not, as John Paterson claims, an unredeemed peasantry who disturb the social order ("*The Mayor*" 105–6). Rather, as Patricia Ingham
observes, they function in the plot to exact retribution for social trans-
gressions.[6] One might read the women's revenge on Lucetta as commercially motivated, a negative advertising campaign masquerading as
moral outrage.[7] Hardy uses the bounded and separated zone of Mixen
Lane not to announce a contrast between modern, up-to-date literacy
and the backward orality of the folk, but to show how the folk's literacy
and power may be exercised to regressive ends.

Published shortly after the passage of the Third Reform Bill, *The
Mayor of Casterbridge* reflects an earlier world in which the judgments
of the people were confined to expression outside the political realm.
The Bill that redistributed seats, regularized districts, and got rid of pocket boroughs controlled by patronage also enfranchised some farm labor-

5. See John Kucich, "Moral Authority in the Late Novels: The Gendering of Art," in *The Sense
of Sex: Feminist Perspectives on Hardy*, ed. Margaret R. Higgonet (Urbana: University of Illinois
Press, 1993), p. 221.
6. *Thomas Hardy*, ed. Sue Roe, Feminist Readings (Atlantic Highlands, NJ: Humanities Press
International, 1990), p. 41.
7. Laurence Lerner sees envy as the main motivation for the skimmington ride and notes that the
inhabitants of Mixen Lane are both criminals and poorer, though still respectable, citizens.
Thomas Hardy's The Mayor of Casterbridge: Tragedy or Social History? (London: Sussex
University Press, 1975), p. 79. Michael Millgate interprets the same events as rooted in class
hostility, in *Thomas Hardy: His Career as a Novelist* (New York: Random House, 1971), p. 224.

ers; due to the Secret Ballot Act of 1872, these new voters would cast their ballots in privacy.[8] Although other historical circumstances are suggested by the fictional world of Casterbridge, most prominently the mechanization of certain aspects of agriculture, this scene is reminiscent of the futile investigations into election fraud that preceded the 1884 Reform Bill, the third of the great extensions of the franchise. How many times did the Parliamentary investigators peer into a pub where everyone knew that the candidate's agents had doled out coins and stood drinks for voters, only to find no evidence of wrongdoing at all?

The link between the mob and the concealing fog reminds the reader that secrecy is risky indeed. Hardy's novel imagines a world in which the common people of Casterbridge make a crucial judgment in the confinement of the annex, one that brings to final ruin the Mayor of the town. The two entrances to Peter's Finger, well-worn slit and locked front, suggest that the space into which the authorities gaze, having entered through the "till then bolted front-door," can also be read as a figurative ballot box, filled with a "mute and inoffensive assembly"— people, having cast their ballots in covert demonstration. In the space of the annex, Hardy creates an alternative zone where prostitutes, poachers, and the homeless demonstrate their engagement in a social world that has habitually regarded them as conventional figures, "of uncouth manner and aspect, stolid understanding, and snail-like movement," with "speech [of] such a chaotic corruption of regular language that few persons of progressive aims consider it worth while to inquire what views, if any, of life, of nature, or society are conveyed in these utterances" ("Dorsetshire Labourer" 252). As I have argued, the views of the individuals in Mixen Lane reinforce conventional morality, though the actions of the mob, staging the skimmington, break the law. As Kingsley does, Hardy combines the residual with the emergent in his narrative annex, figuring class conflict in terms of sexuality, and uneasily revealing the vengeful rustics in the ancient lane of notoriety, in a different light, as metaphorically enfranchised.

8. All male agricultural workers did not become enfranchised until 1918.

Thomas Hardy: A Chronology

1840   June 2: Hardy born in Higher Bockhampton, Dorset ("Mellstock"), first child of Thomas and Jemima Hardy, some five months after their marriage; followed by Mary, Henry, and Katharine, all of whom remain unmarried.

1848   Enters National School in Lower Bockhampton, then, a year later, Isaac Last's Academy in Dorchester, three miles from his home.

1856   Leaves school to become apprenticed to a Dorchester architect, John Hicks, and later becomes his assistant. Observes the hanging of Martha Browne for the murder of her husband. Becomes friendly with Horace Moule, eight years his senior, who helps guide his self-education.

1862   Moves to London to work as a draughtsman for architect Arthur Blomfeld. Attempts without success to publish his poetry.

1863   Awarded an essay prize by the Royal Institute of British Architects. Possibly engaged to Eliza Nicholls in the period 1863–67.

1865   Publishes short sketch, "How I Built Myself a House," his first appearance as an author. About this time begins to lose his religious faith, though he retains an affection for the Church of England and its services.

1867   Returns to Dorset to work with Hicks. Begins a novel, *The Poor Man and the Lady*, but is unable to publish it (later destroyed).

1869   Works as an architect in Weymouth.

1870   While in Cornwall to work on restoration of St. Juliot's Church, meets and falls in love with Emma Lavinia Gifford.

1871   *Desperate Remedies* published anonymously, after Hardy advances £75 toward the costs of publication.

1872   *Under the Greenwood Tree* published.

1873   Suicide of Horace Moule. Publishes *A Pair of Blue Eyes*; decides to give up architecture to become a full-time writer.

1874   *Far from the Madding Crowd* published in the *Cornhill*, for which it was written at the request of Leslie Stephen, with whom Hardy forms a good relationship. (All of Hardy's novels from this date are first published in serial form.) Marries Emma Gifford; they spend their honeymoon in France, then set up house in London, before returning to Dorset (Swanage) in 1875.

1875   *The Hand of Ethelberta* published.

1876   The Hardys visit Holland and Germany. They move to Yeovil and then Sturminster Newton. A sympathetic article by Charles Kegan Paul, "The Wessex Labourer," applauds the truthfulness of Hardy's accounts of Wessex life.

1878   *The Return of the Native* published. The Hardys move back to London (Tooting).

1880   *The Trumpet-Major* published. Hardy becomes seriously ill and believes himself close to death; he is unable to work for five months.

1881   *A Laodicean*, mostly written from his sickbed, published. The Hardys return to Dorset (Wimborne Minster).

1882   *Two on a Tower* published.

1883   The Hardys take temporary accommodation in Dorchester.

1884   Hardy becomes a Justice of the Peace.

1885   The Hardys make their final move, into Max Gate, just outside Dorchester, designed by Hardy himself and built by his brother.

1886   *The Mayor of Casterbridge* published.

1887   *The Woodlanders* published. Visit to Italy.

1888   *Wessex Tales*, Hardy's first collection of short stories, published.

1889   Opening parts of *Tess of the d'Urbervilles* rejected by several publishers.

1890   Publishes the essay "Candour in English Fiction," urging the need for greater freedom of expression in the novel.

1891   *A Group of Noble Dames* (short stories) and *Tess of the d'Urbervilles* published; the latter is attacked for its supposed indecency.

1892   Death of Hardy's father. *The Pursuit of the Well-Beloved* serialized in the *Illustrated London News*.

1893   Meets and forms an intense friendship with Florence Henniker, the first of a number of close relationships with society women, often with literary interests. Growing estrangement between Hardy and Emma; while remaining at Max Gate, they lead increasingly separate lives.

1894   *Life's Little Ironies* (short stories) published.

1895   *Jude the Obscure* published; it receives some favorable reviews but is also fiercely attacked for its supposed immorality and frankness, especially about sexual conduct. This contributes to Hardy's decision to abandon novel-writing. In the same year, he begins to publish the first collected edition of his novels, in 16 volumes, with Osgood, McIlvaine (the Wessex Novels).

1897   *The Well-Beloved* rewritten from *The Pursuit of the Well-Beloved* and published as a book (volume 17 of the Wessex Novels).

Hardy writes no more novels after this date. Visit to Switzerland.

1898   Publishes *Wessex Poems and Other Verses*, Hardy's first volume of poems, with illustrations by himself.

1901   *Poems of the Past and Present* published.

1904   Publishes Part I of *The Dynasts*, Hardy's epic-drama in verse about the Napoleonic Wars. Death of Jemima Hardy, perhaps the most significant figure in his life.

1905   Meets Florence Dugdale (1879–1937), his future second wife.

1906   Part II of *The Dynasts* published.

1908   Part III of *The Dynasts* published.

1909   *Time's Laughingstock and Other Verses* published.

1910   Receives the Order of Merit from King George V; receives the freedom of Dorchester, the highest honor the town could bestow upon him.

1912   Death of Emma (November 27); among other poems of love and mourning, Hardy writes the sequence "Poems of 1912–13" over the next few months. The Wessex Edition of Hardy's writings (24 volumes) begins publication.

1913   Revisits Cornwall, the scene of his courtship of Emma. *A Changed Man and Other Tales* published. Receives Litt.D. from Cambridge, and made Honorary Fellow of Magdalene College.

1914   Marries Florence Dugdale (February 10); publishes *Satires of Circumstance*, which includes his love lyrics about Emma.

1915   Death of Hardy's sister Mary. A distant cousin, Frank George, whom Hardy had thought to make his heir, dies at Gallipoli.

1916   *Selected Poems*, chosen by Hardy himself, published. About this time he begins work with Florence on what will later be published under her name as *The Early Life of Thomas Hardy* (1928) and *The Later Years of Thomas Hardy* (1930), in an effort to forestall other biographers.

1917   *Moments of Vision and Miscellaneous Verses* published.

1920   Mellstock Edition of novels and verse, in 37 volumes, published.

1922   *Late Lyrics and Earlier* published.

1923   Florence Henniker dies. Publication of *The Famous Tragedy of the Queen of Cornwall* (verse drama). The Prince of Wales, later Edward VIII, visits Max Gate. Hardy begins friendship with T. E. Lawrence. Other visitors in the postwar years include Siegfried Sassoon, Robert Graves, and Edmund Blunden.

1924   Dramatized version of *Tess* performed at Dorchester; Hardy (now age 84) becomes infatuated with Gertrude Bugler, who plays Tess.

1925   *Human Shows* published.

1928   January 11: Hardy dies at Max Gate. His ashes are buried at Westminster Abbey, his heart in Emma's grave at Stinsford. *Winter Words*, his eighth volume of verse, is published posthumously. His brother Henry also dies this year.

1937   Death of Florence Hardy.

1940   Death of Kate, Hardy's youngest sibling and the last of the family line.

Selected Bibliography

Bibliographies

Davis, W. Eugene, and Helmut E. Gerber. *Thomas Hardy: An Annnotated Bibliography of Writings about Him*. De Kalb, Ill.: Northern Illinois UP, 1973.
———. *Thomas Hardy: An Annnotated Bibliography of Writings about Him, Vol II: 1970–1978 and Supplement for 1871–1969*. De Kalb, Ill.: Northern Illinois UP, 1983.
Draper, Ronald P., and Martin S. Ray. *An Annotated Critical Bibliography of Thomas Hardy*. London and New York: Macmillan, 1989.
Millgate, Michael. "Thomas Hardy." *Victorian Fiction: A Second Guide to Research*, ed. George H. Ford. New York: Modern Language Association of America, 1978.
Purdy, Richard Little. *Thomas Hardy: A Bibliographical Study*. Oxford: Clarendon Press, 1954.

Biographies

Gibson, James. *Thomas Hardy: A Literary Life*. London: Macmillan, 1996.
Gittings, Robert. *Young Thomas Hardy*. London: Heinemann, 1975.
———. *The Older Hardy*. London: Heinemann, 1978.
Hands, Timothy. *A Hardy Chronology*. London: Macmillan, 1992.
Millgate, Michael. *Thomas Hardy: A Biography*. New York: Random House, 1982.
O'Sullivan, Timothy. *Thomas Hardy: An Illustrated Biography*. London: Macmillan, 1975.
Seymour-Smith, Martin. *Hardy*. London: Bloomsbury, 1994.
Turner, Paul. *The Life of Thomas Hardy*. Oxford: Blackwell, 1998.

Life, Letters, and Notebooks

Björk, Lennart A., ed. *The Literary Notebooks of Thomas Hardy*. 2 vols. London: Macmillan, 1985.
Millgate, Michael, ed. *The Life and Work of Thomas Hardy by Thomas Hardy*. London: Macmillan, 1984.
Orel, Harold, ed. *Thomas Hardy's Personal Writings*. New York: St. Martin's Press, 1990.
Purdy, Richard Little, and Michael Millgate, eds. *The Collected Letters of Thomas Hardy*. 7 vols. Oxford: Clarendon Press, 1978–88.
Taylor, Richard H., ed. *The Personal Notebooks of Thomas Hardy*. London: Macmillan, 1979.

General Criticism

• indicates works included or excerpted in this Norton Critical Edition.

Bayley, John. *An Essay on Hardy*. Cambridge: Cambridge UP, 1978.
Berger, Sheila. *Thomas Hardy and Visual Structures*. New York: New York UP 1990.
Brooks, Jean R. *Thomas Hardy: The Poetic Structure*. London: Elek Books, 1971.
Brown, Douglas. *Thomas Hardy*. London: Longmans, Green, 1954; rev. ed. 1961.
Bullen, J. B. *The Expressive Eye: Fiction and Perception in the Works of Thomas Hardy*. Oxford: Clarendon Press, 1986.
Cox, R. G., ed. *Thomas Hardy: The Critical Heritage*. London: Routledge and Kegan Paul, 1970.
• Daleski, H. M. *Thomas Hardy and Paradoxes of Love*. Columbia and London: U of Missouri P, 1997.
Draper, Ronald P., ed. *Hardy: The Tragic Novels*. London: Macmillan, 1991.
Firor, Ruth. *Folkways in Thomas Hardy*. Philadelphia: U of Pennsylvania P, 1931.
Garson, Marjorie. *Hardy's Fables of Integrity: Woman, Body, Text*. Oxford: Clarendon Press, 1991.
Gatrell, Simon. *Hardy the Creator: A Textual Biography*. Oxford: Clarendon Press, 1988.
———. *Thomas Hardy and the Proper Study of Mankind*. London: Macmillan, 1993.
Goode, John. *Thomas Hardy: The Offensive Truth*. Oxford: Blackwell, 1988.

- Greenslade, William. *Degeneration, Culture and the Novel 1880–1940*. Cambridge: Cambridge University Press, 1994.
- Gregor, Ian. *The Great Web: The Form of Hardy's Major Fiction*. London: Faber and Faber, 1974.
  Grundy, Joan. *Hardy and the Sister Arts*. London: Macmillan, 1979.
- Guerard, Albert J. *Thomas Hardy: The Novels and Stories*. Cambridge: Harvard UP, 1949.
  Hands, Timothy. *Thomas Hardy*. London: Macmillan, 1995.
- Howe, Irving. *Thomas Hardy*. New York: Macmillan, 1967.
- Kay-Robinson, Denis. *Hardy's Wessex Reappraised*. Newton Abbott: David and Charles, 1971.
- Keen, Suzanne. *Victorian Renovations of the Novel: Narrative Annexes and the Boundaries of Representation*. Cambridge: Cambridge University Press, 1998.
  King, Jeanette. *Tragedy in the Victorian Novel: Theory and Practice in the Novels of George Eliot, Thomas Hardy and Henry James*. Cambridge: Cambridge UP, 1978.
  Kramer, Dale. *Thomas Hardy: The Forms of Tragedy*. Detroit: Wayne State UP, 1975.
  Kramer, Dale, ed. *Critical Approaches to the Fiction of Thomas Hardy*. London: Macmillan, 1979.
  Langbaum, Robert. *Thomas Hardy in Our Time*. London: Macmillan, 1995.
  Lawrence, D. H. *Study of Thomas Hardy and Other Essays*, ed. Bruce Steele. Cambridge: Cambridge UP, 1985.
  Lerner, Laurence, and John Holmstrom, eds. *Thomas Hardy and His Readers: A Selection of Contemporary Reviews*. London: Bodley Head, 1968.
- Levine, George. *The Realistic Imagination: English Fiction from Frankenstein to Lady Chatterley*. Chicago: University of Chicago Press, 1981.
  Mallett, Phillip V., and Ronald P. Draper, eds. *A Spacious Vision: Essays on Thomas Hardy*. Penzance: Patten Press, 1994.
- Miller, J. Hillis. *Thomas Hardy: Distance and Desire*. Cambridge: Harvard UP, 1970.
- Millgate, Michael. *Thomas Hardy: His Career as a Novelist*. London: Bodley Head, 1971.
  Morrell, Roy. *Thomas Hardy: The Will and the Way*. Kuala Lumpur: U of Malaysia P, 1965.
  Page, Norman. *Thomas Hardy*. London: Routledge and Kegan Paul, 1977.
  Pettit, Charles P. C., ed. *New Perspectives on Thomas Hardy*. London: Macmillan, 1994.
  ———. *Reading Thomas Hardy*. London: Macmillan, 1998.
  Pinion, F. B. *A Hardy Companion*. London: Macmillan, 1968.
  Springer, Marlene. *Hardy's Art of Allusion*. London: Macmillan, 1983.
  Sumner, Rosemary. *Thomas Hardy: Psychological Novelist*. London: Macmillan, 1981.
  Widdowson, Peter. *Hardy in History: A Study in Literary Sociology*. London and New York: Routledge, 1989.
  Williams, Merryn. *Thomas Hardy and Rural England*. London: Macmillan, 1972.
  Wing, George. *Thomas Hardy*. Edinburgh: Oliver and Boyd, 1963.

The Mayor of Casterbridge

Brown, Douglas. *Thomas Hardy: "The Mayor of Casterbridge."* London: Arnold, 1962.
Dike, D. A. "A Modern Oedipus: *The Mayor of Casterbridge.*" *Essays in Criticism* 2 (1952): 169–79.
Draper, R. P. "*The Mayor of Casterbridge.*" *Critical Quarterly* 25:1 (1983): 57–70.
Ebbatson, Roger. *Thomas Hardy: "The Mayor of Casterbridge."* London: Penguin Books, 1994.
Edmond, Rod. "'The Past-Marked Prospect': *The Mayor of Casterbridge.*" *Reading the Victorian Novel: Detail into Form.* Ed. Ian Gregor. London: Vision Press, 1980. 111–27.
Edwards, Duane. "*The Mayor of Casterbridge* as Aeschylean Tragedy." *Studies in the Novel* 4:4 (1972): 608–18.
Grindle, Juliet. "Compulsion and Choice in *The Mayor of Casterbridge.*" *The Novels of Thomas Hardy.* Ed. Anne Smith. London: Vision Press, 1979. 91–106.
Heilman, Robert B. "Hardy's *Mayor* and the Problem of Intention." *Criticism* 5 (1963): 199–213.
———. "Hardy's *Mayor*: Notes on Style." *Nineteenth-Century Fiction* 18:4 (1964): 307–29.
Karl, Frederick. "*The Mayor of Casterbridge*: A New Fiction Defined." *Modern Fiction Studies* 6 (1960): 195–213.
Kiely, Robert. "Vision and Viewpoint in *The Mayor of Casterbridge.*" *Nineteenth-Century Fiction* 23:2 (1968): 189–200.
King, Jeanette. "*The Mayor of Casterbridge*: Talking about Character." *Thomas Hardy Journal* 8:3 (1992): 42–46.
Langbaum, Robert. "The Minimisation of Sexuality in *The Mayor of Casterbridge.*" *Thomas Hardy Journal* 8:1 (1992): 20–32.
Lerner, Laurence. *Thomas Hardy's "The Mayor of Casterbridge": Tragedy or Social History?* London: Sussex UP, 1975.
Maxwell, J. C. "The 'Sociological' Approach to *The Mayor of Casterbridge.*" *Imagined Worlds: Essays on Some English Novels and Novelists in Honour of John Butt.* Eds. Maynard Mack and Ian Gregor. London: Methuen, 1968. 225–36.

- Moynahan, Julian. "*The Mayor of Casterbridge* and the Old Testament's First Book of Samuel." *PMLA* 71 (1956): 118–30.
- Paterson, John. "*The Mayor of Casterbridge* as Tragedy." *Victorian Studies* 3 (1959): 151–72.
  Schweik, Robert C. "Character and Fate in Hardy's *The Mayor of Casterbridge*." *Nineteenth-Century Fiction* 21:3 (1966): 249–62.
- Showalter, Elaine. "The Unmanning of the Mayor of Casterbridge." *Critical Approaches to the Fiction of Thomas Hardy*. Ed. Dale Kramer. London: Macmillan, 1979. 99–115.
  Starzyk, Lawrence. "Hardy's *Mayor*: The Antitraditional Basis of Tragedy." *Studies in the Novel* 4:4 (1972): 592–607.
  Taft, Michael. "Hardy's Manipulation of Folklore and Literary Imagination: The Case of the Wife-Sale in *The Mayor of Casterbridge*." *Studies in the Novel* 13:4 (1981): 399–407.
  Winfield, Christine. "Factual Sources of Two Episodes in *The Mayor of Casterbridge*." *Nineteenth-Century Fiction* 25:2 (1970): 224–31.
- —— "The Manuscript of Hardy's *The Mayor of Casterbridge*." *Papers of the Bibliographical Society of America* 67 (1973): 37–58.